The Lotus Guide to 1 for Windows

LOTUS BOOKS Pathways to Mastery Series

Who Should Read This Book:

For spreadsheet users with any level of experience. This book helps you quickly master 1-2-3 for Windows and the Windows environment.

What's Inside

- Accessible, incisive coverage of all the new features in 1-2-3 for Windows and a wealth of shortcuts, good ideas, and tips to extend your spreadsheet skills

- Hands-on introduction to spreadsheet publishing, with special techniques to dress up your worksheets and produce professional reports

- In-depth look at the SmartIcon palette—how to take advantage of the built-in icons and how to create your own

- Special section on using the Solver to manage the variables, goals, and constraints of your business and make the best financial decisions

About *LOTUS BOOKS*

LOTUS BOOKS, written in collaboration with Lotus Development Corporation, help you derive the most from Lotus software. There are four series within Lotus Books:

Start Here books introduce beginning users to Lotus software with simple step-by-step instructions.

Pathways to Mastery titles provide the authoritative perspective and expertise from Lotus. Each book is a fast-paced, clear, and concise guide that helps you build on what you know and teaches new product features quickly.

Business Solutions books concentrate on using software to meet your specific business and professional needs; they provide essential tools for working faster and smarter.

Technical Reference provide advanced information for experts, programmers, and application developers.

The Lotus Guide to 1-2-3 for Windows

Justin Fielding

Brady Publishing
New York   London   Toronto   Sydney   Tokyo   Singapore

Copyright© 1991 by Justin Fielding.
All rights reserved,
including the right of reproduction
in whole or in part in any form.

 Brady Publishing

Published by Brady Publishing
A division of Simon & Schuster, Inc.
15 Columbus Circle
New York, NY 10023

Manufactured in the United States of America

10 9 8 7 6 5 4 3 2 1

Library of Congress Cataloging-in-Publication Data

Fielding, Justin.
    Lotus guide to 1-2-3 for windows / Justin Fielding.
      p. cm.
      1. Lotus 1-2-3 (Computer program)   2. Windows (Computer programs)
I. Title. II. Title: Lotus guide to one-two-three for windows.
HF5548.4.L67F53   1991
650' .0285'5369—dc20   91–25975
    Includes index.
    ISBN 0-13-529363-4

Acknowledgments

To Mary Jean, Rebecca, and Bobby for being my best friends.

I'd like to thank the many people who made this book possible: Dick Ridington and Jennifer Smith of Lotus Publishing Corp.; Gideon Ansell, Janice Brown, Frank King, Lisa Landa, Mike McDade, Alice Meade, Mark Scappichio, Debbie Stolper, Paul Stroube, and Alexandra Trevelyan of Lotus Development Corp.; Carol Barth and Greg Reynolds of Modern Design; and Tom Dillon, Mike Violano, and all the folks at Brady Books.

I'm much indebted to the contributors who provided excellent material for several chapters: Stephen Londergan, Kelly Conatser, Nick Delonas, Merle Braley, and Pat Freeland.

Stephen and Kelly also made their mark on the book overall, as did Ann Kremers of Lotus Publishing Corp. and Scott Tucker of Lotus Development Corp. Their patience, hard work, and sage advice were truly invaluable.

And Susan Hunt, my tireless and insightful editor, deserves a raise. Her herculean efforts and incisive comments made a world of difference. This book is as much the result of her efforts as my own.

Thanks also to everyone who has encouraged me over the years, especially James Morrow, John Campbell, James Campbell, Carol Chestnut, Barry Cote, and the Fischer family. And special thanks to Mark Fischer for getting me off to a good start.

I would also like to extend my appreciation to Tandon Corporation. The Tandon 386/SX computer with its fast hard disk and all-around dependable operation was a stalwart throughout the process of working with 1-2-3 for Windows and writing this book. If Windows runs that well on Tandon's 386/SX, it must be a dream on their 386/DX and 486 systems. To get my work from the screen to the printed page, I had the privilege of using an NEC Silentwriter printer. After years of less-than-hospitable relationships with printers, it was a very pleasant surprise. It was easy to set up, and whether I used the PostScript or the Laserjet-compatible mode, it made sure that what I saw was what I got.

Finally, thanks to Lotus Development Corp., Microsoft Corp., Corel Systems Corp., Micrografx, Inc., and Zsoft Corp. for providing software for use in the development of this book.

Portions of this book have appeared in LOTUS magazine in another form. The @function reference is adapted from The Quick Guide to 1-2-3 Financial Formulas by Steve Adams. The Macro Reference is adapted from Inside 1-2-3 Macros by Scott Tucker. Both of these titles are part of the Lotus Books series.

Limits of Liability and Disclaimer of Warranty

The author and publisher of this book have used their best efforts in preparing this book and the programs contained in it. These efforts include the development, research, and testing of the theories and programs to determine their effectiveness. The author and publisher make no warranty of any kind, expressed or implied, with regard to these programs or the documentation contained in this book. The author and publisher shall not be liable in any event for incidental or consequential damages in connection with, or arising out of, the furnishing, performance, or use of these programs.

All brand and product names mentioned herein are trademarks or registered trademarks of their respective holders.

Contents

Introduction / xviii

Foreword / xxi

Part I: Getting Started / 1

Chapter 1 About 1-2-3 for Windows . . . / 3

The Benefits of Microsoft Windows / 3
   The Graphical Advantage / 3 • Combine and Conquer / 4
SmartIcons and Macros / 5
Graceful Graphics / 6
1-2-3's Greatest Hits / 7
The Best of Both Worlds / 10
The Benefits of 1-2-3/W / 11

Chapter 2 Essential Windows Skills / 13

Starting Windows / 13
Mouse Basics / 15
A New Order / 19
Application and Document Windows / 19
   The Active Window / 21
Managing Window Clutter: Minimize, Tile, and Cascade / 21
   Control Menus / 23
Using Control Menus / 24
Scrolling / 26
Windows Menus / 28

Dialog Boxes / **30**
Keyboard Essentials / **33**
  More Keyboard Tips / **35**
Simple Text Editing / **36**
Clipboard Basics / **38**
Moving Among Applications / **39**
DOS Meets Windows / **41**
Customizing Windows / **42**

Part II: Creating Worksheets with 1-2-3/W / **45**

Chapter 3 Build a Worksheet the Windows Way / **47**

Starting a 1-2-3/W Worksheet / **48**
Editing Cells in 1-2-3/W / **53**
  The Edit Line and the EDIT Key / **54** • Edit Mode / **55** •
  Making the Changes / **56** •
Entering Formulas and Copying Ranges / **59**
SmartIcon Shortcuts / **64**
Format Basics / **67**
Basic Printing / **70**
File Management Basics / **73**
Two Files for Every Document / **75**

Chapter 4 Make It Look Good / **77**

Why Neatness Counts / **77**
Font Basics / **80**
Applying Fonts to Your Worksheet / **81**
Borders, Shades, and Colors / **87**
  Adding a Border / **87** • Putting On Shades / **89** •
  Colorizing the Worksheet / **90** • Aligning Labels / **92** •
  New and Unusual Label Techniques / **93** •
Column Widths / **95**
  Row Heights / **99**
Finishing Touches / **100**
Finishing the Sales Worksheet / **101**

Part III: More Worksheet Essentials / **103**

Chapter 5 Learning Your Way Around / **105**

Learn How to Learn 1-2-3/W / **106**
    Using 1-2-3/W's Help System / **106** •
    What's On the Help Menu? / **109** • Be a Browser / **110** •
Use a Safety Net / **112**
Use the Right Tools / **113**
Navigating the Worksheet / **114**
    Mouse Movements / **114** • Keyboard Navigation / **115** •
    The End Key / **116** • The GOTO Key and Range Go To / **117** •
    Range Roving—Anchor Away / **118** •
    Keyboard Preselection / **119** •
Function Keys / **120**
Not Supported in 1-2-3/W / **121**
    The Same But Different / **122**

Chapter 6 Labels, Values, and Formulas / **123**

Label Essentials / **123**
    Label Prefix Basics / **124** • Preventing Prefix Problems / **127** •
Value Essentials / **129**
    From Formula to Value / **130**
Formula Essentials / **130**
    What Makes a Formula? / **131** • String Formulas / **135** •
    Logical Formulas / **135** • Time and Date Formulas / **137** •
Cell Formats / **138**
    Formatting Ranges of Cells / **138** •
    Common Cell Formats: Comma, Currency, Fixed,
    General, and Percent / **140** • Date and Time Formats / **141** •
    Other Formats: Scientific, +/–, Text, Hidden,
    Automatic, and Label / **142** • Parenthetically Speaking / **143** •
    Don't Let the Format Fool You / **144** •
All About @Functions / **145**.
    Database / **147** • Date and Time / **147** •
    Financial Functions / **148** • Logical Functions / **149** •
    Mathematical Functions / **150** • Special Functions / **151** •
    Statistical Functions / **155** • String Functions / **157**

Avoiding Formula Failures I   /   **160**
   Mistaken Identity   /   **160**   •   Circular References   /   **161**   •
   Hierarchy of Operations   /   **161**   •   Formulas That Count   /   **162**   •
   When a Range Has to Be a Range   /   **163**   •
   Other Formula Problems   /   **163**   •

Chapter 7 Copying, Moving, Inserting, and Removing   /   165

Copying   /   **165**
   Edit Copy, Edit Paste   /   **166**   •   Edit Quick Copy   /   **167**   •
   Range Transpose   /   **171**   •   /Copy   /   **174**   •
   :Special Copy   /   **174**   •   /Range Value   /   **174**   •
   /Range Transpose   /   **175**   •   Other Ways to Copy   /   **175**   •
Moving   /   **175**
   Edit Cut, Edit Paste   /   **176**   •   Edit Move Cells   /   **177**   •
   /Move   /   **179**   •   :Special Move   /   **179**   •
Clearing Data   /   **179**
   Edit Cut   /   **180**   •   Edit Clear   /   **180**   •
   Edit Clear Special   /   **181**   •   /Range Erase   /   **181**   •
   :Format Reset   /   **182**   •   :Graph Remove   /   **182**   •
   Other Removal Commands   /   **182**
Inserting Rows, Columns, and Sheets   /   **182**
   Inserting a Row or Column   /   **183**   •   Inserting Sheets   /   **185**   •
Deleting Rows, Columns, and Sheets   /   **185**
Avoiding Formula Failures II   /   **186**
   Relative and Absolute References   /   **186**   •
   Keep It in the Range   /   **189**   •
   Other Cell-Reference Problems   /   **190**   •

Chapter 8 Mastering the Sheet   /   193

Range Names   /   **193**
   Assigning a Range Name   /   **193**   •   Using a Named Range   /   **195**   •
   Range Names and Macros   /   **196**   •   More Range-Name Tips   /   **197**   •
Global Settings and System Defaults   /   **198**
   Worksheet Global Settings   /   **198**   •   Tools User Setup   /   **202**   •
   Window Display Options   /   **205**   •   Other Ways to Customize the Sheet
      and the Environment   /   **208**
Panes and Titles   /   **209**
   Panes   /   **209**

Chapter 9 Building Effective Applications / 215

Creating and Using 3D Worksheets / 215
    Adding Sheets / 216 • Perspective View / 217 •
    Navigating Among Sheets / 219 • Using 3D Ranges / 220 •
    Group Mode / 221 • Entering the Third Dimension / 222 •
    A Few Adjustments / 225 •
    Adventures in the Third Dimension / 226 •
    Changing the Sheets / 228 • A Summary Place / 229 •
    Three on a Printout / 230 •
Using Two or More Worksheet Files at the Same Time / 231
    File-Linking Formulas / 231 • Working with Multiple Files / 233 •
    Where's the File? / 236 • Simple Multifile Formulas / 237 •
    Making Your Files Work Together / 237 •
Other Ways to Link and Combine Data / 245
    File Combine / 246 • File Extract To / 247 •
    File Import From / 247 • Copy Commands / 248 •
    DDE / 249 • DataLens / 249 •
    Translate / 250 • Protecting Your Data / 250 •
File Access on a Network / 250
Strategies and Tactics for Application Design / 251
    Assessing the Needs / 252 • Learning the Options / 253 •
    Designing, Building, and Testing / 253 •

Chapter 10 Printing with 1-2-3 for Windows / 257

Why Are There So Many Ways to Print?! / 258
    When and Why to Use Each Command / 259
    How to Print / 260
Printing That Monster! / 261
    Print Preview: The Show-Me State / 262
The Print Dialog Box / 263
Give Me a Break! / 264
File Page Setup / 266
Print It Again, Sam: Headers and Footers / 267
What Happened To My Column Headings?! Or,
    Why You Need To Use Borders / 269
Condense, Constrict, Constrain, Compression! / 271
Margins / 271
The Fine Art of Orientation / 272
Options / 272
Let's Print in 1-2-3/W / 274
Questions and Answers / 283

Part IV: Tapping the Full Power of 1-2-3/W   /   287

Chapter 11 Creating Graphs with a Message   /   289

Picture This   /   289
   Are You a Graphic Artist?   /   290
Analytical Versus Presentation Graphs   /   290
   1-2-3/W Graphs are the Best of All Worlds   /   290
   Why are 1-2-3/W Graphs Such Effective Analytical Tools?   /   291
How Are Your Graphs Stored in the Worksheet and Format Files?   /   293
Six Critical Points to High-Impact Graphing   /   294
Creating and Managing Graphs   /   295
   Creating Your First Graph   /   295   •
   Columnwise vs. Rowwise Data   /   297
Placing Your Graphic in the Worksheet   /   298
   A Distorted Impression?   /   300
Let's Add Detail   /   300
   Titles and Subtitles   /   301   •   Notes and 2nd Notes   /   301   •
   X Axis and Y Axis Titles   /   303   •   Data Labels   /   303   •
   Scale Indicator   /   304   •   Grid Lines   /   305   •
Each Graph Type Conveys a Different Message   /   305
   Line Graphs   /   305   •   Area Graphs   /   307   •
   Bar Graphs   /   308   •   Horizontal Bar Graph   /   309   •
   Mixed Bar and Line Graph   /   310   •   XY Graphs   /   311   •
   Pie Charts   /   312   •   High-Low-Close-Open (HLCO) Graphs   /   314   •
Where do we go from here?   /   315

Chapter 12 Enhancing Graphics   /   317

What are Graphics in 1-2-3/W?   /   317
Put Graphics from Other Sources Into Your Worksheet   /   318
Adding a PIC file   /   319
   Adding a Metafile or Other Graphics   /   319
Moving a Graphic   /   319
Duplicating a Graphic   /   320
Adding Graphic Objects to the Worksheet   /   320
   What Do We Do First?   /   321   •   Adding Explanatory Text   /   321   •
   Using Lines and Arrows   /   322   •   Circles in the Sheet   /   323   •
   Box It Up   /   323   •

Editing Graphic Objects   /   **324**
Annotating a Range of the
Worksheet with a Blank Graphic   /   **324**
Graphic Destruction   /   **325**
    Sometimes You Really Do Want to Remove a Graphic   /   **325**
    Changing a Column Width or Row Height   •   Also Changes the
    Graphic   /   **325**   •   What Happens to a Graphic If You Hide Some or All
    of Its Columns?   /   **325**   •   Inserting and Deleting Rows and Columns:
    What Can Go Wrong?   /   **326**
Copying Graphics from Another File   /   **326**

Chapter 13 Introduction to 1-2-3/W Databases   /   **329**

Sorting Data   /   **331**
    Click'n Sort   /   **333**
Finding Records   /   **333**
Extracting Records   /   **336**
Deleting Records   /   **338**
    Rapid-Fire Queries   /   **339**
Computed and Aggregate Columns   /   **340**
    Instant Columns   /   **341**   •   Database Statistics Without
    @DFunctions   /   **342**
Joining Two Tables   /   **344**
Managing Data from Mainframes and Other Programs   /   **346**
Parsing Data   /   **348**
Data External   /   **349**
    Introducing DataLens   /   **350**   •   Query External Tables with
    1-2-3/W   /   **350**

Chapter 14 Data Analysis with @DFunctions   /   **357**

The @DGET Function   /   **361**

Chapter 15 Creative Criteria   /   **363**

Operators   /   **364**
Multiple Conditions   /   **365**
Formulas in the Criteria range   /   **367**
    Common Solutions   /   **367**

Chapter 16 In-Depth Data Analysis / 371

Data Tables for What-If Modeling / 371
Two-Way What-If Tables / 375
Three-Way What-If Tables / 376
Cross-Tabulating Data / 378
Frequency Distributions / 381
Histograms / 382
Matrix Multiplication for Advanced Problems / 383
   What is a Matrix? / 384 • Change a Column by a Percentage / 385
Simultaneous Equations / 387
Business Applications of Matrix Math / 389
Regression Analysis / 390
   Predicting Results / 393 • Multiple Regression Models / 395 •

Chapter 17 Macros / 399

When Should You Use a Macro? / 400
Creating and Using Macros / 401
   A Very Simple Macro / 401 • A Macro that Moves / 403 •
   An Inquisitive Macro / 404 • Ask Nicely / 405 •
   Subroutines, Tests, Loops, and Lotteries / 407 •
1-2-3/W's New Macro Commands / 417
   Window Control / 417 • Clipboard/Edit / 418 •
   Dynamic Data Exchange (DDE) / 419
   Data External Commands / 419 • Miscellaneous / 420 •
   New Ways to Navigate Menus, Dialog Boxes, and Worksheets / 420 •
Troubleshooting Macro Problems / 422
The Secrets of Macro Success / 422

Chapter 18 Mastering the SmartIcon Palette / 425

Using a SmartIcon / 426
Altering the Palette / 426
   Moving, Hiding, and Resizing the Palette / 427
   Choosing the Current Icons / 430
Creating Your Own SmartIcons / 434
   Anatomy of a SmartIcon / 435 •
   The Big Picture / 437 • A SmartIcon Challenge / 437 •
   To Build a Bitmap / 438 • Breaking the Barrier / 447 •
   Copy Down and Right: Smarter Than the Average Icon / 449
How to Use the Other Ranges / 453

Back to the Sheet / **454**
Paintbrush Tips / **458**
    How to Get a Bigger Canvas / **458** •
    Use Both Mouse Buttons / **459** • Instant Icons / **459** •
    All BMPs are Not Alike / **460** •

Chapter 19 Solver and Backsolver / **463**

The Backsolver / **463**
Backsolving Through A Budget Projection / **466**
Solving Simultaneously for Several Variables / **467**
The Solver / **468**
A Simple Optimization Problem / **469**
Modeling a More Complex Problem / **474**
Building the Worksheet / **475**
The Answer / **477**
Changing the Problem / **477**
Inconsistent Problems / **477**
Tabling the Answers / **478**
Solving with Macros / **480**
A Problem That Knows No Bounds / **481**
Forcing a Whole-Number Solution / **482**
Introducing the Whole-Number Requirement / **485**
Disadvantages of Forced-Integer Solutions / **486**
Getting Comfortable with the Solver / **486**

Part V: Appendices / **489**

Appendix A: Working Templates and Applications Ideas / **491**

The 1-2-3 Check Register / **492**
    About the Check Register / **492** • Building the Check
    Register / **492** • Using the Check Register / **493** •
Reconciling the Checkbook / **494**
    Building the Reconciliation Template / **494** • Using the
    Reconciliation Template / **495** •
Amortizing Loans / **496**
    Building the Amortizing Loan Template / **497** • Using the
    Amortizing Loan Template / **497** •
Calculating Present Value / **498**
    Building the Present-Value Template / **499** • Using the
    Present-Value Template / **499** •

Calculating Depreciation   /   **500**
    Building the Depreciation Template   /   **501**   •   Using the Depreciation Template   /   **502**   •
The Compound Growth Template   /   **502**
    Building the Compound-Growth Macro   /   **503**   •   Using the Compound-Growth Macro   /   **504**

Appendix B: @Functions   /   **505**

Financial Functions   /   **506**
    Compound Interest   /   **506**   •   Annuities   /   **507**   •   Internal Rate of Return and Net Present Value   /   **509**   •   Depreciation   /   **512**
Math Functions   /   **515**
    Basic Math   /   **516**   •   Logarithms   /   **518**   •   Trigonometric Functions   /   **519**   •
Statistical Functions   /   **523**
    Basic Statistical Functions   /   **523**
Standard Deviation and Variance   /   **525**
The Mathematics of Standard Deviation and Variance   /   **526**
Standard Deviation and Variance @Functions   /   **528**
Database Statistical Functions   /   **530**
    Database @Function Arguments   /   **531**
Date and Time Functions   /   **538**
Logical Functions   /   **544**
String Functions   /   **549**
Special Functions   /   **554**

Appendix C: /   **569**

Getting Started   /   **569**
    Macro Key Names   /   **569**   •   Macro Commands   /   **571**
Controlling the Screen   /   **573**
Allowing Keyboard Interaction   /   **579**
Controlling Program Flow   /   **592**
Manipulating Data   /   **605**
File Manipulation   /   **614**
DDE Commands   /   **624**
Window Control   /   **631**
External Tables   /   **633**
Edit/Clipboard   /   **634**

Index   /   **641**

Introduction

To quote an early user, "1-2-3 for Windows is awesome." Lotus Development Corporation's long-awaited Windows version of 1-2-3 has something for everybody. It's a uniquely powerful and convenient spreadsheet, and it's compatible with the world's most popular software—Lotus 1-2-3 and Microsoft Windows. 1-2-3/W is your ticket to the exciting world of Windows computing, yet it preserves the value of your prior skills and knowledge, and your existing files and macros, too.

But you didn't trade up to 1-2-3 for Windows just to do things the old-fashioned way. *The Lotus Guide to 1-2-3 for Windows* is for you because it will help you exploit 1-2-3/W's "awesome" array of new techniques and tools. You'll learn to harness the power of 1-2-3/W and the Windows environment to turn your most challenging business problems into brilliant business solutions.

Who Should Use This book?

If you can build a worksheet in 1-2-3 or another spreadsheet program and want to make the most of 1-2-3 for Windows, this book is for you. It will help you capitalize on your existing skills and develop the new skills that will enable you to work with 1-2-3/W as efficiently and effectively as possible.

You'll probably like the book's quick pace. Elementary skills are reviewed briskly, and almost immediately you'll learn new and interesting features in 1-2-3/W. You'll learn how 1-2-3 for Windows differs from the version or versions you've used before, Release 2.01, 2.2, 2.3, 3.0, 3.1, or 3.1+. And you'll find everything you need to know about moving your existing worksheets, graphs, and macros—as well as text and pictures from your word processing, database, and graphics software—into and out of 1-2-3/W.

This book is primarily for people who have some experience with Lotus 1-2-3 or another spreadsheet package.

In this chapter you will learn:
- *Who this book is for*
- *How this book is organized*

If you're a 1-2-3 power user, this book will turn you into a 1-2-3/W power user. If you have a bit of 1-2-3 experience but still consider yourself a beginner, don't worry. *The Lotus Guide to 1-2-3 for Windows* contains all the information you need—just follow the book from the beginning. No important steps are left out.

About This Book...

The trick to learning 1-2-3 for Windows is to use the skills you already have and to explore 1-2-3/W's new and better techniques. This book will help you do both.

The Lotus Guide to 1-2-3 for Windows helps you master the basics of 1-2-3 for Windows and then lets you proceed, at your own pace, to delve deeper into 1-2-3/W's powerful new features.

You'll start by creating basic worksheets with the new Windows-style menu commands and SmartIcons, and with a host of new mouse and keyboard shortcuts. In no time, you'll master the techniques for creating highly productive applications, and you'll learn techniques that will help you continually enhance your skills.

Once you know the lay of the land, you can let your curiosity and business needs steer you to the 1-2-3/W topics you want to explore next. The exercises on intermediate and advanced subjects are designed to allow you to jump in at almost any point and learn the particular skills you need.

You'll learn how to make 1-2-3/W do what Windows does best: create great-looking graphics and share data across multiple files and applications. And you'll find out how to fashion your own SmartIcons, from the actual design and creation of the icon to building "smart" macros that you'll just have to brag about. You'll also want to show off the many undocumented and unsung features you'll learn along the way.

Chapters on sophisticated features such as spreadsheet publishing, graphics, databases, and macros outline strategies and tactics for effective results. Then you'll move directly into hands-on exercises that put theory into practice. You'll learn the essential concepts *and* the most useful applications. You'll also learn how these features differ from those in traditional versions of 1-2-3.

Of course, not all of 1-2-3/W's great features are brand new. This book shows you which "1-2-3 Classic" commands can one-up their newfangled counterparts. And it assumes no prior expertise in such relatively new features as 3D worksheets, Solver, Backsolver, and spreadsheet publishing, but it does give special instructions to experienced users of these features. For good measure, you'll also find sections on essential spreadsheet topics that some users overlook.

Throughout the book, easy-to-understand examples illustrate the techniques that will help you solve *your* business problems. And if you'd rather use a working model than develop your applications from scratch, check out the collection of ready-to-use templates in the back of the book. These and all the other worksheets, macros, and SmartIcons in this book are available on disk. You'll find information on ordering this disk in the back of the book.

Throughout the book are sidebars on relevant topics, and in the margins you'll find tips related to the main discussion.

How This Book Is Organized

The book is organized in five parts. Part I, *Getting Started* consists of an overview of the features and benefits of 1-2-3/W, and a brief refresher on using Microsoft Windows—Chapter 2, *Essential Windows Skills*. This chapter, or your prior Windows experience, prepares you to get instantly productive with 1-2-3/W. You can use this Windows overview as a crash course in Windows, by way of some simple 1-2-3/W exercises, and as a browsable guide to Windows fundamentals.

Part II, *Creating Effective Worksheets with 1-2-3/W*, covers the basics of building and using 1-2-3/W spreadsheets. You'll learn how to use 1-2-3/W's new menu commands, shortcuts, and the SmartIcon palette to create, polish, organize, and print effective worksheet applications with the greatest of ease.

Chapter 3, *Build a Worksheet the Windows Way*, shows you how to build a 1-2-3/W worksheet in just minutes. It also introduces many of the distinctive techniques that enable you to use 1-2-3 for Windows as much more than a mere "1-2-3 clone." In Chapter 4, *Make It Look Good*, you'll learn how to turn the plain worksheet you created in the previous chapter into a handsome presentation.

Chapter 5, *More Worksheet Essentials* rounds out your understanding of 1-2-3/W worksheet basics. It presents strategies that help you "learn how to learn" 1-2-3 for Windows, and it shows how to perform such common worksheet tasks as entering @functions and applying all types of cell formats. This chapter also reviews such core concepts as: using string, date, and logical formulas and preventing common formula mistakes; choosing a default worksheet directory and other settings; and copying your 1-2-3/W files—without losing your worksheet styles.

Chapter 9, *Building Effective Applications* shows you how to improve your applications by using multiple files and 3D worksheets, as well as effective organization within the sheet.

In Chapter 10, *Printing* you'll learn how to get what you want out of your printer. In this chapter you'll explore: 1-2-3/W's printing commands and ways to troubleshoot printing problems.

Part IV, *Tapping the Full Power of 1-2-3/W*, includes chapters that show you how to harness 1-2-3/W's graphics, database, and macro-programming capabilities.

Chapters 18 and 19 introduce two of 1-2-3/W's most powerful new features: customizing 1-2-3/W with your own SmartIcons, and solving complex business problems with Solver and Backsolver. In the former chapter, you'll learn how to choose among 1-2-3/W's ready-made SmartIcons and how to create your own. In the latter, you'll learn how to use goal-seeking and optimization techniques to find the best possible answer to challenging problems.

Following Part III, you'll find a valuable collection of appendices. First is a set working models that use 1-2-3/W to solve a variety of common business problems. You can run them as-is, or you can use them as a starting point for creating your own custom business applications.

Concluding the book are two handy reference lists: a complete listing of 1-2-3/W's @functions and macro keywords.

A Note About Style

This book observes the following conventions:

- Instructions that begin with the word *Type* mean to type the appropriate keystrokes, but not to press the Enter key.

- Instructions that begin with the word *Enter* mean to type the appropriate keystrokes and then press the Enter key.

- Keystrokes that include a hyphen are pressed simultaneously. For example, if instructed to press Alt-W, hold down the Alt key and press W.

> Note that both Windows and 1-2-3 for Windows are highly customizable, so the results on your screen may not exactly match the ones described and illustrated in the book. Except as noted, the examples assume the use of initial default settings for Windows and 1-2-3/W. For example, the book may say to click the left mouse button, but you'll have to use the right mouse button if you've swapped the mouse-button assignments with Windows' Control Panel utility.

Foreword

The publication of this guide celebrates one of the most exciting, intensive, and memorable product development efforts in Lotus history. Delivering Lotus 1-2-3 for Windows involved more than 100 top technical, quality assurance, marketing and other professionals; incorporated input from hundreds of customers worldwide; and challenged our creativity.

As we learned from working with our customers, applications software has to play a critical role in helping users make the transition to Windows. By being consistent and compatible across platforms (both Windows and non-Windows), applications can let users make the move to GUI without breaking everything they've learned. The best Windows applications will allow users to be immediately productive, work seamlessly with others throughout their enterprises, and—perhaps most importantly—help them tap the real power of Windows by giving them new ways to work with information and with each other.

These types of goals meant that our development challenges for Lotus 1-2-3 for Windows were aggressive: "make it better, but make it the same." It had to be a great Windows application, but it also had to be 100 percent 1-2-3. These two seemingly inconsistent goals became the creative driving force behind 1-2-3 for Windows, and, I'm pleased to say, resulted an innovative product appealing not only to seasoned 1-2-3 users but also to first-time spreadsheet users and Windows fans.

Inspired by users' enthusiasm over icons and what other Windows applications—such as Ami Pro—provided, our team really pushed the icon concept to make spreadsheet functions even more accessible. For a while, icons became almost a religion for the development team. The result of this effort, SmartIcons, is a Windows innovation that not only makes our spreadsheet easier to use, but also provides a set of common tools that link our suite of Windows applications in ways very beneficial to users.

Compatibility, of course, was also key. Our customers demanded that their investments—not only users' keystroke knowledge, but files, macros and even spreadsheet formatting—be fully protected in moving to 1-2-3 for Windows. Our development team responded with the 1-2-3 Classic menu (which actually labored under the code name, "Same-As-It-Ever-Was," for some time). Now included in both 1-2-3 for Windows and Macintosh, 1-2-3 Classic protects users' investments by letting them access the original 1-2-3 menu, yet it is totally unobtrusive to the GUI.

I'd like to take this opportunity to thank the customers who served as our design partners for this project. I'd also like to acknowledge the Lotus 1-2-3 for Windows development team, whose commitment to our customers, creativity, and energy have resulted in a terrific product. In particular, they include Ed McNierney, director of development; Jeffrey Beir and Paul Stroube of product management; managers Debbie Stolper, Jim Wilson, Susan Esher, Alice Meade, Judy Duff, and Dan Toomey; and all of their staffs.

The Lotus Guide to 1-2-3 for Windows carries on this tradition of empowering spreadsheet users. It's a practical, useful guide that will help you make the most of the product.

Frank King
Senior Vice President
Lotus Development Corporation

About the Author

Justin Fielding is a Product Design Manager with Lotus Development Corporation. He works on macros, @functions, and usability enhancements for future Lotus spreadsheet products. In his previous job, he was a Senior Editor at *LOTUS* Magazine and oversaw the magazine's tutorial and technical sections. His spreadsheet experience dates back to the days of VisiCalc. In the past decade he has used spreadsheets to create a wide variety of business applications for corporate clients. He has also trained over 4,000 people how to get the most out of 1-2-3.

About the Contributors

Merle Braley is a Senior Design Verification Engineer at Lotus and has worked extensively on the graph annotator for Lotus 1-2-3 for Windows. With his comprehensive computer experience, he is much in demand as computer trainer and support person in a variety of fields and professions—including legal, manufacturing, education and insurance. He lives in the mountains of Goffstown, NH, with his wife and four children.

Kelly Conatser is a contributing editor for *LOTUS* Magazine, with a specialty in business applications for Lotus 1-2-3. He also works as a business consultant and is the author of two forthcoming Lotus Books: *Spreadsheets for Smalll Business*, and the *Lotus Guide to 1-2-3 for Macintosh*.

Nick Delonas, with an MBA and a MS/MIS degree, is a Senior Writer and the macro columnist for *LOTUS* Magazine. He also is an experienced software developer—his most recent product on the market is a financial analysis program called RatioMaster. He works as a small business and financial consultant in the Boston area and he recently co-authored another Lotus Book: *The Lotus Guide to 1-2-3 Release 2.3*.

Pat Freeland is a Design Verification Engineer at Lotus for 1-2-3 for Windows. He is also a frequent contributor for *LOTUS* Magazine. He has been a computer software instructor for many years.

Steven Londergan works at Lotus and has been teaching people how to use computers for seven years. Until recently he was on the Quality Assurance team for Lotus 1-2-3's DOS spreadsheet division. Now, he is working with the Lotus Notes group and teaches classes on Notes across the United States. He lives in Dorchester, MA with his wife and two children.

Part I
Getting Started

About 1-2-3 for Windows...

1-2-3 for Windows, commonly known as "1-2-3/W," makes the familiar Lotus 1-2-3 spreadsheet a full citizen in the world of Microsoft Windows 3.

1-2-3/W lets you create highly customized applications with dazzling graphics, and its countless ease-of-use enhancements help you speed through your work. 1-2-3/W also provides superior tools for analyzing and organizing your worksheets. And it gives you all the power and convenience of Windows computing, without sacrificing your investment in 1-2-3 knowledge, worksheets, or macros.

The Benefits of Microsoft Windows

A lot of the excitement behind 1-2-3 for Windows is provided by the Windows environment itself. Windows extends the DOS operating system to improve the power and ease of use of software on IBM-compatible computers.

The Graphical Advantage

Like the Apple Macintosh computer, Windows provides a graphical user interface (GUI). A GUI, pronounced "gooey," is based on pictures, or icons, and on a standard menu structure. One application designed for Windows operates much like any other, and the icons provide easy-to-learn shortcuts for common tasks.

In this chapter you will learn:
- *What 1-2-3 for Windows is*
- *What Microsoft Windows is*
- *The benefits of using 1-2-3/W and other Windows applications*

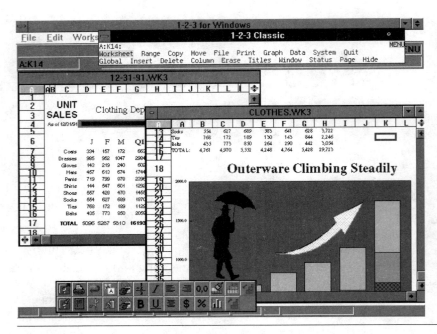

Figure 1.1. 1-2-3 for Windows. A host of new features await you on the Windows-style menus at the top of the screen and on various icons throughout the 1-2-3/W workspace. But if you prefer to fire-off a series of familiar 1-2-3 keystrokes, just press the slash key and up pops the 1-2-3 Classic menu.

Because all Windows applications are graphical, you can say goodbye to the era when smart-looking output was a special feature. With Windows software, you can view graphics and text side-by-side, and text appears on-screen in your choice of styles. Windows applications make it easy to design a handsome document on-screen, and a simple command gets you a printout that looks just as good. And you get these high-quality results without the use of complex setup strings, graph-printing utilities, or add-in software, and without needing an intimate knowledge of your printer.

Combine and Conquer

Windows' biggest payoff is for people who use more than one application. It lets you run several programs at once, and the techniques and data that you develop with one Windows application are reusable in most others.

For example, you can use the Windows Clipboard facility to copy text or graphics within 1-2-3/W. The exact same commands let you copy data in any other Windows application. But the power and consistency don't stop there: The Clipboard also helps you copy data across applications.

If you use a Windows word processor, such as Word for Windows, Ami Pro, or WordPerfect for Windows, it's a breeze to copy selected text into your 1-2-3/W spreadsheet—and vice versa. Design a great-looking logo with Corel-DRAW or Freelance Graphics for Windows? With a couple of quick commands, the logo can embellish your 1-2-3/W worksheet.

Windows' Dynamic Data Exchange (DDE) feature takes this copy-and-paste concept even further. DDE lets you link 1-2-3/W with other applications so that when you change the data in one file, other files are automatically updated. Instead of constantly updating financial information in your worksheet, you can use a DDE link to feed the latest corporate data right into your 1-2-3/W application.

Microsoft Windows is chock full of useful features, including Program Manager and File Manager, which help you locate and organize files and run applications; Print Manager, which allows you to keep working while you print; and the Control Panel utility, which lets you customize the Windows environment. Many people enhance Windows further with software utilities that improve on or complement the built-in utilities.

Since Microsoft shipped approximately five million copies of Windows 3 in the year following its release, it's no wonder that virtually every major software vendor, along with scores of entrepreneurial developers, has either shipped or announced Windows applications. With the arrival of Windows versions of popular DOS applications like 1-2-3, businesspeople can now outfit their machines with a full suite of Windows applications—applications that work alike and work together.

SmartIcons and Macros

Windows' power and simplicity make the world's most popular spreadsheet better than ever. But Windows compatibility is just one of the benefits of 1-2-3 for Windows.

The most exciting innovation in 1-2-3/W is the SmartIcon palette, which gives you instant access to the most frequently used spreadsheet, graphics, and database features. Instead of wading through a series of menus to perform such tasks as aligning column headings or saving a file, you just click the mouse on a SmartIcon.

Figure 1.2. 1-2-3/W's SmartIcon palette gives you a wide array of point-and-click shortcuts for frequently used commands. You can even add your own SmartIcons.

If you dream up SmartIcons that Lotus didn't include, you don't have to wait for the next release, just make your own SmartIcons. You design the way they work and the way they look. By "attaching" your macros to SmartIcons, you can create highly automated applications that are fun to use. Chapter 18, *Mastering the SmartIcon Palette*, shows you how.

Even if you don't plan to build SmartIcons, you can take advantage of 1-2-3/W features that make it easy to create and fine-tune macros. You'll find that tools like the Transcript window and the Macro Trace window take a lot of the guesswork out of creating and testing spreadsheet programs.

More than a dozen new macro commands help you tap the power of Windows. For example, the new {LINK} macro commands tap Windows' DDE feature to let your 1-2-3/W worksheets share data with other applications. Several other new commands help your macros invoke Windows-style menu commands. As always, macro programs can do almost anything you can do via the keyboard or mouse—and then some.

Graceful Graphics

Since the Windows environment is renowned for its graphics features, it's no surprise that 1-2-3 for Windows boasts richer graphics than Releases 2.x and 3.x. You can choose from several new 3D chart styles, and you can enhance your presentations with pictures from almost any Windows graphics program.

1-2-3/W advances the art of spreadsheet publishing beyond the Allways and WYSIWYG add-ins of earlier releases. 1-2-3/W supports all the key features of Allways and WYSIWYG, and it makes these capabilities far more accessible.

Spreadsheet publishing is fundamental to 1-2-3/W, so you don't need to load an add-in to get sharp-looking output. You also don't have to switch into a special mode to enhance your worksheet and then switch back out again every time you want to perform typical 1-2-3 tasks, such as editing data, as you do in Allways. And, unlike both Allways and WYSIWYG, 1-2-3/W's spreadsheet publishing features are available from the program's main menu system.

In 1-2-3 for Windows, as in Allways and WYSIWYG, you can place graphs anywhere in a worksheet and annotate them with arrows, freehand drawings, and more. You can also dress up your work with lines, boxes, shades, colors, and text enhancements, like bold, italics, and underlines.

So your text will look as good as your graphics, 1-2-3/W includes Adobe Type Manager (ATM) software. ATM simplifies the use of fancy fonts both on screen and on paper. ATM exploits the near-typeset quality of today's printers to give you printouts that show you mean business. ATM lets you adjust your fonts up or down to almost any size. And unlike other font systems, the fonts never look "jaggy," and you don't have to fill your hard disk with files that contain various sizes of each font. ATM instantly scales fonts to the appropriate size.

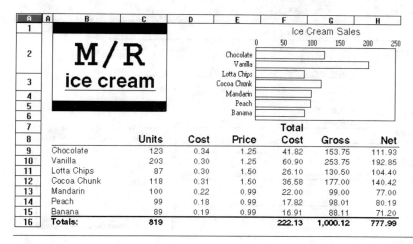

Figure 1.3. Choose from a rich set of tools to enhance the look of your worksheet, including enhanced charts and graphs; graphic images from almost any Windows application; borders and shaded cells; bold, italic, underlined, and colored text; and a wide variety of fonts that look good in any size.

1-2-3's Greatest Hits

1-2-3/W delivers several features found in some releases of 1-2-3 but not in others. Virtually all the Release 2.x and 3.x features you know and love are present and accounted for.

If you've never used 1-2-3 Release 3.x, trading up to 1-2-3/W is the ideal way to put to use Release 3.x innovations such as 3D spreadsheets and external database access. Thanks to Windows' graphical user interface, these features are now much easier to use.

3D Spreadsheets. Organizing different parts of your work on separate sheets can enhance almost any application. You can, for example, keep data for each department or each month of the year on its own sheet. Separate sheets can also help organize the data that you usually don't need to view: macros, interim calculations, lookup tables, database Criteria ranges, and so on. These workhorse ranges are safer when you stash them away from the main sheet or sheets, and your applications look much neater.

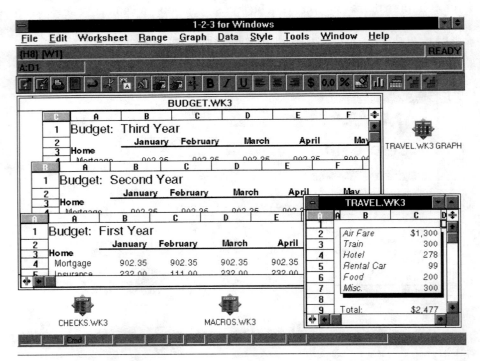

Figure 1.4. With 1-2-3/W, you can view several 3D and single-sheet worksheet files at one time. This greatly simplifies working with applications that span over many sheets and files.

Multifile Applications. 1-2-3/W's use of the Windows environment makes short work of applications that require data that is stored in separate worksheet files. You can arrange several 3D and single-sheet worksheet files on the screen and you can build file-linking formulas with a click of the mouse.

Database Enhancements. 1-2-3/W's Data External commands employ Lotus' DataLens technology to let you use dBASE, Paradox, and SQL Server databases as if they were database ranges in your 1-2-3 worksheet. And the relational database features and computed and aggregate columns will help you perform much more sophisticated queries. Four macro keywords previously found only in Releases 2.3 and 3.x further enhance database applications, helping you create simple data-entry forms.

Solver and Backsolver. 1-2-3 for Windows also provides Solver and Backsolver features, similar to those of Release 3.1+ and 1-2-3/G. These tools perform "what-if in reverse," which means that you specify a desired result and 1-2-3/W figures out how to change your data to achieve that result. Instead of resorting to trial and error to find the ideal combination of values (perhaps to balance your budget or determine the best mix of products to sell), use Solver and Backsolver. In a matter of seconds you'll solve problems that formerly took hours.

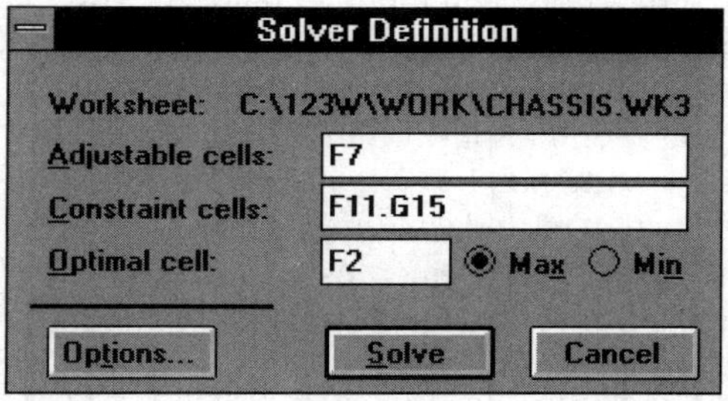

Figure 1.5. 1-2-3/W's Solver solves complex business problems that involve multiple variables. Its cousin, Backsolver, speeds through simpler "how to" problems.

Rich @Function Library. 1-2-3/W supports all 1-2-3 @functions, including the newer @functions from Release 3.x. For example, 1-2-3/W includes @INFO which identifies such important information as the amount of available memory, @SOLVER which tracks Solver's progress, and a slew of enhanced statistical, financial, and database functions.

Hidden Power. Also in the bargain come a host of subtle but useful enhancements: advanced graph options; easier entry of dates, @functions, and macro keywords; the ability to annotate cells and ranges with descriptive comments; and the "Automatic" cell format, which determines the correct format based on the way you enter numeric data.

Compatible Files. 1-2-3/W uses the same file formats as 1-2-3 Release $3.x$, and it can easily trade files with other versions, such as Releases 1A, 2.01, 2.2, and 2.3, as well as all releases of Symphony. 1-2-3/W is compatible with these releases' spreadsheet publishing "style" files as well as worksheet data files.

The Best of Both Worlds

In every sense, 1-2-3 for Windows acts like 1-2-3 *and* like a conventional Windows application. 1-2-3/W supports two menu systems, the GUI menus, which are standard Windows-style menus, and the 1-2-3 Classic menus, which are traditional 1-2-3 menus.

The GUI menu bar is 1-2-3/W's main menu system, and only its menus support 1-2-3/W's new commands. Like the menus in any Windows application, they stay on-screen at all times, and they're accessible via Alt-key combinations or a mouse.

The GUI menus include all the conventional Windows commands for cutting, pasting, printing, exiting, and so on. Many of the GUI menu choices are identical or similar to conventional 1-2-3 commands, but Lotus scrupulously avoided compromising the Windows interface. For example, you won't find Copy on the GUI menu bar; it appears under the Edit menu, as it does in all other Windows applications. With few exceptions, all traditional 1-2-3 features are available from the GUI menus, but many have new names and several boast new options.

The 1-2-3 Classic menus pop up the familiar 1-2-3 menu system at the press of a slash (/) key, and you can type a colon (:) to perform spreadsheet publishing operations using the same commands as in WYSIWYG. In addition to letting you fall back on your prior 1-2-3 and WYSIWYG skills, the 1-2-3 Classic menus let your existing macros run without a hitch—and without conversion.

You can use either menu system at any time, so you can exploit the new menus without having to go "cold turkey." Sometimes it's faster to fire off a series of long-memorized 1-2-3 Classic commands than to look for the new equivalent command on the GUI menus. But if you bypass the GUI menus altogether, you'll lose out on most of 1-2-3/W's new features. Likewise, you rarely *have to* use a mouse with 1-2-3 for Windows, but you'll miss out on a lot of the advantages of Windows computing if you don't warm up to the little critter.

For navigating the worksheet, 1-2-3/W supports both Windows and 1-2-3 techniques. As in any Windows application, you can use scroll bars to navigate via the mouse. You can also use all the familiar 1-2-3 navigation keys, such as the PageUp and PageDown keys, the Arrow keys, the End key, and the GOTO key (the F5 key).

Almost all the other function keys behave as they do in Releases 2.x and 3.x. In addition, 1-2-3/W supports all standard Windows accelerator keys.

The Benefits of 1-2-3/W

As you master 1-2-3 for Windows, you'll get great-looking printouts that include superlative graphics; you'll learn powerful new ways to organize, access, and analyze data; you'll customize 1-2-3/W so you can breeze through your work; and you'll exploit the full power of Windows.

With 1-2-3 for Windows, your spreadsheets will be more effective than ever. And thanks to Windows' rich graphical environment, you'll probably even have some fun.

2

Essential Windows Skills

This chapter is a crash course in Windows fundamentals. Its goal is to steep you in Windows' essential techniques and terminology. If you already know your way around the Windows environment, skip ahead to Chapter 3.

In this chapter, you'll learn how to start Windows and use Windows' Program Manager to locate and run 1-2-3/W and your other applications software. You'll also learn dozens of mouse and keyboard tricks for maneuvering through the windows, menus, and dialog boxes that are common to all Windows applications, and you'll learn basic editing techniques. You'll also find tips that help guide your further explorations of Windows' vast array of features.

Even if you're a veteran DOS user, you might be overwhelmed by Windows' innumerable rules, features, and shortcuts and by its mysterious-sounding terminology. Browse through this chapter to reinforce and expand your knowledge of Windows basics. But don't worry about mastering or memorizing the finer points. Other than the most basic information, such as how to click the mouse, all necessary details are repeated in the chapters that follow.

In this chapter you will learn:

- *How to use Program Manager to run Windows applications*
- *How to use the mouse and keyboard in Windows*
- *How to use windows, menus, and dialog boxes*
- *Windows editing basics*
- *How to switch among applications*
- *How to access DOS commands and DOS applications from Windows*
- *How to customize Windows*

Starting Windows

When you start Windows, the screen becomes a gray workspace called the *desktop*.

The desktop would be a pretty boring place without some software that lets you do something. To get your work done, you'll fill this desktop with applications programs, such as 1-2-3/W. But how do you tell the desktop that you want to run a program?

The bad news is, you can't.

The good news is that an application called *Program Manager* fills this void, and it starts up automatically when you run Windows. Figure 2.1 shows a typical view of Program Manager.

You use Window's Program Manager to locate and run programs.

When Program Manager starts up, it usually appears as a window, just like any other application. Program Manager, though, is no ordinary application. It serves as a kind of main screen for Windows, helping you organize and run your other software. Program Manager stays active as long as you use Windows; when you exit Program Manager, you exit Windows.

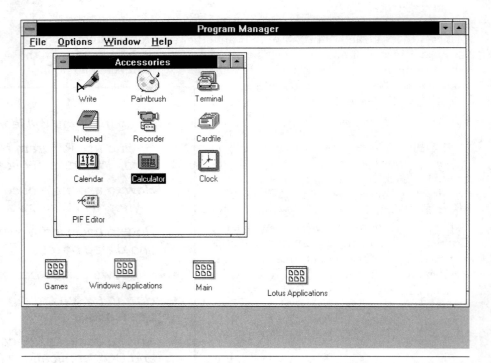

Figure 2.1. The Windows Program Manager, with typical group icons. In this example, the Accessories group window is open, showing icons you can use to run such applications, as the Calculator accessory.

To start Windows, enter *WIN* at your computer's DOS prompt. In a few moments, your screen should look something like Figure 2.1, with the gray desktop visible at the bottom of the screen and with the Program Manager window open.

When you want to run a Windows program, such as 1-2-3/W, you find its icon in one of Program Manager's *groups*. Groups are like file folders, but instead of paper files they contain the icons you use to run your applications.

These groups may appear as open windows, such as the Accessories group in Figure 2.1, or as group icons, like the Lotus Applications group in this figure. When a group is open, you can see the *program item icons* it contains—you use these to start a program. In the Accessory *group window* in Figure 2.1 are icons you can use to run Calculator, Paintbrush, and other applications.

Program Manager organizes applications into groups.

When a group appears not as a window, but as a *group icon*, such as the Lotus Applications group, you must open it to access its icons. In other words, you must turn it into a window to use the program-running icons it contains.

The simplest way to open a group icon, and to run a program from its icon, is to position the mouse pointer on the icon and quickly click the left mouse button twice. In the next section, *Mouse Basics*, we'll use this technique, known as *double clicking*, to open the Lotus Applications group and run 1-2-3/W.

Group Consciousness

Note that the Program Manager window in Figure 2.1 contains several groups: Accessories, Lotus Applications, Main, Windows Applications, and Games. Your copy of Windows probably contains different groups, depending on the software you've installed and whether anyone has created, deleted, or renamed groups on your system. To learn how to perform these group-management tasks, see the *Customizing Windows* section near the end of this chapter.

Your copy of Windows probably *does* contain the Main group, the Accessories group, and the Lotus Applications group. The Main group includes a set of indispensable Windows utilities, and the Accessories group contains the productivity applications that come with Windows. The Lotus Applications group is created by 1-2-3 for Windows' installation program to store the icon you use to start 1-2-3/W and one that lets you reinstall the software. Depending on the options you choose when you install 1-2-3/W, there may also be an icon for the Translate program.

Mouse Basics

Even if you prefer to use the keyboard as much as possible, you'll have to face the facts: Many 1-2-3/W and Windows features are easier with a mouse. A few features, such 1-2-3/W's SmartIcon palette, are accessible *only* via a mouse.

The mouse makes life with Windows much easier.

Windows is all about pointing to things on the screen—icons, menu choices, buttons, and so on. And with Windows' heavy emphasis on graphics, you need a tool for drawing, moving, and altering pictures. These activities are slow and awkward with the keyboard.

The mouse, however, is an ideal tool for these tasks: You roll the mouse on the desk to zip the mouse pointer about the screen. When the pointer is on the object you want to select or manipulate, you perform such operations as *clicking*, *dragging*, and *double-clicking*. These and other mouse techniques are described below.

You're in good company if you find the mouse unwieldy at first. But if you give it a bit of practice, you'll soon find the mouse extremely handy for selecting cells, resizing windows, customizing graphics, and more.

If you've never used a mouse before, you'll need to master a few simple operations:

- **Click** To select something—such as an icon, a menu choice, or a spreadsheet cell—you click it. Roll the mouse until the tip of the mouse pointer is on the item you want to click. Then, without moving the mouse, press and release the left mouse button. Usually when you select something you deselect any previous selection. A few special operations—such as calling up a description of a 1-2-3/W SmartIcon—require clicking with the right mouse button.

- **Double-click** Many Windows shortcuts call for double-clicking. For example, you can start an application such as 1-2-3/W by double-clicking its icon. When you're editing text, you can select an entire word by double-clicking it. To double-click, position the mouse pointer on the appropriate item and then quickly click the left mouse button twice. If you wait too long between clicks, Windows will treat them as two separate clicks, not as a double-click.

- **Drag** Dragging the mouse is essential to a variety of operations, including moving and resizing on-screen objects, drawing pictures, and selecting a group of items, such as a range of spreadsheet cells. To drag the mouse, position the mouse pointer where you want to start dragging, press and hold down the left mouse button, and move the pointer to the location where you want to stop dragging. Finally, release the mouse button. Sometimes dragging is referred to as "clicking and dragging." A common use of this technique is to resize a window by dragging one of its sides or corners.

- **Shift-click, Ctrl-click** Some operations require you to hold down either the Shift or Ctrl key while you click the mouse. In many programs, you Shift-click to extend a selection: To Shift-click or Ctrl-click, position the mouse pointer on the item you want to select. Then, hold the Shift or Ctrl key and click. Note that the Caps Lock key does not turn a simple click into a Shift-click.
- **Shift-drag, Ctrl-drag** Just as some procedures involve a Shift-click or Ctrl-click, some require you to hold Shift or Ctrl while you drag. In many graphics programs, holding the Shift key while you drag helps you move the mouse pointer in a straight line. In some programs, including Program Manager, Ctrl-drag is a shortcut for copying.

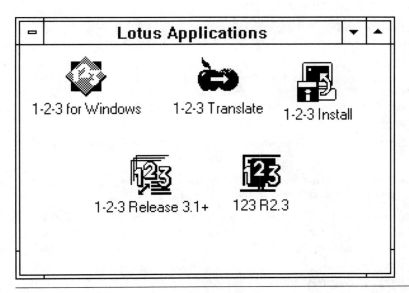

Figure 2.2. The Lotus Applications Group as an open window. After you install 1-2-3/W, this group contains at least two program item icons: one you use to start 1-2-3 for Windows and one you use to change settings you selected during installation. In this example, other Lotus software appears in the group, as well.

Try It: Using the Mouse and Starting 1-2-3/W

Let's try a few typical mouse maneuvers. We'll start by moving the mouse pointer and resizing a window. Then we'll use the mouse to run 1-2-3/W and put some data in a spreadsheet.

1. Roll the mouse until the pointer is on the lower-right corner of the Program Manager window. If you run out of room in which to roll the mouse, you can pick it up, move it to a place where you have more room, and continue rolling.

2. Note that when the mouse pointer is on the corner of a window, it turns into a diagonal double-arrow; this indicates that you can *resize* the window, both horizontally and vertically. Press the left mouse button, and drag the mouse slightly towards the upper-left, and then release the button. Program Manager's window should be slightly smaller.

3. Now do the reverse of the previous operation. Drag the corner of Program Manager's window to return it, more or less, to its previous size.

4. Let's hunt for the 1-2-3 for Windows icon unless its already visible. Click the mouse once on the group that contains the 1-2-3/W icon—usually the Lotus Applications group. A menu pops up with a list of window-management commands. Click the Restore command to open the group window. A faster way to do this is to double-click the icon.

5. Double-click the 1-2-3 for Windows icon. The 1-2-3 for Windows application appears, with an "Untitled" document window inside it.

6. Move the mouse pointer to cell B2. Remember that the cell pointer doesn't move until you click the mouse. Click to move the cell pointer to cell B2.

7. Note that the Control Panel above the worksheet indicates that the current cell is A:B2. The A: indicates that you are in sheet A; if you add more sheets, creating a 3D application, subsequent sheets will be named B, C, D, and so on.

8. Now let's try dragging the mouse to select a range of cells. Hold the left mouse button while you move the pointer from cell B2 to cell D5, and then release the mouse button. Range B2..D5 is now selected.

9. Let's put some data in the selected range. Click the mouse on the Data menu, which appears at the top of the 1-2-3/W window. Then click on the Fill command. Finally, click the OK button.

A series of numbers now appears in range B2..D5.

To resize a window, drag it by one of its edges.

Note that the mouse pointer often changes to reflect its current use. For example, it looks like an arrow when you're navigating a worksheet, but it turns into an I-beam when you use it in text editing. Sometimes the pointer becomes an hourglass, which indicates that Windows is busy and that you have to wait until it finishes a task.

A New Order

In virtually all Windows applications, you select data *before* you issue a command. In contrast, when you choose a traditional 1-2-3 command, such as /Range Erase, you usually choose the command first and then you select the cells that the command should affect.

The Windows method is known as selection-action or noun-verb, because you *preselect* the object and then say what to do with it. The classic 1-2-3 approach is called action-selection or verb-noun, meaning you say what you're going to do, and then you say where you're going to do it.

The advantage of the Windows preselection method is that you can keep a group of data (such as a range of cells) selected while you issue a series of commands that affect the data. For example, you can select a range of spreadsheet cells, and without reselecting you can perform a series of commands to change their color, font, alignment, and border style.

For most commands, 1-2-3/W gives you both options: You select data either before or after you issue a command. If just one cell is selected when you issue a 1-2-3/W command, you get a prompt that lets you select a larger range. If a range of two or more cells is selected, 1-2-3/W assumes it's the selection you want, and it processes the command immediately—unless it's a command that requires two or more ranges. Note that 1-2-3/W's Edit Copy, Edit Cut, and Edit Paste, are an exception; these are standard Windows commands that never prompt you for a selection after you invoke them.

In the *Mouse Basics* exercise, you preselected worksheet cells before issuing a Data Fill command. If you hadn't preselected the cells to fill, 1-2-3/W would have prompted you to do so.

Because 1-2-3/W is a Windows application, you can select a range before you issue a command.

Application and Document Windows

Microsoft Windows is aptly named, because as you use it, you fill your screen with windows of various types. The two most common types are *application*

Each spreadsheet file you open appears in its own document window inside the 1-2-3/W application window.

windows and *document windows*. You'll have the right idea if you think of the application window as the typewriter and the document window as the paper.

Figure 2.3 shows three application windows: 1-2-3 for Windows, Calculator, and Clock. Inside 1-2-3/W's window are two document windows, VIDEO.WK3 and CD.WK.

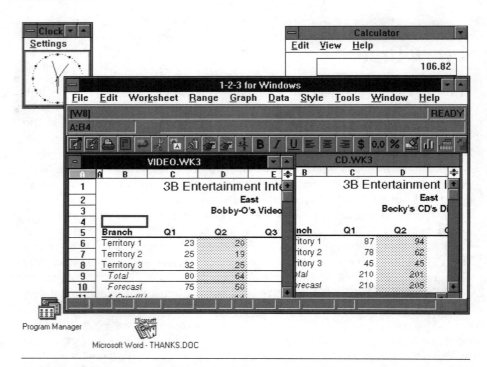

Figure 2.3. Three application windows are open: Calculator, Clock, and 1-2-3/W. Two document windows, VIDEO.WK3 and CD.WK3 are open inside the 1-2-3/W application window.

When you run a program, such as 1-2-3/W, it usually appears in a window—a separate section of the screen. The 1-2-3/W application window provides a workspace where you open one or more document windows. Each spreadsheet file you open becomes a document window.

Not all application windows contain document windows. For example, the Calculator and Clock accessories, shown in Figure 2.3, do not use documents. 1-2-3/W, on the other hand, always contains at least one document.

The Active Window

Just as you need to know where the 1-2-3 cell pointer is before you enter data, you need to know which window is *active*. Windows assumes you're referring to the active window if you issue a command, such as File Save.

Only one Windows application may be active at a time. If the active application includes document windows, one—and only one—of these is active as well. The *title bar*, the area at the top of a window that includes the window's name, is dark when the window is active.

Note that in Figure 2.3, 1-2-3 for Windows is the active application window and that VIDEO.WK3 is the active document window. If the window you want to activate is visible, you can switch to it with a click of the mouse. In this example, to activate the Calculator, you could click anywhere within its window. The Calculator would then become the active application, and it would appear on top of 1-2-3/W's window. Or you could click in the document CD.WK3; 1-2-3 for Windows would remain the active application, but CD.WK3 would become the active document.

Just click in a window to make it active.

Managing Window Clutter: Minimize, Tile, and Cascade

If you want to keep an application running but you don't want its window cluttering the screen, you can *minimize* it so that it appears as an *application icon* at the bottom of the Windows desktop. You can even minimize Program Manager. The simplest way to minimize an application is to click its *minimize icon*, the down arrowhead in the window's title bar.

In Figure 2.3, both Program Manager and Microsoft Word for Windows are minimized. Program Manager and Word for Windows are still running, because minimizing an application is not the same thing as closing it. The simplest way to *restore* a minimized application is to double-click the application icon that appeared when you minimized it

Some programs, including 1-2-3/W, let you minimize documents as well as applications. The minimized document icons appear within the application window rather than on the desktop.

Another way to eliminate clutter is to display windows in a *cascade* or *tile* arrangement. For example, when you choose Program Manager's, or 1-2-3/W's Window Cascade command, the open group or document windows are ar-

To shrink a window to the size of an icon, click its minimize button.

To restore a minimized window to its former size, double click it.

ranged in an overlapping fashion, like a spread-out deck of cards. When you choose Window Tile, each group or document window becomes visible, without any overlapping, like the tiles in a floor.

Avoid Icon Confusion

A minimized program's application icon is different from its program item icon. The application icon of a minimized application always appears at the bottom of the desktop; the program item icon, which you use to start an application, always appears in a group window.

Why is this distinction important? If you mistakenly try to restore a minimized application by double-clicking its program item icon, Windows tries to run another "copy" of the application. You can run only one copy of 1-2-3/W at a time, but some other applications allow you to run multiple sessions. This wastes memory and adds confusion. However, the ability to run multiple sessions can be useful for applications that, unlike 1-2-3/W, can only display one document at a time.

Try It: Organizing Application and Document Windows

In this exercise, we'll explore techniques for cleaning up the Windows workspace.

1. Prepare to name the Untitled document by clicking the File menu, then choosing the Save As command. As explained in the *File Menu Commands Box*, this is not the same as the File Save command.

2. 1-2-3 for Windows suggests a generic file name, such as C:\123W\WORK\FILE0001.WK3. To replace this name, type *TESTDOC* and then press Enter. The word Untitled in the document window's title bar is replaced with TESTDOC.WK3.

3. Click the File menu. Then choose the New command. Note that the document windows appear in a cascade fashion, with the new document, FILE0001.WK3, stacked on top of the original Untitled window. If there are already files with FILEXXXX-type names in the current directory, your new document may have a different number, such as FILE0002.WK3.

4. To activate TESTDOC.WK3's document window, click the mouse in the visible portion of its window. TESTDOC.WK3 moves to the front, and its title bar darkens to indicate that it's the active document.

(continued)

Essential Windows Skills

> *(continued)*
>
> 5. To view both documents side by side, click the Window menu and choose the Tile command.
> 6. To minimize TESTDOC.WK3, click TESTDOC.WK3's minimize icon, which is the down-arrow icon in its title bar. TESTDOC.WK3 remains open, but it now appears as an icon within 1-2-3/W's window.
> 7. To restore TESTDOC.WK3 to full size, double-click its icon.
> 8. Now, let's minimize 1-2-3/W's window. Click its minimize icon. Now 1-2-3/W, documents and all, shrinks down to an icon at the bottom of the desktop.
> 9. To restore 1-2-3/W, double-click its icon.

Control Menus

Most windows have a Control menu, which is indicated by a large or small dash-like icon on the left side of the window's title bar. These icons are sometimes called Control icons, Control-menu boxes, or ventilators. Control menus include commands for manipulating windows, for example changing a window's size or location, closing a window, or switching to a different window.

Applications, such as Program Manager and 1-2-3/W, have an application Control menu, which is the larger dash. Document windows and group windows also have Control menus, and these have the smaller dash. Each group you open in Program Manager and each open 1-2-3/W document has its own Control menu.

The Control icon is at the top left of a window title bar. Click on it to access window control features.

Figure 2.4. The 1-2-3 for Windows application Control menu. Alt-spacebar (or Alt and then a space) is the accelerator key for accessing an application Control menu. Choosing Close from this menu closes the application. Note that the menu's icon resembles a spacebar.

Figure 2.5. A 1-2-3 for Windows Document Control menu. Alt- (Alt-hyphen) is the accelerator key for accessing an application Control menu. Choosing Close from this menu closes the document window. Note that the menu's icon resembles a hyphen.

Using Control Menus

You can close a window by double clicking its Control icon.

If you use a mouse, you can activate a Control menu by clicking once on the Control icon. With the keyboard, you can access an *application* Control menu by pressing Alt-space. To activate a *document or group* window's Control menu via the keyboard, press Alt- (Alt-hyphen). It's easy to remember these keystrokes if you think of the the larger dash as a picture of the spacebar and the smaller one as a hyphen.

Mouse users can choose from two ways to close a window via the Control menu: Click on the Control icon and then select Close, or simply double-click the Control icon.

Ctrl-F4 closes the active document window. Alt-F4 closes the active application window.

Keyboard users can choose three ways to close a window. First, you can press Alt-space or Alt- (alt-hyphen) and then use the Arrow keys and to select Close, and press Enter. Second, you can choose Alt-space or Alt- and type C. Third, you can close the current document window by pressing Ctrl-F4, and you can close the application window by choosing Alt-F4.

Control menus usually include the following choices:

- **Close** Closes the window.

To expand a window to its largest possible size, click on its maximize icon or double click its title bar.

- **Maximize** This command lets you use the menu, rather than the *maximize icon* (the up arrowhead on the right of the title bar), to enlarge the window. If you maximize an application window, it expands to cover the entire screen. If you maximize a document or group window, it expands to fill the application window, and its Control icon moves into the menu bar. Another way to maximize a window is to double click its title bar.

- **Minimize** This command lets you use the menu, rather than the minimize icon (the down arrowhead on the right of the title bar), to "iconize" the window. In many applications, this option appears only in the application's Control menu, not in the documents' Control menus.
- **Move** This command lets you use the keyboard to reposition the window. Dragging a window by its title bar is an easier way to perform this operation.
- **Next** This command appears in document and group control menus, but not in application menus. It lets you switch among open windows in the active application.
- **Restore** This command restores a window to its former size if you have either maximized it or minimized it. When you maximize a window, its maximize icon changes to a restore icon, which is a button with up and down arrowheads. After you restore a maximized window, the restore icon is replaced by a maximize icon. You can also restore a maximized application window by double clicking its title bar.
- **Size** This command lets you use the keyboard to change the dimensions of the window. It's usually easier to resize a window by dragging the edge of the window. Note that you can't size a window when it's maximized or minimized.
- **Switch To** This command appears only in application Control menus. It helps you switch to another active application. The section *Moving Among Applications* details its use.

Click on the Restore icon to return a maximized window to its former size.

Try It: Window Control

Let's use Control menu commands to manage document windows.

1. Click TESTDOC.WK3's document Control icon (the dashlike icon on the left of its title bar).
2. Click the Next command. FILE0001.WK3 is now the active document window.
3. Click FILE0001.WK3's document Control icon, and then choose the Close command. Click the No button when 1-2-3/W asks if you want to save this file. Since no other documents are open, TESTDOC.WK3 once again becomes the active document.

(continued)

> *(continued)*
>
> 4. Double-click TESTDOC.WK3's document Control icon. This is a shortcut for closing the window. Click the No button when 1-2-3/W asks if you want to save this file. Since no other documents are open, 1-2-3/W displays a new Untitled document.

Scrolling

Scroll bars let you move through a window either gradually or by leaps and bounds.

Usually, there's more information in a document than is visible in its window. When this is the case, Windows provides *scroll bars* to help you use the mouse to bring the appropriate data into view. The scroll bars not only provide a very fast way of cruising around the document, they also indicate where you are within the document.

A window may have vertical and/or horizontal scroll bars. Figure 2.6 displays a vertical scroll bar and a horizontal scroll bar.

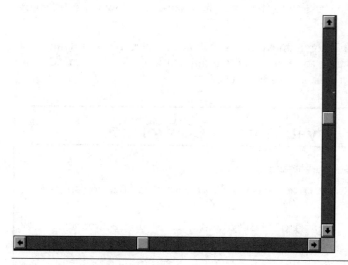

Figure 2.6. Horizontal and vertical scroll bars.

Both types of scroll bars have five parts: two *scroll arrows* (one at either end), the *scroll box*, and the space (at either end) between the scroll box and the scroll arrow. The scroll box indicates the current position within the document. When you're at the beginning of a document, the vertical scroll box is at the top of the scroll bar. If you're in the middle of the document, the vertical scroll box is in the middle of the scroll bar.

Use the following techniques to navigate with the scroll bars:

- Click the up or down scroll arrow in a vertical scroll bar to scroll one worksheet row or line of text up or down.

- Click the right or left scroll arrow in a horizontal scroll bar to scroll one worksheet column or one character to the right or left.

- Hold down the left mouse button when the mouse pointer is on a scroll arrow to gradually scroll in the direction of the arrow.

- Click the space (if any) between a scroll arrow and the scroll box to scroll one screenload in the direction of the arrow.

- Hold down the left mouse button when the pointer is in the space between a scroll arrow and the scroll box to gradually scroll in the direction of the arrow, one screenload at at time.

- Drag the scroll box to jump anywhere, horizontally or vertically, in the document.

In some applications, moving via the scroll bars doesn't move the cursor or cell pointer. In 1-2-3/W, however, the cell pointer moves anytime that a scrolling operation would otherwise move it off the screen.

Try It: Scrolling

Try out a variety of ways to use the scroll bars to navigate the spreadsheet.

1. To scroll down one line at a time, repeatedly click the vertical scroll bar's down-arrow icon.

2. Keep the mouse pointer on the down-arrow icon and hold down the left mouse-button. This lets you scroll gradually through the document.

3. Click in the space between the vertical scroll box and the down-arrow icon. This, like pressing the PageDown key, scrolls down a screenload at a time.

4. Drag the vertical scroll box to the top of the scroll bar. This brings row 1 back into view. In a large worksheet, you'd drag the scroll bar to jump large numbers of rows or columns.

(continued)

> *(continued)*
> 5. Practice scrolling to the right and left of the document via the horizontal scroll bars.
> 6. When you're through, click the A that appears in the upper-left of the sheet; this brings you to the home position in the worksheet.

Windows' Menus

1-2-3/W's menu bar includes a mix of familiar 1-2-3 and Windows menu commands, and some new ones, too.

The list of menu names that appears at the top of a window is called the *menu bar*. As shown in Figure 2.7, 1-2-3/W's menu bar contains the following choices: File, Edit, Worksheet, Range, Graph, Data, Style, Tools, Window, and Help.

| <u>F</u>ile <u>E</u>dit <u>W</u>orksheet <u>R</u>ange <u>G</u>raph <u>D</u>ata <u>S</u>tyle <u>T</u>ools <u>W</u>indow Help |

Figure 2.7. 1-2-3/W's menu bar. The menu names include all the typical Windows menus, such as File, Edit, Window, and Help, along with the Worksheet, Range, Data, and Graph menu names that are well known to 1-2-3 users. These menus, as well as the new Style and Tools menus, offer a mix of new features and variations on familiar themes.

To access a Windows menu via the mouse, click the mouse pointer on the desired item in the menu bar. You can then click on a choice from the menu that appears. To close a menu without choosing a command, click the mouse on the menu's name or anywhere outside the menu.

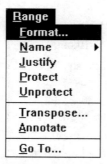

Figure 2.8. 1-2-3/W's Range menu, with the Format command highlighted. Note the ellipses following the Format, Transpose, and Go To commands. The ellipses indicate that a dialog box appears if you choose these commands. The arrowhead to the right of the Name command indicates that a cascade menu will appear if you highlight the command.

Essential Windows Skills

To pick a menu choice with a single click, hold down the left mouse button when you select the menu name, and drag down until you you select (highlight) the desired menu choice. When you release the mouse button, the menu choice will execute.

Some menu choices display a check mark next to indicate an active setting; each time you select the choice again, you deactivate or reactivate the setting. Menu choices that appear in a dim gray are not applicable to the current task.

Two types of menu choices don't execute immediately. Menu choices that contain an arrowhead are cascade menus. When you select these items, a related menu drops down. Menu choices that end with an ellipsis (...) call up a dialog box. 1-2-3/W's Range menu, shown in Figure 2.8, includes a cascade menu choice, Name, and three choices that call up dialog boxes: Format, Transpose, and Goto.

Slashing Through the Classics

Although 1-2-3/W's Windows-style menus are the road to its new capabilities, it's good to know that you can use the old, familiar route whenever you want. If you can't find the command you want on 1-2-3/W's main menus, or if you want to cut a fast path through the old commands, press the slash key (/) or colon (:) for conventional 1-2-3 menus. As shown in Figure 2.9, the 1-2-3 Classic menus appear in the form of a window.

Just as in other versions of 1-2-3, you press the first letter of a menu choice or use the arrow keys and press Enter to choose a command, and you press Ctrl-Break or tap the Escape key one or more times to exit the menus. Note that you cannot use a mouse to navigate the 1-2-3 Classic menus.

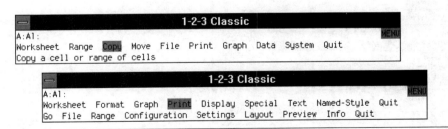

Figure 2.9. The 1-2-3 Classic menus. Although these menus don't support 1-2-3/W's new features, it's reassuring to know that familiar 1-2-3 commands are but a slash key (/) or colon (:) away.

To name an Untitled document choose File Save As and assign it an appropriate name. From then on, use File Save to quickly store it to disk.

File-Menu Commands

Most Windows applications, including 1-2-3/W, contain the following File menu commands. These commands perform critical tasks, such as opening, saving, and printing a file, and exiting an application:

- **File New** Opens a new document window in the active application.
- **File Open** Helps you locate and open an existing document.
- **File Save** Saves the active document, using the name specified in its title bar. If the document is Untitled, the application may ask you to specify a name, just as in the File Save As command. Other applications, including 1-2-3/W assign a generic file name, such as FILE0001.WK3, if you issue a File Save command with an untitled document.
- **File Save As** Also saves the active document, but it lets you specify a new name. You usually use this command the first time you save a document and any time you want to save the current document to a new name while leaving the previously saved version intact.
- **File Print** Sends a printout to the default printer. This and other File-menu commands let you control a variety of printer settings.
- **File Exit** Closes all open documents, prompting you to save any changes, and it quits the application. To exit Windows, choose Program Manager's File Exit command.

Dialog Boxes

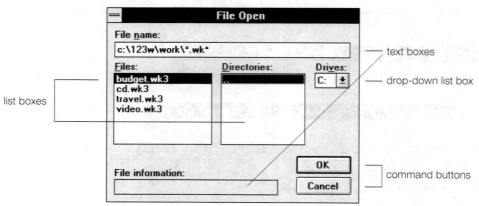

Figure 2.10. 1-2-3/W's File Open dialog box. This dialog box contains many types of controls, including text boxes, command buttons, list boxes, and a drop-down list box.

Essential Windows Skills

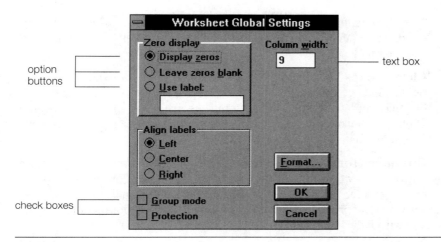

Figure 2.11. 1-2-3/W's Worksheet Global Settings dialog box. This dialog box contains examples of option buttons, check boxes, and a button (Format) that calls up another dialog box.

Windows' *dialog boxes* are like the settings sheets of 1-2-3 Release 2.2, and like the 1-2-3 dialog boxes that superseded them in Release 2.3. They allow you to specify several settings at once.

Many 1-2-3/W commands bring up dialog boxes, so it's important to know how to navigate and use their various *controls* to select options from them. In general, the mouse is faster than the keyboard for working with dialog boxes.

Take the time to read carefully the options suggested by a dialog box. Before you confirm or cancel a dialog box, make sure you're choosing or refusing the appropriate options.

Dialog boxes may contain a combination of the following:

- **Command buttons** Command buttons are icons that you click to choose an option. Most dialog boxes have at least two buttons, OK and Cancel, both of which exit the dialog box. You click OK to accept all the current settings in the dialog box. Click Cancel to exit the box without carrying out any changes. Some dialog box buttons—the ones whose names end with an ellipsis—bring up an additional dialog box.

- **List boxes** List boxes display a series of items, such as the names of documents in a directory. Some list boxes have buttons you can use to scroll up and down the list.

- **Drop-down list boxes** Some list boxes, such as the Drives box in Figure 2.10, expand to full size at the click of a button.

The buttons and other clickable items in a dialog box (or a window) are called controls. Using a mouse is more convenient, but you can also use the Tab and BackTab keys to move around the controls in a dialog box.

- **Text boxes**, or **fields** Text boxes are entry blanks in which you enter or edit such information as the range of worksheet cells that a command should affect.
- **Check boxes** You click in a check box to activate or deactivate a particular setting. A setting is active when an X appears in the box, and it's inactive when the box is empty. Some check boxes appear gray, instead of either checked or empty; this means that present status is unknown or ambiguous.
- **Option buttons** or **radio buttons** Option buttons are groups of round buttons. They differ from check boxes in that they allow you to activate only one choice at a time. Selecting an option button automatically deactivates the previously selected button. The active option button is the one with a dark circle inside it.

Try It: Dialog Boxes

Bring up the File Save As dialog box for a more in-depth look.

1. Click in the FILE0001.WK3 window to activate it.
2. Now try the click-and-drag method of menu selection. Position the mouse pointer on the File menu, and hold down the right mouse button as you drag down to the Save As command. When Save As is highlighted, release the mouse button.
3. Let's try out a check box. Click in the box to the left of the words Password Protect, and an X appears in the box. Click in the box again to remove the X. If you save the file with the Password Protect box checked, 1-2-3/W asks you to enter a password.
4. Click the down-arrow icon underneath the word Drives: to see a list of accessible disk drives. When you need to switch to another drive, you click on the appropriate drive letter. Click the button again to close the list.
5. The File and Directories list boxes show the names of worksheet files and directories that reside within the current directory. To choose one of these file names or directories you double-click it.
6. Click the Cancel button to exit the dialog box without saving the file.

Keyboard Essentials

Most anything you can do in Windows with the mouse you can also do with the keyboard. Except as noted, 1-2-3/W supports all the keyboard techniques listed in this section and in the following section, *More Keyboard Tips*.

If you're partial to using the keyboard for menu, dialog box, and navigation tasks, you'll learn a great many of these tips as you master Windows. However, there are far too many to learn at once. In the meantime, browse the lists in this and the following section to get some idea of the possible keyboard operations.

Keyboard tips you should know from the start include the following:

- **Alt and F10, Arrow keys to use menus** Press the Alt or F10 key to activate the left-most menu name. In 1-2-3/W and most other applications, File is the left-most menu name. Then use the Right- and LeftArrow keys to highlight the desired menu name in the menu bar. Finally, you can use the Down- and UpArrow keys to select a desired menu item, and press Enter to execute it. To close a Windows menu without choosing a command, press Alt or F10 again or press Escape.

- **Alt and underlined letters for shortcut keys** Most menu choices have an underlined character, which indicates a shortcut key. For example, the F in the File menu's name is underlined and the O in the File menu's Open command is underlined. Pressing Alt-F selects the File menu, and then typing an O selects Open. Because Windows uses the Alt key for this purpose, 1-2-3/W uses the Ctrl key, instead of the Alt key to run macros.

- **Enter to confirm** In Program Manager, the Enter key opens the currently selected group icon or, if a program item icon is selected, it runs the program. In most dialog boxes, a particular button—usually the OK button—is darker than other buttons and/or has a dotted-line box; this indicates that Enter is the shortcut for the button. Also, as stated above, Enter executes the current choice in a menu.

- **Escape to cancel** Pressing Escape in a dialog box is the equivalent of clicking Cancel. Also, as stated above, if a Windows menu is open, Escape closes it.

- **Arrow keys to navigate Program Manager** Press the Arrow keys to move among the icons in the active group window.

- **Ctrl-Tab and Ctrl-F6 to navigate documents** Press Ctrl-Tab or Ctrl-F6 to cycle through document windows and minimized documents—including group windows and group icons.

Since Windows reserves the Alt key for menu commands, 1-2-3/W uses the Control key, instead of Alt, to invoke macros.

- **Tab and Shift Tab to navigate a dialog box** Pressing Tab cycles through the elements of a dialog box. Shift-Tab moves backwards through the dialog box.

- **Spacebar to select a control** Press the spacebar in a dialog box to select the currently highlighted button or to toggle (select or deselect) a check box.

- **Shift and navigation keys to select** To select data via the keyboard—instead of by dragging the mouse—hold the Shift key while you press the Arrow keys or other navigation keys, such as PageUp or PageDown.

- **Ctrl-F4 to close document** Press Ctrl-F4 to close the active document in 1-2-3/W, Program Manager, and other applications. If you haven't saved changes to the document, a dialog box asks you if you want to do so.

- **Alt-F4 to close application** Press Alt-F4 to close the active application in 1-2-3/W, Program Manager, and other applications. If you haven't saved changes to one or more open documents, a dialog box asks you if you want to do so. Pressing Alt-F4 from Program Manager exits Windows.

Try It: Keyboard Techniques

Find out how to use the keyboard for a variety of 1-2-3/W and Windows tasks.

1. Let's use the keyboard to switch from the FILE0001.WK3 window back to TESTDOC.WK3. First, press the Alt key to highlight the first menu choice, which is File.

2. Before proceeding, note that two commands in the menu bar, Worksheet and Window, each start with the letter W. The underlined character in each word identifies the shortcut key: K for Worksheet, and W for Window. Type W to select the Window menu.

3. Now, use the Arrow keys to highlight the name TESTDOC.WK3, and press Enter to make it the active window.

4. Use the Arrow keys to select cell B2.

5. Now try pressing the Alt-key simultaneously with a menu shortcut key: Press Alt-S to choose the Style menu, and then press Enter to choose Font, the first choice on the menu.

(continued)

(continued)

6. Press Alt-B to choose the Bold option, and then press Tab repeatedly until the Range text box is highlighted.
7. Press the DownArrow key three times to select the range B2..B5 and press Enter.
8. Press Enter again to confirm the dialog box settings.

More Keyboard Tips

The following list details more keyboard shortcuts. Again, refer to the cheat sheet that comes with this book for a complete list.

- **Accelerator keys** Some menu choices have accelerator keys, such as Ctrl-Insert for Edit Copy. The accelerator key, if any, for a given menu command appears to the right of the command.
- **Dialog box shortcuts** Options in dialog boxes often have shortcut keys that you can access by typing Alt and the underlined letter. As long as a text box or list box isn't currently selected, the Alt is optional.
- **Arrow keys in dialog boxes** The Arrow keys let you move among the members of a group of option buttons. These keys also let you move among the items in a list box.
- **Alt-DownArrow to open drop-down list box** To open a drop-down list box, such as the Drives box in 1-2-3/W's File Open command, press Alt-DownArrow. Then you can use the Arrow keys to move among the entries.
- **Alt-Backspace for Undo** Alt-Backspace is the accelerator key for the Edit Undo command. In 1-2-3 for Windows, you can't redo a command that you undo, so don't choose this option unless you're sure you want to undo the last command.
- **Ctrl to extend navigation range** The Ctrl key extends the scope of the navigation keys. For example, the RightArrow key moves one character to the right, while Ctrl-RightArrow moves one word or several worksheet columns to the right. Note, however, that some Ctrl-key combinations, such as Ctrl-End have special meanings in 1-2-3 and 1-2-3/W.
- **F1 for Help** In most Windows applications, including 1-2-3/W, function key F1 brings up Help for the current task.

> ### Should I Press or Should I Click?
>
> Like many Windows users, you may find that the mouse is the most convenient way to get around Windows applications and their menus. But it's worth knowing keyboard techniques, too, as many 1-2-3 veterans can attest.
>
> Windows Accelerator keys can help you speed through tasks, and moving though text character-by-character with the Arrow keys can be easier than gingerly moving the mouse. Also, knowing how to get around via the keyboard is essential when you use 1-2-3/W on a computer that doesn't have a mouse.
>
> And note that 1-2-3/W macros navigate the Windows menus and dialog boxes using the same techniques you'd use from the keyboard. For this reason, a basic knowledge of keyboard navigation is important to understanding 1-2-3/W macros.

1-2-3/W's Edit mode takes advantage of editing features that are common to most Windows applications.

Simple Text Editing

Text-editing operations in most Windows applications have several features in common. All these techniques apply when you modify text in 1-2-3/W's Edit mode:

- A flashing cursor called the *insertion point* indicates where the next character you type will go.

- The Backspace key deletes the character to the left of the insertion point.

- The Delete key deletes the character to the right of the insertion point.

- If text is selected the Delete or Backspace key removes the entire selection.

- If text is selected, the next character you type replaces the entire selection.

- When you move the mouse over editable text, the pointer becomes an I-beam. You use the I-beam to select text or to reposition the insertion point. When moving the insertion point, remember to click at the new location; simply moving the I-beam does not reset the insertion point.

- To select several characters, words or lines, either drag the mouse or hold the shift key while you use the navigation keys.

- Double-clicking is a common shortcut for selecting a word.
- Pressing Shift-click extends the selection.
- In most applications, Home and End move the insertion point to, respectively, the beginning or the end of the current line.

Try It: Text-Editing

Enter some text in a cell and alter it with Windows-style editing techniques.

1. In cell A1 of TESTDOC.WK3, type *This is text that I am going to edit* and press Enter. The text you entered appears in the Edit line above the worksheet.

2. Click the mouse in the Edit line to invoke Edit mode; this is like pressing 1-2-3/W's EDIT key (F2), except that the cursor flashes at the location where you clicked, rather than the end of the text.

3. Double-click on the word *going* and then press the delete key.

4. Double-click on the word to and type the word *done* and press the spacebar once. The selected word, to, disappears as soon as you type the letter *d* in done.

5. Press Ctrl-RightArrow to move one word to the right—after the word edit. Alternatively, you could have pressed End, which always takes you to the last character in the line in Edit mode.

6. Now type *ing* and press Enter. Cell A1 should now contain the text, *This is the text that I am done editing*.

7. If you prefer the way the text was before you edited it use the Undo command. Click the Edit menu to view the commands it contains. Note that several commands have accelerator keys to their right, including Alt-Backspace for Undo. You could just click on the Undo command, but let's try using an accelerator key. Press the Alt key to close the menu and then press Alt-Backspace. The text is restored to its former self. Think twice before you Undo: in 1-2-3/W you can't reinstate the work that you undo.

Clipboard Basics

The Clipboard is a facility that remembers data that you cut or copy. You choose Edit Paste to copy the contents of the Clipboard back into a document.

Three editing commands are common to most Windows applications: Edit Cut, Edit Copy, and Edit Paste.

When you Cut or Copy text or graphics, the selected data is placed on Windows' *Clipboard*. When you choose Edit Paste, the Clipboard's contents are duplicated at the current location, for example the current spreadsheet cell or at the insertion point in a word-processing document.

The term *cut-and-paste* is commonly used to describe *copy-and-paste* operations, but it's important not to confuse copying with cutting. Edit Cut removes the original selection before placing it in the Clipboard. Edit Copy leaves the original selection in place, *and* it copies the selection on the Clipboard.

Some other Clipboard details:

- Ctrl-Insert is the shortcut for Edit Copy.

- Shift-Delete is the shortcut for Edit Cut.

- Shift-Insert is the shortcut for Edit Paste.

- When you cut or copy something to the Clipboard, or when you exit Windows, the Clipboard "forgets" its previous contents.

- Many applications provide an Edit Clear command. This command, like pressing the Delete key, erases the current selection but does not affect the Clipboard.

- You can paste the same Clipboard contents as many times as you like.

- The Clipboard isn't just a holding area—it's a real application. The Clipboard utility is in the Main group, and it displays the Clipboard's current contents in a variety of formats, and it lets you save the contents directly to a file.

Try It: Clipboard Basics

Let's try out Windows' essential editing commands.

1. Enter the word *Windows* in Cell A1.

2. With the cell pointer in cell A1, choose Edit Copy (select the Copy command from the Edit menu).

(continued)

> 3. Move the mouse pointer to cell A8, and click and drag to cell A9. Range A8..A9 should be selected.
> 4. Choose Edit Paste. The contents of cell A1 should now also appear in cells A8 and A9.
> 5. Click the mouse in cell A9 to make it the current cell. Choose Edit Cut from the menu. The contents of cell A9 disappear, but they are stored in the Clipboard.
> 5. Click the mouse in cell A10. Press Shift-Insert, which is the accelerator key for Edit Paste. The text you cut from cell A9 now appears in A10.
> 6. Click the mouse in cell A13, and press Shift-Insert again. Remember that you can keep pasting the same data from the Clipboard until you cut or copy something else.

Moving Among Applications

The easiest way to switch from 1-2-3/W to another application, such as Program Manager, is to click the other application's window. Unfortunately, open application windows may obscure your view of the application that you want to switch to. Rather than minimizing or resizing your application windows, you can call on the Task List to help you make the switch.

When you select the Switch To command from an application Control menu, the Task List appears. The Task List presents a list of all open applications.

Windows provides two shortcuts that also bring up the Task List: pressing Ctrl-Escape or double-clicking the desktop. Remember that the desktop is the area under the open windows; double-clicking within a window, even the Program Manager's window, won't call up the Task List. Also, double-clicking the desktop won't call up the Task List if Program Manager is the only application in use.

One of the great things about Windows computing is that you can easily switch between applications.

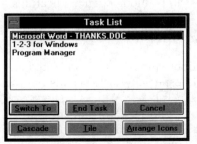

Figure 2-12. The Windows Task List. Pressing Ctrl-Esc is an easy way to bring up a list of your currently running applications. Double click on any item in the list to switch to that application.

Once the Task List appears, use the Arrow keys to highlight the appropriate application's name and press Enter. Or double-click the name.

Try It: Switching Tasks, Closing Applications, and Exiting Windows

Let's use the Task List to move from application to application. Then we'll try two different techniques for closing an application. When we finish, we'll exit Windows and return to a DOS prompt.

1. Click 1-2-3/W's application Control icon (the large dashlike icon on the left of its title bar). Note the accelerator keys, Alt-F4 for Close and Ctrl-Escape for Switch To.

2. Click the Switch To command.

3. The Task List should contain at least two entries, 1-2-3 for Windows and Program Manager. Double-click on Program Manager's name to make it the active application.

4. Press Ctrl-Escape to bring up the Task List. Double-click on 1-2-3/W's name to make it the active application. Or if 1-2-3/W is visible underneath Program Manager, click within its window.

5. Press Alt-F4 to close (exit) 1-2-3/W. Click the No button when 1-2-3/W asks if you want to save all files.

6. Double-click Program Manager's application Control icon to exit Windows. Note the check box option Save Changes. If this is checked, Program Manager will remember changes—such as resizing group windows—that you made in this session with Windows. Choose OK to return to a DOS prompt.

Windows provides two additional ways to switch among open applications:

- Alt-Escape switches to the next application window or minimized application icon.

- Alt-Tab switches to the next application window, and it restores any minimized applications. This option is especially fast, because if you keep holding the Alt key and release the Tab key, Windows shows you just the title bar of the next application. It doesn't "repaint" the rest of the window, so you can keep pressing Tab to rapidly cycle through the open applications as long as the Alt key remains depressed.

> It's not uncommon for one application to "hang up" Windows, forcing you to reboot the computer by pressing Ctrl-Alt-Delete or by turning the computer off and then on again. Because of this risk, it's a good idea to save your documents frequently, especially before you switch applications.

DOS Meets Windows

Most DOS applications can run under Windows. Some run without a hitch and others require special accommodations. For details on configuring DOS applications to run successfully under Windows, see the *More About Applications* chapter of the Windows User's Guide.

To make the most of DOS applications under Windows and to troubleshoot problems, you may need to use a PIF file (Program Information File). The PIF editor in the Accessories group lets you create and modify PIF files. A PIF file specifies many technical details about how a given DOS application should run under Windows.

If you plan to run DOS applications, note the following:

- If you know the precise file name and directory location of the DOS application, you can run it via Program Manager's File Run command.
- If you don't know the file name, you can use Windows' File Manager to locate and run the application.
- To get to a DOS prompt without exiting Windows, open the Main group and run the DOS Prompt application. Type *Exit* at the DOS prompt to return to Windows.
- If you want to return to Windows without quitting the DOS session, use one of the windows-switching methods described in the previous section.
- Beware of utilities that alter DOS's File Allocation Table! This includes DOS's CHKDSK/F command and some file-recovery utilities. Make sure the disk utility you're planning to use is Windows-safe. Otherwise files may be lost or damaged. If you're not sure whether a program performs low-level disk operations, play it safe: exit Windows, rather than calling up a DOS window, before you run the program.
- Don't reboot! Although your screen might look like an ordinary DOS screen, you may have several Windows applications and documents open. If you reboot, your work may be lost or damaged.

Windows doesn't mean giving up all of your old DOS applications or the familiar DOS Command line.

The DOS prompt utility in the Main group lets you perform command-line file management. You type exit to return to Windows.

- Pressing Alt-Enter toggles a DOS window between full-size and windowed display.

- When you use Windows to run a DOS program in a full-screen mode, you can bring up an application Control Menu by pressing Alt-space. Note the additional menu choices, Edit and Settings, which help Windows trade data with DOS applications and allow you to change the way the DOS session works, for example, making the DOS application appear in a resizable window. Another important feature of the Settings menu's dialog box is the Terminate button. If your DOS application locks up, you can use this feature to quit DOS and return to Windows—without rebooting.

- DOS applications that run in graphics mode—including Harvard Graphics, Lotus Freelance for DOS, 1-2-3 Release 3.x, and even 1-2-3 Release 2.x when you use the WYSIWYG or Allways add-in or when you display a graph—do not display properly in a resizable window. Run these in a full-screen mode only.

- Avoid running TSR (terminate-and-stay-resident) DOS utilities with Windows. These are DOS programs that stay in memory and pop up at the press of special keys, and they can conflict with Windows. If you are hooked on a particular TSR program, check with its publisher to see if it behaves well under Windows.

Customizing Windows

You can customize the Windows environment to suit your needs and tastes.

As you get more comfortable with Windows, you'll probably want to explore the many ways of customizing the environment.

The following hints should help you get you started:

- The Control Panel utility in the Main group gives you several options for customizing Windows. For example, it lets you switch among currently installed printer drivers, set the speed of communications ports, and change Windows' color scheme. It even lets you choose a graphics file to use as "wallpaper," to dress up the Windows desktop.

- The Windows Setup utility lets you load Windows drivers that you neglected to choose during Windows' installation process. For example, if you need to run Windows with a different kind of printer or network than you initially specified, run Windows Setup and select the appropriate drivers. Make sure you have the Microsoft Windows disks handy, because the Windows Setup program may need files from these disks.

- Program Manager's File New command lets you create your own groups and add program item icons. You can add program item icons for DOS applications, as well as for Windows applications.

- Program Manager's File Properties command lets you change settings, such as the name, of a group or program item icon.

- The File Properties command also lets you assign a different icon to an application and it lets you indicate the equivalent DOS command that Windows should execute when you "run" the icon. A program item icon can invoke COM, EXE, BAT, or PIF files. It can even load a document, if the application lets you specify a startup document in the command line.

- You can create multiple Program items icons for the same application, each of which calls a different startup document. However, if you run more than one of these program item icons, Windows will try to run an additional "session" of the application.

- You can copy a program item icon if you want to invoke it from various group windows. For example, you might want fast access to the DOS prompt from the Lotus Applications group window. To copy a program item icon, hold Ctrl while you drag the icon from one group window to another group window or group icon. If you don't hold the Ctrl key while you drag the icon, you move rather than copy the icon.

Program Manager Pointers

When you're just starting out with Windows, Program Manager can be a bit confusing. These tips will help you keep on track:

- Although Program Manager is central to many Windows functions, it behaves much like any Windows application program. But remember that when you close Program Manager, you exit Windows.

- Avoid confusing Program Manager's window with the group windows it may contain. Group windows always appear within Program Manager's window. It's frustrating, for example, to close Program Manager when you really intended to close a group window.

(continued)

(continued)

- Program Manager is much easier if you control it with a mouse rather than with the keyboard.

- The About Program Manager command in Program Manager's Help menu displays important status information. It identifies, for example, how much memory is available and which version of Windows you have. It also indicates whether Windows is running in 386 Enhanced mode or in the less-sophisticated Real or Standard modes. Ordinarily, Windows runs in the most advanced mode possible on a given machine: 386 Enhanced mode on all 386- and 486 series computers; Standard mode on 286 -class machines; and Real mode on 8088/8086-class machines. For more on Windows' operating modes, see the Windows User's Guide.

- The Program Manager's File Delete command simply removes a group or program item icon. It does not erase applications or documents from the disk.

- If you need to copy, delete, locate, or otherwise maintain documents or applications, use Windows' File Manager application, which you'll find in the Main group. Note that in File Manager you can double-click on the name of a WK3, WK1, or WKS file to run 1-2-3/W and open that file.

Part II
Creating Worksheets with 1-2-3/W

3

Build a Worksheet the Windows Way

Many worksheet projects require only a handful of operations. You usually need to enter and edit text (labels), numeric values, and formulas and to perform basic formatting. And, of course, you'll want to save and print your work.

Even if you're relatively new to 1-2-3, you probably know how to use traditional 1-2-3 keystrokes to perform these basic worksheet tasks. But to exploit 1-2-3/W's special features, you need to master some new techniques.

In this chapter on spreadsheet basics, and in the following one on spreadsheet enhancements, you'll learn how to make a functional worksheet using 1-2-3/W's Windows-style menu commands, SmartIcons, and keyboard shortcuts and then how to turn the worksheet into a professional-looking report. In the process, you'll develop a set of core skills that will prepare you for the advanced features that lie ahead.

Once you know the new Windows-oriented methods along with the 1-2-3 Classic commands, you can choose whichever methods are most convenient and most effective for the task at hand. But if you overlook 1-2-3/W's new worksheet essentials, you'll miss out on the finer points that make 1-2-3/W a truly superior spreadsheet, and you'll be ill-prepared to master the more advanced techniques.

The example for the next two chapters is a simple sales worksheet for a manufacturer of baseball bats. When you complete the exercises in these chapters, the spreadsheet will look like Figure 3.1.

In this chapter you will learn:

- *How to enter and edit labels, values, and formulas in a 1-2-3/W worksheet*

- *How to copy and clear data in 1-2-3/W*

- *How to open, save, and print a 1-2-3/W worksheet*

- *How to use SmartIcons and other shortcut techniques*

	Bubba's Bat Corporation					
Material	Units	Cost	Price	Total Cost	Gross	Net
Oak	130	$8.00	$14.00	$1,040.00	$1,820.00	$780.00
Pine	200	9.95	13.00	1,990.00	2,600.00	610.00
Aluminum	350	5.00	6.50	1,750.00	2,275.00	525.00
Graphite	120	9.50	15.00	1,140.00	1,800.00	660.00
Total	800			$5,920.00	$8,495.00	$2,575.00

Source: September Flash Report

Figure 3.1. The BATS.WK3 sales worksheet example. In this chapter you'll learn how to use 1-2-3/W's new techniques to make this simple worksheet. In the next chapter, you'll learn how to enhance the worksheet with a variety of type styles, borders, and shades.

Starting a 1-2-3/W Worksheet

It's time to fire up 1-2-3/W and get some data into the worksheet.

If you want to start Windows with 1-2-3/W already running, enter win c:\123w\123w. *If you installed 1-2-3/W in a different directory, type its path instead of C:\123w.*

1. Run Microsoft Windows.

   To run 1-2-3/W you must first start Windows.

   If your computer automatically loads Microsoft Windows upon startup, proceed to step 2. If your computer starts up with a DOS prompt, such as C> or C:\>, type *win* and press Enter.

   Windows should start up, and the Program Manager window should be visible.

1-2-3 for Windows

Figure 3.2. The 1-2-3/W program item icon. Double-clicking this icon starts 1-2-3/W.

2. Find the 1-2-3/W program item icon which is shown in Figure 3.2.

   Before you can run 1-2-3/W, you need to open the group that contains the 1-2-3/W application icon. Ordinarily, this is the Lotus Applications group.

   Mouse: Position the tip of the mouse pointer on the Lotus Applications group and double-click. The group window should now be open, and the 1-2-3/W icon should be visible. If you can't see the 1-2-3/W icon, scroll down the window by clicking the mouse pointer repeatedly on the window's ScrollDown arrow until the icon appears.

   Keyboard: Press Ctrl-Tab or Ctrl-F6 until the Lotus Applications group icon is selected, and then press Enter. If you can't see the 1-2-3/W icon in the group window, scroll down the window by pressing the Down-Arrow key repeatedly until the icon appears.

3. Start 1-2-3 for Windows.

   Mouse: Double-click the 1-2-3/W program item icon.

   Keyboard: Use the Arrow keys to select the 1-2-3/W icon and press Enter.

   1-2-3/W should start up, and an Untitled worksheet should be open as shown in Figure 3.3.

4. Save first.

   It's a good habit to name a new file as soon as you create it. Then you won't run the risk of forgetting to assign it an appropriate name later on. Use 1-2-3/W's File Save As command, rather than File Save. If you save a new (Untitled) worksheet with The File Save command, 1-2-3/W assigns it a generic file name, such as FILE0001.WK3.

   Mouse: Click the mouse on the File menu choice at the top of the 1-2-3/W window, and click on the Save As command. Type *BATS* and then click the OK button (or press Enter).

   Keyboard: Press Alt-F to select the File Menu. Then choose A for Save As. Type *BATS* and press Enter.

   The title bar of the document window now says BATS.WK3.

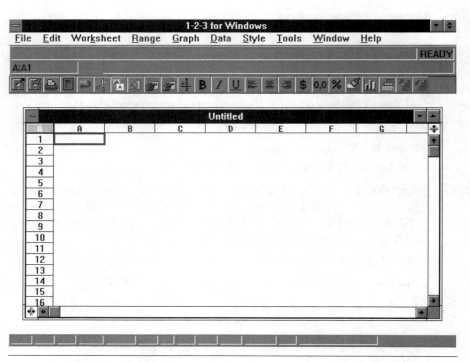

Figure 3.3. 1-2-3/W with an Untitled worksheet.

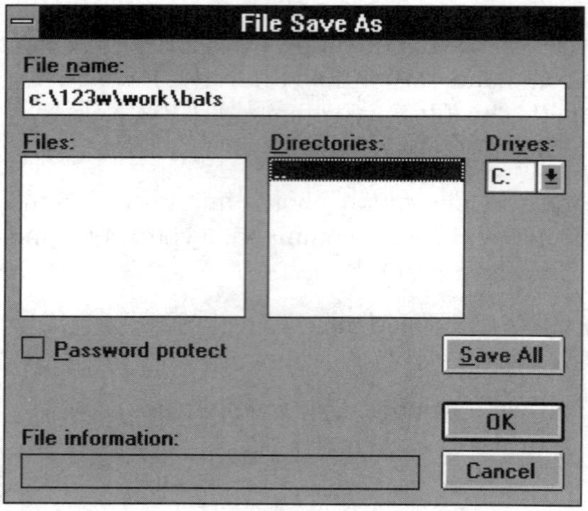

Figure 3.4. The File Save As dialog box.

Name That File

When you choose File Save As to name a new worksheet, 1-2-3/W suggests a default file specification: a drive, directory path, and file name, such as C:\123W\WORK\FILE0001.WK3. This file specification disappears as soon as you start to type a new file name. If you enter a file name without a drive and directory path, 1-2-3/W saves your new file in the default location. The File Save As dialog box is shown in Figure 3.4.

If you want to replace only part of the file specification, drag the mouse to select the part you want to replace. The selected text will disappear when you press Delete or type a character.

If you're schooled in the 1-2-3 Classic File commands, such as /File Save, you may find Windows' file-management dialog boxes a bit frustrating. In particular, you'll have to go easy on the Escape key: If you use it to clear a file specification, you'll discover that it cancels the dialog box altogether.

But as you work with more Windows applications, you'll appreciate having a standard way of naming and finding files. And you'll find that these file-related dialog boxes are quite convenient. In the box titled "Conversing with a File Dialog Box," we'll explore how these dialog boxes help you specify drives, directories, and file names.

---

5. Enter the row headings.

   Let's enter some labels in column A of the BATS worksheet.

   Enter the labels shown in range A1..A6 of Figure 3.5. After you type each label, use the DownArrow key to move the cell pointer down the column. To enter the label in cell A6, type two spaces, type *Total*, and press Enter.

   If you want to cancel an entry you've started typing, press Escape. If you want to delete the character you've just typed, press Backspace. If you catch a mistake after you enter data in a cell, you can always re-enter the cell; the new entry will replace the old one. Later in this chapter, you'll learn how to edit cell contents in 1-2-3/W.

6. Enter the column headings.

   Now we'll enter labels in row 1. To start, we need to move the cell pointer to cell B1.

   Mouse: Click in cell B1. If the computer beeps, you probably didn't finish entering the label in cell A6, so press Enter and try again.

   Keyboard: Press the Home key and then press the RightArrow key once.

Now enter the labels shown in range B1..F1 of Figure 3.5. Don't worry if you can't see all of the text in cell E1. We'll fix that in a moment.

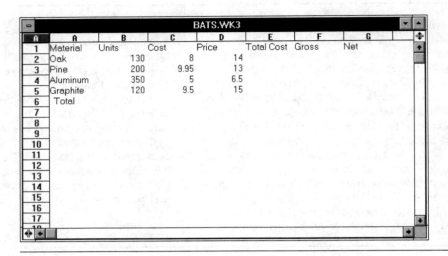

Figure 3.5. The row and column headings for the sales worksheet.

7. Get back home.

    We need to move the cell pointer back to cell A1.

    Mouse: Click the letter A that appears above the row numbers.

    Keyboard: Press the Home key.

8. Enter the values.

    Now enter the data in range B2..D5. A little bit later, we'll reformat these cells so the numbers align better.

9. Save the file again.

    Since we've already named this file by choosing File Save As, we can save it faster this time, by choosing File Save.

    Mouse: Click File and then click Save.

    Keyboard: Press Alt-F to call up the File menu and then press S to select save.

The worksheet is beginning to take shape. We've completed the basic layout and entered all the headings and numbers.

But if we need to change these entries, how can we avoid completely retyping them? In the next section, we'll explore cell-editing techniques, 1-2-3/W–style.

What Is That Letter in the Corner?

The letter that appears in the upper-left corner of a 1-2-3/W worksheet is not a column letter. It's a sheet letter. BATS.WK3 has only one sheet— sheet A. You create 3D worksheets by inserting sheets B,C,D, and so on, into your 1-2-3/W files.

In 1-2-3/W, and in 1-2-3 Releases 3.x, a sheet letter precedes references to cells and ranges.

For example, cell A1 in this sheet is actually named A:A1, and range A1..A6 is really A:A1..A:A6. However, to simplify typing, you can leave off the sheet letter when you refer to cells and ranges that reside in the current sheet.

Save Early and Often

Occasionally, Windows or an application running under Windows may make your computer "crash" or freeze up, forcing you to reboot. The error message *Unrecoverable Application Error* has spelled doom for untold hours of work.

If you're in the habit of saving frequently, restarting Windows is no big deal. The periodic time-out you take to save your files will save you a lot of time and frustration in the long run. You should save your file or files after you enter more data than you'd want to retype, especially before you switch applications and before you print. You should also save after you specify a series of settings, such as cell formats and graphics and print settings. And, of course, you should save your work before you close the document or exit the application.

The only time you shouldn't save is when you're not sure you want your latest revision to overwrite the version on disk. In such cases, use File Save As instead of File Save.

Editing Cells in 1-2-3/W

Data entry isn't an exact science. Sometimes you catch a mistake or change your mind after you press the Enter key.

To the rescue are 1-2-3/W's *edit line* and the EDIT key (F2). They let you alter cell entries without retyping everything in the cell.

1-2-3/W merges traditional 1-2-3 editing methods with those of Windows to provide a number of new editing features. In the exercises ahead, we'll explore a variety of shortcuts for fixing, instead of replacing, your cell entries.

The Edit Line and the EDIT Key

The edit line comprises the fourth line in the *control panel*, the area at the top of the 1-2-3/W workspace. The left side of the edit line contains the *address box*, which identifies the location, format, and style of the current cell. The *edit box* takes up most of the remainder of the edit line, extending to the right-hand edge of 1-2-3/W's window.

When you enter or edit information in a cell, your typing appears in the edit box, and two buttons appear in the edit line: a green check-mark and a red *X*. These are the *Confirm* and *Cancel buttons*. You click the check-mark to enter the contents of the edit box into the cell. To abandon your changes, you click the X. These buttons are simply point-and-click equivalents for, respectively, the Enter and Escape keys.

When you need to select a particular cell, use the address box to make sure the cell pointer is in the appropriate location.

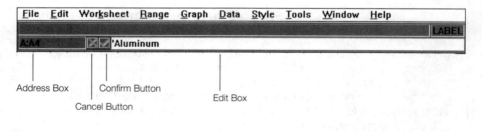

Figure 3.6. Like Caesar's Gaul, the edit line is divided into three parts: the address box, the Confirm and Cancel buttons, and the edit box.

When you're not entering or editing data, the edit box displays the contents of the current cell. If the cell contains a formula, the edit line displays the formula, not the value it calculates. The easiest way to determine whether a cell contains a formula is to position the cell pointer in the cell and look in the edit line.

> ### An Entire Novel in a Single Cell?
>
> 1-2-3/W, like Release 3.x, lets you enter up to 512 characters in a cell, more than twice the 240-character limit of earlier releases. But unlike Release 3.x's edit line, 1-2-3/W's edit box does not expand to multiple lines to help you view long labels. So you may want to keep cell entries to a moderate length.
>
> In any case, it's rarely desirable to cram large numbers of characters into one cell. It's hard to read or fix a formula or label that goes on for dozens, let alone hundreds, of characters.
>
> Instead, use multiple cells to construct your epic formula or label, and then reference these in the cell where you want to put them all together. For more on numeric and string (label) formulas, see Chapter 6, *Labels, Values, and Formulas*.

Edit Mode

Edit mode lets you use the mouse or navigation keys to move character-by-character. In Ready mode, which is 1-2-3/W's normal mode, you move cell-by-cell.

1-2-3/W offers two mouse techniques for invoking Edit mode, in addition to the traditional EDIT key method. You can double-click a cell, or you can click or drag in the edit box to commence editing.

Double-clicking a cell is like pressing EDIT (F2): The insertion point, Windows' flashing vertical cursor, appears at the end of the text. When you invoke Edit mode by clicking the mouse in the edit box, the insertion point appears wherever you click the mouse.

No matter what method you use to start Edit mode, you can use any of the editing keys listed in Table 3.1. Note that in 1-2-3/W, Tab, Ctrl-Right, Shift-Tab, and Ctrl-Tab move you one word at a time, regardless of the word's length. In other versions of 1-2-3, these keys move you five characters at a time.

Most often you switch into Edit mode from Ready mode, but you can also invoke it from the number- and formula-entering modes, Value and Point, or from the text-entry mode, Label. Also, if you enter an "illegal" formula, such as @PIE instead of @PI, 1-2-3/W forces you into Edit mode so that you can make amends.

When 1-2-3/W behaves "strangely," it's often because you are not in the mode that you thought you were in. To find out what the current mode is, see the Mode indicator above the right-hand side of the edit line.

You can turn a formula into the value that it currently displays by using the EDIT key: Select the cell, press EDIT (the F2 key), and then press CALC (the F9 key). After you press Enter or click Confirm, the cell's value will no longer change automatically.

Key	Effect
RightArrow	Moves one character to the right
LeftArrow	Moves one character to the left
Home	Moves to the first character
End	Moves to the last character
Tab or Ctrl-Right	Moves one word to the right
Shift-Tab or Ctrl-Left	Moves one word to the left
Delete	Deletes the character to the right of the insertion point or the current selection
Backspace	Deletes the character to the left of the insertion point or the current selection

Table 3.1. 1-2-3/W Editing keys.

Unlike the cursors in other versions of 1-2-3/W, the Windows insertion point always appears *between* characters, not *under* a character. You press Backspace to delete the character to the left of the insertion point, and you press Delete to remove the character to the right.

If you want to delete or replace several characters, click and drag through the characters or hold down the Shift key while you press navigation keys such as RightArrow and LeftArrow. Once the characters have been selected, they disappear as soon as you type a character or press Backspace or Delete. If you make the wrong selection, deselect by clicking the mouse elsewhere in the edit box or by pressing the RightArrow or LeftArrow key, without the Shift key.

Making the Changes

In 1-2-3/W, you can invoke edit mode by double-clicking a cell.

Now let's try out a variety of 1-2-3/W editing techniques.

1. Get ready to edit.

    We learn that our pine bats are now being marketed to an upscale clientele, so the product is now called Executive Pine. Let's edit cell A3 to add the word *Executive*, instead of retyping the entire label.

    Mouse: Double-click the mouse on cell A3.

    Keyboard: Use the Arrow keys to highlight cell A3 and press the EDIT key (F2).

1-2-3/W goes into Edit mode, and the insertion point appears after the word *Pine*.

2. Get to the start of the cell entry.

    Note that the first character is an apostrophe label prefix, which indicates that this cell contains a left-aligned label. We need to add the new text to the right of the apostrophe. For more on label prefixes, see the following chapter.

    Mouse: Click in between the apostrophe and the letter P. Now type the word *Executive* and one space.

    Keyboard: Press Home, and then move the insertion point one character to the right by pressing the RightArrow key. Now type *Executive* and one space.

    The edit line now displays the new product name, *Executive Pine*.

3. Confirm the entry.

    We're through editing this cell. Let's tell 1-2-3/W to go ahead with the changes.

    Mouse: Click the Confirm button (the green check-mark).

    Keyboard: Press Enter

    A3 now contains the label *Executive Pine*.

4. Replace selected characters.

    The boss calls to inform you that the company sells *granite* bats, not *graphite* bats. Let's make the requisite change in cell A5.

    Mouse: Click cell A5 to select it. Move the mouse pointer to the edit box and drag to select the *ph* in *Graphite*. Now type the letter *n* and click the Confirm button.

    Keyboard: Use the Arrow keys to select cell A5, and press EDIT (F2). Press the LeftArrow key three times, and then hold down the Shift key while you press LeftArrow two more times. Now type the letter *n* and press Enter.

    Our editing alchemy has turned *Graphite* into *Granite*.

> ## What to Do to Enable Undo
>
> Exercises throughout this book assume that you have 1-2-3/W's Undo feature enabled. Enabling Undo helps you survive all manner of worksheet mistakes. The Tools User Setup command lets you see whether Undo is enabled and adjust the settings as you see fit. Unless your machine is severely constrained in available memory, you'll want the convenience and safety of the Undo feature available at all times. If Undo is not enabled, choose the Enable Edit Undo option, and then choose the Update button from the Tools User Setup dialog box and select OK.

5. Undo the change.

   The company president overheard the boss's call. She fires him on the spot and puts you in charge. Your first duty is to put a stop to this silly business about granite bats. Since it was the very last change, you can simply undo it.

   Mouse: Choose Undo from the Edit menu.

   Keyboard: Press Alt-Backspace.

6. Delete a selection.

   As your first official act, you start a back-to-basics program and nix the Executive Pine campaign.

   Mouse: Click cell A3 to select it. Double-click the word *Executive* in the edit line to select it. Note that the space following *Executive* is selected as well. Now press the Delete key to delete the selection, and click the Confirm button.

   Keyboard: Use the Arrow keys to select cell A3. Press EDIT (F2) and then the Home key. This sets the insertion point at the beginning of the text, to the left of the apostrophe label prefix. Press the RightArrow key once, and press Shift-RightArrow enough times to select the word *Executive* and the space after the word. Press the Delete key to delete the selection, and press Enter to confirm it.

There are a few editing commands we haven't tried yet. In the next set of exercises, we'll use Edit Clear, which is a variation on the 1-2-3 Classic command /Range Erase.

> ## What Else Is in the Control Panel?
>
> The first four lines of the 1-2-3/W workspace are 1-2-3/W's control panel, not to be confused with Windows' Control Panel utility. As explained earlier, the fourth line of 1-2-3/W's control panel is the edit line. But what are the others?
>
> The first line, the title bar, displays the application's name: 1-2-3 for Windows. On the left of the title bar is the 1-2-3 for Windows Control menu icon. On the right side of the title bar are icons for minimizing 1-2-3/W and for either maximizing the window or restoring it to a non-maximized size. When you browse through menu options, 1-2-3/W uses the title bar to display long prompts, which describe the highlighted menu choice.
>
> The second line in the control panel is the menu bar, which displays the main menu names: File, Edit, etc.
>
> The third line is the format bar, which displays formatting information for the current cell. The format bar shows such details as the column width, numeric format, and font of the current cell.

You'll learn about the Edit Clear Special and Edit Move Cells commands in Chapter 7. Edit Clear Special lets you remove certain cell attributes, such as the numeric format or type style, without removing the data. This command is a hybrid of the 1-2-3 Classic /Range Erase and /Range Format Reset commands and the Allways and WYSIWYG commands that remove styles and graphics from a cell.

The Edit Find command lets you search for, and optionally replace, labels and formulas. This command operates much like the Range Search commands of later versions of 1-2-3. For example, you might use Edit Find to locate a cell that contains an @SUM function. You could also use Edit Find to make an identical change to several values or formulas, for example, to replace *Fiscal Year 1994* with *Fiscal Year 1995* throughout a large worksheet. To see Edit Find in action, do the *Performing the Lookup* exercise in Chapter 9.

When you want to share data between 1-2-3/W and other applications, such as a word processor or a graphics program, use the Edit Paste Link and Link Options commands. For tips on using these commands, see the end of Chapter 9.

Entering Formulas and Copying Ranges

Let's enter a few formulas into the worksheet and then try some techniques—old and new—for copying them to other cells.

Don't forget the numeric keypad. On the right side of most keyboards is a keypad that features a large plus sign and other arithmetic operators. This keypad is especially convenient for right-handed mouse users.

1. Enter the first formula, total cost.

    We need to enter into cell E2 of the BATS.WK3 worksheet a formula that multiplies the units sold (cell B2) by the cost-per-unit (cell C2) to obtain the total cost of the oak bats.

    Mouse: Click in cell E2 and type a plus (+) to indicate that a formula follows. Then click on cell B2, type a multiplication symbol (*), and click on cell C2. Click the Confirm button, which is the green check-mark icon above the worksheet. If you make a mistake while building the formula, click the Cancel button, which is the red X icon, and start again.

    Keyboard: Type a plus (+) to indicate that a formula follows, and press the LeftArrow key three times to highlight cell B2. Then type a multiplication symbol (*) and press the LeftArrow key twice to highlight cell C2. Finally, press Enter. If you make a mistake while building the formula, press the Escape key and start again.

2. Enter the second and third formulas, gross sales and net profit.

    In cell F2 of the BATS.WK3 worksheet, now enter the formula for gross sales of bats. This time the formula should be units times price-per-unit: +B2*D2. To start, move the cell pointer to cell F2. Repeat the process in step 1, clicking on or highlighting cell D2 instead of cell C2.

    Next, enter the formula for net profit. Move the cell pointer to cell G2. Then enter the formula, which is gross sales minus total cost: +F2-E2.

	A	B	C	D	E	F	G
1	Material	Units	Cost	Price	Total Cost	Gross	Net
2	Oak	130	8	14	1040	1820	780
3	Pine	200	9.95	13			
4	Aluminum	350	5	6.5			
5	Graphite	120	9.5	15			
6	Total						
7							

Figure 3.7. The BATS.WK3 worksheet.

3. Copy with the Windows Clipboard.

    1-2-3/W's Edit menu offers two kinds of copying. One uses the Clipboard and the Edit Copy and Paste commands; the other, Edit Quick Copy, sidesteps the Clipboard. In this step, we'll try the former method.

> ## Clipboard Memory Tricks
>
> Possibly the three most commonly used accelerator keys are Ctrl-Insert for Edit Copy, Shift-Delete for Edit Cut, and Shift-Insert for Edit Paste. Memorizing these can save you a lot of time. But how do you remember which is which?
>
> It's easy to remember that Shift-Delete is the Edit Cut shortcut, because Edit Cut deletes the current selection before placing it in the Clipboard. You're more likely to mix up the other two, but If you remember that both Ctrl and Copy start with C and that both Shift and Paste include an S, you'll be able to keep them straight.

When you select a cell or a range of cells and choose Edit Copy or Edit Cut, Windows stores a copy of the selection in a holding area called the Clipboard. To copy the Clipboard's contents to another location, you select the place to copy to and then choose Edit Paste. All Windows applications support the Clipboard.

We want to copy the total cost formula we entered for oak bats so that we can find the total cost of each of our products.

Mouse: Click cell E2, the cell that contains the formula we want to copy. Choose the Copy command from the Edit menu. Next, drag the mouse to select range E3..E4. (We could also select E5, but just select E3..E4 for now.) Then choose Edit Paste. Now select cell E5, and choose Edit Paste again.

Keyboard: Use the Arrow keys to select cell E2, the cell that contains the formula we want to copy. To choose the Edit Copy command you could press Alt-E for Edit and then C for Copy, but this time try the standard Windows accelerator key for this command: Ctrl-Insert. Then move the cell pointer to cell E3. Press ABS (the F4 key), and press the DownArrow key two times and press Enter. Range E3..E4 should now be selected. (We could also select E5, but just select E3..E4 for now.) Next press Shift-Insert, which is the accelerator key for Edit Paste. Now move the cell pointer down to cell E5, and press Shift-Insert again.

This last step illustrates one of the benefits of using the Clipboard. You can paste the Clipboard's contents as many times as you wish. The data that you cut or copy to the Clipboard stay there until you copy or cut something else.

Instead of pointing to each cell when building a formula, you can simply type the formula into the cell. But pointing ensures that you reference the right cells.

To preselect a range using the keyboard, press the ABS key (F4) from Ready mode, hightlight the range, and press Enter.

If a dialog box is on top of cells you need to select, reposition it by dragging its title bar.

4. Make a Quick Copy.

   1-2-3/W's Edit Quick Copy command resembles the 1-2-3 Classic menu's Copy command. It works in a single step, and it does not use the Windows Clipboard. It presents a dialog box, in which you specify the Copy From and Copy To ranges.

   Let's use this command to copy the gross sales formula. Start by moving the cell pointer to cell F2.

   Mouse: Choose Quick Copy from the Edit menu. The From range, F2..F2, is correct, but this range is also the suggested To range. Since we want to copy to a new location, select the suggested To range to prepare to change it. Now, move the mouse pointer back to the worksheet and drag to select range F3..F5. (The dialog box hides temporarily when you start dragging, and it reappears when you release the mouse button.) Then click OK.

   Keyboard: Press Alt-E and then Q to choose Quick Copy from the Edit menu. The From range, F2..F2, is correct, so press Tab to highlight the To range. Press the DownArrow key. The dialog box temporarily disappears, and the cell pointer moves to cell F3. Type a period to anchor the range, and press the DownArrow key twice. Finally, press Enter twice—once to enter the To range, and once to choose OK.

When you use navigation keys to specify a range in a dialog box, the dialog box temporarily hides while you point to the appropriate cells. When you press Enter, the dialog box reappears.

5. Make a Classic copy.

   Now you've tried two new kinds of copying: using Edit Copy and Paste, and using Edit Quick Copy. Let's copy the net profit formula the old-fashioned way, using the /Copy command. Note that you cannot use the mouse to navigate the 1-2-3 Classic menus, but you can use the mouse to select the ranges that these commands ask you to specify.

   Move the cell pointer to cell G2. Then press the slash key (/). The 1-2-3 Classic menu window appears. Note that the greater-than (>) key also brings up the 1-2-3 Classic menus. Press C to choose Copy.

   Mouse: Click G2 to confirm it as the Copy From range. The Copy To prompt appears. Drag to select range G3..G5. The command is completed when you release the mouse button.

   Keyboard: The Copy From range is correct, so press Enter. Press the DownArrow key once, and anchor by typing a period. Then press the DownArrow key twice more and press Enter.

	A	B	C	D	E	F	G
1	Material	Units	Cost	Price	Total Cost	Gross	Net
2	Oak	130	8	14	1040	1820	780
3	Pine	200	9.95	13	1990	2600	610
4	Aluminum	350	5	6.5	1750	2275	525
5	Graphite	120	9.5	15	1140	1800	660
6	Total						

Figure 3.8. The BATS.WK3 worksheet after the total cost, gross sales, and net profit formulas in E2.G2 have been copied. With simple copying three formulas have begotten nine more.

6. Sum the sales.

   Now we need a formula to total the number of bats sold. Move the cell pointer to cell B6, which is where this formula belongs.

   We could use a lengthy addition formula to find out how many bats we sold: +B2+B3+B4+B5. But this would be a nuisance to type, especially if we had dozens of products to sum.

   As most 1-2-3 users know, the solution is the @SUM function. 1-2-3's many @functions help perform all manner of calculations, and 1-2-3/W supports all of them, along with a couple of new and enhanced ones. But for many applications, the only @function you need is @SUM. If we enter the formula @SUM(B2..B5) in cell B6, we'll find out the total units of all kinds of bats.

   First, let's enter the formula the conventional way.

   Mouse: Type *@SUM(* in cell B6, then drag to select range B2..B5. Finally type a close parenthesis (*)*), and press Enter or click the Confirm button.

   Keyboard: Type *@SUM(* in cell B6 and press the UpArrow key once. Next, type a period to anchor the range in cell B5. Press the End key once, and then the UpArrow key. (For more information on using the End key, see *Navigating Around the Worksheet* in Chapter 5.) Now press the DownArrow key once. If you want the range reference to read B2..B5 instead of B5..B2, press the period key twice, but this isn't necessary. Finally, type a close parenthesis (*)*) and press Enter.

   The total number of bats, which is 800, should appear in cell B6.

If you type an "at" sign (@) and then press NAME (the F3 key), 1-2-3/W displays a list of @functions.

6. Erase a cell—with a single key.

      In the next step, we'll try another method for building an @SUM formula. First, let's clear cell B6.

      With the cell pointer in B6, press the Delete key. Delete is the accelerator key for Edit Clear, which removes the selection but does not place it in the Clipboard.

SmartIcon Shortcuts

You can speed up many 1-2-3/W operations by clicking on an appropriate icon from the SmartIcon palette. Clicking an icon is usually faster than navigating the menus and dialog boxes.

This collection of icons may be displayed along the left, right, top, or bottom of the 1-2-3/W window, or it may appear as a floating window. It may also be hidden.

Figure 3.9. The SmartIcon palette. A simple click can perform a wide variety of 1-2-3/W tasks. If someone has customized the palette in your copy of 1-2-3/W, the collection of icons and its arrangement may differ.

By default, the SmartIcon palette appears at the top of the 1-2-3/W window. If the palette is not visible, choose Tools SmartIcons. When the palette is hidden, an X appears in the Hide Palette check box. To unhide the palette, remove the X by clicking the check box or by pressing Alt-H. Then click OK or press Enter.

No Mouse, No SmartIcons

If you don't use a mouse, you can't use the SmartIcon palette, which is described in the next exercise. Since you won't be rebuilding the @SUM formula via the SmartIcon palette, you need to bring back the formula you just deleted. Choose Edit Undo: Either press Alt-E for Edit and U for Undo, or use the accelerator key, Alt-Backspace.

The next couple of steps show how you can zoom through familiar tasks—such as entering an @SUM formula and copying cells—by clicking on a SmartIcon.

1. Sum with a SmartIcon.

   Locate the SmartSum icon, which is shown in Figure 3.10, and click it. 1-2-3/W automatically figures out which cells to sum, and it enters the correct formula, @SUM(B2..B5), into cell B6.

Figure 3.10. The SmartSum icon. Click this to automatically enter an @SUM formula into a cell. 1-2-3/W "guesses" which cells you want to sum. In most cases, this guess will be exactly the formula you want. If not, you can edit the formula, which is still faster than entering an @SUM from scratch.

2. Copy with a click.

   To get the grand totals for the total cost, gross, and net profit columns, we need to copy the formula from cell B6 into range E6..G6.

   But we don't want to copy the formula into cells C6 and D6. Summing unit costs doesn't make any sense, although the *average* cost and price might be useful data.

Figure 3.11. The icons, from left to right, for common editing commands: Edit Undo, Edit Cut, Edit Copy, Edit Paste, Edit Quick Copy, and Edit Move Cells.

Let's use the icon palette to speed up our copying. There are SmartIcons for Edit Copy and Edit Paste, as well as for Edit Quick Copy. Since we need to copy this formula only once, we'll use the Edit Quick Copy icon. If we needed to paste this formula into various parts of the worksheet, we would put it in the Clipboard via Edit Copy.

Make sure the cell pointer is in cell B6. Locate the Edit Quick Copy icon, which is the fifth icon in Figure 3.11. To make copying with the Edit Quick Copy icon as fast as possible, you don't see a dialog box when you click on the icon. Instead the current cell or selection is treated as the

From range and the mouse pointer turns into a pointing hand that resembles the SmartIcon you clicked. You can then click the pointer on one cell or drag it through a range of cells to define the To range. When you release the mouse button, the copies will appear in the selected range.

Now click the Edit Quick Copy icon with the left mouse button. The Mouse pointer turns into a pointing hand. When you release the mouse button, the copying is complete.

Next, drag the mouse to select range E6..G6.

This, indeed, is a very quick way to copy.

SmartIcon Tips

If you're unsure what a particular SmartIcon does, click it with the *right* mouse button. Remember that you use the left mouse button to run the icon. A prompt appears in 1-2-3/W's title bar describing what the icon does. If you drag through the palette with the right button depressed, you'll see prompts for all the icons in the palette.

If you want to change the position of the SmartIcon palette, choose Tools SmartIcons, select one of the Palette position options, and then press Enter or click OK.

If the SmartIcon palette on your screen is configured as a floating window, you can move the window by clicking anywhere within the palette and dragging it. If you click without dragging, though, you'll invoke the icon you clicked on. You can also change the size and shape of a floating palette by clicking and dragging one of its sides or corners.

The SmartIcon palette is highly configurable. You can decide which of the dozens of icons that come with 1-2-3/W should be in the palette, and you can even create SmartIcons of your own. See Chapter 18, *Mastering the SmartIcon Palette*, for more details.

More Help for the Mouseless

If you don't use a mouse, you'll have to perform this exercise a different way. Position the cell pointer in cell B6, press Alt-E and then Q to choose Edit Quick Copy. The From range, cell B6, is correct, so press Tab to move to the To range. Press the RightArrow key three times to get to cell E6, and then anchor the range with the period key. Press the RightArrow key two more times, and press Enter twice.

Format Basics

In the next chapter, you'll learn how to dramatically improve the appearance of the worksheet. In the meantime, a few enhancements will make this work-in-progress a little easier on the eye. First, we'll resize the window in which it appears and assign some proper formats to the numbers. We'll also align the column headings and widen the column with the longest label.

1. Widen the window.

    The BATS.WK3 window is not quite big enough to display all the data in the worksheet. Let's bring the entire worksheet into view.

    Mouse: Drag the right edge of the window to the right until all of column H is visible.

    Keyboard: Press Alt- (Alt-hyphen) to open BATS.WK3's Control menu. Type *S* for size. Press the RightArrow key several times (about eight), until the window is wide enough to display column G, and press Enter.

2. Format the numbers.

    The numbers in column B look fine, but the decimal alignment C2..G6 look pretty ragged. Let's see how the worksheet looks after we assign this range the Currency format with two decimal places. We'll use the Range Format command, which brings up a dialog box full of formatting options. But note that clicking the $ SmartIcon is a shortcut for choosing the Currency format with two decimal places.

    Mouse: Drag to select range C2..G6. Choose Range Format and select Currency from the Format list box. The default of 2 decimal places is appropriate, so click OK.

    Keyboard: Position the cell pointer in cell C2. Press ABS (F4) to anchor the range, and press End and then the RightArrow key. Press End again, then press the DownArrow key. Range C2..G6 should be selected. Press Alt-R for Range and F (or Enter) for Format. The Format list box is already highlighted, so press C to highlight Currency. The default of 2 decimal places is appropriate, so press Enter to choose OK.

When the mouse pointer turns into a double-arrow icon, you're in the right spot to resize a window. When you drag from the corners, the arrows are diagonal, indicating that you can change both the height and width of the window.

	A	B	C	D	E	F	G
				BATS.WK3			
	A	B	C	D	E	F	G
1	Material	Units	Cost	Price	Total Cost	Gross	Net
2	Oak	130	$8.00	$14.00	$1,040.00	$1,820.00	$780.00
3	Pine	200	$9.95	$13.00	$1,990.00	$2,600.00	$610.00
4	Aluminum	350	$5.00	$6.50	$1,750.00	$2,275.00	$525.00
5	Graphite	120	$9.50	$15.00	$1,140.00	$1,800.00	$660.00
6	Total	800			$5,920.00	$8,495.00	$2,575.00
7							

Figure 3.12. The Currency format clears up the decimal-alignment problem. But all the dollar signs clutter up the worksheet.

3. Fine-tune the format.

   The ragged-decimal problem is taken care of, but the data would be less cluttered if there weren't so many dollar signs. Let's replace the Currency format with the Comma format with two decimal places for rows 2 through 5.

   Mouse: Drag to select range C3..G5. Choose Range Format and click on the Comma format in the Format list box. The default of 2 decimal places is appropriate, so click OK.

   Keyboard: Position the cell pointer in cell C3. Press ABS (F4) to anchor the range, and press End and then the DownArrow key. Press End again, then press the RightArrow key and press Enter. Range C3..G5 should be selected. Press Alt-R for Range and F (or Enter) for Format. The Format list box is already highlighted, so type a comma to select the Comma format. The default of 2 decimal places is appropriate, so press Enter to choose OK.

If some or all of the data in a column appear as a series of asterisks, the column is too narrow. Either you need a wider column, or some erroneous data are causing unusually large numbers to appear.

A Roundabout Shortcut

Formatting the whole range and then reformatting the "middle" rows may seem inefficient, but it actually saves a step. If you assigned the Currency format to the first row, then assigned the Comma format to the middle rows, and finally assigned the Currency format to the last row, you would have performed three Range Format operations instead of two.

4. Align the headings.

   The worksheet will be easier to read if the headings are right-aligned over the numbers.

Figure 3.13. The Right-alignment SmartIcon. Click this to align a label along the right edge of a cell.

Mouse: Drag to select range B1..G1. Click the Right-alignment SmartIcon, shown in Figure 3.13, or choose Style Alignment, click the Align Label Right option, and click OK.

Keyboard: Move the cell pointer to cell B1. Press ABS (F4) to anchor the range, and press End and then the RightArrow key and press Enter. Range B1..G1 should be selected. Press Alt-S for Style and A for Alignment. Choose Alt-R for Right label-alignment, and press Enter.

The headings should now be more or less aligned with the numbers below them.

5. Change a column width.

   If you've changed 1-2-3/W's default font, you may not be able to see all of the column heading in cell E1, *Total Cost*. Even if you don't have any trouble viewing all of column E, try this exercise to learn how to widen columns in 1-2-3/W.

   Mouse: Position the mouse pointer in the worksheet frame, between the column letters E and F. When the pointer is in the correct position, it turns into a double-arrow. Drag to the right to widen the column—enough to allow two more characters to appear in column E.

   Keyboard: Move the cell pointer to any cell in column E. Note that both *Window* and *Worksheet* start with the letter *W*. Since the *k* in the Worksheet menu's name is underlined, Press Alt-K to choose Worksheet, and type *C* for Column Width. Press Tab to move to the box where you specify the width, type *11*, and press Enter.

   Note that unlike Releases 2.x and 3.x, 1-2-3/W provides a single menu command for changing the width of one or several columns. However, only the 1-2-3 Classic commands /Column Set-Width and/Column-Range Set-Width let you use the Arrow keys to adjust the width character by character.

> ### First Things First
>
> Often you have to make a few adjustments to label alignments and column widths to make the worksheet readable while you develop it. But don't spend a lot of time getting fancy. Just as you wouldn't paint and carpet a new house before the plumbing and wiring were finished, it's important to do spreadsheet tasks in the right order.
>
> The rules were different before the advent of spreadsheet publishing. It used to be that as soon as the headings, formulas, and sample data went in, the next task was to fiddle with column-widths and the alignment of labels.
>
> If you plan to take advantage of 1-2-3/W's font enhancements, however, you should postpone this tinkering. Different fonts, font sizes, and font enhancements all affect the alignment and width of data. The carefully customized alignments and widths that seem perfect at first will likely be wasted effort.
>
> Chapter 4, *Make It Look Good*, introduces a variety of techniques you can use to turn a drab worksheet into a handsome report.

Basic Printing

Printing in 1-2-3/W is at once similar to 1-2-3 printing and also quite different. You use Print ranges of cells as in other releases, but the look, feel, and features of 1-2-3/W's printing capabilities come directly from Windows. For example, 1-2-3/W's Install program doesn't ask you to identify your printer or printers, because 1-2-3/W uses Windows' printer drivers.

If your copy of Windows is properly configured, you're ready to print. Usually, you just issue a File Print command. But let's check out a few of 1-2-3/W's printing options enroute to the printout.

1. Check the printer setup.

    First, we'll use the File Printer Setup command to select, and if necessary, reconfigure the printer.

    You typically use the File Printer Setup command to switch among different printer settings if, for example, your computer is connected to more than one printer, or if your printer can switch among different printing modes, such as HP LaserJet emulation and PostScript. You also use this command to install new printer drivers. If your current printer settings are appropriate, you do not need to use this command before you print.

Mouse: Choose File Printer Setup. Click OK to confirm the setup.

Keyboard: Press Alt-F for File and T for Printer Setup. Press Enter to confirm the setup.

This command is an alternative to using Windows' Control Panel utility to specify print settings. Whether you choose these settings from the Control Panel utility or from 1-2-3/W, they remain in effect until you change them, even if you switch to another application or exit and restart Windows.

2. Check the page setup.

We'll use the File Page Setup command to check the way this document is set to print—landscape (sideways) or portrait.

Mouse: Choose File Page Setup. Click the Landscape option in the lower-right corner of the dialog box. Click OK.

Keyboard: Press Alt-F and G for File Page Setup. On the lower-right side of the dialog box are option buttons for landscape or portrait printing. Unless Landscape is already selected, press Alt-D to select it. Press Enter to choose OK.

3. Preview the printout.

We'll use the File Preview command to preview the printout on screen.

Mouse: Choose File Preview or click on the File Preview SmartIcon. If the dialog box is in the way of the range we want to print, range A1..G6, drag it aside by its title bar. Then drag the mouse to select range A1..G6 and click OK.

Keyboard: Press Alt-F and V for File Preview. Press the Home key and anchor the range with the period key. Now press End and then Home to highlight the "last" cell in the worksheet. Then press Enter twice.

Figure 3.14. The File Preview SmartIcon. You click on this icon to see on screen how your printout will look.

The preview shows a functional, if unassuming, worksheet. In the next chapter, we'll explore how to effectively arrange the worksheet on the page, but for now this worksheet does the job.

Material	Units	Cost	Price	Total Cost	Gross	Net
Oak	130	$8.00	$14.00	$1,040.00	$1,820.00	$780.00
Pine	200	9.95	13.00	1,990.00	2,600.00	610.00
Aluminum	350	5.00	6.50	1,750.00	2,275.00	525.00
Graphite	120	9.50	15.00	1,140.00	1,800.00	660.00
Total	800			$5,920.00	$8,495.00	$2,575.00

Figure 3.15. The completed sales worksheet. In Chapter 4, you'll learn how to enhance this worksheet by using simple spreadsheet-publishing techniques.

4. Print the worksheet.

   Now we'll use the File Print command to see our work on paper. Make sure your printer is turned on and on-line. If you don't have a printer available, you can bring up the File Print dialog box, but choose Cancel or press Escape instead of completing the command.

   Mouse: Choose File Print. Note that this command remembers the Print range we specified in the Print Preview command. Click OK.

Figure 3.16. The File Print SmartIcon

Keyboard: Press Alt-F for File and P for Print. Note that this command remembers the Print range we specified in the Print Preview command. Press Enter.

In a few moments, your printout should appear. If the worksheet does not print out, see Chapter 10, *Printing with 1-2-3 for Windows*.

File Management Basics

In addition to the work you do inside your documents, you have to manage the documents themselves. You've saved a file several times in this chapter, but you also need to know how to close and reopen a file and how to exit 1-2-3/W and Windows. You'll learn how to do all these operations in the exercises ahead.

Another important aspect of file management is understanding how 1-2-3/W stores your work. This knowledge helps you copy your worksheets to another disk without losing formatting information. It also helps you exchange files between 1-2-3/W and other versions of 1-2-3. At the end of this section is a discussion of these issues.

1. Close the file.

    Let's save the file one last time and then put it away.

    Mouse: Choose File Save. Then double-click the Control icon (the dashlike symbol) on the left of BATS.WK3 title bar.

    Keyboard: Press Alt-F for File and S for Save. Then choose Alt-F for File and C for Close, or use the accelerator key, Ctrl-F4.

    Note that if you try to close a file without saving your changes, 1-2-3/W will ask whether you want to save the file. It's safer, though, to save first, in case you click the wrong button as you close the file.

2. Open the file.

    You save your work, of course, so that you can use the file in the future. Let's use 1-2-3/W's File Open command to retrieve BATS.WK3. Like Release 3.x's File Open command, 1-2-3/W's File Open command opens an existing file without closing files that are already open. The older File Retrieve command closes the current file before it loads another.

    Mouse: Choose File Open. The file name BATS.WK3 should be visible in the Files list box. You could click on the file name and then click OK, but let's use a shortcut: Double-click the file name.

    Keyboard: Press Alt-F for File and O for Open. Then choose Alt-F to activate the Files list box. If BATS.WK3 is not the first file listed in your default directory, press the DownArrow key until the file name BATS.WK3 is highlighted. Then press Return.

    BATS.WK3 should reappear on your screen.

How To Converse With A File Dialog Box

Several 1-2-3/W commands—including File Open, File Save As, and File Combine From—bring up a dialog box. These dialog boxes contain a File Name box, in which you can type the desired file specification.

To navigate your disk drives a little more easily, you can use three controls that help you specify a file name and location: Files, Directories, and Drives.

The Files list box lets you specify the name of an existing file by double-clicking it. The specified name then appears in the File Name box.

The Directories list box lets you switch among directories. To switch to a subdirectory of the current directory, double-click the subdirectory's name. To back out one directory level, click the .. entry in the Directories list box.

To switch to a different disk drive, click on the Drives button. A list of drive names appears. Click on a drive name to select it.

If you have a file-access dialog box on screen and you want to use the keyboard to identify a file, press Alt and the underlined letter—F for Files, D for Directories, and V for Drives—or press Tab repeatedly to get to the desired control. Then use the Arrow keys to select an item. When the directory you want to switch to is highlighted, press Enter. But don't press Enter anywhere else in the dialog box until you finish specifying the file; outside the Directories list, Enter is the same as clicking OK.

3. Exit 1-2-3/W.

   Mouse: Double-click 1-2-3/W's Control icon.

   Keyboard: Press Alt-F for File and X for Exit, or use the accelerator key, Alt-F4.

   Since we haven't changed BATS.WK1, 1-2-3/W doesn't ask us if we want to save the file.

   You should now see Windows' Program Manager. If you want to exit the Program Manager and return to the DOS prompt, repeat the procedure you just used to quit 1-2-3/W. Then click OK or press Enter to confirm the dialog box that asks if you want to exit Windows.

Congratulations! If you've performed all the exercises in this chapter, you have all the basic skills needed to create a simple worksheet. The next chapter shows you how to beautify the worksheet with simple spreadsheet publishing.

Two Files for Every Document

In 1-2-3/W, *every* document consists of two files: the WK3 worksheet and the FM3 format file. If, for example, you save a file under the name CASHFLOW.WK3, 1-2-3/W also saves a file called CASHFLOW.FM3. The data and basic settings like column widths and cell formats are stored in the WK3 file. Other settings, such as row heights, type styles, borders, and graph enhancements, are stored in the FM3 file.

Whenever you copy files from disk to disk or from directory to directory, *make sure you copy both the worksheet file (WK3) and the format file (FM3)*. Do this even if you haven't consciously done any spreadsheet publishing. As you use 1-2-3/W, you'll want to adjust font styles and row heights, and you'll probably want to use in-sheet graphics as well. These and almost all the other techniques that you'll learn in the following chapter and in Chapter 12, *Enhancing Graphics*, use the settings maintained in the FM3 file.

If you use the worksheet file without its FM3 file, the document and its formatting are likely to get out of synch. 1-2-3/W creates a new FM3 file to go with the WK3 file you copied, and you can lose hours of styling work.

Copy Files Two-by-Two

If you use the DOS COPY command to copy a worksheet file, type a wildcard character for the file extension. For example, the command *COPY BUDGET95.* A:* copies both the WK3 file and its companion FM3 file. If you've saved a version of your worksheet in Release 2.x-compatible WK1 format, this command will also copy that version and its companion format file. To copy just the 1-2-3/W versions, type ??3 for the file extension. For example, type *COPY BUDGET95.??3 A:*.

For information on exchanging worksheets between 1-2-3/W, other versions of 1-2-3, and other leading applications, see Chapter 9, *Building Effective Applications*.

4

Make It Look Good

In the previous chapter you learned how to create a complete, functional worksheet with 1-2-3 for Windows. In this chapter, you'll explore techniques that will make your worksheet beautiful as well as brainy.

Why Neatness Counts

You're completely prepared for the board meeting. You've slaved over the numbers, and you're armed with spreadsheets that show how the company can save over $250,000 a year. Unfortunately, no one's listening to your eloquent presentation because they're too busy snickering at your bib overalls and wading boots.

Odds are you know how to dress for work. But do you know how to dress up your spreadsheets? Now that laser printers—with their near-typset-quality output—are the printing tool of choice, a plain-Jane spreadsheet can look plain amateurish. Even if a laser printer is beyond your budget, you can get similar results out of today's ink-jet and dot-matrix printers.

Compare the spreadsheets in Figures 4.1 and 4.2. The data are exactly the same, but the one in Figure 4.2 is much more pleasing to the eye. It uses a variety of fonts and font enhancements to draw attention to titles, totals, and such. And the borders around the data help the reader scan the rows and columns.

The dressed-up worksheet simply has more pizazz than its ill-clad predecessor. You can't help but think the analyst who put it together has a little more on the ball than the one who tossed off the indifferent one in Figure 4.1.

> *In this chapter you will learn:*
> - *How to use a variety of fonts and font styles*
> - *How to use borders, shades, and colors*
> - *How to use label prefixes to align text*
> - *How to set column widths and row heights*

Material	Units	Cost	Price	Total Cost	Gross	Net
Oak	130	$8.00	$14.00	$1,040.00	$1,820.00	$780.00
Pine	200	9.95	13.00	1,990.00	2,600.00	610.00
Aluminum	350	5.00	6.50	1,750.00	2,275.00	525.00
Graphite	120	9.50	15.00	1,140.00	1,800.00	660.00
Total	800			$5,920.00	$8,495.00	$2,575.00

Figure 4.1. The unadorned bat-sales worksheet, BATS.WK3.

Bubba's Bat Corporation

Material	Units	Cost	Price	Total Cost	Gross	Net
Oak	130	$8.00	$14.00	$1,040.00	$1,820.00	$780.00
Pine	200	9.95	13.00	1,990.00	2,600.00	610.00
Aluminum	350	5.00	6.50	1,750.00	2,275.00	525.00
Graphite	120	9.50	15.00	1,140.00	1,800.00	660.00
Total	800			$5,920.00	$8,495.00	$2,575.00

Source: September Flash Report

Figure 4.2. The bat-sales worksheet, with font enhancements, borders, and shading. The label alignments and column widths have also been fine-tuned.

> ### De Gustibus Non Disputandum Est
>
> The worksheet used in this chapter is simply an example. You probably have your own ideas about what makes a good-looking report, and by experimenting with 1-2-3/W's features, you'll soon be able to make spreadsheets that suit your taste.
>
> While there's a broad range of possibilities in spreadsheet design, there are three guidelines commonly accepted.
>
> - Figure out what you want to say, and emphasize that message. For example, if you want people to pay special attention to a given row or column, use shading, borders, or type styles to highlight that section.
> - Don't use too many different typefaces. Your spreadsheet will look like a ransom note if you use Helvetica, Times New Roman, Zapf Chancery, and New Century Schoolbook all in the same sheet. Instead, use different sizes and enhancements (such as bold or italic) of one or two type faces.
> - Don't use too many design elements. A spreadsheet riddled with every color, shade, and border design in the world can look more like a circus poster than a business report. Remember that the goal is to entice and impress your readers, not to shock them with special effects.

In this chapter, you'll learn the essential skills for making a good-looking spreadsheet with 1-2-3/W. Chapter 10 tells you how to exploit 1-2-3/W's printing features and how to troubleshoot printing problems. Chapter 11 introduces 1-2-3/W's extensive graphics tools.

And in Chapter 12, you'll learn how to add a variety of graphic elements, such as lines, arrows, and circles—along with "clip art" pictures—to get your messages across with style.

Before we get underway, it's worth pointing out that you can very easily get carried away with spreadsheet enhancement. This may sound unlikely to you, but it won't when you're up to two in the morning trying to get the styles *just right* before the big presentation. A refined spreadsheet helps deliver your message, but don't expect much sympathy if the accuracy of your spreadsheet or the quality of your analysis suffers because you're spending too much time becoming the Wyeth of the worksheet.

Now it's time to go wild jazzing up the worksheet. But not *too* wild.

Font Basics

Times and Times New Roman are serif fonts. Serifs are extra little strokes, such as the lines that may appear at the top and bottom of a capital I. (See Figure 4.3). The fonts Helvetica and Arial for example, are sans serif, meaning they do not include serifs. A well-accepted design idea is to use a sans serif font for titles and headings and a serif font for the body of a document, or vice versa.

1-2-3/W, like the WYSIWYG and Allways add-ins, lets you use up to eight fonts in a worksheet. For most practical purposes, you'll find that eight fonts are more than enough.

But what is a font anyway?

Arial 12 Point

Times New Roman 18 Point

Dom Casual 24 Point

Brush Script 32 Point

Bodoni Bold Cond. 40 Point

Figure 4.3. Samples of fonts that come with 1-2-3/W.

Definitions vary, but to 1-2-3/W a font is a typeface, such as Arial (or Helvetica), in a given type size, such as 10-point. That is, Arial 10-point is one font, Arial 18-point is another, and Times 12-point is yet another. (A point is a printing measure, approximately 1/72 of an inch.)

The fonts you choose add personality—appropriate or otherwise—to your printouts. 1-2-3/W comes with 13 Adobe fonts, including such as the stately and conservative Times New Roman (nearly identical to the well-known Times Roman) and the clean, modern-looking Arial (a variation on Helvetica), giving you a wide range of possibilities.

You can bolster this type collection with any of the several thousand Type 1 PostScript-compatible fonts that are available from Adobe and other vendors.

1-2-3/W's Style Font dialog box lets you choose one of the current set of fonts, and its Replace button lets you substitute a different font for one of the current eight. You select one of the available typefaces on your system and specify the desired size. Your fonts can range from a tiny 6 points to a massive 72 points.

You can use up to 8 fonts on a worksheet.

Applying Fonts to Your Worksheet

In the following set of exercises, you'll find out how to select among 1-2-3/W's default fonts and how to replace a currently loaded font with a different one of your choosing. You'll also learn various techniques for applying styling such as boldface and italics.

1. Get the worksheet ready.

    Retrieve the sales worksheet you created in the previous chapter by choosing File Open. See the box "Conversing with a File Dialog Box," near the end of the previous chapter, if you are unable to open the file. To make the worksheet easier to work with, let's maximize it so that it fills the entire 1-2-3/W window.

    Mouse: Click the Maximize icon, which is the up-arrow on the right side of the BATS.WK3 title bar.

    Keyboard: Press Alt- (Alt-hyphen) to activate the BATS.WK3 Control menu. Type X for Maximize.

    When you maximize the worksheet, its Control icon moves up into the menu bar, underneath 1-2-3/W's Control icon. At the right end of the menu bar is the Restore icon, which you can use to restore BATS.WK3 to its previous size.

2. Make room at the top.

    To make room for a title for this worksheet, insert three blank rows at the top.

    Mouse: Click and drag to select range A1..A3. Because three rows are selected, 1-2-3/W will insert three rows before the first row in this range, which is row 1. Choose Worksheet Insert, and since the Row option is selected, choose OK.

    Keyboard: Press Home to move the cell pointer to cell A1. Press ABS (F4) to anchor the range, press the DownArrow key two times and press Enter to select range A1..A3. Because three rows are selected, 1-2-3/W will insert three rows before the first row in this range, which is row 1. Press Alt-K to select the Worksheet menu (remember that W is reserved for the Window menu), and type I for Insert. Since the Row button is automatically selected, press Enter to choose OK.

Rows 1 through 3 are now blank (as shown in Figure 4.4), and the first cell with data is cell A4.

	A	B	C	D	E	F	G
1							
2							
3							
4	Material	Units	Cost	Price	Total Cost	Gross	Net
5	Oak	130	$8.00	$14.00	$1,040.00	$1,820.00	$780.00
6	Pine	200	9.95	13.00	1,990.00	2,600.00	610.00
7	Aluminum	350	5.00	6.50	1,750.00	2,275.00	525.00
8	Graphite	120	9.50	15.00	1,140.00	1,800.00	660.00
9	Total	800			$5,920.00	$8,495.00	$2,575.00
10							

Figure 4.4. The BATS.WK3 document after 3 rows have been inserted at the top.

Unless you assign a font to a cell, it is styled with the first font that appears in the Style Fonts dialog box.

3. Check out the styles.

   Let's select the column headings and then bring up the Style Font dialog box to see what fonts are available.

   Mouse: Click and drag to select range A4..G4. Then choose Style Font.

   Keyboard: Move the cell pointer to the cell A4. Then press ABS (F4) to anchor the range, press the End key and the RightArrow key and then press Enter to select range A4..G4. Then press Alt-S for Style and type F for Font (or press Enter).

   Note that the first font in the list is used in all cells, except those to which you assign a different font. If you replace the first font, all cells without a specific font assignment automatically change to the new font.

Make It Look Good 83

Don't Fire Until You See the Dark Selection Bar

It's easy to misunderstand the dotted-line box that appears around the first item in some dialog boxes. Such a box surrounds the first item in the Fonts list in the Style Fonts dialog box as shown in Figure 4.5.

The dotted-line box indicates that the Fonts list is the focus, or the active area, of the dialog box. But it does not mean that choosing OK will select the font that appears within this box. Immediately clicking OK after you bring up such a box is the same as choosing Cancel.

An item in the list is selected only when a dark bar highlights it. To select an item, you must click it with the mouse, use the navigation keys, such as DownArrow, or type the first character of an item in the list.

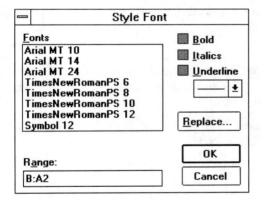

Figure 4.5. The Style Fonts dialog box. The Fonts list shows 1-2-3/W's currently available fonts. The Replace button allows you to replace any of these fonts.

---

4. Choose a style.

    Let's see how the column headings look in Times 12.

    Mouse: Click Times 12 in the Fonts list to select it, and then click OK.

    Keyboard: Press the DownArrow key enough times to select Times 12, and press Enter.

    The column headings in row 4 are now in the Times 12 font.

5. Make it bold.

    Let's see how the column headings look in boldface. Note that range A4..G4 is still preselected.

> **Changeable Times**
>
> Depending on how you've installed 1-2-3 for Windows and Adobe Type Manager, the widely used serif font generally known as Times Roman may be called either Times or Times New Roman. In the exercises that follow we will refer to either of these fonts as Times.

Many styling features are available from the SmartIcon palette. For example, you click the dark B icon for Bold, the slanted I icon for italics, or the underscored U for underlined text.

Figure 4.6. The SmartIcon palette contains icons for common styling tasks: B for bold, I for italics, and U for underline. Click once to select the style, click again to deselect it.

Mouse: The SmartIcon palette includes an icon for boldface type. This icon has a large, dark letter B. Click this icon or choose Style Font, then click the Bold check-box, and click OK.

Keyboard: Press Alt-S for Style and type F for Font. Press Alt-B to select the Bold check-box, and then press Enter to choose OK.

The column headings now appear in Times 12 bold.

6. Choose a simple style for the data.

   Next, let's select a less flashy style for the bulk of the data: Times 12, without the bold.

   Mouse: Drag to select range A5..G9.

   Keyboard: With the cell pointer in cell A5, press the ABS key (F4), the End key, and then the RightArrow key. Next, press End and then the DownArrow key, and press Enter. Range A5..G9 should be selected.

   Now choose the Times 12-point font, just as you did in steps 3 and 4, by invoking the Style Font menu and choosing Times 12.

   After you choose OK, range A5..A9 should appear in the same font as the column headings above this range, but in a lighter weight.

7. Make a subtle comment.

   This report comes courtesy of the corporate *Flash Reports* for the month of November. Let's identify this in our worksheet, in a style that sets it apart from the main data.

   In cell G11, enter *Source: November Flash Report*.

   Next, invoke the Style Font command and select Times 10 *and* the Italics check-box. Then choose OK.

8. Top it off with a title.

   We're going to type a title for the worksheet in cell A2. It may seem strange to put the title way off to the left, but as we'll see later on, this is the most efficient way to center a title above a 1-2-3/W worksheet. In the meantime, let's enter the title and assign it an appropriate font, 24-point Times.

   Move the cell pointer to cell A2, and enter *Bubba's Bat Corporation*. Your worksheet should look like Figure 4.7.

   Later in this chapter, in the Aligning Labels section, you'll use the labels from exercises 7 and 8 to perform some useful and little-known label-alignment tricks.

9. Customize the font set.

   In this step, we'll replace a default font that we don't need for this worksheet with one that we do need.

   First, choose Style Font. Alas, there is no Times 24. Fonts you don't need for this sheet, including puny little Times 6, get their own slots. But why not our Times 24? Don't get mad, get even: We'll replace the Times 6 font with Times 24.

   When you want to replace a font, don't bother to select it from the Style Font dialog box's Font list. That's not where you identify the font you want to replace. Instead, use an identical list called Current fonts, which appears after you choose the Replace button. To start, select the Replace button to bring up the Style Font Replace dialog box, which is shown in Figure 4.8. Choosing from this dialog box is much easier with a mouse, but keyboard instructions are included in case you don't have a mouse.

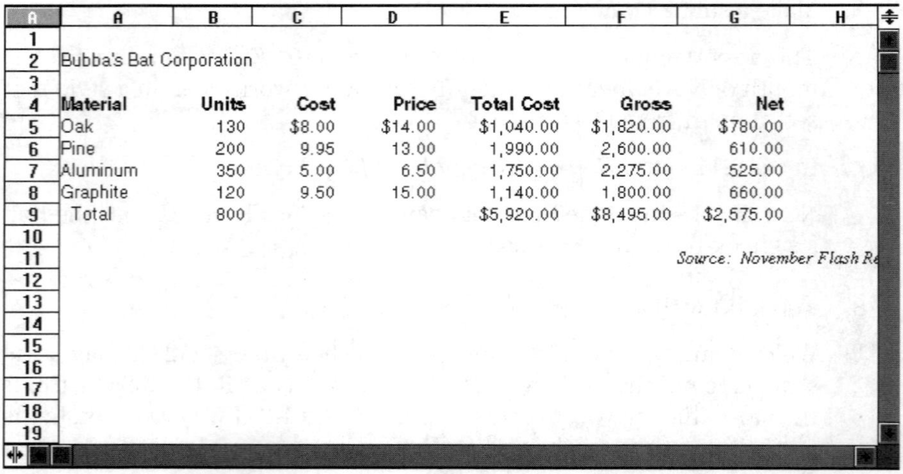

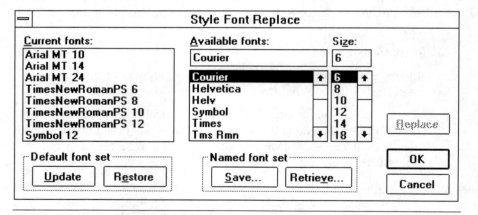

Figure 4.7. The BATS.WK3 sales worksheet so far. To make an impressive-looking title, we want to use the Times 24 font. Since it's not part of the default set, we need to customize the font set.

Figure 4.8. The Style Font Replace dialog box. Here you can substitute the default fonts with your own choices.

Mouse: Click Times 6 in the Current fonts list. Then use the scroll arrows to the right of the Available fonts list to locate the word *Times*. Click Times in this list, and then scroll the Size list to find the number 24. Now click Replace, and then click OK. If you fail to click Replace, choosing OK does not carry out the replacement.

Keyboard: From the Style Fonts dialog box press Alt-R for Replace. Press the DownArrow key enough times to select Times 6. Now press Tab two times to get to the Available fonts list. Press T to select Times. If another font beginning with T is loaded, you may have to press the UpArrow or DownArrow key to select *Times*. Press Tab once, type the number 24, press Alt-R for Replace, and then press Tab enough times to highlight the OK button. Then press Enter to choose OK. Note that if you fail to choose Replace, choosing OK does not carry out the replacement.

Perhaps you were wondering why we had to choose Replace twice. The first Replace button invokes the Style Font Replace dialog box. The second Replace button actually performs the font replacement.

10. Now choose Times 24 from the Font list, select the Italics dialog box, and then choose OK. The venerable corporate name is now in a hearty but stylish font.

Borders, Shades, and Colors

Three stylistic enhancements—borders, shades, and colors—help direct the reader's eye to points of interest in your report and add sizzle to your spreadsheets. In the following steps, you'll see how to apply these enhancements to make the data more readable and more eye-catching.

The data and headings in range A4..G9 will look a bit tidier if we add some borders and shades. If you have a color monitor, and especially if you have a color printer, you can further increase the visual interest of your application with some well-selected hues.

Adding a Border

It's sometimes hard to read up and down or across entire lines of data without losing your place, especially in a large worksheet. Applying borders to the data makes it much easier to scan the sheet's rows and columns.

1. Get ready to add a border.

   The Style Border dialog box presents a wide variety of border options. Before we choose one, let's see what the options are.

   Mouse: Select range A4..G9. Then choose Style Border.

   Keyboard: Move the cell pointer to cell A4. Press ABS (F4) to anchor the range. Next, press the End key and then the RightArrow key, and press End again and then the DownArrow key and press Enter. Range A4..G9 should now be selected. Press Alt-S for Style and then B for Border.

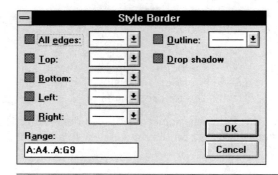

Figure 4.9. The Style Border dialog box. You get to decide which parts of a cell or range receive which kind of border—a single, double, or thick line. You can also add emphasis to the entire selected range by applying a drop-shadow effect.

The Style Border dialog box shown in Figure 4.9 contains seven check-boxes. Next to each of the first six is a drop-down list box that lets you choose from three line styles: a single line, a double line, and a thick line.

Choosing the first check-box, All edges, is the same as choosing the next four. These, respectively, establish borders on the top, bottom, left, and right edges of the cell.

After these is the Outline check-box, which may sound like it does the same thing as All edges. The difference is that the Outline border option puts borders only around the edges of a selection. If you apply this option to a range of cells, you get a rectangle around the range, instead of the grid-like border you get with All edges.

The last check-box in the Style Border dialog box is Drop shadow. This option creates a shadowing effect along the bottom and right edges of the selection.

2. Put single-line borders and a shadowed box around the data.

   Add a border along all the edges of each cell, and use a drop-shadow effect to create a forceful look.

   Mouse: Click the check-box next to All edges and the one next to Drop shadow. An X should appear in each box. Then click OK.

   Keyboard: Press Alt-E to select the All edges check-box. Note that Alt-R activates Right, and in turn Alt-A activates Range; thus Alt-E, rather than Alt-A, is the shortcut for All edges. Then press Alt-D for Drop shadow and press Enter.

   A border now appears around the data, complete with a shadow effect.

Putting On Shades

There are a number of reasons to apply a shade to cells. Shading gives them a special emphasis, breaks up the monotony of large sections of data, and blocks out areas of the worksheet that are not applicable.

Range C9..D9 looks a bit odd with nothing in it, so let's apply a light shade to these two cells as in Figure 4.10. If we wanted to, we could have chosen instead a dark shade or a solid shade.

1. Select a shade.

   Mouse: Select range C9..D9. Select Style Shading. The option Light is selected, so click OK.

   Keyboard: Move the cell pointer to cell C9. Press ABS (F4) to anchor the range, press the RightArrow key one time and press Enter. Now press Alt-S for Style and then S for Shading. The Light option is selected, so press Enter to choose OK.

You may find it easier to view a worksheet that contains a border if you turn off 1-2-3/W's gridlines. To do this, choose the Window Display Options command, and uncheck the Grid box.

7	Aluminum	350	5.00	6.50	1,750.00	2,275.00	525.00
8	Graphite	120	9.50	15.00	1,140.00	1,800.00	660.00
9	Total	800			$5,920.00	$8,495.00	$2,575.00
10							
11						Source: November F	
12							
13							

Figure 4.10. The unneeded cells for total unit cost and total unit price are now "greyed out."

Experiment with different shading patterns to see which looks best with your printer. In particular, you'll want to know how readable the results are when you apply a shade to a cell that contains text.

Colorizing the Worksheet

As the twister in *The Wizard of Oz* did for Dorothy, 1-2-3/W's Style Color command takes your worksheets into a world full of color.

If you use your spreadsheet for on-screen presentations, or if you have access to a color output device, you'll want to illuminate your worksheet with a color scheme that is aesthetically pleasing and that visually organizes the data. You'll also find that having the numbers literally go into the red makes a much stronger impact than simply using minus signs or parentheses to indicate negative values.

1. Check out the color selection.

   Since most people have black-and-white printers, this exercise describes the one color enhancement that everybody can use: turning ordinary black-on-white text into white-on-black. We'll use this enhancement to make the worksheet's title stand out.

   For now, let's try changing the foreground and background colors for the body of the BATS.WK3 spreadsheet. Start by selecting the range A4..G9.

   Mouse: Choose Style Colors. Click on the down arrow beside the Cell Contents option to see the drop list of available colors. Select a color of your choice. Now click on the Background down arrow to select a background color from the drop down list. Click OK.

   Keyboard: Press Alt-S for Style and then C for Colors. Press Alt-C to select Cell Contents from the Select Colors dialog box. Now press the down arrow repeatedly to cycle through the available colors. Select one of your choice. Next, press Alt-B for Background, (or Tab to the Background option) and press the down arrow key to cycle through the background color options. Once you've made your choice, press Enter to make the change.

   Voila! You now have a technicolor worksheet. You'll notice that the style Colors command presents a dialog box that contains two drop-down list boxes, each of which displays a palette of seven colors. The first list box lets you specify the color for the cell's contents, and the second lets you choose the cell's background. Also in the Style Color dialog box is a check-box which, when activated, makes negative numbers in the range appear in red.

The seven choices in the Style Color palettes are only a sampling of the 512 colors available. To substitute a different color for one of the current seven, choose Window Display Options Palette and select the Palette Button.

The Window Display Options command also lets you select colors for all cell contents, backgrounds, and negative numbers in the entire worksheet. In addition, you use this command to set the colors of such screen elements as the worksheet frame and the borders around cells and ranges. For more on setting worksheet defaults, see Chapter 8, *Mastering the Sheet*.

Bubba's Bat Corporation						
Material	Units	Cost	Price	Total Cost	Gross	Net

Figure 4.11. Even with a black-and-white printer, you can enhance your text with color changes—specifically, by printing white text on a black background.

2. Try reverse text (white text on a black background).

   Since most people have black-and-white printers, this exercise describes the one color enhancement that everybody can use: turning ordinary black-on-white text into white-on-black. We'll use this enhancement to make the worksheet's title stand out. The easiest way to do this is to use the Wysiwyg menu.

   Select the range A2..G2. Now choose :Format Color Reverse to give the range a black background with white letters.

   Bubba's Bat Corporation should be reversed as in Figure 4.11. Reverse text can make items on your page stand out, but remember that it is harder to read than black text on a white background. If you reverse text make sure that it is large enough and bold enough to read.

Aligning Labels

As in other versions of 1-2-3, 1-2-3/W uses label prefixes to control the appearance of labels.

Labels that start with the apostrophe (') label prefix appear left-aligned in a cell. By default, 1-2-3/W enters this prefix at the start of each label you enter.

The quotation mark (") prefix indicates right-alignment, and the caret (^) indicates center-alignment. Labels that start with a vertical bar (|) don't print if the label is in the first column of a Print range. Labels that start with a backslash (\) repeat as many times as will fit in the cell.

You can choose a label prefix any of several ways: by typing the prefix before typing the label; by editing the label and substituting a different prefix; or by choosing Style Alignment, /Range Label, or :Text Align, although the latter is for "unconventional" label alignments; or by clicking on a label alignment Smart Icon.

If you performed the exercises in the previous chapter, you've already reassigned label formats in 1-2-3/W by way of the Style Alignment commands. If you move the cell pointer to any cell in range A1..A6 and look in the edit box, you'll see that these cells have an apostrophe (left-alignment) prefix.

1. Center the headings.

    The cells in range B4..G4 are right-aligned. After we fine-tune the column widths, these cells will look better centered.

Figure 4.12. Label Alignment SmartIcons. You can left, center, or right align by clicking on one of the alignment icons.

Mouse: Drag the mouse to select range B4..G4. Choose Style Alignment, select the Align label Center option, and choose OK. Or, you can click the center-alignment SmartIcon after you select the range.

Keyboard: Move the cell pointer to cell B4 and press ABS (F4) to anchor the range. Press the End key and then the RightArrow key to select range B4..G4 and press Enter. Then press Alt-S for Style and A for Alignment. Then press Alt-C for Center Alignment.

The labels in range B4..G4 are now centered within each cell. After we adjust the column widths, they'll look better aligned with the data below them.

If you plan to type a large number of labels that use a prefix other than the apostrophe, you can change the default by choosing Worksheet Global Settings Align labels. But this doesn't affect previously entered labels, and it's usually no more efficient than using Style Alignment.

New and Unusual Label Techniques

1-2-3/W provides some new and little-known label-alignment features that resemble those of the WYSIWYG and Allways add-ins. You can align a label across multiple columns, create a label that spills over into the cell to its left, and create a label that spills over into the cells on the right and the left. In the exercises ahead you'll learn these techniques, and you'll learn even more label tricks in Chapter 6, *Labels, Values, and Formulas*.

1-2-3/W's Style Alignment command includes a check-box called Align over columns. You can easily center a label by selecting a range that includes the full width of your data, choosing Center, and choosing the Align-over-columns option. This is the equivalent of using WYSIWYG's :Text Align Center command.

A	A	B	C	D	E	F	G	H
2								
3								
4				The double-caret (^^)	label-prefix	lets a centered label		
5					overlap cells to the right and left.			
6					(These labels are in column E)			
7								
8				The Style Alignment	options Center and			
9			Align over columns let you center a label across					
10					its neighboring cells to the right.			
11			(These labels are in column B and aligned over columns B through G)					
12								
13				The double-quote ("") label-prefix lets a				
14			right-aligned label overlap cells to the left.					
15					(These labels are in column E)			
16								

Figure 4.13. Examples of lesser-known label-alignment techniques: letting a long, centered label spill over into cells on the right and left; centering a label across multiple columns; and letting a long, flush-right label spill over into the cell on the left. With conventional label-alignment techniques, you can center a label over only one column, and centered and right-aligned labels spill over into the cell on the right, but not the left, when they're too long to fit in one cell.

1. Select the title.

   The title of this worksheet would look much better centered over the data. In 1-2-3/W you no longer have to use trial-and-error to accomplish this.

   Mouse: Select range A2..G2. Choose Style Alignment, click the Align label Center button, and click the Align-over-columns option. Then click OK.

   Keyboard: Press Alt-S for Style and A for Alignment. Then press Alt-C for Center and Alt-O for Align over columns. Note that Alt-R activates Right, and in turn Alt-A activates Range; thus Alt-O, rather than Alt-A, is the shortcut for Align over columns.

   The corporate name is now centered over the worksheet. But how does this work?

   If you move the cell pointer through the cells in range A2..G2, you'll see that each of these cells has a {Text} attribute. As in the WYSIWYG add-in, cells with this attribute have special properties. In this case, we see that a centered cell, cell A2, becomes centered within a range cells that all contain the {Text} attribute.

2. Create a flush-right label.

   The Source label in cell G11 would look better if its last character aligned with the right edge of cell G1. In early versions of 1-2-3, right-aligning a label that was too big for the cell you wanted it aligned in was a tiresome task. You had to move the label to a cell to the left, and then insert a series of spaces after an apostrophe label prefix.

   And remember that newer spreadsheets like 1-2-3/W—and 1-2-3 Release 2.x and 3.x with spreadsheet-publishing add-ins—use proportional (variably spaced) fonts instead of uniformly spaced typewriter-style fonts. This means that different letters have different widths, so aligning with spaces leads to unpredictable results.

   Fortunately, 1-2-3/W supports a technique that came in with the WYSIWYG add-in: Type two right-alignment prefixes (quotation marks) at the beginning of the cell.

   Use any of the mouse or keyboard techniques discussed in the previous section to invoke Edit mode, then delete the apostrophe prefix and replace it with two quotation marks. Before you enter the changes, the

Although inserting spaces right after the label prefix or at the end of a label is not the recommended way to align text, sometimes it's a handy trick for moving a label just a hair to the right or left.

revised cell entry should look like the following, including the quotes but not the period: ""*Source: November Flash Report*.

After you enter this change, the *Source* label should now be aligned with the right edge of column G.

3. Create one more variation.

   In addition to setting a long label flush right, you can center long labels so that they spill over both the right and left edges of the cell. We don't need this for our worksheet, but let's take a look at this unusual technique for future reference.

   We want to experiment in a cell that doesn't have any data, so move the cell pointer to cell C1. Incidentally, since this technique pushes a label out both sides of the cell, it's of no use in column A.

   Type the following, including the caret (^) symbols but not the period: ^^ *This is a very long and strangely centered cell.*

   If this label had a "normal" centering prefix, just one caret, it would appear no different than if it had a left-alignment prefix, because it's too long for conventional centering. If you're not sure how this would look, edit cell C1 and remove one of the carets.

   The tricky thing about editing labels like the ones you created in these three exercises is remembering which cell actually contains the label. Again, when in doubt, check the edit line.

   To erase the practice data in cell C1, go to C1 and press Delete.

   To learn more about working with labels, see Chapter 6, *Labels, Values, and Formulas*.

Column Widths

Few worksheets look perfect without some tinkering with the column widths. For at least some of your columns, 1-2-3/W's default width will probably be too wide or too narrow.

You may recall that in Chapter 3, you adjusted the width of column E. You may also recall being warned against investing much time in fine-tuning column widths until most other spreadsheet enhancements were done. If you set the widths before you determine such factors as the number of characters in a column and the text sizes and enhancements, you'll probably have to adjust the widths again later on. Now that we've entered and formatted the data and dressed up the worksheet with fonts, borders, and such, it's clearer which width adjustments are desirable.

But there's one more consideration: possible increases to some of the values in a worksheet. If we sell a few more units next month, Units could grow into a four-digit column. Likewise, the Cost and Gross figures are close to rolling over into another digit. So that you, or other people who use your spreadsheet, don't get bothered by cells that overflow and display as asterisks, why not anticipate these changes? By entering test data that trigger the problem, you can solve it before it becomes a real problem.

1. Save the real data.

    The solution is to enter some reasonable values that result in the extra digit. But first, we want to preserve the data we've entered.

    In this example, we'll plug some higher numbers into range B6..D6. We don't need to, and shouldn't, mess with cells that contain formulas. These will automatically reflect the larger numbers we type in other cells.

    Mouse: Select range B6..D6 and choose Edit Copy. Then click in cell A1 and choose Edit Paste.

    Keyboard: Move the cell pointer to cell B6. Press ABS (F4) and press the RightArrow key two times and press Enter. Choose Edit Copy from the menu or use the accelerator key, Ctrl-Insert. Now press the Home key, and then choose Edit Paste or press Shift-Insert.

    With the data at the top of the worksheet, we're sure not to forget that we've been toying with the numbers.

2. Enter some high-end values.

    In cell B6, enter *400*, and in cell C6, enter *17.95*. We don't have to change the value in cell D6, because we already accomplished the mission: The totals in columns B, E, and F have each grown by a digit.

    Our assessment? When the Units grow over 999, they'd look better with a comma. The hasty adjustment we made to column E in the previous chapter turned out to be a good hunch, so we don't need to change it further. But the Gross column (column F) needs a bit more width. Also, in case we ever sell our products at a loss, it's comforting to know that the Net column is wide enough to accommodate the negative values. Negative numbers are indeed a factor worth considering before you set widths.

	A	B	C	D	E	F	G
1	200	9.95	13.00				
2	*Bubba's Bat Corporation*						
3							
4	Material	Units	Cost	Price	Total Cost	Gross	Net
5	Oak	130	$8.00	$14.00	$1,040.00	$1,820.00	$780.00
6	Pine	400	17.95	13.00	7,180.00	5,200.00	(1,980.00)
7	Aluminum	350	5.00	6.50	1,750.00	2,275.00	525.00
8	Graphite	120	9.50	15.00	1,140.00	1,800.00	660.00
9	Total	1000			$11,110.00	$11,095.00	($15.00)
10							
11					Source: November Flash Report		
12							

Figure 4.14. The results of increases in cell values. Note that with four digits, the Units total would look better with the Comma format. Also, the Gross total has outgrown its current width, so its numbers display as asterisks.

3. Change the width.

   First, let's widen column F. Move the cell pointer into any cell in column F, such as cell F1. If you specify a width for a column, the width does not change when you change the worksheet's default width via the Worksheet Global Settings command. The 1-2-3 Classic method is included, because it offers the advantage of letting you see the number of characters in the column while you try out a variety of widths.

   Mouse: Drag the line between the letters F and G until column F is a slightly generous width. A width of 11 characters is optimal. After you release the mouse button, look in the control panel to see the current width. It displays [W11] when the current cell's width is 11.

   Keyboard: Press Alt-K for Worksheet and C for Column Width. Then press Tab, enter the number 11, and press Enter.

   1-2-3 Classic: Choose /WCS for Worksheet Column Set-Width, and use the Right- and LeftArrow keys to try out different sizes. When the column width is 11, press Enter. Note that to change multiple column widths via the 1-2-3 Classic menus, you must choose /Worksheet Column Column-Range Set-Width.

In 1-2-3/W, the number of characters representing a width is an approximate value. Because different fonts and characters have different widths, more or fewer characters may fit in a cell than the number specified as the column width.

4. Copy the cells back.

   Let's put the real data back into cells B5..B9.

   Mouse: Select range A1..C1. Choose Edit Quick Copy. The From range is correct, but we need to identify B6 as the To range. If the Edit Quick Copy dialog box is hiding this cell, move the dialog box by dragging its title bar. Click cell B6 and then choose OK. A fast alternative is to click the Edit Quick Copy SmartIcon after you select the range, then click cell B6 to complete the command.

   Keyboard: Press Home and then ABS (F4) to anchor the range. Press the RightArrow key two times and press Enter, then press Alt-E for Edit and Q for Quick Copy. The From range is correct, but we need to identify B6 as the To range. Use the Arrow keys to highlight cell B6, then press Enter twice.

   You might think that you'd save a step by using the Edit Move or Move command to put the contents of range A1..C1 back into B6..B8. But as you'll learn in Chapter 7, moving cells, instead of copying them, can have an unexpected effect on borders and other style attributes.

5. Clear the duplicate data.

   Now that the test is done and the original data are restored, we no longer need the copy of the data that's in range A1..C1.

   Mouse: Select range A1..C1. Choose Edit Clear.

   Keyboard: Press Home and then ABS (F4) to anchor the range. Press the RightArrow key two times and then press Delete.

   Row 1 is now empty again.

6. Change the other column widths.

   You've tried several different methods for changing column widths. Experiment with different widths for this worksheet. The ones that appear in Figure 4.15, the completed version of this worksheet, are listed in Table 4.1 below.

Column	Width	
A	11	
B	6	
C	7	
D	9	(the default width)
E	11	
F	11	
G	10	

Table 4.1. Recommended column widths for the sales worksheet.

Row Heights

1-2-3/W, along with the 1-2-3 releases that contain spreadsheet-publishing add-ins, lets you control row heights as well as column widths.

1-2-3/W automatically adjusts the height of a row to accommodate the largest font in the row. If for any reason you're not satisfied with the "automatic" row height, you can change it much as you change a column width: Drag the border between the row numbers that appears in the worksheet frame, or choose Worksheet Row Height.

Note that row heights are measured in points, and they should be at least one or two points higher than the largest font in the row. Be aware that rows to which you assign a "custom" row height do not automatically adjust to accommodate changes in font size. Choose the Reset height button from the Worksheet Row Height dialog box if you wish to have 1-2-3/W resume automatic resizing of the height.

Note also that each row must be at least one point high, thus you can't completely hide a row. However, you can get nearly the same effect by selecting a height of one point and assigning all data in the row the Hidden format, via the Range Format command.

Since 1-2-3/W usually takes care of row heights automatically, you probably won't need to take matters into your own hands. But this feature comes in handy when you want to center your worksheet on the screen, and when you want to create ample distances between various parts of the worksheet.

1-2-3/W automatically adjusts row heights to fit the largest font in the row.

To move the heading a bit further down from the top of the screen, we'll change the height of row 1 to 36 points.

The 1-2-3 Classic method is included because it offers the advantage of letting you see the point size of the column while you try out a variety of heights.

Start by moving the cell pointer to the Home position (cell A1).

Mouse: Drag the line between the sheet letter A and the row number 1 until row 1 is about half an inch deep. Since there are 72 points in an inch, this should be approximately 36 lines. After you release the mouse button, look in the control panel to see the current height. It displays [H36] when the current cell's height is 36.

Keyboard: Press Alt-K for Worksheet and R for Row Height. Then press Tab, enter the number 36, and press Enter.

1-2-3 Classic: Choose :WRS for Worksheet Row Set-Height, and press Enter to specify the current row as the one to resize. Now use the Up- and DownArrow keys to try out different sizes. When the row height is 36, press Enter.

Finishing Touches

A few more adjustments and our worksheet will be ready for prime time.

This last set of worksheet-enhancement exercises gives you the chance to try 1-2-3/W commands without the training wheels. Each step repeats a technique you've already performed one or more times.

Enough information is provided for you to perform these tasks, but instead of getting step-by-step instructions, you'll have to figure out which selections to make and which items to choose from the dialog boxes. If you get stuck, take a peek at the "Learn How to Learn 1-2-3/W" section in the next chapter for advice on finding your way out of a jam.

Before you proceed, save your file via the File Save command. If anything goes wrong, you can choose Edit Undo or press its accelerator key, Alt-Backspace. If that doesn't restore your work, close the file via the File Close command—without saving the changes—and then open it again

If you're a keyboard user, remember how to preselect ranges: Move the cell pointer to the first cell in the range and press ABS (F4). Then use the navigation keys to highlight the appropriate cells and press Enter. If you don't have a handle on the End-key tricks, save those until the following chapter, which explains how they work. And remember how to get around a dialog box: Press Tab or press Alt plus the appropriate underlined letter.

Finishing the Sales Worksheet

The following enhancement exercises let you further improve the look of your worksheet while giving you a chance to practice the techniques you've learned thus far. Take your time and refer back to the relevant sections of this and the previous chapter as needed.

1. Add a blank column before column A. The command is Worksheet Insert. This command causes all data to move one column to the right.
2. Set the width of the new column A to 4 characters, then set the width of column I to 4 characters, as well. Use one of the techniques described in the "Column Widths" section.
3. Set row 3 to a height of 25 points. Use one of the techniques described in the previous section, "Row Heights."
4. Set the label *Total* (not *Total Cost*) to Italic format. The command is Style Font.
5. Change the *Source* attribution to say *September* instead of *November*. Use one of the editing techniques described in the section "Editing Cells in 1-2-3/W" in Chapter 3.

Bubba's Bat Corporation

Material	Units	Cost	Price	Total Cost	Gross	Net
Oak	130	$8.00	$14.00	$1,040.00	$1,820.00	$780.00
Pine	200	9.95	13.00	1,990.00	2,600.00	610.00
Aluminum	350	5.00	6.50	1,750.00	2,275.00	525.00
Graphite	120	9.50	15.00	1,140.00	1,800.00	660.00
Total	800			$5,920.00	$8,495.00	$2,575.00

Source: September Flash Report

Figure 4.15. The enhanced bat-sales worksheet.

6. Place a double-line border around the entire worksheet (range A1..I13). The command is Style Border. This one's tricky: See the section "Borders, Shades, and Colors" for help.

7. If your worksheet looks pretty much like the one in Figure 4.15, you're all set! Save the file and then print it via the File Print command. Don't forget that the worksheet now spans from cell A1 through I13. And don't forget to save your file again after you print. Otherwise, 1-2-3/W will forget your revised Print range. If you need help on printing, see the printing exercise you performed near the end of Chapter 3, or see Chapter 10 on printing.

Onward and Upward

Congratulations, once again. You've taken your humble but accurate worksheet and turned it into a printout that you'd be proud to present. Take a moment to recall the techniques you've put to productive use in these past two chapters:

Entering labels, values, and formulas

Using a variety of tools to duplicate, erase, and move data

Saving, opening, and printing a file

Using SmartIcons and accelerator keys

Formatting numbers

Editing cell contents

Aligning text

Choosing fonts and font styles

Applying borders, shades, and colors

Adjusting column widths and row heights

If you've performed the exercises in Chapters 3 and 4, you have all the skills needed to create effective worksheets in 1-2-3/W. And now you're ready to shift into a slightly higher gear, since you're an old hand at such fundamentals as selecting cells, menus, and dialog-box items in 1-2-3/W.

As you proceed through the book, you'll build on these skills to truly master the 1-2-3/W worksheet environment. The next several chapters show you how to speed up and improve the accuracy of your work. You'll go beyond the basics to learn how to design extremely powerful and efficient worksheet applications and how to develop habits that will help you learn unfamiliar features.

And while there's more to effective spreadsheets than just fancy presentations, you may be chomping at the bit to learn more about spreadsheet publishing. By following the chapters in sequence, you'll learn numerous skills that will help prepare you for advanced spreadsheet publishing. But if you want to press on towards spreadsheet publishing glory post haste, by all means, jump ahead to Chapter 11, *Creating Graphics* and Chapter 12, *Enhancing Graphics*.

Part III
More Worksheet Essentials

5

Learning Your Way Around

In the preceding chapters, you learned the essential steps for creating a simple application with 1-2-3/W. With these skills, you will be productive with 1-2-3/W right from the start. But to use the software as efficiently and effectively as possible, you need to dig a bit deeper into 1-2-3/W's rich set of spreadsheet features.

This and the next several chapters are designed to round out your core spreadsheet skills. You'll learn essential concepts and hidden tricks for building superior spreadsheets with a minimum of effort. You'll also learn a slew of shortcuts for working with your spreadsheets once they're set up. And along with the techniques you'll want to apply, you'll learn about common pitfalls and how to avoid them.

This chapter shows you how to get around in 1-2-3/W, that is, how to find and use the commands and special keys for a given job, and how to cruise around the worksheet. In short, it shows you how to work smarter and faster with 1-2-3/W.

Topics in the first section of this chapter include making the most of 1-2-3/W's extensive on-line Help system and experimenting with new commands.

The second section shows you how to navigate the worksheet with a variety of mouse and keyboard shortcuts. Knowing how to move quickly through the worksheet will save you time—every time you use 1-2-3/W.

The last section in the chapter is a guided tour of 1-2-3/W's function keys. You'll learn to use these valuable resources, and you'll find out how they differ from those in earlier releases of 1-2-3.

In this chapter you will learn:

- *How to use 1-2-3/W's Help system*
- *How to learn more about 1-2-3/W*
- *How to navigate the worksheet*
- *How to use function keys in 1-2-3/W*

Together, these concepts, skills, and tools will speed up both your use of 1-2-3/W and your further learning of its capabilities.

Learn How to Learn 1-2-3/W

It seems obvious: When you're unsure how to use a particular spreadsheet command, you should slow down, read the available options, and then choose the one that sounds right. Many people, however, race through new commands, as if going fast will somehow fool the program into doing the right things.

Of course, you'll want to go fast through rote tasks, such as moving the cell pointer and using commands you know inside and out. But to hurtle quickly into unfamiliar terrain is courting confusion if not disaster. The best way to get the desired results is to think before you press or click.

With 1-2-3 for Windows, it's easy to get caught speeding, especially if you're a long-standing veteran of earlier releases and of good old DOS. Because both 1-2-3/W and Windows are built on software that you've used before, your expertise is an invaluable foundation. But remember that it took patience and practice to get you this far. A bit more of the same will help you scale the heights of Windows wizardry.

Here's a litmus test to see if you're an impatient user: Have you used 1-2-3/W's on-line Help system yet? If the answer is no, then you haven't yet mastered the art of Windows-style computing. 1-2-3/W, like many Windows applications, provides much of its documentation in on-line form. This Help system provides a ready reference for all manner of subjects, and ambling through it is an excellent way to shop around for features that will save you time in the long run. If you fail to exploit this and other resources, you probably won't get the most out of your software.

Read on to learn how to use the Help system and several other tools and tactics to continually enhance and expand your 1-2-3/W skills.

Using 1-2-3/W's Help System

1-2-3/W Help appears in a separate, resizable window, and it provides exhaustive information about virtually every aspect of the software. This on-line Help facility is based on Windows' WINHELP system, so you'll find it similar to the Help tools in other Windows programs. 1-2-3/W's Help facility, however, is one of the most extensive.

How to Get Help

There are two ways to activate the Help system. You can press the HELP key (F1), just as in other versions of 1-2-3. Or you can choose Help from 1-2-3/W's main menu. Although you can, directly or indirectly, get to all the same Help topics either way, each method of invoking Help has its advantages.

Pressing the HELP key (F1) brings up context-sensitive help. For example, if you press HELP when a dialog box or error message is active, you'll get help on that topic. You can also get help on any @function or macro command by typing the @function or command keyword and then pressing HELP.

You can invoke Help only from the main menu when you're in Ready mode, but this menu offers the convenience of a short list of essential Help topics: Index, Using Help, Keyboard, @Functions, Macros, How Do I?, and For Upgraders.

Most of these are self-explanatory, but the final two choices warrant discussion. The Help How Do I? command presents a large alphabet. Clicking one of these letters calls up a list of tasks that start with that letter. For example, choosing the letter C directs you to help on such tasks as canceling the last action or command or centering labels.

Help For Upgraders is a highly useful menu choice for experienced 1-2-3 users. It tells you which new Windows-style command is similar to a given slash (/) or colon (:) menu command.

From 1-2-3/W's main menu, choose Help For Upgraders to find out which 1-2-3/W main-menu commands effectively replace 1-2-3 Classic commands.

How to Navigate Through Help with Push Button Controls

Press HELP (F1) to see the Help window. When you press HELP from Ready mode you go directly to the Help Index, an extensive list of popular Help topics.

Note that you often need to scroll to see the complete text of a Help topic. Use the Help window's scroll bars, or use navigation keys such as PageDown, to move through the text on a given subject.

If the Help topic you have chosen doesn't contain all the information you need, you can jump to a related topic. Throughout most Help screens are underlined items in green text. To switch to help on the underlined topic, you just click it.

Other items appear in green text with a dotted underline. You click these for brief definitions or examples.

As shown in Figure 5.1, the top of the Help window contains five push-button controls, just underneath the window's menu bar. The buttons give you numerous ways to locate the help you need.

Don't forget to scroll through the Help window. There's often more text than is visible in the window.

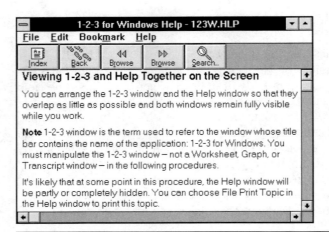

Figure 5.1. The 1-2-3/W Help window. Note the buttons near the top of the window: Index, Back, Browse backward, Browse forward, and Search.

Index Click the Index button or press Alt-I to bring up a list of main topics. You can choose one of these general topics and then navigate through a series of related subjects. For example, you might choose Graph Window from the Help Index, and from the screen about the Graph Window you could choose the Draw topic; from there, you might branch to help on drawing a rectangle. In a few easy steps, you can find all the information you need.

Back Click Back or press Alt-B to return to the last Help screen you read.

Browse backward Click Browse backward or press Alt-R to cycle backward through Help screens on related topics.

Browse forward Click Browse forward or press Alt-O to cycle forward through Help screens on related topics.

Search Click Search or press Alt-S to bring up a dialog box that includes the Search-for box, a long list of key words that represent categories of Help topics. You can scroll through this list, or you can jump right to the item that interests you by entering the first few characters of the key word into the text box above the list. The Help system then displays related topics in the Topics Found list. From this list, you can select the Help screens that suit your needs.

Figure 5.2 shows the Search dialog box with *CLI* entered in the Search-for box. 1-2-3/W responds with the key words *Clipboard* and *Clipboard Macros*, along with other key words in that part of the alphabetical listing. Selecting Clipboard from the Search-for list brings up a dozen Clipboard-related topics. You can then use the Topics Found list to choose one of these subjects, such as *Clipboard, Defined*.

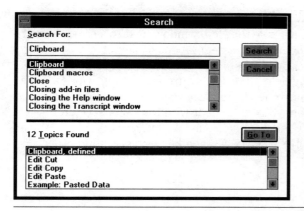

Figure 5.2. The results of a search for Clipboard information. All you do is click the Search icon and enter CLI in the Search-for box. To jump to the Help topic that best fits the bill, select it from the Topics Found box.

What's on the Help Menu?

The Help window's menu commands provide a number of useful features. Once you find the information you need, you can print it, or you can copy it and then paste it into a spreadsheet, word-processing, or other kind of document. You can also insert a *bookmark* to help you return to the topic, and you can even add your own commentary to the Help screens.

The menu names and their options:

File *Open* another program's Help system; *Print* the current topic; change the *Printer Setup*; *Exit* Help.

Edit *Copy* the current Help topic to the Clipboard, so you can paste it into 1-2-3/W or into a Windows word processor; *Annotate* the Help screens with your own comments. (Help screens you annotate display a paper-clip icon. To view your comments, click this icon.)

Bookmark *Define* and access a list of topics that you plan to use frequently.

Help Get information about using Help.

Spend some time touring the Help system. You'll probably uncover some features you were unfamiliar with, and you'll get in the habit of using this invaluable resource. And take advantage of conveniences like bookmarks to speed your access to oft-needed topics, and the ability to copy and print the Help text to make the information even more accessible.

Windows Help allows you to copy entire Help topics, but not selected parts of a topic.

A great way to use 1-2-3/W's Help feature is to keep the Help window open, but in a moderate size. If you arrange the Help window next to a sized-down 1-2-3/W window, you can read the Help screen about a new or tricky feature while you perform the steps it describes.

When you're finished with Help, choose Exit from the Help window's File menu or double-click its Control icon. Because the Windows Help facility is actually a separate application, you can close it with the same accelerator key you use to close 1-2-3/W or Windows itself: Alt-F4. But, try as you might, you can't exit Windows Help by pressing the Escape key, as you can in other versions of 1-2-3.

Be a Browser

Read the screen! These three words are the best advice for a user of any version of 1-2-3. Most often, the information you need is right under your nose.

But you have to train yourself to actively browse through the available information. If things happen unexpectedly, look around the screen for hints. Maybe the mode indicator in the upper right shows that you're in Edit mode when you thought you were in Ready mode. Or maybe the critical clue is a status indicator at the bottom of the 1-2-3/W window, showing that the ScrollLock key was inadvertently pressed.

In addition to being a careful observer of on-screen hints, you should actively prowl for information. If a formula isn't working, select the cell it's in; then inspect the formula in the Edit line at the top of the 1-2-3/W window. And read the Help screens for useful tips about 1-2-3/W. There are many other places to snoop as well. When you have trouble finding a menu command, browse through the menus by dragging the mouse or by pressing Alt and navigating with the Arrow keys. This brings up long prompts at the top of the 1-2-3/W window that tell you a bit more about a feature than the menus do. You won't see these prompts if you choose menu commands by clicking instead of dragging, or by using shortcut keys instead of navigating through the menus.

If the option you want isn't on the main menu, perhaps it's stashed away in a dialog box or submenu. Items in the menu that end with an ellipsis (...) call up a dialog box, and items that feature a right arrowhead call up a cascade-style submenu.

For example, if you want to copy just the styles of a range but not the data, you won't find a command for that on the menu. But if you look in the Edit Quick Copy dialog box, you'll find a check-box that provides this option. Similarly, if you want to locate the macro-debugging tools, you'll find them not on the main menu but in a cascade that branches off the Tools Macro command.

Also note that certain 1-2-3/W features use windows that contain a distinctive set of menu choices. Specifically, these are the Help window, the Graph window, and the Transcript window. Such menus are an easily overlooked resource. The Help menu is described earlier in this chapter. For more on the Graph and Transcript windows, respectively, see Chapter 11, *Creating Graphics*, and Chapter 17, *Macros*.

If you're unfamiliar with the WYSIWYG spreadsheet-publishing add-in, or the Allways add-in with which it shares many features, press the colon (:) and tour the WYSIWYG menus. This gives you an alternate interface to the available spreadsheet-publishing options, and it even shows you a few features that aren't available from any other menu, such as the :Text Edit command, which lets you do rudimentary word processing in your worksheet.

And if you're new to the features of 1-2-3 Release 3.x, check out the / (slash) menu options. This gives you a different look at some of the newer 1-2-3 options that are integrated into 1-2-3/W's main menu, especially a host of advanced database and graphics features. Here, too, are a handful of older 1-2-3 features that you won't find on the main menu, such as the /File Erase and /System commands. These commands, respectively, let you delete a file from the disk, and allow you to switch temporarily to the DOS prompt (you get back to 1-2-3/W by entering the word *exit*).

The SmartIcon palette is yet another place you should window shop for useful features. If you want to confirm what an icon does before you invoke it, click it with the right mouse button, rather than the usual left button. A prompt describing the icon's use appears at the top of the 1-2-3/W window. You can also browse quickly through all the prompts by dragging through the palette while pressing the right mouse button.

And when you know how to customize the palette, as explained in Chapter 18, *Mastering The SmartIcon Palette*, you'll want to peruse the many SmartIcons that come with 1-2-3/W but that aren't on the default palette. If you find a "hidden" SmartIcon that you need, add it to the palette with two clicks of the mouse. As with other features, if you don't seek them out, you won't find them.

One more browsing tool deserves mention: the NAME key (F3). When you use named ranges, which are described in Chapter 8, *Mastering the Sheet*, you can bring up a list of current names by pressing the NAME key. You can do this any time you need to specify a range. For example, after you type @SUM(, press the NAME key to bring up the list of named ranges, then select a range name from the list to add it to your formula.

The NAME key also helps you enter @functions and macro commands. If you type an "at" sign (@) or a left brace ({) and then press the NAME key (F3), a list of @functions or macro commands appears. You can scroll through the list, or you can type a letter to jump to the functions or commands that start with that letter. If you choose an item from this list, it automatically appears in the Edit line.

You can also use the NAME key with 1-2-3 Classic File commands. For example, you can press NAME after choosing /File Open After to enlarge the list of available file names.

Use a Safety Net

You'll feel more comfortable experimenting with novel features if you've taken the necessary precautions with your data.

For starters, enable the Edit Undo feature, as long as you're not running out of memory. If you are running low on memory, buy some more. Odds are, it's cheaper than the time you'll waste if you lose critical worksheet data. Besides, having a well-configured system will help you exploit the features that made you trade up to Windows in the first place. To check and change the status of the Undo feature use the Tools User Setup dialog box.

On the other hand, don't be too hasty with the Edit Undo command. Unlike Releases 2.2 and 2.3, 1-2-3/W does not let you "redo" something that you undid.

Also, there are some things you can't undo, such as moving the cell pointer, printing, or saving a file. If you choose Edit Undo after doing one of these things, you may undo the activity you did before one of these operations. For example, if you copy a range and then press the GOTO key (F5) to move the cell pointer, pressing Undo doesn't undo the pointer movement, it uncopies the range.

Save your files frequently, especially before you try something new. But don't rush to save after you experiment, lest you save a mangled version of your worksheet over the good one on disk. Files that are very important to you shouldn't reside only on your hard disk. Keep well-marked copies on floppy disks. And don't forget to copy the FM3 format file along with the WK3 file, as mentioned at the end of Chapter 3.

Using the File Save As command is an easy way to save your file under another name. However, remember that this command closes the original file without saving it. So issue a File Save command first if you want to store your latest work under the old name, before you "clone" the file with File Save As.

Also, when you try out unfamiliar features, use remote sections of your file. For example, when you use a command like Range Name Paste Table, which enters data into a number of cells, don't select a range that's near some valuable data. The safest place to experiment in a worksheet that contains data is below and to the right of the data. Then, commands that affect the current cell and its neighbors below and to the right, as well as commands that affect the current row or column, cannot harm your data.

Once you know how to use 3D worksheets, adding an extra sheet to experiment in is an excellent way to avoid damaging existing work. However, use great care with the Group mode feature. It causes changes you make in one sheet to ripple through all the other sheets in the file—a very useful feature, but not when you're toying with unknown commands. For more on 3D spreadsheets and Group mode, see Chapter 9, *Building Effective Applications*.

Finally, know when to bow out gracefully. It's safer to press Escape or click Cancel than to carry out the wrong command. If neither of these does the job, try pressing Ctrl-Break.

Use the Right Tools

It's important to understand 1-2-3/W's limitations as well as its advantages. 1-2-3/W is not, for example, a word processor or a desktop-publishing system. While you can use 1-2-3/W as these or other types of software for small tasks, it's often more effective to buy software that was made expressly for such applications, and to use these alongside 1-2-3/W.

The secret to using 1-2-3/W successfully isn't to turn your spreadsheet into a blender. It's in connecting your spreadsheet to the blender. Windows is about getting applications to work together.

1-2-3/W is at its best when you surround it with a host of tools that complement its strengths. You'll create rich, multifaceted applications when you combine 1-2-3/W with graphics programs, word processors, full-featured databases, and communications software that can trade data with 1-2-3/W via the Clipboard, DDE, and DataLens features.

1-2-3/W's great flexibility and programmability give you a lot of room to innovate. But invest your time in pushing the envelope of 1-2-3/W's true capabilities, not in jury-rigging features that you could get in earnest from an inexpensive companion product.

Navigating the Worksheet

Most likely, the bulk of your time, keystrokes, and mouse movements in 1-2-3/W will be spent moving the cell pointer and selecting data. Thus, one of the best ways to speed up your work is to hone your pointer-movement skills. You'll shave seconds off each and every command when you know the fastest way to get from here to there.

The techniques that follow show you how to move effectively around a single worksheet. To learn how to move among multiple windows and among the sheets in a 3D worksheet, see Chapter 9, *Building Effective Applications*. And to learn how to navigate and select text in Edit mode, see the section "Editing Cells in 1-2-3/W" in Chapter 3.

Mouse Movements

The mouse was built for speed. But a lot of 1-2-3 users are so handy with the keyboard, they don't take advantage of the rolling rodent. You don't have to use it to the exclusion of the keyboard, but if you don't use the mouse for what it's best at, you're wasting valuable time.

The mouse is usually the fastest way to hop around the visible portion of the worksheet.

Mouse Basics You can move the cell pointer quickly by clicking the mouse pointer in any visible cell. Usually, this is the fastest way to hop around the visible portion of the worksheet. The keyboard, however, is usually more convenient for moving a cell or two in any direction.

The Mouse Goes Home Clicking the sheet letter in the upper-left corner of the worksheet frame moves the cell pointer to the home cell. The home cell is usually cell A1 of the current sheet. See the Home-key discussion below for more details.

Mouse Scrolling When you want to see or move to a location that isn't visible in the window, you can use the scroll bars that appear on the right and bottom edges of the window.

You can click the scroll arrows to move one row or column at a time, or you can hold the mouse down on these arrows to scroll smoothly. You can drag the scroll box to jump to anywhere in the active worksheet, and you can click in between the scroll box and the arrows to move a screenload in the direction of the arrows. For more information on these Windows-style scrolling options, see Chapter 2, *Essential Windows Skills*.

The Mouse Goes Deep It's easy to select a two-dimensional range with the mouse: you drag the mouse from one corner of the range to the opposite corner. But how can the mouse burrow from one sheet to the next, for example, to select B:C5..E:H9? The trick is to select a *two-dimensional* area in the first or last sheet of the range, such as B:C5..B:H9, and then to use a sheet-switching option like Ctrl-Page Up or Ctrl-Page Down —or their SmartIcon equivalents— to extend the selection.

Keyboard Navigation

You can use the keyboard to navigate within a 1-2-3/W worksheet much as you do in other versions of 1-2-3. The major difference is an enhanced GOTO feature that is accessible from a menu as well as from the keyboard. But if you don't know all of 1-2-3's pointer-movement tricks, you should take the time to learn them. They're as useful in 1-2-3/W as they are in other releases.

The Arrows The UpArrow, DownArrow, RightArrow, and LeftArrow keys move the cell pointer from cell to cell. The Arrow keys are the most convenient way to move small distances within the worksheet. And combined with the End key, which is described below, they can jump large ranges as well.

PageUp and PageDown The PageUp and PageDown keys scroll up or down a screenful of data. In 1-2-3/W, the number of lines that you scroll up or down depends on how large the window is and how high the rows are.

BigRight and BigLeft The BigRight and BigLeft keys are like sideways versions of PageUp and PageDown. BigRight, better known as Tab or Ctrl-RightArrow, takes you one screenload to the right. BigLeft, alias Shift-Tab (Back-Tab) and Ctrl-LeftArrow, moves you one screenload to the left. How many columns do you move? That depends on the width of the window and of the columns.

The Home Key To go to the first cell in the worksheet, press the Home key. Alternatively, you can click the sheet letter, which is the letter that appears in the upper-left corner of the worksheet frame. In a single-sheet file, this letter is always A.

The home cell is usually, but not always, cell A1 of the current sheet. If you use the Worksheet Titles command, as described in Chapter 8—or if you hide column A, as described in Chapter 9—the Home position becomes the upper-leftmost cell outside of the titles or hidden columns.

The End Key

Take the time to master End-key shortcuts. They help you zoom around your data.

1-2-3/W's End-key combinations give you several great shortcuts for moving around the sheet. These techniques are easy to use, but some of them are a bit hard to understand at first.

Unlike the Alt, Shift, and Ctrl keys, the End key is not pressed simultaneously with another key. You press and release the End key, and then you press one of several navigation keys, such as Home or an Arrow key.

When you press End, the END status indicator appears at the bottom of the window, letting you know that the next navigation key you press will perform differently than usual. If you accidentally press End, press it a second time. The indicator disappears, and normal navigation will occur.

End Home Just as every worksheet has a home cell, marking its first accessible cell, it also has a last cell. This is the lower-right corner of the active worksheet, the area that extends from cell A1 to the intersection of the last row and column right that contains an entry, format, or style. If, for example, you want to expand a Print range to include the lower-right corner of the active area, pressing End Home will get you there in a hurry. In the worksheet in Figure 5.3, pressing End Home would take you to cell E9, presuming there are no active cells below or to the right of that cell.

End UpArrow, End DownArrow, End RightArrow, End LeftArrow Most worksheets contain clusters of data—groups of cells that contain labels, values, or formulas. You often need to move the cell pointer to one edge or another of such a cluster, for example, to highlight a series of contiguous cells. You also may want to hop from one group of data to the next.

If you're confused, you're in good company. A lot of people fail to use this handy feature because it's hard to learn from just reading about it. To understand the End key, try it out in the worksheet shown in Figure 5.3. Enter labels and values as shown. If you wish, use the Data Fill command to enter a sequence of numbers in ranges A1..E5 and B9..E9.

With the cell pointer in cell B2, pressing End RightArrow gets you to cell E2, because cell E2 is the next cell to the right that abuts an empty cell. From cell E2, pressing End DownArrow takes you to cell E5. Another End DownArrow shuttles you down to cell E9. From cell E9, End LeftArrow brings you to cell B9.

Learning Your Way Around   **117**

```
              Untitled
      A      B      C      D      E      F
  1   0      5      10     15     20
  2   1      6      11     16     21
  3   2      7      12     17     22
  4   3      8      13     18     23
  5   4      9      14     19     24
  6
  7
  8
  9          0      1      2      3
 10
 11
 12
```

Figure 5.3. Use this sample worksheet to try out the End key. The End key is a fast way to move to the end of a group of cells that contain data.

When you press End and then an Arrow key that heads in a direction where there's no more data, you move to the last possible cell in that direction, be it column A or IV or row 1 or 8192. Pressing End DownArrow with the cell pointer in cell B9, for example, moves you to cell B8192. Press Home to return to the civilized section of your worksheet.

Moving quickly through your chunks of data makes short work of highlighting ranges for @functions and for such tasks as printing, styling, formatting, and label alignment.

As you'll see in Chapter 18, *Mastering the SmartIcon Palette*, 1-2-3/W includes SmartIcons that mimic End-key shortcuts. However, these are not part of the default group of icons, so you must customize the SmartIcon palette if you want them on hand.

The GOTO Key and Range Go To

If you want to get to a particular cell, especially one that's not visible in the current window, you can beam yourself over to that cell. To get your express ticket to another cell, press the GOTO key (F5) or choose the Go To command from the Range menu.

In either case, you get a dialog box that lets you specify the cell you want to jump to. Enter the cell location, and 1-2-3/W takes you right there. If the cell you're going to was already visible in the window, the cell pointer moves, but the worksheet doesn't scroll. If the cell was not previously visible, the worksheet scrolls so that the cell you specified appears in the upper-left cell of the window. And note that if you use a range reference or range name as the location to go to, the cell pointer moves to the first cell in that range.

The GOTO key and the Range Go To command let you zip the cell pointer to a designated location.

Range Roving—Anchor Away

Where would you be without spreadsheet ranges?

If you had to issue a separate command to alter each cell, it would take ages to format a large worksheet. And @functions, like @SUM, that use data from a range of cells would be just a pipedream.

Of course, range references are an essential part of 1-2-3/W, as they are in any spreadsheet. But though you may know the value of using ranges, do you know how to specify a range as easily as possible?

When you want to point to a range of cells you need a way to stretch the cell pointer to highlight more than a single cell. You do this by *anchoring*, identifying the first cell in a range. Then as you use the navigation keys, you expand the highlight to identify the opposite corner of the range.

You anchor a range by identifying its first corner. The range is automatically anchored for some commands, such as Edit Quick Copy. In other words, its notation refers to a range of cells, such as A1..A1, rather than to a single cell, such as A1.

Taking off the 3 D Glasses

Remember that since 1-2-3/W is a 3 D worksheet environment, its range references include a sheet letter. In other words, cell A4 of sheet A is actually cell A:A4. Cell A4 of sheet B is B:A4. To simplify notation, however, the sheet letters are omitted in this section, since all references are to sheet A.

As in other versions of 1-2-3, you press the period key to anchor the range from Point mode. 1-2-3/W goes into Point mode when you move the cell pointer while building a formula and also when 1-2-3/W requests that you specify a range.

The anchored cell becomes one corner of the range reference. You identify the opposite corner of the range by moving the cell pointer to that corner or by entering the cell address of that corner.

If you want to expand or contract the range, you can use the navigation keys to move to the last-specified corner of the anchored range—the *free corner*. To make a different corner the free corner, press the period key until that corner becomes the latter part of the range reference as shown in 1-2-3/W's Control panel.

For example, say you're using Point mode to enter the formula @COUNT(C2..E5) into cell E6 of a worksheet, such as the one in Figure 5.3. You move the cell pointer to cell E6 and type *@COUNT(*. Then you move the cell pointer to cell C2 and type a period to anchor the range. Next, you move to cell E5 to extend the selection, but you don't finish entering the @function just yet.

You decide that this function should count the number of entries in range B1..C5—a slightly larger range than C2..C5. Fortunately, you can fix the formula with a couple of quick steps. Press the period key two times to make C2 the free corner. Then move the cell pointer up and to the left to highlight cell B1. If, before you enter a closing parenthesis, you want to change the reference back to the original order, you can do so by pressing the period twice more. This last step isn't necessary, but many people like their references to start with the upper-left cell in the range, such as B1..E5, rather than with the lower-right cell, such as E5..B1.

> ### Do Mice Use Anchors?
> When you use a mouse to specify ranges, you usually don't speak of anchoring the range. You select the range by dragging the mouse from one corner of the range to its diagonal opposite. But the effect is the same: a range reference or selection that spans from one cell to another.

Keyboard Preselection

If you've tried any of the exercises in chapters 2, 3, or 4, you know that 1-2-3/W lets you select cells before, as well as during, a command.

Dragging the mouse is one way to preselect. But do you recall how to use the keyboard to preselect cells?

Though the period is the traditional key for anchoring while in Point mode, it won't do for selecting cells from Ready mode. This is because 1-2-3/W assumes that when you type a period in Ready mode, you're starting to enter a decimal number, rather than trying to preselect cells.

The answer: 1-2-3/W keyboard users can anchor a preselection by pressing ABS (F4). Note, however, that this doesn't let you anchor from Point mode.

To preselect with the keyboard press ABS (F4) from Ready mode. Then highlight the range and press Enter.

When you press ABS from Ready mode to begin preselecting, 1-2-3/W goes into Point mode, allowing you to use navigation keys to expand the selection. If need be, you can use the previously discussed method for reshaping a range—typing a period one or more times if necessary to respecify the free corner, and then navigating to expand or shrink the range. Once you've identified the selection press Enter. You can also preselect by pressing ABS (F4) and then typing a range reference or range name and pressing Enter.

Remember that when you issue a command, 1-2-3/W uses the preselected range to complete the command. If the command displays a dialog box that requests more than one range, the preselection becomes the first range in the dialog box.

> ### Hold That Cell
>
> If you press the ScrollLock key, the cell pointer resists moving as you scroll the sheet, whether you use navigation keys or the scroll bars. However, the cell pointer's position does change anytime it would otherwise scroll off the screen. To turn off ScrollLock "mode" press ScrollLock a second time.

Function Keys

1-2-3/W's function keys are largely a combination of traditional 1-2-3 function keys and traditional Windows function keys. Table 5.1 shows how 1-2-3/W uses the function keys by themselves and when modified with the Alt and Shift keys.

Other than Alt-F4, Ctrl-F4, and Ctrl-F6, which are standard Windows accelerator keys, 1-2-3/W's function keys are largely similar to those supported by Releases 2.01, 2.2, 2.3, and 3.x. But there are a few differences worth noting.

> ### Other Speed Keys
>
> 1-2-3/W supports several other Windows accelerator keys, along with ones based on the function key ones: Alt-F4, Ctrl-F4, and Ctrl-F6. For a complete listing, see the cheat sheet supplied at the back of this book.

	Key	Alt-Key	Ctrl-Key
F1	HELP	COMPOSE	
F2	EDIT	STEP	
F3	NAME	RUN	
F4	ABS	Close application window	Close document window
F5	GOTO		
F6	PANE	ZOOM	Next document window
F7	QUERY	ADDIN 1	
F8	TABLE	ADDIN 2	
F9	CALC	ADDIN 3	
F10	MENU		

Table 5.1. 1-2-3/W function keys. The first column shows the effect of pressing the key by itself. The second and third columns show the result of pressing the key simultaneously with, respectively, the Alt and Ctrl keys.

Not Supported in 1-2-3/W

The only major 1-2-3 function key that 1-2-3/W doesn't support is the GRAPH key (F10 in other releases). Windows reserves this key as an alternative to using Alt to bring up a menu. While there isn't a GRAPH key in 1-2-3/W, there is a SmartIcon you can use to create a graph based on selected data.

Unlike Releases 2.x and 3.x, 1-2-3/W does not use Alt-F10 as the add-in key. It uses the Tools Add-in command instead. Also, unlike Release 2.x, 1-2-3/W doesn't let you assign an add-in program to the Alt-F10 key. It does, however, let you assign 1-2-3/W add-ins to Alt-F7, Alt-F8, and Alt-F9, as in Releases 2.x and 3.x.

And a minor point for Release 2.3 mavens. Release 2.3's use of Ctrl-F1 as the BOOKMARK key, which revisits the last-viewed Help topic, is not supported in 1-2-3/W. However, 1-2-3/W's Help does provide a Bookmark feature of its own.

The Same But Different

Some of 1-2-3/W's function keys have different names or do different things. And some provide relatively new features that are supported by some, but not all, releases of 1-2-3.

In 1-2-3/W, the F6 key is known as the PANE key, rather than the WINDOW key, as it is in other versions of 1-2-3. The key was renamed to prevent confusion between in-sheet "windowing" features, which this key supports—and which are discussed in Chapter 8—and the application, document, and other types of windows that are part of the Microsoft Windows environment.

As in Release 3.x, Alt-F6 in 1-2-3/W is the ZOOM key. This key, like the PANE key, helps you work with in-sheet "windows." After you use the Window Split command to break a worksheet into multiple views, you can temporarily restore a full-screen view by pressing ZOOM. To return to split-screen view, you press ZOOM once more.

Variations on a Symphony

Symphony users will experience a bit of déjà vu with these "new" 1-2-3/W keys: F10 as the MENU key, F6 as the PANE key, and Alt-F6 as the ZOOM key. Lotus's integrated package has always applied these names to these keys, although they operate somewhat differently in Symphony than in 1-2-3/W.

And as in Releases 2.2 and higher, the RUN key (Alt-F3) in 1-2-3/W starts a macro—even if the macro has a long range name or no name at all. For more on macros, see Chapter 17.

As mentioned earlier in this chapter, you can use 1-2-3/W's NAME key (F3) to bring up a list of @functions and macro commands. This use is also supported in Release 3.x. To learn about other uses of the NAME key, see Chapter 8.

Likewise, the ABS (F4) now boasts an added use that was described earlier in this chapter: It serves as a preselection key when 1-2-3/W is in Ready mode. The ABS key performs this task in the WYSIWYG add-in of Releases 3.1 and 3.1+ and in Release 2.3 with or without the add-in. The traditional use for this key, for specifying absolute references, is described in Chapter 7.

6

Labels, Values, and Formulas

One of the hallmarks of a spreadsheet is how much it does with so little. Its three essential elements—labels, values, and formulas—take you all the way from beginner to expert. No matter how simple or sophisticated your application, this terrific trio stands you in good stead.

In this chapter you'll learn tricks to use and traps to avoid when entering labels, values, and formulas. You'll also learn how to use exotic types of data, such as dates and times, and the full range of data-formatting options. And to exploit the full power of formulas, you'll learn how to make sense of 1-2-3/W's extensive library of @functions.

This section presumes that you know how to edit cell entries. If you need to learn more about cell-editing techniques, see the section "Editing Cells in 1-2-3/W" in Chapter 3.

Label Essentials

For the most part, entering labels simply means moving the cell pointer and typing text. This makes adding headings and other text into your worksheet a very easy task.

But occasionally you'll run into problems when entering labels, and you'll want to know how to avoid or resolve them. And there are a host of alignment features you can use to make your text appear where and how you want it.

> *In this chapter you will learn:*
> - *The effective use of labels, values, and formulas*
> - *How to use non-numeric formulas, such as date, logical, string formulas*
> - *How to avoid common formula errors*
> - *How to format numeric data*
> - *How to use @functions*

The exercises in the section "Aligning Labels" in Chapter 4 reviewed some of the basics of label prefixes and touched on some lesser-known features. Here, we'll explore these and other label techniques in more depth.

Label Prefix Basics

As you probably know from previous worksheet experience, when you enter a label, it automatically gains a label prefix. The prefix determines how the label is displayed.

1-2-3/W recognizes eight label prefixes. These are listed in Table 6.1.

Prefix	Result	Result if Label is Wider than Column
'	Left-aligned label	Overflows into cell to the right
"	Right-aligned label	Overflows into cell to the right
^	Centered label	Overflows into cell to the right
|	Nonprinting label	Overflows into cell to the right
\	Repeating label	Displays only as many characters as fit in the cell
^^	Centered label	Overflows into cells to the right and left
""	Flush-right label	Overflows into cell to the left
"|	Even spacing	Overflows into cell to the right

Table 6.1. 1-2-3/W's label prefixes are listed in the first column. The second column describes the ordinary effect of the prefix, and the third column shows what happens when the label is too wide for the column it's in. Note that the last three prefixes in the table were introduced with the WYSIWYG add-in of Releases 2.3 and 3.1.

How to Pick a Prefix

Unless you specify otherwise, all labels you enter start with an apostrophe label prefix, the prefix that left-aligns a label. You can choose a different prefix by any of seven methods:

- Type the prefix when you start entering the label.
- Edit the label and substitute one prefix for another.
- Choose the Style-Alignment command.
- Click one of the label-alignment SmartIcons.
- Use the 1-2-3 Classic command /Range Label-Alignment.
- Use the 1-2-3 Classic command :Text Alignment.
- Select a different "default" prefix by using the Worksheet Global Settings command.

The first two options let you change only one label's prefix. The next four options let you change several labels at once.

The last option, changing the global prefix, lets you set 1-2-3/W to insert a particular prefix when you enter labels. This does not alter the prefixes of existing labels, and you can always override this setting by typing another prefix.

Also note that the :Text Alignment command is the WYSIWYG command for choosing newer prefix options, such as the double-caret prefix described below. It complements the /Range Label-Alignment command, which supports the more common prefixes that are described in the following section.

1-2-3/W offers seven different ways to align a label.

The Common Prefixes: Left, Center, and Right Alignment

The first three prefixes listed in Table 6.1 are the most commonly used: the apostrophe ('), quotation mark ("), and caret (^) prefixes. Respectively, they left-align a label, center a label, and right-align a label.

Figure 6.1. The left-, center-, and right-alignment SmartIcons. A fast way to align a group of labels is to select them and click one of these icons.

These three prefixes are the only ones that have icons in the default SmartIcon palette. The icons for left-aligning, centering, and right-aligning a label are shown in Figure 6.1.

If a label with one of these prefixes is too wide to fit in a cell, its contents spill over into the neighboring cell, or cells, to the right. However, if the neighboring cell contains an entry, characters that don't fit into the current cell are not displayed—except in the Edit line. As with any label, the entire label is stored in the cell you enter it in, even if it appears to continue into other cells.

Nonprinting Text: The Vertical Bar Prefix

The vertical-bar prefix (|) behaves similarly to the apostrophe prefix, except when it's in the first column of a Print range. In earlier versions of 1-2-3, this prefix is used to embed special print codes and page breaks into the worksheet. These techniques, however, are generally not used in printing in 1-2-3/W. For more on how to print in 1-2-3/W see Chapter 10.

Another Way to Center: The Double-Caret Prefix

The double-caret prefix (^^) is a variation on the caret prefix (^) for centering a label. The difference is in what happens if the label is too wide to fit in a cell. A long label with a single-caret prefix fills the current cell and overlaps into the cell to the right, just like a label with an apostrophe prefix. But a label with a double-caret prefix, remains centered, even when it exceeds the width of the column.

    Oversized labels with this prefix spill out into neighboring cells on both the right and left of the cell. However, if there is an entry in the neighboring cell, or if the label is in the first or last column in the worksheet, some characters may not be visible.

Flush-Right Labels: The Double-Quote Prefix

The double-quote prefix ("") has the same relationship to the quote prefix (") that the double-caret prefix has to the caret prefix. Whereas the regular quotation-mark prefix right-aligns text only if it fits neatly in the cell, the double-quote prefix keeps the label right-aligned, even if it has to spill over into its neighbor on the left to do it.

Even Alignment: The Apostrophe Vertical Bar Combination

The apostrophe vertical-bar prefix even-aligns a label. Ordinarily, Windows uses proportional spacing, meaning that characters vary in width. The characters in an even-aligned label are spaced evenly within the cell.

You choose even alignment by selecting 1-2-3/W's Style Alignment command with the Align-over-columns option and the Even-alignment option. When you complete the command, the apostrophe vertical-bar combination becomes the label prefix, and all selected cells are formatted with the Text attribute.

Aligning Over Columns and the Secret of Text

The Align-over-columns option in the Style Alignment command applies the Text attribute to all selected cells. Left-aligned, centered, right-aligned, and even-aligned cells align themselves within the range of cells to their right that have the Text attribute.

For example, let's say you have a label in cell B2. If you select range B2..D2 and you choose Style Alignment with the Center and Align-over-columns settings, the label will be centered over all those columns. If you move the cell pointer through range B2..D2, you'll see in the control panel that each of these cells has the Text attribute. In the event that the Text attribute is removed from cell D2, the label would then be aligned within range B2..C2.

The Text attribute is common to 1-2-3/W and 1-2-3 Releases 2.3 and 3.x with the WYSIWYG add-in. The Text attribute allows you to perform a variety of word-processing-like operations in the worksheet. This attribute, incidentally is not related to the Text cell format, which displays the formula of a cell rather than its current value.

You can directly apply the Text attribute to one or more cells by choosing :Text Set, and you can remove it by choosing :Text Clear or by selecting the Styles option of the Edit Clear Special command.

Preventing Prefix Problems

Following are common label-prefix problems and ways to prevent or fix them.

Macro Names in the Worksheet

It's common practice to identify a macro with a label. The most common macro names consist of a backslash and a letter. Because the backslash is a label prefix, you have to think twice before entering such a label.

For example, to enter the macro name \M into a cell, you must precede it with a prefix, such as an apostrophe. If you enter \M in a cell, 1-2-3/W fills the cell with M's. If you enter '\M, the entry appears, correctly, as \M. For more on macros, see Chapter 17.

Extra Prefixes

When you edit a label, be careful not to put additional characters to the left of the label prefix. Otherwise, the prefix will be displayed.

Consider a left-aligned label containing the word *Total*. What would happen if you entered *Sub-* before the apostrophe? The label would appear in the worksheet as *Sub-'Total*. In the edit line, it would appear as *'Sub-'Total*.

When you add characters before the apostrophe, or before any other prefix, it ceases to be a prefix. Therefore, 1-2-3/W supplies a new label prefix.

Occasionally, though, you might want to use an extra prefix. You need to enter two apostrophes to display the labels *'Tis the season* or *'Til the pond freezes over*. And as noted above, 1-2-3 lets you double up on caret and quotation-mark prefixes for special types of alignment.

Labels in Disguise

To enter a label that starts with—or looks like—a number or formula, precede it with a label prefix such as the apostrophe (').

You don't have to type a prefix to enter a label that looks like a label, such as *Grand Total* or *Five-Thousand Accordion Favorites*. However, you need to forewarn 1-2-3/W when you want to enter a label that starts with a number or with a character that ordinarily starts a formula: for example, *5,000 Accordion Favorites*, *@ the Hop*, or *#9 Dream*.

Some of these camouflaged labels make 1-2-3/W throw up its arms. If you enter *100 Pound Bag*, 1-2-3/W wonders, "What does this person want from me? Is this a label, a formula, or what?" Stumped by your ambiguous entry, it puts you into Edit mode to clarify your intentions. You can resolve the situation either by inserting a prefix at the beginning of the label or by otherwise changing the entry into a typical label, value, or formula.

Other times, you enter what looks exactly like a number, such as 1999, but you want it treated as a label. 1-2-3/W accepts the entry, but in the form of a value: It appears towards the right of the cell, and you can't use label-alignment commands to reposition it within the column. If you want to turn it into a label, you must edit the cell and insert a label prefix.

And what if you want to start a label with a slash (/), a less-than sign (<), or a colon(:)? All of these characters bring up the 1-2-3 Classic menu, rather than signalling the start of a label.

To avoid all of these ambiguous situations, you can type a prefix before you enter such a label. Or you can assign the cell either the Automatic or the Label format *before* you enter the data, although this latter technique won't let you enter labels that start with menu-access commands. For details on selecting numeric, date, and other formats, see the "Cell Formats" section later in this chapter.

Labels That Won't Quit

As described throughout this section, labels that are too long to fit in a cell usually overflow into neighboring cells. This allows you to write long labels in a single cell without having to change the width of the entire column or break the label into sections, one in each cell.

It's important to remember that the entire label resides in the cell in which you entered it, no matter how many other cells the label overlaps. Even seasoned 1-2-3 veterans occasionally get mixed up and try to edit, restyle, or otherwise change the cells in which the label spills into, only to realize after a bit of frustration that it is the cell in which the label was entered that needs the attention.

The solution? When in doubt, look up in the Edit line to see if it displays the label that you *think* is contained in the current cell.

Incidentally, there is one case in which the settings of another cell affect a label that's entered in an adjoining cell. This is when you align a label over multiple columns. See the box "Aligning Over Columns and the Secret of Text" for more details.

Labels that are too large to fit into one cell spill over into neighboring cells; however, the entire contents of the label are actually stored in the cell where you entered it.

Value Essentials

Easy as it is to enter labels, entering values is even easier. There are no prefixes to enter, and few special rules.

The most common value-entry mistake is attempting to enter formatting characters, such as dollar signs and commas, with the values. While you do enter a period to specify decimal values, you generally don't type other formatting characters.

You add formatting by using the Range Format command. You can type dollar signs, but in most cases 1-2-3/W will ignore them. Commas, on the other hand, are usually not allowed.

Of course, to enter negative numbers, you type a minus sign immediately before the number. And as in 1-2-3 Release 3, you can also enter negative numbers by enclosing them in parentheses, but this is less convenient than using a minus sign.

There are four other exceptions to the rule of not typing formatting characters. First, you can enter dates in a form such as *mm/dd/yy*, for example, 8/15/63. The resulting value is a date serial number, the use of which is explained later in the chapter in the "Cell Formats" section.

Second, you can instantly turn a number into its percentage value—in other words, divide it by 100—by entering a percent sign after it. For example, you can enter *45%* in a cell to put the value .45 in the cell.

Third, in a little-known innovation that comes from 1-2-3 Release 3.x, you can enter numbers in a fractional form. For example, you can enter *8 1/2*, with a space between the eight and the one. This enters the value 8.5 in the cell.

Automatic format dynamically assigns a cell format based on the way you enter the data.

Finally, if you use the Automatic format—also from Release 3.x and also described in the "Cell Formats" section—you can and should enter formatting symbols, such as dollar signs. Cells with Automatic format use these characters to figure out an appropriate format to convert to. For example, if you enter *98.6%* in an Automatic formatted cell, 1-2-3/W divides the number by 100 for you and it sets the format to Percent with one decimal place.

From Formula to Value

Sometimes you want to change the result of a formula into a value. For example, you might want to preserve a current set of formula results for future analysis. Or you might want to do some quick arithmetic in a cell and then convert the result to a simple value.

To convert a formula to a value, you edit the cell and press the CALC key (F9). In the Edit line, you can see that the formula is replaced by its current value. To store this value, press Enter.

To convert a range of formulas to values, you use the Edit Quick Copy command's Convert-to-values option, or the 1-2-3 Classic /Range Values command. For more details, see Chapter 7.

Formula Essentials

Remember the first time you saw what 1-2-3 could do? It was nothing short of magic.

It's hard to believe you ever worked the old way—punching the same numbers into a calculator, again and again. Every time you made a change. And every time you weren't *sure* the numbers were correct. When that muscle-bound spreadsheet drove up in its sleek new PC, your calculator was crushed, devastated, totaled.

You warmed up to the worksheet by laying out your text and numbers in neat little rows and columns. So far, so good.

But the magic took hold when you began entering formulas. You waved the cell pointer over the cells you wanted multiplied, summed, averaged, and so on. And the spreadsheet did the rest. Your calculator never stood a chance.

It got even better the next time you did the same task. As soon as you typed in the new data, the work was done. 1-2-3 remembered all the formula tricks you taught it the last time. It was almost like cheating—as if you found an algebra book that had all the answers.

In this section you'll learn formula features that many users overlook. These techniques complement your knowledge of formula fundamentals, such as addition and multiplication, which you used in the exercises in Chapter 3, and which you probably use frequently in your own work.

Do you know, for example, which characters you can use to start a formula? And do you know the *operators* that lie beyond addition, subtraction, multiplication, and division, and how they can help you make smarter applications?

Like a lot of experienced 1-2-3 users, you may also be new to 1-2-3/W's more exotic formula types. These include *date*, *time*, *logical*, and *string* formulas.

Why are these important? If you know how to use date formulas, you can, for example, determine how many days a payment is overdue. Logical formulas can help you find out whether an account is paid in full. And you can use string formulas to create customer codes based on other data you enter.

Note that these formula tips are just a part of the story. Formulas work in concert with cell formats to make percentages look like percentages, dates look like dates, and so on. And 1-2-3/W's library of @functions enriches your formulas with calculations that would otherwise be difficult or impossible for the spreadsheet to perform. Cell formats and @functions are discussed in subsequent sections.

In addition to knowing the ideal uses of formulas, you should know how to sidestep common formula problems. So be sure to check out the section "Avoiding Formula Failures I" at the end of this chapter.

If you understand the full breadth of 1-2-3/W's formula features, you can streamline and enhance your applications.

What Makes a Formula?

Although formulas can perform an almost limitless variety of tasks, every formula does one of two things: It displays a label or it displays a value.

What differentiates a formula from a simple label or value is that it uses one or more calculations to determine the appropriate string or number to display. Labels and values, on the other hand, always display the same data until someone, or some macro, changes them.

In this section we'll explore the components of a formula.

Starting a Formula

A lot of 1-2-3 users are in the habit of starting formulas with a plus sign (+). It's not a bad habit, because it eliminates a common entry error: entering a label when you mean to enter a formula.

If, for example, you want to enter a formula that multiplies cells G2 and G3, you should start it with a plus sign: +G2*G3. If you forget to type the plus sign, 1-2-3/W interprets the first "G" as the beginning of a label; so it enters G2*G3, preceded by a label prefix, into the cell. Because it's a label, it's not going to multiply numbers or perform any other sort of calculation. Fortunately, you can use Edit mode to replace the label prefix with a plus sign, so you don't need to reenter the entire formula.

One time that there's no need for a plus sign is when you enter an @function. 1-2-3/W knows that an entry that begins with an at sign is a formula. In fact, if you start a formula with a plus sign followed by an @function, 1-2-3/W doesn't bother to store the plus sign.

You can use a few other characters to start formulas. Except for the at sign and the pound sign, these characters can also start off simple numeric values.

The valid formula-starting characters are listed in Table 6.2.

Character	Example
Number	7
Currency symbol	$
Plus sign	+
Minus sign	-
Period	.
Open parenthesis	(
At sign	@
Pound sign	#

Table 6.2. Characters that can start a formula.

Despite the variety of options, starting all formulas with a plus sign or an at sign is a worthwhile technique. As you move the cell pointer through the sheet, you only have to watch for these two characters in the Edit line to spot the cells that contain formulas. And automatically starting off your formulas with the plus sign keeps you from accidentally entering formulas as labels, as described above.

Formula Entries

All formulas contain one or more of the following types of entries: numeric values, character strings, references to one or more cells, and @functions. These items are, in a sense, the bricks that give substance to your formulas. Table 6.3 details the types of entries that you may put in a formula.

Type of Entry	Example	Formula Example	Result of Example
Value	11	+B3*11	Adds 11 to the value of cell B3
String	"Dear"	+"Dear "&B5	Combines *Dear* and the label from cell B5
Cell reference	C19	+C19*14	Multiplies the value of cell C19 by 14
Range reference	C19..C25	@SUM(C19..C25)	Sums the values in all cells from C19 through C25
Range name	*salary_list*	@MAX(*salary_list*)	Finds the highest value in the range named *salary_list*
@function	@MAX()	See above	See above

Table 6.3. Examples of valid formula entries in 1-2-3/W.

Operators are the mortar that glues these pieces into a cohesive whole. Operators determine the relationships among the entries, such as whether one item is added to or subtracted from the following item. 1-2-3/W's operators are listed in Table 6.4.

Symbol	Purpose	Example	Result of Example
+	Addition	+D18+9	Adds 9 to the value of cell D18
-	Subtraction	+D7-D8	Subtracts the value of cell D8 from the value of cell D7
/	Division	+G82/100	Divides the value of cell G82 by 100
*	Multiplication	+H18*H24	Multiplies the value of cell H18 by the value of cell H24
^	Exponentiation	+G17^2	Squares the value of cell G17
=	Equals	+B2=7	Returns 1 if the value of cell B2 is 7; otherwise, returns 0
>	Greater than	+B2>7	Returns 1 if the value of cell B2 is greater than 7; otherwise, returns 0
<	Less than	+B2<7	Returns 1 if the value of cell B2 is less than 7; otherwise, returns 0
>=	Greater than or equal to	+B2>=7	Returns 1 if the value of cell B2 is greater than or equal to 7; otherwise returns 0
<=	Less than or equal to	+B2<=7	Returns 1 if the value of cell B2 is less than or equal to 7; otherwise, returns 0
<>	Greater than or less than	+B2<>7	Returns 1 if the value of cell B2 does not equal 7; otherwise, returns 0
#NOT#	Not condition	#NOT#B2=7	Returns 1 if the value of cell B2 does not equal 7; otherwise, returns 0
#AND#	Both conditions 1 and 2	+B2=7#AND#B3=2	Returns 1 if the value of cell B2 equals 7 *and* the value of cell B3 equals 2; otherwise, returns 0
#OR#	Either condition 1 or 2	+B2=7#OR#B3=2	Returns 1 if the value of cell B2 equals 7 *or* if the value of cell B3 equals 2; otherwise, returns 0
&	Concatenation	+"Dear "&B3	If cell B3 contains the label *John*, returns *Dear John*

Table 6.4. 1-2-3/W's arithmetic, logical, and string operators.

If you're unfamiliar with creating formulas that include the equal sign, or any of the operators listed below it, you'll learn about them shortly. The last item on the list, the ampersand (&) operator is used in string formulas. And the logical, or relational operators, like the equal sign and #NOT#, are key elements in logical formulas.

String Formulas

String formulas sound like a contradiction in terms. Usually, strings, or labels, as you call them when you enter them in cells, are the things that you don't perform calculations on. But string formulas provide a lot of benefits. They can display an appropriate snippet of text based on data in the worksheet, and they can merge text and numbers to create a unique product code.

For example, if you enter your age in cell B8, you can put the following formula in another cell to see if you're old enough to be president of the United States: @IF(B8<35,"Sorry, kid, you can't be president","You've got my vote, friend"). If the value of cell B8 is less than 35, you get the string that appears after the first comma; otherwise, you get the second string.

That was a logical formula that displayed a string in a cell. Other formulas actually alter strings of text. For example @PROPER("e.e. cummings") displays the string as *E.E. Cummings*, while @UPPER("please be quiet") converts its string to *PLEASE BE QUIET*.

You can also use cell references in a string formula. For example, if you have the label *Oil* in cell B15 and *Water* in cell B16, the following formula will combine them to say *Oil and Water don't mix*: +B15&" and "&B16&" don't mix." The ampersands (&) combine, or "concatenate," the strings, and the spaces within the quotes surrounding the word *and* separate the words.

To make the most of string formulas, you need to make use of 1-2-3/W's string-related @functions. @PROPER and @UPPER are but two small examples. See the section on @functions to learn how to perform such trickery as counting the number of characters in a string, borrowing a few characters from a label, and turning values into labels, and vice versa. And for the complete rundown of string functions, see the @function reference in the back of the book.

You can joins strings of text in a formula with an ampersand (&).

Logical Formulas

Logical formulas let your worksheets change with the "whether." They test whether or not one or more conditions are true. If the conditions prove true, you get one result; if they prove false, you can get another.

Logical formulas let your applications identify and act on the status of your data.

The business applications are innumerable. You can have a cell display a warning message if a certain situation exists—for example, if a department's expenses exceed its budgeted amount. And you can choose to charge a lower price if the size of an order exceeds a specific volume.

The @IF function shown in the previous section is representative of the many logical tests you can perform in 1-2-3/W. @IF, like all other logical operations in 1-2-3/W, uses a simple scheme to tell true from false.

To 1-2-3/W, the number 1 means true and 0 means false. To see this in its simplest form, type *2=9* in a cell. 1-2-3/W displays 0, because this statement is false: 2 does not equal 9.

Enter *2=2*, and you get the number 1. The 1 indicates that 2 does equal 2.

This simple behavior allows you to test for a variety of conditions. Because it can tell the difference between what is and what isn't, your worksheet can behave quite intelligently.

Of course you don't need to ask 1-2-3/W whether 2 equals 2, but you might want to know if the interest rate in cell G19 exceeds 12%. Thanks to 1-2-3/W's logical thinking, you can create a formula like @IF(G19>.12,"Sell","Buy").

Or perhaps you want to offer a special rate to your customers who come from Indiana. If the two-letter state code is in cell B3, and the regular rate is in cell G3, you could use this formula to give your Hoosier clients a 25% discount: @IF(B3="IN",G3*.75,G3).

@IF is probably the most commonly used logical @function, but there are several others. For details on logical functions see the section on @functions later in this chapter, and for the complete story see the @function reference in the back of the book.

As Table 6.4 shows, a large number of 1-2-3's operators are built for logical, or relational, operations. Most of them perform simple comparisons, such as determining whether one item is greater than or equal to another.

#AND# and #OR# operators let you test for two conditions in the same formula.

Three others let you alter or combine other logical operations different: #NOT#, #AND#, and #OR#. #NOT# determines whether a condition is not true. It is a variation on <>. #NOT# takes a regular logical test and turns it upside down. For example, the statement #NOT#2=2 yields a 0 (false). The #NOT# turns the question, *Is it true that 2 = 2?* into the question, *Is it untrue that 2=2.?*

#AND# lets you test whether two conditions are both true. You put conditions on either side of this operator. If either the first or the second condition is false, the result of this formula is false (0). For example, the statement 2=2#AND#3=4 returns a 0 (false), because the latter condition is untrue.

#OR# lets you confirm that at least one of two conditions is true. As with the #AND# operator, you put conditions on either side of this operator. If either the first or the second condition is true, or if both are true, this formula returns a 1 (true). For example, 2=2#OR#3=4 returns 1, because the first condition is true.

Time and Date Formulas

1-2-3/W uses a numeric scheme to keep track of dates and times. January 1, 1900, is date 1, and each date thereafter has its own number. January 1, 2001, for example, is date number 36892.

Times are recorded as fractions of a day. For example, noon is 0.5, and 3 P.M. is 0.625.

Traditionally, you had to use @functions to enter dates in 1-2-3. Unfortunately, few among us know such simple facts as the day we were born or even today's date, at least not by serial number.

1-2-3/W, like 1-2-3 Release 3.x, liberates you from having to use @DATE or @DATEVALUE functions for each date you want to enter. In 1-2-3/W, you can enter a date in the *mm/dd/yy* form, such as 11/16/85, and the software understands that you're not trying to divide 11 by 16 by 85. Instead, it translates your entry into a serial number. Then all you have to do is format the number with one of 1-2-3/W's date formats.

It's easy to enter date serial numbers. You just type the date in a form such as 06/24/91.

You can also enter dates in the forms *dd-mmm-yy* or *dd-mmm*, for example 16-Nov-85 or 16-Nov. Note that if you leave the year off, as in the *dd-mmm* form, 1-2-3/W assumes the current year.

And if you want to refer to dates in the 21st century, specify a four-digit year, for example, 16-Nov-2085 or 11/16/2085.

Similarly, you can enter times in such common formats as 3:15:02 PM. This spares you the task of entering it as either 0.63544 or @TIME(15,15,02).

Treating dates and times as serial numbers makes possible all sorts of useful calculations. For example, to find out how far overdue someone's account is, take today's date (@TODAY) and subtract from it the date due. Or to find out when you'll be 100 years old, take your birthday and add 36525 to it (100 times 365 1/4 days).

See the following sections on formats and @functions to learn more about making dates and times with 1-2-3/W. And be sure to check out the @function list in the back of the book for an exhaustive list of date and time @functions.

Cell Formats

In the exercises in Chapter 3, we tried out two numeric formats: Comma and Currency. These are but two of the 1-2-3/W formats that you can apply to a value or a formula that results in a value.

The right format makes your data say what it's supposed to say. It can control the number of decimal places displayed, and it can accent the data with currency symbols, commas, or parentheses.

Some formats do such tricky things as showing the text of a formula rather than its result, displaying numbers in a date format like 6/24/91, and hiding data from view. Newer formats, such as Automatic and Label, are even more dynamic, helping alter the way 1-2-3/W handles the data you input.

So don't just get fixated on Fixed format or go comatose with the Comma format. Check out the full range of options. 1-2-3/W's formats are listed in Table 6.5.

Formatting Ranges of Cells

A wide range of numeric formats lets you display your data as you see fit.

True to its name, the Range Format command lets you format a range of cells. The dialog box shown in Figure 6.2 it brings up is a one-stop place for choosing all the formatting details of a range of numbers: format type, decimal places, and the option of putting parentheses around the numbers.

Alternatively, you can use the 1-2-3 Classic equivalent, /Range Format. But this command is somewhat less convenient because some of its options are tucked away in submenus.

A handful of popular formats have SmartIcon formats shown in Figure 6.3. These can be the fastest way to change how your numbers display, but you should note that they assign a preset decimal precision. If you want to have it your way, use the Range Format command, with or without the slash.

To change the format of all cells—except for those that you have already formatted—you use the Format button in the Worksheet Global Settings dialog box. Or you can use the 1-2-3 Classic command /Worksheet Global Format. To learn more about setting formats globally, instead of by range, see Chapter 8, *Mastering the Sheet.*

Format Name	Description
Fixed	Displays a fixed number of decimal places (a number between 0 and 15) and a minus for negative numbers
Scientific	Displays numbers in exponential notation
Currency	Displays a fixed number of decimal places, along with a currency symbol, such as a dollar sign ($)
Comma	Separates thousands with commas
General	Displays a variable number of decimal places, with no commas (the default format)
+/-	Displays a small graph in the cell, such as +++ to represent the value 3, and — — for -2
Percent	Displays the number multiplied by 100, followed by a % sign, with up to 15 decimal places
Text	Displays the text of a formula, such as +B2*C2, rather than the result of the formula
Hidden	Makes the cell's contents invisible, although they appear in the Edit line when the cell pointer is on the cell, unless you activate 1-2-3/W's Worksheet Global Settings Protection option
Automatic	Changes its format based on the way you enter data. For example, if you enter data in a Currency format, the cell's format converts to that format
Label	Treats all entries as labels, even if they start with numbers or mathematical operators
Date and Time formats (choices 1-9)	Displays a date or time serial number in a variety of common formats such as 07-May-87 or 05/07/87

Table 6.5. 1-2-3/W Range Formats.

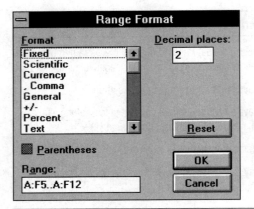

Figure 6.2. The Range Format dialog box. Here you can choose a format to apply to a range of numeric values and/or formulas that result in values. In addition to selecting a format, you can choose the number of decimal places you want to display, and you can choose to surround each value in the range with parentheses.

Figure 6.3. These SmartIcons let you quickly assign some of the most popular formats to a selected range of cells. From left to right, they assign a two-decimal Currency format, a no-decimal Comma format, and a two-decimal Percent format.

Common Cell Formats: Comma, Currency, Fixed, General, and Percent

Comma, Currency, Fixed, General, and Percent are the most commonly used formats. With the exception of General, they all let you choose the number of decimal places to display.

Comma format uses a comma—or another separator appropriate to a given country—to break up large numbers. If you deal in thousands or millions, this is a very useful format. Negative numbers in Comma format are enclosed in parentheses. Note that both Comma and Currency start with the same letter, so you select this option from the Format list box or the Range Format menu by typing a comma (,) rather than a C.

Currency format uses the monetary format you select with the Tools User Setup command, which is the same way you choose the separator for large numbers. In U.S. editions of 1-2-3/W, the currency symbol is a dollar sign ($), unless you specify otherwise. Currency format also displays negative numbers in parentheses.

Fixed format, like Comma format, is a relatively simple way to display values with a fixed number of decimal places. The differences are that no separators are used, and negative numbers in this format start with a minus sign.

General format is the usual default setting in 1-2-3/W. It displays numbers with as many decimal places as needed. And if the integer part of a number is too large to fit in a column, the number appears in Scientific notation. If the integer fits in a cell but one or more decimal places don't, the number appears to be rounded off.

Percent format multiplies the number by 100 and displays the result with a percent sign. For example, the number .5 appears as 50%.

Format Facts

It's easy to find out what format a cell is currently set to. Just move the cell pointer into the cell and look in the control panel at the top of the 1-2-3/W window. The format of the cell is described within parentheses.

For example, a cell that is assigned the Currency format with two decimal places displays (C2) in the control panel. A cell that is assigned the Date 1 format appears as (D1), and so on.

Cells that don't display any format in the control panel do not have an assigned format, so they'll change if you use the Worksheet Global Settings command to select a new global format. Ordinarily, the default format is General.

If you want to unformat a cell or range of cells, don't change them to General format. That would make them stay as General even if you chose a new global format. Instead, select the cell or cells and choose the Reset button from the Range Format dialog box.

Date and Time Formats

You can choose from one of nine different *Date* and *Time* formats. As described in the earlier section on date formulas, 1-2-3 stores dates as numbers, ranging from 1 (January 1, 1900): up to 73050 (December 31, 2099). And each portion of a day is a decimal value: for example, 12 noon is .5. Thus, June 24, 1990 at 6pm is stored as 33048.75.

This approach to handling dates and times gives you a lot of mathematical flexibility. But it doesn't present this data in a way most people can use.

Although 1-2-3/W stores dates and times as numbers, you can format them to make them easy to read.

When you apply date and time formats to these mysterious numbers, they turn into readable dates and times. Table 6.6 lists the available date and time formats.

Date/Time Format	Example
1	07-May-87
2	07-May
3	May-87
4	05/7/89
5	05/07
6	02:14:00 PM
7	02:14 PM
8	18:10:12
9	18:10

Table 6.6. 1-2-3/W's date formats.

Note that some of these formats generate a lot of characters. If you select the format and the data appears as a series of asterisks, its too wide for the current column width. If this happens, you need to choose a different format, widen the column, or select a small font size.

Other Formats: Scientific, +/–, Text, Hidden, Automatic, and Label

Most lay people don't use *Scientific* format, but it is a useful way to represent very large or small numbers in a small space. For this reason, values in cells assigned the General format display in Scientific format if they get too large to fit in the cell. An example of Scientific notation is 1.5E+04. This is a shorthand way of saying 1.5 moved four decimal places to the right, or 15000.

The +/- format lets you make a crude bar graph in a cell. For example, The number 7 in this format displays as seven plus signs (+++++++). The number -3 appears as three minus signs (– – –).

Text format displays formulas in the worksheet in the same form as they appear in the Edit line. You may want to use the Text format to temporarily display a series of formulas while you try to decode them. Note that this format works for string formulas and for formulas that return values.

Hidden format displays no data at all. This is helpful when you want to print a report while keeping a few pieces of information out of the printout. Note that unless you use other security features, you can still view the contents of a hidden cell by positioning the cell pointer in it and looking in the Edit line. For more details on hiding and protecting data, see Chapter 9. This format works for all types of entries, labels, values, and formulas.

Automatic format is an innovation that came in with 1-2-3 Release 3. Cells that you assign this format will automatically convert to one of the other formats, depending on how you enter data. For example, if you enter *$2.00* in a cell assigned the Automatic format, the cell's format instantly converts to Currency format with two decimal places. Note that once the format changes to Currency, Date 1, or whatever, the cell no longer has the Automatic format. You need to reassign Automatic format to the cell if you want it to perform this trick again.

Label format adds a label prefix to any data that you subsequently enter into the cell, even if that data looks like a value or formula. This is useful if you have to enter a lot of labels that look like or begin with numbers or formulas; otherwise, you'd have to type a prefix, such as an apostrophe, at the beginning of each entry. Assigning Label format to a cell that already contains a numeric entry does not turn the entry into a label. Instead, the value appears in General format.

Label format lets you display the formula as you entered instead of the results of the formula.

Parenthetically Speaking

Another option that came in with Release 3 is the ability to assign parentheses to all values in a range. This is not the same as displaying negative numbers in parentheses, as in the Comma and Currency formats.

This allows you, for example, to use positive numbers to represent expense items but to display them as if they were negative. Use this option sparingly, if at all, because it can confuse your readers. They may not be able to tell which values are negative. And if you apply parentheses to a range that includes negative numbers in Comma or Currency format, they'll appear with an extra set of parentheses, such as ((300.25)).

Don't Let the Format Fool You

A common mistake is to assume that changing a format changes the value. Although a change in format can completely change the way the data looks, it does not affect the value. For example, if you enter the number 5 in a cell and change it to Date 1 format, Percent format, +/- format, and then Currency format, it will evolve first into 05-Jan-00, and then into 500.00%, +++++, and $5.00.

Confusion about the Percent format is common. Consider this scenario: Your boss tells you your salary is about to be multiplied by a surprising amount. You'll be a might bit pleased when she shows you the worksheet. You're going to get five times your current pay! But before she prints the salary report, she decides to make one small change, displaying your salary multiplier in Percent format. The bubbles would go out of your champagne dreams pretty fast if your salary was multiplied by 5% instead of 5, just because she reformatted the number.

It's simple mathematics: The number 5 equals 500%. Although Percent format nominally divides a number by 100, by including the percent sign (%), it compensates by multiplying the number by 100. Thus, as in all other formatting changes, the value remains unchanged.

Remember that changing the format of a value does not actually change the value.

The Percentage Solution

If you want to enter 5%, enter .05 in a cell assigned the Percent format. Alternatively, you can include the percent sign (%) as you type. If you enter *5%* in a cell, 1-2-3/W automatically converts the value to .05. To make the number appear as *5%*, assign the cell the Percent format with two decimal places.

Some formats display numbers as rounded, but internally they are stored in full precision

A related pitfall is mistaking the appearance of rounding for actual rounding. Some numeric formats—specifically Comma, Currency, Fixed, Percent, Scientific, and General—may display numbers in rounded-off form. However, the actual value may differ from the displayed value by some decimal amount.

This becomes a concern if you need to do a logical comparison or if your work is sensitive to the finest decimal precision. For example, if you enter *38.47* into cell D8 and assign it the Fixed format with one decimal place, it appears as *38.5* in the cell. But if you enter the formula +D8=38.5 in cell D9, it will return 0 (false), because 38.47 does not equal 38.5. The formula +D8=38.47, on the other hand, would return a 1 (true).

You can solve the problem by using the @ROUND function, which lets you round a value—or a reference to a value—to a specific number of decimal places. If you enter @ROUND(38.47,1) in cell D8, the actual value of cell D8 becomes 38.5. Alternatively, you can use rounding in your test and leave the original value at its full precision: The formula *@ROUND(D8,1)=38.5* yields a 1 (true), because cell D8, rounded to one decimal place, does equal 38.5.

All About @Functions

It's no secret to most 1-2-3 users that Lotus's spreadsheets boast a broad array of built-in calculation functions. The exercises in Chapter 3, like most 1-2-3 worksheets, used the @SUM function to total a range of values. But how do you learn what lies beyond the simple sum?

Dozens of other functions help you with other database, date, time, financial, logical, mathematical, special, statistical, and string operations. If you don't know what's available, you can spend hours trying to reinvent the wheel, or you can miss out on a feature that could make your worksheet more accurate, more detailed, more automated, or more efficient.

Most @functions are easy to use. You simply type an at sign (@), the name of the function, an open parenthesis, and one or more arguments separated by commas. Then you wrap it up with a close parenthesis. The arguments are usually references to cells or ranges or values you type right into the function. The trickiest part is remembering the spelling of the @function's name and the number and type of arguments the function takes.

The entries you place within the parentheses of a string are called arguments. The value or label the @function derives is called the return value.

Born in a Barn?

1-2-3/W unlike other releases automatically enters a () at the end of your @function formula in case *you* forget to enter one.

1-2-3/W's Help system provides extensive information about @functions. As stated in the previous section, you can type an @function and then press the HELP key (F1) for details on how it works. Or you can choose either general @Function information or the @Function Index. Both of these are available directly from the Help Index.

Another way to find the @function of your dreams is to type @ and then press the NAME key (F3). You can scroll through the list that appears, or you can tab into the list and type a letter to jump to the functions that start with that letter. If you choose a function from this list, it automatically appears in the Edit line.

The mouse can also lead you to this @function list. But you must first add the at-sign SmartIcon to the icon palette. To learn how to customize the SmartIcon palette, see Chapter 18.

A New @Function and Some New Uses for an Old One

1-2-3/W supports all the @functions from 1-2-3 Releases 2.x and 3.x, including a number of new ones that came in with Releases 3. And it includes one new @function, @SOLVER, and new uses for Release 3's @INFO function.

@SOLVER is one @function you've never seen—unless you've used 1-2-3 Release 3.1+ or 1-2-3/G. @INFO("selection") is a new use of an @function that came in with Release 3.

To use @SOLVER, you need to know how to use Solver. Solver performs linear and nonlinear calculations to figure out the optimal solution for a complex numeric problem. It is a great tool for answering such questions as, Which mix of products would be the most profitable? When you're using Solver, you can use the @SOLVER function to track its progress and help analyze its results. To learn how to use Solver and @SOLVER, see Chapter 19.

@INFO("selection") identifies what cells are currently selected. @INFO has been around since 1-2-3 Release 3, but the *selection* argument is a new wrinkle.

For example, enter @INFO("selection") in a cell, use the mouse or keyboard to select a range, press the CALC key (F9), and the cell with the formula reports what cells are selected.

Who cares, you may ask, whether an @function can identify the selected range? If you write macros, you'll certainly care. As shown in the SmartIcon macro examples in Chapter 18, your macros need to be able to identify which cells a user has selected. Until the advent of @INFO("selection"), there was no way to do this.

For users of the Data External commands, there are three more @INFO innovations. @INFO("dbreturncode") tells you the most recent error code returned in an external database operation. @INFO("dbdrivermessage") results in the most recent message sent by a DataLens driver, the software that links 1-2-3/W with the external database system. And @INFO(dbrecordcount) identifies the number of records extracted, modified, or inserted from the last query. To learn about 1-2-3/W's database features, see Chapters 13 through 16.

Following is a look at some of the types of calculations these functions can perform for you. For a complete list of 1-2-3/W @functions, see the @function reference in the back of the book.

Database

Most database functions are a hybrid of the statistical @functions, which are described below, and 1-2-3/W's data query features. To use these, you need a solid understanding of 1-2-3/W's database techniques. You'll learn how to use 1-2-3/W databases, including the use of the so-called @D functions, in Chapters 13 through 16.

Date and Time

Date and Time functions help make it easy to work with dates in your spreadsheet. For example, @TODAY generates a number that identifies today's date.

As discussed earlier, 1-2-3's numbering scheme treats January 1, 1900, as date number 1, January 31, 1993, as date number 34,000, and so on. @functions that make it easier to enter and manipulate these strange-looking dates are an essential tool in time-sensitive applications.

Two date @functions help you enter the current date, and optionally, the time. @TODAY gives you both today's serial date and the decimal value of the current time. @NOW returns an integer representing only the date.

Exploring Date and Time Functions: @NOW, @TODAY, @MONTH(*date-number*) @DAY(*date-number*)

Let's use @NOW and @TODAY to put current date and time information into your spreadsheet. Then, we'll use @DAY and @MONTH to extract the day of the month and the month number from a date.

1. Starting with a new spreadsheet, set the width of column A to 10.
2. Enter @*NOW* in cell A1 and @TODAY in cell A2. Notice that the serial date number returned by @NOW contains a decimal portion, while @TODAY simply returns an integer. That's because @NOW returns date (the integer) *and* the time (the decimal portion), while @TODAY returns only the date.
3. Select A1..A2, and format them as dates by choosing Range Format 1.
4. Now click on cell A1 and reformat it to display the time, by choosing Range Format 6.

5. In order to get the latest date and time information, you must recalculate the spreadsheet. Press CALC (F9), and you'll see A1 change to the current time (assuming your computer's clock is set correctly).

6. In A3, enter *@DAY(A1)*. This formula derives the day of the month from the date number in cell A1.

7. In A4, enter *@MONTH(A2)*. This function calculates the month number from the date number in cell A1.

Does the Computer Really Know What Day It Is?

If you rely on date or time information, be sure your computer clock is set correctly. To reset the clock, use the Windows Control Panel utility or type *date* or *time* at a DOS prompt.

If the computer doesn't keep the correct time between work sessions, perhaps the battery is dead, or perhaps you have an older computer that doesn't keep track of the time when it's not on. Check your owner's manual for details.

Financial Functions

1-2-3/W's financial @functions help you analyze investments, annuities, depreciation, cash flows, and loans. Examples include @PV to calculate present value, @NPV to calculate net present value, and @PMT to calculate the number of payments required to pay off a loan.

Exploring the @PMT(*principal,interest,term*)

Financial Function @PMT is one of the most commonly used financial functions. It returns a periodic payment based on the principal, interest rate, and the term of loan. We'll create a table listing these values and then use @PMT to calculate the payment.

Let's say we want to calculate a monthly loan payment based on a principal of 20,000, a 12% interest rate, and a term of thirty-six months.

1. In a new worksheet, enter the labels shown in range A1..A5 of Figure 6.4.

2. Enter the values shown in range B1..B3.

3. Assign the following cell formats: Comma format with no decimal places in cell B1, Percent format with two decimal places in cell B2, and Currency format with two decimal places in cell B5.

4. In cell B5, enter the formula *@PMT(B1,B2/12,B3)*. The interest rate is divided by 12, because we are calculating monthly payments and therefore need to use the monthly interest rate.

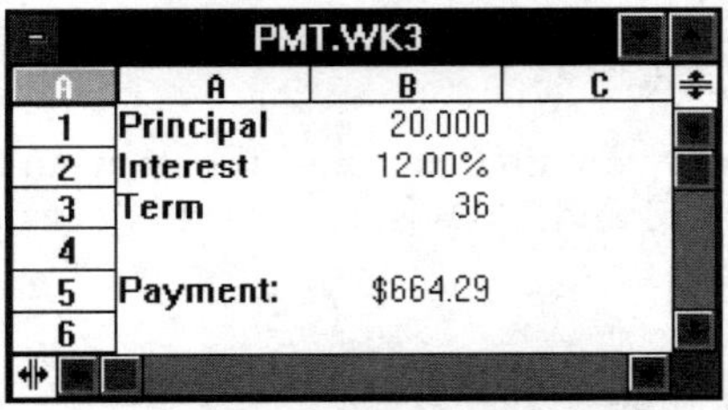

Figure 6.4. A loan-payment worksheet. @PMT formula in cell B5 figures out how much each monthly payment must be to pay off the principal at the specified rate and in the specified time.

Logical Functions

Logical functions identify various conditions as true or false. For example, @IF(B2=C2,5,9) tests whether the contents of cell B2 equal those of cell C2. If the condition is true, the cell containing this formula displays a 5, otherwise it displays a 9. In logical operations, 1-2-3/W considers the value 1 to be true and the value 0 to be false. This means that the statement @IF(0,5,9) would always return the value 9, because the test at the start of the function would always prove false.

Exploring the @IF(*condition,x,y*) Logical Function

Let's use @IF to let the worksheet make decisions based on the value of specific data. This example concerns a clothing store that needs to calculate luxury tax. The tax rate is 5 percent, but it is only applied to luxury items that cost $300 or more.

1. Start with a new spreadsheet
2. Enter labels as shown in ranges A1..A6 and B3..C3 of figure 6.5
3. Enter values as shown in range B4..B6.
4. In cell C4, enter the formula *@IF(B4>=300,B4*$B$1,0)*.
5. Format cell B2 as Percent with two decimal places, and range B4..C6 as currency with two decimal places.
6. Set the width of column A to 10.
7. Copy cell C4 to the range C5..C6.
8. Notice that cells C3 and C4 now contain 0, because the items in B3 and B4 are under 300. On the other hand, C5 posts a sales tax because the condition B5>=300 evaluates to true.

	A	B	C
1	Sales Tax:	5.00%	
2			
3	Item	Price	Tax
4	Socks	$4.95	$0
5	Bowling Shirt	$29.49	$0
6	Armani Suit	$800.00	$40

Figure 6.5. The sales-tax worksheet. The @IF formulas in range C4..C6 test whether the prices in column B exceed the $300 non-taxable limit.

Mathematical Functions

1-2-3/W supports a wide assortment of standard mathematical operations, including @INT to find the absolute value of a number, @ROUND to round off a number to a specified number of decimal places and @SQRT to find the square root of a number.

Exploring the INT(x), @ROUND(x,n), @SQRT(x) Mathematical Functions

Let's try out three of the most commonly used mathematical functions.

1. Start with a new spreadsheet.
2. In cell A1 enter 3.61.
3. In cell B1, enter *@INT(A1)*. As you can see from the results, @INT(A1) returns 3; it has removed the decimal portion of A1.
4. Enter *@ROUND(A1,0)* in cell B2. In this case, we've asked to round the number in cell A1 to 0 decimal places, so 1-2-3/W rounds this value up to 4.
5. Finally, enter *@SQRT(A1)* in cell B3. 1-2-3/W finds the square root of 3.61, which is 1.9.

Special Functions

These @functions provide information about the state of the spreadsheet environment, such as the location of the cell pointer, the type of entry in the current cell, or the release number of the software, as well as finding an appropriate value in a lookup table.

Functions like @INFO, @CELL, @CELLPOINTER, and @COORD let your applications detect what's going on in the worksheet and act accordingly. The @HLOOKUP function matches a given value, such as a part number, against a horizontal table. It then enters information about that item—such as its price—into the cell. The @VLOOKUP function matches a value against a vertical table. And @INDEX returns the contents of a specified location within a range.

Exploring Special Functions for Worksheet-Environment Information: @INFO(attribute) and @CELLPOINTER(attribute)

These functions are typically used in macros to make decisions based on the current state of the spreadsheet, but we can try them out in the worksheet to see what sort of information they provide.

Note that you need to press CALC when you want these formulas to display the most up-to-date information. And also note that the *attributes* listed in these examples are only a few of the ones supported by 1-2-3/W.

1. Start with a new spreadsheet.
2. Enter *@INFO("totmem")* in cell A4. This function shows the total memory currently available on your computer. The available memory changes as you add or delete data in your spreadsheet or do other activities in Windows.
3. Enter *@INFO("system")* in cell A5. This function returns the name of the computer's operating system.
4. Enter *@INFO("osversion")* in cell A6. This displays the version number of the operating system.
5. Enter *@INFO("selection")* in cell A7. This function identifies the coordinates of the currently selected range. This use of @INFO is new with 1-2-3/W. Don't worry that the result is ERR—you haven't selected a range yet. After entering this function, click and drag to select a small range. While the range is still selected, press CALC (F9). @INFO("selection") now returns the coordinates of the current selection.
6. Enter *@CELLPOINTER("address")* in cell A8. This function tells you the address of the cell pointer as of the last time the spreadsheet was calculated. Try putting the pointer in various cells and pressing CALC (F9). The function updates itself to display the new location.

Exploring Special Functions That Perform Lookups: VLOOKUP(*x,range,column offset*) and @CHOOSE(*offset,list*)

In this example, we'll use @VLOOKUP to pick the appropriate per-mile billing rate for a messenger service, based on a rate table. This table lists different rates for different delivery zones.

Note that @VLOOKUP, as well as such functions as HLOOKUP and @CHOOSE includes an *offset* argument. The offset identifies a location relative to the first item in a range or formula. For example, in @VLOOKUP, an offset of 0 means to look in the very first column of the range, 1 means one column to the right of the first column and so on. As you'll see in the exercise on @CHOOSE, the offset identifies which item in the list the function should return; the first item in the list is 0, the second is 1, and so on.

	A	B	C	D	E
1	Zone	Per Mile			
2	1	$0.75			
3	2	$1.25			
4	3	$1.75			
5	4	$2.00			
6					
7					
8					
9	Customer		Zone	Mileage	Per Mile	Amount
10	ABC		1	12	0.75	$9.00
11	Acme		3	23	1.75	$40.25
12	Zinc., Inc.		2	15	1.25	$18.75
13					

Figure 6.6. The formulas in range D10..D12 use a VLOOKUP function to match the zone information in range B10..B12 to the table of zones and rates at the top of the worksheet.

1. In a new spreadsheet, enter the labels and values shown in range A1..B5 of Figure 6.6.

2. Now enter the labels shown in ranges A9..E9 and A10..A12 of the figure.

3. Enter the values shown in range B10..C12.

4. Apply the Currency format with two decimal places to ranges B2..B5 and E10..A12.

5. Right align the labels in ranges A1..B1 and B9..E9.

6. In cell D10, enter the formula *@VLOOKUP(A10,$A$2..$B$5,1)*. This tells 1-2-3/W: In the table A2..B5, look in the leftmost column for an entry that matches the contents of cell. If you find it, return the item that's in the same row and that's one column to the right. This gives us the rate per mile.

7. In E10 we'll calculate the bill by multiplying the rate per mile by the total mileage. Enter the formula +*B10*C10*.

8. Finally, copy D10..E10 to D11..D12 to enter the formulas for the rest of the table.

Next we'll use @CHOOSE, which is an abbreviated lookup function. Rather looking up values in an on-sheet range, as @VLOOKUP does, @CHOOSE stores a list of items right in the cell. The first argument is an *offset-number*, *n*, that @CHOOSE uses to return the nth item in the list.

For example, @CHOOSE(A1,"Yes","No" "Maybe") returns "Yes" if A1 equals zero, "No" if it equals 1, and "Maybe" if it equals 2.

Suppose we have three sales divisions: North East, South East, and West. We would like to use these in reports but don't want to type them over and over again. By entering a code-number to identify each division, and using @CHOOSE, we can simplify the data entry.

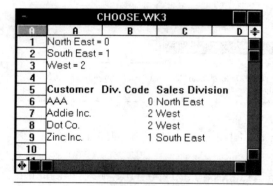

Figure 6.7. Each formula in range C6..C9 uses an @CHOOSE function to display the appropriate division name based on a division code entered in column B.

1. In a new worksheet, enter the labels shown in range A1..A9 of Figure 6.10

2. Next, enter the values shown in range B6..B9 of the figure.

3. In cell C6, enter @CHOOSE(B6,"North East","South East","West"). The function returns *North East* because B6 contains the code 0, and North East is the first item in the list. Keep in mind that first entry in the list has an offset of zero. An offset of 1 returns the second item from the list, and so on.

4. Now copy cell C6 to range C7..C9 to see @CHOOSE display the names of the other divisions.

Statistical Functions

In addition to the old standby @SUM, 1-2-3/W functions include @AVG, which tells you the arithmetic mean of a range; @COUNT, which tells you how many entries a range contains; and @MIN and @MAX, which determine the lowest and highest values in a range.

For more advanced statistical applications, you can use @STD and @STDS, which calculate the population and sample standard deviations; @VAR and @VARS, which determine the population and sample variances; and @SUMPRODUCT, which multiplies lists of values.

Exploring the statistical functions: @SUM(list), @MAX(list), @MIN(list), @AVG(list), @COUNT(list), @STD(list), @STDS(list), @VAR(list), @VARS(list), and @SUMPRODUCT(list)

1. Before we see what statistical functions 1-2-3/W can perform, we'll need some data to analyze. Enter the values shown in range A1..B3 of Figure 6.8

2. Now enter in range B6..B15 each of the functions as shown in A6..A15. If you want to label each function as in the figure, enter the labels in range A5..B5 and then enter each item in range A6..A15, preceded by an apostrophe label prefix.

```
              STATS.WK3
           A           B        C
  1                1        5
  2                2       -2
  3                3       10
  4
  5  Function           Result
  6  @SUM(A1..B3)           19
  7  @MAX(A1..B3)           10
  8  @MIN(A1..B3)           -2
  9  @COUNT(A1..B3)          6
 10  @AVG(A1..B3)      3.166667
 11  @STD(A1..B3)      3.715583
 12  @STDS(A1..B3)     4.070217
 13  @VAR(A1..B3)     13.80556
 14  @VARS(A1..B3)    16.56667
 15  @SUMPRODUCT(A1..B3)    19
 16
```

Figure 6.8. All of 1-2-3/W's statistical functions in action. The entries in range A6..A15 are labels that identify the @functions in use in column B.

3. @SUM, which is shown in cell B6, is the sum of all the values in the list.

4. @MAX, which is shown in cell B7, displays the largest value in the list.

5. @MIN, which is shown in cell B8, displays the smallest value in the list.

6. @COUNT, which is shown in cell B9, calculates the number of non-blank cells in the list.

7. @AVG, which is shown in cell B10, calculates the average of all the values in the list.

8. @STD, which is shown in cell B11, calculates the population standard deviation of the values in the list.

9. @STDS, which is shown in cell B12, calculates the sample standard deviation of the values in the list.

10. @VAR, which is shown in cell B13, calculates the population variance of the values in the list.

11. @VARS, which is shown in cell B14, calculates the sample variance of the values in the list.

12. @SUMPRODUCT, which is shown in cell B15, multiplies the values in each row to then calculates the sum of the products.

13. Experiment with different numbers in A1..B3 and watch the various statistical functions change, based on the current data.

> ### Make a List
>
> Some @functions, like @SUM and @COUNT, will take a list of arguments, allowing you to include multiple ranges. Thus, you can use these functions on noncontiguous sections of data: @SUM(M7..M19,M25..M82,M85..M99), or @COUNT(B:C12..B:C52,D:R52..R90).

String Functions

You can use any of several 1-2-3/W functions to manipulate strings. Strings are simply alphanumeric entries, such as labels, entered into a formula within quotes. Examples of string functions are @LEFT, which returns a specified number of characters from the beginning of a string; @STRING, which converts values into strings (labels); and @CHAR, which lets you display any character that 1-2-3/W recognizes, including several that don't have keyboard equivalents.

Exploring String Functions :@ CHAR(*x*), @CODE(*string*), @FIND(*substring,string,start-number*), @LEFT(*string,n*), @MID(*string,start-number,n*), @LENGTH(*string*), @LOWER(*string*), @REPEAT(*string,n*), @STRING(*x,n*), @VALUE(*string*), @EXACT(*string1,string2*)

Let's try a variety of string functions to see how you can use formulas to manipulate text in 1-2-3/W.

```
              STRING.WK3
         A              B          C         D        E
 1  Adeline Ansell             String Formula:
 2  02124                      ADEANS02124
 3                 123
 4
 5  Function           Result
 6  @CHAR(A3)          {
 7  @CODE("a")              97
 8  @FIND("d",A1,0)          1
 9  @LEFT(A1,4)        Adel
10  @MID(A1,5,2)       ne
11  @LENGTH(A2)              5
12  @LOWER(A1)         adeline ansell
13  @REPEAT("X",10)    XXXXXXXXXX
14  @STRING(A3,2)      123.00
15  @VALUE(A2)            2124
16  @EXACT("Adeline Ansell",A1)  1
17
```

Figure 6.9. All of 1-2-3/W's statistical functions in action. The entries range A6..A15 in column A are labels that identify the @functions in use in column B.

1. In a new spreadsheet, set the width of column A to 22.

2. In cell A1, enter the label Adeline Ansell.

3. In cell A2, enter the label '02124—a ZIP code. Note that the apostrophe label prefix allows you to enter the ZIP code as a label. Without it, the number is entered as the value 2124.

4. In cell A3, enter the number 123.

5. Now enter in range B6..B16 each of the formulas shown in range A6..A16. If you want to label each function as in the figure, enter the labels in range A6..A16, preceding each entry with an apostrophe label prefix.

6. @CHAR, which is shown in cell B6, displays the LMBCS character associated with the specified value. LMBCS (Lotus Multibyte Character Set) is a numbered list of characters you can display in 1-2-3/W. This list of characters goes from character number 32 to character 383. See Appendix B of the 1-2-3 for Windows User's Guide for a complete list of LMBCS characters, or enter @CHAR functions that show you the results of all values from 32 to 383.

7. @CODE, which is shown in cell B7, produces the LMBCS code for the leftmost character in the range.

8. @FIND, which is shown in cell B8, searches for a sub-string within a string and returns the position number if it is found.

9. @LEFT, which is shown in cell B9, returns the leftmost characters of a string. The number of characters is specified by the *length* argument.

10. @MID, which is shown in cell B10, returns a specified number of characters from a string, beginning with the character identified by the *start -number* 1.

11. @LENGTH, which is shown in cell B11, calculates the number of characters in a string.

12. @LOWER, which is shown in cell B12, converts all alphabetic characters in a string to lower case.

13. @REPEAT, which is shown in cell B13, repeats a string a specified number of times.

14. @STRING, which is shown in cell B14, converts a value to a string, with a given number of decimal points.

15. @VALUE, which is shown in cell B15, converts a string that contains only numeric characters to a value.

16. @EXACT, which is shown in cell B16, returns a 1 if the two specified strings match, 0 if they don't.

Now that you've tried these string functions, we'll combine a few of them, along with the concatenation operator (&) to create a string formula.

Let's say we need 1-2-3/W to generate a customer code based on the first 3 letters of the customer's first name, the first three letters of the last name, and the customer's ZIP code. For example the code for Mary Rutkowski with ZIP code 12345 would be MARRUT12345.

Using the name and ZIP code you entered in A1 and A2, let's build the formula.

1. Set the width of column C to 12.

2. In cell C2, enter the label *String Formula*.

3. In cell C2, enter the formula: @UPPER(@LEFT(A1,3)&@MID (A1,@FIND(" ",A1)+1,3)&A2).

4. The tricky part of this formula is using @FIND(" ",A1)+1 inside of @MID to locate the position of the first character of the last name. Once found, we use @MID to get the next three characters.

5. Try changing the data in cells A1 and A2 to see the results of the string functions change.

Avoiding Formula Failures I

There's a tendency to believe that any information that comes from a computer is completely accurate. But it's only accurate if you make it so. The old saying, "Don't believe everything you read in the newspaper," goes double for computerized data.

For the most part, if you start with accurate data and you enter it carefully, and if you understand the formula you're trying to enter, you have only one major consideration left to grapple with: making sure your formulas reference the right cells.

Using an inappropriate formula, such as multiplying when you should have added, and referencing the wrong cells are probably the most common causes of formula mishaps. But there are others, such as circular references and misunderstanding of the hierarchy of operations. These are more subtle, but they can render your formulas useless—or worse.

Mistaken Identity

If the formula you enter references the wrong cells, or if it is mathematically or logically flawed, you'd have to be pretty lucky to get the desired result. Make sure you understand your formulas, and test them with numbers that prove whether they work. If you know that a certain calculation turns 212 into 100, enter *212* to see if you get the expected result. The more testing you do, the more certain you can be of the integrity of your formulas.

There are two good ways to make sure that your formulas refer to the right cells or ranges. First, use Point mode to build your formulas: Specify cells by moving the mouse or navigating with the keyboard, instead of typing references. Identifying the cells visually is much safer than trying to remember their addresses and hoping you enter them without error.

Second, use easy-to-remember range names to identify cells. It's a lot easier to remember the range name *data* than the range reference B:A17..G:M920. To learn how to use range names, see Chapter 8.

Circular References

Popeye is famous for saying, "I am what I am." For the cartoon sailor, this is a bold declaration of pride. In a formula, it's a recipe for confusion.

If, for example, cell B2 contains the formula +B2 or the formula +B2*B3, you're asking 1-2-3/W to chase its own tail. The formula tries to determine what it should contain by seeing what it contains. Very Zen, but in most worksheets, not very useful.

When your worksheet includes a circular reference—a cell that references itself—the *CIRC* indicator appears at the bottom of the 1-2-3/W window. This is usually a sign that you made a mistake when entering a formula.

If you have trouble locating the self-absorbed cell, choose About 1-2-3 for Windows from the Help menu. This command's dialog box tells you the location of the cell containing the circular reference.

After you go back to the worksheet and fix the circular reference, the CIRC indicator may still appear. That means that you have one or more other circular references to fix. If you can't find the next circular reference, look again in the About 1-2-3 for Windows dialog box for its location.

In some rare cases, you may actually want circular references. For example, you can use circular references to perform recursive calculations, calculations that, in fact, refer to themselves. Usually, however, you can do these more effectively with one or more conventional formulas.

If you want to use circular references, don't worry about the CIRC indicator. It doesn't mean that your worksheet won't compute. But note that each time the worksheet calculates, it recalculates the circular reference. If you want to determine how many times 1-2-3/W performs each circular calculation, use the Iterations box in the Worksheet Global Settings command.

To locate a circular reference, choose About 1-2-3 for Windows from the Help Menu.

Hierarchy of Operations

One of the fundamental rules of mathematics is one of the fundamental rules of 1-2-3/W: There is a preset order in which calculations are performed. This is known as the hierarchy of operations or the order of precedence. You don't

If you want to control which parts of a formulas are calculated first, use parentheses

have to memorize this order if you use parentheses liberally, because they bypass the usual order.

The most commonly used operators work in the following order of precedence: Exponents are calculated first, then come multiplication and division from left to right, then addition and subtraction from left to right.

Why should you care? Consider the following formula: +4+4/8. What's the answer, 1 or 4.5? If you apply the standard rules, it's clear that 1-2-3/W must divide 4 by 8 before adding 4 to it. If you intended to add the first two values and then divide the total by 8, this formula puts wrong data in your worksheet. To solve the problem, use parentheses: +(4+4)/8. Then, you can be sure that the addition comes first.

The complete hierarchy of operations in 1-2-3/W is listed in Table 6.7.

Operator	Precedence Number
^	1
-, + (when used to identify a number as positive or negative)	2
*, /	3
+, - (when used for addition or subtraction)	4
=, < >, <, >,<= ,>=	5
#NOT#	6
#AND#, #OR#, &	7

Table 6.7. 1-2-3/W's hierarchy of operations. Unless you use parentheses to override this order, 1-2-3 performs the operations with the highest precedence first, from left to right, on down through the list.

Formulas That Count

@Functions such as @COUNT, @AVG, @DCOUNT, and @DAVG determine how many entries there are in a range. But what qualifies as an entry?

Cells that are truly blank do not count in a counting or averaging function, but cells with any kind of entry do, even cells that contain a "blank" label, such as a single apostrophe. This is why the common technique of "erasing" cells by entering a space over the current contents is a dangerous habit. You can inadvertently raise a count or bring down an average by littering your worksheet with such pseudoblank cells.

Note that if you use one of these counting functions with a single cell, that cell counts, even if it is blank.

When a Range Has to Be a Range

In certain situations 1-2-3/W expects a range reference, such as G19..G24, or even G19..G19, instead of a single cell reference. To turn a single cell reference into a range reference, you can precede it with an exclamation point. For example, !G19 is treated as G19..G19.

@functions such as @count and @AVG count the number of entries in a range. They include any cell with an entry—including a label—in the count

Other Formula Problems

Many formula problems occur not when you first build a formula but when you copy, move, or erase ranges, or when you insert or delete rows. The impact of these operations on formulas is discussed at the end of Chapter 7. There you'll learn how to protect your formulas with absolute references.

Also take heed of the warnings in the Cell Formats section of this chapter. Specifically, changing the way a value is displayed does not alter the data itself. Thus, rounding errors can creep in if you don't use @ROUND or @INT formulas appropriately.

Err Pollution

Sometimes a formula evaluates to ERR. This indicates that the cell contains or references an illegal formula. For example, dividing by zero is a mathematical impossibility, so a formula such as +B2/0 that attempts to do results in ERR. Note that any formula that references an ERR-generating cell also evaluates to ERR.

Another common cause of ERR conditions is opening a worksheet that contains file-linking formulas that link to files that are unavailable.

This can happen if the other files are not present in the directory where 1-2-3/W looks for them, or a linked-to sheet is password-protected.

For more on file-linking, see Chapter 9: Building Effective Applications.

7

Copying, Moving, Inserting, and Removing

Copying, moving, inserting, and removing data are 1-2-3/W techniques that you should know inside and out. Using them well saves you a great deal of time, and using them badly can make a mess of your worksheet.

Undoubtedly, you've performed some or all of these tasks before. But there are many tricks to learn—and traps to avoid.

In this chapter, you'll learn the best ways to reuse, reposition, and remove the labels, values, formulas, formats, and styles, in your worksheet.

Copying

Outside of moving the cell pointer, copying is probably the single most common 1-2-3/W procedure. Just as the Eskimos have a rich vocabulary for describing snow, Lotus has given 1-2-3/W an impressive array of copying commands—to reflect the frequency and importance of the task. These commands are listed in Table 7.1. You can perform almost any copying task quickly and efficiently if you know which tool to use.

Copying is a great time saver, but keep in mind that you need to exercise some caution when copying formulas. See "Avoiding Formula Failures II" at the end of this chapter to learn how to prevent unwanted side-effects when you copy.

> *In this chapter you will learn:*
> - *How to copy data, formats, and styles*
> - *How to move data, formats, and styles*
> - *How to clear (erase) data, formats, and styles*
> - *How to insert and delete rows, columns, and sheets*
> - *How to avoid worksheet errors when copying, moving, clearing, inserting, and deleting*

There are many ways to copy data in 1-2-3/W, each with its own unique abilities.

Command	Shortcut
Edit Copy	SmartIcon, Ctrl-Insert , Alt-E C
Edit Paste	SmartIcon, Shift-Insert, Alt-E P
Edit Quick Copy	SmartIcons, Alt-E Q
Range Transpose	Alt-R T
/Copy	/C
:Special Copy	:SC
/Range Transpose	/RT
/Range Value	/RV

Table 7.1. 1-2-3/W commands that copy data and spreadsheet styles.

Edit Copy, Edit Paste

The Edit Copy command puts selected information into the Windows Clipboard. You choose Edit Paste to copy the Clipboard's contents to a selected location. You've seen these commands in action if you've performed the exercises in Chapters 2 and 3 or if you've used other Windows applications.

The accelerator keys for Edit Copy and Edit Paste, respectively, are Ctrl-Insert and Shift-Insert. Both commands have SmartIcon equivalents, as shown in Figure 7.1

Figure 7.1. The SmartIcons for the Edit Copy and Edit Paste commands. The icon on the left puts a copy of selected text into the Clipboard. The icon on the right pastes a copy of the Clipboard's contents at the current location.

Note that Edit Copy copies not only the contents of a range, but all of its styles, numeric formats, etc. It's the only copy command that lets you copy a graph that you've inserted into the worksheet.

Clipboard Basics

You can paste the Clipboard's contents as many times as you wish. If, for example, you need to copy a particular set of column headings to several locations, you can enter them once and copy them into the Clipboard. Then you can move about your worksheet or worksheets, pasting these headings as needed.

The Clipboard forgets its current contents when you use the Edit Copy or Edit Cut commands to copy or cut something else. These are the only commands that alter the Clipboard; none of the other copying, moving, and deleting commands discussed in this chapter affect the Clipboard.

The Clipboard's contents disappear entirely when you leave Windows. You can, however, use the Clipboard utility in Windows' Main Group to store and retrieve text and graphics from the Clipboard, in the form of CLP files.

You can paste the Clipboard's contents as many times as you like, without having to choose Edit Copy again.

Copying Across Programs

Wherever you travel in the Windows environment, you'll find the Edit Copy/Edit Paste combination. This not only gives you familiar commands in various programs, it lets you trade data between programs. You can copy data from 1-2-3/W and paste it into another application—and vice versa.

All you need to do is copy text or graphics from one program, switch to the other program, select the destination, and then paste. For details on switching among Windows applications, see Chapter 2, *Essential Windows Skills*.

The Edit Paste Link command works in conjunction with the Edit Copy command to let you create hotlinks. When you use Edit Paste Link to copy data from one program to another, Windows' DDE feature keeps the copy in touch with the original so that when you make changes to the original, the linked copy is updated either automatically or upon request. This feature lets you, for example, share 1-2-3/W data with a word-processing document without having to manually revise the document when the spreadsheet changes.

You can use the combination of Edit Copy and Edit Paste to copy data from one Windows program to another, as well as from within 1-2-3/W.

Edit Quick Copy

The Edit Quick Copy command is a single command copying method, as opposed to the conventional Windows combo of Edit Copy and Edit Paste. In many ways, it resembles the 1-2-3 Classic /Copy command, which is discussed in the next section.

Edit Quick Copy is 1-2-3/W's most versatile copying command.

The versatile Edit Quick Copy command not only does the job of the /Copy command, it provides two check boxes that deliver the features of two other 1-2-3 Classic copying commands: /Range Values and :Special Copy. And for the quickest of quick copies, you can choose from three very handy SmartIcon equivalents.

Like the /Copy command, the Edit Quick Copy command requires two pieces of information: the range you're copying from and the range you're copying to. The location you're copying from is known as the *From* range or the *source*. The range you're copying to is known as the *To* range, the *target*, or the *destination*. When you choose Edit Quick Copy, it presents the dialog box shown in figure 7.2.

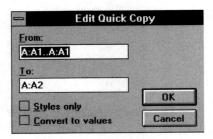

Figure 7.2. The Edit Quick Copy dialog box. This command is the Windows-menu equivalent of the /Copy command. The Styles-only and Convert-to-values boxes let this command also do the work of the /Range Values and :Special Copy commands.

Note that Edit Quick Copy duplicates not only the contents of a range, but all of its styles and numeric formats as well. It will not, however, copy graphs that you've inserted into the worksheet. Of course, if you choose the Styles-only option, it copies only the styles.

Quick Copying Basics

If only a single cell is selected when you choose Edit Quick Copy, the dialog box opens with the From range highlighted. You specify the From range, click or tab to the To range, and specify the destination. Then you choose OK.

If two or more cells are preselected when you start the command, 1-2-3/W treats the selection as the From range. To save you a step, the dialog box opens with the To range, instead of the From range, highlighted.

The SmartIcon shown in Figure 7.3 makes for extremely quick copying. It automatically treats the current selection as the From range, even if it's a single cell, and it lets you identify the To range with a click or drag of the mouse. When you use this icon for quick copying, 1-2-3/W doesn't present a dialog box. Thus, you don't even have to press Enter or click OK. Instead, the mouse pointer changes into a pointing hand, and the copying takes place as soon as you release the mouse button.

Figure 7.3. A SmartIcon for quick copying of a range of cells. Select a range to copy, and click this icon. The mouse pointer changes to resemble the pointing hand from the icon. You click or drag this pointer to identify the cell or cells to copy to. When you release the mouse button, the copying is done.

The SmartIcon in Figure 7.3 makes for very fast copying. Select a source to copy from, click this icon, and click or drag the destination. You don't even have to press Enter or click OK in a dialog box.

Fill 'Em Up

Another valuable quick-copying SmartIcon fills a selected range with the contents of the current cell. If for example, you want to copy a formula from cell B2 into range B2..B18, you select range B2..B18 and click this icon. Instantly, the range fills with copies of the formula. You can use this icon to copy the contents of a cell across a row, such as B2..H2, or throughout a two-dimensional range of cells, such as B2..H18.

Figure 7.4. This handy copying icon comes with 1-2-3/W, but it's not in the default palette. Add it to your SmartIcon palette to copy a single cell into all other selected cells.

Add the SmartIcon from Figure 7.4 to your default SmartIcon palette to copy from one cell to several neighboring cells with a single click.

This icon is not one of the default icons, so to use it, you must first choose Tools SmartIcons Customize to add it to your palette. For more on customizing the SmartIcon palette, see Chapter 18, *Mastering the SmartIcon Palette*.

Note that with this icon, the *current cell*, the cell within the selection where the cell pointer resides is the From range. To confirm which cell is current, check the control panel at the top of the 1-2-3/W window.

The method you use to preselect the range determines which cell is the current cell. If you preselect by using the mouse, the cell in which you start dragging is the current cell. When you preselect with the ABS key (F4), the last cell you select is the current cell unless you press the period key one or more times to make a different corner of the range the current, or free, cell.

Remember that this icon duplicates a single cell, not a range of cells. If you need to copy several cells down or across, use one of the other copying methods, such as Edit Quick Copy or the pointing-hand copy icon.

Copying Styles

The Edit Quick Copy command's Styles-only box lets you copy such styling as borders, colors, fonts, and font enhancements from one range to another. You use this option to copy only the styles, and not the data or numeric formats, from the From range to the To range.

Using the Styles-only box makes the Edit Quick Copy command the functional equivalent of the :Special Copy command of Allways and WYSIWYG. If you like doing it the old way, you can choose :Special Copy from the 1-2-3 Classic menu.

The SmartIcon in Figure 7.5 makes copying styles even quicker than either menu command. Like the pointing hand copy icon, it copies from the current selection and changes the mouse pointer to resemble its icon—in this case, a paintbrush. To copy the styles to one or more cells, click or drag the mouse.

The "paintbrush" icon shown in Figure 7.5 is a fast way to copy the styles, but not the data, from one range to another.

Figure 7.5. This icon is a shortcut for choosing Edit Quick Copy with the Styles-only option. It lets you copy the borders, fonts, font enhancements, colors, and shading of a selected range and apply it to another. The mouse pointer turns into a paint brush, and you drag it through a range to spruce it up with the styles of the original selection. The data in the destination range is unchanged.

You can build a library of styles that you plan to use repeatedly, assigning them descriptive names. Then you can apply these named styles as needed. For details on using named styles, see Chapter 4, *Make It Look Good*.

Converting Formulas to Values

The Edit Quick Copy command has one more impersonation in its repertoire. By way of the Convert-to-values check box, it can ape the /Range Values command. This option lets you copy the current *values* from a range of cells that contain *formulas*.

Consider a worksheet that lets you enter monthly data and that sums these values in a year-to-date column. What if you want to perform a lengthy analysis of the totals through August? When the September data comes in, the year-to-date totals will change, ruining the through-August totals. A simple solution is to use the Convert-to-values option to copy the August data instead of the formulas that derive the current year-to-date totals.

Whenever you need to copy only the values and not the underlying formulas, converting to values makes sense. Since formulas usually adjust when you copy them (see the section "Relative and Absolute References" later in this chapter), copying formulas may not get you the current values; instead you'll get formulas that mimic the logic of the formulas you copied. Also, formulas take up more memory than values; if you never need to recalculate the values, you're wasting resources to keep them as formulas.

Note that you can use the Edit Quick Copy command's Convert-to-values option, or the /Range Values command, with formulas that return strings as well as with those that return numeric values.

1-2-3/W's Edit Quick Copy command's Convert-to-values option does the work of the /Range Values command.

Range Transpose

The Range Transpose command on the 1-2-3/W main menu, like its 1-2-3 Classic menu equivalent, lets you stand your data on end. You copy a selected range, and when you enter the destination the data in the rows takes to columns, and vice versa.

On the face of it, this command is very straightforward to use, because it resembles a simple copying command. Like the Edit Quick Copy command, it takes you right to the To prompt if you preselect a From range of two or more cells.

There's one trick, though: making sure there's enough room in the destination. This takes a bit of thinking, because the dimensions of the transposed copy are the opposite of the original dimensions. To better understand this, see the example in Figure 7.6.

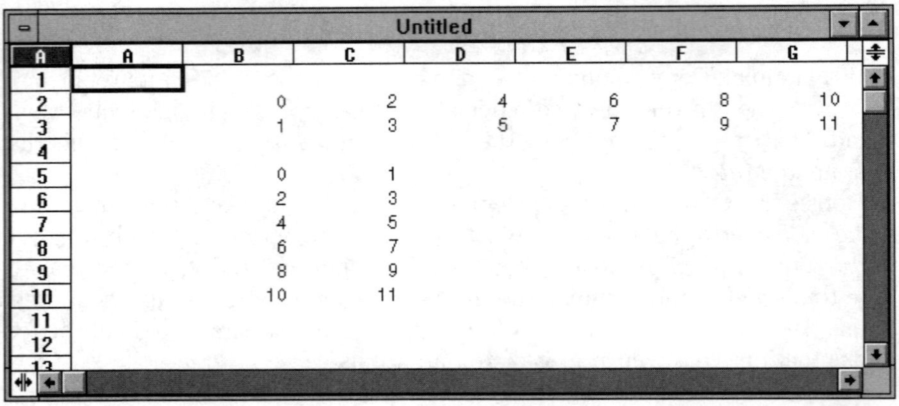

Figure 7.6. An example of using Range Transpose. The data in range B2..G3 has been transposed to B5.

The figure shows the results of transposing data from range B2..G3 to B5. Where the source of the copy had six columns by two rows, the transposed version has two columns by six rows. If there had been data in cells B10 and above, they would have been overwritten.

Note that 1-2-3/W's Range Transpose and /Range Transpose commands differ from the /Range Transpose command of 1-2-3 Releases 2.01 and earlier. In those releases, formulas you transpose remain as formulas. In Releases 2.2 and higher, formulas you transpose convert to their current values.

Pattern Copying: A Weird and Wonderful Trick

A favorite trick of 1-2-3 mavens is using a single copy command to duplicate one or more cells in a pattern—such as putting the label *Quarter* in every fourth column, or putting a series of formulas in every other row.

This is one technique you have to see to believe. Let's try to number every other row in a range. We want cell A3 to show the number 1, cell A5 to display the number 2, and so on, up to the number 6. And we want to do this with a single copy command.

Start with a new worksheet and enter the formula +A1+1 in cell A3. This adds the value of cell A1, which is 0, to the number 1. Why would we make such a sorry formula? When we copy this formula, it will add the number two rows above it, to come up with the next number in the sequence. For example, when this formula is copied to cell A5, it will read +A3+1, and it will put the number 2 in the cell.

(continued)

(continued)

But how can we get this formula into cells A5, A7, A11, and A13 in one fell swoop? There are two parts to this trick. First, you have to "overselect" the Copy From range to include both the source range and the entire destination range. We want to copy the formula from cell A3 into range A5..A13, so we need to select this entire region, range A3..A13 as our From range. Now, select range A3..A13 and choose Edit Quick Copy.

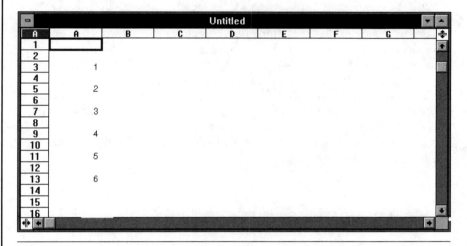

Figure 7.7. Range A5..A13 shows the result of a pattern copy. A single command duplicated the formula in cell A3 into every other cell in the column.

The second part of the trick is to move down or across the number or rows of columns that you want to alternate by. In other words, if you want copies in every third column, move the cell pointer three columns to the right. In this case, we want copies in every second row, so we'll move down two rows, to cell A5. Select A5 as the To range and choose OK.

Voilà! We get our wish—copies in every other row.

This technique also works with the /Copy command. It even works with the Range Values command if you specify a destination range that is also contained in the source range. Also note that you can "pattern-copy" more than one cell at a time.

/Copy

Note that the /Copy command does not copy borders and graphs. Use Edit Quick Copy to copy borders along with your data. Or use Edit Copy, which copies not only data and borders, but graphs as well.

The /Copy command is probably the one that flies from your fingers faster than any other.

A lot of beginners stumble on this command, because they don't understand that there are two parts to it, just as in the Edit Quick Copy command. If you've used 1-2-3 much at all, you probably got over this hurdle long ago, and you know that you start this command by entering the From range and finish it by entering the To range.

As you've seen, Edit Quick Copy provides a number of useful options, and its SmartIcon equivalents are fast and powerful. However, there's no reason to stop using /Copy for those tasks it does just fine. And it shares with Edit Quick Copy the feature known as pattern copying, explained in the box above.

The /Copy command copies all cell attributes except for borders and graphs. Its inability to copy borders can be an advantage or a nuisance. Just remember to use this command when you don't want or don't need to copy borders, and rely on commands like Edit Copy and Edit Quick Copy when you need to copy borders.

:Special Copy

The 1-2-3 Classic command :Special Copy is the WYSIWYG menu command for copying styles—but not data or numeric formats—from one range to another. See the "Edit Quick Copy" section above for more details.

/Range Value

The 1-2-3 Classic command /Range Value has the same effect as the Convert-to-values option of 1-2-3/W's Edit Quick Copy command. See the "Converting Formulas to Values" section above.

/Range Transpose

The 1-2-3 Classic command /Range Transpose has the same effect as the new Range Transpose command on the Windows menu. Both versions of this command in 1-2-3/W convert formulas to values, along with changing the orientation of the data you copy. See the "Range Transpose" section above for more details.

Other Ways to Copy

One could argue that other 1-2-3/W commands belong in a discussion about copying. For example, the Combine From, Import From, and Extract To commands on the File menu put copies of data from one place into another. Also, the Data Query command, with its Extract and Extract-unique-only options, copies data from one place to another. Then, of course, there are the 1-2-3 Classic equivalents of all these commands.

Though all of these are copy commands of a sort, they introduce a number of other issues that are best described elsewhere. To learn about the aforementioned File commands see Chapter 9. And to learn about Data Query, see Chapter 13.

Moving

Sometimes you don't want to duplicate your data, you just want to put things in different places. A variety of moving techniques help you rearrange your worksheet to your satisfaction. Commands that move data are listed in Table 7.2.

As explained later in this chapter, moving cells is often more dangerous than copying them. Moving affects formulas differently than copying does. If you move a cell that contains a formula, the formula's references will not adjust to the new location.

What happens when you move a cell that's referenced by a formula? If there's a cell somewhere in your worksheet with the formula @SUM(B8..B99), for example, that formula will sum a lot larger range if you move cell B99 to cell G1490. But if you move a cell that's within the formula's range, such as B98, no such change will occur.

You can choose among five different ways to remove the contents, styles, or formats from a range.

Command	Shortcut
Edit Cut	SmartIcon, Shift-Delete , Alt-E T
Edit Paste	SmartIcon, Shift-Insert, Alt-E P
Edit Move Cells	SmartIcon, Alt-E M
/Move	/M
:Special Move	:SM

Table 7.2. 1-2-3/W commands that move data and spreadsheet styles.

What if you do both things at once, move a formula *and* the cells that the formula refers to? The formula will update, which is probably what you wanted, because the cells it refers to are no longer in their old locations. Therefore, it's usually safe to move an entire table of data, as long as no cells outside the region you're moving refer to its cells.

The moving commands have side effects that can be dangerous only if you don't understand them. See "Avoiding Formula Failures II" at the end of this chapter for tips on safe moving.

Still, because of the risks of corrupting your formulas, it's often better to copy cells to a new location and then remove the originals. But if you need to relocate a group of labels, or if you're otherwise sure that you're not going to foul up any formulas, you'll want to know how to move data in 1-2-3/W.

Edit Cut, Edit Paste

The Edit Cut command, like Edit Copy, puts selected information into the Windows Clipboard. You then choose Edit Paste to copy the Clipboard's contents to a selected location. The only difference between Edit Cut and Edit Copy is that Edit Cut removes the selected information from its original location while it copies it to the Clipboard. Thus the combination of Edit Cut and Edit Paste is a way to move cells from one place to another.

Figure 7.8. The SmartIcons for the Edit Cut and Edit Paste commands. The icon on the left puts a copy of selected text into the Clipboard. The icon on the right pastes a copy of the Clipboard's contents at the current location.

The accelerator keys for Edit Cut and Edit Paste, respectively, are Shift-Delete and Shift-Insert. Both commands have SmartIcon equivalents, as shown in Figure 7.8.

Note that Edit Cut carries with it not only the contents of a range, but all of its styles, numeric formats, etc. You can also use it to move a graph that you've inserted into the worksheet. If any part of the graph is in the selected range, Edit Cut moves the graph to the Clipboard along with any selected worksheet data.

See the "Clipboard Basics" and "Copying Across Programs" sections earlier in this chapter. Most of the Clipboard rules about copying apply to cutting as well. The only difference is that you can't use Edit Paste Link to build a DDE link. After all, how can you link data when you just removed the original? And you'll also rarely want to cut data in order to copy it into another application. If the data is important enough to copy to another application, it's probably important enough to save in its source program.

The Edit Cut command not only takes the data from a range of cells, but it also snags the formats, styles, and graphs from the range, and puts them in the clipboard.

Edit Move Cells

Edit Move Cells does for /Move and :Special Move what Edit Quick Copy does for 1-2-3's copying features: It combines them into a single command and adds them to 1-2-3/W's Windows-style menus. And it brings the convenience of a SmartIcon equivalent.

Edit Move Cells resembles Edit Quick Copy in that it's a single command alternative to a pair of conventional Windows Clipboard commands—in this case, Edit Cut and Edit Paste. And it shares many traits with its 1-2-3 Classic equivalent, the /Move command, which is discussed in the next section.

Like the /Move command, the Edit Move Cells command requires two pieces of information: the range you're moving from and the range you're moving to. When you choose Edit Move Cells, you get the dialog box shown in Figure 7.9.

Note that Edit Move Cells moves not only the contents of a range, but all of its styles and numeric formats as well. It does not, however, move graphs that you've inserted into the worksheet, unless the graph is completely contained in the From range. To move only the styles from a range, choose the Styles-only option.

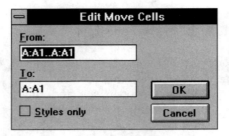

Figure 7.9. The Edit Move Cells' dialog box. This command is the Windows-menu equivalent of the /Move command. The Styles-only box lets this command also do the work of the Special Move command.

Edit Move Cells Basics

If only a single cell is selected when you choose Edit Move Cells, the dialog box opens with the From range highlighted. You specify the From range, click or tab to the To range, and specify the destination. Then you choose OK.

If two or more cells are preselected when you start the command, 1-2-3/W treats the selection as the From range. To save you a step, the dialog box opens with the To range, instead of the From range, highlighted.

The SmartIcon in Figure 7.10 is a very fast shortcut for moving ranges of cells. Select a source to move from, click this icon and click or drag the destination. You don't even have to press Enter or click OK in a dialog box.

Figure 7.10. A SmartIcon for fast moving of a range of cells. Select a range to move, and click this icon. The mouse pointer changes to resemble the pointing hand from the icon. You click or drag this pointer to identify the cell or cells to move to. When you release the mouse button, the moving is done.

The SmartIcon shown in Figure 7.10 lets you move cells very quickly. It looks like, and it functions quite similarly to, the quick-copying icon shown in Figure 7.3.

It automatically treats the current selection as the From range, even if it's a single cell, and it lets you identify the To range with a click or drag of the mouse. When you use this icon to move data, 1-2-3/W doesn't present a dialog box. Thus, you don't even have to press Enter or click OK. Instead, the mouse pointer changes into a pointing hand, and the moving takes place as soon as you release the mouse button.

Moving Styles

The Edit Move Cells command's Styles-only box lets you move the borders, colors, fonts, and font enhancements from one range to another. When you use this option, you move only the styles, and not the data or numeric formats.

Using the Styles-only box makes the Edit Move Cells command a functional equivalent of Allways' and WYSIWYG's Special Move command. As an alternative, you can choose :Special Move from the 1-2-3 Classic menu.

/Move

The /Move command is very similar to the new Edit Move Cells command. Like its Windows equivalent, it moves the data, formats, and styles of a range, and it can move graphs around the worksheet, as long as the From range selects them in their entirety.

:Special Move

The 1-2-3 Classic command :Special Move is the WYSIWYG menu command for moving styles—but not data or numeric formats—from one range to another. It's the functional equivalent of the Edit Move Cells command's Styles-only option.

Clearing Data

Most of the time you're trying to get stuff into your worksheet—data, formulas, descriptive headings, formats, styles, graphs, and more. But sometimes you need to take out the trash.

Maybe you entered the wrong data and want to get rid of it, or maybe you need to wring the old data out of the worksheet before you key in the new. Whatever the reason, you need ways to get the lead out of your worksheets. Table 7.3 lists the 1-2-3 commands that remove data from a range of cells.

Command	Shortcut
Edit Cut	SmartIcon, Shift-Delete , Alt-E T
Edit Clear	SmartIcon, Delete, Alt-E E
Edit Clear Special	Alt-ER
/Range Erase	/RE
:Format Reset	:FR
:Graph Remove	:GR

Table 7.3. 1-2-3/W commands that remove data and spreadsheet styles.

The commands for removing data are by definition destructive. The goal, of course, is to remove the offending data while steering clear of the good data.

In addition to the data-removal commands listed in Table 7.3 is the Worksheet Delete command, which removes not only the data from the cells but also the rows, columns, or worksheets that the data reside in. See the "Deleting Rows, Columns, and Sheets" section later in this chapter for details.

Edit Cut

One way to remove data from the worksheet is to use Edit Cut, but without its colleague Edit Paste. However, if you don't plan to paste it elsewhere, you're probably better off clearing rather than cutting the selection.

If the Clipboard contains something that you *do* want to paste, choosing Edit Cut will blow it away. Also, the Clipboard uses up memory, so if you're removing a large amount of data, you're wasting system resources by storing it there.

For more details, see the the discussion about the Edit Cut command earlier in this chapter.

Edit Clear

Edit Clear is the Windows-style menu equivalent of the /Range Erase command. The Edit Clear command removes selected information, but it does not use or affect the Clipboard's contents.

This command removes not only the contents of a range, but all of its styles and numeric formats as well. It also removes any graphs that are partially or completely contained in the selected range.

Figure 7.11. The SmartIcon for the Edit Clear command. This icon removes the current selection, but it does not use the Windows Clipboard.

The accelerator key for the Edit Clear command is the Delete key. The SmartIcon equivalent is shown in Figure 7.11.

You can delete a selection simply by pressing the Delete key.

Edit Clear Special

The Edit Clear Special command presents a dialog box that lets you selectively delete contents and attributes of a range of cells.

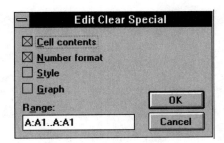

Figure 7.12. The Edit Clear Special dialog box. You can choose any combination of four elements to delete from a range: its contents, numeric formats, styles, or graphs.

When you choose Edit Clear Special, the Cell contents and Number format options are selected, but you can select any combination of elements to delete.

/Range Erase

This is another command that most 1-2-3 users can blaze through in a fraction of a second. It continues to be useful in 1-2-3/W, but you should note that you cannot use it to delete a graph.

If you preselect a range of cells, this command erases them immediately. Otherwise, it prompts you to enter the range to erase.

:Format Reset

The 1-2-3 Classic command :Format Reset is the WYSIWYG menu command for clearing the styles—but not the data or numeric formats—from a range of cells. Thus, it performs one of the functions of the Edit Clear Special command described above.

:Graph Remove

This 1-2-3 Classic command is the WYSIWYG command for removing a graph that you've inserted into the worksheet. It does not, however, destroy the settings from the graph. For more on working with graphs see Chapter 11, *Creating Graphics*.

Other Removal Commands

Some attributes, such as whether a cell is unprotected, aren't affected by 1-2-3/W's erasure commands. Look in the menu or dialog box where you assign these attributes to find the command that resets them.

The commands described above remove the visible contents from a cell, such as labels, values, cell borders, and graphs. Many of them also reset attributes, such as numeric formats and bold type.

If you need to reset some other attribute, check the command that sets the attribute. That command's dialog box, or a neighboring menu choice, should provide a way to undo the setting.

For example, to reset the numeric format of a range of cells, select Range Format and the Reset button. And to reset a range to protected status from unprotected, choose Range Protect, which is on the Range menu along with the Range Unprotect command.

Inserting Rows, Columns, and Sheets

Sometimes you need to make room for data. That's when you need the Worksheet Insert command.

Inserting a row or column is much like moving all the data in a row or column down or to the right. The main differences are that it's faster to insert than to select and move a large group of data, and when you insert, you don't have to worry about whether you remembered to move some data that's off in a remote part of the worksheet. Perhaps the most important difference is that inserting one or more sheets is how you turn a two-dimensional worksheet into a 3D one.

Inserting a Row or Column

Inserting a row or column is easy. You just select one or more cells and select Worksheet Insert or the Classic command /Worksheet Insert. Then you choose the Row or Column option. The number of rows or columns in the range that you select—or that you specify after you start the command—is the number that will be inserted.

Figure 7.13. The SmartIcons for inserting a row, a column, and a single sheet.

The first two SmartIcons in Figure 7.13 let you insert, respectively, a selected number of rows and columns into the worksheet. The SmartIcon on the right lets you insert a single sheet after the current sheet. None of these icons is part of the default SmartIcon palette, so if you want to use them you must first choose Tools SmartIcons Customize to add them to your palette.

Figures 7.14 shows the original worksheet, and Figure 7.15 shows the result of inserting rows in range B3..B6.

There are two important details to keep in mind about inserting. First, as with other worksheet-maintenance commands, you have to consider how the inserted rows, columns, and sheets affect formulas. The section "Avoiding Formula Failures II" at the end of this chapter shows how to avoid calculation problems that can result from inserting data at the wrong location.

The other issue is understanding how to select the desired number of rows, columns, or sheets to insert. Again, Figure 7.15 shows what happens when we insert four rows at range B3..B6. We would have gotten the same result, however, had we inserted at range A3..B6 or range AK3..FP6. In other words, the column or number of columns selected is irrelevant to a row insertion.

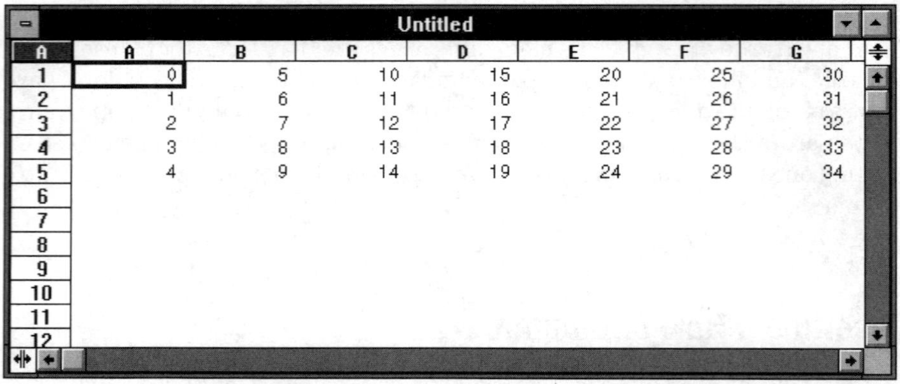

Figure 7.14. To add four rows to this worksheet, with the first new row as row 3, select any range that includes rows 3 through 6, such as range B3..B6, and choose Worksheet Insert Row.

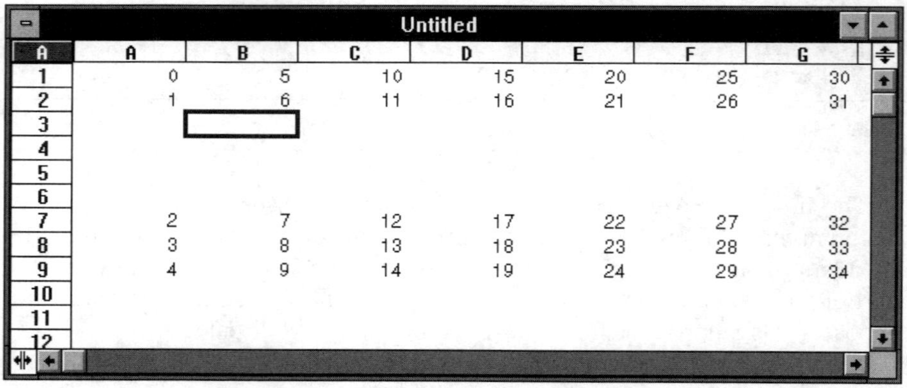

Figure 7.15. The worksheet after inserting four rows at range B3..B6.

Inserting columns, which you perform by choosing Worksheet Insert Column, works by all the same rules, but of course from a different angle. The number of columns you select is the number that is inserted when you invoke this command. For example, to add two blank columns after column B, you could select range C1..D1, range C99..D99, or perhaps range C19..D57, and then choose Worksheet Insert Column.

Inserting Sheets

3D worksheets are covered in detail in Chapter 9. But since you create 3D worksheets with the same command that you use to insert rows and columns, let's take a brief look at how you add this extra dimension.

One difference between the commands for inserting rows and columns and the command for inserting sheets is that you don't start the latter command by preselecting a range. You choose Worksheet Insert Sheet, and you type in the Quantity of sheets and whether the sheets should be added Before or After the current sheet.

If you have a file with only one sheet, sheet A, and you want to add two blank sheets after that sheet, choose Worksheet Insert Sheet and select After and a Quantity of 2. When you complete the command, you'll be in sheet C.

To move to a previous sheet, press Ctrl-PageDown. To move to the next sheet, press Ctrl-PageUp. To move to the first cell of the first sheet, press Ctrl-Home.

All it takes to turn a two-dimensional application into a 3D one is to add sheets via the Worksheet Insert Sheet command.

Deleting Rows, Columns, and Sheets

As you'd expect, the Worksheet Delete command is the opposite of the Worksheet Insert command. Like its 1-2-3/W Classic equivalent, /Worksheet Delete, it carves rows, columns, and sheets out of your worksheet documents.

The mechanics of this command are nearly identical to those of Worksheet Insert. You select a range, and when you complete the command, all rows or columns in the range are deleted. The major difference is that you also delete sheets by selecting a range, rather than by specifying a quantity, as you do when you insert sheets.

This, of course, is an extremely dangerous command. Use it with caution, and take all the necessary steps to protect your data in case of a mishap, such as saving the file first and immediately inspecting the result of this command so you can undo it if need be.

As you do when you insert rows and columns, you have to think clearly about what you're selecting when you use Worksheet Delete—and the potential damage is far greater with this command. If, for example, you want to delete rows 5 through 7, you could select range C5..C7. But if you mistakenly choose Worksheet Delete *Column* instead of *Row*, you'll wipe out column C. And you'd wipe out the whole sheet if you chose Worksheet Delete Sheet!

When deleting, be careful to select the right options. If you're not careful, you could delete a row when you need to delete a column.

Think of this command as a chain saw that carves out large chunks of data. If you use it carefully, the Worksheet Delete command is a terrific power tool. But if you use it recklessly, you can massacre your data.

Deleted But Not Forgotten

The 1-2-3/W Classic command /Worksheet Delete has one option, File, that's not included in the 1-2-3/W main-menu version of the command. /Worksheet Delete File deletes a file from memory, but not from the disk—presuming you saved the file at some point. In other words, it closes the file without saving it.

This variation of the /Worksheet Delete command was introduced in 1-2-3 Release 3 to let you close a single file, as opposed to clearing all files by choosing /Worksheet Erase Yes Yes. In 1-2-3 for Windows, you can close a file more easily by choosing File Close or by double-clicking a document's Control icon.

Avoiding Formula Failures II

In the previous chapter, you learned about a number of potential formula fiascoes and how to avoid them. Most of these involved setting up your formulas properly.

Sometimes commands that copy, move, insert, and remove data can turn good formulas into faulty ones. Read on to learn how to prevent errors from creeping into your worksheet when you perform these maintenance tasks.

In addition to these more subtle issues, keep in mind the importance of not copying over, moving over, clearing, or deleting valuable formulas or cells that contain data needed by a formula. It takes a lot longer to rebuild your formulas than it does to look around the worksheet and inspect cells that you think might have formulas or data that's part of a formula.

It's usually helpful that 1-2-3/W adjusts formulas when you copy them. Use absolute references when you don't want your cell references to change when you copy a formula.

Relative and Absolute References

If you create worksheets without understanding the difference between absolute and relative references, you could be building serious errors into your applications.

A lot of self-taught spreadsheet users can get pretty far with their worksheets until they stumble across an absolute-referencing problem. What makes this problem hard to spot is that it shows up not when you build your formulas, but when you copy them.

A Relatively Bad Formula

Consider this salary scenario: Pete, Lincoln, and Julie are all in line for raises. This time, everybody is supposed to get the same raise, which is 10%. The boss puts together the worksheet in Figure 7.16 to calculate the new salaries.

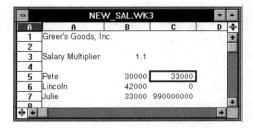

Figure 7.16. A worksheet that requires the use of absolute references. The formula in cell C5 (+B5*B3) worked just fine for Pete's new salary. Why did Lincoln lose every penny, and why did Julie make a mint when the formula was copied to cells C6 and C7? The answer: This formula needs an absolute reference.

Enter the labels in column A, and enter the values in column B. Then enter the formula +B5*B3 in cell C5. This formula multiplies Pete's old salary by 1.1, yielding the desired 10% increase. Copy this formula to range C6..C7. If Julie's new salary in column C appears as a series of asterisks, make column C wide enough to display her prodigious new pay rate.

Why did the formula that succeeded in cell C5 flop in cells C6 and C7? Look at the formulas in the latter two cells to see why.

When you copied the formula down column C, the references to the rows increased by one. In other words, the 5 in B5 turned into a 6, and the 3 in B3 turned into a 4 for Lincoln's new salary. This is the way any ordinary formula behaves, because 1-2-3/W usually works with relative references. 1-2-3/W thinks of Pete's new salary formula not as +B5*B3, but as the value in the cell to the left times the value in the cell that's one column to the left and two cells up.

This relative referencing makes it possible to copy formulas, as well as insert and delete rows, columns, and sheets, without having to update your formulas manually. In fact, the first part of this formula, which finds the employee's current salary in the neighboring cell, works just fine with a relative reference.

The reference to the salary multiplier, however, should be absolute. We don't want to take each person's old salary and multiply it by the value that's two cells above it. We want each and every old salary to be multiplied by the value in cell B3, and only cell B3.

The trick is to include dollar signs ($) in the reference. To fix this fiscal mess, change Pete's new-salary formula to +B5*$B$3, and then copy it down column C to cells C5..C7. Each member of the squad is now getting the same raise.

Note that you can make partial absolute references, such as +B$5 or $B5, as well as full absolute references, like the aforementioned +$B$5. The expression +B$5 "locks in" the row reference but not the column reference. No matter where you copy or move the formula, it will always refer to row 5. But if you put this formula in a different column, the column reference will change. The expression +$B5, in contrast, preserves the column reference, but not the row reference.

Remember that in a 3D worksheet, there's another dimension beyond rows and columns: the sheet. If you want to make the sheet references in your formulas absolute, 1-2-3/W is happy to oblige. Just throw in a dollar sign before the sheet reference. For example, if you enter the formula +$B:A13*100, the reference to sheet B does not change, even if you copy or move this formula to another sheet. Also be aware that if you enter a two-dimensional reference, such as $G$4, that when you copy it to another sheet 1-2-3/W assumes you want to make the sheet reference absolute as well.

Absolute Convenience

The ABS key (F4) makes it easy to enter the dollar signs that signify an absolute reference.

The ABS key (F4) is a shortcut for entering the dollar signs. This is the same key you use to start preselecting with the keyboard when you're in Ready mode. When you're building a formula in Point, Value, or Edit mode and you press the ABS key, the sheet, column, and row of the current cell reference take on dollar signs.

For example, imagine that you're entering the formula +A:B2*A:C2. With the insertion point (cursor) positioned anywhere within—or immediately before or after—the reference to cell C2, press ABS (F4). The latter cell reference changes to $A:$C$2. If you press ABS again, the reference changes to $A:C$2—with absolute sheet and row references and a relative column reference. See Table 7.4 to find what happens with each subsequent press of the ABS key. Note that if you press the ABS key a total of eight times, all the formula's references become relative again.

Number of Presses	Effect	Example
1	All references absolute	+$B:$C$2
2	Sheet and row absolute	+$B:C$2
3	Sheet and column absolute	+$B:$C2
4	Sheet absolute	+$B:C2
5	Column and row absolute	+B:$C$2
6	Row absolute	+B:C$2
7	Column absolute	+B:$C2
8	All references relative	+B:C2

Table 7.4. Each time you press the ABS key when you're working on a formula in Point, Value, or Edit mode, different combinations of dollar signs make different portions of a reference absolute.

Keep It in the Range

A typical mishap could befall the worksheet in Figure 7.17 when it's time to add a new expense item. Range B2..B9 contains a list of expenses, and the formula in cell B10, @SUM(B2..B9) tallies up your outlay. You need an extra line item, and you want it at the bottom of the expense list, right before the total line. But if you're not careful, the data you add won't be reflected in the expense total.

If you add a blank row after row 9, the @SUM formula below it will not expand to accommodate the new row. That's as it should be, because you don't want formulas to take on additional cells arbitrarily. 1-2-3/W does, however, adjust formulas when you insert or delete rows *within* the range that the formula refers to.

It certainly won't do us any good to enter an expense item if 1-2-3/W isn't going to add it to the total. And we're not interested in rebuilding formulas, especially if there were a series of @functions in this row.

The trick is to insert a line before the last line, in this case between the current rows 8 and 9. Then copy the data in the last row of the range into the new blank row above it. Now enter the correct data for your new expense item in the final row.

Range references expand when you insert rows, columns, or sheets within the referenced range, not when you append new data in neighboring cells.

	EXPENSES.WK3	
	B	B
1		
2	Salaries	$650,000
3	Rent	374,000
4	Equipment	400,000
5	Taxes	200,000
6	Interest	185,000
7	Legal	87,500
8	Consultants	92,450
9	Travel	10,000
10	Total Expenses:	$1,998,950
11		

Figure 7.17. The @SUM formula in cell B10 totals range B2..B9. If you insert or delete a row within this range, the formula will adjust automatically. If you insert a row before or after this range, the formula will not adjust to include the new row. And if you move either cell B2 or cell B9, the reference in the formula will "move" with it.

Other Cell-Reference Problems

Use caution when deleting or moving cells that serve as the "corners" of a formula's range reference. Such changes will expand or contract the reference.

The previous examples, on copying relative and absolute references and on inserting rows into a table, showed two common problems that you can run into while you maintain a worksheet.

Following are a couple of variations on this theme. In a some cases these "side effects" may be the desired results, but you should think twice about these and other activities that can alter your formulas.

Moving a Referenced Cell

If you move a cell that's referenced in another cell's formula, the reference changes to reflect the new cell address. For example, if you move the contents of cell D12 to cell D14, a formula that reads +C12*D12 changes to +C12*D14. Likewise, a formula that reads @SUM(B12..D12) changes to @SUM(B12..D14).

Deleting a Referenced Row, Column, or Sheet

If you delete a row, column, or sheet that's referenced in a cell, the results vary, depending on whether the formula refers to an individual cell or a range. If you delete column C or row 2, a formula that reads +B1*C2 evaluates to an error; when you edit the cell, the formula appears as +B1*ERR. This error occurs because 1-2-3/W has no way to determine which cell you'd prefer to substitute for the one whose row or column you deleted.

However, if you delete column C or row 2, a formula that reads @SUM(B1..C2) shrinks to exclude the missing row or column. The same rules apply to deleting a referenced sheet: Cell references result in an error, and range references shrink to exclude the deleted sheet.

8

Mastering the Sheet

This chapter covers several 1-2-3/W features that are important but easy to overlook: range names, customizable default settings, panes, and titles. You will rarely have to use any of them, but each can greatly improve the usability of your applications.

Range names make your formulas easier to enter and read, and they open the door to the power of 1-2-3/W macros. A slew of default settings let you change entire worksheets—and even the 1-2-3/W environment—with a single command. And panes and titles let you view data from more than one part of your worksheet at any time.

Once you learn how to use these features, you'll wonder how you ever created spreadsheets without them.

Range Names

A range name serves no immediate benefit. It's simply a nickname for a block of one or more cells. Yet range names are vital for spreadsheets of even modest complexity, and they're virtually required in the creation of macros.

You can use a range name just about any time you specify a cell or a range reference. The most obvious advantages are that range names are easier to remember and easier to read in formulas.

Assigning a Range Name

To assign a range name, you choose Range Name Create and specify both the name and the range that the name identifies. There are a few rules about range names. They can be no longer than 15 characters, you should

> *In this chapter you will learn:*
> - *How to create and use named ranges*
> - *How to customize the 1-2-3/W environment*
> - *How to use panes and titles*

avoid starting them with numbers or an exclamation point, and you shouldn't use spaces, semicolons, commas, periods or the following characters in the name: +, *, -, /, &, >, <, @, #, or {. Also, don't create range names that look like cell references, such as A1, Q4, or FY99. Technically, you can break some of these rules, but you may get unpredictable or undesirable results.

You can use an underscore (_) to separate words in a range name.

One special character that *is* recommended is the underscore (_), which you can use to separate words. For example, you can name a range *fifty_something* instead of *fiftysomething*. Also note that range names are case-insensitive. Thus MYRANGE, *myrange*, *MyRange*, and so on, all refer to the same range.

Figure 8.1. The Range Name Create dialog box. Here you specify a range name and the location of the cells that will bear the name.

A named range, like any range, cannot have an irregular shape, such as two cells from one row and three from another. However, a named range can span multiple sheets in a 3D worksheet, such as A:A1..G:E17.

A Formula for Naming

If you create a range name via the /Range Name Create 1-2-3 Classic menu command, you can type a short formula when 1-2-3/W prompts you for the name. If you press the CALC key (F9) before you press Enter, 1-2-3/W turns the formula into a label.

For example, if the label *Distribution* is in cell B6, you can type +B6 and press the CALC key to choose *Distribution* as a range name. Next, you press Enter and then enter the range you want to apply this name to.

The other way to assign a range name is to choose Range Name Label Create. This command lets you assign the label in one cell as the name for one of its neighboring cells.

When you need to assign several names, you can use the Create button in the Range Name Create command's dialog box. This lets you assign a name without closing the dialog box. When you name the last of a group of ranges, you choose OK.

Try It: Assigning Range Names

Let's try assigning some range names. We'll use these names in subsequent exercises.

1. Start up 1-2-3/W and use the Untitled worksheet that appears. If 1-2-3/W is already running, and the worksheet on screen is not empty, choose File New to create a blank worksheet.
2. Enter the label *Under* in cell A1 and the label *The Greenwood Tree* in cell A2. Enter the numbers 4, 7, and 9 in, respectively, cells C1, E1, and F1.
3. Select cell C1 and choose Range Name Create. Note that the Range box at the bottom of the dialog box indicates range C1..C1. Type *luckynum* and select OK.
4. Select range E1..F1 and choose Range Name Create again. Now the Range box specifies range E1..F1. Type *data* in the Range name box and choose OK.
5. This time we'll use the label in one cell to name the cell below it. Select cell A1, choose Range Name Label Create, select the Down button from the dialog box, then choose OK. The tricky part is that we specified cell A1, because it's the cell with the label, but the named cell will actually be the cell below it, cell A2.

Using a Named Range

Now let's put these range names to use. Press the GOTO key (F5), and a dialog box appears, presenting a list of range names. Either type *data*, tab down the list of ranges and press the DownArrow key, or click the name *data*. When you choose OK, the cell pointer jumps to cell E1, which is the first cell in the *data* range. The upper-left cell in the range is used for any operation, like using the GOTO key, that expects a single cell instead of a range.

Next, use the GOTO key again, this time to jump to *luckynum*. In this small worksheet, using the GOTO key to jump from cell to cell isn't much of a time-saver, but in a large worksheet it can save a lot of scrolling.

Now lets use our range names in some formulas. Select cell A4, and enter the following formula: @SUM(data). The total of the data range, E1..F1, magically appears.

Next, move to cell B4 and type a plus sign (+), and then press the NAME key (F3). The list of range names appears. Choose *luckynum* and select OK. Add the expression *2 to the formula, to multiply *luckynum* by 2. Enter the formula, and cell B4 displays the value 8.

Remember how we used the Range Name Label Create command to assign the label in cell A1 as the name for the cell below it? Let's put that name to use, too. In cell C4, enter the formula +*under*. The label *The Greenwood Tree* appears in the cell.

Note that you can use absolute references if you want to preserve a range name reference in case you copy the formula. For example, the formula @SUM($data) will continue to refer to the *data* range even if you copy it to a new cell.

Also note that if you enter a reference to a named cell or range, 1-2-3/W does not automatically convert the reference to the name (1-2-3 Release 2.x does). But if you press the NAME key (F3) while entering or editing such a reference, it converts the reference to its name. For example, if you typed the formula +B4 and pressed the NAME key, the formula would read +*luckynum*.

The NAME key (F3) is also useful for bringing up a list of range names in almost any situation in which you'd use a name. This list resembles the one that appears when you press the GOTO key. For example, when you're entering a formula or specifying a range to copy from, you can press the NAME key and choose the range name from the list. Using range names saves you from having to memorize cell and range references; using the NAME key saves you from having to memorize range names. Note that you cannot use the NAME key from Ready mode.

When you need to enter a range name, you can press the NAME key (F3) to bring up a list of names.

Range Names and Macros

Range names are essential for macro programming. Typically, you use a range name to identify a macro. If you assign a name that consists of a backslash (\) and a single letter to a cell, the label in that cell (and all cells directly below it until the next blank cell) becomes an easy-to-run macro. In 1-2-3/W you activate such a macro by pressing the Control key (instead of the Alt key, as in other releases) plus the letter name.

You should also use range names within your macros in place of ordinary range or cell references. Otherwise, the macro may lose track of the cells as they relocate after such operations as inserting, deleting, moving, and copying. Cell and range references in macros, unlike those in formulas, don't automatically adjust when the ranges move. Macros are simply labels that store keystrokes and Advanced Macro Commands—those special macro commands, such as {PUT}, that appear within braces. For more on macros, see Chapter 17.

More Range-Name Tips

Here are a few helpful hints on using range names:

Keep them short. It's a lot easier to enter *@SUM(cost)* than to enter *@SUM(cost_of_goods)*. On the other hand, make them as long as necessary—up to the 15-character limit—to be understandable.

Use one per file. Note that you cannot use the same range name twice in a 3D file.

Put first things first. If you want to access a particular range name frequently, give it a name that's early in the alphabet, such as *a_summary*. That way it appears near the beginning of the list of names.

Put last things last. Use characters late in the alphabet or allowable special characters, such as ~, to start range names that you want to put at the end of the name list.

Name it later. 1-2-3/W, like Release 3.x, lets you enter formulas that include names that don't exist yet. If you enter a formula, such as *@AVG(sales)*, 1-2-3/W accepts the entry and displays ERR if there is no *sales* range. As soon as you assign the name *sales*, the formula displays the appropriate value. You cannot use nonexistent range names in formulas in Releases 2.x and earlier.

Unname unused ranges. Use the Range Name Delete command to delete names you're no longer using. This saves a bit of memory, and it saves you from wading through a list of irrelevant range names.

Make a table. Place a list of current range names in your worksheet by choosing Range Name Paste Table. Make sure there's enough room in your worksheet for the table, so that it doesn't overwrite any data. The table is two columns wide by as many rows as you have range names. A printout of the table of names makes a handy reference.

Annotate the names. The 1-2-3 Classic command /Range Name Note lets you assign comments to describe the range names. This is a useful way to document the logic of your applications. Commands from the /Range Name Note menu let you create, delete, reset (clear all), and paste a table of range name notes. The table you create with this command is one column wider than the one generated by the Range Name Paste Table command.

Global Settings and System Defaults

In 1-2-3/W, global settings are options that affect an entire worksheet or file. Other settings, known as defaults, change the 1-2-3/W environment—for the current work session only or for future sessions as well.

Central control for most of 1-2-3/W's global settings is, appropriately enough, the Worksheet Global Settings command. To establish a wide range of 1-2-3/W default settings, you use the Tools User Setup command. And you can customize the look of either the current file or the 1-2-3/W environment by way of the Window Display Options command. Each of these three commands presents a dialog box with a variety of options.

Global settings you can control include the format of all "unformatted" numeric cells and the protection status of the worksheet. Default settings you can change include the preferred directory for saving and opening files and the way 1-2-3/W performs calculations. The colors that are available for screen display and printing can be established as global settings or the default settings.

Note that the difference between the terms *global* and *default* is somewhat inexact, because global settings for a worksheet are sometimes called defaults—the term that's also used to describe system-wide settings. Ultimately, the terms are not terribly important, but it is important to understand the scope of the changes you make.

In this section, you'll learn which changes you can make within a given worksheet or file and which changes reconfigure the way 1-2-3/W works with all files. In practice, you may find it useful to press the HELP key (F1) when you're selecting options from the Worksheet Global Settings, Tools User Setup, and Window Display Options commands. That way you'll be able to determine the domain of the settings you choose.

Worksheet Global Settings

The Worksheet Global Settings command lets you control settings for an entire worksheet.

The dialog box that this command brings up is reminiscent of the 1-2-3 Classic /Worksheet Global menu. The main differences are that it does not let you alter printer settings and it doesn't offer a default option. As in other Windows applications, you use File-menu commands to change 1-2-3/W's printer settings. And to set default options in 1-2-3/W, you use either Tools User Setup or Window Display Options.

The options in the Worksheet Global Settings dialog box and the 1-2-3 Classic /Worksheet Global menu share the same general scope. Except for both commands' Group-mode setting and the slash command's Default command, all options apply to the current worksheet only.

Global versus Local

Many global commands are big brothers to commands you perform on a cell-by-cell or range-by-range basis. These smaller-scale commands are sometimes called local commands.

When you need to assign a setting to a large portion of the worksheet, global commands offer two advantages over equivalent local commands. First, its faster to specify a global setting than to highlight the entire sheet and issue a local command. Second, global commands are more memory-efficient; 1-2-3/W has to remember only one setting, rather than settings you've placed into each and every cell or column.

Powerful as they are, most global commands respect the independence of local commands. For example, if you set the width of a particular column, setting the global column width won't affect it—it will change only those columns you haven't specifically widened or narrowed.

The same goes for numeric formats. Ranges to which you've assigned formats don't change their tune when you choose a global format.

But what if you use a local command to set a column width or a numeric format but then later want the cell or range to get back in step with the rest of the worksheet? In other words, how do you make it respond to global settings? The answer is to reset the attribute, for example, by choosing the Reset option of the Worksheet Column Width or Range Format commands.

A common mistake is to try to reset such attributes by changing them to match the current global settings. That technique still leaves these columns or cells with special attributes, so they won't adjust the next time you change the global settings.

Following are descriptions of the options you can choose from the Worksheet Global Default Settings dialog box, which is shown in Figure 8.2.

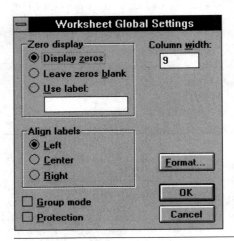

Figure 8.2. The Worksheet Global Settings dialog box. Here you determine settings for the current worksheet.

Zero Display

This option lets you choose among three ways to display zeros in your worksheet. The first choice, Display zeros, is the default setting. It makes zeros look like zeros. The second, Leave zeros blank, suppresses display of all zero-value cells in the worksheet, so they appear as blank cells. The third option, Use label, lets you substitute a label for any cells that equal zero. If you wish, you can precede this label with a label prefix, such as the caret (^) for a centered label.

Note that this command affects only cells that contain a value of zero or cells that contain a formula that evaluates to zero. The benefit of this command is that it lets you present a cleaner screen if it's currently riddled with zeros from data that aren't yet available, and it lets you flag formulas as N/A or ERR if they evaluate to zero.

There is no local equivalent for these zero-handling options, but you can use an @IF formula, such as @IF(B2=0,"",B2) to suppress the value of a cell if it's zero. And to put a message in a zero-value cell, you can use a variation such as @IF(B2,0,@ERR) or @IF(B2,0,"Zip, zilch. Nothing, nada. You got bupkis, pal.").

Align Labels

You can use this command if you want your labels to be automatically centered or right-justified, instead of the usual left alignment. For the most part, this option is unnecessary, because you can easily realign a range of labels with the Style Alignment command.

Also, it can be disconcerting to other people who use the worksheet to enter labels and have them appear in unexpected alignments. However, this setting can be useful if you need to enter a large number of centered or right-aligned labels, especially if they are not all in a single, easy-to-realign range.

Note that this option does not change the alignment of existing cells. It affects only the entry of new labels.

Group Mode

If you use the Worksheet Global Settings command's Group option, the current worksheet's global and local settings are automatically applied throughout the other worksheets in the file. *Be forewarned: Group mode has many powerful side effects* that can be extremely useful or extremely dangerous, depending on your application's needs. See the section on Group mode in Chapter 9 before tinkering with this high-powered command.

Protection

When you enable this option, all cells with the *protected* attribute are locked up so that you cannot alter their contents. This is a useful way to ensure against accidental changes to the worksheet. And combined with other security features, it can also help protect against unauthorized tampering.

If you're a new 1-2-3 user, you may be surprised to find that all cells are protected unless you choose otherwise, by selecting the Range Unprotect option. If you turn on global protection without having unprotected any cells, you will be unable to alter any cells in the worksheet.

This command can be a nuisance while you're developing or maintaining your worksheet, because it prevents you from making changes. But when the worksheet is in normal use, it's a blessing, especially if your application is sometimes used by spreadsheet novices.

Unless other worksheet-protection tools are in use, you can toggle this protection mode on or off by means of its check box. For more details on creating secure applications, see Chapter 9.

By default all 1-2-3/W cells are "protected." When you activate global protection, they can't be altered unless you've used Range Unprotect.

Column Width

This command is a fast way to reset the width of all the columns in your worksheet, except for those whose widths you've specifically changed. To use this option, you simply enter a number in the Column-width box.

Instead of changing the setting in this manner, you may prefer to use the 1-2-3/W Classic command /Worksheet Global Col-Width. Its advantage is that it lets you press the RightArrow or LeftArrow key to gradually change the global column width, previewing the result of the new width before you confirm it.

Format

If you choose the Format button from the Worksheet Global Settings dialog box, up pops a dialog box that's nearly identical to the one from the Range Format command.

If you prefer, for example, to see most of your worksheet's numbers presented in fixed length with two decimal places, it's more efficient to make the change here, instead of reformatting large ranges of cells.

For more about the available format choices, see the section on cell formats in Chapter 6.

Tools User Setup

The Tools User Setup command lets you select default settings for the current work session. You can select the default directory for saving and opening worksheets, allocate memory so that you can undo commands, and determine whether the software will automatically run a macro named \0, should you retrieve a file that contains such a macro.

To turn these settings into permanent 1-2-3/W defaults, choose the Update button. Then the revised settings will be in effect each time you start up 1-2-3/W.

Beep On Error

The Beep-on-error option lets you determine whether the computer beeps at you in case of an error. If you like things nice and quiet, you might turn the beeping off, but it's usually advantageous to let 1-2-3/W alert you to errors.

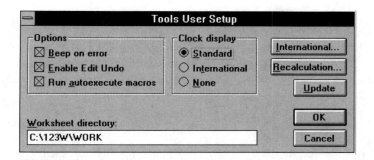

Figure 8.3. The Tools User Setup dialog box. Here you determine settings for the 1-2-3/W environment. These options are similar to those of the 1-2-3 Classic command /Worksheet Global Default.

Note that if you turn the beeping off, the macro command {BEEP} is silenced as well.

Enable Edit Undo

Early in the book you were advised to keep the 1-2-3/W Undo feature enabled. Deselecting the Enable Edit Undo option lets you forgo one of 1-2-3/W's best features: the ability to undo the result of a command.

Why would you do such a thing? Well, it's not recommended, but if you're running low on memory, you may have to disable Undo to free some of your computer's RAM. It takes a lot of memory to remember the way the worksheet looked before the last command as well as after it. Thus, absolving 1-2-3/W from the former responsibility unleashes a substantial amount of memory.

Most likely, your work is more valuable than the humble sum you'd pay to add more memory to your system. So instead of working without this safety net, you'd be better off investing in a few extra memory chips.

Run Autoexecute Macros

The Run Autoexecute Macros option lets you enable or disable the 1-2-3 feature that automatically runs a macro program named \0 as soon as you load any worksheet that contains one.

Such macros are a handy way to make a highly automated system, one that performs from the moment it appears on your screen. However, sometimes you want to open such a file without having the autoexecuting macro do its stuff. By disabling this option, you suppress this automatic running feature.

Clock Display

The Clock Display option lets you decide whether the time and date appear at the bottom of the 1-2-3/W window. You can choose from a Standard or International date and time format, or you can choose to have no clock display.

International

The International button brings up a dialog box that lets you determine how values, currency, dates, and times are displayed. The option that lets you determine the style for values also lets you determine which character, such as a comma or semicolon, is used to separate arguments in @functions, macro commands, and such. Two other options let you choose preferred character formats for imported and exported files.

Recalculation

The Recalculation button brings up a dialog box that allows you to alter the way 1-2-3/W calculates data. The default is Natural recalculation, which is appropriate for most worksheet tasks. In rare situations, you may choose to have 1-2-3/W calculate Columnwise (column-by-column) or Rowwise (row-by-row) instead of letting it figure out the "natural" order of the calculations.

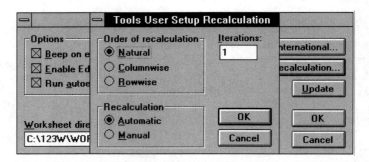

Figure 8.4. The Tools User Setup Recalculation dialog box. These options control how 1-2-3/W recalculates the Worksheet.

For most people, the most frequent choice is between Automatic and Manual recalculation. Switching from Automatic to Manual recalculation mode lets you speed through tasks in a worksheet that has a lot of formulas, and it lets you preserve a current set of results until you desire to have the numbers updated.

Unlike Release 2.x, 1-2-3/W supports background recalculation, so you don't have to wait until calculations finish in order to proceed with the next task. But when you have a lot of data to enter, you may find it distracting to have 1-2-3/W go through its recalculating paces with each entry.

If you set recalculation to Manual, the CALC indicator appears at the bottom of the screen to warn you when values have changed and the current formula results may no longer be accurate. To update the calculations, you press the CALC key (F9). The CALC key does not restore Automatic calculation. To do this, you must use the Tools User Setup command.

Iterations

In the unlikely event that you want to build circular references—formulas that refer to the cells that contain them—you may want to use the Iterations option. This feature lets you select a specific number of times 1-2-3/W will run through these circular calculations. For more on circular references, see Chapter 6.

Worksheet Directory

Like the 1-2-3 Classic command /Worksheet Global Default Dir, this option lets you determine which directory 1-2-3/W assumes when you issue a File-menu command, such as File Open, File Save, or File Save As.

If, for example, you want to store all your files in a directory called C:\MARTIN or C:\SHEILA\BUDGET, you can specify this name in the Worksheet Directory text box and then use the Update command to make 1-2-3/W remember that this is the preferred directory for future work sessions.

Window Display Options

The Window Display Options command lets you change the look of the 1-2-3/W environment. You can alter the way a particular file looks, and you can permanently change 1-2-3/W's default display settings. These settings are especially handy if you use 1-2-3/W to make on-screen presentations, and if you simply want to redecorate the 1-2-3/W workspace. Even if you're not concerned with the niceties of screen colors and such, you can use this command to see more information on the screen, or to zoom in to view part of the screen in greater detail.

> *When the formulas are out of date because automatic recalculation is disabled, a CALC indicator appears at the bottom of the screen. This lets you know that the currently displayed values don't reflect the latest calculations. Press the CALC key (F9) to update the calculations.*

> ### A Private :Display
>
> Note that the :Display command in the 1-2-3 Classic WYSIWYG menu offers a different way to change display options. Since it also provides a few options not available with Window Display Options, you'll find this menu worth exploring. For example, it lets you change the cell pointer from a solid box to an outline. To make permanent any changes you select from the :Display menu, choose :Display Default Update.

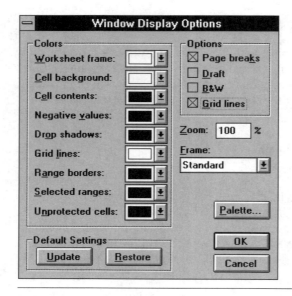

Figure 8.5. The Window Display Options dialog box. Here you customize your view of your worksheet and the worksheet environment.

Colors

The Colors options provide a series of palettes from which you select the color of such items as the cell pointer, the worksheet frame, and the contents and background of cells. These latter two options change the color of all cells that you don't explicitly color via the Style Color command.

Options

The Options section of this dialog box is a group of check boxes for a variety of settings. They let you turn on or off the display of grid lines and page breaks, they let you choose either draft-quality or graphics display, and they let you choose either monochrome or color display.

Zoom

The Zoom setting lets you either shrink down the worksheet to see more data at one time or blow up a section to see it more easily. A Zoom value of 100% generates a normal view.

You can zoom down to as small a size as 25%—one quarter the size of a normal display. And you can zoom up as much as 400%, four times the normal size.

Zooming down is particularly useful if you have multiple worksheets on the screen or simply a lot of data in one worksheet. It lets you view enough data to make sense of the sheets. Zooming up makes the characters more readable, and it can help you tune out all but a small part of the worksheet.

Frame

The frame is the so-called inverted L that defines the top and left side of the worksheet, home of the sheet letter, column letters, and row numbers. You can choose from several frame options: a standard 1-2-3/W frame, or a ruler-style frame that measures the worksheet by number of characters, inches, centimeters, or points and picas.

If you want the ultimate clean-screen look, you can choose to have no frame at all. This is handy for presentations, but it makes normal worksheet operations difficult.

Palette

To alter the set of seven colors that are available for enhancing cell contents and backgrounds and the worksheet environment, choose the Palette button. Then select one of the current items in the palette and replace it with one of the 512 available colors.

Update

To make the current settings permanent, and to apply them to all other open worksheets, choose the Update button.

Restore

If you want to use the colors that a worksheet had when you last saved it, as opposed to the current system defaults, select the Restore button.

For Hackers Only

Permanent changes you make to 1-2-3/W are stored in the file 123W.INI, which you'll find in your Windows directory. Power users may want to view and alter the settings in this file. You can accomplish this by editing it with a text editor such as Window's Notepad accessory.

If you decide to tinker with this file, be careful. You may mess up settings that will require you to reinstall 1-2-3/W. For the most part it is safe to choose default settings via 1-2-3/W's menu commands and dialog boxes—and let *them* make the changes to 123W.INI.

Other Ways to Customize the Sheet and the Environment

Some of the local settings you choose have options that let you turn them into global settings or defaults. For example, if you select the Default button from the Style Font Replace dialog box, the current settings become the system defaults.

Also, remember that you set print options for either the current worksheet or for 1-2-3/W in general by way of File-menu commands. For example, File Page Setup's Default button lets you apply the current print settings to all worksheets in the current file. And File Printer Setup lets you set printing defaults for 1-2-3/W and other Windows applications. For more about printing, see Chapter 10.

For the ultimate in custom worksheet functionality, you can create your own clickable SmartIcons. See Chapter 18, *Mastering the SmartIcon Palette*, for details.

Panes and Titles

Since its first release, 1-2-3 has possessed some rudimentary windowing capabilities. These were, and still are, available via the 1-2-3 Classic commands /Worksheet Windows and /Worksheet Titles. These commands, and their new Windows-style equivalents—Window Split and Window Titles—give you a variety of ways to display different parts of a file at the same time.

Panes

To avoid confusion with the other sorts of windows in the Microsoft Windows environment, the split sections of a worksheet are now called panes instead of windows. The Window Split command gives you a variety of ways to divide your worksheet window into multiple panes.

Pane Basics

Splitting your worksheet file into panes lets you compare sections of data that otherwise would not fit on-screen together. This assists you in analyzing your worksheet, and it helps you build formulas that include cells in remote locations.

No matter which pane option you choose, you can switch from pane to pane by using the PANE key (F6). In earlier releases, this was known as the WINDOW key.

You can temporarily switch to a normal, full-screen view by pressing the ZOOM key (Alt-F6). To switch back to the pane view, you press ZOOM again. Note that the ZOOM key is unrelated to the Zoom option in the Window Display Options dialog box.

With any of these splitting options, you can choose to have the panes synchronized or unsynchronized. If they are synchronized, any scrolling you do in one pane is reflected in the other pane(s). Otherwise, scrolling in one pane does not affect the other.

To permanently return to an unsplit view, choose Window Split Clear.

Horizontal and Vertical Panes

As in 1-2-3 Releases 2.3 and earlier, you can divide a worksheet into two horizontal or vertical sections. Figure 8.6 shows a horizontally split worksheet. Figure 8.7 shows a vertically split worksheet.

To split the worksheet in two, move to a cell in the row or column where you want to divide the worksheet view. Then choose Window Split and select the Horizontal or Vertical option.

Or you can drag the splitter icons shown in Figure 8.8. This was introduced in WYSIWYG with Releases 2.3 and 3.1. In those releases, you drag the frame to the left of column A or above row 1. In 1-2-3/W, these icons make it easier to remember how to split the worksheet.

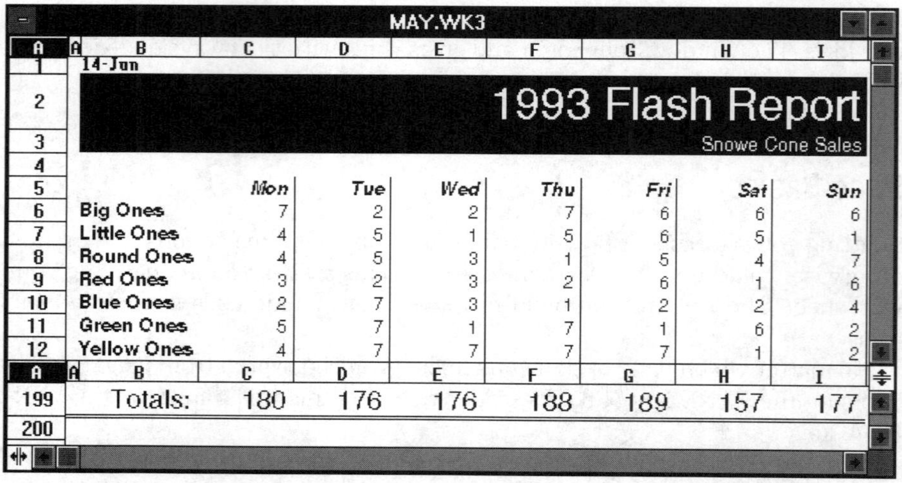

Figure 8.6. A worksheet split into horizontal panes. This view lets you move freely about the worksheet in the upper pane, while keeping the bottom line on display in the other.

To make a horizontal split, you drag the horizontal splitter towards the right. To make a vertical split, you drag the vertical splitter down. To restore the unsplit view of the worksheet, drag either splitter as far as possible in the opposite direction.

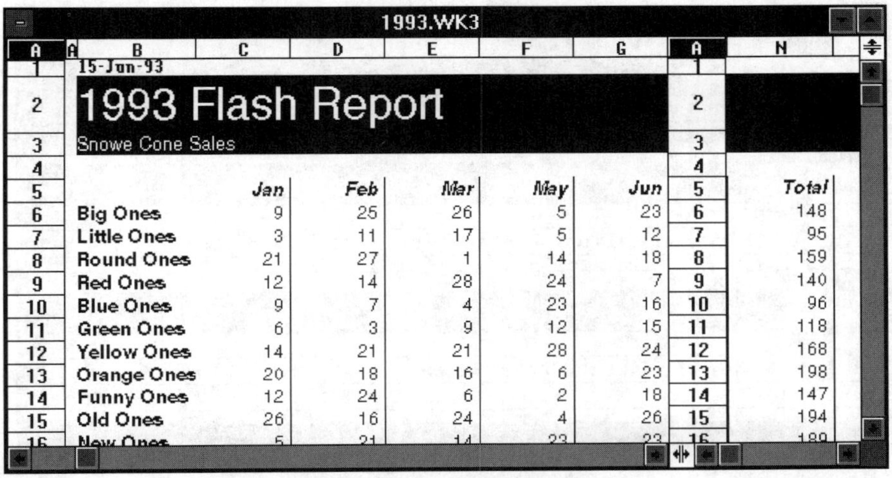

Figure 8.7. A worksheet split into vertical panes. This view lets you see several rows in each pane while you peruse columns from different parts of the worksheet.

Figure 8.8. These splitter icons appear at the beginning of, respectively, the horizontal and vertical scroll bars. When you drag the horizontal scroll bar's splitter to the right, you break the window into two vertical panes. When you drag the vertical scroll bar's splitter down, you create two horizontal panes. To restore a full-screen view, you drag the splitter back in the opposite direction.

Perspective View

Like Release 3.x, 1-2-3/W lets you simultaneously view up to three worksheets in a file. Figure 8.9 shows a 3D worksheet in Perspective view.

A fast way to switch into and out of Perspective view is to use the icon shown on the left side of Figure 8.10. Click it once to switch the current window to Perspective view. Click it again to switch back to a full-screen view.

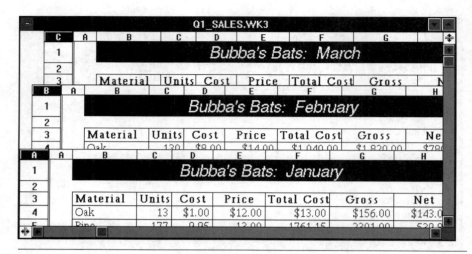

Figure 8.9. A worksheet split into a three-sheet Perspective view.

You use the other two icons in Figure 8.9 to move among worksheets, whether or not they're part of a 3D worksheet in Perspective view. Another way to move from worksheet to worksheet is simply to click the mouse in another visible worksheet in Perspective view. For more on moving among worksheets, see Chapter 9, *Building Effective Applications*.

Figure 8.10. Three icons that help you work with 3D worksheets. From left to right, these let you switch into and out of Perspective view, move to the next worksheet, and move to the previous worksheet. These latter two icons, incidentally, work even when you're not in Perspective view.

Titles

The column and row headings you create are invaluable. They tell you what the data in a particular column and in a particular row are all about.

The problem is that as you scroll down or across the worksheet, you lose sight of these titles. The worksheet becomes like a sports section that tells you scores, such as 7-0 and 12-3, without telling you what teams were playing.

To the rescue is the Window Titles command. This command lets you keep the column or row headings—or both—on display, even when you scroll to other parts of the worksheet.

To use it, place the cell pointer in the first data cell below the column headings and/or to the right of the row headings. Then choose Window Titles. If you choose the Row option, the rows above the cell pointer stay locked on-screen as you scroll down the sheet. If you choose Column, the columns to the left of the cell pointer stay locked on-screen as you scroll to the right. If you choose Both, the row and column stay fixed as you move about the worksheet.

In addition to helping you see what row and column you're in, the Titles option helps prevent accidental changes to the headings. You can't move directly into the title area with the mouse or the cell pointer.

In fact, even pressing the Home key doesn't get you up into the titles. When you have Titles in use, the worksheet's home position changes from cell A1 to the first cell below and to the right of the titles. For example, if you select Worksheet Titles Both when the cell pointer is in cell B4, cell B4 becomes the home position.

To move to a cell that's within the title area, use the GOTO key (F5) or the Range Go To command. For example, press GOTO and enter A1 to get to the traditional home cell when Titles are in use.

To disable the Titles feature, choose Window Titles Clear.

Use the Worksheet Titles command to keep row and column headings on-screen as you scroll through the sheet.

9

Building Effective Applications

This chapter will help you make applications that not only work, but work well. In particular, you'll learn how to organize your spreadsheet projects into easy-to-maintain sections: multiple sheets within a file and separate files that work together.

In the pages that follow, you'll learn how and when to use 3-D worksheets and linked files. And you'll get to explore, hands-on, the process of building a sophisticated application that exploits these features. Along the way, you'll also use range names, titles, cell protection, @IF and @VLOOKUP formulas, global settings, and hidden data. The result is a powerful worksheet system that's both efficient and easy to use.

Following these sections on 3D and multifile techniques are discussions of ways to get data from one file into another, how to create security applications and how to use files on a network. The concluding section gives you advice on managing spreadsheet development process. These suggestions will help you make any spreadsheet project into a solid, successful application—with a minimum of effort.

> *In this chapter you will learn:*
> - *How to use 3-D worksheets*
> - *How to use two or more worksheet files at the same time*
> - *How to navigate among multiple sheets and files*
> - *How to protect worksheet data*
> - *How to combine, import, and extract worksheets*
> - *Strategies and tactics for worksheet management*

Creating and Using 3D Worksheets

Had Christopher Columbus been born 500 years later, perhaps he'd set out to prove that spreadsheets aren't flat after all. Some people haven't yet gotten the news about the exciting new world of 3D spreadsheets, so Chris could still make some headlines.

If you've never worked with 3D worksheets, take the plunge. They can enhance small applications and cut big applications down to size..

If you're like a lot of spreadsheet users, you have yet to set sail into the third dimension that was opened up by 1-2-3 Release 3.x and its fleet of sister products, such as 1-2-3 for Windows, 1-2-3 for Macintosh, 1-2-3 for OS/2, and 1-2-3 for Sun. Once you make the trip, though, odds are you'll never go back to the old world.

There are two main reasons to use 3D worksheets. 3D is ideal when you have multiple tables, or pages, in a worksheet. And it lets you set aside ranges, such as macros, that you want to keep off the main worksheet.

Perhaps the quintessential 3-D application is one that includes several tables that resemble each other. For example, you may have a 13-sheet file with monthly data on each of 12 sheets and annual totals on the final sheet. Or you may have several divisions—or several budget scenarios—each on its own sheet.

Suppose that you have to enter and total expense data for three cost centers. You could arrange the data for each of these cost centers within a single 1-2-3/W worksheet.

But it would be much easier to organize the application in separate sheets. Sheets A through C would contain the three cost centers' data. And Sheet D would total up this data.

For one thing, it's easier to sum all the occurrences of a line item if they're in the same location in several sheets—(for example, @SUM(A:C18..C:C18), than if they're in several tables scattered throughout a single sheet. You can also speed through formatting, copying, and so on, when similar cells are in the same location in each sheet.

A separate, and optionally hidden, sheet is an excellent place to stash macros, lookup tables, and other utility components of your application. If you've ever lost macros because you deleted a row or column, you'll appreciate this feature—as long as you're careful about the use of Group mode, a powerful feature you'll learn about shortly.

Adding Sheets

Adding worksheets to a file isn't much more complicated than inserting rows or columns into the worksheet. You start with the same command, Worksheet Insert, or with its 1-2-3 Classic equivalent /Worksheet Insert.

Then you select the Sheet option, choose whether the new sheet or sheets should appear before or after the current sheet, and specify the quantity of sheets that you want to add. Just as a worksheet has 256 columns, from A to IV, a 3-D worksheet can have up to 256 sheets, also named A to IV.

Figure 9.1. The SmartIcon for inserting a single sheet. If you add this icon to your palette, you can add a sheet—after the current one—with a click of the mouse.

There is a SmartIcon for inserting a single sheet after the current one, but it's not one of the default SmartIcons, so you'll have to add it to the SmartIcon palette before you can use it. This icon is shown in Figure 9.1. To learn how to customize the palette, see Chapter 18.

To delete one or more sheets, you select a range that spans the sheets you want to remove. Then you choose Worksheet Delete and specify the Sheet option. Of course, you want to be quite sure there's no valuable data on any of the sheets in the range before you issue the command. Deleting whole worksheets is not an operation to take lightly. For more on the Worksheet Insert and Worksheet Delete Commands, see Chapter 7.

Perspective View

To view three consecutive sheets in a file simultaneously, use 1-2-3/W's Perspective view feature. In addition to helping you see different parts of a file at the same time, this option gives you some perspective on how 3-D worksheets are organized.

As shown in Figure 9.2, the sheets are arranged from the bottom to the top. In this case, sheet A is in the bottom slot, sheet B is in the middle, and sheet C is on top. Since you can see a bit more data in the bottom sheet, you'll usually want to keep the current sheet in this position, with the next two sheets visible above it.

Navigating from one sheet to the next, which is detailed in the following section, means moving *up* through the worksheet. For example, you move up into the file to go from sheet B to sheet C. If you're inclined to picture this as moving *down* through the sheet, you're liable to choose the wrong navigation key and move down to sheet A when you want to move up to sheet C. As long as you picture the Perspective view, in which the next sheet appears *above* the current sheet, you'll remember which way is up.

Remember that moving from one sheet to the next means moving up into the file.

To use Perspective mode, select Worksheet Split and choose the Perspective option. If you choose the Synchronize option, the other sheets will scroll when you scroll through the current sheet.

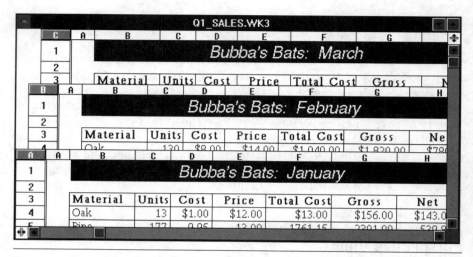

Figure 9.2. Three sheets in Perspective view. This option lets you see three consecutive sheets in a file—such as sheets A through C, or sheets J through L—at the same time.

The SmartIcon in Figure 9.3 makes it easy to switch between three-sheet Perspective view and a normal single-sheet view.

As described in the worksheet panes section in Chapter 8, you can use the PANE key (F6) and the ZOOM key (Alt-F6) with Perspective view. The PANE key moves you from one sheet to the next. The ZOOM key lets you temporarily expand the current sheet to full size. To return to Perspective view, you press ZOOM again.

Figure 9.3. This SmartIcon splits the window so that you can see three sheets in Perspective view. If you click it a second time, a normal view is restored.

Navigating Among Sheets

The easiest way to move among the sheets in a file is to use two simple mouse techniques. First, if the sheet you want to switch to is visible in a Perspective view, you can get to that sheet by clicking anywhere within it.

Figure 9.4. These SmartIcons, respectively, move you to the next sheet and to the previous sheet.

The SmartIcons in Figure 9.4 make it easy to move from sheet to sheet.

Second, if you want to scroll upward to the next sheet, you can click the SmartIcon that appears on the left in Figure 9.4. To scroll down to the previous sheet, click the SmartIcon on the right.

There are several keyboard techniques for moving from sheet to sheet. The simplest are using Ctrl-PageUp to move to the next sheet, and Ctrl-PageDown to move to the previous sheet. These, incidentally, will move you not only among sheets in a file but through sheets that are open in other windows as well.

Two other easy-to-remember sheet-navigation combinations are Ctrl-Home, to move to the Home position in the first sheet (usually A:A1) and Ctrl-End, to move to the last active cell in the file. Table 9.1 lists all the keys for navigating among sheets in a 1-2-3/W file.

Key	Moves Cell Pointer
Ctrl-Home	To the Home cell of first sheet—usually A:A1
Ctrl-PageUp/Ctrl-PageDown	Up to next sheet or down to previous sheet. Unless Group mode is in use, the cell pointer appears in the cell it was in last time the sheet was active.

Table 9.1. You can use these keys to navigate among the sheets in a 3D spreadsheet. *(continued)*

Key	Moves Cell Pointer (continued)
End Ctrl-Home	To the last active cell in the file.
End Ctrl-PageUp/Down	The next or previous worksheet that contains data in the current cell location and that is next to a blank cell.

Table 9.1. You can use these keys to navigate among the sheets in a 3-D spreadsheet.

Using 3-D Ranges

As you've surely seen in your use of 1-2-3/W thus far, cell and range references have an additional dimension. The worksheet frame itself proclaims the name of the current sheet, at the intersection of the column letters and the row numbers.

And as you can see in the 1-2-3/W control panel, the current cell is indicated not just by row and column coordinates, but by sheet letter as well. B2 isn't B2 any more, but A:B2, or G:B2, or RJ:B2.

As you've also seen throughout the book, when you refer to cells that reside on the current sheet, you don't have to specify a sheet letter. For example, you can enter the formula @SUM(H8..H14) in sheet A and let 1-2-3/W put in the sheet letters. When you look in the Edit line, you'll see the formula @SUM(A:H8..H14).

To specify 3-D cells in a formula or dialog box, use this same format: the sheet letter, a colon, and the column and row locations—for example, G:A19. To specify a 3-D range, use two 3-D addresses, separated by two periods—for example G:A19..Q19.

To preselect a 3-D range with the mouse, select a two-dimensional range and use the next sheet or previous sheet icon shown in Figure 9.4.

To preselect from the keyboard—when the worksheet is in Ready mode—press the ABS key (F4), and then use keyboard-navigation techniques. When you've highlighted the appropriate range, press Enter.

Group Mode

Group mode is a feature that's almost too hot to handle. For those who dare, it's got the raw power to transform a series of sheets with rapier-like speed. But if you misunderstand and misuse it, you can trash your worksheet in seconds flat.

When you enable Group mode—by choosing it from the Worksheet Global Settings Options dialog box—all sheets in the file take on the styles, formats, column widths, row heights, page breaks, and other attributes of the current sheet. This happens even if you immediately turn Group mode off again. When Group mode is active, the GROUP indicator appears at the bottom of the 1-2-3/W window.

To see what Group mode can do, imagine that you've gone wild in dressing up range D12..K99 of sheet C: Using Percent format with two decimal places; a double-line border with drop shadow; the Dom Casual 12-point font with bold, italic, and underline styling; a column width of 15 and a row height of 24; and magenta text on a yellow background. If this sheet is current when you enable Group mode, every range D12..K99 in the file will pick up these garish attributes. The same goes for any other such attributes you've applied elsewhere in sheet C.

If all sheets in your 3-D file are arranged identically, this is an incredible time-saver. All you need do is style and format one sheet. Then you can reformat all the others, simply by invoking Group mode. It's like teaching the sheets to sing in unison.

If, on the other hand, the sheets in your file are not similar, then Group mode will cause more harm than good. It will apply the settings and, as you'll see, the commands that make sense in one sheet to sheets that are entirely different. It would be like instructing every member of the football team to throw the ball—instead each is supposed to perform in a different manner. The result would be chaos.

Not only are the current settings applied through the other sheets, but any changes you make while Group mode is active ripple through the entire file. If Group mode is active when you assign the Currency format to cell B2 of the current sheet, all its little B2 cousins in the other sheets get dollar signs in their eyes, too. Select a font, a style alignment, or shading pattern, and the sibling cells in the other sheets go wild for the new fashion craze.

To see why keeping Group mode enabled can be dangerous, consider what happens when you delete a row or column. Although it looks like you're carving some data out of a single sheet, you're really chainsawing the same row or column out of all of the file's sheets.

If this is what you want to do, you can't do it any more conveniently than with Group mode. But if you forget that Group mode is enabled, you can wreak havoc throughout your application without even seeing it happen. It may be too late when you view one of the other sheets and see the damage you've done.

When you want to reign supreme over all the sheets in your file, this option gives you incredible power. For safety's sake, though, turn it off when you don't need it any more.

Entering the Third Dimension

3-D worksheets are easier to understand after you've used them. This section describes, step-by-step, how to create and use a multisheet application.

What's the Problem?

In this exercise, you'll learn how to create a 3D worksheet that consolidates data from multiple departments.

You're the spreadsheet whiz at the Eastern-branch office of 3B Entertainment International. You've been enlisted to create a spreadsheet system that tracks revenues generated by your branch.

Rumor has it that the company's CEO is very interested in the results of this project. Being the corporate climber that you are, you want to create a system that will do you proud.

The Northern, Southern, and Western branches don't have spreadsheet users of your caliber. So when you're done, you'll share your worksheet format with your colleagues in the other offices. It will take a few seconds of work to turn your worksheet into a template for use by others, and you'll become renowned across the nation.

Like the other branches, the Eastern branch acts as a wholesaler for two product lines, Becky's CD's and Bobby-O's Videos. You need a spreadsheet system to track each product line's revenues on a quarterly and year-to-date basis.

In addition to the actual revenue figures, your worksheet needs to identify the forecasted revenues. And it should show how the actual results compare with the forecast.

Because the product lines are managed independently, the local branches report their actual performance in two separate printouts, one for CD's, and one for videos. 3B's CEO wants to see how each branch performs overall, so we'll need a third worksheet to report total branch revenues—the *combined* revenues from CD's and videos.

Setting Up the First Sheet

This job calls for a 3D worksheet. We need three lookalike sheets, one for CD's, one for videos, and one for the branch total.

To get things started, let's set up the CD revenue worksheet.

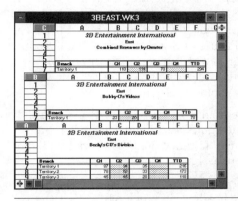

Figure 9.5. A look at the finished 3D worksheet for the Eastern division of 3B International. Three sheets are visible in the window because the Window Split Perspective option is selected. The Window Display Options Zoom feature lets you view your spreadsheets in a magnified or reduced size; the window in the figure is "zoomed down" to 60% of its normal size.

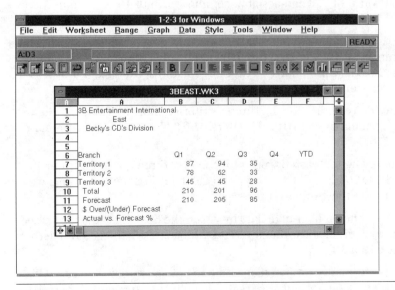

Figure 9.6. The labels and values of sheet A, which shows quarterly revenues for the East region of a CD wholesaler. The completed application will compare forecasted revenues with actual income.

1. Start with a new file. And before you enter anything into the worksheet, assign a name to the file. Choose the File Save As command and save the file under the name; 3BEAST, for 3B Entertainment's East branch. The name 3BEAST appears at the top of the document window.

2. Enter the labels *3B Entertainment International*, *East*, and *Becky's CD's Division*, in, respectively, cells A1, A2, and A3. Because the label in cell A1 begins with a number, precede it with a label prefix, such as a caret (^). Then select range A1..F3, select Style Alignment, and choose the Center and Align-over-columns options. If you want the style of the headings to match the figure, set the style of cell A1 to Arial or Helvetica 14-point italic bold, and assign the bold stye to range A2..A3.

3. Enter the following labels in range A6..F6: *Branch*, *Q1*, *Q2*, *Q3*, *Q4*, and *YTD*. To match the text style in the figure, assign the bold style to range A6..F6 and assign centered alignment to range B6..F6. But wait until the worksheet is fully functional before assigning the border styles.

4. Enter the row headings: *Territory 1*, *Territory 2*, and *Territory 3* in range A7..A9. Precede each of the headings in range A10..A13 with two blank spaces to indent them slightly: *Total*, *Forecast*, *$ Over/(Under) Forecast*, *Actual vs. Forecast %*. Assign italic style to range A10..A12. To improve readability, choose Worksheet Global Settings and select a column width of 7. Then assign a column width of 19 to column A, via the Worksheet Column Width command.

5. Enter the data for each quarter. For the first quarter, enter *87*, *78*, and *45* in range B7..B9. For the second quarter, enter *94*, *62*, and *45* in range C7..C9. For the third quarter, enter *35*, *33*, and *28* in range D7..D9. The fourth-quarter data aren't in yet, so we'll leave this column blank.

6. To total the revenues for the three territories, start by entering the following formula in cell B10: *@SUM(B7..B9)*. Then copy the formula to range C10..F10.

7. Now enter the forecasted values for the first three quarters. Enter *210* in cell B11, *205* in cell C11, and *85* in cell D11. For the meantime, we'll leave out the fourth-quarter forecast.

8. To find out the number of dollars by which the East exceeded or missed the forecast, enter the formula *+B10-B11* in cell B12, then copy it across to cells C12..F12.

9. To see performance against plan as a percentage, rather than as a dollar amount, enter the formula *+B10/B11* in cell B13, then copy it across to cells C13..F13.

10. To see the year-to-date totals, add up the quarters we've entered thus far by entering the formula @SUM(B7..E7) in cell F7. Then copy this formula down to range F8..F11.

11. Now choose File Save to store the work you've done so far.

A Few Adjustments

The top worksheet for the CD division in the Eastern branch is now functional, but it needs a few improvements before we replicate it to work for the video division and to serve as a template for the branch-total worksheet.

	A	B	C	D	E	F
1	3B Entertainment International					
2	East					
3	Becky's CD's Division					
4						
5						
6	Branch	Q1	Q2	Q3	Q4	YTD
7	Territory 1	87	94	35		216
8	Territory 2	78	62	33		173
9	Territory 3	45	45	28		118
10	Total	210	201	96	0	507
11	Forecast	210	205	85		500
12	$ Over/(Under) Forecast	0	-4	11	0	7
13	Actual vs. Forecast %	1	0.98049	1.12941	ERR	1.014
14						
15						

Figure 9.7. The CD worksheet. The basic setup is fine, but now it's time to make it more presentable.

The data in row 13 aren't looking too sharp, and they don't have the requisite percent signs. Select range B13..F13, and use the Range Format command to assign it the Percent format with one decimal place.

The reformatting improves the raggedness of data in this row, but any cells in which we haven't yet entered a forecast—in this case, cell E13—display an error, because dividing by zero is a mathematical impossibility. To solve this, let's enhance the formula in cell B13 and copy the revised formula across the row. Edit, or replace, the formula in cell B13 so that it reads: @IF(B11=0,0,B10/B11). If there is a zero or no data in cell B11, this formula will place a zero in cell B13; otherwise, it will divide the value of cell B10 by the value of cell B11. Now copy this formula to cells C13..F13.

Also, we decide that the calculations that result in zeroes are a bit misleading, because most of these reflect the lack of available data, rather than data

The worksheet Global Settings Zero display option lets you decide how zero values appear.

that really equal zero. The zero in the *$ Over/Under Forecast* column also seems less appropriate than, say, a dash to indicate that there is no difference between the forecast and the actual income.

To rectify this, we'll choose Worksheet Global Settings, and under the Zero display option, we'll choose Use Label and specify a label that consists of a caret (^) and 11 hyphens (-). This will turn the zeros into dashed lines. Note, however, that this does not affect cells that are simply blank.

Now that the CD worksheet is in good working order, you may want to dress it up with borders and shades. To replicate the borders and shades of Figure 9.8, issue the following commands: for range A5..F13, select Style Borders Top and Bottom with thin lines, and Left and Right with thick lines. After you choose OK, issue another Style Borders command for range A5..F13, but this time choose Outline with a thick line. Then select range A7..F7, and select a double line for the Top line. To select the shading in range C7..C13, highlight the range and choose Style Shading Light. Repeat this process to place similar shading in range E7..E13.

Choose File Save again to store these changes.

	A	B	C	D	E	F
1	3B Entertainment International					
2	East					
3	Becky's CD's Division					
4						
5						
6	Branch	Q1	Q2	Q3	Q4	YTD
7	Territory 1	87	94	35		216
8	Territory 2	78	62	33		173
9	Territory 3	45	45	28		118
10	Total	210	201	96		507
11	Forecast	210	205	85		500
12	$ Over/(Under) Forecast	-----------	-4	11		7
13	Actual vs. Forecast %	100.0%	98.0%	112.9%		101.4%

Figure 9.8. Now the CD worksheet is ready to be copied to become the basis of the video and branch-total worksheets.

Adventures in the Third Dimension

We need to add two sheets to our file, one for the video product line, and one that totals the revenues of the CD and video lines. Choose Worksheet Insert Sheet, and select the After option and the Quantity of 2. When you choose OK, worksheet B appears on the screen. Because you chose the After option, the

CD sheet is still sheet A. Had you chosen the Before option, the CD worksheet would now be sheet C, and A and B would be blank.

To switch among the sheets, press Ctrl-PageUp and Ctrl-PageDown. Other sheet-navigation keys and SmartIcons are listed in Table 9.1. Remember that moving "deeper" into the file's worksheets, from A to B and from B to C, is considered moving *up* in the sheet.

Choose Window Split, select the Perspective option, and leave the Synchronize option selected. 1-2-3/W displays the three sheets, one above the other. When you're in Perspective mode, you can use the PANE key (F6), known as the WINDOW key in other releases, to switch among the sheets.

You can't see very much data in each of the three sheets, but Perspective mode is a handy way to compare similar areas in a 3-D worksheet. If you choose Perspective mode without the Synchronize option, you can scroll to different parts in different sheets.

We want to see as much data as possible in Perspective mode, so maximize the 3BEAST.WK3 worksheet by clicking the Maximize icon (the up-arrow in its title bar), or press Alt- (Alt-hyphen) and type an X, the shortcut key for Maximize.

Not satisfied with this view, we'll fit even more of our 3-D sheet on the screen: Choose Window Display Options, select Zoom, and specify 55 as the percentage to zoom to. This displays the worksheet at 55% of its normal size, which should be small enough to view the entire CD worksheet, range A:A1..A:F13.

Select range A:A1..A:F13, and choose Edit Quick Copy. Specify range B:A1..C:A1 as the range to copy to, and choose OK. Instantly, you have three lookalike worksheets.

But there is one difference: When you copy cells, you don't copy the column widths; so column A of sheets B and C is not as roomy as Column A in sheet A. Here's a chance to tap the power of Group mode. Choose Worksheet Global Settings, and choose Group mode. When you choose OK, the A columns in the other sheets fall into line. Now choose Worksheet Global Settings again, and deselect Group mode. When you choose OK, the Group mode indicator at the bottom of the 1-2-3/W window disappears.

We need to do a bit of work to change sheets B and C into suitable worksheets for the video business and the branch summary, and we need to return to a more spacious view of our data.

Move the cell pointer into sheet B by clicking in it or by pressing the PANE key (F6) or Ctrl-PageUp. Then choose Window Split, and choose Clear. When you choose OK, sheet B should fill the 1-2-3/W window.

Now choose Window Display Options and restore the Zoom option to 100%. When you choose OK, the worksheet should be back to a normal size.

Choose File Save to store your most recent work.

It's a good idea to maximize a worksheet window when you use Perspective view. This lets you see as much of the three visible sheets as possible.

Changing the Sheets

The sheet for Eastern revenues for Bobby-O's Videos was nearly complete to begin with. All we need to do is change the heading and the raw data. All the formulas and formats are satisfactory. Before you proceed, make sure that sheet B is the current sheet. The risk of having lookalike sheets is that you may change the wrong one.

Let's start by making the sheets less alike. Edit or reenter the label in cell A3 so that it says *Bobby-O's Videos* and is preceded by a caret (^) label prefix.

We need to replace the CD data for each quarter with the revenues for video sales. For the first quarter, enter *23*, *25*, and *32* in range B7..B9. For the second quarter, enter *20*, *19*, and *25* in range C7..C9. For the third quarter, enter *35*, *33*, and *28* in range D7..D9. Again, we don't yet have the fourth-quarter data, so we'll leave that column blank.

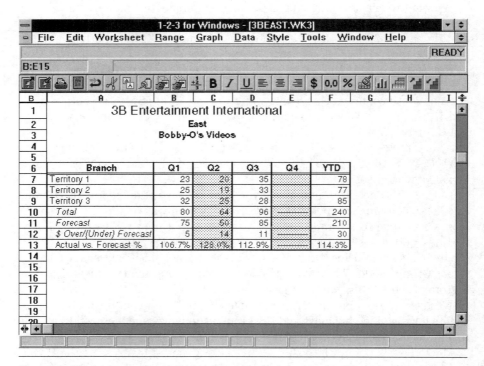

Figure 9.9. Now the video worksheet is finished. Since it started out as a copy of the CD worksheet, it was a pretty fast job.

Now enter the forecasted values for videos in the first three quarters. Enter *75* in cell B11, *50* in cell C11, and *85* in cell D11. Again, we'll leave out the fourth-quarter forecast.

That was pretty fast, so let's save our work again and move on to the summary sheet. Press Ctrl-PageUp to move to sheet C.

A Summary Place

Now we want to give sheet C the power to sum up the data from sheets A and B.

Once again, let's start by giving a proper heading to our new sheet. Replace the heading in cell A3 with the following label, preceded by a caret (^) label prefix: *Combined Revenues by Quarter*.

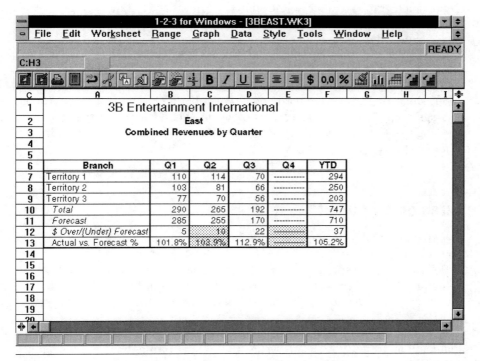

Figure 9.10. The branch-total worksheet. Because all three sheets share the same design, it's not only easy to set up this summing worksheet, but it's easy to build the totaling formulas. The branch total in a given cell is simply the summation of cells that are in the same location in the other sheets.

We're not going to enter any data in this sheet, since its purpose is to tally the data from the other sheets. Let's put the first of our new summary formulas in cell B7. To sum up first-quarter sales in Territory 1, enter the formula *@SUM(A:B7..B:B7)*. We could have opted for a simple addition formula, A:B7+B:B7, but an @SUM formula is more flexible. Suppose that we want to slip a new sheet between sheets A and B, perhaps if we start distributing Bubba's Baseball Bats, another fine product of 3B Entertainment International. The range reference in the @SUM formula will automatically expand to accommodate the new sheet.

Now copy the formula in cell B7 to range B7..E11. At a glance, we can see that year-to-date revenues for the branch are 98.3% of the forecasted amount. Not too bad, but we'll have to do better in the fourth quarter. Spurred by our findings, we might extend the worksheet to analyze how far we have to go over the fourth-quarter forecast to meet or exceed our plan. Or we might want to create some graphs to analyze the shortfalls. But that's for another day.

And in our excitement about the arrival of this useful data, we overlooked what happened to our borders when we copied cell B7. The tops of all the cells in range B7..E11 picked up the double-line style from cell B7.

Group mode can come to the rescue again. Instead of carefully reconstructing the appropriate borders, press Ctrl-PageDown to move to the previous sheet, sheet B. Turn Group mode on—remember it's in the Worksheet Global Settings dialog box—and then turn it off again. When you return to sheet C, by pressing Ctrl-PageUp, you see that sheet B's formats have been applied to the other sheets.

Three on a Printout

Now that our 3-D worksheet is in good shape, let's prepare to print out the data from sheets A, B, and C.

Select the entire spreadsheet range. The easiest way is to go to the first cell in the file, A:A1, by pressing Ctrl-Home, anchor by pressing the ABS key (F4), and extend the selection to the last cell in the file, C:F13, by pressing End and Ctrl-Home.

Now choose File Preview. (Remember there are SmartIcons for both this command and File Print.) The result: Everything prints, but not on separate pages. Here's one more job for Group mode. Turn on Group mode, select range A1..F13 in any of the sheets, choose Worksheet Page Break, and choose the Both option. Then turn off Group mode, select the three sheets again, and try File Preview. Each time you press a key, you see the next page of your sheet.

Finally, choose File Print to make a printout. In the next chapter, you'll learn how to fiddle with margins and other details, but you've made a pretty sophisticated worksheet very quickly.

Using Two or More Worksheet Files at the Same Time

3D worksheets are the ticket for applications in which all the data belong in the same file. But sometimes you need data from more than one file.

You could bunch up all your spreadsheet projects into one large 3-D worksheet. But there are several reasons to keep different applications in separate files.

For example, you might need to include the latest sales figures in a profit-and-loss (P&L) worksheet. Other than needing a few numbers from the sales worksheet, the P&L sheet is really a separate application. So it makes more sense to create two separate files, such as PL.WK3 and SALES.WK3, and to use 1-2-3/W's file-linking formulas to connect them, rather than put both worksheets in a single WK3 file.

If you lump both the P&L data and the sales data in a single 1-2-3/W file, only one person can make changes at any given time. Also a massive 3-D worksheet that includes all sorts of data requires a lot of memory, which is a waste of resources if you need to change only one small part of an application. And it probably won't fit on a single floppy disk for easy backup.

There's no need to put all your eggs in one basket, because 1-2-3/W joins the file-linking features of Release 3.x and the multiple-document features of Windows. It's now easier than ever to build applications that collect data from multiple files.

File-Linking Formulas

In the days when 1-2-3 Release 2.01 was king, cell and range references were confined to a single sheet. The only way to get data from one worksheet into another was to go through some not-so-friendly procedure, such as /File Combine Copy.

When you made changes in one file, the other file didn't update to reflect the new figures. So you had to be vigilant to re-combine the files whenever you suspected that changes had been made.

File-Linking Basics

Releases 2.2, 2.3, and 3.x introduced file linking, which lets a formula in one file refer to data in another. The file that contains the linking formula is called the *source*, and the file that you're linking to is called the *target*. File-linking formulas automatically copy the current values from the source worksheet into the target worksheet.

For example, the formula +<<C:\123W\BUDGET\NWTERR.WK3>>G17 copies the data from cell G17 in the source file into the cell that contains this formula. The source file is identified in the double-angle brackets. You don't have to specify the target file, because it is simply the file that includes the formula.

Releases 2.2 and 2.3 don't let you use file-linking references as part of a larger formula. You can, for example, use the formula +<<C:\123R23\COSTS.WK1>>B17, but you can't use the formula +<<C:\123R23\COSTS.WK1>>B17*200 or the formula @SUM(<<C:\123R23\COSTS.WK1>>B17..B19).

1-2-3/W, like Release 3.x, has no such restriction. You can use simple file links as in Releases 2.2 and 2.3, and you can include file-linking references within larger formulas. The formula +<<C:\123W\COSTS.WK3>>B17*200 and the formula @SUM(<<C:\123W\COSTS.WK3>>B17..B19) are legal in these releases. You can even use such formulas to reference cells that are stored in Release 2.x's WK1 files.

Using Range Names with File Links

Range names make file linking easier and safer. It's easier to remember what cells you want to link to if they have a descriptive name. Names like *prime_rate* or *interest_data*, for example, are much simpler to remember than cell and range references such as B:A14 and C:G12..C:G42.

File-linking formulas with named ranges are also less prone to errors. If you make changes in the source sheet—for example, if you move cells or insert or delete rows, columns, or sheets—the location of the source range can change. Thus, linking formulas that use cell and range addresses may refer to the wrong cells. Range names can help guard against these problems.

For example, let's say you need a formula in one sheet to reference an account balance that's stored in another sheet, CHECK.WK3. If the balance information is in cell H95 of that sheet, you could use the formula +<<C:\123W\CHECK>>H95 to copy it into the other sheet. But what if you insert some rows into CHECK.WK3 and the balance is now in cell H104? The linking formula won't know this, and it will copy whatever value is now in cell H95 of CHECK.WK3.

If, on the other hand, your file links are based on range names, they'll always locate the appropriate cells, as long as the range names remain in place. If you assigned the range name *balance* to cell H95 before you altered the sheet, the formula +<<C:\123W\CHECK>>BALANCE will retrieve the correct data, even after you insert rows or otherwise rearrange the sheet.

How Links Are Updated

Whenever you retrieve a file that contains a linking formula, it checks the source files for the latest values. If you want to refresh your sheet with up-to-the-minute information, you can choose File Administration Update Links at any time.

Note that changes that have been made to a source file, but not saved to disk, are not reflected in the target formula. This is true whether you've made changes to the source file in another window or if another user on a common network is altering the file. Also note that you cannot use file links with a file that is password-protected unless you first open that file and issue the appropriate password.

Working with Multiple Files

One of the conveniences of a file-linking formula is that the source files don't have to be open for the formulas to work. Thus, you can draw data from multiple sources without filling your computer's memory with worksheets.

But when you do want to view several worksheets at once, 1-2-3/W makes it easy. It helps you compare data from various sources, and it lets you use mouse and keyboard navigation techniques to set up linking formulas.

When you open a file by selecting File Open or /File Open, or when you create a file by choosing File New or /File New, the worksheet appears in a separate window, inside the 1-2-3/W window. If, however, you choose the old standby /File Retrieve, you're telling 1-2-3/W to close the current window to make way for a different file. (Remember to save your changes before you close the file!) If pressing /FR to retrieve a file is a reflex for you, you'll have to retrain yourself if you want more than one file open at a time.

Open files may appear as windows or, if they're minimized, as icons. You can use all the standard Windows techniques for switching among open files and for minimizing, maximizing, and restoring documents. For example, you can press Ctrl-F6 or Ctrl-Tab to go to the next window, and you can click a document's Control icon (the dashlike icon on the left of the document's title bar) to choose a variety of window-management features. Clicking a minimized document also brings up its control menu.

Below are details on 1-2-3/W's essential window-management features. You may also want to check out Chapter 2 for an exhaustive review of window-management techniques.

Navigating Among Open Worksheets

The easiest way to switch from one window to another is to click the mouse in the other window. The window you click in becomes the active window, and it appears on top of all other windows.

But sometimes, other windows block your view of the window you want to activate, so you can't click the mouse in it. And sometimes, you may simply prefer to use a keyboard technique to switch from one window to another.

As it happens, you have a lot of navigation options to choose from. In addition to standard Windows navigation features, 1-2-3/W supports such sheet-switching keystrokes as Ctrl-PageUp and Ctrl-PageDown, which take you sheet-by-sheet through all worksheets in all open worksheet files.

You can also use the GOTO key or the Range Go To command to move the cell pointer to any cell in any open worksheet. You refer to the other files just as you do in file-linking formulas, by placing the file name in double-angle brackets. For example, if you're in a file called HAM.WK3 and you want to go to cell B:D9 of the worksheet MAYO.WK3, you could press GOTO and specify the destination as <<MAYO>>B:D9. In fact, when you choose the GOTO key or the Range Go To command, a list of open files in double-angle-bracket format appears.

Another way to switch from one open document to another is, appropriately enough, by using the Window menu. At the bottom of the menu is a numbered list of open worksheet files. You can switch to a file from this menu by clicking on the file name or by typing the number that appears before the file name.

Two other window-switching methods are available. Ctrl-F6 or Ctrl-Tab, as in other Windows applications. Ctrl-F6 is the accelerator key for choosing Next from a document's Control menu. Control menus are discussed in the following section and in Chapter 2.

> ### Windows, Windows Everywhere
>
> When you move from one window to the next by pressing Ctrl-F6 or by choosing Next from a document Control menu, you may switch to windows that aren't worksheets. 1-2-3/W graphs are displayed in windows as well, and so is the Transcript, a listing of recently typed keystrokes. If you have any open graph windows or an open Transcript window, these will appear as you cycle through the windows.

Other Window-Management Techniques

Although, strictly speaking, neither is a window-navigation technique, the Window Cascade and Window Tile commands can make it easier to get from one window to the next. Cascading windows leave a small portion of each window visible, so you can easily click on the one you want to activate.

Tiling automatically sizes down all the open worksheet files so they fit together within the 1-2-3/W window, without any overlapping. Again, this makes it easy to click within the window you want to switch to.

Similarly, maximizing, minimizing, and restoring document windows can help you manage the 1-2-3/W workspace. Maximizing a worksheet file makes it fill the current application's window, minimizing it shrinks it down to an icon at the bottom of the window; and restoring converts either a maximized or minimized document to its previous size.

Figure 9.11. The title bar of a 1-2-3/W document contains the Control, Minimize, and Maximize icons. Note that if the document is maximized, the Maximize icon is replaced with a double-arrowhead icon called the Restore icon. You click this icon to return the window to its previous size.

You can perform these operations by choosing Maximize, Minimize, or Restore from the document's Control menu or by clicking the Maximize, Minimize, or Restore icons. You activate a document window's Control menu by clicking the Control icon or by pressing Alt- (Alt-hyphen). If the document is minimized, you can either use the Alt- method, or you can click the document once to get the document Control menu.

In addition to the Minimize, Maximize, and Restore commands, the document Control menu includes the Size and Move options, which let you use the keyboard to resize or relocate the window. However, its easier to resize a window by dragging one if its edges or corners, and its easier to move a document window by dragging its title bar.

The other options on the document Control menu are Next, which is the equivalent of pressing F6 to go to the next document window, and Close, which is the equivalent of pressing Ctrl-F4 or choosing File Close to put away the current document.

Where's the File?

There are three ways to refer to another file in file-linking formulas, GOTO operations, and such. You can specify the complete path, for example, <<C:\RAZORS\CASHFLOW.WK3>>; you can specify the file name without the path, for example, <<CASHFLOW.WK3>>; or you can give a "wildcard" file name, for example, <<?>>.

If you move the target file to another subdirectory, 1-2-3/W will find the source file if you specify the complete path. If you're likely to move or copy the target file to another directory without relocating the source file, complete-path specifications are the way to go.

On the other hand, if you move the source file to another directory, a reference that includes the path won't work. File references that don't include the path do the job, as long as you either keep the source sheet open or store it in the default directory for 1-2-3/W files.

The wildcard file reference, <<?>>, is a convenient way to refer to range names that are in another sheet. If you want 1-2-3/W to find a range referenced this way, the other sheet must be open and the range name should not be duplicated in another open sheet.

If 1-2-3/W cannot locate a reference to a linked cell or range—or if the source file is password-protected—all cells that depend on the linked data evaluate to ERR. As long as you establish your links correctly so that 1-2-3/W can locate the linked files, you shouldn't encounter such an error condition.

To help you keep track of the files that are linked to the current file, you can choose File Administration Paste Table. This command pastes into your worksheet a table of information about active or linked files. If you choose this command, make sure there are several rows and columns of blank cells below and to the right of the current cell so that this table doesn't overwrite any data.

Simple Multifile Formulas

The next section shows you an especially powerful and flexible way of using multifile formulas, building on the application you created in the section on 3-D worksheets.

Before you tackle this advanced application, you should try using a simple file-linking formula. In these next several steps, you'll set up a basic linking formula, even if you didn't create the 3-D worksheet that is necessary for the extended example.

Here, you'll create two new files and build a formula that links them. Try it. It's a lot easier than it sounds!

1. Choose File New to create a worksheet for this exercise.
2. Enter the value *3500* in cell F10 of this new worksheet.
3. Choose File New again to create another new worksheet.
4. With the cell pointer in cell A1 of the new worksheet, type a plus sign, and then press one of the Arrow keys to activate Point mode.
5. Press Ctrl-F6 one or more times until the other new worksheet appears, the one with the value 3500 in cell F10. Use the Arrow keys to highlight cell F10. Press Enter. Now cell A1 of your newest worksheet also contains the value 3500.
6. With the cell pointer in cell A1 of the newer worksheet, look in the 1-2-3/W control panel for the formula in cell A1. It should look something like this: <<FILE0003.WK3>>F10.
7. Choose File Close. We're not going to use this worksheet again, so you don't need to save it.
8. Press Ctrl-F6 until the other new worksheet appears. Again, choose File Close and don't save the file.

As you can see, file-linking formulas are just about as easy to enter as formulas that refer to cells in the current worksheet.

Making Your Files Work Together

The revenue system that you created in the section on 3-D worksheets showed the value of organizing similar worksheets into a single file.

But suppose the CEO of 3B Entertainment International wants you to feed the latest figures from the corporate forecasts directly into your local branch's worksheets. This would be especially convenient, and it would eliminate retyping errors. However, the corporate headquarters' forecasts for the video and CD product lines are stored in separate files.

You guessed it—file-linking formulas are the solution. We could use some simple file-linking formulas, for example, to link a particular forecast cell in the 3BEAST.WK3 file to a forecast cell in the video or CD corporate worksheet. But we want to make it easy to modify this system so that it will also work for the Northern, Southern, and Western branches—as well as for your home base, the Eastern branch. So we'll use a file-linking formula in conjunction with the @VLOOKUP function. File links and lookups are a powerful combination. The target formula actually finds the right value in the source file, rather than simply linking to a specific cell.

We'll also try some other trickery, such as using @IF formulas and Worksheet Global Settings. The application of these various techniques will make our final spreadsheet system both sophisticated and easy to use.

Before we can extend our system to pull the relevant data from the corporate forecast sheets, we need to set up these sheets. To save time, we're going to do only minimal style enhancements to these. Figures 9.12 and 9.13 show the headquarters data for CD and video revenues at the branches.

Open the Windows

Keep the worksheet from the previous exercise open, and since it shares the same four-quarter headings, let's put these in the Clipboard so we can paste a copy of them into our new worksheets. Select range B6..E6 in any one of the sheets in the 3BEAST file, and choose Edit Copy.

Now let's clean up the 1-2-3/W workspace a bit. If the 3BEAST window is maximized, restore it to normal size by clicking the Restore button, the double-arrow icon in its title bar, and then clicking the Minimize button, the down-arrow icon in the 3BEAST title bar. If you prefer to use the keyboard, press Alt-(Alt-hyphen) and then choose Minimize (you can skip the Restore step). The 3BEAST file now appears as an icon near the bottom of the 1-2-3/W window.

Next, choose File New and then select File Save As to assign the name CORPCD to the new file, which will contain corporate forecast information for the CD business.

Before you forget, position the cell pointer in cell B5 and choose Edit Paste. Now the four headings for the quarters appear in the new sheet; then enter *Region* in cell A5 *Total* in cell F5 to complete the column headings. To remove the styles from range B9..E9 select the range, choose Edit Clear Special, and select the Style option.

	A	B	C	D	E	F
			CORPCD.WK3			
1			Becky's CD Sales, Inc.			
2						
3			Sales Forecast by Region			
4						
5	Region	Q1	Q2	Q3	Q4	Total
6	East	210	205	85	225	725
7	North	140	160	110	210	620
8	South	155	150	80	200	585
9	West	205	200	155	230	790
10	Total	710	715	430	865	2720
11						

Figure 9.12. The corporate CD forecasts. With clever use of an @VLOOKUP function, each of several worksheets can locate the data for a given region.

Enter the row headings as shown in range A6..A10 in Figure 9.12, typing two blank spaces before the label *Total* in cell A10. Next, enter in range B6..E9 the values shown.

Now, we want to total the first-quarter's forecasted sales. In cell B10, enter the formula *@SUM(B6..B9)*, and copy it to range C10..F10.

Next, enter the regional-total formula for the Eastern division. In cell F6, enter the formula *@SUM(B6..E6)*, and copy it to range F7..F9.

Preparing for a Lookup

We're going to try something ambitious. We want each division's worksheet to locate its forecast figures in the corporate spreadsheets by finding its name in column A. This will make it easy to modify the Eastern division's worksheet so that it can be used for the three other divisions.

To make it easy to write a formula that looks for the appropriate value, let's assign a range name to range A6..F9: Select this range, choose Range Name Create, and specify *cdfcst* as the range name.

Our corporate CD file is complete! Choose File Save to save it. Then select range A1..F10, and choose Edit Copy. Now a copy of the corporate CD sheet is in the Clipboard, ready to be pasted into our soon-to-be-christened corporate video sheet.

Select File New, then assign a name to the new file by choosing File Save As and specifying the name CORPVID.

With the cell pointer in cell A1 of the new file, choose Edit Paste. Edit the heading in cell A1 so that it says *Bobby-O's Video Co.* and is preceded by a caret (^) label prefix.

	A	B	C	D	E	F
			CORPVID.WK3			
1			Bobby-O's Video Co.			
2						
3			Sales Forecast by Region			
4						
5	Region	Q1	Q2	Q3	Q4	Total
6	East	75	50	85	130	340
7	North	85	100	110	170	465
8	South	155	130	80	200	565
9	West	185	100	95	190	570
10	Total	500	380	370	690	1940
11						

Figure 9.13. The corporate video forecasts. To create a simple lookup to this file, we'll create a unique range name to identify the location of regional data in the sheet.

Then enter in range B6..F9 the values as shown in Figure 9.13. Now assign a range name to range A6..F9: Select this range, choose Range Name Create, and specify *vidfcst* as the range name. Then save the file.

Window Hopping

Right now, you have three documents open: CORPCD.WK3, CORPVID.WK3, and 3BEAST.WK3. The former two are displayed as normal windows, and the 3BEAST.WK3 window is now minimized.

Let's explore some of the ways we can customize our view of these windows.

First, choose Tile from the Window menu. The two "non-minimized" windows appear side-by-side.

Now try choosing Window Cascade. This time the corporate forecast documents are presented in an overlapping arrangement. To switch from one window to the other, click in the visible portion of its window, even if all you can see is the title bar, or just a bit of the right or left side of the window. Try this a few times, and leave CORPVID.WK3 as the active window.

Select CORPVID.WK3's Control menu by clicking the Control icon on the left of its title bar or by pressing Alt- (Alt-Hyphen).

Note that the last two options in the document's Control menu support accelerator keys: Ctrl-F4 to close the current document, and Ctrl-F6 for Next. The former is a shortcut alternative to choosing File Close, and the latter takes you on a tour through the open documents.

Close the Control menu by pressing Escape or by clicking its icon again, and try using Ctrl-F6 to go from window to window. As you cycle through the windows, 1-2-3/W stops at the minimized document icons, as well as the open windows. Incidentally, to restore the size of a minimized document you double

If you click the mouse once on a minimized document, such as the 3BEAST.WK3 spreadsheet, its Control menu pops up.

click it or you select it and then press Alt- (Alt-hyphen) to bring up its Control menu. From there, you choose Restore.

Press the GOTO key (F5) or choose Range Go To, and note that the dialog box displays the names of all open files. You can select one of these from the list. Select CORPCD.WK3.

Let's try yet another way to switch among windows: Select the Window menu. At the bottom of the menu is a numbered list of the open windows. You can switch to another window by typing the number that precedes the window's name or by clicking the name. Choose the CORPVID.WK3 window.

Finally, let's restore the Eastern division worksheet by double-clicking its document icon or by pressing Ctrl-F6 until the icon is selected, then choosing Alt- (Alt-Hyphen) and typing an R for Restore.

Creating a Smart Application

Now that we have all the corporate data available, we can improve on the Eastern-division spreadsheet in two significant ways. First, we can set up the 3BEAST.WK3 file so that it automatically reads in the correct corporate forecast data. Second, we can include the forecast data for future quarters.

This second step will help the Eastern division in planning, but if we include the fourth-quarter forecast in the year-to-date totals, we will get a distorted perspective on our real performance. That is, the *YTD* column would reflect four-quarters of forecasted revenues, but the actual-revenue row in that column would show a three-quarter actual total.

The solution? Display the future forecasts where they belong, but store them as strings. Since strings have no mathematical value, they won't affect the year-to-date totals. The only thing wrong with this plan is that if we look up the data from the corporate sheets and retrieve it in string form, then it will be difficult to use this data if we want to write more formulas, such as one that indicates how much we have to increase sales to overcome a deficit to meet the next quarter's forecast.

So that our spreadsheet will include the forecasts both as strings and as values, we'll create a fourth sheet in 3BEAST.WK3, but one that most users won't see. It will look up all the regional forecast data. Then, formulas in the three main sheets can use these data as either values or strings, depending on whether actual data from the current quarter are in.

To create the new sheet, start by moving to the last sheet in the file. Press End and then press Ctrl-Home. The current sheet should now be sheet C.

Insert a new sheet by choosing Worksheet Insert, selecting the Sheet After option, and a Quantity of 1. After you choose OK, a new sheet, sheet D, appears.

Since most users won't see sheet D, we're not going to spend much time styling it. However, if you invoke Group mode from any of the sheets that include borders, custom column widths, bold text, etc., these will be applied to sheet D. Likewise, if you happen to invoke Group mode from sheet D, the other sheets will lose all their fancy formats and pick up whatever styling we add to this sheet.

Enter the Label *Calculation Area—Do Not Delete* in cell A1. Enter the label *Region:* in cell A3, and enter *East* in cell B3. It's important that the label *East* is entered exactly as it was entered in the corporate spreadsheets. We're going to compare this label with the corporate forecast sheets to look up our regional data.

Now select cell A3, choose the Range Name Label Create command, and select the Right option to assign the range name *region:* to cell B4.

In range A6..F6, enter the following labels: *Line*, *Q1*, *Q2*, *Q3*, *Q4*, and *Total*. If *Q1* through *Q4* are still in the Clipboard, you can paste them into cell B4. If you paste the Clipboard and it doesn't contain these labels, just choose Edit Undo.

	A	B	C	D	E	F
1	Calculation Area—Do not Delete					
2						
3	Region:	East				
4						
5						
6	Line	Q1	Q2	Q3	Q4	Total
7	CD Forecast					0
8	Video Forecast					0
9	Total	0	0	0	0	0
10						

Figure 9.14. Sheet D of the 3BEAST.WK3 worksheet supports the other sheets. Formulas in this sheet do all the file linking, so formulas elsewhere in this application that need this data will be much simpler to write.

Enter the labels *Line*, *CD Forecast*, and *Video Forecast* in range A6..A9, and enter *Total*, preceded by two spaces, in cell A9.

To sum the quarterly data that we look up, which is simpler than looking up the totals from the corporate worksheets, enter in cell F7 the formula *@SUM(B7..E7)*, and copy the formula down to range F8..F9.

To sum the forecasted data for the two product lines, enter in cell B9 the formula *@SUM(B7..B8)*, and copy the formula to range C9..E9.

If you want to format your sheet to match Figure 9.14, apply the bold style to range A1..F6, and choose a single-line border style for all edges of range A6..F9.

Now save your latest work.

Performing the Lookup

With the 3BEAST.WK3 document active, move the cell pointer to cell D:B7—cell B7 of sheet D. If sheet D is not the current sheet, press GOTO (F5) or choose Range Go To and enter D:B7.

Enter the following formula in cell B7:

@VLOOKUP($REGION:,<<?>>CDFCAST,1)

This formula gets the contents of the range named *Region:* (cell B3, which contains the label *East*), looks for it in the range *CDFCAST* (if it can find such a range in an open file), and finds the value one cell to the right of the matching label *East*. If we create a similar worksheet for the Western region and enter *West* in cell B3, the formula will return the first-quarter forecast for the West branch, rather than the East.

Copy the formula from B7 to range C7..E7. The formulas do not adjust to reflect the other quarters, because the number 1 at the end of the formula does not change to 2, 3, and 4 as you copy the formula.

To fix the copied formulas, edit each cell in range C7..E7: Replace the 1 at the end of the formula with a 2 in cell C7, with a 3 in cell D7, and with a 4 in cell E7.

	A	B	C	D	E	F
1	Calculation Area—Do not Delete					
2						
3	Region:		East			
4						
5						
6	Line		Q1	Q2	Q3	Q4	Total
7	CD Forecast		210	205	85	225	725
8	Video Forecast		75	50	85	130	340
9	Total		285	255	170	355	1065
10						

Figure 9.15. Sheet D of 3BEAST.WK3, with the file-linking lookup formulas in place. These formulas use the region name *east* to locate the region's forecasted revenues from the corporate video and CD worksheets.

Copy the formulas from range B7..E7 to cell B8. Now range B8..E8 contains the lookup formulas, but the lookups are for the wrong product line—CDs instead of videos. The fastest way to fix this is with the Edit Find command, which resembles the Range Search command of later releases of 1-2-3.

Select range B8..E8 and choose Edit Find. Type *CDFCAST* in the Search-for box, select the Action option called Replace with, and type *vidfcast*. Set the Search-through option as either Formulas or Both. Then choose Replace All to complete the command.

Save the file once again.

The Edit Find command lets you locate or replace data in labels or formulas, or both, in a specified range.

Putting It Together

The next step is to revise the formulas in the other sheets so they get their forecast data from the corporate data that we pulled into sheet D via file links. Make a note that the quarterly forecast data for CDs start in cell B7 and that the data for videos start in cell B8. This will make it easier to enter the formulas.

Go to cell A:B11 (cell B11 of sheet A) and enter the following formula (including four blank spaces within the first set of quotation marks):

@IF(B10=0,+"   "&@STRING($D:B7,0)&"*",$D:B7)

This formula checks for the presence of a total in the current column. If the total equals zero—that is, if the actual data aren't in yet—this cell displays a string consisting of four blank spaces, a string representation of the quarterly forecast, and an asterisk. If the total in the current column does not equal zero—that is, if there are quarterly revenues—the forecasted value appears in the cell. If the quarterly revenue figures could add up to zero, we would have to use a different test instead of B10=0: for example, @COUNT(B7..B9).

Copy the formula in cell B11 to cells C11..E11. Then copy the formula in cell B11 to range B:B11..C:11, the first-quarter forecast cells in the video and combined revenue worksheets. Next, go to cell B:B11 and edit the two references to cell $D:B7 in the formula so that they say $D:B8, which is the cell where the first-quarter video forecast is stored. Copy this formula across to range C11..E11.

To fix the formulas in sheet C, go to cell C:B11 and edit the two references to cell $D:B7 in the formula so that they say $D:B9. Then copy the formula in cell B11 to range C11..E11.

To clarify the meaning of the asterisks that appear on the future forecasts, enter the following formula in A16 cell (including 30 blank spaces after the first quotation mark):

@IF(E10=0,"   * Forecasts for future quarters are not included in YTD","")

If there is no actual data for the last quarter of the year, this formula displays the note. If there is data for this quarter, this formula displays an empty (null) string.

To make this label resemble the figure, select bold and italic style for cell B16.

Now copy this formula to range A:B16..B:C16.

The shading in range A:C7..C:13 needs a bit of touching up, so select the range and issue the Style Shading command to reapply light shading. Repeat this process for range A:E7..A:E13.

Save the worksheet to preserve your most recent changes. If you want to print all of 3BEAST.WK3, you need to extend the Print range so that it includes the footnote and sheet D. Thus, it should be range A:A1..D:F16.

The multisheet and multifile application is now complete! Remember that to use this application, you must open the three relevant files: 3BEAST.WK3, CORPVID.WK3, and CORPCD.WK3. To make this application even slicker, you might want to create a macro to open up the corporate forecast files automatically whenever you load the Eastern-region file.

	A	B	C	D	E	F
1	3B Entertainment International					
2	East					
3	Becky's CD's Division					
4						
5						
6	Branch	Q1	Q2	Q3	Q4	YTD
7	Territory 1	87	94	35		216
8	Territory 2	78	62	33		173
9	Territory 3	45	45	28		118
10	Total	210	201	96		507
11	Forecast	210	205	85	225*	500
12	$ Over/(Under) Forecast	----------	-4	11		7
13	Actual vs. Forecast %	100.0%	98.0%	112.9%		101.4%
14						
15						
16	* Forecasts for future quarters are not included in YTD					

Figure 9.16. The enhanced version of the Eastern region's corporate revenue sheet. With a few simple adjustments, this worksheet can be turned into a ready-to-run application for any of the three other regions.

All you have to do to make the 3BEAST.WK3 file usable for any of the three other regions is change the region name in sheet D, clear out the Eastern region's actual revenues, and save the file under a new name.

Other Ways to Link and Combine Data

File linking is the simplest way for one worksheet to get the latest data from another worksheet. But there are several other ways to get data from here to there, and different techniques are preferable for different tasks. Some even let you share between 1-2-3/W and other software.

File Combine From

The File Combine From command is a handy way to bring a large section of one 1-2-3/W file into another. This command lets you copy to the current file a specified range, or all cells, from another file. Instead of a simple copy, you can choose to have the incoming values add themselves to or subtract themselves from the values in the target range.

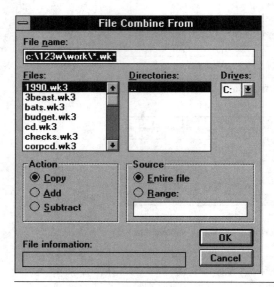

Figure 9.17. The File Combine From command's dialog box. This dialog box lets you bestow upon the current file some or all data from another file.

Note that blank cells in the source file do not overwrite data in the target file. And if you choose Add or Subtract, only the values from the source file are used; the source file's labels and formulas are ignored.

Note also that if you combine a 3D range with more sheets than are available in the target range, you may get unexpected results. For example, don't copy range A:A1..G:K250 into a file that contains only one worksheet.

Since the File Combine From command makes large-scale changes to the target file, it's a good idea to save the target file before you issue this command.

File Extract To

The File Extract To command lets you copy selected data from the current file into another file. If you choose the Formula option, all formulas, labels, values, and worksheet settings are copied to the new file.

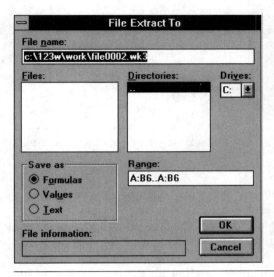

Figure 9.18. The File Extract To command's dialog box lets you copy selected data to a new file, which may be either a worksheet file or a text file.

If you choose the Text option, all data in the selected range is copied to a plain text file. If you choose the Values option, all selected data is copied to a worksheet file, but formulas are converted to the values that they currently display.

File Import From

The File Import From command lets you bring in data from a text file or formatting from another worksheet's ALL, FMT, or FM3 style file.

File Import From Text places each line of text from the source file into a cell in the target worksheet. Although the text may appear to be spread across several cells, each line of imported text is actually a single, long label. To split the data into separate entries in separate cells, you can use the Data Parse command, which is described in Chapter 13.

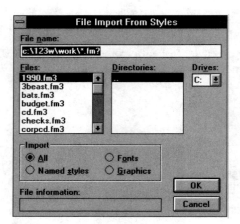

Figure 9.19. The File Import From commands let you import data from text files or borrow spreadsheet publishing styles from another worksheet file.

File Import From Numbers brings the data into separate cells, but its results may not be as satisfactory as the results of the File Import Text and Data Parse com-mands. Since File Import From Numbers requires just a single step, you may want to try it first and then undo the import if you want to try text importing and parsing.

File Import From Styles lets you import another file's spreadsheet-publishing styles. You can import all styles, or just named styles, font sets, and graphics. Be aware that if you copy all styles, that styling may appear in inappropriate places in the target file, unless the file you're importing from is structurally identical to the current file.

The File Import From command can also radically alter the current file, by either writing over valuable data or completely changing the file's spreadsheet-publishing styles. Therefore, save your file before you issue a File Import From command.

Copy Commands

All of the various range-copying techniques described in Chapter 7 let you copy chunks of data between files, as well as within files.

For example, you can use Edit Quick Copy or the Clipboard commands Edit Copy and Edit Paste to copy data from one file to another. As in any copying operation, all you have to do is specify the target location after you copy the source.

One way to identify a target location in another open file is to specify the file and cell location in a dialog box (as in the Edit Quick Copy command) or at a prompt (as in the Copy command). For example, to copy a selected range to cell C23 of an open worksheet called MEMBERS.WK3, you'd indicate the range <<MEMBERS>>C23 after the *To:* prompt. Or you could navigate to the target location in the other sheet before you finished the copying command.

Remember that the Clipboard commands not only let you copy worksheet data, but they deliver almost any kind of text and graphics you can copy from other Windows programs. None of these copying techniques, however, will update the target file when data changes in the source file.

DDE

Windows' DDE feature is similar to both file-linking and simple Clipboard operations. You can use DDE to link data from different applications. The simplest way to accomplish this is to choose Edit Copy in one program, switch to the target file in the target application, and select Edit Paste Link.

Like file-linking formulas, DDE links automatically post the latest data from one file into another. What's more, DDE usually updates the file as soon as you make changes in the source file. If you're using 1-2-3/W with an application that requires manual updating—or if for performance reasons you've used the Edit Link Options Manual feature to postpone DDE updates—you can choose Edit Link Options Update to transmit the latest data.

You can use DDE to share data among 1-2-3/W files, giving you even more up-to-the-minute data. But file-linking commands make smaller demands on the computer's processing resources, and they don't require the source files to be in memory as DDE links do. In general, you'll get the best results if you use file-linking formulas to link data among 1-2-3/W spreadsheets and DDE links to link up with other Windows applications.

DataLens

In 1-2-3/W, as in Release 3.1, you can treat data in an external database program as if it were part of a database in your spreadsheet. If you use database software such as dBase or Paradox, or if you use an SQL Server system, you can exploit Lotus's DataLens technology to make accessing these databases as easy as 1-2-3.

Translate

The translate facility is a separate, character-based application that lets you convert 1-2-3/W's WK3 files into a variety of formats. It's the fastest way, for example, to convert a 3D WK3 file into a series of single-sheet WK1 files. Note, though, that Translate does not convert the FM3 files that store spreadsheet publishing styles and graphics annotations. Remember that you can convert a single-sheet WK# file to a Release 2.x-compatible WK1 file simply by saving it with a .WK1 extension. Along with the WK1 file 1-2-3/W saves an FMT file that stores spreadsheet publishing enhancements in a format you can use with 1-2-3 Release 2.3's WYSIWYG Add-in. Use the :Special Export command to convert a 1-2-3/W FM3 style file to the ALL format that's supported by Release 2.2's Allways add-in.

Note that no conversions are necessary to exchange data between 1-2-3/W and 1-2-3 Release 3.x, or to open files from earlier releases into 1-2-3/W. 1-2-3/W can also open spreadsheets created with Microsoft Excel 2.x.

Protecting Your Data

1-2-3/W provides a number of techniques for protecting your data. You can enable global protection; you can hide cells, columns, and sheets; and you can password-protect files.

By default, every cell in a 1-2-3/W worksheet is protected. If you activate the Worksheet Global Settings Protection option, no one can enter or alter data in the worksheet until Protection is disabled.

To allow entry in certain cells, apply the Range Unprotect option to these cells before you enable global protection. The Window Display Options command lets you assign a color to unprotected cells.

You can hide a cell by choosing the Hidden Range Format, and you can restore it by choosing a "normal" format. The control panel displays the contents of a hidden cell, unless password protection is enabled.

You can hide a column by dragging the right edge of the frame surrounding the column letter, and you can hide either a sheet or a column by way of the Worksheet Hide command. The Worksheet Unhide command restores hidden columns and sheets.

The File Save As dialog box has a Password-protect option that lets you assign a "secret code" for access to a file. If you want to prevent people who know the password from changing critical settings, you can create a higher level of password protection by using the File Administration Seal commands, which are described below.

File Access on a Network

When you use 1-2-3/W in a network environment, a new issue comes up. Can the same file be in two places at the same time? If both Mary Jean and Josephine modify the same file simultaneously, whose changes actually get stored to disk?

1-2-3/W, like all Releases 2.2 or higher, supports a simple file-reservation scheme. Ordinarily, the user who first retrieves a file gets the reservation—the exclusive right to save the file under its current name.

If Mary Jean opens the file first, Josephine can still open the file, but in a "read-only" mode. When you open a file with read-only access, the "RO" indicator appears in the file's title bar. If Josephine makes changes, she *can* save them, but she must use the File Save As or File Save command and specify a new name for her modified version of the file. If Linda, Joanne, and Billy also want to open the file, they can too—but with the same read-only restriction.

The File Administration Network Reserve command's Release button allows you to give up the reservation so another user can get dibs on the file. And its Get button allows you to claim the reservation if it's up for grabs. The Get-reservation-automatically check box lets you decide whether the file reservation goes to the first taker or if, instead, it goes to the first person who chooses File Administration Network Reserve Get.

The File Administration Seal command is a security feature that works in conjunction with the reservation feature. If you choose this command's File-and-network-reservation-status option, the user will need a special password—in addition to any password required simply to open the file—to access the network-reservation options and a variety of other commands. The Reservation-status-only option lets you limit access to the reservation features without limiting access to other commands.

If you choose the former option, not only do you prevent unauthorized access to the reservation feature, you cordon off such features as creating and deleting graphs, choosing Worksheet Global Settings, altering column widths, hiding or unhiding columns, and changing the format of a range of cells. Several of these limitations prevent such security breaches as having a user turn off the Protection mode or displaying a hidden column or ranges that are in the Hidden format.

To "unseal" a file, you choose File Administration Seal and select the Disable-all-restrictions options. After you enter the appropriate password, the file becomes unsealed.

Strategies and Tactics for Application Design

The best thing about a spreadsheet is also the worst: its infinite flexibility.

Doubtless, you'll prize the way 1-2-3/W lets you casually set up small, disposable spreadsheets. But many a simple application grows into a bigger one, and before you know it, your business operations can depend on a worksheet you started on a whim.

A good worksheet requires a fair amount of planning and testing. If you apply sloppy workmanship to important applications, don't expect any miracles. An ill-conceived spreadsheet, like a house with a crumbling foundation, can be a nightmare to maintain.

Unless you start your application with sound planning and check its integrity with thorough testing, you'll have to pay the piper at some point. The cost may be slow performance, lost or inaccurate data, confused users, redundant efforts, or long hours of tinkering for even the humblest changes. Eventually, you may have to scrap most of your work and completely redesign the system.

Next time, you vow, you'll design the spreadsheet before you build and use it. It's pretty hard, though, to delay the gratification of watching your spreadsheet grow labels, values, and formulas as fast as you can type them. But if you can keep those itchy fingers from running away with you, you'll save time in the long run.

Creating successful applications in 1-2-3/W takes at least three things: a good understanding of the business problem you're trying to solve; a working knowledge of the tools at your disposal; and a methodical approach to designing, building, and testing the application.

Assessing the Needs

Many spreadsheet projects start with the goal of automating a manual system. But to create a successful application, you should sets your sights beyond simply replicating a paper-based system. As computer consultant Michael Hammer has said, "If you automate a mess, you get an automated mess." Even if your current reports and procedures seem to do the trick, you'll find that once you put information in computerized form, you and your coworkers will think up numerous ways to make the data work harder.

Ideally, your design will incorporate as many of the application's potentially valuable uses as possible. It's always easier to include features in a new application than to alter a system that's full of data and in constant use.

Before you build a major spreadsheet application, think creatively about its potential uses, and spend a lot of time talking to people who might use—directly or indirectly—the spreadsheet and its data. Ask what features they want and expect from it.

You'll also want to know about the skills of the people who will use the application. Do they already know 1-2-3 for Windows or some other version of 1-2-3? Do they know their way around the Windows environment? Do they need a "foolproof" system that limits their options but prevents mishaps? Or are they power users who want a system that lets them improvise at will?

Odds are, because of time and technical restraints, your application won't fulfill everybody's dreams. But the information and insights you gain will help you make informed decisions about the application's design.

Learning the Options

The more you know about the features of 1-2-3/W, the easier it is to craft solutions to your business problems. Do a little homework before you decide that 1-2-3/W doesn't have a feature you want or before you do headstands to make something work. Chances are there's a solution in the product's arsenal of features.

Before you write an epic formula, check the list of available @functions to make sure there isn't one that meets your needs. If you need to automate a feature, write a macro. If you're having trouble finding the optimal answer for a problem, check out 1-2-3/W's Solver and Backsolver. And by all means, learn how to create multifile and 3-D applications, even if you suspect that your applications are too simple to require them. Once you've seen these powerful features in action, you'll wonder how and why you ever lived without them.

And if you find that 1-2-3/W doesn't have the feature you want, perhaps you need to use your spreadsheet in conjunction with another application, such as a database management program, a word processor, or a dedicated graphics package. In the chapters ahead, you'll also learn how to combine these resources with 1-2-3/W to make powerful multiapplication solutions.

Designing, Building, and Testing

If you create applications for the department you work in, the process and demands can be uncontrolled. The requirements and schedules are certain to be more changeable and more unrealistic than when you commission an application from corporate MIS.

If the person who commissioned the spreadsheet—and that might be you—doesn't provide sufficient time for design and testing, the application will almost surely suffer. 1-2-3/W is a power tool for creating custom applications quickly and conveniently. Quickly and conveniently, however, do not mean instantly and automatically.

If you're inclined to create applications by trial and error, it may sound burdensome to apply a "methodology" to spreadsheet tasks. Indeed, one of the reasons 1-2-3/W is so rewarding to work with is that it doesn't require you to use the stodgy tools of the systems analyst: the flow charts, IPO charts, and such.

But if you don't manage the process of developing large applications, the process will manage you. The methods suggested below will make the process more efficient and productive. When you avoid design and implementation mistakes, you have *more* time for creative work—and play.

Minimize Redundant Data Entry. Organize your applications so that you don't have to enter the same data twice. Redundant data entry wastes time and leads to errors. File-linking formulas and the Edit link command help you reuse data. The File Combine and File Import commands are less-automated but more-memory-efficient alternatives, and the Data External commands let you access data that's managed by a separate database program.

Minimize Redundant Calculations. Avoid having multiple formulas perform the same calculation. If several formulas require the same calculated value, put a formula that derives this value in a remote location—such as another sheet—and reference it in the other formulas. The other formulas will be easier to read, and if you have to change this oft-used formula, you need only change it in one place.

Design and Build First, Enter Later. Try not to put too much data into your worksheet until the overall structure is mapped out. Remember, you've got heavy construction work to do. You won't be able to hammer and saw away at will if the data moves in before you're finished building the application.

Leave Room for Growth. Consider whether the application needs room for more time periods, more line items, and so on. Also, don't make the columns too tight; inflation, acquisitions, and an upturn in business could make your data impossible to fit. Don't wait until a confused user gets a cell or column full of asterisks.

Make It Work Before You Decorate. Don't waste your time with fancy fontwork and borders until you know that the worksheet works. These enhancements can be a nuisance when you try to reorganize the worksheet. And check your column widths *after* you fine-tune fonts and enhancements, because they affect how much data fits in a cell.

Check for Accuracy, Capacity. Test the application with data that are easy to check. Load up the spreadsheet with numbers you already know the "answers" to, and make sure the spreadsheet performs all calculations correctly. And run a full test. The application that works great with a small sample of data may work slowly or not at all when it's fully stocked. Also, enter zeros, negative numbers, and numbers that include decimal places anywhere that they might occur; formulas that work with positive integers may not work properly with these other types of values.

Build for Safety. Unless the worksheet's intended users are all 1-2-3/W experts, use global and range protection; range, column, and sheet hiding; worksheet titles; password protection; and other safety features to protect against mistakes—honest and otherwise. When that isn't enough, use macros to guide users through all the necessary procedures. Also, protect the spreadsheet from common redesign errors: Use range names and absolute references so that cell references aren't mixed up when you insert and delete rows, columns and sheets when you copy and move formulas. And use the Group mode feature judiciously. It's a powerful but dangerous tool for 3-D worksheets. This chapter describes the effective use of all these techniques.

Test for Ease of Use. Before the spreadsheet becomes a going concern, have some typical users try it out. Identify any operations that will be stumbling blocks, then work to simplify or automate these procedures. Get the "user-hostile" tasks ironed out, before anyone tackles data entry in earnest.

Polish It Up. When you're sure the application is fully functional, apply the necessary fit and finish. If the worksheet you're handing out is a template that needs to be copied for each time period, division, or so on, make sure you document or automate the procedure for saving the file under a new name. Remember to clear out any test data, and enter and check any data that should be in the sheet.

Test It Again. Finally, when you think it's perfect, do one last trial run to find out if it is. It's very easy to forget little details or to inadvertently change something that worked at one time. If you're going to hand your application over to someone else to use, make sure it's in full working order. For example, see to it that the current Print ranges, worksheet titles, and cell-pointer locations are appropriate when you save your files. Then when someone starts up the application, the worksheet will be ready to go.

Train the Users. If other people are going to use the worksheet, don't assume they know all the ins and outs of 1-2-3/W and your application. For example, in a multifile application, make sure they know the names of all the files they have to load to run. In a 3-D application, make sure they know how to go from sheet to sheet. And if they have to make backup copies of the files, make sure they know to save the .FM3 files along with the .WK3 files.

Document Your Work. To print out the formulas behind the worksheet, choose File Page Setup and select the Show-formulas option. Along with the Show-worksheet-frame, and Show-grid-lines options, this helps you make a printout that shows the logic behind your spreadsheet. After you confirm these options, select File Print to get a "documented" printout. Remember to return the setup to normal settings. Another documentation trick is to append notes in cells that contain values and formulas by adding a semicolon and an appropriate comment. You can also annotate range names with the /Range Name Note Create command and add a table of these names to your worksheet via the /Range Name Note Table.

Unfortunately, a great many spreadsheets are born in the line of fire. You have a set of data you have to process *now*. But even when you're under the gun, you can apply most of the design and testing methods described above. In fact, the applications you produce under pressure are most likely the ones that require you to be the most careful and methodical.

10

Printing with 1-2-3 for Windows

You've entered your line items, added up your columns, and you even found some extra money for the training budget! Your fonts are just right, and you've used a subtle combination of outlines and shading to make your spreadsheet look as good as it can. It's time to print!

The good news is that printing a 1-2-3 spreadsheet has never been easier, and the output has never looked better. 1-2-3/W lets you preview the page on the screen, and will even automatically compress the printout so that it will all fit on one page. 1-2-3/W even prints in the background, so you can get on with your important work instead of sitting on your hands waiting for the printer to finish.

The bad news is that the paper is still going to jam occasionally, and you're still going to run out of toner, and sometimes it will still take some trial and error until you get the perfect printout.

This chapter gives you a foundation in the vernacular of 1-2-3/W printing, and helps you get the most out of the 1-2-3/W printing options. It includes an exercise for learning how to print with 1-2-3/W. And it gives you the most frequently asked questions and their answers.

In this chapter you will learn:

- *How to print with 1-2-3/W*
- *How to use page breaks*
- *The difference between the various printing commands and options*
- *Strategies for printing large sheets*
- *How to set up the page*
- *The terms and concepts that are important to 1-2-3/W printing*

Why Are There So Many Ways to Print?!

You'll be surprised at how often you find the word *Print* in the various 1-2-3 menus (see Figure 10.1). There's the regular Windows File Print, WYSIWYG's :Print, and the 1-2-3 Classic /Print! One of the most important things you'll need to understand is when and why to use each command.

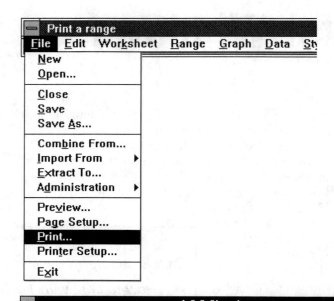

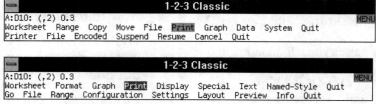

Figure 10.1. 1-2-3/W has three Print commands, but you'll use the one in the File menu most often.

When and Why to Use Each Command

The 1-2-3/W File Print commands and dialog boxes offer the easiest and most direct access to 1-2-3/W's printing features. You should use them (including Preview, Page Setup and Printer Setup) to print in 1-2-3/W unless you have a specific reason to use the 1-2-3 Classic Print commands. For example, you might use the Classic Print commands in an old macro or in a sheet you've embellished with setup strings—sequences of codes that control printouts. Windows-style printing menus you'll never have to add those cryptic codes to your worksheets again. So most or all of your printing from now on will be via the Windows File menu print the Windows Way. But Windows-Style printing is more capable and more consistent across applications. If you can print in any other Windows applications, you can print in 1-2-3/W—and vice versa.

Also note that the WYSIWYG :Print commands and the 1-2-3/W File Print commands often offer very different approaches that result in the *exact* same effect. For example, if you use the WYSIWYG :Print Layout Titles command to create a header, it will automatically show up when you choose File Page Setup. And if you use the 1-2-3/W File menu to turn on Automatic Compression, you'll see that the :Print Settings sheet will already display Compression... Automatic. Set your Print Range through WYSIWYG's :Print Range Set command or by choosing 1-2-3/W's File Print command; it just doesn't matter. Everything you can do with the WYSIWYG :Print menu you can do with the 1-2-3/W's File menu (and then some).

The 1-2-3 Classic /Print commands—and a "general" printer driver—are also included primarily for compatibility with old files. If you have an old spreadsheet in which you've created some print macros and setup strings, retrieve it in 1-2-3/W, press Alt and the name of the macro, and out it will come, setup strings and all. You might also use the /Print options when you need a quick and dirty printout, but keep in mind that you sacrifice your WYSIWYG-style formats—fonts, italics, graphs, etc.—and the handy Windows Print Manager facility whenever you print via the Classic /Print menu.

In summary, use the 1-2-3/W File Print options as the easiest and best way to get your masterpiece on a piece of paper.

Use 1-2-3/W's File Print command to print your spreadsheets.

How to Print

If your spreadsheet is small, printing it with 1-2-3/W is as easy as, well, pardon the expression, 1-2-3. Highlight the range you want to print, choose Print from the 1-2-3/W File menu, choose OK, and out it comes. It may lack many extras, like headers, footers, and page numbers, but you see how easy it is to print.

The normal printing headaches (like which printer port to use, what size paper) are taken care of by Windows. You do need to tell Windows which printers you'll be using and how they'll be configured, but you probably already did that when you installed Windows. In fact, if you've printed with *any* other Windows program (even Paintbrush!), you're already set up and ready to go.

Choosing File Print does not send the entire file to the printer, as it does in most Windows products. You have to tell 1-2-3/W what to print by defining a Print range. The Print range can be a single cell, the entire spreadsheet, multiple sheets, or any combination of the above.

Figure 10.2 shows a simple spreadsheet, one that would easily fit on a single page.

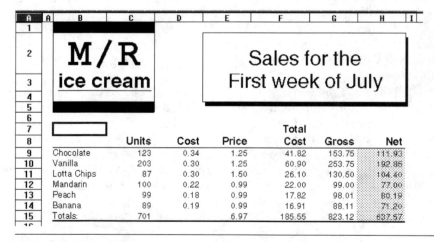

Figure 10.2. This small spreadsheet will easily fit on one page and can therefore be printed quite easily.

To print this worksheet, you'd just click and drag to select range A1..I15, click the Print SmartIcon (as displayed in Figure 10.3), choose OK, and that's that! And the next time you print, it's even easier. Once you have identified the Print range, you just click the Print icon without confirming the range.

Figure 10.3. The Print SmartIcon makes it easy to print your worksheets. Click the icon and you've got instant (well, almost) hardcopy.

Remember that a Print range need not be one block of contiguous cells. To print different parts of a single worksheet or even multiple worksheets, you specify their addresses (or range names), separating them with commas. Let's say you have a document that contains three worksheets, each containing the sales for one quarter of last year.

To print each range from each sheet, you'd specify a Print range like A:A1..A:I45,B:A10..C:B55.

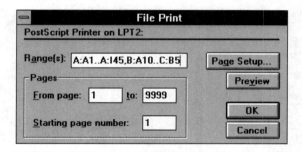

Figure 10.4. To print more than one range, separate the range addresses with a comma in the File Print dialog box.

Printing That Monster!

So far, our discussion has focused on printing small ranges that fit on a single page. But a budget spreadsheet that contains columns for the months and maybe a hundred line items *won't* fit. Do you think you can highlight the whole worksheet, click the Print SmartIcon and hope for the best? If you carelessly print a large document like this, your printout is going to look lousy, you're going to waste a ream of paper, and you'll be *persona non grata* at the network printer station.

Printing a large spreadsheet or a series of ranges from different worksheets demands more planning on your part. In the next several pages, we'll discuss techniques for printing a large spreadsheet. One of the most important (and one of 1-2-3/W's best features) is Print Preview.

Print Preview: The Show-Me State

Use the File Preview command to "try out" your Print range.

To Preview your printout, highlight the Print range (if you haven't established it already), and click the Preview SmartIcon, as shown in Figure 10.5. (Of course, you could choose Preview from the File menu, if you like doing things the hard way). If you have highlighted a new Print range, you'll have to click the OK button, but you don't have to click the OK button if you're previewing a range you've previewed (or printed) before. Figure 10.6 shows a sample Preview screen.

Figure 10.5. The File Preview SmartIcon lets you quickly enter Preview mode. Clicking the File Preview SmartIcon is the same as choosing Preview from the File menu.

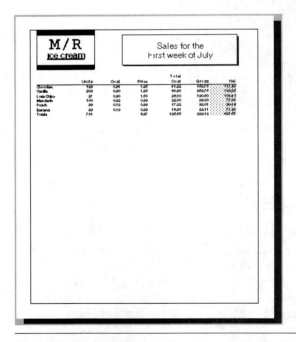

Figure 10.6. With File Preview you get to see what your Print range will look like on a piece of paper. It will also display your headers, borders, etc. Preview will save you a lot of time and paper.

While previewing a page, press any key to display the next page. You can also press Escape anytime to leave Print Preview and return to the worksheet.

The Print Dialog Box

If your range takes more than one page, you may not always need to print all the pages. Maybe you were printing a large spreadsheet, and the printer jammed after page 3. You spent the last hour unjamming the printer, and now you're ready to try again. But you don't need to print the first three pages again —so you use the File Print dialog box, which is displayed whenever you choose Print from the File menu, to tell 1-2-3/W to start printing with page 4 (as displayed in Figure 10.7).

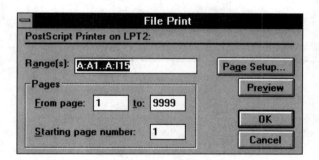

Figure 10.7. In addition to setting that all-important Print range, the Print dialog box is useful when you want to print only certain pages and when you want to start printing after the first page.

Let's say you're preparing a report for your boss that's going to include data from more than one worksheet. You print the range you need from the first worksheet, which ends up taking three pages. (Needless to say, you used the File Page Setup dialog box to make a header that automatically numbers your pages.) You've retrieved the second worksheet, and now you're ready to print it. The problem is that the *first* page that will get printed from this second worksheet is actually the *fourth* page of your report. Unless you tell it differently, 1-2-3/W is going to print *Page 1* in your header, and the pages from the second worksheet will all be numbered incorrectly. Fortunately, you can also use the File Print dialog box to tell 1-2-3/W to start numbering the pages at 4, as we see in Figure 10.7.

Give Me a Break!

A page break tells 1-2-3/W to begin printing on the next page. There are two kinds of page breaks: soft breaks, which 1-2-3/W inserts automatically, and manual breaks, which you insert.

You'll notice that after printing or previewing a range that it becomes surrounded by a dashed line, as displayed in Figure 10.8. This is just one of the clues 1-2-3/W gives you to help you visualize what the worksheet is going to look like when you print it. These broken lines represent page breaks, which show you where 1-2-3/W is going to start printing on the next piece of paper.

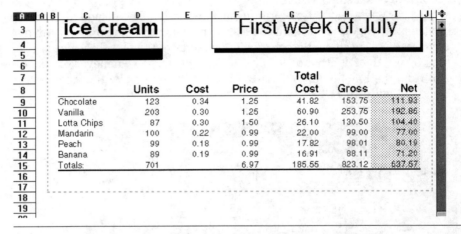

Figure 10.8. 1-2-3/W shows you where the next page will begin with a dashed line, called a page break.

1-2-3/W automatically figures out where to put page breaks from the size of the Print range, the margins, etc. These page breaks that 1-2-3/W has placed for you are often called soft page breaks. You'll see the soft page breaks in your worksheet move as you change fonts, insert and delete rows, etc. It just stands to reason that if you decide to start using a larger font, not as many rows will fit on a page, and the page break will end up in row 45 instead of row 60.

The other kind of page break you need to know about is called a manual page break. You will on occasion need to insert a manual page break to force 1-2-3/W to print the rest of your Print range on the next page, even if the range could fit on the current page. You might insert a page break when printing a range that spans across more than one worksheet so that 1-2-3/W will print sheet A on one page and sheet B on the next. You do this by choosing Page Break from the Worksheet menu, and then choosing the type of page break to be inserted (as displayed in Figure 10.9). If you choose Horizontal, you are telling 1-2-3/W to begin printing the current row on the next page. If you choose Vertical, 1-2-3/W will start printing the current column on the next page.

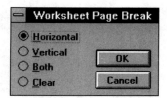

Figure 10.9. Use the Worksheet Page Break dialog box when you want to force 1-2-3/W to start printing part of your Print range on another page.

As we discussed earlier, 1-2-3/W uses a dashed line to show you where the page breaks are. But how do you know if that page break is soft (automatically inserted by 1-2-3/W) or manual (inserted by you)? Well, you'll also notice that when you point to a cell that contains a page break, the format line in the control panel provides a clue. It displays {Page} for soft page breaks and {MPage} for manual page breaks. Figure 10.10 shows a soft page break, and Figure 10.11 shows a manual page break.

Figure 10.10. When you point to a cell that contains a soft page break, 1-2-3/W displays {Page} in the control panel.

Figure 10.11. When you point to a cell that contains a manual page break, 1-2-3/W displays {MPage} in the control panel.

1-2-3/W offers another piece of information: When you point to the first cell in a Print range (or page within a Print range), the control panel tells you what page you're on in the Print range (see Figure 10.12).

Figure 10.12. The control panel tells you that you are on page 1 of a four-page Print range.

When your Print range spans more than one worksheet, insert a manual page break at the bottom of the range on each worksheet if you want 1-2-3/W to print only one range on each page.

If you are printing multiple ranges, 1-2-3/W will not automatically insert a page break between the ranges. The same is true if your Print range is a multi-sheet range. This lets you consolidate several areas of the sheet onto one page. But if you do need page breaks between the ranges, remember to insert manual page breaks at the bottom of each range or sheet.

For those large print ranges, it's important to understand how 1-2-3/W prints the pages. 1-2-3/W prints a multipage range from top to bottom, and then from left to right.

GUI's Get Some of the Breaks

Note that the page breaks described in this chapter—both the page breaks you insert with the Worksheet Page and the soft page breaks 1-2-3/W puts in—are different from the ones you insert with the 1-2-3 Classic command /Worksheet Page. The former, like the page breaks you add with the WYSIWYG command :Worksheet Page work when you use the File Print command. /Worksheet Page breaks only work when you perform the old-fashioned /Print Go command.

File Page Setup

The File Page Setup dialog box, shown in Figure 10.13, is used to set margins, borders, headers, etc.

Most people arrive at a particular mix of Page Setup options and then use them as the default. Let's say you always print on your company's letterhead, which requires a large top margin, and that you always want your name to be printed in the footer. You could establish, say, a 2-inch top margin, enter your footer, and then make that the default by clicking the Update button in the Page Setup dialog box. From then on, 1-2-3/W will use that set of Page Setup options whenever you print, unless you override them, which you can do anytime you want.

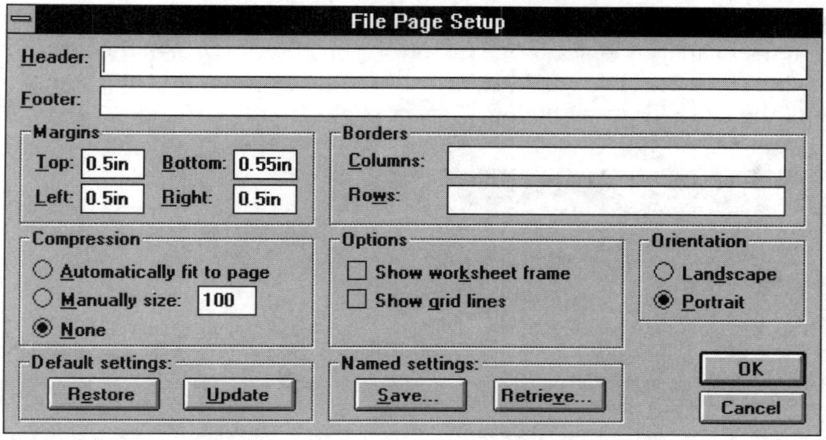

Figure 10.13. Use the Page Setup dialog box to determine your page's layout.

You can use Restore to change the current settings back to the default. So if you really blew it and the margins are all wrong, the header isn't working, and you have the wrong borders, use Restore to start over.

You can also name a particular bunch of Page Setup options, and save them to disk. Say you use two printers. You could select the appropriate settings for your laser printer in the dialog box, choose Save, and call them LASER. Then you could select the settings for your dot-matrix printer, choose Save again, and call those settings DOT. Now whenever you want to switch to the laser printer, you won't have to try to remember the correct margins. You just pick Retrieve, type *laser*, and you're ready to print on the laser printer.

Let's discuss each of the Page Setup options in detail.

Use the Page Setup dialog box's Restore button when you want to use 1-2-3/W's default print settings.

Print It Again, Sam: Headers and Footers

You use headers if you want to print information at the very top of each page in your printout, and you use footers to print information at the very bottom of each page. Headers and footers are in Font 1—the first font in the Style Font dialog box—and they often include the title of the report, the page number, the date it was printed, and so on. Headers and footers can be 512 bytes long (essentially 512 characters) and can include any text, plus some reserved characters such as # and @ that have special meanings for headers and footers. You enter headers and footers by choosing Page Setup from the File menu.

Very often you'll want to number your pages. You need only enter a pound sign (#) in the header or footer. For example, if you enter *Page* # in the header, as shown in Figure 10.14, 1-2-3/W will substitute the appropriate page number in place of the pound sign at the top of every page.

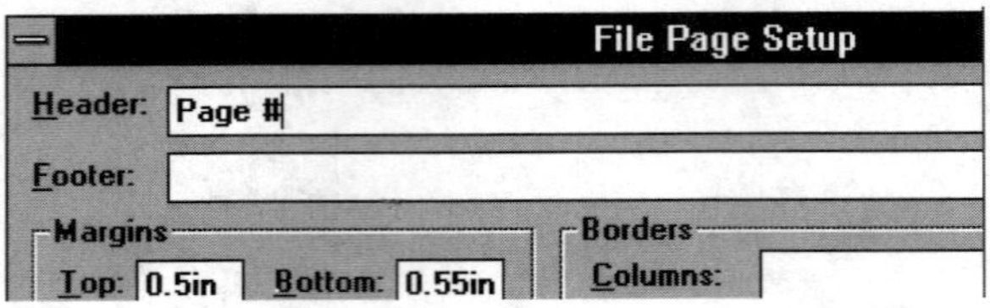

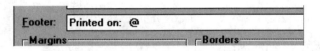

Figure 10.14. 1-2-3/W substitutes the page number for the pound sign (#) in a header or footer.

In a header or footer, type @ to print today's date, # to print the page number, and ¦ to justify the text.

1-2-3/W substitutes today's date for an "at" sign (@) in a header or footer, as in Figure 10.15.

Figure 10.15. If you type an "at" sign (@) in a footer, 1-2-3/W automatically prints the correct date at the bottom of every page.

Finally, 1-2-3/W will print the contents of a cell if you enter a backslash and the cell address (or range name). For example, if you enter *\D2* in the Header box on the Page Setup dialog box, 1-2-3/W will include the contents of cell D2 at the top of each page. Keep in mind that 1-2-3/W will *not* include any formatting you've done to cell D2. Cell D2 could be bold and blue, but in the header it'll just be printed in Font 1.

You can also left-align, right-align, and center text in a header or footer by separating the elements with a split vertical bar (¦). (It's just below the Enter key on most keyboards). 1-2-3 will left-align anything before the split vertical bar, center anything after it, and right-align whatever you type after the second split vertical bar. Let's see that in action. If you were to enter *Printed on: @|Yearly Summary|Page #* as a header, you would get a printed heading that looked something like this:

Printed on 19-Dec-91   Yearly Summary   Page 1

The bad news is that you cannot use the split vertical bar heading symbol with cell contents. Entering \A1 in the footer will print whatever is in cell A1 at the bottom of every page. Entering |Confidential in the Footer will center the word *Confidential* at the bottom of every page. But, entering //\A1 in the footer will not center the contents of cell A1 at the bottom of every page. It will instead right-align the letter A and the number 1 (see Figure 10.19).

Figure 10.19. Unfortunately, you can't use the split vertical bar to justify the contents of a cell. If you enter a cell address after the split vertical bar, 1-2-3/W prints the cell address instead of the cell's contents.

What Happened To My Column Headings? Or, Why You Need To Use Borders

When you work with a larger Print range that spans several pages, you'll learn very quickly that the column and row headings don't get re-printed on each page—unless you use borders. You can tell 1-2-3/W to print certain rows at the top of each page and certain columns at the left of each page. You might say that borders are the Print command's answer to Worksheet Titles.

Let's say you've got a budget spreadsheet, as illustrated in Figure 10.20. Row 1 contains the labels *January* through *December*. If you include the *Total* column, it goes all the way out to column N. Column A contains the line items, all the way down to row 200. Print Compression would make the spreadsheet so small that it would be unreadable, so you'll have to live with a 2- or 3-page printout. Simply defining A1..N200 won't do, because you'll never know what those columns of figures are on page 2, nor will you know what the rows are on page 3. It's borders to the rescue! 1-2-3/W will print the border columns and rows at the top and at the left of every page.

In the Page Setup dialog box, you could enter cell A1 as both the border column and the border row, as illustrated in Figure 10.17. 1-2-3/W knows that when you specify cell A1 as the border column, you mean the whole column, range A1..A200. The same thing goes for entering the Border rows. If you enter *A1 ..A3* as the Border rows, 1-2-3/W knows you *really* mean A1..N3.

To cure headless rows in columns and rows in your printouts, use the Borders option..

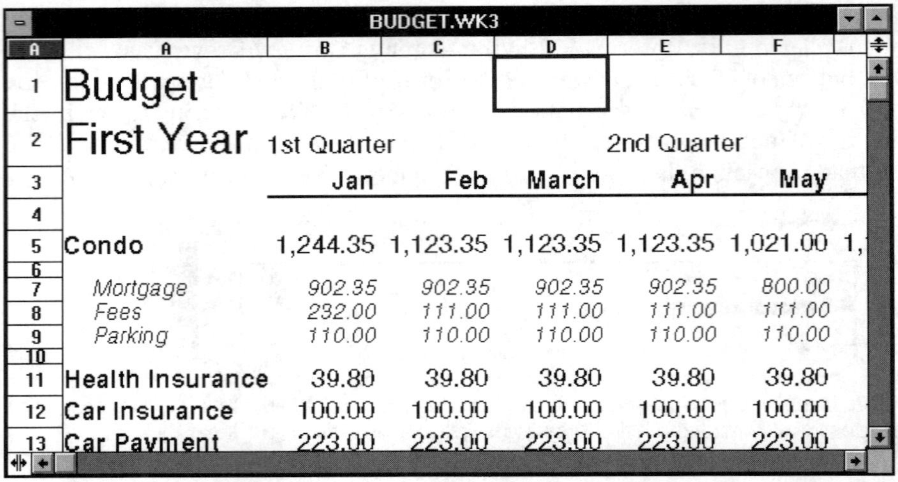

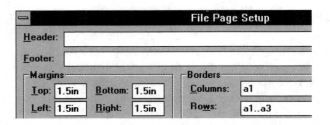

Figure 10.16. Because this spreadsheet is so wide and long, we'll use borders to re-print the column and row headings on each page.

Figure 10.17. You use the Page Setup dialog box to tell 1-2-3/W to print borders on every page. Make sure you don't include the borders in the Print range!

If a border or column row is included in the Print range, 1-2-3/W will print them twice.

A common mistake is to include the borders in the Print range. If you make this mistake once, you'll never make it again. 1-2-3/W will print column A and row 1 twice on the first page—once as the border, and then again as the first part of the actual Print range.

Condense, Constrict, Constrain, Compression!

The Compression options within the File Page Setup box are reason enough to use 1-2-3/W (although they are also in 1-2-3 Releases 2.3 and 3.1 and 3.1+). This feature lets you change the size of the printed worksheet to anywhere from 15% of its original size (really, really small) all the way up to 1000% of its original size. Thus, *Compression* is a bit of a misnomer: You use this feature to make your printout bigger, too. (See Fig-ure 10.18.)

Use Automatically Fit to Page to make your entire Print range fit on one page.

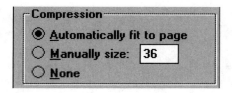

Figure 10.18. 1-2-3/W can reduce a printout to 15% of its original size or enlarge it by as much as 1000%. The biggest Time-saver is to choose Automatically fit to page, which tells 1-2-3/W to figure out how to reduce it to make it fit on one page.

You can enter the factor by which the printed worksheet is to be changed manually, but if you choose Automatically Fit to Page, 1-2-3/W will figure out how much it should reduce the worksheet to fit the *whole* thing on one page. 1-2-3/W displays the percentage it used when you next return to Page Setup.

Margins

There isn't much about margins that isn't obvious. If you specify a margin of 3, 1-2-3/W assumes you mean 3 inches. You can enter *3mm* if you want 3 millimeters, or *3cm* if you want 3 centimeters. Just be careful that your right and left margins combined don't exceed the length or width of the page.

By adjusting the margins, you can get that extra bit of space you need to fit larger spreadsheets on a single page. If you have a worksheet that *almost* fits, maybe you can make the margins a little smaller.

The Fine Art of Orientation

1-2-3/W lets you print in either Landscape or Portrait orientation. If you're printing on an 8½-inch-by-11-inch page and you choose Portrait orientation, the text will run parallel to the 8½-inch side.

The Mona Lisa is taller than it is wide—a portrait.

The typical landscape or seascape painting is wider than it is high. Choose Landscape orientation, and 1-2-3/W will print parallel to the 11-inch side. Landscape orientation is particularly useful if you have a very wide worksheet. In fact, you'll often be able to fit your entire Print range on one or two pages if you flip it on its side (see Figure 10.5).

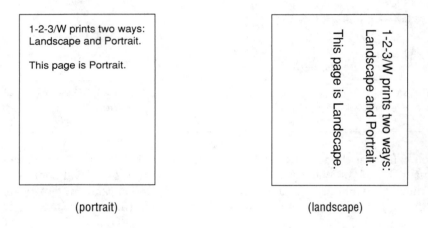

Figure 10.19. The worksheet on the left was printed in Portrait orientation; the one on the right was printed in Landscape orientation.

Options

The two choices offered under the Options section of the File Page Setup dialog box can be explained quickly.

When you choose Show worksheet frame in the Page Setup dialog box, 1-2-3/W prints the column letters and the row numbers, as in Figure 10.20. This is useful if you want to print a "map" of your spreadsheet so that you'll know exactly which cell contains which value, etc.

Printing with 1-2-3 for Windows

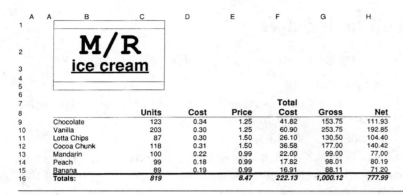

Figure 10.20. When you choose Show worksheet frame in the Page Setup dialog box, 1-2-3/W prints the column letters and row numbers.

If you choose Show grid lines in the Page Setup dialog box, 1-2-3/W outlines each cell in the Print range (see Figure 10.21).

	Units	Cost	Price	Total Cost	Gross	Net
Chocolate	123	0.34	1.25	41.82	153.75	111.93
Vanilla	203	0.30	1.25	60.90	253.75	192.85
Lotta Chips	87	0.30	1.50	26.10	130.50	104.40
Cocoa Chunk	118	0.31	1.50	36.58	177.00	140.42
Mandarin	100	0.22	0.99	22.00	99.00	77.00
Peach	99	0.18	0.99	17.82	98.01	80.19
Banana	89	0.19	0.99	16.91	88.11	71.20
Totals:	819		8.47	222.13	1,000.12	777.99

Figure 10.21. When you choose Show grid lines in the Page Setup dialog box, 1-2-3/W outlines each cell in the Print range, as if you had chosen Border from the Style menu.

Let's Print in 1-2-3/W

The following exercise illustrates the key topics discussed in this chapter.

1. Get the worksheet ready.

   Save your file(s), and then use the /Worksheet Erase command from the 1-2-3 Classic menu to start from scratch.

2. Create a small range of values.

   Mouse: Select range A1..H20, choose Data Fill, and click OK. Then click the Maximize icon in the upper-right corner so that the worksheet fills the screen.

   Keyboard: Press Alt-D (for Data), then F (for Fill). Then type A1..H20 and press Enter. Press Alt-(Alt-hyphen) to open the document Control menu, and choose Maximize.

3. Change Font 1 to 18-point Helvetica.

   Mouse: Select Style, then choose Font. Choose Replace. Click on Arial (or Helvetica 10) in the Left Font window, and then click on Arial (or Helvetica) and 18 in the Right Font window. Then click OK twice.

   Keyboard: Press Alt-S to choose Style, and then press Alt-F to choose Font. Press Alt-R to choose Replace. Press the DownArrow key to highlight Arial 10 (or Helvetica 10) in the Left Font window, and then press Tab twice to move to the list of Available Fonts. Move the up or down arrow key to select Arial (or Helvetica) and press Tab twice to move to the Point-size box. Type *18* and press Enter. Then press Tab to move to the OK button, and press Enter.

   Your worksheet should now match Figure 10.22. Note how the rows have expanded to accommodate the new, larger font.

	A	B	C	D	E	F	G	H
1	0	20	40	60	80	100	120	140
2	1	21	41	61	81	101	121	141
3	2	22	42	62	82	102	122	142
4	3	23	43	63	83	103	123	143
5	4	24	44	64	84	104	124	144
6	5	25	45	65	85	105	125	145
7	6	26	46	66	86	106	126	146
8	7	27	47	67	87	107	127	147
9	8	28	48	68	88	108	128	148
10	9	29	49	69	89	109	129	149
11	10	30	50	70	90	110	130	150

Figure 10.22. The worksheet's columns and rows are bigger, now that Font 1 is 18-point Helvetica.

4. Preview the range.

   Mouse: Click and drag to select range A1..H20, and then click on the Print Preview icon (the fourth from the left).

   Keyboard: Press Home to move the cell pointer to cell A1. To select the range to be printed, press ABS (F4) to anchor the range, and press the End key followed by the DownArrow key and press Enter. Then press the End key followed by the RightArrow key. Press Alt-F to choose File, then press V to choose Preview. Press the Tab key to move to the OK button, and press Enter.

   The screen should look like Figure 10.23. The Print range is small, so it all fits on one page.

   Press Escape to return to Ready mode.

5. Print the range.

   Since everything checked out on the Preview, we'll print the range.

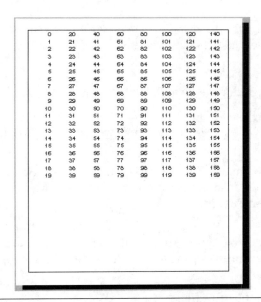

Figure 10.23. Even with 20 rows of 18-point type, the Print range fits on one page.

Mouse: Click on the Print icon, the third from the left. A dialog box will appear briefly (Figure 10.26). Then the printer should produce a hard copy of range A1..H20.

Keyboard: Press Alt-F to choose File, then press P to choose Print. Press the Tab key to move to the OK button, and press Enter. A dialog box will appear briefly (Figure 10.24) giving you the option of canceling the printout. Then the printer should produce a hard copy of range A1..H20.

Figure 10.24. The Cancel Print dialog box allows you to interrupt your printing.

We'll use the Preview option for the rest of this exercise, but if you want to print any of the examples, just choose Print instead of Preview.

6. Add a header.

Let's spruce up the top of each page by adding a Header.

Mouse: Choose File, then Page Setup. Type *This is my First Header* in the Header box and click OK. Now click the Preview icon to see how it looks.

Keyboard: Press Alt-F to choose File, then G to choose Page Setup. Type *This is my First Header* in the Header box and press Enter OK. Then press Alt-F to choose File, press V to choose Preview, and press Enter.

Your screen should look like Figure 10.26. The numbers in range A1..H20 show up in the page preview, and the header appears at the top of the page, in Font 1.

7. Add another worksheet to the Print range.

Let's complicate the situation by adding another worksheet and including part of it in our Print range.

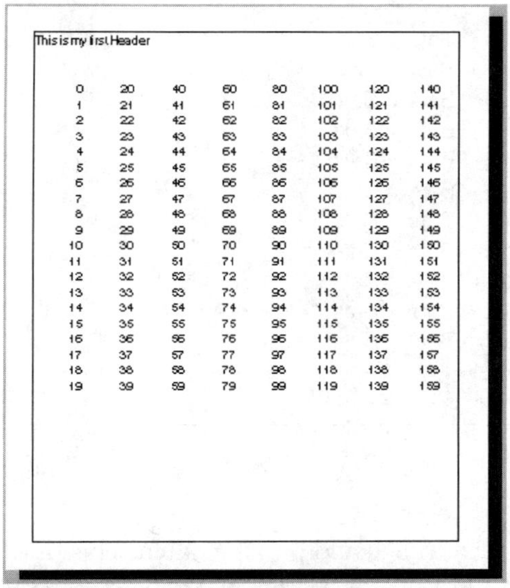

This is my first Header

0	20	40	60	80	100	120	140
1	21	41	61	81	101	121	141
2	22	42	62	82	102	122	142
3	23	43	63	83	103	123	143
4	24	44	64	84	104	124	144
5	25	45	65	85	105	125	145
6	26	46	66	86	106	126	146
7	27	47	67	87	107	127	147
8	28	48	68	88	108	128	148
9	29	49	69	89	109	129	149
10	30	50	70	90	110	130	150
11	31	51	71	91	111	131	151
12	32	52	72	92	112	132	152
13	33	53	73	93	113	133	153
14	34	54	74	94	114	134	154
15	35	55	75	95	115	135	155
16	36	56	76	96	116	136	156
17	37	57	77	97	117	137	157
18	38	58	78	98	118	138	158
19	39	59	79	99	119	139	159

Figure 10.26. The header appears at the top of each page, even if your Print range is only one page long.

Mouse: Choose Worksheet, then Insert. Click the Sheet button, and click OK you should now be in Sheet B. Then press Home to move to cell A1. Type *Bats* and press Enter. Copy the label in cell A1 to the Clipboard by choosing Edit, then Copy. Click and drag to highlight range A1..H20, and choose Edit, then Paste to fill the range with the word *Bats*.

Keyboard: Press Alt-K to choose Worksheet, then press I to choose Insert. Press the RightArrow key to choose Sheet, and then press Enter. Now press Home to move to cell A1, type *Bats*, and press Enter. Copy the label in cell A1 to the Clipboard by pressing Control-Insert. Press ABS (F4), then press the End key followed by the DownArrow key. Press the End key followed by the RightArrow key to highlight range A1..H20 and press Enter. Press Shift-Insert to paste the contents of the Clipboard to the highlighted range.

The word *Bats* should appear in range A1..H20 of sheet B, as in Figure 10.27.

	A	B	C	D	E	F	G	H
1	Bats	Bats	Bats	Bats	Bats	Bats	Bats	Bats
2	Bats	Bats	Bats	Bats	Bats	Bats	Bats	Bats
3	Bats	Bats	Bats	Bats	Bats	Bats	Bats	Bats
4	Bats	Bats	Bats	Bats	Bats	Bats	Bats	Bats
5	Bats	Bats	Bats	Bats	Bats	Bats	Bats	Bats
6	Bats	Bats	Bats	Bats	Bats	Bats	Bats	Bats
7	Bats	Bats	Bats	Bats	Bats	Bats	Bats	Bats
8	Bats	Bats	Bats	Bats	Bats	Bats	Bats	Bats
9	Bats	Bats	Bats	Bats	Bats	Bats	Bats	Bats
10	Bats	Bats	Bats	Bats	Bats	Bats	Bats	Bats
11	Bats	Bats	Bats	Bats	Bats	Bats	Bats	Bats

Figure 10.27. Range A1..H20 in sheet B contains some labels.

8. Add the cells to the Print range.

   Let's add the new cells to the Print range and preview them. This time, we'll have to use the menu to Print Preview. If we use the Print Preview icon, we won't be able to add the new cells to the Print range.

   Mouse: Choose File, then Preview. Type *A:A1..B:H20* to include the new sheet in the Print range, and click OK.

   Keyboard: Press Alt-F to choose File, and then press V to choose Preview. Type *A:A1..B:H20* to include the new sheet in the Print range, and then choose OK.

   Press Enter after the first page has been displayed to see the second page.

   Notice that 1-2-3/W prints the cells from sheet B immediately underneath those from sheet A (see Figure 10.28). And since the Print range is much larger, it takes up two pages with the header at the top of both pages.

9. Add a page break.

   Let's add a manual page break at the bottom of the Print range in sheet A so that the cells from sheet B will print on page 2 instead of at the bottom of page 1.

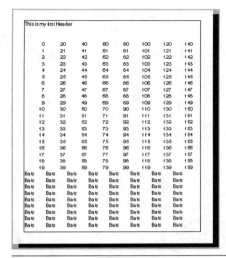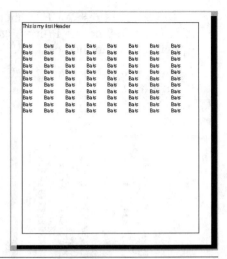

Figure 10.28. If your Print range includes ranges on different worksheets, 1-2-3/W prints the range from the second worksheet immediately underneath the range from the first. The Print range now takes two pages. Notice that the header is printed at the top of both pages.

Mouse: Press Ctrl-PageDown to return to sheet A, and then press Home to move to cell A1. Press End, then press DownArrow three times to move to cell A23. Insert the page break by choosing Worksheet, then PageBreak. Horizontal is the default, so click OK.

Keyboard: Press Ctrl-PageDown to return to sheet A, and then press Home to move to cell A1. Press End, then press DownArrow twice to move to cell A22. Insert the page break by pressing Alt-K to choose Worksheet, and then P to choose Page Break. Horizontal is the default, so choose OK.

10. Reset the Print range.

    For this new page break to take effect, it must become part of the Print range.

    Let's reset the Print range to include the new row, and Preview the new range.

    Mouse: Choose Preview from the File menu. Redefine the Print range by typing A:A1..B:H22 in the Preview dialog and then click OK.

Keyboard: Press Alt-F to choose File, and then type V to choose Preview. Re-define the Print range by typing A:A1..B:H23 in the Preview dialog box and then click OK.

Press a key to see the second page. Your preview pages should look like Figure 10.29.

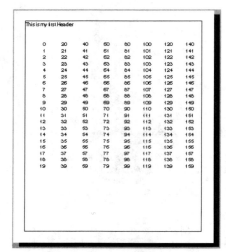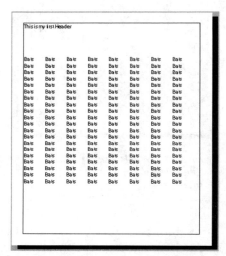

Figure 10.29. Because of the manual page break at the bottom of the range on sheet A, 1-2-3/W prints only the first range on page 1, and it prints the range from sheet B on a new page.

11. Change the header and add a footer.

    Let's make the header a little more sophisticated, and let's add a footer so that the page number prints at the bottom of each page.

    Mouse: Choose File, then Page Setup. Type |*Printing Exercise*|@ in the Header box, type ||Page # in the Footer box, and click OK.

    Keyboard: Press Alt-F to choose File, then press G to choose Page Setup. Type |*Printing Exercise*|@ in the header box, type ||*Page* # in the Footer box, and press Enter.

    Now click the Preview icon to preview the range.

Your screen should look like Figure 10.31. Look at that header and footer! 1-2-3 substituted today's date for the @ and the page number for the #. Also note how the split vertical bars aligned the text.

12. Remove page breaks.

    Let's print the entire Print range on our page. Before we can do that, though, we have to remove the manual page break in cell A21.

    Mouse: Click on cell A21, then choose Worksheet. Choose Page Break, and then click the Clear button. Now click the OK button.

    Keyboard: Press Alt-K to choose Worksheet, then press P to choose Page Break. Press C to choose Clear, and press Enter.

    Your screen should now look like Figure 10.30. The dashed line that represented the page break is now gone.

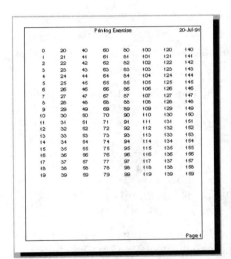
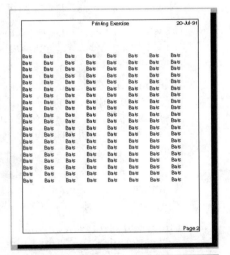

Figure 10.30. 1-2-3/W substitutes today's date for the @ in the header, and automatically changes the page number in the footer when you use the # sign.

	A	B	C	D	E	F	G	H
16	15	35	55	75	95	115	135	155
17	16	36	56	76	96	116	136	156
18	17	37	57	77	97	117	137	157
19	18	38	58	78	98	118	138	158
20	19	39	59	79	99	119	139	159
21								
22								
23								
24								
25								

Figure 10.31. The worksheet no longer includes a manual page break.

13. Compress the Print range.

    Now you can make 1-2-3/W fit the entire Print range on one page.

    Mouse: Choose File, then choose Preview. Choose Page Setup. Choose Automatically Fit to Page, and then click OK. Click OK again to preview the range.

    Keyboard: Press Alt-F to choose File, then press V to choose Preview. Press G to choose Page Setup. Press the Tab key eight times to move to the Compression group of options, press A to choose Automatically Fit to Page, and press Enter. Press Tab, then press Enter to preview the range.

    Your preview should look like Figure 10.32. 1-2-3/W has fit the entire Print range on one page. You should probably get rid of the Footer; you don't need a page number if there's only one page.

To print a real spreadsheet, you'll follow the same steps we used in this exercise. You'll determine the Print range, and you'll select Preview. You'll decide you need a header, and you'll select Preview again. Maybe you'll decide you need borders. You'll keep refining your printout, selecting Preview each time to see the results. When you arrive at a perfect mix of the Page Setup options, you'll choose Print instead of Preview.

Printing with 1-2-3 for Windows

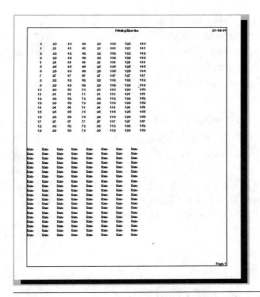

Figure 10.32. No matter how big your fonts, margins, columns, etc., 1-2-3/W will fit the entire Print range on one Page if you choose Automatically Fit to Page from the Page Setup dialog box.

Questions and Answers

Question: How can I control the order in which Windows processes pending printouts? And how can I cancel a printout once 1-2-3/W has finished its part of the printing procedure.

Answer: Switch to Window's Print Manager Utility which should already be running as a minimized application—as long as there are still print jobs left to finish. For more on using Print Manager, see the Windows User Guide.

Question: When I print, both the the computer and the printer seem to slow down. Why?

Answer: Some printers use fonts that are resident in memory or on a font cartridge. This speeds up printing because these fonts don't need to be downloaded from the computer. If you have installed Adobe Type Manager fonts with 1-2-3/W, you may not be taking advantage of these resident fonts. Run the ATM Control Panel accessory from the Accessories group (see the ATM documentation if you have trouble locating the ATM Control Panel icon) and select Use Pre-built or Resident Bitmap Fonts. This may increase performance by reducing the amount of printer memory required. You do not have to restart Windows after turning this option on or off.

Also, if you are using Adobe Type Manager fonts, you may not have allocated enough memory for the font cache—memory that's used to keep font information quickly accessible to Windows and to your printer. Try increasing the font cache size on the ATM control panel to reduce the printer's access to the disk. Of course, as you increase the font cache size, you decrease the amount of RAM available for 1-2-3/W and other Windows applications. Try a few different settings to see how performance is affected.

Question: Why don't the Adobe Type Manager fonts appear on my Font menu?

Answer: Either the fonts were installed incorrectly or the currently selected printer driver does not know that the ATM fonts were installed. Try reselecting your printer from the 1-2-3/W Printer Setup dialog box. If this doesn't work, add the fonts again using the ATM control panel.

Question: My fonts and other embellishments are not printing. My printer produces just a plain spreadsheet. What did I do wrong?

Answer: You may have used the 1-2-3 Classic /Print command. Use the 1-2-3/W File Print command instead. Also, make sure that you didn't choose Draft in the Printer Setup dialog box.

Question: Why is my worksheet printing with the wrong fonts?

Answer: Check to see that the right font cartridge is plugged into your printer. It's also possible that the fonts displayed on the screen are not available on your printer. Try a different font to see if the printer can match it more closely.

If you are using a PostScript printer and you're printing with fonts that aren't built into your printer, you may need to edit the WIN.INI file in the Windows directory to identify the fonts that need to be downloaded to the printer. These are identified as .PFB and .PFM files. See the Adobe Type Manager documentation for details.

Question: Why won't anything come out of the printer when I click the icon or choose Print from the menu?

Answer: Also, make sure that the printer is assigned to the proper printer port: Switch to the Windows Control Panel utility, choose Printers, and pick the correct port.

Finally, check the Windows Control Panel Printer dialog box to make sure that your printout is going to the printer and not to a file.

Question: Why does my Print range print on more than one page, even when I choose Automatically Fit to Page?

Answer: There may be a manual page break in your worksheet. You can hunt around to find it, or you can highlight the entire Print range and select Page Break Clear from the Worksheet menu.

Question: Why does my Print range suddenly grow or shrink?

Answer: Be sure you have selected the right Print range and that it was not changed when you moved some material around.

Question: Why did my page print sideways?

Answer: You may have inadvertently chosen Landscape from the Page Setup dialog box or the Printer Setup Setup dialog box.

Question: Why did the top row and the first column of my worksheet print twice?

Answer: You included the border in the Print range. Respecify the Print range to omit the border.

Question: How do I print more than one copy of my worksheet?

Answer: The easiest way is to use the WYSIWYG :Print command and choose Settings, then Copies. (You can also choose Printer Setup from the File menu.)

Question: Why does the printer keep printing garbage that doesn't look anything like my Print range?

Answer: You have probably selected the wrong printer. Choose Printer Setup from the File menu and make sure you have chosen the correct printer (and corresponding printer port).

Question: Can I convert my worksheet to a plain text (ASCII) file so that I can easily import it into another program?

Answer: If you want to export part of a 1-2-3/W worksheet into another Windows application (like Microsoft Word or Ami Pro), the easiest way to use Edit Copy and Edit Paste. If you are sure you need to convert it to an ASCII file, use the Classic /Print File command.

Part IV
Tapping the Full Power of 1-2-3/W

11

Creating Graphs with a Message

Out of all the people using Lotus 1-2-3 to crunch numbers, surprising number do not take advantage of the high impact of graphs. Now with the full-featured graphical user interface of 1-2-3/W it is easier than ever to create presentation-quality graphical representations of your worksheet data.

Picture This

You have a marketing idea that could revolutionize your company in the baseball bat industry. No one has ever done it that way before. You're breaking new ground. You know it's a great idea. You know that profits will soar. But you've got to convince every vice president in the company that your idea is worthwhile. Time is limited. You're allowed five minutes to make your presentation in the monthly management meeting. You figure that you must capture their attention within the first minute and persuade them that your idea is worth considering.

How do you do it? Do you inundate them with numbers and rattle on about the significance of each piece of data? Do you spend your time telling funny stories? Or do you sketch graphs on the board, or do you employ a graphic artist to help you make your point?

In this chapter you will learn:

- *Basics of effective graphing.*
- *Strengths of various graph types.*
- *How to match the graph with your message.*
- *How minor adjustments can change the whole message.*

Are You a Graphic Artist?

You don't need to hire a graphic artist to become one yourself to present your ideas quickly and memorably in graph form. With just a few clicks and drags of the mouse across your worksheet data, you can display market share as slices of a pie, profit and loss as rising and dropping lines, contribution margin as a three- dimensional bar chart. But we're not going to stop there.

We are going to analyze why one graph may be more effective when making a particular point and another graph for another point. We are also going to look at ways to bring attention to certain areas of the graph for emphasis and even how to create misleading graphs. Create misleading graphs? Well, just so we can avoid using the techniques, of course.

Analytical Versus Presentation Graphs

Until recently there was a great distinction between analytical (or "business") graphs and presentation-quality graphs. The software packages were separate. One for analyzing, one for presenting conclusions. Analytical graphs would show you the results in standard unadorned line, bar, and pie charts. You could use them to do what-if analysis but then you had to redo them in another program that produced finer output.

Graphs have changed, most remarkably starting with 1-2-3 Release 3.1 with WYSIWYG and then 1-2-3 Release 2.3 with an increase in the use of the graphical user interface (GUI). And now, 1-2-3/W represents a significant development from analytical graphs to presentation-quality graphs and has made high-quality graphics even easier for everyday use. Now even analytical graphs are suitable for presentations. More quality. More flexibility. More options. More impact.

1-2-3/W Graphs are the Best of All Worlds

1-2-3 for Windows retains all the analytical capabilities that have made it the most popular analytical graphics software in the world. Now with the incorporation of spreadsheet-publishing capabilities, it has improved as an analytical tool and it has become a superior presentation-graphics tool.

Thinking Tool

You can now more easily than ever add graphs to your suite of analytical tools. The 1-2-3/W worksheet gives you the numbers. And graphs can show trends and relationships that may otherwise be overlooked.

Effective use of graphs necessitates a clear understanding of the strengths and weaknesses of each major graph type. You may like the looks of a pie graph, but does it convey the message effectively? Would a bar graph be more appropriate for the specific data set?

Through examples, we will see which graph is most effective in showing the information you need.

Negotiating Tool

Negotiation skills are critical in a fast-paced market. Effective negotiation requires information. Combine your negotiation skills with 1-2-3/W's what-if analysis capabilities. You'll get instantaneous feedback from 1-2-3/W worksheets and graphs for a winning combination.

Persuasive Tool

A well conceived graph offers a quick summary of detailed data and creates a favorable, finished impression to management, co-workers, clients, or whomever the audience might be.

As you read this chapter and study the examples within, you will learn many tricks to turn an otherwise inferior graph into a high-powered statement.

You'll learn how to of decide when a graph is appropriate, which graph type to use to get your point across, and how to customize an otherwise ordinary graph.

Why are 1-2-3/W Graphs Such Effective Analytical Tools?

We should think of 1-2-3 for Windows graphs as an ever changing, dynamic representation of our organization, our ideas, and our plans. 1-2-3/W graphs are fluid. They are made up of a collection of settings describing characteristics of the graph, including pointers to specific data in the worksheet. When the worksheet changes, the graph responds by changing the size of the wedges of the pie, the angle of the lines, or the height of the bars, for example.

This is good for what-if graphing. What if we add another sales person? What if that sales person sells 5,000 units per month? What will that do to our profits? What will that do to our market share? Our marginal costs? We can see it all on the screen. All at the same time.

Graph are Simply Settings

Graph settings are stored in the computer's internal memory while you are working with 1-2-3/W graphs. Each graph has a collection of settings describing the graph. The settings tell 1-2-3 what type of graph it is (pie, line, bar, etc.); what ranges of the worksheet are represented by what wedge of the pie, line, or bar; what are the titles, footnotes, data labels, and legends on the graph; how are the X and Y axes scaled and formatted; are there borders and grids, colors, or hatch patterns; what fonts and line styles are used? You can change these initial settings by using the Chart cascading menu when first creating a graph with Graph New or editing an existing graph with Graph View. These settings for the graph are saved in the worksheet file when you select File Save.

In the early versions of 1-2-3, you were limited to seeing only one graph on the screen at a time. You could see the graph on the screen or the worksheet data on the screen. Never both at the same time. Now we have *live* in-sheet graphics: The graphic and the worksheet share the same screen. We can even have several live in-sheet graphics on the screen at the same time, showing the impact of a change in the worksheet from several perspectives. Figure 11.1 shows two live in-sheet graphics (one bar and one pie chart) comparing sales performance of bats over a three-month period. 1-2-3's internal graph settings link the graphic with the data ranges in the worksheet. When you change the data, as on the right half of the figure, the graphic reflects your change.

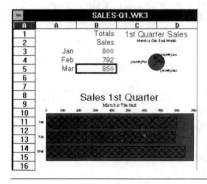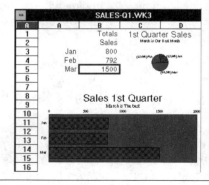

Figure 11.1. The two live in-sheet graphs are updated immediately after the sales data is changed, as shown on the right.

What Happened to the F10 Graph Key?

In early versions of 1-2-3, only one collection of graph settings could be specified at once. The graph associated with those current settings was called the current graph. The F10 key would show the current graph in full screen display. To see another graph, you would have to make another one current by either creating a new graph or recalling an existing named graph with the /Graph Name Use menu. You could have several named graphs, but only one could be current at a time.

Now in 1-2-3/W, you are not limited to seeing only one graph. For example, you can load several graphs into the graph editor in separate windows with Graph View and then select Window Tile or Window Cascade menus. Or you can place several graphics into the worksheet at the same time by selecting the Graph Add-to-sheet menu. You are not limited to only one active graph at a time.

1-2-3 for Windows retains most of the Classic methods of working with current graphs for compatibility with older versions of 1-2-3. However, in 1-2-3/W, the F10 key accesses the GUI menu for keyboard operation (in case you don't have a mouse attached to your computer).

How Are Your Graphs Stored in the Worksheet and Format Files?

Until a graph is added to a specific range in the worksheet using either the Graph Add-to-sheet menu or :Graph Add, it is stored only as settings in the worksheet file. The graphic image, location, and any annotation added to it is stored in a format file associated with the worksheet. Any annotations you make such as text, lines, arrows, polygons, rectangles, ellipses, freehand drawings, and coloration will also be stored in the format file. (Annotations will be covered in the next chapter.) So keep the files together. Whenever you copy your worksheet from one computer to another, copy the format file. The format file contains all those features that dress up the worksheet display.

Six Critical Points to High-Impact Graphing

You can quickly learn how to create graphs just by toying with 1-2-3/W's SmartIcons. But the real art in graphing is to create graphs that make an instant impression—that tell you clearly whether business is good, bad, or stable —and that attract and lead the viewer's attention to specific details.

There are 6 critical points to creating a high-impact graph. Without them your graph will lack sizzle.

Understand Your Data This may sound obvious. The best graphs are created by those who understand the data and who have the tools and artistic skills to communicate those numbers graphically.

Clarify Your Message You must be clear about the message you wish to convey with the graph. You can't expect a graph to rescue a poorly thought out message.

Visualize Your Graph You'll have an easier time creating effective graphs if you have a mental picture of the finished product. What is the X data range? What do you want along the X axis of the graph?

What are the A-F data ranges? What data are you going to plot to correspond with each point along the X axis? You can plot up to 6 sets of data (A, B, C, D, E, and F). But would your message get lost if too many lines or bars are used in the graph?

Are there titles, notes, legends, or other data to link to the worksheet? Do you want them to automatically change when you modifying worksheet entries, or do you want them to remain static? How can they aid in getting your message across?

Know What You Want to Emphasize Should the worksheet data be sorted before graphing? Should you put the most salient data first to help control the viewer's attention?

What about changing the Y-scaling factor to emphasize change or perhaps stability? If you know your data and the significance of a change in your organization, then you can make that determination.

Should some data be grouped into an "other" category to cause the viewer to focus on the three or four most important factors, thereby reducing clutter and confusion?

Know What Graph Type is Most Appropriate What is the most appropriate graph to communicate your message? Each type of graph has its strengths and weaknesses. A line graph can't replace a pie chart. Even within each type, there are variations that affect the impact. You can't just pick any graph and get away with it. Your message may not get communicated. Or worse, the wrong message could be given.

Where and How Will You be Adding the Graph to the Worksheet
Once a graph is created, you can add it to the worksheet by using Graph Add-to-sheet. What range size and shape should you choose for the graph?

What is the effect of a narrow graph? A short wide graph? The range that you allot to a graphic chart affects its appearance and message considerably.

Creating and Managing Graphs

You have your worksheet, you know what data needs to be graphed, and you know what message you want to convey. Let's create a graph and at the same time look at the anatomy of a graph.

Creating Your First Graph

You have entered the sales performance analysis worksheet shown in Figure 11.2 comparing sales of wooden baseball bats to sales of metal baseball bats. Now you want to see how sales of the two bat types have changed over the last six months. You decide to use a line graph because the lines will connect the points plotted on the graph and give a clear impression of change over time. The graph could also uncover some trend that would otherwise not be seen when looking at the worksheet.

What Are Graph Data Ranges?

There are six data ranges that can be graphed (A, B, C, D, E, and F) plus data range X. Graph data ranges are ranges in the worksheet containing values or labels represented in the graph as bars, lines, or wedges of a pie chart. The X data range is used for the labels on the *x* axis of most graphs. On pie charts the X data range provides the labels for each wedge of the pie. On an XY chart, the X data range is used to calculate the *x* axis scale. When displaying a graph, 1-2-3 matches corresponding values or labels from each range based upon their relative positions in the range. For instance, the first value or label in range X corresponds with the first value in range A and the first in range B and so on.

Notice that in Figure 11.2, the X data range includes the names of the months. This data will be placed along the *x* axis (horizontal axis) of the graph. The two other data ranges (A and B) will be plotted as lines on the graph above the *x* axis. Each point in data range A and B will be plotted above the corresponding point on the *x* axis. For example, the *330* at the top of data range A will be plotted over *Jan*, the *332* will be over *Feb*, and so on. This graph will contain two lines because two data ranges will be selected (A and B). A maximum of six lines (A-F) can be included in a 1-2-3/W graph.

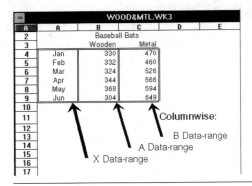

Figure 11.2. Sales performance analysis worksheet showing the bats to be graphed.

Try It: Create a Line Graph

In just two steps you can create a line graph representing the data in the worksheet shown in Figure 11.2.

1. Preselect (click and drag) the data to be graphed. In Figure 11.2, that is range A4..C9.
2. Click on the graph SmartIcon as shown in Figure 11.3 below

Figure 11.3

Several chnages occur in the 1-2-3/W workspace. A window appears showing a line graph with the months along its x axis. Also the 1-2-3/W menu bar changes to display a set of graph-related menu names and the SmartIcon palette now displays a set of tools for enhancing graphs.

Keep Pace with Lotus Books

Available at your local book or computer store or order by telephone: (800) 624-0023

A Limited Time Special Offer from Lotus Books

Solutions From The Source

Sign up for The Lotus Guide to 1-2-3 for Windows Definitive Supplement

Let author Justin Fielding give you an insider's view of spreadsheet publishing, printing, and Dynamic Data Exchange using 1-2-3 for Windows, and the latest breaking advances and hidden features of the software.

Absolutely free but hurry! Offer limited to first 5000 customers!

☐ Lotus Guide to 1-2-3 for Windows Supplement/Update

☐ Lotus Books Catalog
Yes, please send me a Lotus Books Catalog

Name _____
Address _____
City _____ State _____ Zip _____
Name of Book Purchased _____
Date of Purchase _____

70-52936

MICROSERVICES
200 Old Tappan Road
Old Tappan, NJ 07675

ATT: Carol Youngling

Place First Class
Postage Here
Post Office
Will Not Deliver
Without Postage

Columnwise vs. Rowwise Data

This example took only two steps. That's because the data was organized in a columnwise fashion. Data ranges X, A, and B were vertically arranged. If your data is horizontally arranged, as in Figure 11.4, you must let 1-2-3/W know.

	A	B	C	D	E	F	G	H	I	J
1	Sales first 6 months, 1995							Rowwise:		
2	Baseball Bats									
3			Jan	Feb	Mar	Apr	May	Jun	——— X Data Range	
4	Wooden		330	332	324	344	368	304	——— A Data Range	
5	Metal		470	460	526	566	594	649	——— B Data Range	
6										

Figure 11.4. This is the same data as in Figure 11.2, except that the data ranges are in rows.

Try It: Graph Data in a Row

To graph data that is organized in rows you start the same way as with columns. But you finish by telling 1-2-3/W that your data is rowwise.

1. Preselect (click and drag) the data to be graphed. In Figure 11.4, that is range B3..G5.

2. Click on the graph SmartIcon.

   Notice that the graph does not look right. It has *Jan*, *330*, and *470* on the *x* axis.

3. Tell 1-2-3 that your data is organized in rows: Select Chart Ranges from the Graph Menu Bar. Click Group Range. Click Rowwise, then click OK twice.

You should have a line graph just like the one created when you graphed the data in Figure 11.2.

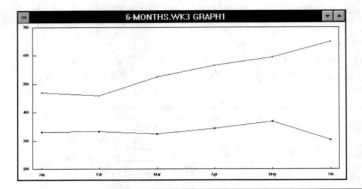

Figure 11.5. Line graph from the bat sales worksheets shown in Figures 11.2 and 11.4. They both produce the same graph, even though the data in the first was columnwise and the data in the second was rowwise.

At this point you should see the line graph in its own window, as shown in Figure 11.5. You can now change the graph type or add standard graph enhancements, such as data labels, headings, and legends, using the Chart menu. Instead of using the menu, you can select the graph type by clicking the desired SmartIcon with the appropriate picture (line, bar, horizontal bar, mixed line and bar, pie, area, HLCO, or three-dimensional versions of those). The best way to select the type of graph is to choose Chart Type.

From the Chart Type dialog box, select the type and orientation. Most graph types have various ways of displaying. So when you select the graph type, you may need to click the example graph type that displays in the top right of the dialog box.

Whenever a graph window is displayed, you're in a *draw layers*, and you can add graphic annotations such as text, lines, arrows, rectangles, polygons, ellipses, and freehand drawings. You can access these tools with SmartIcons or you can use the Draw menu. You will learn more about this in the next chapter.

Placing Your Graphic in the Worksheet

Now let's place the graph we have created in the worksheet. When a graph is placed in the worksheet, the graph is still associated with a range in the worksheet, but the settings that maintain the location of the graphic are stored in the format file. Once you add a graph to the sheet and save your work (File Save, File Save As, or /File Save), all the settings pertaining to the added graph are saved in the format file (the file with the FM3 extension). All worksheet formulas, numbers, and labels are stored in the worksheet file (the file with the WK3 extension).

A graph may be added to any range associated with the worksheet even if the worksheet has data and or other graphs already added. Any graphs or data in cells *behind* the graph will not be visible unless you change the graph to transparent by choosing Graph Style Display Options Transparent. Any labels, numbers, and formulas underneath the graph are not affected by the added graph.

Adding a graph to the worksheet is as simple as selecting the range and identifying the graph you want to add.

Try It: Add a Graph to the Worksheet

Refer to Figure 11.6 to see what the graphs should look like.

1. Close the Graph from the previous exercise by clicking on its Control-menu box and selecting Close.
2. Preselect (click and drag) the area to receive the graph. In Figure 11.6 that is range E2..F10, narrow range.
3. Select Graph Add-to-sheet (or :Graph Add Named).

    Note that if you choose add to sheet without selecting a range, you get the entire graph pasted into the current cell—in absurdly small size for a graph.

4. Make sure the correct graph name is chosen, then select OK.

    The graph shows that sales of the metal baseball bats (top line) are increasing dramatically.

5. Now let's add another copy of the same graphic.
6. Preselect range J2..H7.
7. Select Graph Add-to-sheet.
8. Select the graph, then click OK. Notice that the metal bats are doing well, but not as well as in the first graph.
9. Now let's try it one more time. Preselect range F12..J14, a low, wide range.
10. Select Graph Add-to-sheet.
11. Select the graph, then click OK. Notice that with the same data and same graph, the differently shaped range produces a graph showing that business is fairly stable.

When adding a graphic, specify a single-sheet range. If you specify a three-dimensional range, 1-2-3/W will place the graphic in the first worksheet of the range anyway.

Once you place a graph in the worksheet, its size will change if column widths or row heights are changed, or if rows or columns are added or removed with the Worksheet Delete or Worksheet Insert command.

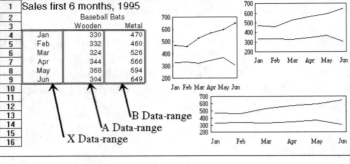

Figure 11.6. Three graphs and three messages, all from the same graph settings. The only difference is the shape of the range they are added to.

A Distorted Impression?

When you add a line graph to a narrow range, fluctuations in the data are emphasized. When you add a line graph to a low, wide range, stability is emphasized. When planning a graph, consider the shape it will take in the worksheet. Always leave enough space and leave the right dimensions.

In Figure 11.6, you can see that placing the graph in ranges of differing shapes creates very different impressions. Which is right? That will depend upon your professional opinion. You will have to decide if the change in sales is a significant factor. If it is, then emphasize it with the narrow range. In a small company a change of a few thousand dollars may be very important and therefore should be emphasized. The same few thousand dollars in a large company would be insignificant; therefore, you may decide that stability should be emphasized and use a low, wide range for the graph.

You can't add a graph to a worksheet with Worksheet Global Protection enabled unless the range to which you want to add it is unprotected with Range Unprotect. The graph can't be removed from a protected range. A graph can't be moved to a protected range.

Let's Add Detail

Now that you have created a graph and placed it you should add descriptive information in the form of titles, subtitles, and notes. 1-2-3/W provides several fill-in-the-blank enhancements that you can add with the Chart Headings command. If used properly, the fill-in-the-blank enhancements will provide fast and effective commentary for many of your graphs.

Titles and Subtitles

All graphs need some form of documentation that indicates the purpose of the graph. To make your graphs informative, place the topic in the first title and messages in the subtitle. Compare the messages conveyed with the two graphs in Figure 11.7. The graph on the left leaves interpretation to the viewer. The one on the right uses the titles clearly to say that metal bats are selling better than before.

Notes and 2nd Notes

Notes are like titles, except that they appear tucked away in a bottom corner of the graph, as in the note "First 6 Months" in Figure 11.7.

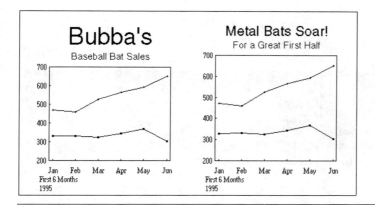

Figure 11.7. A line graph with a title, subtitle, note, and 2nd note.

Whenever possible use range names when filling in the Chart Headings dialog box. This will ensure that if data is moved in the worksheet, the graph settings for titles, subtitles, notes, and 2nd notes will remain correct. The graph titles and notes shown in Figure 11.7 could have been produced with any of the three sets of entries displayed in the Chart Headings dialog boxes in Figure 11.9. Each set of entries produces the same initial result. The dialog box on the top left in Figure 11.9 contains fixed text. It will not change because it is not linked to the worksheet data. The top right dialog box uses cell addresses to tell 1-2-3/W that it should use the contents of these specified cells in the titles and notes. (Figure 11.8 shows the worksheet.)

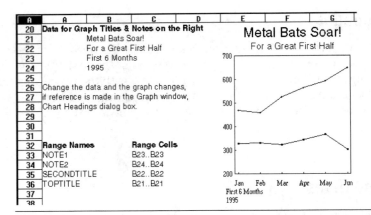

Figure 11.8. A worksheet containing data that can be used in titles and notes on the graph in Figure 11.7. Notice that the cells have been assigned range names. A range name table is included so that you can see where Figure 11.9 gets its range names.

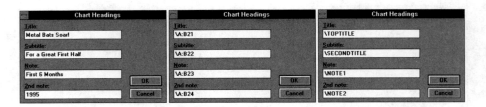

Figure 11.9. There are various ways to enter titles and notes. This figure shows three dialog boxes that would produce the same titles and notes. The left one is not linked to the worksheet. The middle uses cell references to the worksheet (Figure 11.8) so that if the data changes, the titles and notes change. The bottom one also gets its data from the worksheet by using range names.

X Axis and Y Axis Titles

x-axis and *y*-axis titles are descriptive text for the graph axes, as shown with the labels "Expected Demand" and "Months" in Figure 11.10. They are entered using the graph editor's Chart Axis Options dialog box. Just as with the titles and notes, you can use named cells or cell addresses to refer to in-sheet data for *x*-and *y*-axis titles, thereby ensuring that they will reflect any changes in the worksheet. However, *x*- and *y*-axis titles do not tend to change often so simply entering the desired text is appropriate.

To magnify text, select the Graph Style Font dialog box or the Classic command :Graph Edit Other Font-magnification.

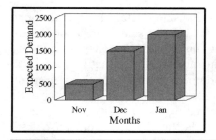

Figure 11.10. Bar graph with *x*-axis and *y*-axis titles added using the graph editor's, Chart Axis Options box.

Data Labels

Data labels describe the data or numeric points on the *x* axis. They are applied with the graph editor's Chart Data Labels command. Just as with the titles and notes, you may use cell addresses or range names for entries. In Figure 11.11 the use of the single data label forces the viewer's attention to a specific month in the graph.

You can rotate the graph clockwise by 90 degrees using the Chart Type orientation or /Graph Type Features commands. Normally the x axis is the horizontal line, and the y axis is the vertical line.

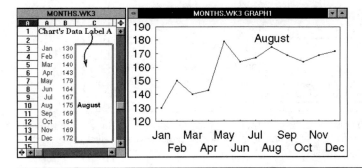

Figure 11.11. This graph uses only one data label. Notice how it makes you look for the month of August.

Scale Indicator

The scale indicator specifies the order of magnitude (hundreds, thousands, millions) of the y-axis scale. 1-2-3 automatically scales the graph based on the data ranges you are graphing.

You can override the y-axis scaling on all graphs but pie charts. On XY graphs you can also control the x-axis scaling. Use Chart Axis X or Chart Axis Y to change to manual scaling and select lower and upper limits. In general, if the difference between the two limits is small, the lines or bars will magnify any change.

The line graphs in Figure 11.12 both use the same data. The X data range contains the months. The A data range contains the sales corresponding to those months. Both show change over time, but the first emphasizes stability while the second creates an impression of instability. Notice that in the second graph, the difference between the lower and upper limits on the y axis is small.

The two graphs create very different impressions. In one, sales appear to be constant. In the other, sales seem to be fluctuating dramatically.

You must decide how to scale the graph. Is the change significant? If so, emphasize it. If not, then minimize it. The y-axis scaling depends on the importance of the change. For example a variation in sales of 200 baseball bats would be insignificant to a large company with many products. The same variation in a small company may mean the difference between making money and losing money. The intention is not to trick your audience. It is to help them understand the meaning of the change in the graph without additional explanation. If you need to be there to explain your graphs, then you are doing them wrong.

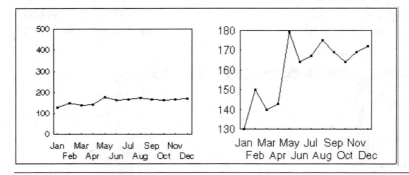

Figure 11.12. These two graphs contain the same data but show very different messages. The y-axis scaling in the second one has been changed from Automatic to Manual, and its lower and upper limits are numerically closer together.

Grid Lines

Grid lines are horizontal and/or vertical lines that cross the graph. You tell 1-2-3/W to display grid lines with the Chart Borders/Grids command. The number of grid lines displayed depends on the x-axis or y-axis scaling. Notice that the horizontal grid lines in Figure 11.13 help to show the value of each point on the line graph.

Grid lines may clutter the graph, making it unattractive and difficult to see the lines and any annotation that you have added. Use grid lines sparingly. Use very rarely on printed output for a presentation.

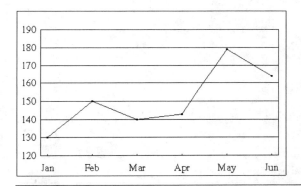

Figure 11.13. The horizontal grid lines in this graph help the readers see where the points on the line graph are in relationship to the *y* axis.

Each Graph Type Conveys a Different Message

Before you can decide which graph type to use, you must know what you want to convey. What is your message? What specific point do you want to make? What do you want to emphasize about your data?

Line Graphs

Line graphs are most commonly used to show changes in data over time, such as the increase or decrease in profits or sales over several months or years; production changes over a period of time; or changes in temperature or rainfall. Line graphs emphasize movement, and the angles of the lines indicate the speed of change.

A basic line graph represents each value with a point above the x axis. The X data range represents what will display along the x axis of the graph. Data ranges A through F are used for each set of data you want represented as a line on the graph. 1-2-3/W automatically places a numerical scale along the y axis.

Consider the worksheet in Figure 11.14, which shows sales of baseball bats for April, May, and June. The line graph is used because it connects the three months. No other graph type makes change so visible.

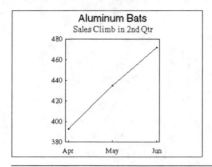

Figure 11.14. Baseball bat sales for the second quarter of the year.

As a general rule horizontal line graphs are confusing and should be avoided. If you wish to rotate your graph clockwise 90 degrees, a horizontal bar graph is generally more effective at conveying the message.

Lines in a line graph are not very thick. By using a three-dimensional line graph you can improve the appearance and the readability of the graph.

A line chart that contains all six data ranges (A-F) can look like a tangled mess (see Figure 11.15). Figure 11.15 shows the sales for your company and four of your company's competitors. You want to compare performance of your company to all the rest, so you decide to use a line graph; however, the same data is much better presented as a series of line graphs, as in Figure 11.16—where the message can be more easily interpreted.

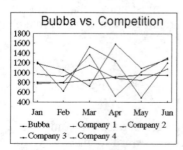

Figure 11.15. A line graph of the sales for your company and its four closest competitors is confusing and conveys no clear message.

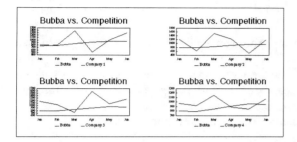

Figure 11.16. A group of line graphs, each comparing your company with a different competitor, is easier to understand than a single line graph with five line. Each competitor's data is in data range A.

Avoid using a line graph for more than three sets of data.

Area Graphs

An area graph is a variation on a line graph. Unlike a line graph where each line is plotted independently, the lines in an area graph are cumulative—the second data series is stacked above thef first data series, and so on. Area graphs are useful when each data range represents part of a total value; for example, you can expense items. The top line of the graph indicated the total expenses. The area between each pair of lines in an area chart is filled with either a shaded, colored, or hatched pattern.

A three-dimensional line graph isn't necessarily more informative, but it can be more attractive and more interesting. If you can get your audience to look at your graph, you have a better chance of getting your message across.

The graph in Figure 11.15 can be changed into an area graph to show total sales for each month for all companies combined (See Figure 11.17). It can be used to show how the industry as a whole is doing in your geographic area.

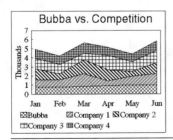

Figure 11.17. This stacked area graph shows sales of all companies. Notice that your company is placed next to the x axis so that you can more easily read your sales. All other companies figures are measured from a slanted line.

When creating area graphs, place the most important line at the bottom, since it is the only line that is measured against a straight line.

Bar Graphs

Bar graphs are used to emphasize differences between data items, often at a fixed point in time.

A basic bar graph represents each value with a vertical bar with varying heights above the horizontal x axis. Just as with line graphs, the X data range is for the x axis and ranges A through F are each represented with a bar. 1-2-3/W automatically places a numerical scale along the vertical y axis.

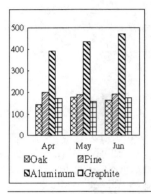

Figure 11.18. A bar graph of the baseball bats sold over three months.

Figure 11.18 shows Bubba's Bat Corporation sales by bat type for three months. It is easy to see which bat sold most in any month. But how did your company as a *whole* do each month? What are the total baseball bat sales for April, for example? Figure 11.19 uses a stacked bar graph to add all sales for each month in one larger bar.

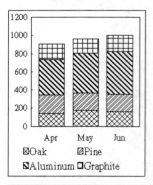

Figure 11.19. Stacked bar graph of baseball bats sold for three months.

A standard bar graph is a variation on a bar chart. Like the area chart, the stacked bar chart shows cumulative values of two or more data ranges. Each segment with in stacked bar represents a particular value, and the overall height of the bar represents the sum of the values. For example, a stacked bar could show you the mix of products sold in different divisions. Each region total sales would be represented by one bar and the colored, shaded, or hatched segments within each bar represent that region's sales for a particular product.

Horizontal Bar Graph

A horizontal bar graph has a horizontal y axis and a vertical x axis on the left side of the graph. The axes are rotated clockwise 90 degrees.

Sorting the data before creating a horizontal bar graph can dramatically improve its value in communicating the intended message. For instance, you could show the range of sales for each type of baseball bat, from highest to lowest. Figure 11.20 shows the sales of baseball bats unsorted and sorted. Figure 11.21 shows the graphs from the unsorted and sorted data.

	A	B	C	D	E
1	Unsorted data:				
2		Oak	Pine	Aluminum	Graphite
3	Apr	143	201	393	173
4	May	179	189	435	159
5	Jun	164	192	472	177
6	Total:	486	582	1300	509
7					
8					
9	Sorted by number of bats sold:				
10		Aluminum	Pine	Graphite	Oak
11	Apr	393	201	173	143
12	May	435	189	159	179
13	Jun	472	192	177	164
14	Total:	1300	582	509	486

Figure 11.20. Baseball bat sales, unsorted and sorted.

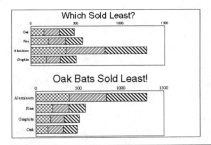

Figure 11.21. Baseball bat sales, unsorted and sorted.

Mixed Bar and Line Graph

A mixed bar and line graph includes both lines and bars. A mixed graph can include up to three lines and three sets of bars. The bars are data ranges A, B, and C. The lines are data ranges D, E, and F.

From the data in Figure 11.22 you may want to show *Expected Demand* as a line connecting estimates for each month, and you may want to show *Must Produce* as a bar for each month on the same graph. You can show both with a mixed bar and line graph by selecting data range A for *Must Produce* and data range D for *Expected Demand*. Notice how easy it is to distinguish the two sets of data in the graph.

	A	B	C	D
1		Nov	Dec	Jan
2	Expected Demand	500	1,500	2,000
3	10% Ending Safety Stock	150	200	100
4	TOTAL NEEDS	650	1,700	2,100
5				
6	10% Begining Safety Stock	50	150	200
7	MUST PRODUCE	600	1,550	1,900

Figure 11.22. This worksheet shows the marketing department's expected demand (data range D) and the manufacturing department's production schedule to meet the demand (data range A).

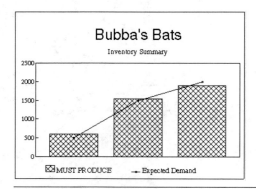

Figure 11.18. This mixed bar and line graph depicts the worksheet in Figure 11.17. Two separate departments can use the same graph. The manufacturing department uses the graph to plan production according to the marketing department's projections.

XY Graphs

XY graphs show relationships between two sets of data. An XY graph looks much like a line graph except that there is a numerical scale along the horizontal x axis as well as the vertical y axis. XY graphs must have numerical values in the X data range.

1-2-3/W pairs each value from the X data range with corresponding values from ranges A through F. The values in ranges A through F are plotted on the y axis. The data points in each line are identified by a different symbol.

Figure 11.19 shows a worksheet with gas mileage results for your delivery vehicles in 24-hour increments. Figure 11.25 clearly shows that your company's fuel efficiency would be maximized if each truck drove at about 45 to 50 miles per hour.

MPH	Mileage Car 1	Mileage Car 2	Mileage Car 3	Mileage Car 4
5	6	5	4	3
10	11	11	10	8
15	16	16	17	17
20	23	22	21	22
25	25	25	24	21
30	26	26	23	22
35	27	25	26	24
40	27	25	24	25
45	30	29	30	29
50	31	31	30	29
55	28	26	25	25
60	25	24	22	22
65	22	22	23	21
70	21	20	20	17

Figure 11.24. This worksheet shows gas mileage rates in 5-mile-per-hour increments.

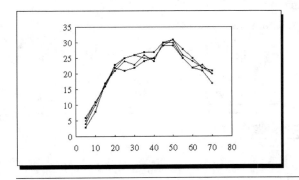

Figure 11.25. This XY graph shows the relationship of miles per hour to gas mileage.

Pie Charts

A pie chart is best suited to showing parts of a whole. Each wedge of the pie is clearly a percentage of the whole: for example, a department's contribution to the company as a whole, or the company's market share as a percentage of the whole market.

By convention, the X data range contains labels for each pie wedge, and the A data range contains the values represented by the pie wedges. In early versions of 1-2-3 it was necessary to use the B data range to add cross-hatching or color to the pie wedges. Now in 1-2-3/W, the pie wedges are automatically displayed in color. You *can* include a B data range to specify your own colors. Just be sure that when you add a B data range, you use only numbers from 1 to 15 for each cell corresponding to a cell in the A data range. The number you put in determines the color of each wedge of the pie.

If you want to explode or pull out a wedge for emphasis, you must set up a B data range. Add 100 to the color code (1 to 15) of the wedge that you wish to explode. For example, the wedge you want to explode is coded 9, enter the number 109 if you want to use the color associated with number 9. To hide a slice, enter a negative number in the B range.

Note that by default the label for each slice of a pie chart lists its percentage value compared to the whole as shown in Figure 11.27. To suppress this display, assign your chart a C range that includes a 0 value for each data point for which you don't want to see a percentage value.

The worksheet in Figure 11.26 shows sales of baseball bats for April, May, and June. An easy way to demonstrate each months sales as a percentage of the whole is to use a pie chart, as in Figure 11.27

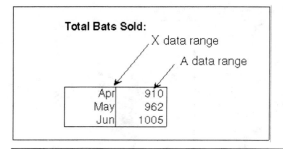

Figure 11.26. Baseball bat sales for the second quarter of the year.

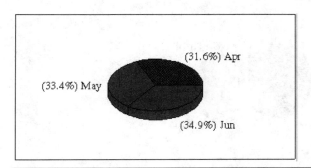

Figure 11.27. This 3D pie chart shows the percentage of sales that each bat type represents, using only the X data range and the A data range from Figure 11.26.

Pie charts that have more than six wedges are difficult to read. If you have more than six components to graph, select the five most important components and group the remainder into an "others" category. You may have to create formulas in a blank area of the worksheet to add those values representing the "others" group. Figures 11.28 and 11.29 demonstrate how to consolidate the data.

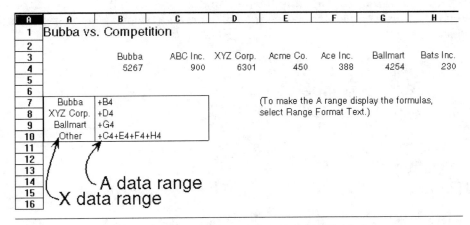

Figure 11.28. This worksheet contains formulas that consolidate data for use in "others" category.

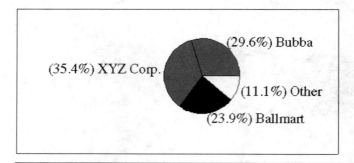

Figure 11.29. This pie graph was created from the worksheet in Figure 11.28.

High-Low-Close-Open (HLCO) Graphs

The High-Low Close-Open graph is also called the stock market graph. It tracks measurable fluctuation during a specific period of time. HLCO graphs are commonly used to depict daily stock market fluctuations or daily air temperature.

Your baseball bat factory's climate control system is malfunctioning and you want to show the fluctuation in temperature. Figure 11.30 is a worksheet of temperatures recorded for one week, and Figure 11.31 shows a graph of these fluctuations.

Factory Temperatures

		Mon	Tue	Wed	Thu	Fri	Sat	Sun
Opening	07:00 AM	62	64	59	67	66	64	68
	11:00 AM	88	83	84	82	83	85	80
	03:00 PM	103	107	103	102	103	106	85
	07:00 PM	101	104	88	91	98	99	99
	11:00 PM	99	97	104	105	107	109	90
Closing	03:00 AM	89	90	93	93	92	95	88
High		103	107	104	105	107	109	99
Low		62	64	59	67	66	64	68
Average		90	90	88	90	91	93	85
Variation		41	43	45	38	41	45	31

Figure 11.30. Factory temperatures for one week.

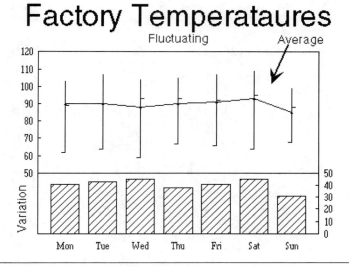

Figure 11.31. This HLCO graph shows fluctuations in temperatures.

Where do we go from here?

In the next chapter you will move from graphs into graphics. You will learn how to add enhancements such as color and geometric objects, and you will learn how to resize and reshape graphic objects.

12

Enhancing Graphics

In the previous chapter you learned what the various graph types were and how you could most effectively communicate your message by selecting the correct graph type, and by scaling and resizing the graph.

What are Graphics in 1-2-3/W?

As we learned in the previous chapter, a graph is a pictorial representation of data. Once a 1-2-3/W graph is placed on the worksheet, it is a graphic to which we can add colors and shadings and that we can reshape and illustrate with various graphic objects, such as pictures, charts, symbols, and other elements, including type, to make a visual statement.

The focus of the previous chapter was on 1-2-3/W *graphs*, the pictorial representation of data and their fill-in-the-blank enhancements such as headers, legends, and data labels. The spreadsheet-publishing capabilities of 1-2-3/W use images of 1-2-3/W graphs for placement in the worksheet as malleable *graphics*. These images, or graphics, inherit from the 1-2-3/W graph its "live" link with the worksheet data. Consequently, when placed in the worksheet, these live in-sheet graphics are immediately updated when the worksheet data changes.

There are *static* in-sheet graphics as well. These include blank graphics created with the Range Annotate command; PIC files and Metafiles (CGM) created with previous versions of 1-2-3 and other commercially available programs that can be imported into 1-2-3/W using the Graph Import menus; and many other Windows programs via the Windows Clipboard. These static graphics are independent of the worksheet data.

In this chapter you will learn:

- *How to add graphic objects to your worksheets and graphs*
- *How to resize, move, copy, and delete graphic objects.*

Whether the graphic is the image of a 1-2-3/W graph, a blank graph, or an image from the Clipboard, PIC, or CGM file, it can be annotated with *graphic objects* such as text, lines, arrows, rectangles, polygons, ellipses, and freehand drawings. You can modify the shape, size, orientation, and color of these objects and the underlying graphic by using the Graph editor menu options or the SmartIcons that display when you edit a graphic and its objects. Figure 12.1 displays the uncustomized SmartIcons that appear when the Graph window is active.

Figure 12.1. The graphics SmartIcon palette. 1-2-3/W's collection of point-and-click shortcuts changes to an array of graphics-related tools when you create or edit a graph.

Click It

Be sure to check out the wide assortment of SmartIcons that help you speed through graphics tasks. When you create or edit a graph, the SmartIcon Palette changes from a set of worksheet-related tools to a collection of graph-building and graph-editing tools.

To find out what a given icon is for, click it with the *right* mouse button, instead of the usual left button. This brings up a prompt describing the icon's use. To put the icon to work, click it with the left button.

As you'll see in Chapter 18, *Mastering the SmartIcon Palette*, you can customize the palette. The icons visible in the palette are only a few of the icons you can keep handy for ultrafast shortcuts for graphics and spreadsheet work. You can change the size and location of the palette, and you can hide it if you don't plan to use it.

Put Graphics from Other Sources Into Your Worksheet

In the last chapter you learned how to place a "live" in-sheet graphic in your worksheet using the Graph Add-to-sheet command. Here we'll explore ways of adding graphics from other sources into a 1-2-3/W worksheet.

Adding a PIC file

PIC files are created in earlier releases of 1-2-3 or Symphony. PIC files are files with a .PIC extension. They store graphs for future printing. The /Graph Save command, which was used to create the PIC file, is not available in 1-2-3/W. To copy 1-2-3/W graphics to another application, you use the Clipboard instead. And since you insert graphs into the sheet, you don't need to create PIC files in order to print with the now-obsolete PrintGraph utility.

To add an existing PIC file to your worksheet, select Graph Import, select the file type PIC, and select a file to import.

Adding a Metafile or Other Graphics

Metafiles are files with a .CGM extension. CGM stands for Computer Graphics Metafile. It is an industry-standard graphics format that can be created using Lotus Freelance Plus or other programs, including 1-2-3 Release 3.x.

Choose Graph Import or :Graph Add Metafile to place a CGM graphic in the worksheet.

Once a graphic has been added to the sheet you can get a full-screen view of the graphic by using the 1-2-3 Classic :Graph Zoom command. You can also use the New Graph View command and then click on the Maximize button.

To avoid adding the wrong PIC or CGM graphic, you can display a full-screen view of the graphic before adding the graphic to the sheet with the 1-2-3 Classic :Graph View command.

Moving a Graphic

Most worksheets need to be changed from time to time. The initial location of a graphic may not be its permanent home. It may be moved to another location by various means. Some methods are specifically designed to move graphics, others move the graphic as a byproduct. See "Graphic Destruction" later in this chapter.

To move a graphic from one location in the worksheet to another while retaining its same dimensions, you must first remove the graphic from the worksheet. Place the cell pointer in one cell of the graphic range or preselect the whole range. If you select more than one cell but not all cells, the graphic will be unaffected by the command. Select Edit Cut to remove the graphic from the worksheet and place it in the Windows Clipboard.

If you use PIC or CGM files for graphics in your worksheet, you should keep them with your worksheet if you copy the worksheet to another computer. If you do not copy the CGM and PIC files to the other computer, the range for those graphics will merely be blank.

Once the graphic has been removed from the worksheet with Edit Cut, you must relocate the cell pointer to the upper-left corner of the range in which you want the graphic to appear. If, instead, you highlight a range of cells for the graphic to be moved to it will resize to the range you select. Select Edit Paste to place the graphic in the worksheet. It will have the same dimensions as the original if you selected one cell as a target, or it will be the size of the selected range.

The 1-2-3 Classic :Graph Move and :Graph Settings Range commands can also move a graphic. Although :Graph Settings Range is meant for resizing a graphic, you may select its new range anywhere in the worksheet.

Duplicating a Graphic

There are times when you want to have several copies of the same graphic in the worksheet. They can be put in different parts of the worksheet or they can overlap. They can even be different sizes. To make a copy, first position the cell pointer on the graphic you want to copy. Then select Edit Copy to put a copy of the graphic in the Clipboard. Next, position the cell pointer to the upper-left corner of the range in which you want the copy to appear and select Edit Paste. The copied graph will have the same dimensions (same number of rows and columns) as the original.

If the rows in the destination range have a different height than the original graphic's rows or the columns have a different width, the new graphic will adjust to fit the new size. The new graphic will occupy the same number of rows and columns unless you explicitly specify otherwise.

If you want to change the graphics dimensions, you must preselect the new graphic's range before you select Edit Paste. You can make the graphic larger, smaller, wider, narrower, higher, or lower. The graphic and any added graphic objects will change shape.

Adding Graphic Objects to the Worksheet

Graphic objects are text, geometric shapes, or freehand drawings placed on top of the graphic using the Graph (New or View) Chart command. You can even manipulate the underlying graphic image from a 1-2-3 graph, PIC, or CGM file.

What Do We Do First?

To add objects to the graphic, first use the Graph New or Graph View command, or double-click on the graphic that has already been added to the worksheet. It doesn't matter what method you—use you get the same menus and SmartIcon palette.

You can select Draw and choose any of the graphic objects listed in the menu: text, line, arrow, rectangle, polygon, ellipse, or freehand. The Draw menu appears in Figure 12.2. All of the graphic objects have an associated SmartIcon. The pictures on the icons are intuitive, but if you are unsure of their purpose, point to them with the mouse and press the right button to get a short description of their functionality at the top of the screen. Once you select the object, the rest is just a matter of clicking and dragging of the mouse.

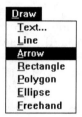

Figure 12.2. The Draw Menu. When you work in a Graph window, you can choose any of these annotation tools.

Adding Explanatory Text

To create a 1-2-3 graph, you use the fill-in-the-blank titles, notes, legends, and other annotations. Those options, however, are limited and have fixed predefined locations within the graph. Text objects and other geometric shapes, on the other hand, can be added anywhere. The Graph window's Draw Text dialog box gives you this flexibility. You can alternately click on the SmartIcon shown in Figure 12.3 to add text.

Figure 12.3. This SmartIcon lets you add text to annotate your graphics.

You can change the font of your added text with the Style Font dialog box or the Classic :Graph Edit Edit Font command. Changing the font in this way does not affect the graph's title, subtitle, notes, 2nd note, data-labels, or legends. It only affects selected text objects you've added with the "abc", SmartIcon, or the Draw Text or :Graph Edit Add Text commands.

Using Lines and Arrows

The graph SmartIcons shown in Figure 12.4 make it easy to add a line or arrow to your worksheet. Alternatively, you can choose line or arrow from the Draw menu. After you choose the tool, you drag it in the Graph window to draw a line segment. If you want to continue drawing connected segments, click and keep clicking at each point where you want to start a new segment. To complete drawing a line, double-click. To undo the last segment you added, click the *right* mouse button. Note that when you draw an arrow, the arrowhead appears where you double-click.

Figure 12.4. These SmartIcons make it easy to add a line to a graphic.

Change an arrow to a line or a line to an arrow with the graph editor's Style Lines or :Graph Edit Edit Arrowheads commands.

If you want to draw freely in the Graph Window use the Draw Freehand command or the SmartIcon:

Figure 12.5. This tool lets you draw freely in the Graph Window.

It takes a very steady hand to draw presentation-quality output with Draw Freehand. However, using Draw Line, you can add a line that approximates the curvature you want. Then smooth the angles by using the graph editor's Style Lines Smoothing command or the 1-2-3 Classic :Graph Edit Edit Smoothing Medium command.

Circles in the Sheet

Ellipses, circles, and ovals attract attention and help to pull elements of the graphic together. It's easy to add a circle with the graph SmartIcon.

Figure 12.6. The Ellipse-drawing tool lets you add circles and ovals to your graphics.

You can change a circle or ellipse into a square or rectangle with the graph editor's Style Lines or :Graph Edit Edit Smoothing None command.

When stretching the bounding box that defines the edges of the circle, hold down the Shift key; otherwise, the circle will become an oval.

Box It Up

Rectangles visually group the objects in a graphic. The graph SmartIcon makes it easy to add a rectangle:

Figure 12.7. To add squares and rectangles click this SmartIcon and drag it in the Graph Window.

As in making a circle, when adding a rectangle hold down the Shift key if you wish to make a square.

Editing Graphic Objects

The SmartIcon shown in Figure 12.8 is a useful shortcut for resizing a the graphic or an added graphic object. You click this icon and then move the mouse to resize the object. When you're satisfied with the altered graphic, click twice—once to confirm the size, again to indicate that you don't want to move the object. Note that this SmartIcon is a custom icon, which means you can choose to add it to your palette (it isn't visible by default) and you can even change the macro file that makes it work. See Chapter 19 for details on choosing and customizing SmartIcons.

Figure 12.8. Add this icon to your palette to make it easy to resize a selected object.

Annotating a Range of the Worksheet with a Blank Graphic

The Range Annotate command lets you add graphic objects over the worksheet data or text. Since the graph editing window is not transparent while you are adding the annotation, you should move the annotation window off the range that is being annotated. Move the window by either clicking and dragging or by using the Window Tile command. Then you can work in one window and see the results in another. Once you finish adding annotations, any text underneath will show through because the blank graph you create with Range Annotate is transparent.

```
        Sales first 6 months
           Baseball Bats
         Wooden    Metal
   Jan     330      470
   Feb     332      460
   Mar     324      526
   Apr     344      566
   May     368      594
   Jun     304      649

  Total:  2002     3265
```

Figure 12.9. "Circling" data is a time-honored method for drawing the reader's eye to pertinent information.

Graphic Destruction

A graphic may accidentally change size even when you don't want it to. Make sure you know and respect the effects of the following commands. They are very useful and very powerful.

Sometimes You Really Do Want to Remove a Graphic

To remove a graphic use the Edit Cut command, the Edit Clear Special command or the 1-2-3/W Classic :Graph Remove command. If you want to remove only one graphic from the worksheet, place the cell pointer in the graphic you wish to remove. If you want to remove more than one graphic, select a range that includes those you wish to remove.

Changing a Column Width or Row Height Also Changes the Graphic

You can change worksheet columns and rows in several ways. If a column that contains a graphic is widened, the graphic will widen; if narrowed, the graphic will narrow. All graphic objects will change geometrically. The changes in the graphic will be proportional, a circle may become an ellipse; a square may become a rectangle.

If you increase the font size in a data range, the height of the whole row (the entire width of worksheet) will increase to accommodate the larger font. Any graphic in that row will be resized whether you want it to or not.

When you change the width of a column the whole column is affected, from top to bottom. Therefore, a graphic in that column will be affected, even if it is not on the screen.

What Happens to a Graphic If You Hide Some or All of Its Columns?

If you hide columns with Worksheet Column Hide, the graphic will remain intact, but it will be distorted. Figure 12.12 shows what happens to the graphics proportions when a few columns are hidden.

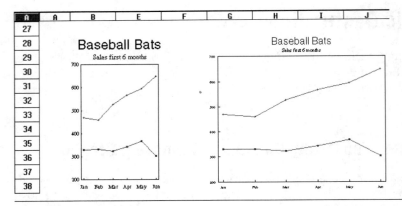

Figure 12.10. The graph on the left changes proportions dramatically when you hide columns, as on the right.

Inserting and Deleting Rows and Columns : What Can Go Wrong?

The Worksheet Insert Column and Worksheet Insert Row commands may push a graphic off the visible worksheet. If you insert too many rows or columns, the graphic will be pushed off the right side or bottom of the worksheet.

If a row or column contained within a graphic's range is deleted, the graphic will resize proportionately. Beware! If you delete all rows or columns of the graphic the graphic will be deleted along with any added enhancements.

If you insert or delete rows above the graphic with the Worksheet Delete Row or Worksheet Insert Row commands, the graphic will move up or down. Likewise, if you insert or delete columns, the graphic moves left or right.

Copying Graphics from Another File

When your worksheet is saved with File Save or File Save As, the format file will store all your graphics associated with the worksheet. A lot of creativity goes into the production of a 1-2-3/W graphic. There will most likely be graphic designs such as a company logo that you create and will want to use again and again.

The 1-2-3 Classic command sequence, :Special Import Graphs, will import all graphs from a format file created by WYSIWYG in 1-2-3 versions 2.3, 3.1 or 3.1+, or by the Impress or Allways addins. If you have created graphics in any of these products you can import them into 1-2-3/W and further modify and enhance them.

13

Introduction to 1-2-3/W Databases

1-2-3/W is ideal for managing small databases. The spreadsheet provides you with a plethora of tools for manipulating and analyzing data. In addition to a wealth of commands for common database operations 1-2-3/W offers a set of statistical @ functions just for databases. It also lets you read and write data to external tables using Lotus's DataLens technology. These tables can be files on your hard disk, a network server, a corporate mainframe, or a CD-ROM. 1-2-3/W comes with drivers that let you access dBase, Sybase (SQL), and Paradox files. Other drivers are available through Lotus and other vendors.

Even without the ability to connect to external data, 1-2-3/W is a great tool for managing and analyzing information. A 1-2-3/W database is really just a collection of one or more tables of information, so don't worry that this subject is too technical. There are a few terms you should know before we start, however.

In 1-2-3/W, a table is simply a range of related information with identifying labels or field names at the top of each column. Figure 13.1 shows an example of a typical 1-2-3/W database table.

Here, the database consists of a single table. The entries in range A4..E11 keep track of some employee information. The table lists employee numbers, first and last names, dates of hire, and current hourly wages.

You enter the information for each employee in a single row called a record. As you

In this chapter you'll learn how to:

- Set up a database in 1-2-3/W
- Sort data
- Find information in a database
- Extract information from a database
- Perform table joins
- Delete records from a database
- Use the QUERY key for fast data queries
- Import data from other programs
- Link to external database tables
- Parse text files

can see, each record stores information in the same way. In every record, column A holds the employee number, column B holds the employee's first name, and so on.

The columns in a 1-2-3/W database are called *fields* and the first row of every database contains the *field names*. So here, the labels *Emp. #*, *Fname*, *Lname*, *Hired*, and *Wage* name the fields of this database.

	A	B	C	D	E
1					
2					
3					
4	Emp. #	Fname	Lname	Hired	Wage
5	154	Raul	Jones	18-Mar-80	$12.59
6	175	Auo	Reed	09-Dec-80	$10.88
7	295	Reisha	Cosmo	02-Oct-81	$9.98
8	446	Pedro	Jones	25-Jun-82	$9.85
9	547	Grumph	Pontiac	22-Apr-83	$9.51
10	585	Sallis	Aphrus	19-Jun-89	$6.86
11	734	Gertrude	Woko	20-Jan-90	$5.70

Figure 13.1. Here's an example of a simple 1-2-3/W database, a table that stores employee information. You can use the database tools in 1-2-3/W to sort, analyze, and manipulate the database in a variety of ways.

Try It: Set Up the Database

Let's create this database to use again later.

1. Enter data in columns A through C as shown in Figure 13.1.

2. Enter the dates in column D as shown, and then format them with the Range Format option.

3. Enter the wages in column E and format them for currency with 2 decimal places.

4. Use the Range Name Create command to assign the name *database* to range A4..E11.

5. Save the file as DATABASE.WK3.

Sorting Data

Sorting is to databases what adding is to calculators. Arranging the records in your database in some logical order is one of 1-2-3/W's most useful capabilities.

The records in Figure 13.1 are sorted by employee number. That also happens to be in ascending order of the date of hire. Now, suppose you want the list sorted alphabetically by employee name. In such a small database, it would be easy enough just to move the records around by using the Move command. But what if this were a table containing hundreds of employee records?

A better way to sort a data table in 1-2-3/W is to use the Data Sort command and fill in the Data Sort dialog box:

- Specify the data range that contains the records you wish to sort. The range should *not* include the field names at the top of the data table, since you don't want them sorted along with the data records. Be sure to include all the columns of the database. This is very important. If you sort without including all columns, you will corrupt the database, since the excluded columns will no longer match the rest of the data.

- Specify the primary key field to tell 1-2-3/W which field to use to sort the data.

- Select ascending or descending alphanumeric sort order. Ascending order is from 0 to 9 or from A to Z; descending is the reverse.

- Specify a secondary key (*optional*) to order records that have identical primary keys, and select ascending or descending order.

- Specify additional sorting keys (*optional*) to order records that have identical primary and secondary keys.

The Date Sort command lets you put a range of data in alphabetical or numerical order.

Figure 13.2 shows you how to set up the Data Sort dialog to sort the records shown in Figure 13.1, alphabetically by the employees' last name.

Sorting our database this way works, but there's a problem, as you can see in Figure 13.3. Raul and Pedro Jones are in the wrong order. That's because 1-2-3/W sorted only the on last name field. Raul and Pedro have the same last name, so 1-2-3/W treated the two records as equivalent.

To solve this kind of problem, specify a secondary key. In this case, you just need to specify the first name field as a secondary key and re-sort.

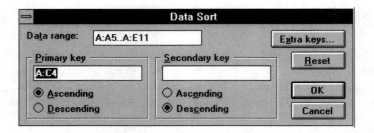

Figure 13.2. At first glance, the Data Sort menu and dialog box can be intimidating. But just take it one step at a time, and you'll find that sorting data in 1-2-3/W is really very easy.

Try It: Sorting Records

Let's sort the records in our example database so that they appear alphabetically by last name.

1. Retrieve the example worksheet, DATABASE, that you created in the previous section (if it's not already loaded).

2. Select range A5..E11. Leave out row 4, since we don't want to sort the field labels with the data.

3. Choose the Data Sort command and enter A:C4 as the primary key.

4. Click the Ascending radio button in the primary key box.

5. Click OK to sort the data.

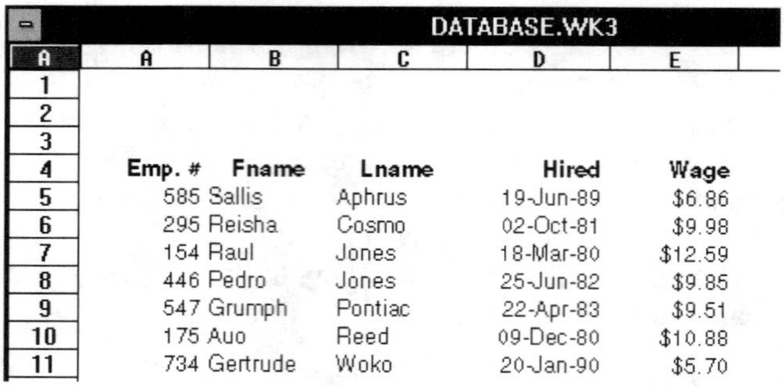

```
                    DATABASE.WK3
      A        B         C          D           E
1
2
3
4   Emp. #   Fname     Lname       Hired       Wage
5    585     Sallis    Aphrus      19-Jun-89   $6.86
6    295     Reisha    Cosmo       02-Oct-81   $9.98
7    154     Raul      Jones       18-Mar-80   $12.59
8    446     Pedro     Jones       25-Jun-82   $9.85
9    547     Grumph    Pontiac     22-Apr-83   $9.51
10   175     Auo       Reed        09-Dec-80   $10.88
11   734     Gertrude  Woko        20-Jan-90   $5.70
```

Figure 13.3. With the Data Sort command, it was easy to sort this database. But because we sorted only by last name, Pedro and Raul Jones are missorted. To sort by first and last names, you must specify both a primary and secondary key.

> ### Try It: Sorting With a Secondary Key
>
> Let's sort the records in our example database so that they appear alphabetically by last name and first name.
>
> 1. Choose the Data Sort command and enter A:B4 as the secondary key. The other dialog settings should be the same as before.
> 2. Click the Ascending radio button in the secondary key box.
> 3. Click OK to sort the data.

This time Pedro and Raul are in the right place. The secondary key tells 1-2-3/W how to sort records when their primary keys are the same.

Click'n Sort

The simplest way to sort is to select a range and click on one of the SmartIcons shown in Figure 13.4. The one on the left sorts in ascending order; the one on the right sorts in descending order. To learn how to add these or any other available SmartIcons to your Palette, see Chapter 18.

Figure 13.4. Add these two SmartIcons to your palette to sort a selected range with a simple click. The one on the left sorts from lowest to highest, the one on the right sorts from highest to lowest.

Finding Records

Sorting a small database like the one in our example is very fast. Of course a database containing 2,000 records takes longer to sort. If you just want to find a particular record, then sorting the whole database to help with your search is impractical.

Fortunately, 1-2-3/W provides another solution. You can simply ask 1-2-3/W to find a record that satisfies some search criterion. To do this, you first have to set up a Criteria range in your worksheet. The Criteria range must consist of a row containing some or all the field names used in your database. It must also contain at least one row below those field names where you enter the criteria for the database search.

The Criteria range is a range you use to instruct 1-2-3/W to use only certain records in a database operation.

This may sound complicated, but it's not that hard once you get the hang of it. Figure 13.5 shows you how to set up a Criteria range for the employee database. The most important thing to remember is that the field names in the Criteria range must be the same as the field names in the database. To avoid making small mistakes, your best bet is simply to copy those field names. You could also use a reference formula, such as +A4 in cell A1 in this example.

	A	B	C	D	E
1	Emp. #	Fname	Lname	Hired	Wage
2					
3					
4	Emp. #	Fname	Lname	Hired	Wage
5	585	Sallis	Aphrus	19-Jun-89	$6.86
6	295	Reisha	Cosmo	02-Oct-81	$9.98
7	446	Pedro	Jones	25-Jun-82	$9.85
8	154	Raul	Jones	18-Mar-80	$12.59
9	547	Grumph	Pontiac	22-Apr-83	$9.51
10	175	Auo	Reed	09-Dec-80	$10.88
11	734	Gertrude	Woko	20-Jan-90	$5.70
12					

Figure 13.5. To set up a Criteria range in row 1 for the employee database, first copy the field names from row 4. Next assign the name *crit* to range A1..E2. Finally, choose Data Query and enter *crit* as the Criteria range.

Try It: Create a Criteria Range

Let's set up a Criteria range in our employee database.

1. Use the Edit Quick Copy command to copy range A:A4..A:E4 to cell A:A1.

2. Choose Range Name Create and assign the name *crit* to range A1..E2. You don't have to use range names to use the Data Query commands, but they make the operation easier to understand.

In the next exercise we'll put this criteria range to work.

Once you have a Criteria range, you can query the database using a variety of criteria. To find a particular record, you enter an identifying characteristic in one or more of the cells underneath the field labels in the Criteria range. For example, if you want to find employee number 175, you enter *175* under the *Emp.#* field in the Criteria range, then issue the Data Query Find command.

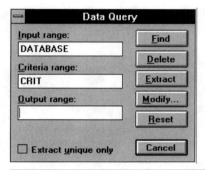

Figure 13.6. The Data Query dialog box helps you manage and manipulate databases.

Try It: Find a Record

Let's use 1-2-3/W to find the record for employee number 175.

1. Enter *175* in cell A2. This tells 1-2-3/W to find the records with an employee number of 175.

2. Choose Data Query. Assign the Input range and Criteria range as shown in Figure 13.6. The Input range should always encompass the whole database, including the field names.

3. Click Find. 1-2-3/W highlights the record for Auo Reed. Just press Return and choose Cancel to get out of Find mode.

Experiment by using different entries in the Criteria range (*crit*). For example, erase cell A2, enter Jones in cell C2, and reissue the Data Query Find command. Two records match this criterion.

When you use the Find command, 1-2-3/W puts you into Find mode, as you can see by the mode indicator in the upper-right corner of your screen. 1-2-3/W highlights the first record in the data table that matches the criterion, if there is

Data Query Find puts 1-2-3/W in a special mode when the arrow keys move you only through records that match a set of criteria.

one. If more than one record matches the criterion, press the DownArrow to move to the next matching record. You can scan all matching records by pressing UpArrow or DownArrow. You cannot, however, move the cell pointer onto records that do not match the criterion while you're in Find mode.

Locating records isn't the only thing you can do with the Find command. You can also edit the records you find. Suppose Raul Jones just got a 5% raise. Use the Find command to locate Raul's record, then edit that record. To do that, just press the RightArrow key four times to select the *Wage* field, then edit Raul's salary as you would edit any cell.

Extracting Records

Suppose you want to analyze a subset of database records. Before you do that, you should extract the records to an Output range. Then you can examine, manipulate, and analyze the subset of records copied from the database.

To do that, you first set up an Output range in much the same way that you set up the Criteria range.

Try It: Create an Output Range

Let's create an Output range to which we can extract records that match a criterion.

1. Copy the labels from range A1..E1 to cell I1 in the DATABASE worksheet, as shown in Figure 13.7.

2. Assign the range name *out* to range I1..M1.

3. Choose Data Query and enter *out* as the output range, as shown in Figure 13.8.

Once you have specified the Input, Criteria, and Output ranges in the Data Query dialog box, you're ready to extract all the records that match your Criteria range. If, for example, you want to look at all the employees named Jones, enter the label *Jones* in cell C2 and use the Data Query Extract command.

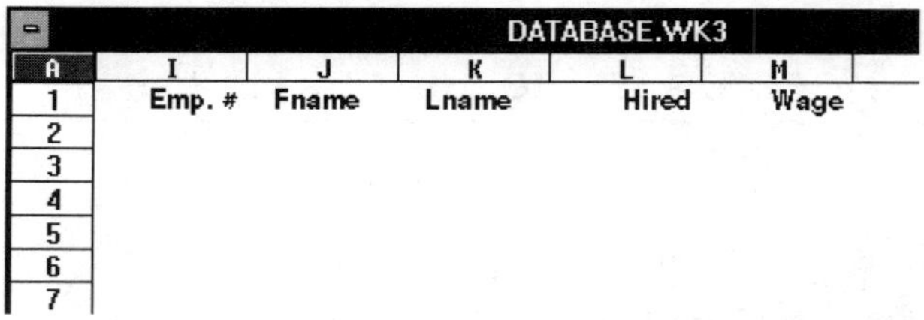
DATABASE.WK3
A
I
J
K
L
M
Emp. #
Fname
Lname
Hired
Wage
1
2
3
4
5
6
7

Figure 13.7. Copy the field names from the Criteria range to create an Output range. Make sure there is ample room below the field-name labels in the extract range. Allow for all the database records that you may extract with the Data Query Extract command.

If you change the criterion and reissue the Data Query Extract command, 1-2-3/W will overwrite the old extract. If you use the Data Query Extract command when the second row of the Criteria range is empty, 1-2-3/W will extract all the records in the database.

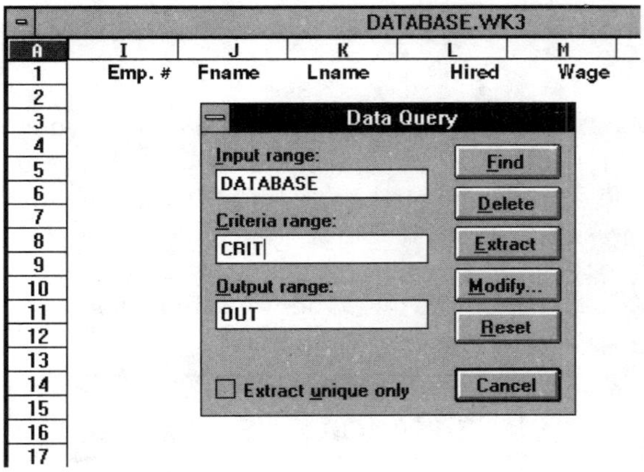
DATABASE.WK3
Emp. #
Fname
Lname
Hired
Wage
Data Query
Input range:
DATABASE
Criteria range:
CRIT
Output range:
OUT
Find
Delete
Extract
Modify...
Reset
Cancel
Extract unique only

Figure 13.8. Before you can extract records from the database, you must specify all three Query Ranges: Input, Criteria, and Output.

> ### Try It: Extract Records to the Output Range
>
> Let's extract the records of all employees whose last name is Jones.
>
> 1. Enter *Jones* in cell C2 as the criterion.
> 2. Choose Data Query and select Extract to copy all the records that match the criterion to the area below the Output range.
> 3. Select Cancel to see the extracted records. 1-2-3/W extracted the records for all employees whose last name is Jones. Note that these are copies of the records in the database, not the records themselves. So you can change or even erase the records in the Output range without affecting the original records in the database.

Deleting Records

Deleting records is as easy as extracting them. You just use the Data Query Delete command to remove all records that match a criterion. Use this command with caution. If you use the Delete command when the second row of the Criteria range is blank, you'll erase the entire database. So make it a habit to extract records before you delete them. That way you can look over the records you're about to delete to make sure they're the ones you want removed.

> ### Try It: Delete a Record
>
> Let's use the Data Query Delete command to remove Pedro Jones from the employee database.
>
> 1. Enter *Jones* in cell C2 and *12.59* in cell E2.
> 2. Choose Data Query and select Delete. 1-2-3/W will ask you to confirm the deletion. If you do, 1-2-3/W will remove Pedro Jones from the employee database.
> 3. Choose Edit Undo (if it is enabled) to reverse the Data Query Delete command.

Rapid-Fire Queries

Once you get used to 1-2-3/Ws Data Query commands, there's almost no end to the ways you can look at data. But going back and forth between changing criteria and running through the Data Query menu commands can get tedious. Fortunately, 1-2-3/W provides a handy short-cut: the QUERY key (F7).

The QUERY key repeats the last Data Query command you executed. This makes it easy to change criteria rapidly and see the results without going through the menus. Suppose, for example, you wanted to do an ad hoc analysis on a table of students, shown in Figure 13.8.

This database is slightly different from the previous example and shows that you don't have to use every single field label in the Criteria and Output ranges. The Criteria range, A1..B3, contains only two of the field labels. That's perfectly fine. Your Criteria range can use whichever fields you want and exclude those you don't need. Similarly, the Output range, F1..H1, contains only three of the original four field labels. 1-2-3/W ignores blank rows in the Criteria range as long as one of the rows contains some data; otherwise, it matches all records in the database. If there is a criterion in each of two rows, 1-2-3/W searches for all records that match the criterion in the first row *or* the criterion in the second row. For example, if you enter *phi* in cell A2 and *cs* in cell A3, you'll get the records of students whose major is either philosophy *or* computer science.

This database lets you perform a wide variety of queries using varying complex criteria. And the QUERY key lets you do it fast.

	A	B	C	D	E	F	G	H
1	Major	Numeric				Name	Major	Letter
2								
3								
4								
5	Name	Major	Letter	Numeric				
6	Allen	PYS	B+	3.33				
7	Blake	PHI	A	4.00				
8	Brown	CS	C-	1.67				
9	Casner	PHI	D+	1.33				
10	DeCocker	CS	A	4.00				
11	Kirby	CS	B	3.00				
12	Oakley	BUS	C-	1.67				
13	Peterson	MUS	B-	2.67				
14	Scott	PHI	C-	1.67				
15	Smith	MUS	C+	2.33				
16	Su	CS	B-	2.67				
17	Warner	PHI	C	2.00				
18	Wolosen	CS	A	4.00				

Figure 13.9. 1-2-3/W lets you look at a database of final grades for a college class in a variety of ways.

> ### Try It: Rapid Queries
>
> Let's experiment with the QUERY key.
>
> 1. Enter data as shown in Figure 13.9.
> 2. In the Data Query dialog box, assign range A1..B3 as the Criteria range, range A5..D18 as the Input range, and range F1..H1 as the Output range.
> 3. Choose the Extract command and exit the dialog box.
> 4. Enter '>3 under the *numeric* field in the Criteria range, and press the QUERY key (F7) to extract the records of students with better than a 3.0 numeric grade.
> 5. Experiment with different criteria in both rows 2 and 3 using the QUERY key.

Almost as quickly as you can enter labels in the Criteria range, you can extract matching records into the Output range using the QUERY key. If you use the Data Query Find command, then the QUERY key lets you search for records in the database as fast as you can create new criteria. Every time you press QUERY, you go straight into Find mode.

Exercise caution when using the QUERY key to delete records. If the last query you made was a deletion, then the next time you press the QUERY key, all the records matching the criterion will be deleted without warning. This could result in substantial data loss. It's safer to use the Data Query commands through the menus when deleting records. That way you can examine the records before issuing the Data Query Delete command.

Computed and Aggregate Columns

1-2-3/W can automatically create columns that perform calculations on data you extract.

Most database programs can perform calculations as part of the query process. A single command can list the products you sold in three months and, simultaneously, generate a column that projects a full year's sales. 1-2-3/W also lets you create columns that aren't simply extractions from the database. For example, you can use the Extract command to list records for employees and calculate a salary field that is 10% greater than the salary in the Input range. To do that, you create a computed column. You can also tell 1-2-3/W to extract records in summary form. For example, you can extract the sum of salaries in each department. To do that, you create an *aggregate column*.

Or you can get a report that lists each unique value in the database along with a summary of relevant data. For example, suppose your database has a separate record for each sales transaction. If a customer makes multiple purchases, data about his or her account will appear in many records. You can produce a summary report that lists the name of each customer along with that customer's total purchases.

1-2-3/W's computed-column and aggregate-column features make it easy to calculate values from records in a database. Just enter an appropriate formula in the top row of the Output range and issue the Data Query Extract command.

Instant Columns

The simplest computed columns are generated from values in the records you extract. For example, in the database of employees in Figure 13.10, column G of the Output range calculates a 10% increase in each employee's salary.

Cells E4 and F4 in the Output range contain conventional database field names, *Name* and *Dept*, entered as labels. Cell G4, however, contains a formula. When you issue the Data Query Extract command, 1-2-3 uses this formula to multiply each salary by 1.1.

When you issue an Extract command for a computed column (contained in the Output range), you might be surprised to see that the Data Query Extract command recognizes field names, such as *Salary*, when it encounters them in a formula in the Output range. Normally, formulas that use field names, such as the one in cell G4 of Figure 13.10, evaluate to ERR because the field-name labels are not range names. This ERR indication isn't important, but if you don't want to see it, change the formats of the cells that contain such formulas to Text so that the formulas are displayed instead of ERRs.

	A	B	C	D	E	F	G
1	Name	Dept	Salary				
2							
3							
4	Name	Dept	Salary		Name		Dept +SALARY*1.1
5	Collins	10	30000				
6	Kaye	20	25000				
7	Phillips	10	40000				
8	Banks	30	19000				
9	Squire	10	20000				
10	Wood	20	30000				

Figure 13.10. Column G is a computed column.

> ## Try It: Create a Computed Column
>
> Let's create a computed column to see how this feature works.
>
> 1. Set the widths of columns A and E to 10, columns B and C to 7, column D to 12, and columns F and G to 13.
> 2. Enter the labels in range A1..C1, then copy that range to cells A4 and E4.
> 3. Replace the label in cell G4 with the formula +Salary*1.1. For now, ignore the *ERR* that appears in that cell.
> 4. Enter the labels and values in range A5..C10.
> 5. Choose Data Query and specify range A4..C10 as the Input range, range A1..C2 as the Criteria range, and range E4..G4 as the Output range.
> 6. Issue the Data Query Extract command. Remember that when you specify a one-row Output range, such as range E4..G4, 1-2-3/W treats all the cells below that range as part of the Output range.

Database Statistics Without @D Functions

Aggregate columns are computed columns that help you create summary reports. In Figure 13.10, the output of the Data Query Extract command is a list of each unique department number and its corresponding salary total. Like the Data Query Unique command, the aggregate-column feature produces a list of the unique labels or values in selected database fields. But an aggregate column also computes summary statistics for the rows that you output, as in the Output range shown in Figure 13.11.

	A	B	C	D	E	F
1	Name	Dept	Salary			
2						
3						
4	Name	Dept	Salary		Dept	@SUM(SALARY)
5	Collins	10	30000		10	90000
6	Kaye	20	25000		20	55000
7	Phillips	10	40000		30	19000
8	Banks	30	19000			
9	Squire	10	20000			
10	Wood	20	30000			

Figure 13.11. Column F is an aggregate column.

> ## What's Unique
>
> A record is unique if no other record has identical data in all the fields whose names appear as labels in the Output range. In the example in Figure 13.10, if the Output range had included both the *Name* field and the *Dept* field, the out-put would have contained all six records. No two people in the database share both the same name and the same department.

> ## Try It: Create an Aggregate Column
>
> Let's change the previous example to create an aggregate column that shows the sum of salaries in each department.
>
> 1. To convert the previous example to the one shown in Figure 13.11, start by erasing range E4..G10.
> 2. Enter the label *Dept* in cell E4 and the formula *@SUM(Salary)* in cell F4.
> 3. Assign the Text format to cell F4.
> 4. In the Data Query dialog box change the Output range to range E4..F4, then issue the Data Query Extract command.

How does 1-2-3/W differentiate between aggregate columns and other computed columns? Aggregate-column formulas contain any of five statistical @functions: @AVG, @COUNT, @MAX, @MIN, or @SUM. When 1-2-3/W encounters one of these @functions in a computed-column formula, it treats the query in a special way. In database parlance, an aggregate column gives you a summary report rather than a detail report.

As you experiment with computed columns, you should consider a few details. For all practical purposes, you cannot use both aggregate columns and other computed columns in the same query. It is technically possible, but with severe restrictions. One computed column cannot reference another, so you cannot create a query that, for example, calculates total departmental salaries *and* a 10% increase in each department's total. Also, imagine you were to use an Output range whose top row contains the following labels and formulas: *Dept, @SUM(Salary), + Salary*, and *+ Salary* 1.1*. Unfortunately, by including the Salary field, the aggregate-column feature considers each record to be unique, because in this database, no two people work in the same department

Besides being easy to use, aggregate columns work faster than @D functions such as @DSUM and @DAVG.

at the same salary. Therefore, the Query Extract includes all records and the aggregate column becomes meaningless. Also, though the preceding examples used blank Criteria ranges, computed columns do support the use of criteria.

> You should be aware that the results of aggregate queries can sometimes differ from the results of equivalent @D functions. That can happen if your database contains blank cells or cells with ERR or NA values. @D functions ignore blank cells, but aggregate columns do not. @D functions evaluate to ERR or NA if they reference any cell that includes those values, whereas aggregate queries treat ERR and NA as zeros.

Joining Two Tables

One of the most useful database features in 1-2-3/W is its ability to join two database tables in an extract. In database lingo, a *join* uses some criteria to create a table from two other tables. The new table consists of all the possible unified pairs of records, one from each of the two original tables.

For example, consider the two database tables shown in Figure 13.12. The first database table, *parts*, lists all parts in inventory. The second database table, *orders*, lists recent stock orders. Given these two tables, it's easy to generate a third table that lists order numbers, part numbers, part names, and total price (computed column).

You create such a table using the Data Query Extract command. The trick is to create special Criteria and Output ranges, as shown in Figure 13.13. Here, the criteria range is A18..A19. It contains the field label *orders.order* and the criterion formula +*orders.part=parts.part*. The Output range is A21..D21. It contains the field labels *orders.order*, *orders.part*, *parts.pname*, and the computed column formula +quantity*price. Lets look at how this works.

As in any Criteria range, the first row holds the field names and the second row holds the criteria. When doing a join, you have to specify the table name along with a field name. So the field name in cell A18 is *orders.order*. This specifies the *order* field of the database table named *orders*.

	A	B	C
	\multicolumn{3}{c}{PARTS.WK3}		
	A	B	C
1	PART	PNAME	PRICE
2	108	Silk Cloth	$14.50
3	216	Pillow	$11.95
4	324	Quilt	$75.95
5	540	Lace	$7.00
6	648	Basket	$21.00
7			
8	ORDER	PART	QUANTITY
9	1100	108	9
10	1101	216	9
11	1102	324	3
12	1103	540	2
13	1104	648	4
14	1105	108	5
15	1106	216	7
16	1107	324	3

Figure 13.12. Here are two database tables. The first one in range A1..C6 is named *parts*, and it lists stock items. The second table in range A8..C16 is named *orders*, and it lists recent parts ordered.

	A	B	C	D
18	ORDERS.ORDER			
19	+ORDERS.PART=PARTS.PART			
20				
21	ORDERS.ORDER	ORDERS.PART	PARTS.PNAME	+QUANTITY*PRICE
22				

Figure 13.13. To prepare for a join, you have to create specialized Criteria and Output ranges, as shown here. You use the range name of each table followed by the field name, separated by a period, to specify the table and field you're interested in.

The second row of the Criteria range contains the formula +*orders.part=parts.part*. This formula tells 1-2-3/W to create a join such that the *part* field in the *orders* table equals the *part* field in the *parts* table. Note that you cannot do a join unless both tables contain at least one field with the same name. This is sometimes called a common key field. Also note that this formula returns ERR unless you assign the Text format to the cell.

The Output range contains the field names we want in the join table. These names can be any of the fields from either table. One of them must be the common field. Here, the common field is *part*, and we've specified that field in the second column of the Output range. Note that column D is a computed column. We're using it to calculate the total price of each order (unit price x quantity).

Once you have the ranges set up, all you do is fill in the dialog box, as shown in Figure 13.14, and then select Extract.

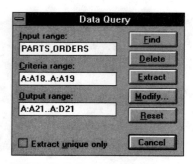

Figure 13.14. When doing a join extract, be sure to specify the range names of the two database tables, separating them with commas, as shown here.

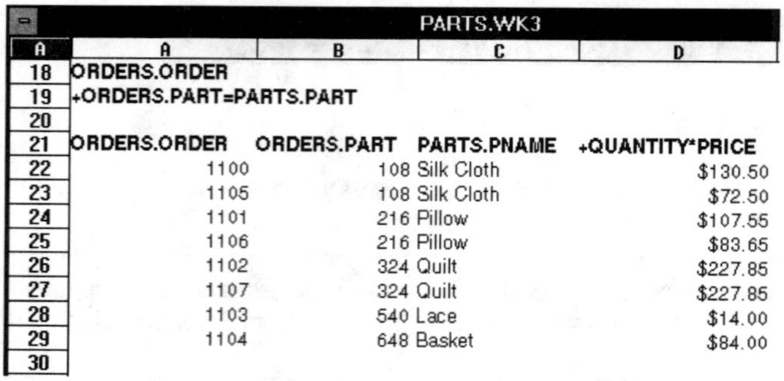

```
                        PARTS.WK3
         A              B              C              D
18  ORDERS.ORDER
19  +ORDERS.PART=PARTS.PART
20
21  ORDERS.ORDER   ORDERS.PART   PARTS.PNAME   +QUANTITY*PRICE
22          1100           108   Silk Cloth            $130.50
23          1105           108   Silk Cloth             $72.50
24          1101           216   Pillow                $107.55
25          1106           216   Pillow                 $83.65
26          1102           324   Quilt                 $227.85
27          1107           324   Quilt                 $227.85
28          1103           540   Lace                   $14.00
29          1104           648   Basket                 $84.00
30
```

Figure 13.15. Joining *parts* and *orders* provides this useful list of orders and price. Once you learn how to do joins in 1-2-3/W, you'll find many uses for this valuable feature.

Managing Data from Mainframes and Other Programs

Once you get used to 1-2-3/W, you may want to use its analytical powers on data that's currently in other programs or on your company's mainframe. That's understandable, and often not a problem. For example, you can use 1-2-3/W's

Translate utility (see the 1-2-3/W documentation) to translate data from 1-2-3 Releases 1A, 2, 2.01, and 2.2; dBase II, III, and IV; DIF files; Enable 2.0; Multiplan (SYLK); SuperCalc4; Symphony Releases 1.0 - 2.0; and VisiCalc. That might be all the translating power you need. If not, you can connect to external data via the Data External commands, which we'll cover in the next section. 1-2-3/W also lets you import simple text (ASCII) files that you download from mainframes or output from other programs.

To analyze a text file, you have to import the file into 1-2-3/W, then separate the text into discrete cells. Sometimes this is easy, and sometimes it's not.

If the text file consists of columns of numbers separated by spaces, the job is elementary, though not always trouble-free. Consider the following text held in an ASCII file named TEMP.PRN.

```
Sales
Jan Feb    March April May
139000     668400
898500     666900
990500     424500
642400     175600
817400     962900
```

To import such a file, you could perform the following three steps:

- Choose File Import From Text and indicate TEMP.PRN. 1-2-3/W imports the file as a set of seven long labels.

- Choose File Import From Numbers and again indicate TEMP.PRN. 1-2-3/W reimports all the numbers in the file, breaking them into discrete columns and cells.

- Manually break up the long labels into discrete cells. Here, that would mean splitting a label containing the months, so that each column of values has the correct month at the top.

If your text file is mostly numbers (numbers without commas), this technique works pretty well. That's because the File Import From Numbers command assumes that the file you're importing is a *delimited* file. Now, our example TEMP.PRN file, strictly speaking, is not a delimited file. But since the numbers are in columns separated by spaces, 1-2-3/W treats it as if it were. If the columns of numbers contain commas, however, 1-2-3/W treats the comma as a de-limiter and separates a number with a comma into two cells.

If you use this tricky combination of the File Import Text and File Import Numbers commands, however, you're usually stuck with column labels all strung together in one single cell. Since the File Import Numbers command ignores labels unless they're delimited with quotation marks, the months in TEMP.PRN remain a long label from the previous File Import Labels command. In this case, it would be easy enough just to reenter those labels by hand. But sometimes you're left with hundreds of long labels that you have to separate into columns. In such cases, the Data Parse command can often solve the problem.

Parsing Data

1-2-3/W's Data Parse command gives you a convenient dialog box where you define how to divide up long labels.

Few things are more frustrating than seeing information on your screen but not being able to use that information in your program. You run into this problem when you have long labels of data that need to be separated into individual cells. 1-2-3/W's solution is the Data Parse command, which separates a column of run-on labels into separate columns of individual entries.

1-2-3/W improves on the previous versions of this command by letting you set up the parsing in a dialog box, rather than by performing a series of on-sheet steps. If you want to do it the old-fashioned way, use the 1-2-3 Classic command /Data Query Parse.

In the TEMP.PRN example, let's use Data Parse to separate the long label into discrete cells. To do that you would:

- Move the cell pointer to the long label containing the names of the months separated by spaces.

- Choose Data Parse and select Create. 1-2-3/W displays a definition label or format line in the dialog box—above the long label text. The label will contain a string in the following format: L>>***** L>>*****.

- The Input-Column is the range containing the data you want to parse. In this case you have already selected the cell you want to parse.

- Output-Range is where the parsed data should be placed in the worksheet. In this case we want the parsed data to replace the input data.

- Choose OK. 1-2-3/W separates the long label into the appropriate cells.

The Data Parse command separates long labels according to the format line created with the Create command. The format line includes Data Parse symbols that show how the command will separate the long labels. Letters show the type of data the Parse command expects. The other symbols indicate the width of each piece of data. For example, the format L>>***** tells the Parse command to treat the characters in the first portion of a long label as a label and to include up to 9 characters in the first label. There is no functional difference between > and *. The > characters simply show the number of characters that were present in the long label used to create the format line. In this case, the format line will look something like this:

L>>******L>>******L>>******L>>******L>>******

Figure 13.16 shows a format line containing most of the data-type symbols. The symbols are L for labels, V for values, D for dates, and T for times. Data Parse also recognizes the S data-type. The S data-type symbol tells 1-2-3/W's parser to skip a block of characters. You can use this data type in a format line to throw out columns of data you don't want.

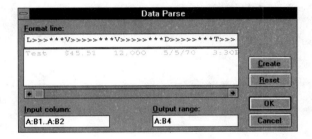

Figure 13.16. This illustration shows a format line above a long label in cell B2. The resulting, unformatted, parsed data is in range B4..F4.

Data External

What if all the data you want to analyze is in a corporate database? Or in a dBase IV database on a LAN? It used to be that you had to import that data into 1-2-3 before you could do anything with it. But 1-2-3/W lets you connect to many external databases directly from the worksheet. Not only can you bring data into the worksheet for analysis, but you can even write data back to the database. All this capability comes to you courtesy of Lotus's DataLens technology.

Introducing DataLens

If you ever have had to convert data files from one program to another, you know it usually isn't easy. Data conversions often require you to switch back and forth between programs, perform extensive file alterations, and use special conversion utilities. Then you have to clean up the results without too much manual intervention.

Lotus's DataLens technology offers a more sophisticated link between 1-2-3/W and other database application files than you get with conventional importing and exporting. For example, it lets you modify data created in a separate database package, even if the information resides on a remote mainframe computer or on a network file server.

1-2-3/W's Data External commands let you use DataLens by way of 1-2-3/W menu choices. 1-2-3 Release 3.x also supports DataLens.

Lotus markets a toolkit that helps software publishers make DataLens drivers, which are programs that oversee the translation of data and commands. One benefit of DataLens is that a given driver works with all DataLens-compatible software on the same system. If you have a DataLens driver for your database program, you can use your database files with any other program that supports DataLens.

The drivers included with 1-2-3/W give you access to dBase IV, Paradox, and SQL tables, but if you use a different database program, you'll need to acquire the appropriate driver. Lotus provides a toll-free number For information about the availability of DataLens drivers; call Lotus's toll-free number, 800-343-5414, from 8:30 A.M. to 8:00 P.M. Eastern time.

Query External Tables with 1-2-3/W

If you use database software other than 1-2-3/W, you may want to import selected data into a spreadsheet. Chances are your database program can't match 1-2-3/W's aptitude for calculations. And few, if any, database programs are as flexible as 1-2-3/W for manual control of report formats.

Unfortunately, importing and exporting data can be cumbersome and frustrating. 1-2-3/W offers a convenient and powerful alternative to traditional data import and export.

With 1-2-3/W's Data External commands, you can treat an external database table as if it were a conventional 1-2-3/W database Input range. You use ordinary Criteria and Output ranges to extract the desired records and fields from a table. The database you query can be of almost any size, but the information that you extract into the worksheet cannot exceed 1-2-3/W's constraints on memory size and the numbers of fields and records.

The Data External commands let you manipulate the database itself. Within 1-2-3/W you can create, delete, and modify tables in a database. Like other features of 1-2-3/W, the Data External commands support multiple-table, or "relational," databases. You can even issue commands in the command language of the program that created the database.

What You Need to Know

To use the Data External commands, you need to understand 1-2-3/W databases, as well as the program that created your database. Although the examples here import data from dBase III files, you don't have to know dBase III to do the exercises.

1-2-3/W comes with DBASE, a driver that helps the spreadsheet work with dBase IV files. It also comes with a dBase practice file called EMPLOYEE.DBF.

If dBase is your main point of reference for database terminology, a few terms used by the Data External commands may need explanation. dBase IV stores each table of data in a separate file. You generally identify a dBase database by the names of its component files.

The Data External commands use terminology that is more familiar to users of SQL-based relational databases, such as Oracle. These systems are based on tables rather than files. The actual names and structures of the files are neither apparent nor relevant to the user. What Oracle users call a database is somewhat analogous to a subdirectory that contains all of the files in a dBase application. To the Data External commands, a database is the location where the data is stored.

It's important to recognize 1-2-3/W's terminology because it can be confusing. In 1-2-3/W, the term *database table* is often used instead of *database* or *Input range*, simply because the database you query may consist of more than one table. An *external table* is the part of a database that you access via Data External commands.

Stepping through the Connect to External dialog box helps you build a full table name, which consists of the names of a driver, an external database, and an external table. The full table name is the combination of these elements, separated by spaces. Some database systems require one additional element, an owner name, but this is not needed with dBase files and the DBASE driver.

Once you have established a link to the external table, you need to build your Criteria and Output ranges. You could type in the field names, but that would require you to remember the exact spelling of the field names in the dBase file.

Instead, you can choose the Data External Options Paste Fields command. This command requests the range name of the external table and enters a table definition into the worksheet.

Try It: Setting Up a Link

Let's use the DBASE driver and the EMPLOYEE.DBF file to see how Data External commands work.

1. Start with a blank worksheet with the cell pointer in cell A1. Since you're just going to use worksheet A, you don't need to use 1-2-3/W's 3D notation (for example, specify A1 instead of A:A1).

2. Choose Data Connect to External and 1-2-3/W will take you through the steps of identifying the table you want to use. The names of the drivers you have installed appear in the dialog box. Select DBASE by double-clicking it or by clicking Connect.

3. Identify the database. For dBase databases, this is the subdirectory that contains the database file. If you installed 1-2-3 with the default settings, subdirectory C:\123W contains the dBase test file EMPLOYEE.DBF. Select C:\123W, or whichever directory contains your copy of EMPLOYEE.DBF. If the default is correct, just click Connect.

4. Select the table (or *file* in *dBase* parlance) named EMPLOYEE and click Connect. You now have access to an external database table.

5. Select *employee* as the range name for the table, and select Cancel.

Try It: Get a Table Definition

Let's ask 1-2-3/W to create a table definition for the example EMPLOYEE.DBF file.

1. With the cell pointer in cell A1, choose Data External Options.

2. Choose Paste Fields, select EMPLOYEE, and click OK. You should now see a table definition in range A1..F6.

The table definition that you import with the Data External Options Paste Fields command contains six columns of information about the external table. Not all of the columns are relevant to all external programs and their related drivers. The DBASE driver uses only the first three and the last: field names, data types, field widths, and field-creation strings. The other two columns, D and E, are for column labels and field descriptions.

The only column that you should be concerned with at this time is column A, which contains the field names. You need only the field names because all of 1-2-3/W's Data Query commands rely solely on information related to the field names in the Input, Criteria, and Output ranges. Since 1-2-3 arranges the field names vertically, you need to do a bit of reorganizing if you want to use them in Criteria and Output ranges. Start by erasing the other columns and transposing the remaining labels so that they fall in a single row. Then copy those labels to create the labels for the Output range. Finally, assign the two sets of labels as the Criteria and Output ranges for data queries.

Try It: Create Data Query Ranges and Extract Data from a dBase File

Let's continue with the EMPLOYEE.DBF example and create Criteria and Output ranges in the worksheet. Then we'll extract data from that file into the worksheet.

1. Erase range B1..F6.

2. Select range A1..A6, choose Range Transpose, and click OK. Now, the field names are in a row, ready to be used as a Criteria range.

3. Erase range A2..A6.

4. Copy the labels in range A1..F1 to cell A5. Now you're ready to specify the location of the various database ranges.

5. Choose Data Query and specify A1..F2 as the Criteria range.

6. Specify range A5..F5 as the Output range. Remember that any data entered below the Output range will be erased if you perform a Data Query Extract or Data Query Unique command.

7. Select the Input-Range box and press the NAME key (F3) for the list of range names. You need to identify the location of the Input range. Here's where you start to see the Data External facility in action. Instead of identifying cells in the current worksheet, you identify the external table as your Input range. Select EMPLOYEE and OK. From here on out, you can use the external table like any other 1-2-3/W database Input range.

8. Choose Extract. Because there are no criteria in the Criteria range, your Output range now contains a copy of the entire contents of EMPLOYEE.DBF.

If you're a seasoned user of 1-2-3 databases, you may see a potential problem with using an Input range that's not on the worksheet. Formulas in a Criteria range, such as +Z99<1987, often refer to the second row of the Input range (the first row that contains data). Also, many people use the Range Name Labels Down command to assign the field names at the top of the Input range to the first data row, so they can write formulas like +deptnum>3000. Since the external table doesn't actually reside in the worksheet, there's no way to assign range names to parts of it. Although the Data External Use command does not assign range names to the fields, criterion formulas can use field names from the external table as if they were range names.

Try It: Use Formulas in Criteria

Let's extract all the records from the EMPLOYEE.DBF file that have a department number greater than 3,000.

1. Move the cell pointer to cell F2 and enter the formula *+deptnum>3000*. An ERR indicator appears in cell F2, but don't worry about it. 1-2-3/W treats this formula as an error because it refers to a range name that doesn't really exist. The formula, however, is used in a Data Query command.

2. Press the QUERY key to perform another Data Query Extract operation. Your Output range now contains a list of employees whose department number is greater than 3,000.

Keep in mind that in large databases, some queries might require a larger Output range than 1-2-3/W can accommodate. Some database commands, such as the Data Query Find command, aren't practical with an external table. And remember that some of the more advanced Data External features aren't supported by the DBASE driver.

Extra Commands via the Classic /Data Menu

There are three Data External commands that are available only on the 1-2-3 Classic menu. You access these simply by pressing the slash key (/) and selecting Data External. You can use these commands to get a list of all the external data tables in the current directory; to set 1-2-3/W so that it periodically updates all @D functions and Data Queries involving external tables; and to change the character set 1-2-3/W uses when extracting data from an external table.

/Data External List Tables enters a list of the names, owners, and descriptions of all the tables in an external database into a range in the worksheet. The first column of the resulting table contains the names of the external tables. The second column contains the owner names. The third column contains the descriptions of each table.

/Data External Other Refresh tells 1-2-3/W to refresh @D functions and Data Queries for external data tables. This is a handy feature for people who are sharing database files with others on a network because it helps ensure that your data is current.

When you select /Data External Other Refresh, 1-2-3/W gives you three menu options: Automatic, Manual, and Interval. If you select Automatic, 1-2-3/W will automatically update all relevant @D functions and the last Data Query operation every second. To turn this automatic updating off, select Manual. If you select manual, you have to reissue the Data Query commands. If you want an automatic interval other than one second, select Interval and enter the number of seconds you want between updates.

/Data External Other Translation lets you select a character set for use with external tables. You'll need this command when the character set of the database table doesn't match 1-2-3/W's current character set. If you see nonstandard characters in records when you extract them into 1-2-3, try selecting a character set using this command. The character set you select remains in effect for all the tables in that database until you select another character set or end the 1-2-3 session.

Using @DQUERY to Access External Database Functions in Queries

@DQUERY is an unusual @function. It works like the Data External Options Send Command command, letting you send a command to an external database program. The difference is that you use @DQUERY as part of a Criteria range when you want to conduct queries against the external data table. Its syntax is @DQUERY(*function, external_arguments*).

For example, suppose you have an external database that contains average temperatures for cities around the world. This database stores all the temperatures as Centigrade, but you want to query the table using Fahrenheit temperatures. Let's say the external database program has a function called CENTI-

GRADE that converts Fahrenheit temperatures to Centigrade. You could then use the @DQUERY function to use that external database's function for your queries. You might, for example, enter the formula @DQUERY("centigrade", 70) in a Criteria range to extract records from an external table that match the temperature in Centigrade that is equivalent to 70 degrees Fahrenheit.

1-2-3/W will recalculate @DQUERY formulas whenever you select Data Query Delete, Data Query Extract, Data Query Modify Extract, or Data Query Modify Replace. It does not recalculate @DQUERY formulas when the worksheet normally recalculates other @function formulas, such as when you press the CALC key.

@DQUERY and the Data External commands represent the advanced end of 1-2-3/W's database spectrum. A lot of database users will never need to do anything more complicated than a simple Data Sort or Data Query Extract.

But other @D functions, such as @DSUM, are valuable in most any database. You'll learn about these in the following chapter.

14

Data Analysis with @D Functions

How many employees earn over $50,000 a year, and what is the sum of their salaries? What was the lowest unit sales amount for a selected product? What was the average revenue generated by reps in the quarter? These are typical of the questions you might want to answer with information stored in a database. You answer such questions by applying statistical @functions.

Statistical @functions fall into two categories. The first includes @functions that evaluate all the values in a range. The @SUM function falls into this group. The other includes @functions that evaluate a subset of the values in a database.

In this chapter we'll quickly review the statistical @functions that work with all values in a range. Then we'll explore their counterparts—the @D statistical functions, which let you analyze only data that meet certain criteria.

Figure 14.1 shows a worksheet that can serve as a convenient reference for some of the most commonly used statistical @functions.

In the figure, column D contains labels that show the type of information you can glean by using 1-2-3/W's built-in @functions. The labels organize the formulas you'll enter according to the two categories of statistical @functions. You probably already know how to enter some of these functions.

If you feel comfortable with the @SUM function, learning the rest of the @functions in the All category should be a piece of cake. To figure out the average (mean) purchase amount, use the @AVG function. To count the nonblank cells in a range, use @COUNT.

> *In this chapter you'll learn how to:*
>
> - Find the largest value in a range or database
> - Find the smallest value in a range or database
> - Find the average or mean value of a range or database
> - Find the standard deviation of values in a range or database
> - Find the variance of values in a range or database

	A	B	C	D	E	F
1	Date	Customer	Amount	Records	All	Criteria
2						
3				Average:		
4	Date	Customer	Amount	Count:		
5	02/03/91	Big Co. W	$9,567	Maximum:		
6	02/19/91	Small Co.	$3,034	Minimum:		
7	04/08/91	Big Co. E	$847	Standard deviation:		
8	05/22/91	Big Co. E	$8,847	Sample standard deviation:		
9	05/23/91	Small Co.	$6,124	Sum:		
10	06/13/91	Big Co. W	$3,135	Variance:		
11	07/27/91	Small Co.	$4,145	Sample Variance:		
12	09/02/91	Big Co. E	$6,147			
13	10/31/91	Small Co.	$5,455			
14	11/10/91	Big Co. E	$6,132			

Figure 14.1. Create this sample database to test some of 1-2-3/W's statistical @functions. After you've entered all the pertinent @functions into column F, this worksheet will serve as a reference.

Try It: Create the STATFUNC.WK3 Worksheet

Let's create the worksheet shown in Figure 14.1 to serve as a reference of statistical @functions.

1. Enter the dates, labels, and values, as shown in Figure 14.1.

2. Set the width of column D to 22 and the widths of columns E and F to 11.

3. Use the Worksheet Global Setting Format command to assign the Currency format with no decimal places to the whole worksheet. Use the Range Format command to assign the Long Intl Date format to range A5..A14.

4. Use the Range Name Create command to assign the name *crit* to range A1..C2. Assign the name *database* to range A4..C14. Assign the name *column* to range C5..C14.

5. Select range A4..C4 and choose Range Name Label Create Down to assign those labels as names for the cells below them.

6. Select range D3..D11 and choose Style Alignment Right.

7. Select range D3..D11 and choose Style Font Bold.

8. Save the file with the name STATFUNC.WK3.

Try It: Enter Statistical @Functions

Let's enter all the statistical @functions for the All column.

1. Enter the formula @*AVG(column)* in cell E3 to determine the average value in the range named *column*.

2. Enter the formula @*COUNT(column)* in cell E4 to find the number of nonblank cells in *column*. Format this cell as General with the Range Format command.

3. Enter the formulas @*MAX(column)* and @*MIN(column)* in cells E5 and E6, respectively, to determine the highest and lowest amounts in *column*.

4. Finding the standard deviation is just as easy. Enter the formula @*STD(column)* in cell E7.

5. Enter the formula @*STDS(column)* in cell E8 to determine the sample standard deviation.

6. Enter the formula @*SUM(column)* in cell E9 to calculate the sum of values in *column*.

7. Enter the formula @*VAR(column)* in cell E10 to determine the population variance of the values in *column*.

8. Enter the formula @*VARS(column)* in cell E11 to determine the sample variance of the values in *column*.

Calculating statistical measures for all the values in a given range is very easy. Doing the same thing for a subset of records in a database is only a little harder. The database-statistical or @D functions all use the same syntax. They each take three arguments: *input, field name (or offset)*, and *criteria*. The first and last of these arguments are already familiar, since they're the same as the Input and Criteria ranges for the Data Query commands. In the STATFUNC worksheet, the Input range is *database* and the Criteria range is *crit*. The *field name* argument tells the @function which column to evaluate in the database. In the STATFUNC worksheet the field name we want to analyze is *Amount*. Note that you can also specify the Amount column by its offset number. The offset is the number of columns to the right of the first column in the database. In STATFUNC, you're analyzing the data in column C. That column is two columns to the right of the first column in the *database* range. Can you see how that works? Column A is offset 0, and column B is offset 1, and column C, *Amount*, is offset 2.

Except for the three arguments, the @D functions are the same as the regular statistical @functions. So using the arguments *database*, *Amount* and *crit*, you can easily create the equivalent @D functions in the Criteria column (column F) shown in Figure 14.1.

Try It: Enter @D Functions in STATFUNC

Let's enter all the equivalent @D functions in column F of the STATFUNC.WK3 worksheet. Since the Criteria range is blank, the @D functions match all the records in the database, so they will return the same answer as the equivalent @ functions in the E column.

1. Enter the formula *@DAVG(database,"Amount",crit)* in cell F3. It returns the average of all the values in column C of *database* because there's no criterion in the Criteria range, *crit*.

2. Enter the formula *@DCOUNT(database,"Amount",crit)* in cell F4, *@DMAX (database,Amount,crit)* in cell F5, *@DMIN(database,"Amount",crit)* in cell F6, *@DSTD(database,"Amount",crit)* in cell F7, *@DSTDS(database,"Amount", crit)* in cell F8, *@DSUM(database,"Amount",crit)* in cell F9, *@DVAR(database, "Amount",* crit) in cell F10, and *@DVARS(database,"Amount",crit)* in cell F11.

3. Assign the General format to cell F4.

4. Now move the cell pointer to cell B2 and enter the label *Small Co.*, as shown in Figure 14.2. Note how the values returned by the @D functions change.

A	A	B	C	D	E	F
1	Date	Customer	Amount	Records	All	Criteria
2		Small Co.				
3				Average:	$5,343	$4,690
4	Date	Customer	Amount	Count:	10	4
5	02/03/91	Big Co. W	$9,567	Maximum:	$9,567	$6,124
6	02/19/91	Small Co.	$3,034	Minimum:	$847	$3,034
7	04/08/91	Big Co. E	$847	Standard deviation:	$2,527	$1,192
8	05/22/91	Big Co. E	$8,847	Sample standard deviation:	$2,664	$1,376
9	05/23/91	Small Co.	$6,124	Sum:	$53,433	$18,758
10	06/13/91	Big Co. W	$3,135	Variance:	$6,386,760	$1,420,235
11	07/27/91	Small Co.	$4,145	Sample Variance:	$7,096,400	$1,893,647
12	09/02/91	Big Co. E	$6,147			
13	10/31/91	Small Co.	$5,455			
14	11/10/91	Big Co. E	$6,132			

Figure 14.2. The @D functions let you glean statistical information on a subset of records in a database. You just have to enter the criterion for the records you want to analyze.

The @D functions intimidate many 1-2-3 users, but as you can see, they're really not so hard to use. You just have to know how to set up a Criteria range and understand the meaning of the three arguments. Save this worksheet and refer to it if you forget how the @D functions work.

The @DGET Function

Like the @DQUERY function, which we discussed in Chapter 13, @DGET doesn't really belong with the rest of the statistically oriented @D functions. Neither of these functions performs a statistical calculation, which is why we didn't include them in the previous discussion. But this doesn't mean that these @D functions aren't useful. Let's see what you can do with the @DGET function.

The @DGET function simply returns a value or label from a data table that matches a criterion in the Criteria range. It is similar to the @VLOOKUP function except that it uses a database Criteria range rather than matching a variable with the entries in the first column, the way @VLOOKUP does.

The syntax for this function is @DGET(*input,field,criteria*). For example, if you enter the label *Small Co.* in cell B2 and the number *6124* in cell C2 of the worksheet shown in Figure 14.2, the formula @DGET(A4..C14,"DATE",A1..C2) returns the date value for 05/23/91. That's because the record in row 9 is the only record that matches the criteria and the second argument of the formula specifies the data field. You would get the same result with the formula @DGET(A4..C14,0,A1..C2), since you can specify fields in a database by either column offset or by name.

Note that @DGET returns an answer if there is one and only one matching record. If no records match the criteria, @DGET returns ERR. If more than one record matches the criteria, @DGET also returns ERR.

Since @DGET is useful only for matching unique records, you'll find that it's most useful in databases that have a unique key. It's handy for looking up employee names given an employee number, for example.

15

Creative Criteria

Whether querying a database or applying @D functions, only your ability to create meaningful criteria limits what you can learn. To see how you might devise creative criteria, use the STATFUNC.WK3 worksheet that you created in Chapter 14. If you didn't work through that section, you might want to go back and create the STATFUNC.WK3 worksheet.

For the most part, we've used only simple criteria when discussing the use of 1-2-3/W databases and @D functions. But what if you want to match records using more complex criteria? Well, 1-2-3/W lets you do just that.

For example, to get stats on all of Big Company—east and west—just set up a logical formula in the Criteria range that specifies that criteria. The easiest way to do that is to enter the label *B** in cell B2, as shown in Figure 15.1. This tells 1-2-3/W that you want to look at all labels that start with the letter B. That works here since you know that only *Big Co. E* and *Big Co. W* start with B. If you didn't know that, you could narrow the search by entering the label *Big Co. ?*.

Both these criteria make use of wild-card characters. The asterisk (*) tells 1-2-3/W to match all remaining characters. So the string *B** tells 1-2-3/W to match all entries that start with B, regardless of subsequent characters. The criteria *B*, without the asterisk, selects only entries that contain the letter B alone.

The question mark (?) tells 1-2-3/W to match any single character. So the criteria *Big Co. ?* selects any records that start with *Big Co.* followed by a space and any character. 1-2-3/W would not match records that started with *Big Co.* but that had no following letter. Similarly, it also wouldn't match records that started with *Big Co. West*. If you wanted such records selected, you would use the asterisk: *Big Co. **.

> **In this chapter you'll learn how to:**
> - Create complex logical criteria for data queries
> - Use wild-card characters in criteria
> - Use logical operators in criteria
> - Create multiple conditions as criteria
> - Use formulas in criteria
> - Match records by searching for strings in a field
> - Match records by date, day, month, or time values in fields

	A	B	C	D	E	F
1	Date	Customer	Amount	Records	All	Criteria
2		B*				
3				Average:	$5,343	$5,779
4	Date	Customer	Amount	Count:	10	6
5	02/03/91	Big Co. W	$9,567	Maximum:	$9,567	$9,567
6	02/19/91	Small Co.	$3,034	Minimum:	$847	$847
7	04/08/91	Big Co. E	$847	Standard Deviation:	$2,527	$3,037
8	05/22/91	Big Co. E	$8,847	Sample Standard Deviation:	$2,664	$3,327
9	05/23/91	Small Co.	$6,124	Sum:	$53,433	$34,675
10	06/13/91	Big Co. W	$3,135	Variance:	$6,386,760	$9,222,827
11	07/27/91	Small Co.	$4,145	Sample Variance:	$7,096,400	$11,067,392
12	09/02/91	Big Co. E	$6,147			
13	10/30/91	Small Co.	$5,455			
14	11/10/91	Big Co. E	$6,132			

Figure 15.1. You can get @D functions and Data Query commands to operate on records that match a variety of criteria. Here, you use a wild-card character to select Big Company East and Big Company West.

Operators

You can create criteria for database queries and @D functions using the following logical operators in labels:

Operator	Matches fields that are:
<*string*	Less than *string*
<=*string*	Less than or equal to *string*
<>*string*	Not equal to *string*
=*string*	Equal to *string*
>*string*	Greater than *string*
>=*string*	Greater than or equal to *string*
~*string*	Not *string*

You can use these operators on fields that are either values or labels. For example, if you enter '>C in cell B2 of the STATFUNC worksheet, you'll get all the Small Co. records. That's because those are the only records that are "greater than" the label *C*. In other words, these are records that 1-2-3/W would sort after the label *C*.

You use an operator for a value field the same way. For example, if you enter '>6000 in cell C2, you'll get the top five records in the database.

Experiment with the operators to see how each works. Just remember to start the label with a label prefix followed by the operator and the string.

Multiple Conditions

There are times when a single condition is not enough. Say, for example, that you want to examine all records with sales amounts less than 8,000 and more than 1,000. To set up that kind of criterion, you need to create a logical formula in the Criteria range.

To do that you use a logical formula that performs a test on a field as identified by its field name—such as *+amount<8000+#AND#amount>1000*.

Try It: Create a Compound Criterion

Let's use the Criteria range in the STATFUNCS worksheet to match all records with sales amounts less than 8,000 and greater than 1,000.

Erase range A2..C2 and enter the formula *+C5<8000#AND#C5>1000* in cell C2. This formula tells 1-2-3/W to find all records whose Amount field is less than 8,000 and greater than 1,000. Note: In this type of logical formula, both conditions must be true to get a match.

You can also create logical formulas that refer to the first record—as a representative record in your database—when you want to create a criterion involving the operator #AND# for the same field as in +C5<8000#AND#C5>1000. And while 1-2-3/W lets you create a formula like +B5="Small Co."#AND#C5<8000, its better to enter '=*Small Co*. in cell B2 and '*<8000* in cell C2. By putting them in the same row in the criteria range, they effectively function like a logical #AND#. Such constructs are clearer and easier to modify later.

Some 1-2-3/W professionals like to assign the fields names as range names for the first record of a database. You can do that easily. Just move the cell pointer to the first name (here, cell A4), choose Range Name Label Create Down, and indicate all the field names (A4..C4). If you use the field names as range names, you can enter less cryptic formulas like +amount<8000#AND#amount>1000 and not have them evaluate to ERR.

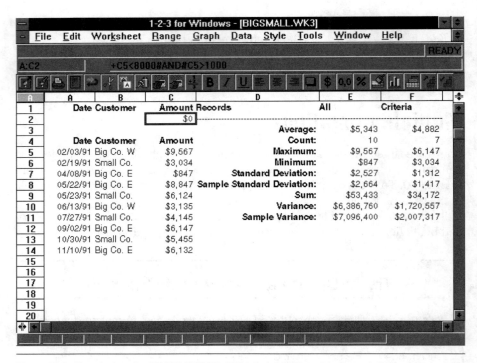

Figure 15.2. Here, the formula +C5<8000#AND#C5>1000 tells 1-2-3/W to match all records that have a value in the *amount* field that is less than 8,000 and greater than 1,000. The logical formula returns 0 (false) or 1 (true) based on its evaluation of the first record in the database. Here, that record does not meet the criteria.

To create criteria involving the logical operator #OR#, you should add rows to the Criteria range. In the STATFUNC worksheet, that would mean reassigning the Criteria range, *crit*, using the Data Query command. Then, the @D functions with reference to *crit* in the criteria column F3..F11 would automatically reflect the new values.

Once you have two rows for entering criteria, you just enter any #OR#-type criteria in the second row. Each row in the Criteria range is treated as an *or* condition. Your database command or function will use all values that meet the first row's Criteria, *or* the second row's and so on. For example, you could enter '*B** in cell B2 and '>*5000* in cell C3 if you expanded the Criteria range in the STATFUNC worksheet. That would find all records with a customer name that starts with the letter B, or all records that have an amount greater than 5,000.

Formulas in the Criteria range

The number of ways you can use the Criteria range to match records in a database is limited only by your imagination. If you understand how 1-2-3/W uses formulas in the Criteria range, it's easy to find a formula to fit your particular needs.

Again, the thing to remember is that you set up a formula that references the field names (or the first record) in the database. Note that first record acts as a reference record. 1-2-3/W examines all subsequent records, replacing the cell reference to the first record with an appropriate new address. For example, if you clear the Criteria range in the STATFUNC worksheet and enter the formula +C5>5000 in cell C2, the formula returns 1 (true), since the value of the first record in cell C5 is greater than 5,000. Now the @D functions and the Data Query functions replace the C5 reference with C6, C7, and so on, to evaluate the condition against each record in the database. 1-2-3/W selects or matches all records for which the formula returns any value other than 0 or ERR.

If you entered the formula +C5-9567 in cell C2, all records would match the criterion except the first one, since 9567-9567 is 0. Experiment with complex criteria. To understand better how 1-2-3 works, you can temporarily change the first record to see how your formula in the criteria range evaluates different entries in the field(s) you're referencing.

Common Solutions

Simply understanding how 1-2-3/W uses a Criteria range doesn't mean that you realize all the querying power you have. How do you find all the records that contain *Inc* anywhere in the company name? How do you match all the records for a particular date? The answers to these and other common questions follow.

Find a specific string

Say that you want to select all records that contain a particular string in a particular field. You can create a criterion using the @FIND formula to do just that. For example, enter the formula *@FIND("mall",B5,0)+1* in cell B2 of the STATFUNC worksheet. With that criterion, the @D functions find all the records whose *customer* field contains the string *Small Co.*, as shown in Figure 15.3.

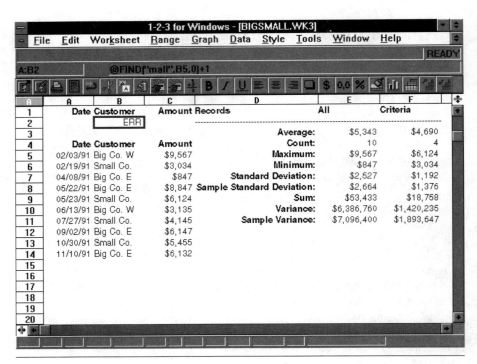

Figure 15.3. You can use the @FIND formula in the Criteria range to match records that have a particular string anywhere in a particular field. Here, the @D functions match all records whose *customer* field contains the string *mall*.

You have to end the @FIND formula with the expression +1 so that 1-2-3/W matches records starting with the string you're trying to match. For example, if one of the customers in the database in Figure 15.3 were named Mallwart, the @FIND formula alone would return 0, since the string *mall* starts at offset 0. And since the @FIND function returns ERR if the string isn't present, we can safely add to the @FIND function without causing the formula to match unwanted records. If the record doesn't contain the string, the formula returns ERR and 1-2-3/W doesn't match it. If the record does contain the string, all we have to do is make sure that it doesn't return 0.

You don't have to enter all the conditions of a formula in the Criteria range. For example, you could enter the formula @FIND($H$1,B5,0)+1 and then enter the strings you want found in cell H1. Any formula criterion can refer to a cell in the worksheet. Just remember to use absolute cell references.

You can also compare fields with each other. For example, you might want to compare one quarter's results with another's, as shown in Figure 15.4.

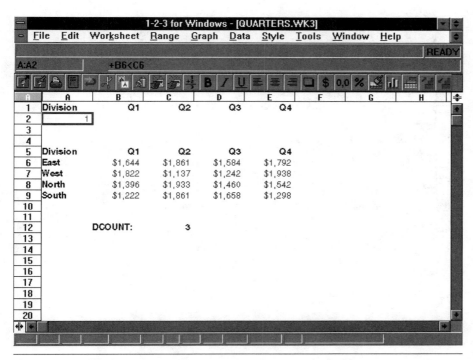

Figure 15.4. To match records by comparing one field to another, enter a representative formula for the first record anywhere in the Criteria range. Here, the @DCOUNT formula in cell C12 matches all records in which the *Q2* amount is greater than the *Q1* amount. The formula that expresses this condition is in cell A2, but it could be anywhere in the Criteria range.

To match all records in which the *Q2* amount is greater than the *Q1* amount, you just need to enter the formula +B6<C6 anywhere in the Criteria range. Note that these are both relative cell references. If you entered the formula +B6<$C$6, 1-2-3/W would match all records in which the *Q1* amount is less than the *Q2* amount for the East division.

Find a Specific Date

There are many ways to find records that contain specific dates. One way is to create a logical formula that references the date field in the database. For example, consider the database in Figure 15.5. The criterion formula +A5>@DATE(91,5,24) in cell A2 selects all records containing a date value greater than that returned by the formula @DATE(91,5,24).

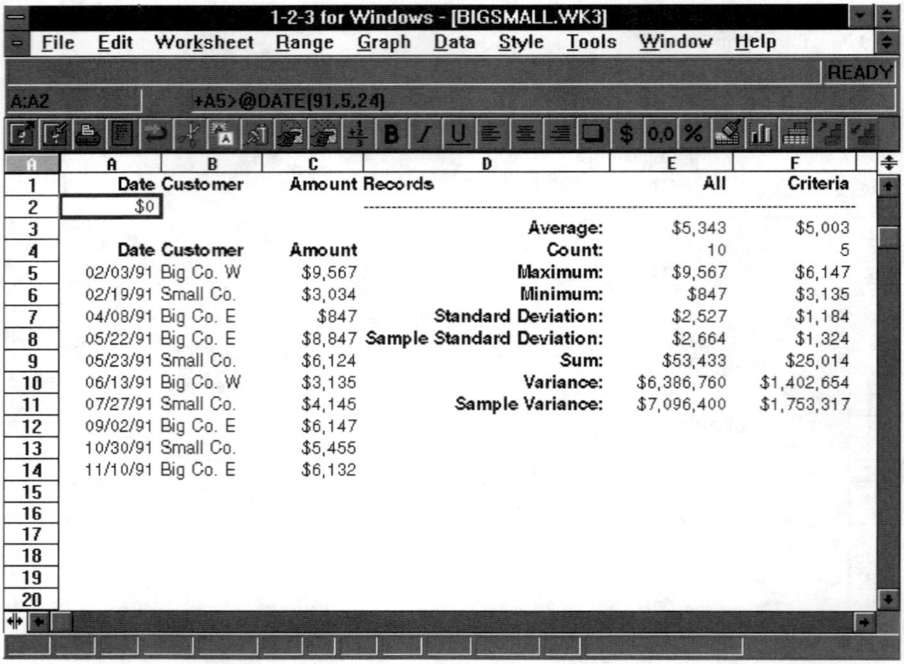

Figure 15.5. To use dates as a criterion, you can create a logical formula using the @DATE formula to reference a date field.

You can use any time-related @functions in the Criteria range. For example, the formula @DAY(A5)=3 matches all records in which the date is the third day of the month. The formula @MONTH(A5)=2 matches all records with a February date. The formula @YEAR(A5)=91 matches all records with dates in 1991.

In some databases, you may enter dates using the @NOW function. That makes comparisons to @DATE formulas a little more complex, since the @NOW formula includes a fractional amount for the time of the day. When you want to make comparisons in such databases, just use the @INT function to trim the fractional portion of the date values from the field values. For example, the formula +@INT(A5)=@DATE(91,5,22) will find any record whose date is May 22, 1991, regardless of whether the date serial number in the database includes a decimal component.

16

In-Depth Data Analysis

What if you spent $50,000 on advertising in the next quarter? Or $45,000? Or $60,000? What happens if you increase the percentage of potassium in the fertilizer mix by 5%? What if the increase is 7%? Or 8%? Is there a relationship between the color of a product and how well the product sells? Does the amount spent on advertising in a particular market actually affect sales? And if so, by how much?

There is no end to the questions you might ask when analyzing your business. When you understand the tools that let you perform what-if analyses, frequency distributions, and regression analyses, you can use 1-2-3/W to answer these questions. Even if you don't know what a frequency distribution or a regression analysis is, follow along. You will gain some insights that will let you begin doing your own in-depth data analyses. For some analytical problems, 1-2-3/W's Solver and Backsolver tools are simpler and more flexible than these "traditional" 1-2-3 techniques. So, be sure to check out Chapter 19 which shows you how to use 1-2-3/W's new problem-solving techniques.

> **In this chapter you'll learn how to:**
> - **Perform what-if analysis with one-, two-, and three-way data tables**
> - **Cross-tabulate data in a database**
> - **Calculate frequency distributions and plot them as histograms**
> - **Use the Matrix Multiply command to solve simultaneous equations**
> - **Perform regression analysis to make predictions based on historical data**

Data Tables for What-If Modeling

It's easy to set up financial analyses in 1-2-3/W. You can happily plug in numbers until the worksheet tells you what you want to know. But what if the numbers aren't accurate? Projections are especially prone to error, and that can mean disaster if you make the wrong financial decision.

To help you deal with an uncertain world, 1-2-3/W includes commands for conducting what-if and sensitivity analyses. You can see how the bottom line varies as your assumptions change.

Imagine that your company is considering buying a wax injector machine that has a useful life of just 11 months. The machine costs $100,000, and you believe it will have a salvage value of about $95,000 because its parts are so valuable. While you have it, you think the wax injector will generate about $1,200 of profit per month. To clarify the situation, you might produce a worksheet like the one shown in Figure 16.1.

	A	B
1	Hurdle:	0.58%
2	Profit:	$1,200
3	NPV:	$1,383
4	IRR:	0.70%
5		
6	Period	Cash flow
7	0	($100,000)
8	1	$1,200
9	2	$1,200
10	3	$1,200
11	4	$1,200
12	5	$1,200
13	6	$1,200
14	7	$1,200
15	8	$1,200
16	9	$1,200
17	10	$1,200
18	11	$1,200
19	12	$95,000

Figure 16.1. A quick analysis based on projections shows that the machine purchase is worthwhile. The NPV is positive and the IRR is higher than the hurdle rate. But are the projections accurate?

In this figure the "hurdle rate" in cell B1 is the monthly return that you'll receive if you invest the $100,000 elsewhere. The @NPV formula in cell B3, @NPV(B1, B&..B19), uses the hurdle rate to discount the cash flows you receive in future months. The result is a net present value that tells you how much better off you'll be by investing in the wax injector. The @IRR formula in cell B4, @IRR(B1, B7..B19), uses the hurdle rate to help calculate the internal rate of return of the cash inflows and outflows associated with the wax injector investment

In this case, @NPV and @IRR formulas tell us that the purchase is a go. The @NPV in cell B3 is $1,383—the amount that you'll gain, in current dollars, by investing in the wax injector. The @IRR in cell B4 is 0.71—a better rate of return than the 0.581 you could get by investing elsewhere.

But you wonder about the risk involved. The biggest question in your mind concerns the reliability of the $1,200-profit-per-month estimate. What if the machine is more costly to operate than expected? How bad would it be if the profit per month were $1,175? $1,150? $1,000?

You could plug in different values to see how they affect the NPV, but that's time consuming and hard to document. Fortunately, there's an easier way. Just use the Data What-if Table command. With the Data What-if Table command, you can create a range of cells that show the results of changing one or two variables in a specified formula. To see how this works, follow the instructions in the box titled, Try It: Create a What-If Table.

	A	B	C	D	E
1	Hurdle:	0.58%			NPV
2	Profit:	$1,200			+B3
3	NPV:	$1,383			$950
4	IRR:	0.70%			$975
5					$1,000
6	Period	Cash flow			$1,025
7	0	($100,000)			$1,050
8	1	$1,200			$1,075
9	2	$1,200			$1,100
10	3	$1,200			$1,125
11	4	$1,200			$1,150
12	5	$1,200			$1,175
13	6	$1,200			$1,200
14	7	$1,200			$1,225
15	8	$1,200			$1,250
16	9	$1,200			$1,275
17	10	$1,200			
18	11	$1,200			
19	12	$95,000			

Figure 16.2. To use the Data What-if Table command, first create a column of values that represent alternate projections.

Try It: Create a What-If Table

Let's create the worksheet shown in Figure 16.2 and create a one-way what-if table.

1. Enter labels and values as shown in Figure 16.2.
2. Use the Range Format command to assign the text format to range E2..G2 and the Currency 0 format to range D3..E16.
3. Enter the following formulas in the cells indicated:

   B3: +B7+@NPV(B1,B8..B19)
   B4: @IRR(B1,B7..B19)
   B8: +$B$2 (copied to B9..B18)
   B19: 95000

4. Select range D2..E16 as the Table range, and choose Data What-if Table 1-Way.
5. Indicate cell E2 as the input cell and click OK. 1-2-3/W generates the table shown in Figure 16.3.

When you change just one variable, such as monthly profit, you produce a *one-way* what-if table as shown Figure 16.3. One-way what-if tables let you examine the effect of a change in *one* variable on the result of one or more formulas. In this example, IRR also depends on the profit per month. You don't have to create another what-if table to see how changes in the profit variable affect the result of that formula. You can simply add more columns to the current what-if table. Just create more formulas as column headers, reissue the Data What-if Table 1-Way command and expand the Table range to include the new columns. Enter the formula +B4 in cell F2 and the formula +B4*12 in cell G2. Then select D2..G16 as the new Table range, choose Data What-if Table 1-Way, and again specify cell B2 as the input cell. Figure 16.4 shows the resulting what-if table.

	A	B	C	D	E
1	Hurdle:	0.58%			NPV
2	Profit:	$1,200			+B3
3	NPV:	$1,383		$950	($1,274)
4	IRR:	0.70%		$975	($1,008)
5				$1,000	($743)
6	Period	Cash flow		$1,025	($477)
7	0	($100,000)		$1,050	($211)
8	1	$1,200		$1,075	$54
9	2	$1,200		$1,100	$320
10	3	$1,200		$1,125	$586
11	4	$1,200		$1,150	$851
12	5	$1,200		$1,175	$1,117
13	6	$1,200		$1,200	$1,383
14	7	$1,200		$1,225	$1,648
15	8	$1,200		$1,250	$1,914
16	9	$1,200		$1,275	$2,180
17	10	$1,200			
18	11	$1,200			
19	12	$95,000			

Figure 16.3. The Data What-if Table command shows how NPV varies when the profit per month varies. You can see that the project is profitable as long as the profit per month doesn't drop much below $1,075.

	A	B	C	D	E	F	G
1	Hurdle:	0.58%			NPV	IRR	IRR*12
2	Profit:	$1,200			+B3	+B4	+B4*12
3	NPV:	$1,383		$950	($1,274)	0.47%	5.60%
4	IRR:	0.70%		$975	($1,008)	0.49%	5.88%
5				$1,000	($743)	0.51%	6.17%
6	Period	Cash flow		$1,025	($477)	0.54%	6.45%
7	0	($100,000)		$1,050	($211)	0.56%	6.73%
8	1	$1,200		$1,075	$54	0.58%	7.02%
9	2	$1,200		$1,100	$320	0.61%	7.30%
10	3	$1,200		$1,125	$586	0.63%	7.59%
11	4	$1,200		$1,150	$851	0.66%	7.87%
12	5	$1,200		$1,175	$1,117	0.68%	8.15%
13	6	$1,200		$1,200	$1,383	0.70%	8.44%
14	7	$1,200		$1,225	$1,648	0.73%	8.72%
15	8	$1,200		$1,250	$1,914	0.75%	9.00%
16	9	$1,200		$1,275	$2,180	0.77%	9.29%
17	10	$1,200					
18	11	$1,200					
19	12	$95,000					

Figure 16.4. By adding more formulas at the top of the what-if Table range, you can see the effect of a change in one variable on the result of several formulas.

Two-Way What-If Tables

You also can analyze data using a *two-way* what-if table. It works the same way as the one-way what-if table except that you vary two input cells instead of just one. Unlike the one-way what-if table, a two-way what-if table lets you see the result of only one formula at a time.

Consider the wax injector example. What if you wondered not just about the profit-per-month projection but also about the projected-salvage value. You can set up a two-way what-if table that varies both these values to see the effect on NPV. Figure 16.5 shows how you might set up such a what-if table.

	A	B	C	D	E	F	G
1	Hurdle:	0.58%		Profit			
2	Profit:	$1,200	Salvage	+B3	$93,000	$94,000	$95,000
3	NPV:	$1,383		$950			
4	IRR:	0.70%		$975			
5				$1,000			
6	Period	Cash flow		$1,025			
7	0	($100,000)		$1,050			
8	1	$1,200		$1,075			
9	2	$1,200		$1,100			
10	3	$1,200		$1,125			
11	4	$1,200		$1,150			
12	5	$1,200		$1,175			
13	6	$1,200		$1,200			
14	7	$1,200		$1,225			
15	8	$1,200		$1,250			
16	9	$1,200		$1,275			
17	10	$1,200					
18	11	$1,200					
19	12	$95,000					

Figure 16.5. The two-way what-if table lets you evaluate only one formula. You enter this formula in the upper-left corner of the what-if table—here, in cell D2. The left column of the what-if table contains the values for the first input cell, as in the one-way what-if table. The top row of the what-if table contains the values for the second input cell.

Once you've prepared the range for the Data What-if Table command, you just use the 2-Way Table command.

Try It: Generate a Two-Way What-If Table

Let's create a two-way table.

1. Modify your worksheet from the previous example, as shown in Figure 16.5.
2. Select range D2..G16 as the Table range, then choose Data What-if Table 2-Way.
3. Enter B2 as input cell 1 and cell B19 as input cell 2. 1-2-3/W generates a two-way table, as shown in Figure 16.6.

	A	B	C	D	E	F	G
1	Hurdle:	0.58%		Profit			
2	Profit:	$1,200	Salvage	+B3	$93,000	$94,000	$95,000
3	NPV:	$1,383		$950	($3,140)	($2,207)	($1,274)
4	IRR:	0.70%		$975	($2,874)	($1,941)	($1,008)
5				$1,000	($2,609)	($1,676)	($743)
6	Period	Cash flow		$1,025	($2,343)	($1,410)	($477)
7	0	($100,000)		$1,050	($2,077)	($1,144)	($211)
8	1	$1,200		$1,075	($1,812)	($879)	$54
9	2	$1,200		$1,100	($1,546)	($613)	$320
10	3	$1,200		$1,125	($1,280)	($347)	$586
11	4	$1,200		$1,150	($1,015)	($82)	$851
12	5	$1,200		$1,175	($749)	$184	$1,117
13	6	$1,200		$1,200	($483)	$450	$1,383
14	7	$1,200		$1,225	($218)	$715	$1,648
15	8	$1,200		$1,250	$48	$981	$1,914
16	9	$1,200		$1,275	$314	$1,247	$2,180

Figure 16.6. The two-way what-if table shows you that the profitability of the purchase is somewhat sensitive to fluctuations in the salvage value of the machine. If the salvage value drops to $93,000, then the what-if table doesn't show a positive NPV until the profit per month reaches $1,250, which is above the current projection.

Three-Way What-If Tables

If a two-way what-if table just isn't enough, 1-2-3/W lets you use its 3-D structure to create a three-way data table. So if you want to see how the NPV results will vary with profit, salvage value, and hurdle rate, you create a three-way what-if table. The three-way table extends across the three dimensions of 1-2-3/W, so you'll have to add additional sheets to accommodate the third variable. Figure 16.7 shows how to set up a three-way data table. This table differs from the two-way table in the previous example in that it shows the effect of a changing hurdle rate. We just copied the two-way table format to a second and third sheet and entered three different hurdle rates in the upper-left corner of each table. Here, we chose to vary the original hurdle rate up and down by six-hundredths of a percent.

The three-way table differs from the one-way and two-way tables in that the formula that includes the varying input(s) is not in the table. You can see that the formula that was in cell A:D2 of the two-way table, +B3 is replaced with one of the hurdle-rate values. Instead, you specify the formula in a dialog box, as shown in Figure 16.8.

Note that the Table range has to include the range in all the spreadsheets. Once you fill in the ranges and the formula cell information, clicking OK fills in the three-way table, as shown in Figure 16.9.

In-Depth Data Analysis   377

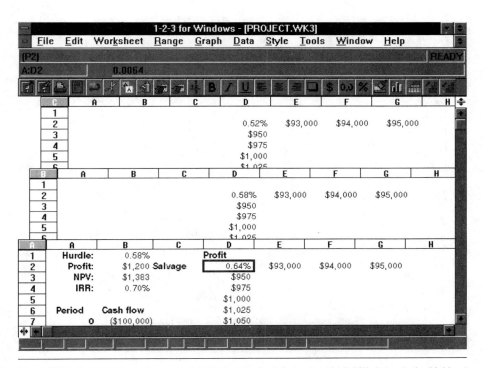

Figure 16.7. You can set up a three-way what-if table using the 3-D structure of 1-2-3/W. Just enter the third input variable in the upper-left corner of the table in each sheet.

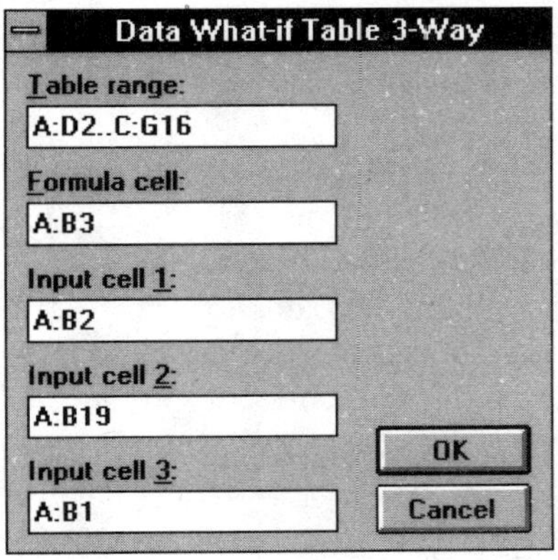

Figure 16.8. You specify the Table range and input cells for a three-way table as you do for a two-way table, but you also need to specify a formula cell, because the formula isn't part of the Table range. Here, we specified cell A:B3, since it contains the @NPV formula we're evaluating.

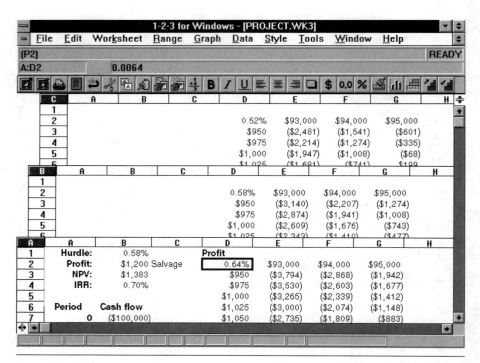

Figure 16.9. The three-way table lets you see the impact of changing three variables. Here there are three hurdle rates, 0.64%, 0.58%, and 0.52%, so there are three sheets for the three-way table. More variables would require more sheets and a deeper 3-D table.

Cross-Tabulating Data

The What-if Table command also provides a good way to analyze information in a database. You can use it to cross-tabulate data according to varying criteria. For example, the database in Figure 16.10 shows data on sales for four retail stores. Suppose you wanted to know the total sales, the average sales per month, and the standard deviation of sales for each store.

The easiest way to get such information from a database is to use the Data What-if Table 1-Way command. You just specify an input cell in the database's Criteria range and use @D functions in the what-if table. There's no secret to using @D functions in a what-if table. The @D functions change their values according to the entries in the Criteria range. As long as you set the input cell that the What-if Table command varies to a cell in the Criteria range, 1-2-3/W will calculate @D function results by varying the Criteria .

In-Depth Data Analysis **379**

	A	B	C	D
1	Store			
2				
3				
4	Store	Month	Sales	
5	Boston	Jan	$528,697	
6	Brockton	Jan	$581,211	
7	Weymouth	Jan	$627,803	
8	Barnstable	Jan	$596,968	
9	Boston	Feb	$620,246	
10	Brockton	Feb	$542,197	
11	Weymouth	Feb	$623,504	
12	Barnstable	Feb	$729,228	
13	Boston	Mar	$725,774	
14	Brockton	Mar	$509,634	
15	Weymouth	Mar	$557,183	
16	Barnstable	Mar	$571,500	
17	Boston	Apr	$671,297	
18	Brockton	Apr	$595,720	
19	Weymouth	Apr	$575,656	
20	Barnstable	Apr	$633,848	

Figure 16.10. This worksheet shows a database of sales for four retail stores for the first four months of the year.

Try It: Cross-Tabulate Data

Let's cross-tabulate the data by store, as shown in Figure 16.10.

1. Enter labels and values as shown in Figure 16.10.

2. Assign the Currency 0 format to ranges C5..C20 and E2..G6.

3. Set up a what-if table, as shown in Figure 16.11, and enter the following formulas in the cells indicated:

   E2: @DSUM(A4..C20,2,A1..A2)

   F2: @DAVG(A4..C20,2,A1..A2)

   G2: @DSTD(A4..C20,2,A1..A2)

4. Select range D2..G6 as the Table range and choose Data What-if Table 1-Way.

5. Indicate cell A2 as the input cell and click OK. 1-2-3/W generates the cross-tabulation shown in Figure 16.12.

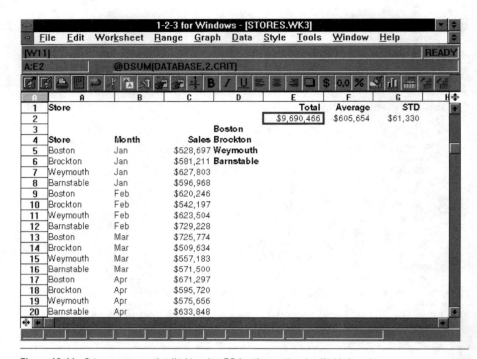

Figure 16.11. Set up a one-way what-if table using @D functions as the what-if table formulas.

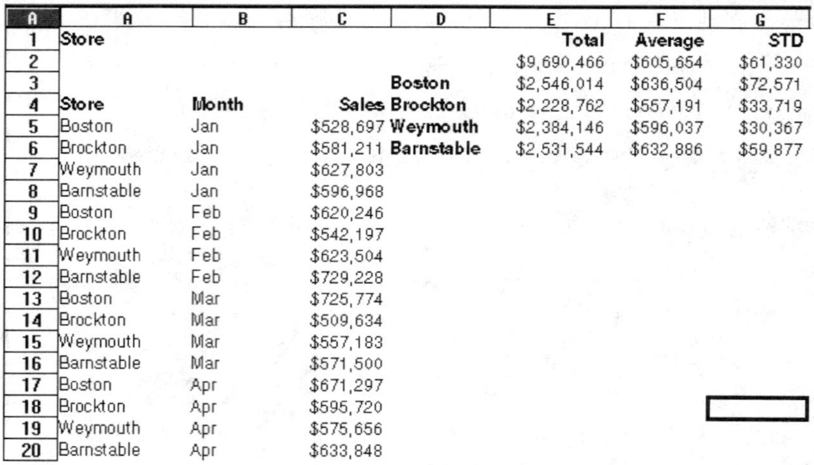

Figure 16.12. The what-if table quickly generates a cross-tabulation of the information in the database. This feature is especially useful for analyzing large databases

Frequency Distributions

One of 1-2-3/W's greatest attributes is its flexibility. You can move numbers and labels, create all manner of formulas and graphs, and juggle, massage, and crunch numbers until you have a handle on your data. This versatility is enhanced by another tool: the Data Distribution command.

The Data Distribution command lets you organize values into ranges or bins. For example, say that you're dealing with highly variable billings for a temp agency. Figure 16.13 shows a table of the hours billed per month for the agency's top 10 customers.

	A	B	C	D	E	F	G	H
1		Temporary Contractor - Hours Billed						
2								
3	Customer	Jan	Feb	Mar	Apr	May	Jun	Total
4	1	323.4	192.5	333.0	267.6	241.3	140.0	1497.8
5	2	579.6	95.2	461.1	218.9	462.9	583.1	2400.8
6	3	305.9	237.3	324.3	290.0	219.6	96.6	1473.7
7	4	286.3	588.7	314.5	465.7	493.3	644.0	2792.5
8	5	592.2	539.0	467.4	440.8	226.3	109.9	2375.6
9	6	252.0	558.6	297.3	450.6	338.6	334.6	2231.8
10	7	138.6	385.7	240.6	364.2	395.3	448.0	1972.4
11	8	641.2	208.6	491.9	275.6	245.9	149.1	2012.3
12	9	420.0	398.3	381.3	370.5	447.5	552.3	2569.9
13	10	69.3	252.0	206.0	297.3	250.1	157.5	1232.2
14	Total	3608.5	3455.9	3517.5	3441.2	3320.8	3215.1	20559.0
15	Average	360.9	345.6	351.8	344.1	332.1	321.5	2055.9
16	St. Dev.	184.3	164.8	92.2	82.4	103.3	206.6	

Figure 16.13. The @SUM, @AVG, and @STD functions can help clarify all this data. But a distribution of the data isn't readily apparent. For example, you might want to know how often a company bills between 400 and 480 hours. To answer such questions, use the Data Distribution command.

There are several ways the Data Distribution command can help clarify these numbers. For example, you might like to know how often you billed a company for 80 hours or less during this period. To answer that, you can generate a data distribution, as shown in Figure 16.14. We created this distribution by first entering the values in range I1..I10. These are the bin values for the number of hours we wanted to look at. Once you have a range of bin values, you choose Data Distribution and enter the appropriate ranges. In this case, range B4..G13 is the Values range and range I1..I10 is the Bin range. When you click OK, the Data Distribution command enters the distribution values in the column next to the Bin range, as in column J in the figure.

	I	J
1	80	11.0
2	160	7.0
3	240	7.0
4	320	14.0
5	400	11.0
6	480	9.0
7	560	5.0
8	640	4.0
9	720	2.0
10	800	0.0
11		10.0

Figure 16.14. The Data Distribution command examines a range of values and tells you how many of those values fall within each bin in the Bin range. A bin is a range of values. Here, the 80 bin represents all values less than or equal to 80. The 160 bin represents all values greater than 80 and less than or equal to 160.

The values in column J are the number of values in range B4..G13 that fall within the scope of the bins identified by the values in range I1..I10. These bins represent a numerical range. For example, the first value in the Bin range is 80. That tells the Data Distribution command to count all values that are less than or equal to 80 in the Values range. The command enters the result in column J next to the 80 bin-value that's in column I. The second value in the bin range is 160. That represents all values that are greater than 80 and less than or equal to 160. The Data Distribution command counts the number of those values and enters the result in the adjacent column.

So the Data Distribution command counts the number of values that fall into each bin and enters that number in the appropriate cell next to the Bin range. Note that the command entered the value 10 in cell J11, which is below the last row of the Bin range. The Data Distribution command always enters a value beyond the last bin. That represents the number of values that didn't fall into any bin. Since, there were 10 values outside the bins in the example, this value is 10.

Histograms

The Data Distribution command is useful for creating what statisticians call a *histogram*. A histogram is simply a bar graph of a data distribution. To create a histogram, you merely create a bar graph of the results of the Data Distribution command. Using the drop-shadow feature on a bar graph makes for an effective histogram.

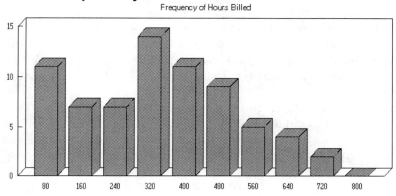

Figure 16.15. The bar graph using the drop-shadow feature makes for an effective histogram.

Matrix Multiplication for Advanced Problems

Inverted matrices, matrix multiplication, simultaneous equations—these sound like good subjects to skip. None of these terms sounds as though it relates in any way to solving business problems. Well, stick around. You may find some uses for 1-2-3's data matrix operations.

The Data Matrix Multiply command lets you quickly increase or decrease a column of numbers by a percentage—for example, to calculate price increases or discounts across an entire line of merchandise. The Data Matrix commands also help you to solve simultaneous equations so that you can learn which process or machine among several is the most, or the least, efficient. Many of these kinds of problems can also be addressed with the Solver utility. Which do you choose? Well, it depends on what's important to you. The Data Matrix commands are likely to be much faster than the Solver. But what the Solver lacks in speed, it makes up for in ease of use. Before we look at applications of the Data Matrix commands, we'll risk boring you a bit with an explanation of what the commands do.

What is a Matrix?

In the spreadsheet world, a matrix is simply a range of contiguous numbers. Mathematicians use matrix multiplication to solve systems of linear equations. That sounds complex because it is complex. But that doesn't mean that mortal business people can't use matrix mathematics to solve real-world problems such as cost allocations and productivity evaluations. You just need to learn the basics of matrices.

Mathematicians talk about matrices in terms of their dimensions. A 5 by 7 matrix has 5 rows and 7 columns. A 1 by 1 matrix has 1 row and 1 column—a single cell. This row-by-column naming convention is important when you're trying to decide whether you can perform matrix math on a particular range of cells.

1-2-3/W handles two kinds of matrix calculations: multiplication and inversion. Multiplying a matrix by another matrix isn't as simple as multiplying one value by another. An explanation of matrix multiplication is beyond the scope of this book. Suffice it to say that when you multiply one matrix by another, you get a third matrix.

Not all matrices can be multiplied, and multiplying matrix A by matrix B doesn't yield the same result as multiplying matrix B by matrix A. In other words, unlike normal multiplication, matrix multiplication is not commutative. While this isn't intuitive, it's similar to the noncommutative property of subtraction: For example, 12 - 4 isn't the same as 4 - 12.

To multiply two matrices, the number of columns in the first matrix must be the same as the number of rows in the second matrix. So if matrix A is 2 by 5 and matrix B is 5 by 7, the two can be multiplied to yield a 2 by 7 matrix.

This is all very abstract, but if you remember that a matrix is a row-by-column range of values, it's simple! To multiply two matrices, the two interior numbers must match. The resulting matrix will have the dimensions of the two outer numbers. For example, you can multiply matrix A (6 by 7) and matrix B (7 by 1) because the interior numbers are the same (7 and 7). The resulting matrix is 6 by 1. But can you multiply matrix B by matrix A? No. The interior numbers are then 1 and 6, which are not equivalent.

The inverse of a matrix is another matrix such that matrix A multiplied by its inverse and its inverse multiplied by matrix A both yield an *identity matrix*. An identity matrix is a special matrix made up of 0s and 1s. It has 1s in the upper-left and lower-right corners, and 0s in the other corners.

Now before you skip ahead to the next chapter, look at some things you can do with matrix operations, even if you don't fully understand the mathematical theory behind them—and most of us don't!

Change a Column by a Percentage

The easiest thing to do with matrix math is to change a column of numbers by some percentage. This is a technique that uses less memory than creating a second column with a formula. It comes in handy in very large worksheets where memory limitations are significant.

For example, consider the data shown in Figure 16.16. Range B2..B11 is a 10 by 1 matrix (rows by columns), and range D2..D2 is a 1 by 1 matrix. You can multiply them because the interior numbers match: The first matrix has the same number of columns as the second matrix has rows. Matrix multiplication here will reduce all the values in range B2..B11 by 20%. That's the same as multiplying each value by .8 or 80%, which is the factor in cell D2.

	A	B	C	D
1	Item	Price		Factor
2	0	$682		0.8
3	1	$660		
4	2	$711		
5	3	$57		
6	4	$112		
7	5	$574		
8	6	$229		
9	7	$681		
10	8	$871		
11	9	$532		

Figure 16.16. Create this worksheet to see how the Data Matrix Multiply command can increase or decrease a column of numbers by a specific percentage.

Try It: Decrease a Column by a Percentage

Let's see how you can use matrix math to change all the values in a column by a percentage.

1. Create the worksheet shown in Figure 16.16.
2. To multiply the matrices, choose Data Matrix Multiply.
3. Indicate range B2..B11 as the first range, cell D2 as the second range, and cell C2 as the Output range.
4. Click OK and 1-2-3/W will enter a column of values that are 20% smaller than the original values. Here, we specified cell C2 as the Output range so that we could compare the results with the original values. When you're trying to save memory, specify the first cell in the original column as the Output range. In this case, you'd select cell B2 as the Output range to overwrite the original values.

Suppose you have two columns that you want to change by a percentage. The easiest way to do that is simply to repeat the above process for the two ranges. In other words, multiply the first column by the 1 by 1 matrix, and then multiply the second column by the 1 by 1 matrix. But if you want to see how to set up the full problem for matrix multiplication, you need to create a second 2 by 2 matrix, as shown in Figure 16.17.

	A	B	C	D	E
1	Item	Price	Price2	Factor	
2	0	$682	$100	0.8	0
3	1	$660	$100	0	0.8
4	2	$711	$100		
5	3	$57	$100		
6	4	$112	$100		
7	5	$574	$100		
8	6	$229	$100		
9	7	$681	$100		
10	8	$871	$100		
11	9	$532	$100		

Figure 16.17. To change two columns by a percentage, you must set up a 2 by 2 matrix, as shown here in range D2..E3. The number by which you multiply the columns must be in the upper-left and lower-right corners of the matrix. The other values must be 0.

Try It: Decrease Two Columns by a Percentage

Let's see how you can use matrix math to change two columns of numbers by a percentage.

1. Enter labels and values as shown in Figure 16.17. All the values in the second column are 100, so you can easily see that the matrix multiplication works.

2. Choose Data Matrix Multiply. Indicate range B2..C11 as the first range and range D2..E3 as the second range. Indicate cell B2 as the Output range.

3. Click OK and 1-2-3/W will overwrite the previous columns with values that are 20% lower.

Simultaneous Equations

When two or more polynomials express relationships of the same variables, the polynomials are called simultaneous equations. Although it may sound unlikely, such equations describe many business problems. For example, the waste output of a group of piece workers should be related to their output of finished product. But does each worker waste the same amount?

Waste and product numbers for three laborers for a three-day period might combine into the following formulas:

Day 1:   10 worker X + 13 worker Y + 11 worker Z = 10 lbs. waste

Day 2:   12 worker X + 10 worker Y + 11 worker Z = 11 lbs. waste

Day 3:   12 worker X + 12 worker Y + 12 worker Z = 11 lbs. waste

Solving these simultaneous equations should reveal how much material each worker generated per finished product in the three-day period.

1-2-3/W's Matrix commands let you solve simultaneous equations. In fact, you can solve for up to 256 variables in 256 equations. To see how, consider a more modest example:

Solve for x and y, where

7x + 11y = 108

and

3x - 11y = 33.

In this example, we have two simultaneous equations with two variables. In general, to solve a set of n simultaneous equations with n variables using matrix math, follow these steps:

1. Create an n by n matrix (A) of the equation coefficients.
2. Create an n by 1 matrix (B) of the equation constants.
3. Use the Data Matrix Inverse command to create the inverse matrix (C) of matrix A.
4. Multiply matrix C with matrix B to yield the solution in matrix D.

In this example, you first need to create a 2 by 2 matrix of the equation coefficients and a 2 by 1 matrix of the equation constants, as shown in Figure 16.18.

	A	B	C	D
1	x	y		constants
2	7	11		108
3	3	-11		33

Figure 16.18. To solve for two variables given two simultaneous equations, start by setting up a 2 by 2 matrix of the variable coefficients and a 2 by 1 matrix of the equations' constants.

The next step is to create the inverse matrix of the coefficient matrix and then multiply the inverted matrix by the matrix of constants.

Try It: Solve Simultaneous Equations

Let's solve for the following equations: $7x + 11y = 108$ and $3x - 11y = 33$.

1. Enter the labels and values shown in Figure 16.18.
2. Choose Data Matrix Invert.
3. Specify range A2..B3 as the range to invert and click OK.
4. Specify cell A5 as the Output range.
5. Choose Data Matrix Multiply.
6. Specify range A5..B6 as the first range to multiply and D2..D3 as the second range to multiply.
7. Specify cell B8 as the Output range and click OK. 1-2-3/W lists the answers in order so that you can enter x in cell A8 and y in cell A9 to clarify the results, as shown in Figure 16.19. A quick verification shows that the procedure worked: $7*14.1 + 11*0.845454 = 108$, and $3*14.1 - 11*0.845454 = 33$.

	A	B	C	D
1	x	y		constants
2	7	11		108
3	3	-11		33
4				
5	0.1	0.1		
6	0.02727273	-0.0636364		
7				
8	x	14.1		
9	y	0.84545455		

Figure 16.19. 1-2-3/W lists the solution in range B8..B9. Enter the variables as labels in range A8..A9 to clarify the answer.

Business Applications of Matrix Math

Matrix math is helpful when you want answers to cost-allocation, efficiency, and productivity questions. Suppose you own a materials-processing plant, for example, and you want to know how efficient each of your three conveyor belts is. First, you enter the amount of material processed by each belt during the last three months. Then you enter the amount of diesel fuel used by the belts during those months. Figure 16.20 shows the worksheet.

	A	B	C	D
1		Tonnage Processed		
2		Belt1	Belt2	Belt3
3	Jan	1,170.6	1,174.3	1,129.8
4	Feb	1,142.2	1,114.4	1,074.2
5	Mar	1,191.7	1,128.8	1,191.1
6				
7		Gallons of Diesel		
8	Jan	4,771.4		
9	Feb	4,566.9		
10	Mar	4,890.8		

Figure 16.20. The tonnage processed by each belt and the total fuel consumed form two matrices. The first is a 3 x 3 matrix, and the second is a 3 x 1 matrix.

To solve this problem you just solve three simultaneous equations. Range B3..D5 is a 3 by 3 matrix (A) of the equation coefficients. Range B8..B10 is a 3 by 1 matrix (B) of the equation constants. If we follow the steps explained in the previous section, the next step is to use the Data Matrix Inverse command to create the inverse matrix (C) of matrix A. To do that we choose Data Matrix Invert, specify range B3..D5 as the range to invert, and specify cell B12 as the Output range.

1-2-3/W creates the inverse of the matrix, as shown in Figure 16.21.

The last step is to multiply matrix C by matrix B to yield the solution in matrix D. Choose Data Matrix Multiply, specify range B12..D14 as the first range, specify range B8..B10 as the second range, and specify cell B17 as the Output range. The results are shown in Figure 16.22.

Figure 16.21. The inverse matrix of range B12..D14 presents apparently meaningless numbers. It simply represents an intermediate step toward an answer.

Figure 16.22. Enter labels next to the resulting matrix to clarify the results of the matrix multiplication. Here you can see that belt 2 is the most efficient and that belt 3 may need servicing or replacement.

Regression Analysis

Suppose you work in a company that administers an aptitude test to all engineers who apply for employment. The company uses the test as one of several factors in deciding whether to hire an applicant, and your boss asks you to find out how well the aptitude test predicts job performance. This type of problem is ideally suited to *regression analysis*.

Regression analysis isn't something you go through on a psychiatrist's couch. It is a statistical technique that lets you make predictions based on accumulated data. You can use 1-2-3/W's ability to perform a regression even if you are unfamiliar with the statistical theory behind the analysis.

To answer the question about test scores, you must first select a *sample* group. If your company is small enough, you can study data on all the engineers employed. But if the company is large, you need to come up with a representative sample. This sample should be *randomly* selected from the entire pool of engineers employed. Also, the size of the sample group should be large enough to yield meaningful results. The larger your sample, the more accurate your analysis will be.

Let's say that you use a set of dice to select 14 engineers randomly from an employee list and that you gather information on those engineers. Then you set up a worksheet like the one in Figure 16.23, with the employees' aptitude test scores in one column and their most recent performance-review ratings in the next column. A perfect score on the aptitude test is 100, and the managers' reviews range from 0 to 5. A score of 5 means that the employee far exceeded expectations. A score of less than 2 means that the employee needs to improve.

Employee	Aptitude Test	Manager's Rating
1	91	4.3
2	78	3.1
3	86	3.7
4	79	2.9
5	98	4.2
6	98	5.0
7	69	2.5
8	69	2.2
9	71	1.9
10	81	3.2
11	84	3.5
12	81	3.1
13	54	1.2
14	100	4.0

Figure 16.23. Each randomly chosen engineer is identified by a number in column A. Column B shows the engineers' aptitude test scores, and column C shows their employee ratings.

The XY graph shown in Figure 16.24 shows that there is a relationship between the aptitude scores and the performance ratings. Regression analysis simply refines this visual assessment and lets you make predictions.

To perform a regression analysis you need to identify two sets of variables: independent and dependent. The goal of regression analysis is to develop a model by which you can predict dependent values based on independent variables. Here, you want to know if you can predict an employee's performance based on his or her aptitude test score. So the performance rating is the dependent variable, since you want to know how reliably it can be predicted from the aptitude test score, the independent variable.

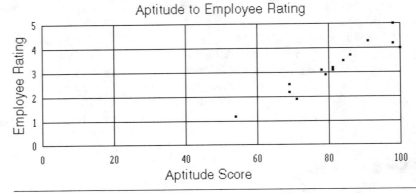

Figure 16.24. The graph shows that there is indeed a relationship between aptitude scores and performance, as your boss suspected. To refine your understanding of this relationship, use 1-2-3/W's regression analysis capabilities.

Try It: Perform a Regression Analysis

Let's see how to do a regression.

1. Enter the labels and values shown in Figure 16.23.
2. Choose Data Regression.
3. Specify range B3..B16 as the X-Range. This is the independent variable range.
4. Specify range C3..C16 as the Y-Range. This is the dependent variable range.
5. Specify cell A21 as the Output range.
6. Click OK to perform the regression analysis, as shown in Figure 16.25.

At first glance, the results of a regression analysis can look intimidating. But once you know what to look for, it's easy to answer basic business questions. For example, the analysis shown in Figure 16.25 yields the answer to your boss's question. The value next to the label *R Squared* tells you the proportion of variation in the dependent variable that the independent variable explains.

Here, the score on the aptitude test explains 90.6942% of the variation in the performance rating. So there is a very strong linear relationship between scores on the aptitude test and later job performance.

	RESULTS.WK3	
	B / C	D
21	Regression Output:	
22	Constant	-2.9168998
23	Std Err of Y Est	0.3261843
24	R Squared	0.9069421
25	No. of Observations	14
26	Degrees of Freedom	12
27		
28	X Coefficient(s) 0.07518577	
29	Std Err of Coef. 0.00695235	
30		
31	Adj. R Squared	0.89918727

Figure 16.25. The Data Regression Go command generates the results of the regression analysis in the designated Output range.

If your boss is statistically sophisticated, he or she may also want to know the adjusted R^2. 1-2-3/W doesn't provide this figure, but it's not difficult to calculate. The equation for adjusted R^2 is as follows:

$$R^2adj = 1 - [\,(1 - R^2) * (n - 1) / (n - 2)\,],$$

where n is the value next to the label, *No. of observations*. The adjusted R^2 considers both the number of independent variables and the sample size. It may provide a better measure of reliability when you have multiple columns of independent variables. In this example, you can calculate the adjusted R^2 by entering the formula 1-(1-D24)*(D25-1)/(D25-2) into cell D31. The result, 89.9187%, again shows a strong relationship between aptitude test scores and job performance.

Predicting Results

Of course, finding that a relationship exists between variables isn't really useful unless you can come up with some kind of model for predicting future results. To do that, you need to create an equation that you apply to an independent variable to predict a dependent variable. Here, you want an equation that predicts a future managerial rating from an applicant's aptitude test score.

The general form of the equation is

$y = \text{constant} + (x \text{ coefficient} * x)$,

where y is the dependent variable (future performance) and x is the independent variable (aptitude test score). So given any aptitude test score, you can plug that score into this equation with the constant and x coefficient to get a prediction of the managerial rating.

In this case the constant is in cell D22, and the x coefficient is in cell C28. You don't have to know how the regression formula was derived or what the constant and the x coefficient represent. Knowing the formula and how to apply it is enough to work with a regression analysis. Here, you just enter the formula +$D$22+$C$28*B3 in cell D3 and copy that formula to range D4..D16, as shown in Figure 16.26.

A	C	D	C	D
1		Aptitude	Manager's	
2	Employee	Test	Rating	Predicted
3	1	91	4.3	3.9
4	2	78	3.1	2.9
5	3	86	3.7	3.5
6	4	79	2.9	3.0
7	5	98	4.2	4.5
8	6	98	5.0	4.5
9	7	69	2.5	2.3
10	8	69	2.2	2.3
11	9	71	1.9	2.4
12	10	81	3.2	3.2
13	11	84	3.5	3.4
14	12	81	3.1	3.2
15	13	54	1.2	1.1
16	14	100	4.0	4.6

Figure 16.26. After generating a regression analysis, you can create formulas that predict a dependent value from an independent value. Here, the predicted values are next to the actual values.

By placing predicted results next to the actual results, you can plot a graph against the actual data, as shown in Figure 16.27. Unless you're a sophisticated statistician, you should always plot regression equations against the actual data to gain a better understanding of how well the regression equation predicts the dependent variable.

Once you have the regression equations, it's easy to make predictions. Say you want to predict the job-performance rating for a new engineer who scored 89 on his aptitude test. Just enter that test score in the independent-variable column, and copy the prediction formula. In this case, you would enter 89 in cell B17 and copy the formula from cell D16 to cell D17. The formula predicts that the employee will earn a manager's rating of 3.8.

Figure 16.27. In this graph, the ratings values generated by the regression are plotted as a line, while data points represent the actual data. You can look at such a graph to see how well your regression equation predicts results. Here, the correlation between aptitude test scores and job performance is very high.

Multiple Regression Models

Suppose you want to look at several independent variables to consider their influence on the dependent variable, job performance. In Figure 16.28, there are three independent variables: aptitude test score, college grade-point average, and sex. You've already seen the results of a regression analysis on the independent variables in column B (aptitude test scores) in Figure 16.25. Figure 16.29 shows the results of simple linear regression analyses on the independent variables in columns C and D.

You can see that the regression analysis on college GPA shows a significant correlation between GPA and future job performance. The R^2 is over 90%. The R^2 for the regression analysis on the applicants' sex shows no significant correlation between sex and job performance. You should note, however, how the variables were set up. Anytime you have a true/false or yes/no variable, use 0 for false or no and 1 for true or yes.

So far the best correlation is between the aptitude test score and job performance. That has an R^2 of about 90.7%, while the R^2 for the GPA regression is about 90.5%. But an even more reliable regression can be done if you use both independent variables. This is called *multiple regression analysis*.

By using both variables in a multiple regression analysis, you can realize an R^2 of over 97%.

	A	B	C	D	E
1		Aptitude	College	Sex	Manager's
2	Employee	Test	GPA	Male?	Rating
3	1	91	3.69	1	4.3
4	2	78	3.28	0	3.1
5	3	86	3.37	1	3.7
6	4	79	3.00	1	2.9
7	5	98	3.39	1	4.2
8	6	98	4.00	0	5.0
9	7	69	2.85	0	2.5
10	8	69	2.57	0	2.2
11	9	71	2.23	1	1.9
12	10	81	3.19	0	3.2
13	11	84	3.51	0	3.5
14	12	81	3.20	1	3.1
15	13	54	1.76	1	1.2
16	14	100	3.23	0	4.0

Figure 16.28. You can examine more than one column of independent variables.

	A	B	C	D	E
41	College GPA				
42			Regression Output:		
43		Constant			-1.9605639
44		Std Err of Y Est			0.32902708
45		R Squared			0.90531298
46		No. of Observations			14
47		Degrees of Freedom			12
48					
49		X Coefficient(s)	1.66969944		
50		Std Err of Coef.	0.15588112		
51	Sex Male?				
52			Regression Output:		
53		Constant			3.35714286
54		Std Err of Y Est			1.0557101
55		R Squared			0.02519783
56		No. of Observations			14
57		Degrees of Freedom			12
58					
59		X Coefficient(s)	-0.3142857		
60		Std Err of Coef.	0.56430078		

Figure 16.29. By entering alternate Output ranges, you can compare the results of simple linear regressions using different independent variables.

Try It: Perform a Multiple Regression

Let's perform a regression using both the test score and the GPA as independent variables.

1. Enter the labels and values shown in range A1..F16 of Figure 16.28.
2. Choose Data Regression and indicate range B3..C16 as the X-Range, the independent variables.
3. Indicate range E3..E16 as the Y-Range, the dependent variables.
4. Indicate cell A21 as the Output range and click OK. 1-2-3/W generates the regression analysis shown in Figure 16.30. Note that 1-2-3/W overwrites any cells in the Output range with the analysis results. You should be sure to include enough room for the analysis. Overwriting previous regression results is not a problem here.

	A	B	C	D
21		Regression Output:		
22	Constant			-2.8672804
23	Std Err of Y Est			0.17818687
24	R Squared			0.97454401
25	No. of Observations			14
26	Degrees of Freedom			11
27				
28	X Coefficient(s)		0.04065363	0.89293832
29	Std Err of Coef.		0.00743272	0.16521163

Figure 16.30. Using two independent variables yields a higher R^2 in this case.

The regression output looks the same as before except that there are two sets of values for the x coefficient and its corresponding standard error. These values let you create a new equation for predicting job performance:

y = constant + (x coefficient1 * x_1) + (x coefficient$_2$ * x_2).

So now you can create an even more accurate formula for predicting job performance. Just enter the formula *+$D$22+$C$28*B3+$D$28*C3* in cell F3 and copy that formula to range F4..F16, as shown in Figure 16.31.

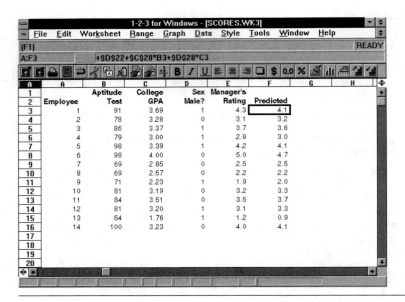

Figure 16.31. Using multiple regression analysis, you can create a more accurate formula for predicting employee performance.

Determining r, t, and z in Simple Linear Regression

If you're a statistical sophisticate, you may want to know how to determine the values for r, t, and z in 1-2-3/W. You can ascertain these values from 1-2-3/W's regression output. The general formulas for these measures follow. Replace the arguments with the values from the regression output when entering these formulas.

To find r, use the following formula:

@SQRT(R^2)*@IF(x coefficient<0,-1,1).

To figure the value of t, use the following formula:

@SQRT(R^2)*@IF(x coefficient<0,-1,1)*@SQRT(df/(1-R^2))

To determine z, if that measure is applicable, use the following formula:

@SQRT(R^2)*@IF(x coefficient<0,-1,1)*@SQRT(N)

17

Macros

Macros are spreadsheet programs. They range from simple lists of keystrokes to complex systems of loops and subroutines. Don't shy away from macros because you're not a trained programmer. Writing a macro is as easy as entering a label in a worksheet. Assign a range name, and your macro is ready to run.

The simplest macros help you automate a series of keystrokes. If you frequently run through the same sequence of keys, you can teach these keystrokes to a macro. And if you do repetitive chores with the mouse, odds are these steps have a keyboard equivalent that you can make into a macro, as well.

A keystroke macro lets a single key-combination, such as Ctrl-A, do the work of a slew of keystrokes. For example, the macro *Mary Chung's{DOWN}World-Class Restaurant~* types a label in one cell, moves the cell pointer down one cell and then enters another label.

{DOWN}, incidentally is a macro keyname, an entry that tells a macro to press the DownArrow key. The tilde (~) tells the macro to press the Enter key.

Most programming languages require considerable know-how for even modestly useful applications. Macros do not. You can learn additional techniques as you need them, and with a bit of practice and curiosity you can build extremely sophisticated—and productive—applications without any formal training.

Once you master the creation of macros that mimic keystrokes, you're ready for the next step: using 1-2-3's programming language, the *Advanced Macro Commands*. Like *key names*, such as {DOWN} and {PGUP}, the commands are surrounded by braces. But unlike macro key names, Advanced Macro Commands do things above and beyond what you can do from the keyboard. Macro commands, for example, can display a prompt on the screen requesting user input, and after the user answers the question, the macro can interpret the entry and decide what to do next.

> **In this chapter you will learn:**
> - *What a macro is and when to use one*
> - *How to create and run a macro*
> - *How to write "smart" macros*
> - *New macro features of 1-2-3/W*
> - *Efficient macro techniques*

Highly skilled macro developers can make customized applications that provide features never dreamed of by 1-2-3/W's creators. At their best, these features are as slick and professional as the built-in ones.

To 1-2-3's great tradition of macro features, 1-2-3/W provides an exciting new capability: You can attach your macros to SmartIcons, to create on-screen buttons that run your custom programs.

Tired of going to the menu for a commonly used feature? Make a SmartIcon to make that feature accessible with a single mouse click. Your SmartIcon macros can perform most of the tasks a conventional macro can, and they can invoke macros that you store in a worksheet. By combining the skills you'll learn in this chapter with the techniques explored in *Chapter 18: Mastering the SmartIcon Palette*, you'll make 1-2-3/W into your own custom worksheet environment.

Whether or not you build SmartIcons, you'll probably want to partake of new macro keynames and commands that let your macros exploit the unique features of 1-2-3/W. These range from {Alt} which lets you invoke the Windows-style menus to a series of commands that manage windows and which access Windows' Clipboard and DDE features.

In this chapter, you'll learn how to create and run keystroke macros and how to enhance your macros with Advanced Macro commands. You'll learn about the macro commands that are new with 1-2-3/W, along with 1-2-3/W's new and improved macro-recording and debugging tools. And to get you off on the right foot, you'll find some pointers on making the most of your macros while avoiding several common mistakes.

When Should You Use a Macro?

There are two common reasons to use a macro: to speed through repetitive tasks and to automate cumbersome procedures.

As you develop and modify a worksheet, you often have to repeat certain operations. For example, you might have to erase every other cell in a column. Without the aid of a macro, you'll just sit at the keyboard pressing Delete and pressing the DownArrow key twice, repeating the procedure until all the deleting is done.

If you're not a robot, this kind of work gets old after a little while. Wouldn't you rather palm off these boring jobs on 1-2-3/W? With a small macro—like *{DOWN}{DOWN}{DELETE}*, or its abbreviated version *{D 2}{DEL}*—you can hold down a macro key-combination, such as Ctrl-D, and let the macro do all the grunt work.

You can also use a macro to automate a lengthy, detailed operation. Perhaps you have a multifile spreadsheet that requires you to load a series of files and arrange them on the screen in a particular fashion. Why not have a macro do the work instead of forcing the user to do all of this setup work. The macro could invoke menu commands, such as /Alt/FO, to open each file, and it could use 1-2-3/W's new Window-management macro commands, such as {WINDOW-ADJUST}, {WINDOW-SELECT}, and {WINDOW-STATE} to determine how the windows appear on the screen.

Another sort of automated procedure is one that takes the novice user step-by-step through an interactive process. For example, you might create a macro that escorts the user through the data-entry process, and when all the data are entered, the macro could present a custom menu of report-printing options. Commands such as {?}, {GETLABEL}, {GETNUMBER}, and {MENUBRANCH} let the user provide entries or choose from a menu of options.

Creating and Using Macros

If you know how to enter a label, you know how to write a macro. In the exercises ahead, we'll build some very primitive macros. Then we'll gradually expand on the fundamentals, adding powerful features as we go.

A Very Simple Macro

If you need to enter the same heading various places in your worksheet, you might save time and reduce spelling mistakes by letting a macro do the typing. Such a macro is easy to set up, and it illustrates techniques we'll use in more substantial macros.

Bring up a new worksheet and enter the label, *Hello* in cell E1. This is a macro that types the characters H-e-l-l-o.

To make the macro easy to run, we'll assign it the range name \H. Macros named with a backslash (\) and a letter are accessible by pressing the MACRO key (Ctrl) plus the letter. In other versions of 1-2-3, the Alt key serves as the MACRO key, but Windows reserves the Alt key for menu commands.

> ### Alt Has Been Altered, So Ctrl is in Control
>
> If you've run macros in other versions of 1-2-3, you're surely in the habit of pressing Alt to run a macro. For example, to run a macro named \R in 1-2-3 Releases 2.x and 3.x, you'd press Alt-R.
>
> But in Windows, Alt brings up the menus, so pressing Alt-R in 1-2-3/W calls up the Range menu. For this reason, 1-2-3/W's MACRO key cannot be the Alt key.
>
> Ctrl, rather than Alt, is 1-2-3/W's MACRO key. To run the macro called \R in 1-2-3/W, you press Ctrl-R.

In cell D1, enter the label \H, preceded with an apostrophe label prefix. If you neglect to type the apostrophe prefix, 1-2-3/W assumes the backslash to be a repeating label prefix, and it fills the cell with H's.

With cell D1 selected, choose Range Name Label Create and select the Right option. This command uses the label in cell D1, \H, to name its right-hand neighbor, E1. To learn more about assigning range names, see Chapter 8.

Now move the cell pointer to cell A1, and run the macro by pressing Ctrl-H.

Sure enough, the macro typed the word "Hello," but it didn't enter it for us. Press Enter to finish the job.

Before you blame 1-2-3/W, consider what the macro in E1 says to do. It says to type the word "Hello," but it doesn't say to press the Enter key. To have a macro press the Enter key, include a tilde (~) in the label.

Edit cell E1, so it reads HELLO~. Then move the cell pointer to cell A2 and run it again, by pressing Ctrl-H.

> ### Run This Way And That
>
> You don't have to give a macro a backslash-and-letter combination for a name. If you give it a longer name, you can run it by pressing the RUN key (Alt-F3) or by choosing the Tools Macro Run command.
>
> You can also invoke Tools Macro Run by clicking on the SmartIcon that has a picture of a group of runners. This SmartIcon does not appear in the palette by default, so you'll need to customize the palette to make it available. See Chapter 18 for details.
>
> Although, you'll usually want to name your macros, you can use any of these methods to run the labels in any range—named or not—as a macro.
>
> And if you name a macro \0 (that's backslash and a zero), 1-2-3/W automatically runs the macro each time you load the worksheet, unless the Run-autoexecute-macros option in the Tools User Setup dialog box has been disabled. Note, however, that you can't run such a macro by pressing Ctrl-0.

This time the macro entered the label without your assistance.

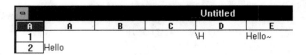

Figure 17.1. The tilde (~) following the word Hello tells the macro to press the Enter key when it finishes typing the word.

A Macro that Moves

Now we want our macro to enter two labels, one above the other. The first should say "Hello," and the second should say "Goodbye." After typing "Goodbye," we want the macro to go down one more time, in case we want to enter the pair of labels once again.

We could keep adding to our macro in cell E1, but it's easier to read modify a macro that's organized in a series of cells. Macros are built to handle this easily. After 1-2-3/W processes the steps in a macro, it looks in the cell below the current macro cell. If there is a label in that cell, the macro keeps chugging through the keystrokes, until a blank cell or one that contains a value is encountered. Keep in mind that 1-2-3/W's macro processor moves to the cell below the current macro entry, not the cell below the cell pointer.

Let's add our new macro keystrokes in cell E2. Enter the following label in cell E2: {DOWN}GOODBYE{DOWN}.

Move the cell pointer to cell A4 and press Ctrl-H two times. Now hold down Ctrl-H for about a second. The macro does its stuff again and again.

You may have noticed that we didn't enter a tilde (~) after the word "Goodbye." Just as *you* can type a label, and then enter it by moving the cell pointer, so can the macro. This is the essential lesson of simple macros: almost anything you can do from the keyboard, the macro can do for you.

The word {DOWN} in curly braces is an example of a macro key name. 1-2-3/W supports a large number of macro entries in curly braces. Some, like {DOWN} are simply the equivalent of keystrokes. Others, such as {FOR}, {IF}, and {GETLABEL} are commands that have no keyboard equivalents—these are the special macro features known as the Advanced Macro Commands, and they give true programming power to your macros. Collectively, macro key names and Advanced Macro Commands are known as *macro keywords*.

Note that you can abbreviate certain macro key names, such as entering {D} instead of {DOWN}, or {R} instead of {RIGHT}. The list of macro keywords in Appendix C includes the acceptable abbreviations.

Instead of writing out the the macro key words for the Arrow keys, you can use single-letter abbreviations, such as {D} for {DOWN}, and {R} for {RIGHT}.

An Inquisitive Macro

Now, we'll create a macro that asks for some data-entry.

In cell D4, enter the label \Q, preceded by an apostrophe label prefix. Enter the following labels in cells E4, E5, and E6:

{GOTO}B1~

How about them Cubs?{d}{?}

{d}You can say that again!{d}

Select cell D4 and choose the Range Name Label Create command and choose the Right option to make \Q the name of cell E4.

This time we don't have to move the cell pointer, because the first step in the macro is to go to cell B1. Press Ctrl-Q to run the macro.

The macro enters its question and then pauses. Type your answer to this question in cell B2, and press Enter. The press of the Enter key is the macro's cue to get back to work. It enters its response in cell B3.

Tell Your Macros Where To Go

It's possible for a macro to destroy itself. For example, if you write a macro that enters, erases, cuts, copies, or deletes data, it can damage itself or neighboring macros cells. This can happen if you invoke the macro while the cell pointer is on or near the macro text.

If you write a macro to does its stuff in the vicinity of the current cell location, you must remember to move the cell pointer away from the macro entries before you run it. For example, imagine that you put the following macro in cell A7: '@NOW{CALC}~. This macro enters into a cell a number representing today's date. If you run this macro with the cell pointer in cell A7, the macro is replaced with the date number. If you try to run the macro again, it no longer works as a macro because a macro entry must be a label, rather than a value.

If the macro always needs to perform its work at a given cell location, include a command that assures the cell pointer is in the right location—prior to any potentially destructive operations. You can, for example, include {GOTO}A:B14~ or {HOME} to tell the macro to move the cell pointer to a specific location. Macro key names like {DOWN} and {TAB} move the cell pointer a certain number cells from its current position, but depending where in the sheet you are, they move the pointer to a different cell.

Stop a Macro in Its Tracks

One thing you need to know about macros is how to stop one that's misbehaving or one that's finished its work but keeps going through its paces. Press Ctrl-Break to stop a macro from running.

A dialog box appears, announcing that an error has occurred. Choose OK to clear the dialog box.

Ask Nicely

This previous example, macro \Q, uses the {?} macro command to pause for user input. It has the basis of a useful data-entry macro, but it's lacking in a few respects.

First, it's hard to tell that the macro is still running, waiting for your input. Also, you really don't want to fill your worksheet with questions that the program asks—it would be better if the macro asked its questions in an off-sheet prompt.

Another weakness is that the {?} macro command is fairly uncontrolled. You can move freely about the worksheet, doing whatever you please, as long as you don't press Enter.

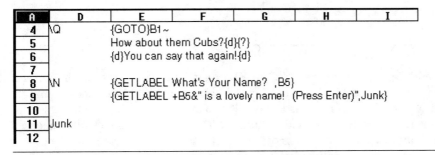

Figure 17.2. Macros \Q and \N demonstrate two ways to prompt the user to enter data.

The {GETLABEL *prompt, location*} and {GETNUMBER *prompt, location*} macro commands provide a useful alternative to the {?} command. They make sure the input is of an appropriate kind—label or value—and they display a prompt at the top of the screen, in the 1-2-3 Classic window. They also enter the user's input at a specified location.

Try It: Using {GETLABEL} for Prompts and for Text Entry

Let's create another input macro, this time using {GETLABEL} to ask for and accept a user-entered string of text, and to present instructions or comments to the user. This macro is shown in range D8..E11 of Figure 18.2.

1. In cell D8, enter the label \N, preceded by an apostrophe label prefix, and enter the label *Junk* in cell D11.

2. In cell E8, enter following label, including two blank spaces after the question mark: *{GETLABEL What's Your Name? ,B5}*.

3. In cell E9, enter the following label, including one blank space after the first quotation mark, and two spaces after the exclamation point: *{GETLABEL +B5&" is a lovely name! (Press Enter)",Junk}*.

4. Now select range D8..D11 and select the Range Name Label Create command and choose the Right option. This assigns \N as the name of cell E8, and *Junk* as the name of cell E11.

5. Now press Ctrl-N to run the macro. The 1-2-3 Classic window pops up, asking you to enter your name.

6. Type your name, but before you press Enter, notice that your typing appears two spaces after the question mark. Had you not included these spaces in macro cell E8, your typing would start right next to the prompt. Press Enter when you finish typing your name.

7. Next, the macro congratulates you on your handsome moniker, and it requests that you press Enter when you're done. Just to be naughty, type something before you press Enter. When you do press Enter, the macro finishes running. This macro is smart enough to put your unwanted entry in the cell named *Junk*.

In addition to the use of {GETLABEL}, macro \N introduces two important techniques, both of which are used in the entry in cell E9. First, the prompt in this {GETLABEL} command is the result of a string formula. 1-2-3/W lets your macros alter themselves based on information in the worksheet. In this case, the prompt inserts the contents of cell B5 into the prompt string. Note that the plus (+) sign and quotation marks are required to identify this string as a formula, and the ampersand (&) concatenates the segments of the string. For more on string formulas, see Chapter 6.

The other noteworthy technique is the use of a named range. The {GETLABEL} command in cell E9 puts any unwanted input the user might provide into the named cell Junk, which is cell E11. Using range names is essential to good macro writing, because various spreadsheet activities could cause a given cell to relocate. For example, if the formula identified the "junk" location as cell E11, rather than as the named cell Junk, the reference wouldn't update as we inserted lines into the worksheet and expanded macro \N to include cells E10, E11, and beyond. If we then ran the macro, the contents of E11 would be destroyed.

If you want to save these macros, choose File Save As and give the file a unique name, such as MYMAC1.WK3, and then close the file.

Subroutines, Tests, Loops, and Lotteries

This next example demonstrates several essential techniques for creating a sophisticated macro, and it uses subroutines, {IF} tests and {FOR} loops to perform steps selectively and repetitively and to organize the macro into functional units.

In creating this macro, \L, we'll also use 1-2-3/W's new macro-recording tools, the Transcript and Trace windows, and we'll use 1-2-3/W's 3D capability to house our macros on a separate sheet. And in addition to these macro features, we'll exploit 1-2-3/W's Data Fill and Data Distribution commands, and a variety of @functions.

Setting Up the User Display

The task is to create a system that produces random numbers for use in a lottery. In this particular lottery, we have to choose a set of six numbers, ranging in value from 1 to 36.

We can actually perform this operation without the aid of a macro. The formula @ROUND((@RAND)*35,0)+1 generates a number between 1 and 36, and if we put this formula in six different cells, we get six random numbers. But how do we make sure no two cells have the same number? That's where the macro comes in.

Start with a new worksheet, and choose File Save As to name it LOTTO.WK3.

In cell A1, enter the label *Press Ctrl-L to Get a New Number*.
Enter the following formula in cell A3, and then copy it to cells B3..F3:

@ROUND((@RAND)*35,0)+1

The first set of random numbers appears. Depending on luck of the draw there may or may not be two identical numbers in the list.

Select range A3..F3, choose Range Name Create and assign the name *Sixnums* to the range.

	A	B	C	D	E	F
1	Press Ctrl-L to Get a New Number.					
2						
3	7	1	3	2	35	6
4						
5						

Figure 17.3. This simple screen is all the user will ever see of this application. The brains behind this worksheet will be cloistered away in another sheet.

Back-Room Macros and Beancounters

"Pay no attention to the man behind the curtain." That's what the Wizard of Oz told Dorothy when she got a peek behind the Wizard's mighty facade. Like the Wizard, your macros may be more impressive if they are heard from but not seen.

Now, there's nothing hush-hush about the workings of the lottery macro. But it can be distracting and confusing to the casual user if the worksheet displays cells that the macro needs to use but which the user needn't worry about.

1-2-3/W's 3D worksheet environment makes it easy to cordon off your macros and related data. Just put them on a separate sheet.

To create a sheet to contain the macros and behind-the-scenes calculations, choose the Worksheet Insert command and select the Sheet After option, and specify a Quantity of 1 sheet. After you press OK, sheet B appears.

In range B:A2..B:B37 we're going to set up a data distribution table. The Data Distribution command, which is discussed in Chapter 16, identifies how many times a given value occurs within a range.

By setting up a list of the possible values that could occur in the *Sixnums* range, and by invoking the Data Distribution command, we can find out if any value is repeated in the current crop of random numbers. Of course, we could check for duplicate values by looking at sheet A, but we want our macro to be able to detect this situation. Then, if it generates a set of numbers that contains duplicates it can generate more sets of numbers, until it comes up with a set of six unique values.

The Data Distribution command needs a "bin" that contains examples of the values we are keeping count of. We'll set up *Bin* range in column A of sheet B. When you perform a data distribution, the number of occurrences of each value are placed in the column to the right of the bin. We'll refer to column B, then, as the *Occurs* column.

In cells A1 and B1 of sheet B, enter the labels *Bin* and *Occurs*.

Then select range A2..A37, and assign it the name *Bin*, by using the Range Name Create command. While we're at it, let's assign the name *Occurs* to range B2..B37. We'll use this range later on to see whether the current batch of random numbers contains any duplicates.

The next step is to enter the numbers 1 through 36 in range A2..A37. The easiest way is to choose Data Fill, select *Bin* as the range and 1 as the Start value—you can leave the Step and Stop values as 1 and 8191, respectively. After you choose OK, the numbers appear in column A.

Now assign a width of seven characters to columns A through C, for example by selecting range A1..C1 and selecting Worksheet Column Width, and specifying 7. Then set column D to a width of 10 and column E to a width of 30.

Choose Data Distribution and specify *Sixnums* as the Values range and *Bin* as the Bin range. After you choose OK, 1-2-3/W enters alongside the BIN column the number of times each value occurs in the *Sixnums* range.

If you scroll down to the end of the *Bin* range, you'll see that an "extra" value appears in cell B38. When you perform a data distribution, 1-2-3/W lets you know how many values exceeded the last value in the bin. In our example, this number should always be zero, since the *Bin* range lists all the values that the *Sixnums* range could contain.

The Transcript Window: Candid Keystrokes

Now that we've set up a data-distribution range we can use to test for duplicates, we're ready to start putting together the macro that will run the show.

The first thing our macro needs to do is to make sure that sheet A is the current sheet. Then it will need to generate a new set of random numbers and update the data distribution to see if the current crop of data has any duplicates.

There's an easy way to put the keystrokes that accomplish these tasks into our macro. You just perform the steps manually and then copy the list of keystrokes from the transcript of these steps that 1-2-3/W maintains as we do our work.

Before we perform these keystrokes, let's take a look in the Transcript window. And we'll clear out its contents so we won't have to sift through the transcript to find the keystrokes to paste into our macro.

Choose Tools Macro Show Transcript. Maximize the Transcript window, so you can see all the keystrokes it contains. All the various menu commands, cell entries, and selections you've performed are remembered here—up to 512 characters worth.

Selection, Natural and Otherwise

If your macro needs to select a specific cell, take steps to ensure that it can find that cell. For example, you can use the Home, Ctrl-Home, or GOTO key to move the cell pointer to a specific location. And then, if need be, you can use navigation keys to move move the cell pointer from there. All of these keystrokes will be recorded in the Transcript.

If you need to have your macro preselect a range, you can do this quite easily by recording—or entering directly into your macros—a press of the ABS key followed by a range reference and a press of the Enter key. For example, {ABS}B4..G18~ preselects range B4..G18. That's a easier than, for example, selecting range B4..G18 with the following sequence: {GOTO}B4~{ABS}{R 5}{D14}~.

Note that you can also make short work out of selecting named ranges. If B4..G18 has been assigned the name *Prices*, you could preselect the range with by entering{ABS}Prices~.

You can chart the progress of keystroke recording by opening the Transcript window and using the Window Tile command to make it share the screen with your open worksheet files.

Choose Window Tile, so you can view the transcript as you work in the LOTTO.WK3 worksheet.

Choose the Edit Clear All command to empty out the Transcript window, and then close the window, and then click somewhere within the LOTTO.WK3 window to activate it.

Just as you watch what you say when you're being tape recorded, you should try to be very deliberate about the keystrokes and mouse-clicks you make while you're recording a sequence of steps to paste into a macro. Otherwise, you'll have to locate and edit out the missteps, lest your macro repeat your miscues each time you run it.

Now, let's perform the first step that we want the macro to do: Press Ctrl-Home to display the first sheet in the file. The transcript records {FC}, the macro abbreviation for the keystroke that takes you to the first cell in the file.

> ## Review the Transcript
>
> In general, use the Transcript to get an approximation of the keys you need for your macro. By going through a dry run of the steps you want your macro to perform, you build a Transcript that will be a good start to creation your macro.
>
> But don't expect the Transcript to precisely match the keystrokes and mouse clicks you performed. 1-2-3/W uses its own shorthand of recording menu commands, cell pointer movements, and so on. For example, you may hop around a dialog box with a sequence of mouse clicks, presses of the Tab key and so on. The Transcripts record, in a minimum of steps, the keystrokes necessary to specify the same settings as you choose; it does not, however provide a blow-by-blow account of how you meandered through the dialog box.
>
> Usually, a macro you copy from the Transcript will work in your macro just as you recorded it. In a different context, however, the steps you recorded may yield unpredictable or unwanted results. Use the Transcript, then, to build a foundation for you macro steps, but make a point to inspect and, as needed, alter the recorded keystrokes.

Stop the Recalculation

Before we perform a Data Distribution, let's anticipate a subtle problem that lies ahead of us. Whenever you perform a Data Distribution, 1-2-3/W recalculates the data in the file. Consider this scenario: you have your macro press CALC to generate a new set of random numbers, and then you have it repeat the Data Distribution command to analyze these numbers. Unfortunately, the random numbers will change automatically the moment that the new distribution is presented. The solution is to turn the recalculation mode to manual.

Choose Tools User Setup, and select the Recalculation button, and choose the Manual Recalculation option. Then Choose OK two times to return to Ready mode.

Now press CALC (F9) to generate a new set of random numbers, and then choose Data Distribution to get the latest report on whether there are duplicate values in *Sixnums*, the random number set. Since the settings you used last time you issued this command are still applicable, you can simply confirm them by choosing OK.

Before we inspect the results of the new distribution, let's copy the current transcript, so we can paste it into our macro. Click anywhere in the Transcript window, and select the entire contents of the transcript, which should start with {FC} for {FIRSTCELL}, the way the Transcript recorded our press of the Ctrl-Page Up key. The latter part of the Transcript should document our execution of the Data Distribution command.

Now choose Edit Copy to put this selection in the Clipboard, and then close the Transcript window. Double-click the Transcript window's Control icon, or choose Close from its Control menu or from the File Menu at the top of the 1-2-3/W Window. Note, however, that choosing Exit from the Transcript window menu exits 1-2-3/W.

With LOTTO.WK3 as the active window, go back to sheet B, by pressing Ctrl-PageUp, and then Maximize the window, by clicking LOTTO.WK3's Maximize Icon, the upward-pointing arrowhead on the right side of its title bar or by choosing Maximize from its Control menu.

Transcript Tidbits

Here's a few more things you ought to know about using the Transcript window:

If you paste text from the Transcript window, and some keystrokes at the end are missing, select a larger range and repeat the Edit Paste command.

You can run a sequence of keystrokes directly from the macro. Just select them and choose Run from the Macro menu.

And if you the Transcript window is open but it's not visible because other worksheet or graph windows are blocking it, press Ctrl-F6 until the Transcript appears.

Select range E1..E10, and choose Edit Paste. The keystrokes from the transcript appear in the selected range. If for any reason the keystrokes you pasted from the Transcript don't match those in Figure 17.5, edit your worksheet to match the figure.

Enter the label \L in cell D1, preceded by an apostrophe label prefix.

With cell D1 selected, choose Range Name Label Create and choose the Right option. This applies the name \L to the macro in cell E1.

Press Ctrl-L to run the macro. If no two of the numbers are the same, press Ctrl-L until this occurs. Make a note of the duplicated number or numbers. Then press Ctrl-PageUp to return to sheet B, and scroll down column B. Since at least one number in the *Bin* range is duplicated in the *Sixnums* range of sheet A (the current batch of random numbers), one or more of the values in column B will be two or higher. This information comes courtesy of the Data Distribution command.

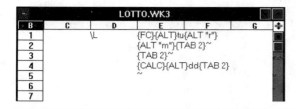

Figure 17.5. The beginnings of the lottery macro. Thanks to the Transcript window, you don't have to memorize the keystrokes that select options from a dialog box. You just try these from the keyboard or mouse and paste them from the Transcript into the worksheet—by way of the Clipboard.

Breaking the Macro into Subroutines

Now we need to teach the macro to recognize and resolve situations when we have duplicate numbers.

Let's strategize a bit before we modify the macro. It's quite possible that duplicate numbers could occur several times in succession, so it would be inefficient to write a macro that contains multiple occurrences of the calculation and testing procedure—how many repetitions of the test would be enough?

A better solution is to have one macro do the testing and have another do the calculating. This concept gives us the opportunity to make the macro more interesting. We can have the macro run through several iterations of random numbers before stopping at one set, even if there aren't duplicates.

\L will continue to be the main part of the macro, but we're going to move some of the existing macro commands to a new location to become part of a subroutine that macro \L can call as needed. The name of this subroutine will be *Newnum*.

In cell D11, enter the label *Newnum*, and then use the Range Name Label Create command to assign the label in this cell as the name of the cell to its right.

Now perform the necessary editing to rearrange your macro so it looks like Figure 17.6. Remember that you can cut parts of a cell-entry to the clipboard by editing the cell, selecting the appropriate text, and pressing Shift-Delete. Then you press Enter to complete editing the cell. To paste the contents elsewhere, click in the target cell and choose Edit Paste or press Ctrl-Insert.

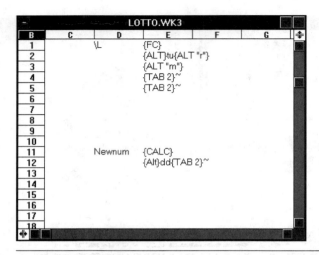

Figure 17.6. The nearly completed lottery macro. With the recalculating set up in a subroutine, the main part of the program will be able to call this procedure as many times as needed.

Making a Smart Macro

Now we need to give our macro the logic that lets it cycle through sequences of numbers and stop when it has a satisfactory collection of unique values.

In the cell E6, the first empty cell at the bottom of the \L macro, enter the following label: *{FOR Counter,1,1000,1,Newnum}*.

This command will to run the *Newnum* routine 1,000 times. It's extremely unlikely that we'll need to try that many times to find a unique set of numbers, but using a very large number like this ensures that the loop won't stop short of its goal. Later on we'll tell the macro that it can break out of this {FOR} loop when a satisfactory set of numbers appears.

To break this command down: *Counter* is a named range (we need to name it), the first 1 indicates the number to start counting from, and the 1000 is the number to count up to. The next 1 means to count one-by-one, and *Newnum* is the routine to execute each time another number is counted off.

To provide a place to put maintain the count, enter the label *Counter* in cell D17, and use the Range Name Label Create command to assign this label as the name of the cell to the right.

To allow the subroutine to determine whether a satisfactory set of random numbers has been generated, we need to add a couple of more commands.

> ## So Much to Know, So Much to Type
>
> One 1-2-3/W feature makes it easy to remember the details of macro commands, and another helps you quickly key in a macro keyword.
>
> If you type a macro command and then press HELP (F1), up pops 1-2-3/W's Help window with information about the command. If you type an open brace ({), you get the Macro Command Index Help screen. Note also that on the Help menu there's a menu choice called Macros, which takes you to a Help screen called Macro Basics. Since there are sometimes lots of details and options involved in a macro command, online Help is especially valuable to the Macro writer.
>
> If you type an open brace ({) and press the NAME key (F3), you get a scrollable list of available macro keywords. When you choose an entry from this list, it appears on the Edit line.

In cell E13, enter *{IF @MAX(Occurs)<2#AND#Counter>5}{FORBREAK}*.

This command checks whether the highest value in the *Occurs* range is greater than 2 and if *Counter* is equal to at least 6. This command makes sure that the macro spins through at least six sets of numbers. If there have been more than five tries and if the set of numbers in the *Sixnum* range on sheet A has no duplicates, the {FOR} loop stops.

As you may recall, *Occurs* is the range that the Data Distribution command uses to identify duplicates in the *Sixnums* range. IF @MAX(Occurs) is greater than one, that means that one of the numbers listed in the *Bin* range has two or more occurences in the *Sixnums* range.

In subroutines, you should signal the end of the procedure by including the {RETURN} command. Enter the label {RETURN} in cell E14.

We need to add only one more step: returning the default mode to automatic recalculation. This time lets use the 1-2-3 Classic command: in cell E8, enter /WGRA, preceded by an apostrophe. This is the keystroke sequence for the command /Worksheet Global Recalculation Automatic.

Now, save the file, and press Ctrl-L to run the macro. But use it at your own risk!

If the macro fails to work as described, check the Troubleshooting Macro Problems section at the end of this chapter. There you'll find tips on rooting the bugs out of your macros.

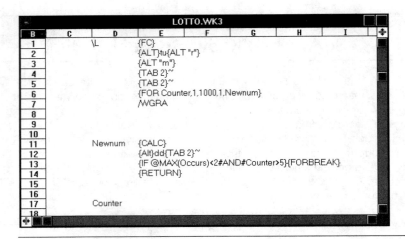

Figure 17.7. The completed lottery macro. As you can see, subroutines, such as *Newnum*, and variable cells, such as *Counter*—along with {FOR} loops and {IF} tests—let your macros go well beyond merely entering a sequence of keystrokes.

See What You've Done!

Let's take stock of what we learned in the LOTTO.WK3 exercise. This macro gave us a chance to sample a wide variety of advanced macro techniques.

We used the Transcript window to teach our macro how to play back menu commands that we chose. And we mixed and matched 1-2-3/W's Windows-style menu commands with 1-2-3 Classic menu commands.

We also tried out some of the most popular of the Advanced Macro Commands, {FOR} and {IF}, which add real programming power to your macros. {FOR} loops let your macro repetitively call a subroutine, and {IF} commands test for a certain condition and then decide what to do under the circumstances.

In case that wasn't enough macro magic, we used a variable cell, which we named *Counter*, to keep track of information that the macro needed to use. And we combined the talents of an @function, @MAX, with the {IF} command.

If you create a lot of macros, odds are you'll use all of these techniques, or variations on them, quite often.

> ## Make Your Own Macros
>
> These examples are intended to stimulate your interest in creating custom macros that suit *your* needs and to show you techniques that are common to most intermediate-to-advanced macros.
>
> The following section outlines the new macro features of 1-2-3/W. If you're an old hand at macro writing, you'll want to know what's new with macros in 1-2-3 for Windows.
>
> In Appendix C, you'll find a detailed list of all of 1-2-3/W's macro commands, both old and new. As you need to expand your macros with new features, peruse the list to find commands that give your macros the power to do everything that you could ask of them.
>
> Also explore the list of @functions in Appendix B. By including @functions such as @cellpointer, @info, @coord, @cell, you can make macros that adjust based on a variety of worksheet conditions. You'll find examples of macros that use many of these techniques in the following chapter, *Mastering the SmartIcon Palette*.

1-2-3/W's New Macro Commands

In addition to a vocabulary that includes the fifty-odd macro commands that are supported by 1-2-3 Release 3.x, 1-2-3/W knows more than a dozen new ones. Most, but not all of these, are built to capitalize on the Windows environment. The new commands fall into the following general categories: Window Control, Clipboard, Dynamic Data Exchange (DDE), Data External, and Miscellaneous commands. Note that the quotation marks that appear in some of the argument examples are required.

Window Control

The window control commands allow you to alter the display of the 1-2-3/W application window and the document (Worksheet, Graph, and Transcript) windows within it.

{APP-ADJUST x-pos,y-pos,width,height} This command lets you alter the size of the 1-2-3/W application window. *X-pos* and *y-pos* are the horizontal and vertical positions, measured, respectively, from the top and left of the screen to the top and left edges of the 1-2-3/W window. *Width* and *height* are the number of pixels from one edge of the window to the opposite edge.

{APP-STATE state} This command lets you alter the status of the 1-2-3/W application window. *State* can be "Maximize", "Minimize", or "Restore".

{WINDOW-ADJUST x-pos,y-pos,width,height} This command lets you alter the size of the active document window, which may be a Worksheet, Graph, or Transcript window. *X-pos* and *y-pos* are the horizontal and vertical positions, measured, respectively, from the top and left of the 1-2-3/W window to the top and left edges of the document window. *Width* and *height* are the number of pixels from one edge of the window to the opposite edge.

{WINDOW-SELECT window-name} This command activates the Worksheet or Graph window identified by *window-name*. You specify the name as it appears in the window's title bar.

{WINDOW-STATE state} This command lets you alter the status of the active Worksheet, Graph, or Transcript window. State can be "Maximize", "Minimize", or "Restore".

Clipboard/Edit

The edit commands, in their simplest form, mimic commands you can choose from the Edit menu. Most of these commands use the Clipboard to perform common editing tasks. You can use these commands as more-readable substitutes for Alt commands, for example using *{EDIT-COPY}* instead of *{ALT}EC*.

Some of these commands have an optional *format* argument. This argument lets you can determine which of several data formats should be used when 1-2-3/W puts information onto the Clipboard or copies it from the Clipboard.

{EDIT-CLEAR [range],[property]} Without the optional arguments, this command is equivalent to the Edit Clear menu command. *Source-range* is the range to be cleared. With the optional *property* argument, this command resembles the Edit Clear Special menu command. *Property* may be one of the following choices: "Contents", "Formats", "Styles", or "Graphs".

{EDIT-COPY [source-range];[format]} Without the optional arguments, this command is equivalent to the Edit Copy menu command. *Source-range* is the range to be copied to the Clipboard. *Format* may include such standard Windows formats as "Text", "Metafilepict", and "Rich Text Format".

{EDIT-COPY-GRAPH} This command is the equivalent of choosing Edit Copy from a Graph window. It copies the current graph to the Clipboard.

{EDIT-CUT [source-range],[format]} Without the optional arguments, this command is equivalent to the Edit Cut menu command. *Source-range* is the range to be cut to the Clipboard. *Format* may include such standard Windows formats as "Text", "Metafilepict", and "Rich Text Format".

{EDIT-PASTE [destination-range],[format]} Without the optional arguments, this command is equivalent to the Edit Paste menu command. *Source-range* is the range to be pasted from the Clipboard. *Format* may include such standard Windows formats as "Text", "Metafilepict", and "Rich Text Format".

{EDIT-PASTE-LINK [destination-range]} Without the optional arguments, this command is equivalent to the Edit Paste Link menu command, which uses the Clipboard to establish a DDE link. Before you use this command, the Clipboard should already have a copy of text or graphics from another Windows application that supports DDE. *Destination-range* is the range into which the linked data should be pasted.

Dynamic Data Exchange (DDE)

In addition to the simple {EDIT-PASTE-LINK} command described above, there are several commands built to help you exploit Windows' DDE feature to create hotlinks between applications. When data changes in the source application, it can automatically update the target application.

These commands fall into two categories: {LINK} commands and {DDE} commands. The {LINK} commands—{LINK-CREATE},{LINK-DELETE},{LINK-ASSIGN}, {LINK-REMOVE}, {LINK-UPDATE}, and {LINK-TABLE}—are largely equivalents of features that are available from the Edit Link Options dialog box.

The {DDE} commands—{DDE-OPEN}, {DDE-USE}, {DDE-CLOSE}, {DDE-ADVISE}, {DDE-UNADVISE}, {DDE-REQUEST}, {DDE-EXECUTE}, and {DDE-POKE} are for the true Windows hacker. They let you manage the conversation between applications at a very low level. These commands provide a greater degree of control over the interapplication communication process, but they are quite cumbersome to use.

Data External Commands

{COMMIT [driver, database]} You use this command if you're working with 1-2-3/W in conjunction with the SQL Server DataLens driver to complete a pending transaction. *Driver* is the name of a DataLens driver, enclosed in quotes, specifically "SQL_SERVER". See Chapter 13 for details on using the Data External commands to link 1-2-3 with external database systems. *Database* is the name, also in quotes, of the database to which you want to commit the transaction. If you don't specify *driver* and *database*, this command commits all pending transactions.

{ROLLBACK [driver, database]} You use this command if you're working with 1-2-3/W in conjunction with the SQL Server DataLens driver to cancel a pending transaction. *Driver* is the name of a DataLens driver, enclosed in quotes, specifically "SQL_SERVER". *Database* is the name, also in quotes, of the database for which you want to cancel the transaction. If you don't specify *driver* and *database*, this command cancels all pending transactions.

Miscellaneous

The {LAUNCH} command is in a category unto itself. Its closest relative is the {SYSTEM} command that allows 1-2-3 and 1-2-3/W to execute a DOS command. {LAUNCH} loads a Windows application and determines the state of its window.

{LAUNCH command-string,[window-command]} This command runs the Windows application specified in the *command-string*. *Window-command* may be "Minimize", "Maximize", or "Restored". If you don't specify a *window-command*, the application you launch is minimized and 1-2-3/W remains the active application.

New Ways to Navigate Menus, Dialog Boxes, and Worksheets

In addition to these commands are new menu-, dialog-box, and worksheet-navigation techniques.

The {ALT}, {MENUBAR}, and {MB} key names are the equivalent to pressing the Alt key to activate the Windows menu bar in 1-2-3/W. You can, for example, invoke 1-2-3/W's Style menu by including *{ALT}S* or *{MB}S* in your macros. Then your macro can use characters, usually letters, or navigation keys and the Enter key to choose options from the menu that appears.

There's another use of the {ALT} key name, which takes the form of {Alt "*letter*"}. The effect is the same as pressing Alt and the letter simultaneously. *{ALT "K"}*, for example, is the same as pressing *ALT-K*.

You can apply {ALT "letter"} to bringing up the menu, but its primary application is to issue shortcut keys within dialog boxes. Unlike when you invoke the Windows-style menus, you can't press Alt and then a letter to choose a dialog-box shortcut. Instead you need to combine them, such as by using {ALT "r"} to choose the Replace button from within the Style Font dialog box.

The {TAB} key name is identical to the long-established {BIGRIGHT} key. Either one is the equivalent of pressing Tab or Ctrl-RightArrow. You might find {TAB} more readable than {BIGRIGHT}, especially in macros that navigate the dialog box. You can also use {TAB} to navigate through the worksheet, just as you'd use {BIGRIGHT}—to scroll one sheet to the right or, in Edit mode, to move one word to the right. There's also a new {BACKTAB} key which is the equivalent of pressing Shift-Tab or Ctrl-LeftArrow.

The {ABS} key name isn't new, but its use in Ready mode as a way to preselect cells is new. As you've done in exercises throughout the book, you can use {ABS} and then a series of navigation keys, a range reference, or range name, and finally a press of the Enter key. (~) to preselect a range in a macro. If you'd rather use a more descriptive keyword for preselection operations, you can substitute the new key name {ANCHOR} for the {ABS} key.

To GUI or Not to GUI?

1-2-3/W poses a major question to macro writers: should you use the new Windows-style GUI menu commands or use 1-2-3 Classic commands?

If you want to share your macros with people who use earlier releases of 1-2-3, or with 1-2-3 for Macintosh, you'll want to build your macros around 1-2-3 Classic commands. These other versions won't know what to make of the {Alt} commands that are the bread and butter of 1-2-3 for Windows.

But if you want your macros to tap the full power of 1-2-3/W, you must rely on the new Windows-style commands. You also won't want to neglect 1-2-3/W's new Windows-related macro commands, which let you access Clipboard and DDE features and give you control over the display of the the 1-2-3/W window and the document windows inside it.

In fact, {EDIT-CUT}, {EDIT-COPY}, and {EDIT-PASTE} *are* also supported in both 1-2-3/W and 1-2-3 for Macintosh. This means that you can share between these two releases macros that use the Clipboard.

If your macros will always run within 1-2-3/W and not in other releases, note that you can use a mix of both GUI and 1-2-3 Classic commands. So if you find /WIC easier to enter and read than its GUI equivalent for inserting a column, *{Alt}ki{Alt "c"}{BIGRIGHT 4}~*, by all means include the 1-2-3 Classic command in your macro. But don't stay so hooked on 1-2-3 Classic commands that your spreadsheets miss out on 1-2-3/W's unique capabilities.

Troubleshooting Macro Problems

Remember that macros are very finicky. If you leave a stray space in a label that contains a macro, that tells the macro to press the spacebar. Read your macros carefully to see if there are any subtle inclusions or omissions.

Also remember that a macro that works with the cell pointer in a particular location, or when a particular dialog box is open, may not work properly in another context. Perhaps you need to add steps to your macro that set up this context, such as going to a certain cell, or invoking Edit mode.

When the problem is hard to spot, choose Tools Macro Debug, and select the Single step and Trace options. These debugging features make it easy for you to go over your macros with a fine-tooth comb. When you invoke your macro with these options in use, you can watch the macro operate in slow motion. Each time you press Enter, the macro performs another step. As you do this, you can study the Trace window to see the location of the current macro commands, and the instructions it is currently performing. When you're done, return to the Tools Macro Debug menu and clear these options.

One common and tricky macro flaw is missing or incorrect range names. If everything else seems to be in order, but your macro still isn't doing the job, move to a remote place in your worksheet and invoke the Range Name Paste Table command. This gives you a list of current range names and the cells they reference. Compare these names and ranges carefully against your worksheet. Perhaps you neglected to assign one of the names referenced in your macros, or maybe the name currently refers to a different range than you think it does.

The Secrets of Macro Success

The most important ingredient in successful macro writing is a firm grasp of 1-2-3/W's spreadsheet, graphics, and database capabilities. If you know 1-2-3/W's built-in features, you'll find it easy to turn your know-how into macro instructions.

For example, if you're well schooled in ways to navigate the worksheet area and in @functions that detect the status of the worksheet, you can write "smart" macros that find their way around the sheet and perform tasks selectively and without user intervention. You can use your expertise with such features as sorting data, you can automate the task so less-skilled users won't have to figure out how to do it—and run the risk of sending the wrong data into orbit.

Your knowledge of built-in functions can also keep you from reinventing the wheel. The idea of macros is to save time, not to write programs that attempt to do things the program can do without a macro, or things that you can't do effectively with a macro.

A rewarding and challenging demand of macros is the need for creative thinking. Invariably, macros start out in burst of lightbulb-over-your-head inspiration. Perhaps you've caught yourself in a rut, issuing the same command repeatedly. Or you've thought, "if only 1-2-3/W had a command that...." When you follow these observations with ideas on how you can make these new-fangled features a reality, a useful macro may be born.

Another hallmark of successful macro writers is a very methodical approach. Macros behave like robots. And like a good robot, your macro does exactly what you ask of it. However, you have to think carefully about what you ask your robot to do. A macro that does the right thing when you execute it with the cell pointer in cell A1 may wreak havoc if the cell pointer is elsewhere. If you think through the scenarios in which the macro might run, you can add steps to ensure the macro's success, such as having it move the cell pointer the appropriate location before it performs a given task.

A related, and obviously essential, requirement is that your macros be accurate. A misspelled letter or missing punctuation mark can render your macro useless or worse. To the rescue are 1-2-3/W's powerful and easy-to-use macro tools. The Transcript window and improved debugging tools help ensure that your macros do what you want them to.

And don't forget that while you use 1-2-3/W, it records an account of the last several operations you performed. Even if you use the mouse, 1-2-3/W records the keystroke equivalent of your activities. You can copy selected keystrokes from this transcript and paste them into a cell.

18

Mastering the SmartIcon Palette

SmartIcons are the most exciting thing to happen to 1-2-3 since a bunch of Hawaiian-shirted men and women gathered in Cambridge, Massachusetts to put spreadsheets, graphics, databases, and macros into one neat little package.

As a user of SmartIcons, you'll find them to be the shortest of shortcuts. You'll also find that they help you work without having to concentrate on menu commands and keystroke combinations. The philosophy behind SmartIcons is *go for it*. One click, and the job is done.

In this chapter you'll learn how to make the most of the SmartIcons that come with 1-2-3/W. You'll want to peruse this vast library to decide which ones to keep handy and to get ideas for SmartIcons that you'd like to create.

Then it's on to the main event: learning how to make your own SmartIcons. In no time, you'll turn 1-2-3/W into your personal spreadsheet domain, outfitted with all the pushbutton shortcuts you could desire. All you need are basic macro skills and a copy of Paintbrush—a graphics program that comes with Windows.

Seeing your own creation become an integral part of 1-2-3/W is Windows computing at its best. It's hard to describe the excitement you'll feel when you make your first Smart-Icon. But it's a safe bet that you'll immediately grab the next 1-2-3/W user you see and show off your creation.

If your home-grown SmartIcon is a real time-saver, your colleague will be dying for a copy. Magnanimous sort that you are, you're glad to oblige. At the right price....

> *In this chapter you will learn:*
>
> - **How to change the location of the SmartIcon palette**
> - **How to use choose among the built-in SmartIcons**
> - **How to use Paintbrush to design your own icons**
> - **How to attach macros to your icons**
> - **Strategies and tactics for effective SmartIcons**

Using a SmartIcon

If you know how to click with the left mouse button, you know how to use a SmartIcon. Like any icon, a SmartIcon is an on-screen button that's identified by a picture.

Because SmartIcons are built for speed, they usually don't bring up a dialog box or a prompt that asks you to specify a range. For this reason, you should make sure to preselect the cells that you want the SmartIcon to copy, style, or whatever.

For example, you can give a range of cells italic styling by preselecting the range and clicking on the slanted-I icon. If you don't preselect a range, clicking this icon italicizes only the current cell.

What sets SmartIcons apart from other icons is that they're customizable and they reside in the SmartIcon palette. The palette may be in any of several locations about the screen, but it's easy to spot because it contains a gallery of little buttons, like the collection shown in Figure 18.1.

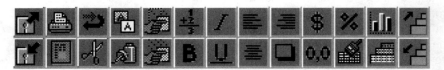

Figure 18.1. The SmartIcon palette. When you install 1-2-3/W, these are the available SmartIcons. By customizing the palette, you can choose from other built-in SmartIcons—and you can add your own.

If you think there's an icon in the palette for the task at hand, look at the pictures to find one that represents the feature you need. After you use a particular icon a few times, finding and choosing it becomes second nature.

Click the Right mouse-button on a SmartIcon to see a prompt that describes what the icon does.

If you're not certain what a SmartIcon does, you can bring up a prompt that clues you in. To do this, click the icon with the right mouse button. A brief description of the icon's use appears at the top of the 1-2-3/W window. If you drag through the palette with the right-button depressed, you can find out what each icon will do.

Altering the Palette

Between the large collection that Lotus includes in the box and the ones that you create, you'll have a lot of icons to choose from. By customizing the palette you can affect the number of icons you can see at once, and you can decide which icons the palette will display.

The basic palette-management options are positioning it at the top, bottom, right, or left of the 1-2-3/W window; making the palette into a resizable, free-floating window; hiding the palette; and choosing which icons to include in the palette. When you master these simple tasks, you'll know how to make the most of the built-in icons and you'll be ready to embellish the palette with your own innovations.

Moving, Hiding, and Resizing the Palette

To change the way the SmartIcon palette is displayed, select Tools SmartIcons. The dialog box shown in Figure 18.2 appears when you choose this command.

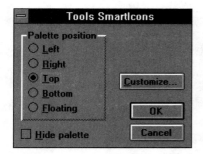

Figure 18.2. Tools SmartIcons dialog box. This dialog box lets you alter the way the SmartIcons are displayed, and its customize button allows you to select which icons appear on the palette.

Figures 18.3 and 18.4 show two views of the palette. When you install 1-2-3/W, the palette is at the top of the 1-2-3/W window. You can instead have the palette appear along the bottom, right, or left side of the 1-2-3/W workspace. Alternatively, you can turn the palette into a floating window or you can hide it from view.

If you want to display the palette along any of the four sides of the worksheet window, there's no ideal choice. Personal taste will be you main guide.

But there are trade-offs. You can see more icons with the palette on the top or bottom than with it on either side, simply because the typical computer screen is wider than it is high.

Note that whatever the palette arrangement, if your current palette contains more icons than there's room to display, 1-2-3/W shows you the first ones in the set. You'll learn how to decide what icons are in the current palette, and the order in which they appear, in a following section.

428 The Lotus Guide to 1-2-3 for Windows

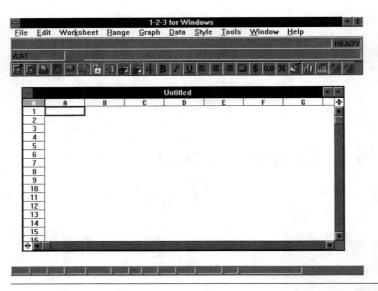

Figure 18.3. By default, the palette appears at the top of the window. When the palette appears at the top or bottom of the window, you can see more than 25 icons.

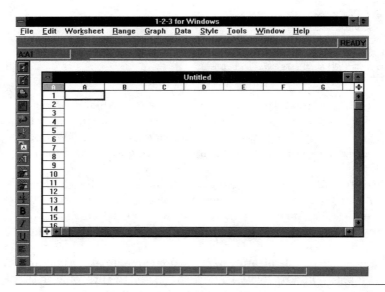

Figure 18.4. When the palette appears on the left- or right-side of the window, fewer icons appear, but if you prefer these locations, it might be worth the trade-off.

Mastering the SmartIcon Palette   **429**

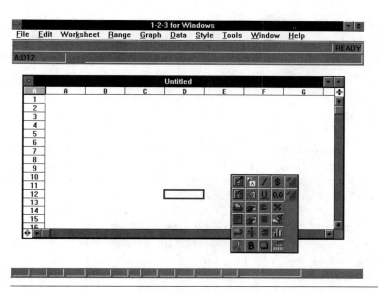

Figure 18.5. When the palette is floating, you stretch it to display a large number of icons. And you can size it down small enough to display but a pair of icons. When you want to move the floating palette, you drag it by one of its icons.

The other two options, displaying it as a floating window or hiding the palette, make a more dramatic difference.

The Floating Palette

Quite literally, the floating palette gives you the most flexibility. You can resize it by dragging its edges, and you can move it anywhere on the screen. This floating palette is at once the most compact and the most expansive palette arrangement.

Using an oversized, floating palette lets you try out the full range of SmartIcon options. You can load up dozens of icons and try them all out.

Then when you learn which icons you find most valuable, you'll want to remove some lesser-used icons from the palette. This will make it easier to find the icons you use most. And if you continue to display the palette as a floating window, keeping it down to size frees up screen space.

Even if the palette is loaded up with a lot of icons, you can keep it from hogging a lot of space. Just like any window, you can resize the floating palette by dragging its edges. You can make it small enough to fit only two icons or large enough to display all the icons in your current palette.

The floating palette arangement lets you see the most icons at a time. And you can size it down to show as few as two icons.

You can move the floating palette by dragging it by one of its icons.

You can also drag the floating palette anywhere you wish on the screen. Simply click within the palette and drag to a new location. Remember that when you click the palette without dragging, you invoke an icon rather than moving the palette.

Hiding the Palette

If you hide the palette, you get a bit more screen space to work with, but you lose all the convenience of the SmartIcons.

Why would you ever hide the palette? First, if you don't use a mouse, the SmartIcon palette will be nothing but a bunch of pretty pictures. If your computer has no such pointing device, you may as well use the screen's real estate for something you can use: more room to view data.

Secondly, you may want to keep the icons away from novice users. Although the icons are easy to use, some are quite powerful, so an untrained or incautious user can damage the worksheet with some reckless clicking. A better alternative, though, is to apply necessary protection to the sheet, such as using the security options described in Chapter 9, and changing the palette to include just those icons you want the beginning user to have access to.

Choosing the Current Icons

The icons that are in the palette when you first run 1-2-3/W provide a lot of valuable shortcuts. As you've seen throughout this book, these icons help with such chores as opening or saving a file; previewing or executing a printout; undoing the last command; copying, moving, and removing data; helping you view and move among multiple worksheets; and changing the styling or format of some data. Others do such neat tricks as automatically summing rows or columns of data and making a graph from a selected range of cells.

Choose Tools SmartIcons Customize to determine which icons are visible in the palette.

These, however, are just the tip of the iceberg. There are many more built-in icons to choose from. You can add some of these to the current palette, and you can free the palette of icons you don't have much use for. And when you create your own icons, the need to choose which icons are visible in the palette will only increase.

To make it easy to explore a large number of the SmartIcons, select the Floating option from the Tools SmartIcons dialog box. Then select the Customize button to bring up the Tools SmartIcons Customize dialog box. This latter dialog box is shown in Figure 18.6.

Figure 18.6. The Tools SmartIcons Customize dialog box. The Current Palette box determines the which icons appear, and in which order. The order of the icons is from top to bottom and from right to left—first icon is the one on in the upper-left of this box, and the next is the one below it.

The Current Palette

The Current Palette box, as the name implies, contains the icons that make up the current SmartIcon palette. For an icon to be available to the user, it must be in the Current Palette. The scroll bar underneath this box lets you scan through all the current SmartIcons if there are more than you can see in the box.

To see what task one of the current icons performs, click it once. A prompt appears in the Description box in the lower left of the dialog box.

To remove an icon from the Current Palette, you double-click it. Alternatively, you can click it once and choose the Remove button. Note that removing an icon from the Current Palette does not permanently delete the icon. You can always add it back, using the techniques described in the following sections.

To clear an icon out of the Current Palette box in the Tools Icon Palette Customize dialog box, you double-click the icon.

> ### Try It: Removing an Icon from the Current Palette
>
> One step in customizing the palette is to remove icons that you don't plan to use. This leaves more room for icons that you find more useful.
>
> 1. Locate the underlining SmartIcon, which looks like a large, underlined letter U.
> 2. Click the underlining SmartIcon once to see its description appear in the Description box. This step is not required, but it helps confirm that you've chosen the appropriate icon.
> 3. Double-click the underlining SmartIcon.
>
>   Remember that removing an icon from the current palette does not destroy the icon. It merely demotes it from being a current choice in the palette.

Note that an icon's presence in the Current Palette box does not guarantee that it will be visible in the SmartIcon palette. When there are more current icons than the present icon-palette arrangement can accommodate, 1-2-3/W displays as many of the current icons as it can; the others are left off.

The Current Palette not only determines which icons appear, but it puts them in order. The order runs from top to bottom and right to left. In other words, the icon in the upper-left of the current palette is the first icon, the icon below it is next. After the last icon in the column, the sequence continues with the topmost icon in the next column, and so on.

This order is important because it determines how the icons are grouped. It's easier to find the appropriate icon when similar icons appear next to each other. And if the palette is too small to show all current icons, this ordering determines which icons are visible. For example, if you're using a palette arrangement that can fit 26 icons, and if you have 28 icons in the current palette, the last two icons won't be visible.

Adding Standard Icons and Custom Icons to the Current Palette

The Current Palette box is one of three groups of SmartIcons that are displayed in the Tools SmartIcons Customize dialog box. The others are the Standard Icons box and the Custom Icons box. Each of these boxes features a scroll bar to help you see icons that aren't visible in the box.

All the icons that are built into 1-2-3/W, including those that are in the Current Palette, appear in the Standard Icons box. Icons that you create—along with a few customizable sample icons that come with 1-2-3/W—appear in the Custom Icons box. Most likely, there are icons in the latter two boxes that aren't in the current palette. To make one of these available, you need to add it to the current palette.

As in the Current Palette, you click a standard icon once to get a description of its functionality. All custom icons, however, have the same description, which is "Macro Button."

Double-clicking an icon from the Standard Icons box or Custom Icon box adds the icon to the Current Palette. If you prefer, you can also add a standard or custom icon to the Current Palette by clicking it once and then choosing the Add button.

To add a Standard or Custom icon to the Current Palette, you double-click it.

Figure 18.7. Three icons you might want to add to your current palette. The one on the left is a shortcut for bringing up the Tools Icon Palette Customize dialog box. The one in the middle copies the contents of the current cell into all the other cells in the selected range. The one on the right enters the names of the months into twelve cells in the current row. You'll find the first two among the 1-2-3/W's standard icons. The third is a sample custom icon that also comes with the software.

You control where in the palette an icon is added. If you click once on an icon in the Current Palette and then add a standard or custom icon, the icon is inserted immediately before the one you clicked. By choosing the location to add new icons, you can keep related icons together and you can control which icons are most likely to be visible even in a smaller palette arrangement.

If you want to move an icon from one place in the Current Palette to another, start by removing the icon from the palette. Then click on the icon before which you want to add back the one you just removed. When you add the icon back to the Current Palette it will appear in the desired location.

One more detail worth noting is that it's possible to put two or more copies of the same icon in the Current Palette. In general, this is a waste of space. If it happens by mistake, you'll want to remove the duplicates. But if you can't get enough of a certain icon, you can choose to fill the palette with as many copies of it as you see fit to include.

> ### Try It: Adding Icons to the Current Palette
>
> Let's add three SmartIcons to the current palette: one that makes it easy to return to the Tools SmartIcons Customize dialog box, one that copies the contents of the current cell into all other selected cells, and one that enters three-letter abbreviations of the names of the 12 months. These icons are illustrated in Figure 18.7.
>
> 1. Locate in the Standard Icons box the SmartIcon that invokes the Tools SmartIcons Customize command. This icon is shown on the left of Figure 18.7.
>
> 2. Click the Icon once to see its description appear in the Description box. This step is not required, but it helps confirm that you've chosen the appropriate icon.
>
> 3. To add this icon to the current palette, double click it.
>
> 4. Repeat this process to add the icon shown in the middle of Figure 18.7, the icon that copies the current cell into the other cells in a selection.
>
> 5. Once again repeat this process to add the icon on the right of Figure 18.7, the icon that enters the names of the 12 months. Note that this icon is found in the Custom Icons box, rather than the Standard Icons box.
>
> 6. Choose OK to confirm the changes to the Tools SmartIcons Customize dialog box, and choose OK again to confirm the changes to the Tools SmartIcons dialog box.
>
> The icon palette now displays the three icons you just added.

Creating Your Own SmartIcons

To get you started in creating your own SmartIcons, Lotus includes a set of customizable icons that you can examine and modify. These appear in the Custom Icons box of the Tools SmartIconsCustomize dialog box. Until you create your own icons, these are the only custom icons that are available.

As we'll see, there are two parts to a custom icon: the picture that gives the button its distinctive look and the macro that 1-2-3/W runs when you click the icon. The icon is a small graphics file in the BMP bitmap format. Among the tools you can use to create and modify a BMP file is Windows' Paintbrush program.

The macro that runs when you click the icon bears a similar name. If you create a SmartIcon called ADDRESS.BMP, the macro that the icon invokes is called ADDRESS.MAC. MAC files are simple text files that you can create from within 1-2-3/W or with a text editor such as Windows' Notepad utility.

In the following sections you'll explore the inner workings of an existing SmartIcon, and you'll learn how to create a BMP file and join it with a macro to make a button does what you want when you want it. And you'll find out little-known tips that will take your SmartIcons well beyond the basics.

Standard Icons versus Custom Icons

1-2-3/W comes with two kinds of SmartIcons: Standard Icons and Custom Icons. The reason that they fall in two categories is that they are intended to serve different purposes.

The standard ones are a built-in part of 1-2-3 for Windows, so you won't find BMP or MAC files for these icons, and you cannot modify they way they work. These icons provide shortcuts for many of the most frequently used features. Even if you could customize these icons, it would be ill-advised, because experienced 1-2-3/W users will assume these icons work the same way in any copy of the software.

A handful of custom icons are included, primarily for the purpose of demonstrating how to build your own icons. Unlike with the Standard Icons, you will find the BMP and MAC files that make these icons work. These sample icons—and the ones that you create—are stored in the SHEETICO subdirectory within the 1-2-3/W directory. For example, if you installed 1-2-3/W in the directory C:\123W, these custom icons are stored in C:\123W\SHEETICO.

Anatomy of a SmartIcon

Let's examine one of the custom icons that comes with 1-2-3/W to see how a SmartIcon is constructed. Since we just added the "Calendar" icon, we'll make it our subject for dissection.

First let's see the Calendar icon in action. With the cell pointer in cell A1 of a new worksheet, click the Calendar icon. Three-letter abbreviations of the names of the months appear in cells A1..L1, and then the cell pointer returns to the original cell. Not a bad deal—you get 12 cell entries with one click of the mouse.

To find out what makes this icon tick, start by clicking the icon that takes you directly to the Tools SmartIcons Customize dialog box. This is another icon that you added in the previous exercise. Alternatively, you can get there by choosing Tools SmartIcons from the menu and then selecting the Customize button.

When the dialog box appears, click the Calendar icon in the Custom Icons box. Note that the Assign Macro button becomes an active option when you click a custom icon. Click the Assign Macro button to see what macro is currently assigned to this icon. Later on, you'll use this same button to associate a macro with a SmartIcon of your own devising.

When you select the Assign Macro button, another dialog box pops up, by name of Tools SmartIcons Customize Assign Macro. Figure 18.8 shows this dialog box with the Calendar icon's macro on display.

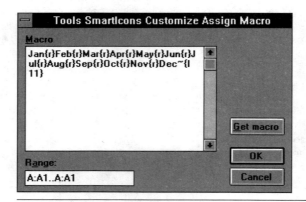

Figure 18.8. The Tools SmartIcons Customize Assign Macro dialog box. In the Macro box is the macro that runs when you click the Calendar SmartIcon.

This macro simply enters a label in a cell, moves a cell to the right, and so on. And when it's done with the last month, Dec, it returns the cell pointer to its previous location—11 cells to the left. It's not a very complicated macro, but a useful one if you frequently need to enter abbreviated date names.

Choose Cancel three times, because we don't need to save any changes we've made in the dialog boxes we opened. You should now be back in the sheet and in Ready mode.

The Big Picture

Now that we've seen what the Calendar icon looks like, what it does, and how the macro behind it works, let's take stock of what this—and any—custom SmartIcon is made of.

Like any custom SmartIcon, it consists of a picture (a small graphics file in BMP format) and a macro file (a plain-text MAC file). In this case, the picture file is called MONTHS.BMP and the macro that runs when you click the icon is called MONTHS.MAC. And like any worksheet SmartIcon files, MONTHS.BMP and MONTHS.MAC reside in the SHEETICO subdirectory off the 1-2-3/W directory.

If you want to confirm the existence of these files with your own eyes, you can issue a /File List Other command and specify the SHEETICO directory. This will list the names of all the custom SmartIcon pictures (BMP files) and macros (MAC files).

A SmartIcon Challenge

When do you write a SmartIcon? Any time you wish there were a push-button control to speed up your use of 1-2-3/W.

For a first SmartIcon-building example, let's add an icon that invokes 1-2-3/W's /System command, the command that takes you to a DOS prompt. This feature lets you perform some fast file-maintenance operations and then return to 1-2-3/W by entering the word *EXIT*.

The /System command is an ideal candidate for a SmartIcon, especially if you like to exit to DOS fairly often. Not only isn't there a built-in SmartIcon for this purpose, but the System command does not appear on the 1-2-3/W's Windows-style menus. So putting this feature in the SmartIcon palette makes it rather more accessible.

It's tempting to get right to work painting the BMP file, the clickable picture that identifies the SmartIcon. But there's one step you should always perform first: make sure the keystrokes or Advanced Macro Commands you've planned for your macro are practical. You can sink a lot of effort into immortalizing your idea with a prize-winning design, but if your dream icon is nothing but a dream it's a waste of time.

If you think that your desired SmartIcon may require keystrokes that a macro can't perform, it's worth testing out the procedure as an on-sheet macro. But for the simple key sequence we need for this operation, we'll skip that step.

Exiting to DOS calls for a terribly simple macro: /S. Press /S to confirm that these keystrokes do, in fact, bring up a DOS prompt. And then type *EXIT* to return to 1-2-3/W. That's all there is to it, a slash to call up the 1-2-3 Classic menu, and the letter S to choose the System command.

You'd never think of creating a keyboard macro this simple, would you? After all, it's about as easy to type /S as it is to press Ctrl-S, or whatever key you'd use for this macro. But as you'll find when you fashion your own SmartIcons, the simplest ones are often the most useful. In fact, many of 1-2-3/W's best built-in SmartIcons are based on the most modest of macros.

Of course, some SmartIcon macros are going to be more technically demanding than this one. If you're dying to advance the science of programming a SmartIcon, don't worry. Later on you'll learn how to make ones that really push the envelope.

To Build a Bitmap

To construct the visible part of the SmartIcon—the unique picture that entices you to click—you need to create a bitmapped graphics file. Unless you have another graphics program that supports the BMP format, this means using the Windows Paintbrush program. Paintbrush is included with your copy of Windows, and you'll find it in the Accessories group.

The exercises that follow do not assume any prior experience with Paintbrush, and this brief overview will help you understand the very basics. The more you know about Paintbrush's many features, though, the easier it will be to create good-looking icons with a minimum of effort. To learn more of the details, see the section on Paintbrush in the Windows User's manual or invoke Help from within Paintbrush by pressing F1 or choosing Help from the menu.

Bitmap Basics

Paintbrush displays an electronic canvas in which you apply dots of colored "paint." Such a collection of dots is known as a bitmap. To make a bitmap for use as a SmartIcon, you store your painting as a BMP file, which is Paintbrush's default format.

Figure 18.9. This icon, which is located in the Accessories group, starts the Paintbrush application.

To start Paintbrush, you open the Accessories Group window from Program Manager and double-click the Paintbrush program item icon. Figure 18.9 shows this icon.

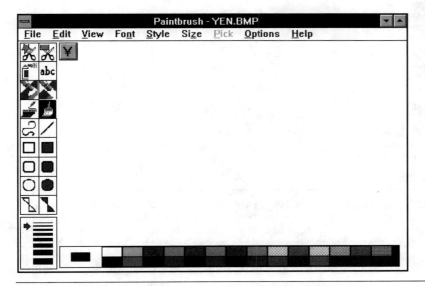

Figure 18.10. The Windows Paintbrush program with the YEN.BMP bitmap file open. The yen-sign icon is one of the customizable SmartIcons that comes with 1-2-3/W.

Figure 18.10 shows the Paintbrush program in action, with a SmartIcon bitmap on screen. With a little skill and a fair amount of patience, you can use Paintbrush to create bitmaps that make your SmartIcons visually stimulating.

Because SmartIcon bitmaps are quite small, a simple, well-defined image—like the yen symbol in the figure—is usually better than one that's too subtle. And though you want the icon to look nice, you should give the highest priority to ensuring that the picture clearly identifies what the icon will do when you click it.

To use a Paintbrush tool, click the tool in the palette. Then move the mouse pointer into the canvas and click or drag the tool on the canvas.

Paintbrush's Tool Palette, which is shown in Figure 18.11, provides an arsenal of ways to paint and edit on the canvas. You invoke one of these tools by clicking it, moving the mouse pointer to the canvas, and then clicking or dragging as appropriate.

Figure 18.11. The Paintbrush Tools Palette gives you several ways to paint and edit dots on the on-screen canvas. To use any of these tools, you start by clicking on the tool, then moving (not dragging) the mouse pointer to the place on the canvas where you want to use it. Then you click or drag as needed to use the tool on a part of the painting.

The tools include the brush, the paint roller, and the ellipse-, box-, and line-drawing tools. And there's even a text tool that lets you "paint" alphanumeric characters by way of the keyboard.

The top two tools in the palette provide different ways to select a section of the painting, so you can perform such editing operations as copying, clearing, and moving. You can erase parts of the painting by using one of two eraser tools or by repainting over an area so it blends in with the background.

And for the finest editing, you can choose View Zoom In and perform dot-by-dot editing and then choose View Zoom Out to return to a normal perspective. Figure 18.12 shows a zoomed view of a painting. To learn how to edit in this zoom mode, see the section on Paintbrush Tips near the end of the chapter.

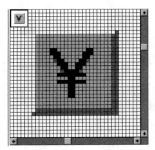

Figure 18.12. The View Zoom In option lets you perform dot-by-dot editing. See the Paintbrush Tips section later in this chapter to find out how to see a blow up of an entire SmartIcon, as shown above.

Most of Paintbrush's tools are fairly self-explanatory, and you'll master the basics quickly with some experimentation and practice. To get a quick rundown on how each tool works, call up Paintbrush's Help system and locate help on Tools.

What's Dot?

The technical term for each dot on the screen is a pixel, which is short for "picture element." A common abbreviation for this term is pels. A collection of pixels is known as a bitmap because if the computer maps out the arrangement of dots by way of a group of bits—those tiny electronic circuits inside the computer's memory chips. So now you know.

No matter what painting tool you use, the color of the paint you add is determined by the color palette at the bottom of the Paintbrush Window. To choose a paint color, you click the left-mouse button on the desired color. To choose the border color for any filled-in object that you paint—note that some tools have an empty, or outlined version and a filled-in one—click a color with the right mouse button.

As you get started with Paintbrush, you'll find that it shares a number of features with 1-2-3/W and other Windows applications. For example, it has similar file-management options, and you can use typical Windows editing techniques such as Edit Undo. Thus, even if you're completely new to Paintbrush, it shouldn't seem totally unfamiliar.

There are a few other things you'll need to know about using Paintbrush, but we'll deal with these as we get on with creating a custom SmartIcon. Let's get to it!

Painting the Icon

Now we're ready to create the picture that will identify our exit-to-DOS Smart-Icon. We'll fire up Paintbrush and make a suitable icon.

Thanks to Windows' ability to run multiple programs at the same time, we can keep 1-2-3/W running while we switch to Paintbrush. To get to Program Manager, press Ctrl-Esc to bring up the Task List, and choose Program Manager from this list. If you're comfortable with other window-switching methods, such as using Alt-Tab or the application Control menu's Switch-To command, any of these will also do the job. However you choose to do it, make Program Manager the current application.

Next, open the Accessories group and run the Paintbrush application. An untitled document will appear, and we could commence painting right away. But hold on one more minute.

If we were making any old painting, we could just start splashing colors on the large canvas that Paintbrush ordinarily displays. A SmartIcon, though, has a special requirement: it has to be 21-dots high and 21-dots wide. If your painting exceeds these dimensions, parts of it may be scrunched or missing when you add it to the palette.

Since counting the dots in a painting is onerous at best, even if you use the View Zoom In command, Lotus provides a sample SmartIcon you can use as a prototype for your own icons. Appropriately enough, this file is called SAMPLE.BMP.

Choose the File Open command and select the SAMPLE.BMP file, which is stored in 1-2-3/W's SHEETICO subdirectory. If you have a typical directory set up, you'll need to back out of Paintbrush's default directory, the \WINDOWS directory on drive C:, and then choose the 123W directory. Finally, select the SHEETICO subdirectory and double-click on SAMPLE.BMP in the Files list. Remember that to back out one directory level, you double-click the "[..]" choice in the Directories list. And if you need to switch to a different drive, you choose the drive's name from the Directories list, as well.

Once you load SAMPLE.BMP, your screen should resemble Figure 18.13. Since we don't want to lose the convenience of having this nice, clean sample icon, let's give our new icon a unique name instead of saving it over SAMPLE.BMP. Choose File Save As and enter the name DOSEXIT.BMP.

The simple, functional icon on the left of Figure 18.14 should do the trick. If you're a seasoned Paintbrush artist, you can attempt a more ambitious icon like the one on the right side of the figure, or another design of your own devising. If you do decide to veer from the steps described in the exercises, be sure to check out the section on Paintbrush Tips later in this chapter. It contains some important information about working with 21-by-21-dot bitmaps.

Mastering the SmartIcon Palette **443**

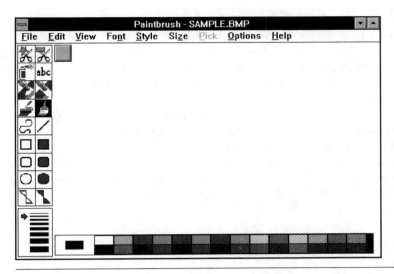

Figure 18.13. The Windows Paintbrush program with the SAMPLE.BMP bitmap on-screen. This "blank" SmartIcon is found in the SHEETICO subdirectory of the directory where you installed 1-2-3/W, and you can use it as a starting point for your own icon designs.

Figure 18.14. Two possible designs you can use to identify the DOSEXIT.BMP SmartIcon.

Click the text tool, which is the "abc" tool in the palette, and click toward the left side of the icon. Next, choose the Font menu and select a clean-looking font, such as Arial, Helvetica, or Helv, and then choose the Size menu and select a size of 10 (points).

Typing on the Canvas

Text tool, which is identified by the "abc" icon in the Tools Palette, lets you add text to your paintings. You choose this tool and then click in the canvas to set the insertion point, and then you type text as needed. To avoid confusion, you need to understand how Paintbrush handles the text that you enter.

While you're in the process of typing, you can perform simple editing, such as changing the font or pressing Backspace to delete the previous character. But once you finish entering text and then choose another tool or another location to enter text, the text becomes stored as a series of dots on the canvas, and not as editable characters.

If you make a mistake when entering text in a painting, backspace to delete it before you do anything else.

There's no immediately visible difference, but once you finish the entry, you can no longer edit it as text—although you can paint over it or otherwise modify it like any other part of the canvas. You can't, however, alter it character-by-character or change it to a new font or style. Because of this, you should make sure you have the right text in the right location and in the right style before you move on to another task.

Now, type *EXIT*, but don't press or click anything else. If the word looks good where you entered it, proceed to the next step. But you typed the word in an awkward-looking location, press Backspace enough times to remove the word, and then click again where you think it would look better. As long as you don't click elsewhere or choose another tool, you can repeat this process as many times as necessary to make the word look right. The finished product should look more or less like the one in Figure 18.15.

Figure 18.15. The DOSEXIT.BMP icon. After you type EXIT on the icon format that you borrowed from SAMPLE.BMP, the icon should look something like the one pictured here.

That's it! The icon is done. Choose File Save to preserve your changes to DOSEXIT.BMP.

Since you might want to do some more painting later on, you can keep Paintbrush open and switch back to 1-2-3/W by pressing Ctrl-Escape to bring up the task list, or by using any other application-switching method. It's a good-enough looking icon. But if it only had a brain, it would be useful, too. Now it's time to make your icon get smart.

Programming the SmartIcon

A simple macro like the DOSEXIT macro is easy to enter directly into the dialog box that displays the SmartIcon's instructions. In a more ambitious macro, you'd want to build and test the macro in the sheet, and then you'd load it into the Macro box of the Assign Macro dialog box.

When you're back in 1-2-3/W, choose Tools SmartIcons Customize, and then click on the picture of the DOSEXIT.BMP bitmap that appears in the Custom Icons box. Then choose Assign Macro so you can tell the icon what do to when someone clicks it.

Mastering the SmartIcon Palette **445**

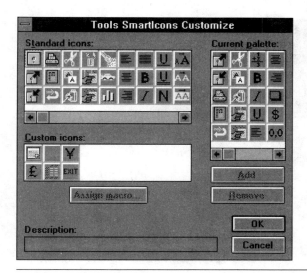

Figure 18.16. The Tools SmartIcons Customize dialog box. Note that the new icon, DOSEXIT.BMP appears with the custom icons. You click it once and then click the Assign Macro button to enter the macro that will run when you use this icon.

In the Macro box, type /S, and then choose OK. Without your having to say as much, 1-2-3/W stashes this macro in a file called DOSEXIT.MAC, and it's now stored alongside its partner, DOSEXIT.BMP, in your SHEETICO directory.

Now double-click your newly coined SmartIcon, to add it to the end of the Current Palette. If you think there are too many icons in the palette to be able to see your new creation, you can remove some lesser-used icons, or you can choose a floating palette when you get back to the Tools SmartIcons dialog box, so the palette can display as many icons as possible.

After you choose OK enough times to return to Ready mode, your SmartIcon should appear in the palette. Figure 18.17 shows a typical collection of Smart-Icons, including the DOSEXIT icon.

Send your icon on a maiden voyage by clicking it once. When you find yourself at a DOS prompt, you'll know it worked. Congratulations: you're an IconMaker.

Enter *DIR* to prove that the power of the DOS command line is but a mouse click away. And then enter *EXIT* to return to 1-2-3.

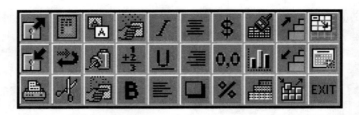

Figure 18.17. The new icon, DOSEXIT.BMP now appears alongside your other icons. Go ahead and click it. Remember that when you want to return to 1-2-3/W from the DOS prompt, you enter *EXIT*.

Review the Process

Once you've been around the Paintbrush program and the Tools SmartIcons dialog boxes a few times, the process of building a SmartIcon will be a breeze. All it takes are the nine steps that are detailed below:

1. Test out the macro that you plan to use.

2. Use Paintbrush to create a 21-by-21 dot painting—optionally using SAMPLE.BMP as a starting point.

3. Save the painting under a unique name in the SHEETICO subdirectory.

4. Choose Tools SmartIcons Customize, move the mouse pointer into the Custom Icons box, and click the icon once to select the icon.

5. Choose the Assign Macro button.

6. Enter the Macro in the Macro box, or choose Get Macro to copy a selected macro from the sheet. Note that Get Macro retrieves the worksheet range identified in the Range box—this is either the range of cells you preselected before you invoked the Tools SmartIcons Customize command or a range you specified directly in the Range box.

7. Choose OK to confirm the new macro entry.

8. Double-click the icon to add it to the SmartIcon palette.

9. Choose OK two times to confirm the changes to Tools SmartIcons Customize dialog box and the Tools SmartIcons dialog box.

As long as the palette is large enough to view your SmartIcon, it's ready to go. All told, this is a pretty easy way to build new features into the spreadsheet, no?

Breaking the Barrier

There's an important difference between a SmartIcon macro in the Macro box and a conventional macro on the worksheet. A macro in the Macro box is, in effect, one very large cell entry. A sheet-bound macro, on the other hand, can be composed of entries hundreds or even thousands of cells.

As you probably know, there's no need to write an extremely long macro in a single worksheet cell. Instead, you key the macro into a series of consecutive cells in a column, and/or you organize it into subroutines. In contrast, the Macro box confines the SmartIcon to a single location.

In a long SmartIcon macro, text wraps around from one "line" of the box to the next, but the appearance of separate lines in the box is a mirage. No matter how much code you put in the box, 1-2-3/W's macro command processor treats the SmartIcon's macro as one long string.

Is a Single Cell Enough?

So the SmartIcon Macro box gives you a single "cell" in which to write your Macro. What does this mean to you?

First of all, if your macro can span no more than one cell, you can't use subroutines. Without subroutines, the only way to run the same procedure eight times is to repeat it eight times in the macro. And you can't have your macro jump to a related macro elsewhere in the box, because there are no named ranges or cell addresses to jump to.

The Macro box also has no place to store variables. If you want to keep track of variable information, such as what the current cell address was when the macro started or the number of seconds that have passed since the user clicked the icon there are no "other cells" in the Macro box to put this data.

There are two ways to deal with the single-celled nature of SmartIcon macros. The simplest solution is to avoid using techniques—such as subroutines and variables—that you can't perform in the confines of one macro cell. Although certain sophisticated procedures may be impossible, or at least tricky, within these constraints, you can create an endless number of useful macros without the aid of such techniques. Most Advanced Macro Commands, and virtually all keystrokes, are callable from the macro box, so you've got a healthy selection of tools to choose from even with these restrictions.

The other solution is to use worksheet cells to provide workspace for your SmartIcon macros. A SmartIcon can call a macro subroutine that's on a worksheet, and it can store and use entries in worksheet cells. What it can't do is organize such entries within the confines of the Macro box.

Should Your Sheets Help Your SmartIcons?

Using a worksheet to store information for use by a SmartIcon macro is an intriguing idea. Doing so can give your SmartIcons the power of subroutines, branches, and variables.

And since you store macros and related information in your sheets all the time, it seems obvious that you would do the same for your SmartIcon macros. Remember, though, that most macros are developed for a particular spreadsheet, while SmartIcons typically are not.

In most cases, a macro is stored in the sheet where you run it. You set aside a separate area in that sheet for macros, macro subroutines, and for any data, such as the number of times you've run a subroutine, that the macro may need to access. The typical SmartIcon, in contrast, is a feature you'd want to run in any worksheet—it's like part of the furniture.

A SmartIcon that works properly only in a given worksheet can be frustrating and dangerous when you run it in another sheet. The first and foremost risk is that your macro could damage the worksheet's data. For example, let's say that you make a SmartIcon with a {FOR} loop that enlists cell H15 to serve as the "counter" cell in a loop. This macro may work just fine in the sheet for which you designed it. But if you click the SmartIcon with the wrong sheet open, you could corrupt that worksheet's data; cell H15 may store some important information.

Then there's the possibility that a file that includes necessary data—subroutines, named ranges, values, labels, and so on—may not be open when you run the macro. A macro that calls a subroutine named {Sort_All_Data} will stop in its tracks if you click it when the worksheet that contains the *Sort_All_ Data* range is not open.

The best way to allocate worksheet space to your SmartIcon macros is to keep a sheet open expressly that purpose. Windows, of course, thinks nothing of keeping multiple files in memory at once. And if you exploit 1-2-3/W's automation features—using an autoloading worksheet and an autoexecuting macro—you won't even have to remember to load the sheet before you use the SmartIcon that relies on it. All you have to do is to avoid closing this macro-storage file until you're ready to exit 1-2-3/W.

The following section describes a SmartIcon that uses these automation techniques to create a sophisticated point-and-click macro—one that exploits variables, subroutines, and more.

Copy Down and Right: Smarter Than the Average Icon

1-2-3/W contains a useful SmartIcon that copies the entry in the current cell into all the other cells in a selection. This icon is illustrated in Figure 18.18.

This tool is ideal when you need to copy the same cell down a single row or column. And it lets you fill a two or three-dimensional range with copies of a single cell.

This icon will not, however, let you copy each cell in the top row of a selection into all the other selected rows. Nor will it copy all the cells in the first column of a selection into the other columns.

So let's create a pair of SmartIcons that complement the functionality of this built-in one. Our new SmartIcons, CPYDOWN and CPYRIGHT, will copy the current row or column across all other selected rows or columns.

What's the Difference?

To get a better sense of what these new icons will do, you should understand the behavior of the copying icon shown in Figure 18.18, which inspired these variations.

This copying icon isn't visible in the palette when you install 1-2-3/W, but if you performed the exercise in the Adding Icons to the Current Palette "Try It" box earlier in the chapter, it should appear in the icon palette on your screen. Let's see how this icon works.

Figure 18.18. The built-in SmartIcon that copies the current cell to all other selected cells in the range. Our two new SmartIcons, CPYDOWN and CPYRIGHT, are variations on this theme.

In a new file, enter *HOLA* in cell B2. Then select range B2..E6 and click the icon shown in Figure 18.18. Instantly, the label "HOLA" appears in all cells in the selected range. Choose Edit Undo (or click the Undo icon) to undo this copying operation.

Now enter *ADIOS* in cell C2, and highlight range B2..E6 again and click the same icon. Note that the entire range fills with copies of the word "*HOLA*," and the "ADIOS" that was in cell C2 has bid us adieu.

The goal of creating the CPYDOWN and CPYRIGHT icons will be to allow us to select a two-dimensional range, such as B2..E6, and to choose to have either the top row or the leftmost column of a selection copied into all other selected rows and columns. If we had our CPYDOWN icon handy, we could copy several rows of HOLAs and ADIOSes with a single click.

How Is It Going to Work?

To create a SmartIcon that copies the current row or column into other rows or columns, we need a macro that not only performs a copying operation, but one that manages several subtle, but important details. To do this, we'll use a worksheet called SMTICONX.WK3 to let the macro jot down and reference data about the selected range and to allow our two SmartIcons to share a subroutine that is needed in each macro.

And since we need to store some of the macro data on-sheet anyway, we'll just put the first few macro commands in the macro box itself. The rest we'll put in a subroutine that we'll call from the macro box.

The two macros will operate almost identically. The only difference is that when the CPYDOWN macro moves the cellpointer down, the CPYRIGHT macro will move to the right, and so on.

Use Paintbrush to create an icon that you feel is appropriate to the CPYDOWN operation. See the *To Build a Bitmap* section earlier in this chapter for details on creating an icon.

One possible design is shown in Figure 18.19. However you choose to style your icon, be sure to save it as CPYDOWN.BMP in the SHEETICO subdirectory.

Figure 18.19. One possible design for the CPYDOWN icon.

Strange Range Names

In the exercise that follows, the range names are deliberately weird. For example, the range that keeps track of the selected cells is called *zzSelect*. If you store SmartIcon macros and macro-related data on a sheet, you should use strange names, too.

Using such names allows you to change the name of the sheet containing these ranges without worrying about whether any of these range names occur in other sheets. If you use terribly normal names, you'll have to include the specific file name, lest you accidentally run a macro or change a cell that bears an name that's identical to one used in your macro.

Setting Up the Sheet

Create a new worksheet, and save it as SMTICONX.WK3.

First, we'll set up a section that lets us track a variety of information about the current selection and other attributes of the worksheet. We'll only use a few of these in the CPYDOWN and CPYRIGHT macros, but you may well use the information in your other SmartIcons. The more your macros know about the worksheet environment, the "smarter" they can be.

Enter the following labels:

Cell	Entry
A1	SmartIcon Scratch Sheet
A3	Coordinates of Selection
A4	zzSelect
A5	zzTop_Left
A6	zzBot_Right

A7	zzFirst_Col
A8	zzLast_Col
A9	zzFirst_Row
A10	zzLast_Row
A11	zzSel_Cols
A12	zzSel_Rows
A14	Other Worksheet Info
A15	zzCurr_Cell
A16	zzFileName
A17	zzOrigin
A18	zzSheet

Select range A4..A12, and choose Range Name Label Create Right to apply these names to the neighboring cells in column B.

Now, we'll set up the formulas that will help us find out what's what in the worksheet: the top-left cell of the selection, the number of columns in the selection, and so on. Note that all of these formulas depend—directly or indirectly—on the existence of a label in cell B4 indicating the selected range. Until you run the macro, which will use the command {LET <<?>>zzSelect,@INFO ("selection")} to put such a label in cell B4, these formulas will evaluate to ERR. If you wish, you can enter into cell B4 a "sample" label, such as *B2..C5*, to see how these formulas work.

Enter the following formulas:

Cell	Entry
B5	+"!"&@CELL("coord",@@($zzSelect)
B6	+"!"&@RIGHT($zzSelect,@LENGTH($zzSelect)-@FIND(".",($zzSelect),0)+2))
B7	@CELL("col",@@($zzTop_Left))
B8	@CELL("col",@@($zzBot_Right))
B9	@CELL("row",@@($zzTop_Left))

B10	@CELL("row",@@($zzBot_Right))
B11	+$zzLast_Col-$zzFirst_Col+1
B12	+$zzLast_Row-$zzFirst_Row+1

Change the widths of columns A and B as you see fit.

How to Use the Other Ranges

Don't enter the following commands, but these are the macro commands that would give you the information for range B15..B18. Use them in your macros as needed, as long as you've created the named ranges, such as zzCurr_Cell in a worksheet that you plan to have open when you use your SmartIcons.

To find the address of the current cell:

{LET <<?>>zzCurr_Cell,@CELLPOINTER("coord")}.

To find the name of the active file:

{LET <<?>>zzCurr_Filename,@CELLPOINTER("filename")}.

To find the origin, the upper-left cell in the window:

{LET <<?>>zzOrigin,@INFO("origin")}

To find the number of current sheet (sheet A is 1, sheet B is to, and so on):

{LET <<?>>zzSheet,@CELLPOINTER("sheet")}

Put a Macro in the Box

Let's look at the operations the macro has to perform. These commands, we'll enter into macro box for CPYDOWN.MAC. Choose Tools SmartIcons Customize and click once on the picture of your CPYDOWN.BMP icon, and then choose Assign Macro. Then type into the Macro box the following macro commands shown in bold. Do not press Enter or include any spaces between one macro entry and the next. *Note: to create a CPYRIGHT icon, follow the same procedure to create CPYRIGHT.BMP and assign a macro to it.*

{LET <<?>>zzSelect,@INFO("selection")} First, the macro needs to take note of what range of cells is selected. Once the macro highlights the current row or column to begin the copying process, the initial selection will be forgotten. If the macro doesn't store information about the initial selection, how will it remember what cells it's supposed to *copy to* after it's through telling 1-2-3/W where to *copy from?* And the experienced 1-2-3/W user expects a selected range to remain selected after you finish a command. Your macro can only reselect the original selection if it recalls what cells it included.

{LET <<?>>zzSelect,@INFO("origin")}{CALC} Secondly, the macro must note what cell is in the upper-left of the worksheet when the macro starts. This cell is known as the origin. If the macro needs to scroll to copy into cells that aren't in the current window, you'll want it to restore the origin to the cell that it was in when you clicked the icon. Having the origin unexpectedly jump to a new cell after you run a macro can be disorienting to the user.

{BRANCH <<?>>zzCopy_Down} Third, the macro branches into the *zzCopy_Down* routine, which we'll enter into the SMRTICONX.WK3 worksheet. *Note: to create the CPYRIGHT macro, you'll change the range reference to <<?>>Copy_Right. You can copy the text of the CPYDOWN macro box into the CPYRIGHT macro, by copying and pasting it via the Clipboard Acelerator keys Ctrl-Insert and Shift-Insert.*

Back to the Sheet

Enter the label *zzCopy_Down* in cell A32, and choose Range Name Label Create Right to assign the name zzCopyDown in cell A32 to neighboring cell B32. *Note: To create the zzCopy_Right macro, enter* zzCopy_Right *in cell A47 and choose Range Name Label Create Right.*

Enter the following in range B32..B42:

Cell	Entry
B32	{LET <<?>>zzOrigin,@INFO("origin")}
B33	{IF +<<?>>Sel_Rows<2}{QUIT}
B34	{WINDOWSOFF}
B35	+"{GOTO}"&<<?>>zzTop_Left&"~"
B36	{ABS}

B37	{R +<<?>>zzSel_Cols-1}~
B38	{ALT}EQ
B39	{IF +<<?>>zzSel_Cols<2}{TAB}
B40	{D}.
B41	{D (+?<<?>>$zzSel_Rows-2)}~~
B42	{Reselect}

Note: To create the CPYRIGHT macro, copy range B32..B42 to cell B47. Then edit the copy of the macro as indicated by the italic text below.

These commands perform the following steps:

{LET <<?>>zzOrigin,@INFO("origin")} This command enters the coordinates of the origin—the cell in the upper-left of the current window—into the zzOrigin cell in the SMTICONX.WK3 worksheet.

{IF +<<?>>Sel_Rows<2}{QUIT} If there are fewer than two rows selected, the selection is not appropriate for a row-copy operation. If this is the case, the macro quits.

{WINDOWSOFF} This command prevents the display of the commands and dialog boxes during macro execution. Including this isn't necessary, but it makes the macro look more professional, since menus and dialog boxes aren't flickering on and off the screen.

+"{GOTO}"&<<?>>zzTop_Left&"~" This command causes the cell pointer to move to the first cell in the selection. Notice that this is a string formula, which combines the {GOTO} keyname, the coordinates of the top-left cell of the selection, and a press of the enter key.

{ABS} A press of the ABS key from Ready mode starts a preselection operation.

{R +<<?>>zzSel_Cols-1}~ This command causes the selection to move to the right enough times to highlight the full width of the selection. The reason that the value one is subtracted from zzSel_Cols is that the cell pointer starts in the first cell of the selection, so that's one right-movement it doesn't need to do. *Note: To convert this macro to the CPYRIGHT macro, change this entry to {D +<<?>>zzSel_Rows-1}~.*

{ALT}EQ This command invokes the Windows menu and chooses Edit Quick Copy.

{IF +<<?>>zzSel_Cols<2}{TAB} If there are fewer than two columns, the selected range to copy from will be a single cell. When only one cell is selected, the Edit Quick Copy dialog box starts with the From range highlighted, thus a tab is needed to switch to the To: box. When more than one cell is selected, the tab is not needed. *Note: To convert this macro to the CPYRIGHT macro, change this entry to {IF +<<?>>zzSel_Rows<2}{TAB}.*

{D}. This command moves the cell pointer down to the first cell of the Copy To: range and then anchors by typing a period. *Note: To convert this macro to the CPYRIGHT macro, change this entry to {R}.*

**{D (+<<?>>$zzSel_Rows-2)}~~** This command moves the cell pointer down as many rows as are in the selection, minus two. Why are two subtracted? First, the To range is one row less than the size of the total selection. And second, you don't need a DownArrow movement to highlight the current row—in other words, to highlight three rows, you move down twice. Note: To convert this macro to the CPYRIGHT macro, change this entry to *{R(+<<?>>$22Sel_ COIS-20}rr.*

{Reselect} This command branches to the routine that reselects the cells that were originally selected and which ensures that the origin is the same as it was when the icon was clicked. By placing these commands in a subroutine, both the CPYDOWN and CPYRIGHT macros can share it.

Cleanup Time

The Reselect subroutine makes the display look the way it did before you clicked the CPYDOWN or CPYRIGHT macro.

To create this routine, enter the label *Reselect* in cell A61 and use the Range Name Label Create command to assign the label in cell A61 as the name of cell B61.

Next, enter into cells B61 and B62 the macro commands that appear in bold below. Note that both entries are string formulas.

+"{GOTO}"&$zzOrigin&"~" This command moves the cell pointer to the cell that was the origin at the time the SmartIcon was clicked. If that cell has scrolled off the screen, it will cause the cell identified in zzOrigin to once again become the origin.

+"{ABS}"&zzSelect&"~" This command reselects the range of cells that was selected when the SmartIcon was clicked.

Make sure you save the file before you test out the macro. Choose File Save, and the file will again be saved under the name SMTICONX.WK3.

Try It Out

To try out the CPYDOWN and CPYRIGHT icons, add them to the palette as described in the Adding Standard Icons section earlier in this chapter.

Then, minimize the SMTICONX document and choose File New to open up a new worksheet.

To test the CPYDOWN icon, enter a variety of labels, values, and formulas in a few contiguous cells in a row. Next, select the data in that row and in several rows of blank cells below it. Then click the CPYDOWN icon to perform the copying operation.

Had you clicked the built-in icon that copies within a selected range, all cells in the range would now resemble the upper-lefthand cell in the range. Thanks to your trusty new CPYDOWN icon, you can copy each entry in the top row of the selection down into the other rows of the selection—all with a single click.

To test the CPYRIGHT icon, set up some entries in a column. Then highlight the data in that column and several blank cells to the right of the data. Click the CPYRIGHT icon to copy sideways.

As long as the SMTICONX.WK3 file is open and these icons are part of the palette, you can use them to copy rows and columns of data into their neighboring cells.

Make It Automatic

If you want 1-2-3/W to automtically load the worksheet that you use to store macros and data for SmartIcons, you need to create a file called AUTO123.WK3 in your default directory for 1-2-3/W files. If one already exists, you can modify it to include a macro like the one described below—although if someone already created the AUTO123.WK3 file, you should make sure such a change won't interfere with the original purpose of your AUTO123.WK3 file.

If you name a macro \0 in the AUTO123.WK3—and if you have it invoke commands such as those described below—you can have SMTICONX. WK3 or another file load every time you start 1-2-3/W.

Macro \0 might contain the following entries:

```
{ALT}FOsmarticonx~
{WINDOW-STATE "minimize"}
{WINDOW-SELECT "AUTO123.WK3"}
{ALT}FC
```

This macro opens the SMARTICONX.WK3 file and then minimizes it. Then it selects the AUTO123W.WK3 file and closes it. You may want to add—before the command that closes AUTO123W.WK3 and hence stops the macro—the entry {ALT}FN. This causes 1-2-3/W to create a blank worksheet.

Paintbrush Tips

A few little-known paintbrush techniques will help simplify the task of creating BMP files for your SmartIcons.

How to Get a Bigger Canvas

Using the SAMPLE.BMP bitmap that comes with 1-2-3/W gives is a quick way to get started with a painting of the right dimensions (21-by-21 dots) for a SmartIcon. But the tiny 21-by-21 dot canvas you get in Paintbrush when you start your icon this way can be constricting.

Most importantly, the View Zoom In feature that gives you a blown-up dot-by-dot view of the image does not work properly in this small space. When the canvas is larger, however, you can see the entire SmartIcon in a single view, and you can simultaneously preview the results on a full-size copy of the zoomed-in area.

To get the best of both worlds—a large, convenient workspace and icons that conform to the 21-by-21 dot requirement, you need to understand how Paintbrush decides how large a canvas a given file should have. The Paintbrush command Options Image Attributes determines the dimensions of the next file you create. By default, this is a width of 6.67 inches and a height of 5 inches. Measured in dots, this is 640 by 480 pixels.

Unless you've changed the Option Image Attributes settings, you'll get a much more generous canvas when you start Paintbrush or open a new file than the small one that appears when you open SAMPLE.BMP. To bring SAMPLE.BMP into this larger workspace, you choose Edit Paste From and specify SAMPLE.BMP in the SHEETICO directory. This allows you more workspace to play in, and you can use View Zoom In to perform dot-by-dot editing.

When you're done with this editing, you need to put your icon back into a small BMP file. To do so, select it with the Pick tool, the tool that looks like a pair of scissors cutting a rectangle, and then choosing Edit Copy To.

The trick to this technique is selecting exactly 21 by 21 pixels. This takes some practice, but at least you can easily tell what size selection you've grabbed. From the Copy To dialog box, you can select the Info Button. A click of this button confirms the width and height of the selection. If you grabbed something other than 21 by 21 pixels, it's back to the drawing board to try again to select just the right number of dots.

At least at first, this trial-and-error way of copying the right number of pixels may seem somewhat awkward. But the advantages of dot-by-dot editing in the View Zoom In mode make it worthwhile.

Another detail of the Copy To dialog box is also worth noting. The Options button lets you control such settings as colors and file formats. If the dialog box you see when you click the Info button suggests that the file will not be a 16 color file, you use the Options button to set things straight.

Use Both Mouse Buttons

A lot of casual users of Paintbrush don't know the secret of using the right mouse button. When you click the color palette at the bottom of the Paintbrush window with either mouse button, you "load" that kind of paint into that button. The right mouse button color is used as the outline color for filled-in objects.

The only time you can use the right mouse button to paint is when you blow up the painting by choosing View Zoom in. And it's especially handy in this mode. For example, if you make the left mouse-button color red and the right mouse-button color the same gray as the SmartIcon's background, you'll have an easy time of painting red dots as needed, and then "erasing" any mistakes by clicking them with the gray paint.

Instant Icons

Windows' built-in screen-capture facility can help you turn something on the screen into a bitmap, so you can use it as the basis of a SmartIcon. For example, you might want to capture a picture of a scroll arrow to turn it into a SmartIcon that scrolls down the sheet. To capture this or any screen element, you press the PrintScreen key.

When you press the PrintScreen key in Windows, the entire screen's contents are copied to the Clipboard in the form of a bitmapped picture. Like any Clipboard entry, this picture stays there until you cut or copy something else or you exit Windows.

Once the captured image is on-screen, you can select the portion that you want to use in your SmartIcon. Then you can choose the File Copy To command or you can copy it to the Clipboard, open another file, and then paste it in.

One common use of this image-capturing technique is to convert an icon from the popular ICO format into a BMP file. You simply display the icon on the screen with any of several commonly available icon editors, and you use PrintScreen to turn the ICO design into a BMP-format bitmap. Another way to display the ICO file on screen is to use Program Manager's File New command and assign the ICO file as the icon for a program; when you open the group that contains this program icon, you can view it and capture it with the PrintScreen key.

All BMPs Are Not Alike

A BMP isn't necessarily the same as a BMP. Windows' BMP format is not compatible with the BMP format used by the OS/2 operating system. If you have an OS/2-based bitmap editor, you cannot use it to create SmartIcons, even though its files bear the identical extension.

To make use of this captured image, you paste it into a new Paintbrush document. After you choose Edit Paste, you can drag the image around the screen to decide which portion you want to view. Note that Paintbrush does not store parts of the pasted image that don't fit on the screen, so you need to make sure the image you want is visible before you deselect the newly pasted picture.

To ensure that you capture the desired image, make a point of moving the item you want a picture of toward the upper-left of the screen before you press PrintScreen. Then it's guaranteed to appear when you paste the captured screen into Paintbrush. To deselect the pasted image, click on one of the selection tools at the top of the Tools Palette.

SmartIcons for Graphics

Although the examples in this chapter focus on the use of SmartIcons within the spreadsheet environment, all the techniques described here also let you customize icons for use in a graph window.

When you create or modify a graph, the SmartIcon palette changes to display a set of graphics-related icons. When you return to Ready mode, the palette again displays the worksheet-related icons.

(continued)

Mastering the SmartIcon Palette

(continued)

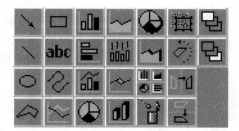

Figure 18.20. When you create and edit graphics, the available set of SmartIcons changes to provide tools for typical graphics tasks. You can customize this palette just as you can the one you use for worksheets operations.

The SmartIcons in Figure 18.20 are the point-and-click graphics tools that are loaded as a default when you install 1-2-3/W. Just as with sheet-oriented icons, you can add or remove standard and custom icons to and from this palette. Even the command to accomplish this is the same: Tools SmartIcons Customize.

The only difference between creating graphics SmartIcons and worksheet SmartIcons is that 1-2-3/W looks for your custom graphics icons in a subdirectory off the 1-2-3/W directory called GRAPHICO. If, for example, your copy of 1-2-3/W is installed in the directory C:\123W, you should put your custom-made graphics icons in the directory C:\123W\GRAPHICO. For more on graphics, see Chapters 11 and 12.

19

Solver and Backsolver

As you've seen in preceding chapters, 1-2-3 for Windows contains a number of powerful problem-solving tools. Some problems, though, are too complex to be handled neatly by traditional spreadsheet analysis. To help you tackle such problems, 1-2-3 for Windows contains two sophisticated problem-solving utilities: the Solver and the Backsolver.

The Backsolver is easy to understand and is applicable to a wide variety of common business and personal-finance problems. The two examples at the beginning of this chapter will introduce you to just some of the ways that you can use the Backsolver to simplify your "what-if" analyses.

The Solver is a good deal more complex. To get a meaningful answer from the Solver, you must correctly identify and model your problem. Therefore, we'll explain the Solver's many features in the context of a two-part tutorial that helps you think about ways to set up Solver problems. A third example provides additional practice while showing you how to force the Solver to return a whole-number solution.

The Backsolver

Have you ever built a model with a specific bottom line in mind, only to find that the results don't quite meet expectations? To achieve the bottom line you wanted, you may have tried the time-honored and time-consuming "what-if" approach known to almost every spreadsheet user: manually plugging in different variable values until you find the right one.

In this chapter you will learn:

- *How to simplify "what if" analysis with Backsolver*
- *How to use Solver simultaneously for several variables*
- *How to use @SOLVER*

If your problem can be expressed as a chain of formulas, the Backsolver can provide a better way to arrive at the desired solution. Consider the common problem of qualifying for a mortgage, shown in simple form in Figure 19.1.

	A	B
1	Salary	$45,000
2	Other Income	$3,000
3	Total Income	$48,000
4		
5	Mortgage	$120,000
6	Interest rate	10.00%
7	Term (months)	180
8		
9	Monthly payment	$1,290
10	Yearly payment	$15,474
11		
12	Payment/Total Income	32.24%
13		

Figure 19.1. A simple Backsolver worksheet

There are five variables in this calculation: salary, outside income, the mortgage amount, the mortgage interest rate, and the term of the mortgage. To build this problem in your worksheet, enter the labels in Figure 19.1. Enter the values in ranges B1..B2 and B5..B7, and add the following formulas:

Cell	Formula
B3	@SUM(B1..B2)
B9	@PMT(B5,B6/12,B7)
B10	+B9*12
B12	+B10/B3

Use the Worksheet Column-Width command to widen column A to 17. Assign ranges B1..B5 and B9..B10 the Currency format with 0 decimal places. Assign cells B6 and B12 the Percent format with 2 decimal places.

The bottom line here, literally and figuratively, is cell B12: the ratio of the mortgage payment to total income. In this case, the ratio of annual payments to annual income is 32.24%. But what if the maximum ratio the bank will allow is 30%?

The Backsolver can tell you exactly how far you'll have to push any of your five variables to get to the 30% solution. Choose Tools from the main menu, then select Backsolver. A definition window requiring three inputs appears as in Figure 19.2. You can specify these inputs by pointing to worksheet cells with the mouse, by using the Arrow keys, or by typing cell names.

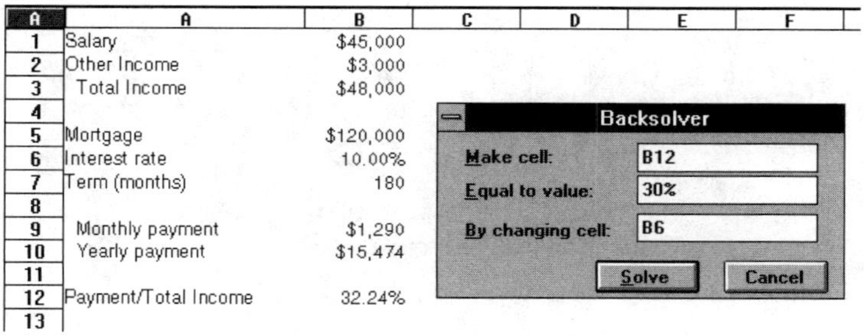

Figure 19.2: Backsolver worksheet with definition window

The fill-in-the-blanks format of Backsolver's definition window makes it almost impossible to misunderstand the process. Put together, the three prompts read:

Make cell _____ equal to value _____ by changing cell _____.

The cursor automatically resides in the first blank (which appears as a box in the definition window). In this case, you want to make the value in cell B12 equal to 30%, so enter B12 in this first box, or use the mouse to click on cell B12 in the worksheet.

Tab to the second box in the definition widow, where you specify the desired value for cell B12. In this case, that's 30%. Type *30%*.

Now Tab to the third box by Changing Cell. Which of your five variables do you want to solve for box. You can choose between any of them. If you want to know what interest rate will qualify this $120,000, 180-month mortgage, given a $48,000 total income, specify cell B6, which contains the interest-rate variable.

When you enter this third input, click on Solve and the Backsolver immediately solves the problem. Cell B6 shows that an 8.76% interest rate will bring the payment-to-income ratio down to 30%, holding all other variables constant.

To test a scenario involving another variable, type *.1* in cell B6 to return it to its original value of 10%. Invoke the Backsolver again. Respecify cell B12 as the Make cell, but this time indicate cell B5 (the mortgage variable) as the cell to change. Click Solve and the Backsolver calculates the mortgage amount, $111,669, that will result in a 30% ratio between mortgage payments and total income.

When the Backsolver changes the value of a variable, other worksheet formulas that depend on that value recalculate automatically. Suppose you had built a monthly amortization schedule linked to the variable in your worksheet. When you use Backsolver to change one of these variables to meet the 30% payment-to-income requirement, the entire amortization schedule recalculates automatically to reflect the new mortgage amount.

> The Backsolver works with almost all @functions, including @IF, @CHOOSE, and all of the spreadsheet financial functions. It can even work backward through a lookup table. However, @D functions, string @functions, time and date @functions, @functions with text strings as arguments, and some special @functions, such as @@, confound the Backsolver. Fortunately, these are functions that you'll seldom use in the "what-if" situations for which the Backsolver is most useful.

Backsolving Through A Budget Projection

Suppose you are thinking about starting a small business that produces ceramic vases for sale in craft shops. You estimate that the company can sell 20,000 vases at a price of $5.00 each in its first year, for a total revenue of $100,000. You also estimate the variable and fixed costs that go along with a year in the vase-making business, as shown in Figure 19.3.

	A	B	C	D
1	Projecting a Profit			
2				
3	Unit sales			20,000
4	Price/unit			5.00
5				
6	Revenue			100,000
7				
8	Variable costs/unit			
9	Materials			0.65
10	Labor			0.35
11	Shipping			0.50
12	Total variable cost/unit			1.50
13				
14	Total variable cost			30,000
15				
16	Gross margin			70,000
17				
18	Fixed costs			
19	Rent			9,000
20	Payroll expense			36,000
21	Insurance			1,500
22	Equipment payments			3,000
23				
24	Total fixed cost			49,500
25				
26	Net profit			20,500

Figure 19.3. A second Backsolver worksheet projecting profits for a ceramics business.

To build this model, enter the labels in column A of the figure. Enter the values in ranges D3..D4, D9..D11, and D19..D22. Then enter the following formulas:

Cell	Formula
D6	+D3*D4
D12	@SUM(D9..D11)
D14	+D3*D12
D16	+D6-D14
D24	@SUM(D19..D22)
D26	+D16-D24

With the Backsolver you can determine how much one of the variable values will have to change in order to reach a certain profit level. How many more sales will it take to reach a profit level of $30,000 instead of the current $20,500? To find out, activate the Backsolver, enter cell D26 as the Make cell, 30000 as the desired value, and cell D3 as the cell to change. The Backsolver calculates the number of sales needed to meet the $30,000 profit goal and places the result, 22,714, in cell D3 of the worksheet.

Solving Simultaneously for Several Variables

Unlike the examples above, some problems involve several variables that change simultaneously. For example, how can a manufacturing manager determine the ideal mix of several products, each with its own demand schedule and profit margin, and all straining for a share of the labor supply and factory time? And how can a money manager minimize the risk when the portfolio grows to dozens of assets, each with its own risk profile?

Real-world scenarios like these, with numerous variables and constraints, are sometimes too unwieldy to be modeled cleanly with traditional spreadsheet commands and formulas, or even with the help of an automatic utility such as the Backsolver. Such problems require mathematical optimization, also known as linear or nonlinear programming. Mathematical optimization tells you how best to allocate resources to various products or projects.

The techniques used in optimization aren't terribly difficult—you can solve small problems with pencil and paper—but for larger models the process becomes so complicated that until recently it had to be done on a mainframe.

> The methodology behind mathematical optimization was developed in the late 1940s by the U.S. military. Air Force strategists used mathematical optimization techniques to prepare cold-war planning models that would allocate America's remaining resources in the event of a nuclear exchange with the Soviet Union.
>
> In the 1950s, mathematical optimization became widely popular in American industry, although even modest-size problems required the computing power of the mainframes of the time. The development of powerful desktop computers in the 1980s has greatly broadened the application of optimization techniques. Today, optimization is used in everything from personnel planning to mass mailings. Many managers have begun to use mathematical optimization to help allocate their capital budgets to different projects. On Wall Street, investment bankers use it to create the best possible portfolios.

The Solver

By incorporating the power of optimization into a spreadsheet environment, the 1-2-3 for Windows Solver helps you grapple with many of the problems that you could almost answer with the spreadsheet's conventional what-if tools: @functions, macros, regression analysis, data tables, and trial and error.

In a departure from most spreadsheet optimization add-ins and stand-alone linear programming software, the Solver doesn't force you to express your problem strictly with linear equations—those that take the format X = A1 + B1. The Solver can analyze nonlinear formulas that require the multiplication of two variables and formulas that involve exponentiation. (The latter capability is especially helpful in financial calculations, because all of 1-2-3's financial @functions rely on exponential values.)

Though the 1-2-3 for Windows Solver can handle fairly large optimization problems, you needn't be an MBA running a multimillion dollar factory to use it. The Solver takes full advantage of the graphical interface of 1-2-3 for Windows to help demystify optimization and make it more widely applicable to everyday problems. If you're new to optimization, though, it helps to know a little bit about the essential concepts before modeling your own problems, large or small. The conceptual framework is actually quite simple. By working through the following examples, you'll be able to decide when and how to best use the Solver.

A Simple Optimization Problem

The diagram in Figure 19.4 illustrates a simple linear optimization problem. Suppose you are the manager of a small foundry that produces two types of chassis for industrial moving equipment. Your specific goal is to determine the product mix that maximizes profits.

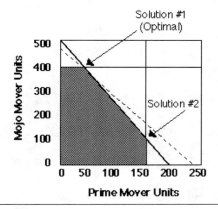

Figure 19.4. Graphical representation of the chassis problem

In this simple example, two factors limit your production options. At full capacity, your company's machinery can turn out either 160 higher-quality Prime Mover chassis, 400 lower-quality Mojo Mover chassis, or some mix of the two each month. In Figure 19.4, these constraints are illustrated by the solid vertical line and the solid horizontal line, respectively.

The other limit on production is a budgetary one: at prevailing wage rates, your monthly budget allows for no more than 5,000 hours of the skilled labor that it takes to produce your products. You know from past experience that it takes 10 man-hours to produce a Mojo Mover chassis and 25 man-hours to produce a Prime Mover chassis. Therefore, monthly production possibilities range from 500 Mojo Mover chassis and 0 Prime Mover chassis to 0 Mojo Mover chassis and 200 Prime Mover chassis. The sloping solid line in Figure 19.4 illustrates this constraint.

These are the only constraints on production in this simple example, so the shaded area in Figure 19.4 represents your company's range of output options. Any product mix that calls for more than 160 Prime Mover chassis, more than 400 Mojo Mover chassis, or more than 5,000 hours of labor falls outside the shaded area and is therefore not feasible.

Your challenge is to maximize profit given these constraints. Each Prime Mover chassis you produce yields a profit of $60, while each Mojo Mover chassis yields a profit of $30. The dashed line in Figure 19.4 illustrates this relationship.

You can see how even a simple problem becomes difficult to solve graphically. Fortunately, it isn't hard to express these constraints mathematically:

1. Prime Mover units <= 160
2. Mojo Mover units <= 400
3. (Prime Mover units*25) + (Mojo Mover units*10) <= 5000

Similarly, profit can be expressed as a formula:

4. (Prime Mover units*60) + (Mojo Mover units*30) = Profit

The verbal translation of these equations is as follows:

1. Prime Mover units cannot exceed 160 (a production-capacity constraint).
2. Mojo Mover units cannot exceed 400 (a production-capacity constraint).
3. Man-hours cannot exceed 5,000 (a budgetary constraint).
4. Profit equals the number of Prime Mover units times $60 plus the number of Mojo Mover units times $30.

Figure 19.5 shows how to set up such a problem in a worksheet. To duplicate this figure in your own worksheet, enter all labels and the two zeros in range C3..C4. Select Range Format Currency, specify 0 decimal places, and indicate range D3..D6.

The production levels in range C3..C4, initially set to 0, are the problem's *adjustable cells*. The Solver will substitute values into these cells, either algebraically or through iteration, until it finds the optimal product mix. Adjustable cells must contain a value and, if global protection is enabled, must be unprotected before you can solve a problem.

	A	B	C	D
1			Number	
2			Produced	Profit
3		Prime Movers	0	$0
4		Mojo Movers	0	$0
5				
6			Total Profit	$0
7				
8	Within Prime Mover production capacity?			1
9	Within Mojo Mover production capacity?			1
10	Less than 5000 man-hours?			1
11				

Figure 19.5. Chassis worksheet for the Solver.

The entries in range D8..D10 express the machine-capacity and labor constraints as logical formulas. Enter the following formulas:

Cell	Formula
D8	+C3<=160
D9	+C4<=400
D10	+C3*25+C4*10<=5000

The formulas in range D3..D4 calculate profit generated by the number of chassis in cells C3 and C4, depending on how much of each kind of chassis the Solver places in those adjustable cells. Enter the following formulas:

Cell	Formula
D3	+C3*60
D4	+C4*30

To add these two profit figures, enter the formula @SUM(D3..D4) in cell D6. You want to maximize this overall profit, so cell D6 is the *optimal cell* in your calculation.

To solve this problem, select Tools and then Solver from the menu. A definition box appears in the worksheet, as shown in Figure 19.6.

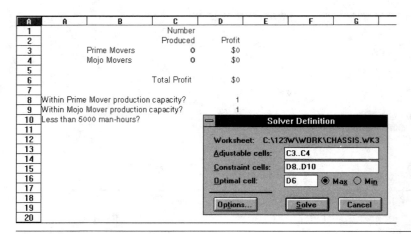

Figure 19.6. Chassis worksheet with Solver definition box

Specify the following ranges:

Prompt	Range
Adjustable cells	C3..C4
Constraint cells	D8..D10
Optimal cell	D6

Because you are maximizing profit, specify the Max setting for the optimal cell, which is the default setting. Select Solve.

A progress window replaces the Solver's definition box. The Solver first analyzes the problem, searching all active files for formulas and inputs that relate directly or indirectly to the problem. Once this analysis is complete, the Solver begins searching for answers, including the optimal answer. The progress window (see Figure 19.7) remains on the screen until the Solver has found a predetermined number of answers (usually 10), or until you purposely suspend or terminate the problem.

In this simple problem, there are only three possible answers. When the Solver has found them, it replaces the progress window with the answer window shown in Figure 19.8. You can use the mouse to move this answer window in the worksheet by clicking on the window title, then dragging it to its desired location.

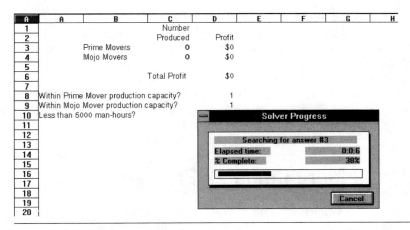

Figure 19.7. Chassis worksheet with Solver progress window

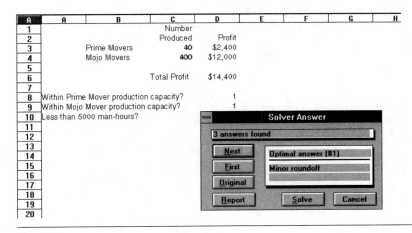

Figure 19.8. Chassis worksheet with Solver answer window

The Solver displays the optimal answer in the worksheet (it enters *40* in cell C3 and *400* in cell C4) and recalculates the worksheet to reflect your optimal profit in cell D6: $14,400. Because the Solver places its answers directly in the worksheet (as shown in Figure 19.8) any cells that depend on the adjustable cells will change as soon as the worksheet is recalculated.

To see the Solver's second-best answer in the worksheet, select Next. The Solver enters *160* in cell C3 and *100* in cell C4, then it recalculates the worksheet to show that this second-best scenario yields a profit of $12,600.

Select Next again to see the third solution. The Solver enters *0* in cell C3 and *0* in cell C4. When you begin your problem with zeros in the adjustable cells, the Solver considers zero production to be a viable answer—unless such an answer violates a constraint.

You can eliminate the Answer window by selecting the Cancel option. To close the Solver completely and return to the worksheet, select Cancel from the Answer window, then select Cancel from the Solver's Definition box.

Modeling a More Complex Problem

Figure 19.9 models a more difficult problem. Suppose you're no longer the manufacturing manager at the chassis company, but have moved on to a start-up company that plans to produce feed for four kinds of wild animals: rabbits, birds, badgers, and peccaries. Each of the company's four secret recipes relies on the same four ingredients: corn meal, a protein supplement, oat bran, and sun-dried tomatoes. However, each calls for a different mix of the four ingredients. For example, a sack of rabbit feed requires 75 pounds of corn meal, 45 pounds of protein supplement, 100 pounds of oat bran, and 50 pounds of sun-dried tomatoes.

	A	B	C	D	E	F	G	H
1			Protein	Oat	Sun-dried	Amount of	Profit per	
2		Corn meal	Supplement	Bran	tomatoes	product	product	Total Profit
3	Rabbit feed	75	45	100	50	0.0	$75	$0
4	Bird feed	60	25	60	0	0.0	$50	$0
5	Badger feed	40	35	80	60	0.0	$90	$0
6	Peccary feed	15	40	25	10	0.0	$25	$0
7								
8						Total Profit		$0
9								
10	Inventory	3000	4000	5000	2000			
11	Used	0	0	0	0			
12								
13								
14	Corn meal used < corn meal inventory?				1			
15	Protein used < Protein inventory?				1			
16	Oat bran used < Oat bran inventory?				1			
17	Tomatoes used < Tomato inventory?				1			
18	Rabbit feed >= 0?				1			
19	Bird feed >= 0?				1			
20	Badger feed >= 0?				1			
21	Peccary feed >= 0?				1			

Figure 19.9. Animal-feed Solver worksheet

In addition, each product has a separate profit level per batch. For example, rabbit feed generates a profit of $75 per sack; bird feed, $50 per sack; badger feed, $90 per sack; and peccary feed, $25 per sack.

What production mix will optimize the profit potential of these culinary creations? You can use the Solver to calculate the answer.

Building the Worksheet

To create the model shown in Figure 19.10, select File New from the main menu to open a second file on your *1-2-3 /W* desktop. Enter all labels from the figure, and enter the numbers in range B3..F6, B10..E10, and G3..G6.

Enter the following formulas:

Cell	Formula
H3	+F3*G3

Copy this formula to range H4..H6

H8	@SUM(H3..H6)
B11	+$F3*B3+$F4*B4+$F5*B5+$F6*B6

Copy this formula to range C11..E11.

E14	+B11<=B10
E15	+C11<=C10
E16	+D11<=D10
E17	+E11<=E10
E18	+F3>=0
E19	+F4>=0
E20	+F5>=0
E21	+F6>=0

To adjust your column widths to match the figure, select a range that includes cells in columns F through H, such as range F1..H1. Then select Worksheet Column Width, indicate 8 as the column-width, and choose OK. Use the same procedure to set the width of column A to 11.

Use the Range Format command to format range G8..H8 for Currency with 0 decimal places. Assign the Fixed 1 format to range F3..F6.

Finally, select Range Name Create, enter the name *adjustable*, and indicate range F3..F6. Repeat this procedure to name the following two ranges:

Use range names to identify your adjustable, constraint, and optimal cells. It' a more intuitive way to keep track of your problem.

Name	Range
constraint	E14..E21
optimal	H8

The formulas in range B11..E11 are the key to understanding this problem. Each time the Solver comes up with a set of inputs for the adjustable cells, 1-2-3/W recalculates the formulas in range B11..E11. The Solver then checks to see if the new result of the formula violates any constraints.

	A	B	C	D	E	F	G	H
1			Protein		Oat	Sun-dried	Amount of	Profit per
2		Corn meal	Supplement		Bran	tomatoes	product	product Total Profit
3	Rabbit feed	75	45	100	50	0.0	$75	$0
4	Bird feed	60	25	60	0	18.1	$50	$905
5	Badger feed	40	35	80	60	21.7	$90	$1,955
6	Peccary feed	15	40	25	10	69.7	$25	$1,742
7								
8							Total Profit	$4,602
9								
10	Inventory	3000	4000					
11	Used	3000	4000	4565.6				
12								
13								
14	Corn meal used < corn meal inventory?							
15	Protein used < Protein inventory?							
16	Oat bran used < Oat bran inventory?							
17	Tomatoes used < Tomato inventory?							
18	Rabbit feed >= 0?							
19	Bird feed >= 0?							
20	Badger feed >= 0?							
21	Peccary feed >= 0?							

Solver Answer
10 answers found
Next — Optimal answer (#1)
First — Minor roundoff
Original
Report   Solve   Cancel

Figure 19.10. Animal-feed worksheet with Solver answer box and best answer found

In this case, the constraints in range E14..E17 come into play. The formulas in range E14..E17 guarantee that the amounts of each raw material used in the manufacturing process don't exceed the supply on hand. The formulas in range E18..E21 force the Solver to substitute only nonnegative quantities of the raw materials into the adjustable cells in range F3..F6.

Select Tools Solver from the main menu and indicate the range names *adjustable, constraint,* and *optimal* in the appropriate boxes in the Solver definition window. Specify Max for the optimal cell, then select Solve. You'll see the Solver Progress box reporting on the Solver's progress as it searches for answers.

The Answer

Your screen should match Figure 19.10, showing a total profit of $4,602. The product mix has changed to 0 sacks of rabbit feed, 18.1 sacks of of bird feed, 21.7 sacks of badger feed, and 69.7 sacks of peccary feed. (For tips on rounding off these numbers, see "Finding a Whole-Number Solution" at the end of this chapter.)

Changing the Problem

Changing a constraint can dramatically affect the outcome of your problem. For example, cancel the Solver edit cell E21, the constraint for peccary feed, to read +F6>=100.

The answer box appears when the Solver has completed the problem indicates that the Solver found only one answer.

The Solver indicates that under these constraints, the only possible solution is to produce 100 batches of peccary feed and nothing else. Range B10..E11 explains this situation. Though this solution uses up only half the corn meal, oat bran, and sun-dried tomatoes on hand, it depletes the protein supplement. This production mix would be less than desirable for the company, because the entire inventory of other materials would go to waste. But it's the only one possible with the specified constraints.

Inconsistent Problems

Select Original from the answer box to restore the original optimal solution to the worksheet. Cancel the Solver, then edit cell E21 to read F6>=110. Then select Solve from the definition box.

After only a few moments, the answer window appears and the Solver reports *No Answers Found. 1 attempt.* The Inconsistent message in the answer box (shown in Figure 20.11) offers a clue.

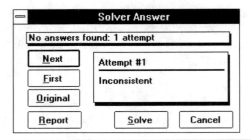

Figure 19.11. Answer box containing Inconsistent option over animal-feed worksheet

To indicate an illogical problem (or perhaps a typo in one of your constraints), the Solver displays the Inconsistent option in its answer box. Never ignore this signal.

What happened here? To find out, select Report from the Answer box then choose Inconsistent Constraints as the type of report and click OK. Click Cancel to close the Solver report dialog box. Choose Cancel two more times to get back to Ready mode. Now where is the report? Solver created a new file for the report called INCONSO1.WK3. Press Ctrl-PgUp one or more times to see the report. The Solver pinpoints the trouble in cell E15, the constraint that ensures that the protein inventory is not exceeded. The minimum of 110 batches of peccary feed in cell E21 will require 4,400 pounds of protein supplement, more than the constraint in cell E15 will allow. The Solver reports the inconsistency between these two constraints.

Let's edit cell E21 to its original formula F6>=0. Choose Tools Solver and select Solve to resolve the problem with its original constraints.

Tabling the Answers

The Solver gives you a full range of reporting options whenever its answer window is active. Among other things, the Solver's built-in reports calculate the differences between answers, tell you what cells and constraints were used to solve the problem, and tell you how much you can tinker with each adjustable cell and still satisfy all constraints.

For example, to see each answer the Solver has generated in tabular form, select Report Answer Table from the Solver's menu. Indicate OK or press Return to create an answer file. This command creates a file named

ANSWER01.WK3 that contains a table with each answer found. (This file exists only in RAM. You can decide later whether you want to save it to disk or discard it.) To see the table, choose Cancel from the Solver Report dialog box and choose Cancel two more times to get to Ready mode. Select Windows from the 1-2-3/W menu and choose the ANSWER01.WK3 file.

For easy reference within the answer table, the Solver structures its report from the range names and labels in your worksheet. For the optimal cell (cell H8), for example, the Solver displays the range name *optimal*, which you assigned the cell. If a cell used in the report doesn't have a range name, the Solver takes its best guess as to what label is assigned to a certain cell.

The Solver's Reports

The Report selection from the Solver's menu allows you to analyze the most recently solved problem from several different angles.

The *Report Answer* table option (described above) displays the adjustable and optimal cell values for each answer found.

The *Report Differences* option compares any two answers that the Solver found, cell by cell. You must specify which two answers you want to compare. (If the Solver has found several answers, it's a good idea to use the Report Answer command first to identify the two you want.) You can also focus the Differences report by telling the Solver only to display cells that differ by a certain amount, say, $1,000 or more.

The *Report Cells Used* option lists all of the adjustable cells and constraint cells the Solver used to solve the problem.

The *Report Unused Constraints* option tells you which constraints the Solver did not need to solve the problem. If your problem returns unexpected results, check the Report Unused Constraints option to see if any constraints were unexpectedly ignored. For example, a constraint that was entered incorrectly as +COST>1000 might be ignored in a problem, whereas the correct constraint, +COST<1000, probably would not.

The *Report Inconsistent Constraints* option can help you pinpoint the problem if the Solver returns with the error message *No answers found* because a problem was set up incorrectly. For a more detailed explanation, see the section titled "Inconsistent Problems" earlier in this chapter.

The *Report How Solved* option provides an extensive listing of answers, constraints, and adjustable cells pertaining to the answer that is currently displayed in the worksheet. The Report How Solved command tells you which constraints are binding, how to make nonbinding constraints binding, and, in the case of inconsistent problems, suggests possible ways to rewrite inconsistent constraints.

The *Report What-If Limits* option tells you what range of values you can enter in an adjustable cell and still satisfy the constraints of the problem. This option is sometimes useful if the Solver returns a best answer found instead of an optimal answer.

Solving with Macros

Like any *1-2-3/W* command, the Solver can be automated with macros. To run the Solver from the current file, you would use the following macro for the original four-product example:

{ALT}TS{ESC}adjustable{TAB}constraint{TAB}optimal~

Note that the {ESC} is necessary if the Solver has been used for the current worksheet. It cancels the Solver Answer dialog box in order to access the Solver Definition box.

If you're experimenting with the parameters of a single problem—dropping or adding adjustable or constraint cells, for example, or specifying a different optimal cell—a short macro such as the one above can quickly recreate your original problem.

If you're not changing parameters, you probably won't need a macro to use the Solver repetitively. Once you've defined your problem, you can change formulas in your worksheet, including those in constraint and optimal cells, without respecifying ranges each time you solve. *1-2-3/W* saves the current parameters of the Solver's definition box when you save your worksheet.

A macro can also take advantage of the @SOLVER function, which monitors the Solver's progress. The syntax of this function is @SOLVER(query_string) where query_string can be one of eight different arguments. For example, the formula @SOLVER("progress") tells you what percentage of the problem the Solver has completed, while @SOLVER("optimal") returns 1 if the Solver has found the optimal answer.

If you're running an iterative macro in a separate worksheet while the Solver is working in the background, you can add the following line of code to your macro so you'll be alerted as soon as the Solver has found the optimal answer:

{IF @SOLVER("optimal")=1}{BEEP 2}{BEEP 3}{BEEP 2}

The eight arguments of the @SOLVER function are as follows:

consistent. @SOLVER("consistent") returns 1 if all constraints are satisfied, 2 if all constraints are not satisfied.

done. @SOLVER("done") returns 1 if the Solver is finished solving the current problem, 2 if the Solver is currently working on the problem, and 3 if the Solver is active but hasn't started solving the problem.

(continued)

> *(continued)*
>
> *moreanswers*. @SOLVER("moreanswers") returns 1 if the Solver has found all possible answers, 2 if more answers might be found.
>
> *needguess*. @SOLVER("needguess") returns 1 if the Solver does not need a guess to solve the problem, 2 if the Solver does need a guess to solve the problem. (See the section below, "Take a Guess," for a more detailed explanation of when the Solver requires a guess to solve a problem.)
>
> *numanswers*. @SOLVER("numanswers") returns the number of answers the Solver found. If no answers were found, @SOLVER("numanswers") returns the number of attempts the Solver made to find an answer.
>
> *optimal*. @SOLVER("optimal") returns 1 if the Solver has found the optimal answer, 2 if the Solver has come up with a best answer found, 3 if the problem is unbounded, and 4 if the Solver could not find an answer or if you have not yet selected Solve. (For an explanation of unbounded problems, see the following section, "A Problem That Knows No Bounds.")
>
> *progress*. @SOLVER("progress") returns the percentage of the problem that the Solver has completed. If @SOLVER("progress") equals .25, the Solver has completed 25% of the problem.
>
> *result*. @SOLVER("result") returns 1 if the Solver has found one or more answers, 2 if the Solver has made attempts but has found no answers.
>
> The @SOLVER function returns ERR when the Solver is not active or has not yet solved a problem.

A Problem That Knows No Bounds

Some what-if problems aren't meant for the Solver. Consider the following example:

Revenue	$10,000
Cost	$5,000
Commissions	$1,000
Profit	$4,000

In this example, revenue and cost are independent variables, and commissions depend on revenue. If your goal is to achieve profits of $5,000 or greater, you might think this is a good time to use the Solver.

But this problem doesn't fit the basic requirements of optimization. Think about how you might depict this problem graphically. You can't. There are no bounds on revenue or costs. For this kind of problem, the Solver returns an error message: *Cannot find optimal answer—the optimal cell is unbounded.*

Take a Guess

The Solver first attempts to solve a problem by setting up a system of equations based on the worksheet formulas you have specified. It then attempts to solve the system of equations using common algebraic, or symbolic, techniques.

Sometimes, however, worksheet equations are too complex for the Solver to complete a problem efficiently with symbolic techniques. In these cases, the Solver turns to an iterative method in which it assigns guess values to the adjustable cells and then adjusts them until it reaches the optimal answer.

Because the variables are often moving in different directions, a large problem can stump the iterative method as well. In this case, the Solver will return with the error message *No answers found* in its answer box.

However, the answer box may also contain the message *Guesses required*. If this is the case, a Guess selection also appears in the answer box. If you select Guess, the Solver opens a guess window and asks you to enter guess values for the adjustable cells that are the most troublesome. You can then attempt to solve the problem again.

None of the examples in this chapter require guess values.

Forcing a Whole-Number Solution

If your problem requires a whole-number solution and you come up with nothing but fractions—or worse, fractions rounded to nonoptimal solutions—your fancy footwork may fetch more flak than flattery. Some problems are defined by constraints that yield a completely different set of answers when you introduce a whole-number requirement into the optimization process. In these cases, you must structure your problem to come up with a whole-number answer. The purchasing worksheet in Figure 19.12 changes radically when a whole-number requirement is introduced.

Suppose you are a buyer for Wholesum Toys, a company that is gearing up for a monthly production of 85,000 Chimp on a Mission action figures. Your job is to find the combination of manufacturers who can supply 85,000 tough-looking chimpanzee heads to your factory each month at the lowest cost. After researching the monthly production and pricing of five different suppliers, you construct the following worksheet:

To build this worksheet, select File New to add another worksheet file to your 1-2-3/W desktop. Enter all labels in ranges A1..H2, A2..A7, F9..F10, and E12. Enter the values in range B3..D7.

	A	B	C	D	E	F	G	H
1		Lot		Portion	Lot size	Lot size	Amount	Item
2	Company	Size	Cost	of Lot	>= 0?	<=1?	to Buy	Cost
3	A	50,000	$35,000	0%	1	1	0	$0
4	B	47,500	$34,000	0%	1	1	0	$0
5	C	37,500	$28,250	0%	1	1	0	$0
6	D	27,500	$20,500	0%	1	1	0	$0
7	E	10,000	$7,250	0%	1	1	0	$0
8								
9						Total Cost		$0
10						Total Item	0	
11								
12					Enough tough heads?		0	

Figure 19.12. Purchasing worksheet before optimization

Enter the following Formulas:

Cell	Formula
E3	+D3>=0
F3	+D3<=1
G3	+B3*D3
H3	+C3*D3

Copy range E3..H3 to range E4..E7.

H9	@SUM(H3..H7)
G10	@SUM(G3..G7)
G12	+G10>=85000

Use the Range Format command to assign the Punctuated format with 0 decimal places to range B3..B7. Assign the Currency 0 format to ranges C3..C7 and H3..H9, and the Percent 0 format to range D3..D7.

Columns A through C contain the results of your research. Column D contains the adjustable cells in this problem—just how much of each supplier's monthly production will you buy? These cells must contain a value at the beginning of the problem, and they must be unprotected if global protection is enabled. Column E contains constraints that ensure that the Solver won't try to purchase a negative amount of a supplier's production, while the constraints in column F limit the maximum purchase to the supplier's maximum monthly volume. (In other words, you can't buy more from a supplier than the supplier can produce.) Column G multiplies the adjustable cell in column D by the supplier's monthly production, while column H multiplies the adjustable cell by the cost of the monthly production.

To find the optimal purchasing mix, shown below, select Tools Solver and identify the following adjustable, constraint, and optimal cells

Input	Range
Adjustable cells	D3..D7
Constraint cells	E3..F7,G12
Optimal cell	H9

A	A	B	C	D	E	F	G	H
1		Lot		Portion	Lot size	Lot size	Amount	Item
2	Company	Size	Cost	of Lot	>= 0?	<=1?	to Buy	Cost
3	A	50,000	$35,000	100%	1	1	50,000	$35,000
4	B	47,500	$34,000	74%	1	1	35,000	$25,053
5	C	37,500	$28,250	0%	1	1	0	$0
6	D	27,500	$20,500	0%	1	1	0	$0
7	E	10,000	$7,250	0%	1	1	0	$0
8								
9						Total Cost		$60,053
10						Total Item	85,000	
11								
12					Enough tough heads?		1	

Figure 19.13. Optimized buying worksheet without the whole-number requirement

Specify that you want to *minimize* optimal cell H9 (total cost), then select Solve.

The Solver finds the following optimal answer: You will buy all of supplier A's production and 74% of supplier B's production. Your company's total cost for this optimal purchase of 85,000 doll heads is $60,053.

Introducing the Whole-Number Requirement

However, this scenario might not work out. You may find that the suppliers have no use for leftover chimpanzee parts and insist that you buy their entire monthly production, instead of just a portion. In that case you must force an integer solution by inserting an extra column into your template:

	A	B	C	D	E	F	G	H	I
1		Lot		Portion	Integer	Lot size	Lot size	Amount	Item
2	Company	Size	Cost	of Lot	Portion	>= 0?	<=1?	to Buy	Cost
3	A	50,000	$35,000	0%	0	1	1	0	$0
4	B	47,500	$34,000	100%	1	1	1	47,500	$34,000
5	C	37,500	$28,250	0%	0	1	1	0	$0
6	D	27,500	$20,500	100%	1	1	1	27,500	$20,500
7	E	10,000	$7,250	100%	1	1	1	10,000	$7,250
8									
9						Total Cost			$61,750
10						Total Item		85,000	
11									
12						Enough tough heads?		1	
13									
14									
15									
16									

Figure 19.14. Optimized buying worksheet with additional column

As Figure 19.14 shows, the new problem requires a far different mix of suppliers. The best solution calls for you to buy 100% of the production of suppliers B, D, and E at a total cost of $61,750. While this cost isn't as low as the optimal cost reached in the first solution, it's the best you can do under the circumstances.

The inserted column, column E, simply contains @INT formulas that take the integer values of the adjustable cells in column D. For example, cell E3 contains the formula @INT(D3). The trick to forcing an integer solution is to use this integer portion of the adjustable cell, rather than the adjustable cell itself, in calculating the amount to buy in column H and the cost in column I.

To create the template in Figure 19.14, place the cell pointer in column E and use the Worksheet Insert Column command to insert a new column. In the newly created cell E3, enter the formula @INT(D3). The constraints in columns F and G remain the same. Edit the formulas in cells H3 and I3 to read as follows:

Cell	Formula
H3	+B3*E3
I3	+C3*E3

Copy cell E3 to range E4..E7, and copy range H3..I3 to range H4..H7. Select Tools Solver. Because the adjustable cells, constraint cells, and optimal cell remain the same, you can select Solve without making any modifications to the definition box.

Disadvantages of Forced-Integer Solutions

The price you pay for an integer solution is increased solving time. In addition, a best answer found, rather than an optimal answer, will almost always be the result when you force an integers-only solution. This outcome occurs because the Solver knows that the optimal answer contains fractional numbers, but also knows that such an answer isn't what you asked for. The only exceptions are problems whose optimal answers also happen to be whole numbers.

Because of the extra calculations, this workaround can bog down on a large problem. Even a relatively small, well-constructed problem that requires an integers-only solution will require a huge amount of RAM and virtual memory. And as with normal problems, an ill-structured integers-only problem will send the Solver into algebraic oblivion—only sooner.

Getting Comfortable with the Solver

If you're new to optimization, you probably shouldn't expect things to go perfectly the first time you set up a problem from scratch. Despite the Solver's easy-to-follow menu structure and on-line help, defining your problem and interpreting the Solver's results won't be as intuitive as using @SUM.

Fortunately, the Solver will generally tell you—either directly with an error message or indirectly with interminable solving time or wildly incorrect answers—when your problem doesn't make sense. And by working through the sample Solver templates in this chapter, you'll quickly grasp the rationale behind the technique. (Additional examples come with *1-2-3/W.*)

The following guidelines will speed you up the Solver learning curve:

Break large problems into smaller pieces. Theoretically, the Solver is limited only by the amount of RAM you have in your PC. For practical purposes, Lotus recommends that you use the Solver only on problems with fewer than 1,000 formulas pertaining to the optimization. Even a problem of this size would take a long time to solve.

Use inequalities as constraints wherever possible. Unless you're using an equality to express a relationship between two variables, there's probably a better way to structure the problem. For example, if *badger_feed* is an adjustable cell and your constraint reads badger_feed=50, then you should simply enter 50 in *badger_feed*, erase the constraint, and redefine your problem so that *badger_feed* is no longer an adjustable cell.

Like the Backsolver, the Solver is not compatible with some @functions, such as the @D functions, string @functions like @TRIM and @MID, and any @function containing a string argument. If formulas anywhere in the problem contain these functions, the Solver will not work. Likewise, logical operators such as #AND# are not allowed.

In addition, try to keep the following @functions out of the problem you're solving: @CHOOSE, @IF, @INDEX, @HLOOKUP, and @VLOOKUP. Even though the Solver supports these functions, they may make the problem nearly impossible to solve.

Don't change any worksheet containing part of the problem while the Solver is working. The adjustable, constraint, and optimal cells in your Solver problem can span up to 15 open worksheet files. But if you change any of the Solver's source worksheets while the Solver is working, the process aborts immediately and all answers are lost.

Finally, if the Solver seems to be taking an extraordinarily long time to come up with answers, check the structure of your problem. Even if you have to change the problem and start the Solver from scratch, the time savings can be tremendous.

Part V
Appendices

Working Templates and Applications Ideas

The exercises in this book give you the hands-on experience you need to become proficient with the many functions and features of 1-2-3 for Windows. However, it's always helpful to have models that are applicable to some immediate problem, whether it's an everyday task such as keeping track of your checking account or a long-term investment question concerning compound interest.

This appendix contains six practical applications that can help you put 1-2-3 for Windows to work immediately. The 1-2-3 check register and the check reconciliation template help you keep your personal or business checking accounts up-to-date and accurate.

The amortizing loan template calculates a home mortgage or business loan payment and constructs a complete amortization schedule that includes a breakdown of payment and interest. The compound-growth macro slices tricky compound-growth questions three ways: you can find out what a CD will be worth in 10 years, how long it will take to reach an investment goal, or what interest rate you need to achieve a goal.

The final two templates address questions that often arise in business: depreciation and present value. The depreciation template creates a depreciation schedule with all four of 1-2-3's depreciation @ functions, including the @VDB function for variable-declining balance depreciation. The present value template helps you evaluate the present value of payments that you'll receive in the future, whether they come in a periodic stream or a single lump sum.

The sections that follow describe each template and tell you how to build and modify it for your own use. All six templates are also available on the 1-2-3 for Windows application disk (which also contains examples from earlier chapters and SmartIcon bitmaps and macro files). You can find order information for the disk at the back of this book.

The 1-2-3 Check Register

The check register template (file REGISTER.WK3) uses some of 1-2-3's simplest arithmetic and @ functions to help you track the transactions in your checking account. Using the deposit and withdrawal information you enter in columns E and F, the template calculates your account balance, as well as deposit, withdrawal, and account-balance statistics.

About the Check Register

The check register uses three range names, *deposits* (range E10..E14), *withdrawals* (range F10..F14), and *balance* (range G9..G14) to help calculate some basic check register statistics. @AVG formulas in range F2..F3 use range names *deposit* and *withdrawal* to calculate the average deposit and withdrawal in the checking account. An @MAX formula in cell F4 returns the maximum checking account balance, and an @MIN formula in cell F5 returns the minimum checking account balance.

	A	B	C	D	E	F	G
1	Check Register						
2				Average deposit		1,000.00	
3				Average withdrawal		416.67	
4				Maximum balance		10,000.00	
5				Minimum balance		8,750.00	
6							
7							
8	Check #	Date	Payor/Payee	Description	Deposit	Withdrwl.	Balance
9							10,000.00
10	1452	08/01/91	Landlord	Rent		750.00	9,250.00
11	1453	08/01/91	Electric Co.	Utilities		250.00	9,000.00
12	1454	08/02/91	GMAC	Truck paymt.		250.00	8,750.00
13		08/03/91	Jo Mama	Pd Inv 451A	1,000.00		9,750.00
14							
15							

Figure A.1. Check register

Building the Check Register

To build the check register, use the Worksheet Global Settings command to set the default cell format to Comma with 2 decimal places. Use the Range Format command to assign the General format to range A10..A14.

Enter the labels in range A1..G8 of the figure. Use the Range Name Create command to enter the following range names:

Name	Range
deposit	E10..E14
withdrawal	F10..F14
balance	G9..G14

Enter the following formulas:

Cell	Formula
F2	@AVG(deposits)
F3	@AVG(withdrawals)
F4	@MAX(balance)
F5	@MIN(balance)
G10	+G9+E10-F10

Copy the formula in cell G10 to range G11..G13.

Using the Check Register

Enter your beginning checking balance in cell G9 and information for your first four checking transactions in range A10..F13. Each checking account transaction should occupy one row. The bottom row of the check register should always be blank, so that ranges *deposit*, *withdrawal*, and *balance* will expand automatically when you add rows.

To add rows for new transactions, move the cell pointer to the blank bottom row of the register (currently row 14). Highlight the number of new rows you want to add to the register, select Worksheet Insert Row from the menu, and click OK. Then copy the last formula in the Balance column (currently cell G13) to column G of the new register rows.

Reconciling the Checkbook

Even if the information in your checkbook or check register is perfectly calculated and up-to-date, your current balance may look nothing like the current balance shown on your bank statement. That's because several days usually elapse between the time the bank generates your statement and the time you receive it.

To make the reconciliation between the two as painless as possible, the check reconciliation template (File BALANCE.WK3) presents the problem in simple ledger form. Transactions pertaining to the checkbook are on the left side of the template (columns A through C), while transactions pertaining to the checking statement are on the right side of the template (columns E through G). Column D is intentionally left blank to provide some spacing between the two sides.

	A	B	C	D	E	F	G
1	Checkbook reconciliation				Status:		Balanced
2							
3							
4	Check register balance		9,500.00		Statement balance		10,040.00
5	Interest		0.00		Outstanding checks		
6	Bank service charge		15.00		#1449		175.00
7	Notes received		500.00		#1450		225.00
8					#1451		50.00
9					Total checks		450.00
10					Deposits in transit		
11					8/5/90--Lowell		200.00
12					8/6/90--Mather		195.00
13					Total deposits		395.00
14	Adjusted balance		9,985.00		Adjusted balance		9,985.00

Figure A.2. Reconciliation template

Building the Reconciliation Template

To build the check-reconciliation template, use the Worksheet Global Settings command to set the default cell format to Comma with 2 decimal places.

Enter the labels in ranges A1..A14 and E1..E14. Begin the labels in ranges E6..E9 and E11..E13 with two spaces. Enter the values in ranges C4..C7, G4, G6..G8, and G11..G12. Then enter the following formulas:

Cell	Formula
C14	@SUM(C4..C5,C7)-C6
F1	@IF(C14=G14,"Balanced","Not Balanced")
G9	@SUM(G6..G8)
G13	@SUM(G11..G12)
G14	+G4-G9+G13

Your worksheet should now match the figure.

Using the Reconciliation Template

To adapt the reconciliation template for your own use, erase the values in ranges C4..C7, G4..G8, and G11..G12. Enter your current check register balance in cell C4. Enter the interest shown on your bank statement in cell C5, and any service charge in cell C6. If the bank made a collection or automatically debited your account for any reason and you have not yet recorded the transaction in your checkbook or check register, enter the amount in cell C7. (Enter collections on your behalf as positive amounts; enter automatic debits as negative amounts.)

On the right side of the template, enter the ending balance from your bank statement in cell G4. Then adjust that balance by entering the checks you have written since the statement was generated in range G6..G8. Change the entries in range E6..E8 to match your transactions. Similarly, enter the deposits you have recorded since the statement was generated in range G11..G12. Edit the entries in range E11..E12 to describe these transactions.

If you have more than three outstanding checks, place the cell pointer in row 8 and insert the number of additional rows you need. If you have more than two outstanding deposits, place the cell pointer in row 12 and insert additional rows. The @SUM formulas currently in cells G9 and G13 will adjust to accommodate your new entries.

If you have fewer than three outstanding checks or two deposits in transit, don't delete rows. Doing so could destroy the @SUM formulas in cells G9 and G13 or erase a vital row from the left side of the template. Instead, erase the data in the unneeded rows, leaving them blank.

When your entries bring the two sides into balance, the adjusted balance figures in cells C14 and G14 contain the same amount, and the @IF formula in cell F1 reads "Balanced." If you want to keep a record of how you arrived at the balance for that month, save the template to a unique file name, such as BAL1_92.

Amortizing Loans

1-2-3's @PMT function provides an easy way to calculate the periodic payments required by a fixed-length, amortizing loan. Almost all home mortgages, as well as many long-term business loans, use the @PMT calculations found in this template (File AMORT.WK3).

To calculate the periodic loan payment, the @PMT function requires three arguments: the principal amount, the periodic interest rate, and the number of periods in the loan. Once you know the periodic payment, you can also construct an amortization table that shows your principal balance at every period in the loan. For example, to find out how much you still owe after five years of monthly payments, scroll to period 60. But be forewarned: The answer is likely to shock and dismay you.

	A	B	C	D	E
1	An amortizing loan with fixed payments				
2					
3	Principal		$100,000.00		
4	APR		9.00%		
5	Periods in loan		120		
6	Periods/year		12		
7	Period interest		0.75%		
8					
9	Payment		$1,266.76		
10					
11	Period	Payment	Interest	Principal	Balance
12	0				$100,000.00
13	1	$1,266.76	$750.00	$516.76	$99,483.24
14	2	$1,266.76	$746.12	$520.63	$98,962.61
15	3	$1,266.76	$742.22	$524.54	$98,438.07
16	4	$1,266.76	$738.29	$528.47	$97,909.60
17	5	$1,266.76	$734.32	$532.44	$97,377.16
18	6	$1,266.76	$730.33	$536.43	$96,840.73
19	7	$1,266.76	$726.31	$540.45	$96,300.28

Figure A.3. Amortization template

Building the Amortizing Loan Template

To build the amortizing loan template, use the Worksheet Global Settings command to set the default cell format to Currency with 2 decimal places. Use the Range Format command to assign the following formats:

Format	Cells
Percent 2	C4,C7
General	C5..C6

Enter the labels in ranges A1..A7 and A11..E11. Enter the values in range C3..C6 and in cells A12 and E12.

Enter the following formulas:

Cell	Formula
C7	+C4/C6
C9	@PMT(C3,C7,C5)
A13	+A12+1
B13	+C$9
C13	+E12*C$7
D13	+B13-C13
E13	+E12-D13

Copy range A13..E13 to range A14..A132. Your worksheet should now match the figure.

Using the Amortizing Loan Template

To adapt the template for your own use, enter your own loan variables in range C3..C6. The template formulas automatically calculate the periodic payment and a new loan amortization schedule.

The periods/year variable in cell C6 lets you calculate loan payments on any schedule—yearly, monthly, even weekly. For annual loan payments, enter 1 in cell C6; for quarterly payments, enter 4. In this example, cell C6 contains the value 12 to calculate monthly payments.

This template contains an amortization schedule for 120 periods (10 years of 12 monthly payments). To extend the amortization schedule (for example, for a 30-year mortgage), copy the formulas in row 132 to as many rows as necessary. If your amortization schedule has fewer than 120 periods, erase the extra periods. They will return negative amortization amounts that could prove confusing.

Calculating Present Value

If someone offers you cash in the future, either as a stream of payments, a lump sum, or both, what's that offer worth today? 1-2-3 lets you calculate the present value of both types of future cash flows.

Suppose someone offers you the following deal for some property you own: $25,000 up front, 120 monthly payments of $1,000 each, and a $25,000 payment at the end of 10 years. The present value template (File PV.WK3) shows you how to evaluate such an offer.

	A	B	C	D	E	F	G	H
1	**The present value of mixed cash flows**							
2								
3	Discount rate		10.00%					
4								
5	OFFER				PRESENT VALUE (PV) OF OFFER			
6								
7	Up-front payment		$25,000		PV of up-front payment			$25,000
8								
9	Period payment		$1,000		PV of periodic payments			$75,671
10	Years in term		10					
11	Periods/year		12					
12								
13	Back-end payment		$25,000		PV of back-end payment			$9,639
14								
15					TOTAL			$110,310
16								

Figure A.4. Present value template

Buildling the Present-Value Template

To build the present value template, use the Worksheet Global Settings command to set the default cell format to Currency with 0 decimal places. Use the Range Format command to assign the following formats:

Format	Cells
Percent 2	C3
General	C10..C11

Enter the labels in ranges A1..A13 and E5..E15, and enter the values in range C3..C13. Enter the following formulas:

Cell	Formula
H7	+C7
H9	@PV(C9,C3/C11,C10*C11)
H13	+C13/(1+C3)^C10
H15	@SUM(H7..H13)

Your worksheet should now match the figure.

Using the Present-Value Template

If the up-front payment is made in the present (a reasonable assumption), then the present value of the up-front payment is equal to the up-front payment. The formula in cell H9 uses 1-2-3's @PV function to calculate the present value of the stream of 120 monthly payments, based on the discount rate in cell C3. The formula in cell H13 also uses the discount rate (this time on an annual basis) to calculate the present value of a lump-sum payment 10 years from now. The formula in cell H15 shows the total present value of the offer in the example, $110,310.

To adapt the present value template for your own use, enter your own inputs in range C3..C13. The formulas in range H3..H15 do the rest. If any of the three types of payment (up-front lump sum, future stream of paymenst, or future lump sum) does not apply to your situation, enter 0 in the appropriate cell in column C. The template will ignore this entry in determining overall present value.

Calculating Depreciation

1-2-3 for Windows offers four depreciation functions: @SLN, @SYD, @DDB, and @VDB. The depreciation template (File DEPREC.WK3) shows you how to apply each function to a hypothetical depreciation problem.

You can use any of these depreciation formulas to calculate an asset's depreciation for your own books. However, the rules for figuring tax depreciation are far more restrictive and complicated. For assets placed in service after 1986, you are restricted to three basic depreciation choices: straight-line, MACRS, and a special 150% election not covered by 1-2-3's @ functions.

In addition, special timing conventions apply to both straightline and MACRS depreciation; in the first year of an asset's life, you are only allowed to take a portion of a full year's depreciation.

Methods of Depreciation

Cost		$50,000				
Salvage		$15,000				
Life		10				
Percent		200%				
Discount		7%				

Year	Tax Rate	Straight Line	S-Y-D	Declining Balance	MACRS	Tax Difference: MACRS - Straight Line
1	28%	$3,500	$6,364	$10,000	$5,000	$420
2	28%	$3,500	$5,727	$8,000	$9,000	$1,540
3	28%	$3,500	$5,091	$6,400	$7,200	$1,036
4	28%	$3,500	$4,455	$5,120	$5,760	$633
5	28%	$3,500	$3,818	$4,096	$4,608	$310
6	28%	$3,500	$3,182	$1,384	$3,686	$52
7	28%	$3,500	$2,545	$0	$3,277	($62)
8	28%	$3,500	$1,909	$0	$3,277	($62)
9	28%	$3,500	$1,273	$0	$3,277	($62)
10	28%	$3,500	$636	$0	$3,277	($62)
11	28%	$0	$0	$0	$1,638	($3,741)
Total		$35,000	$35,000	$35,000	$50,000	$0
Present value of tax savings						$1,404

Figure A.5. Depreciation template

This template uses the simplest MACRS calculation, the half-year convention. The half-year convention allows you to take half a year's depreciation on an asset the first year you place it in service. Depending on your circumstances, the half-year convention may not be a valid way to calculate MACRS depreciation for tax purposes.

Unfortunately, the @SLN function does not allow fractional year arguments—half year or otherwise—so you must use more complex formulas for straightline calculation under MACRS.

Building the Depreciation Template

To build the depreciation template, use the Worksheet Global Settings command to set the default cell format to Currency with 0 decimal places. Set the width of column A to 15 characters and the width of columns B through E to 11 characters. Use the Range Format command to assign the following format:

Format	Cell
General	B5

Enter the labels in ranges A1..A7 and A9..E10, and enter the values in ranges B3..B4. Enter the following formulas:

Cell	Formula
B7	@SUM(B11..B31)

Copy the formula in cell B7 to range C7..E7.

Cell	Formula
B11	@IF(A11>$B$5,"",@SLN(B$3,B$4,B$5))
C11	@IF(A11>$B$5,"",@SYD(B$3,B$4,B$5,A11))
E11	@IF(A11>$B$5,"",@DDB(B$3,B$4,B$5,A11))
F11	@IF(A11>$B$5+1,"",@VDB(C$3,0,C$5,@MAX(A11-1.5,0),A11-.5,@IF($B$5>=15,1.5,2))

Your worksheet should now match the figure.

Using the Depreciation Template

To adapt the template for your own use, enter your own cost, salvage, and life variables in range B3..B5. Worksheet formulas do the rest. Since MACRS calculations ignore salvage value, the template's @VDB functions use 0 as salvage value argument, and total depreciation equals the asset's full cost of $50,000 rather than its depreciable cost of $35,000. However, you must remember that you'll have to pay tax on the asset when you sell it if you've depreciated it past its sales price.

The template accommodates assets with class lives of up to 20 years. (Real estate is not included in this category.) For assets with class lives less than 20 years, worksheet formulas cause irrelevant years to appear blank.

The Compound Growth Template

The 1-2-3 formulas needed to calculate compounding problems—to find a future value, growth rate, or compounding period—are fairly simple but often difficult to remember. The compound-growth macro (File COMPOUND.WK3) uses a fill-in-the-blanks format to let you solve for the variable of your choice, saving you the trouble of returning to a reference book every time the problem arises.

The compound-growth macro assumes that you are starting from a known present value and that you want to calculate one of three quantities:

1. The future value associated with a given growth rate and compounding period

2. The growth rate necessary to reach a given future value over a given compounding period

3. The compounding period needed to reach a given future value, given a certain growth rate

This model contains two worksheets. The four variables are located in the entry area, which is shaded blue and is found on sheet A. The macro occupies sheet B.

	A	B
1	**Projecting growth**	
2		
3	Present value	$50,000
4	Future value	$75,000
5	Growth rate	8.00%
6	Period	5.27
7		

Figure A.6. Sheet A of the compound-growth template

	A	B	C	D	E	F
1	\g	{blank variables}				
2		{menucall main_menu}				
3						
4	main_menu	Future value	Growth rate	Period		
5		Find future value	Find growth rate	Find period		
6		{find_future}	{find_growth}	{find_period}		
7						
8	find_future	{get_present}				
9		{get_growth}				
10		{get_period}				
11		{let future_value,present_value*(1+growth_rate)^period}~				
12						
13	find_growth	{get_present}				
14		{get_future}				
15		{get_period}				
16		{let growth_rate,@rate(future_value,present_value,period)}~				
17						
18	find_period	{get_present}				
19		{get_future}				
20		{get_growth}				
21		{let period,@cterm(growth_rate,future_value,present_value)}~				
22						
23	get_present	{getnumber "Enter present value: ",present_value}				
24						
25	get_future	{getnumber "Enter future value: ",future_value}				
26						
27	get_growth	{getnumber "Enter growth rate: ",growth_rate}				
28						
29	get_period	{getnumber "Enter number of periods: ",period}				

Figure A.7. Sheet B of the compound-growth template

Building the Compound-Growth Macro

To build the compound-growth model, use the Worksheet Global Settings command to set the default cell format to Currency with 0 decimal places. Use the Range Format command to assign the following formats:

Format	Cells
Percent 2	B5
Fixed 2	B6

Enter the labels on sheets A and B. Begin the label in cell B:A1 with an apostrophe.

Using the Compound-Growth Macro

To run the model, make sheet A visible so you can watch the macro fill in the entry area. To start the macro, press Control-G. Select Future value, Growth rate, or Period from the custom macro menu. The macro will then prompt you for the appropriate variable inputs. When you have entered the three variables, the macro will calculate the target value and place it in the entry area.

B

@Functions

Next to mathematical operators, such as +, -, *, and /, @Functions are perhaps the most basic key to 1-2-3 calculations. This appendix is a basic guide to the 1-2-3 @Functions. The functions are divided into the standard categories used in the 1-2-3 manual. Within each category, functions that make similar calculations are grouped together. Otherwise, they are listed alphabetically. The @Functions fall into these categories:

- Financial functions, including compound interest, annuities, internal rate of return and net present value, and depreciation.
- Math functions, including basic math, logarithms, and trigonometric functions.
- Statistical functions, including basic statistical functions, as well as standard deviation and variance.
- Database statistical functions, which allow you to make statistical calculations on records from a database that meet certain criteria.
- Date and time functions, which allow you to make a variety of date and time calculations, such as the interval between two dates or times.
- Logical functions, which calculate the results of conditional (or logical) formulas.
- String functions, which allow you to perform various operations on "strings," which are labels or other strings of characters that are not values.
- Special functions, which allow you to look up data in a table and to set a warning flag when data were not available or a calculation yielded an error. Beginning with Release 2.0, special functions are expanded to perform a variety of other tasks. These are used mostly to determine various conditions in logic formulas and macros.

Financial Functions

All of 1-2-3's financial @Functions involve the time value of money, and all involve at least three of these variables: present value (or principal, in the case of a loan), future value, interest rate, term, and payments. The interest rate and term must always be expressed in the same periods. For example, if interest is compounded monthly, the term must be expressed in months; if the term is expressed in years, you must use an effective annual interest rate. For depreciation, the rate varies from year to year, except in the case of straight-line depreciation.

The financial @Functions fall into four categories:

1. Compound interest functions make calculations involving a lump sum at a fixed interest rate.

2. Annuity functions involve a regular series of payments (an annuity) at a fixed interest rate. All of these functions are designed for ordinary annuities, with payments at the end of each period. However, they can be adapted easily for annuities due, with payments at the beginning of each period.

3. @IRR and @NPV calculate the internal rate of return and net present value of an uneven series of cash flows. While the cash may vary, periods and interest rate must be consistent.

4. 1-2-3 provides @Functions for calculating depreciation using double-declining balance, the sum of the years' digits, and straight-line depreciation. It also includes a function for variable declining balance, which can be adapted to the Modified Accelerated Cost Recovery System (MACRS) method used in the current tax law.

Compound Interest

1-2-3 provides two @Functions for making calculations involving compound interest on a lump sum. @CTERM calculates the term required to reach a future value, given present value and periodic interest rate. @RATE computes the rate required to reach a future value, given present value and term.

@CTERM

@CTERM (*interest,future value,present value*) calculates the number of compounding periods required for a present value to reach a future value at a constant interest rate. The term and the compounding period must be expressed in the same periods. For example, if interest is compounded monthly, you must find the *monthly* interest rate, and the term will be calculated in months.

Example: You have deposited $10,000 at an Annual Percentage Rate of 12%, compounded monthly. How long will it take to accumulate $20,000?

Answer: @CTERM(0.01,20000,10000) = 69.66 months. Because interest is compounded monthly, the periodic interest rate is .12/12 = .01 (or 12%/12 = 1%).

@RATE

@RATE(*future value,present value,term*) calculates the rate required to reach a future value, given the present value and term.

Example: If you deposit $10,000, what monthly interest rate is required for your investment to grow to $20,000 in seven years?

@ANSWER @RATE(20000,10000,7*12) = 0.0082859 = 0.82859%. This is the monthly percentage rate. The advertised annual percentage rate should be 12*0.08259% = 9.94%.

Annuities

Annuities are an even series of payments at a fixed interest rate over a given term. Again, all 1-2-3 @Functions assume that payments come at the end of each period (ordinary annuities), as with loans. Formulas are provided here for adapting the functions to payments that come at the beginning of each period (annuities due).

@FV

@FV(*payment,interest,term*) calculates the future value of an ordinary annuity (end-of-period payments, as with a loan). Interest must be expressed in the same periods as the term. To convert to an annuity due (beginning-of-period payments, as with a lease), multiply by (1+*interest*):

@FV(*payment,interest,term*)*(1+*interest*)

Example: You plan to deposit $10,000 a year at an effective annual rate of 10% for 10 years. How much will you have if you make the deposits at the end of each year? How much if you make the deposits at the beginning?

Answers: @FV(10000,0.1,10) = $159,374.25 and @FV(10000,0.1,10)*(1+0.1) = $175,311.67.

@PMT

@PMT(*principal,interest,term*) calculates the payment of an ordinary annuity (payments at the end of each period, as with a loan). As with all annuity calculations, the interest and term must be expressed in the same period. To convert the function for an annuity due (payments at the beginning of each period, as with a lease), divide by (1+*interest*): @PMT(*principal, interest, term*)/(1+*interest*).

Example: You have a choice of purchasing a $10,000 piece of equipment or leasing it. In either case, payments will be monthly for five years, calculated at 15% APR. Assuming no salvage value, how do the payments compare?

Answers: In both cases, you must convert the annual interest rate to monthly interest (0.15/12) and the term to months (5*12). For a loan the answer is @PMT(10000,0.15/12,5*12) = $237.90. For a lease the answer is @PMT(10000,0.15/12,5*12)/(1+0.15/12) = $234.96

@PV

@PV(*payment ,interest ,term*) calculates the present value of an even series of payments at the end of each period. By definition, the present value of a loan is the principal. To convert the calculation to an annuity due, with payments at the beginning of each period, multiply by (1+*interest*):

@PV(*payment, interest,term*)*(1+*interest*)

Example: You have a choice of purchasing a $10,000 piece of equipment or leasing it. If you take out a loan, the monthly payments will be $238 for five years. If you lease, the monthly payments will be $235 for five years. If your cost of capital is 15%, how do the payments compare, assuming no salvage value?

Answers: In both cases you must convert the annual interest rate to monthly interest (0.15/12) and the term to months (5*12). For a loan the answer is @PV(238,0.15/12,5*12) = $10,004.23. For a lease the answer is @PV(235,0.15/

12,5*12)*(1+0.15/12) = $10,001.60. The difference is insignificant because the loan and lease have been calculated on the same terms. In fact, rounding the payments to the nearest dollar is the only reason the present values differ at all.

@TERM

@TERM(*payment, interest, future value*) calculates the time required to reach a future value, given regular payments at the end of each period (ordinary annuity) and a periodic interest rate. To convert to beginning-of-period payments (annuity due), divide by (1+*interest*):

@TERM(*payment,interest, future value*)/(1+*interest*)

Example: You can save $1,000 a year. The effective annual percentage rate is 8.75%. How long will it take you to accumulate $10,000 if you make your deposits at the end of the year? How long if you make your deposits at the beginning of the year?

Answers: For end-of-year payments the answer is @TERM(1000,0.0875, 10000) = 7.49 years. For beginning-of-year payments the answer is @TERM (1000,0.0875.0875,10000) = 6.9 years.

It will take a few months less to accumulate $10,000 if you make your deposits at the beginning of the year instead of at the end.

Internal Rate of Return and Net Present Value

Internal rate of return and net present value are used to evaluate uneven cash flows. Although the amount of the cash flow may vary, the periods must be regular. If some cash flows occur on a monthly basis, for example, then cash flows (even if 0) must be entered for every month. @IRR calculates the internal rate of return for a series of payments, given an initial outlay. @NPV calculates the net present value of a series of payments, given a specified interest rate.

@IRR

@IRR(*guess, range*) calculates the internal rate of return for an uneven series of cash flow values generated by an investment. Normally the initial outlay—or the first cash flow amount—is a negative value that represents the investment. The cash flows may vary, but they must be for the same periods. For example, you will need to use monthly cash flows if there are cash flows after 1 month, after 6 months, and after 10 months. (The values for the intervening months will be 0.) The IRR will be for the same period. Guess is your estimate of what the IRR might be. In most cases, a guess of 10% (0.01) will work. Range is the range containing the series of cash flows.

Example: You purchase 100 shares of stock at $100 a share. You receive dividends of $3.25 a share the first year, $2.00 the second, $4.50 the third, $4.00 the fourth, and $5.00 the fifth. At the end of the fifth year, you sell at $140 a share, so the total inflow for the year is $145 per share. What is the internal rate of return?

Answer: As shown in Figure B.1, @IRR(0.1,B2..B7) = 10.17%.

	A	B	C
1			
2	Cost	(10,000)	
3	Year 1	325	
4	Year 2	200	
5	Year 3	450	
6	Year 4	400	
7	Year 5	14,500	
8			
9	IRR	10.17%	@IRR(0.1,B2..B7)

Figure B.1. Calculating internal rate of return.

> Note: @IRR assumes that cash flows occur at the end of each period. If the first inflow comes at the same time as the initial outflow, subtract it from the initial cost.

@IRR calculates internal rate of return by trial and error. You will see an ERR message if it cannot calculate the answer within 0.0000001 after 30 iterations. If this occurs, try changing your guess.

@NPV

@NPV(*interest,range*) calculates the value (in today's dollars) of a series of uneven cash flows—given a certain interest rate, sometimes called a hurdle rate. The cash flows must be at even intervals, and the period for the interest must match the intervals of the cash flows. That is, if cash flows are monthly, then you must calculate the monthly interest rate, and thus divide the annual interest rate by 12.

Use @NPV to evaluate an investment or to compare one investment with another. With @NPV you can, for example, figure out the initial investment necessary to achieve a certain cash outflow at a given interest rate (see example below). Or you can calculate the value of an investment where you make an initial cash outlay followed by a series of future cash inflows.

Like @IRR, @NPV assumes that all cash flows come at the end of each period. If you have an initial cash flow that occurs immediately you must *add* it to the @NPV of the remaining cash flows as follows: (Initial Cash) + @NPV (*interest, range with remaining cash flows*). This is because the initial cash is not affected by the interest rate. Here, if your net present value result is greater than 0, go ahead with the investment.

Example: Your daughter Becky is going to college in four years. (She starts at the beginning of the fourth year.) You expect the cost to be $11,000 the first year, $12,000 the second, $13,500 the third, and $14,500 the fourth. How much must you set aside now to cover the cost if you can earn 8% interest per year?

Answer: As shown in Figure B.2, the Total cost is $51,000, but you can cover the expense by setting aside $33,220 now.

	A	B	C
1			
2	Becky's College Plan		
3			
4	Year 1	0	
5	Year 2	0	
6	Year 3	0	
7	Year 4	11,000	
8	Year 5	12,000	
9	Year 6	13,500	
10	Year 7	14,500	
11		========	
12	Total	51,000	
13	@NPV	33,220	@NPV(0.08,B4..B10)

Figure B.2. Calculating the net present value of an uneven series of cash flows.

Depreciation

1-2-3/W includes depreciation @Functions using the following methods: double-declining balance, straight-line, and sum-of-the-year's digits. It also includes a variable declining balance function (@VDB), which can be adapted to the current tax system. With the exception of @VDB, the depreciation functions may require some adaptation to the tax law and business practice.

DDB

DDB(*cost,salvage,life,period*) calculates the depreciation of an asset using the double- declining balance method. DDB is a method of calculating accelerated depreciation commonly used before 1981, but is now of limited use because of changes in the tax laws. Frequently, businesses switched to the straight-line method at the point it yielded a higher depreciation allowance.

Example: A piece of equipment cost $10,000, has an expected useful life of five years, and should have a salvage value of $1,000 when it is fully depreciated. What is the DDB depreciation schedule?

```
Year 1: @DDB(10000,1000,5,1) =   $4,000
Year 2: @DDB(10000,1000,5,2) =   $2,400
Year 3: @DDB(10000,1000,5,3) =   $1,440
Year 4: @DDB(10000,1000,5,4) =   $  864
Year 5: @DDB(10000,1000,5,5) =   $  296
Total                            $9,000
Salvage Value                    $1,000
                                 ======
                                 $10,000
```

@SLN

@SLN(*cost,salvage,life*) computes annual straight-line depreciation for an asset, where cost is the original cost of the item, salvage is the salvage value at the end of the period, and life is the item's useful life.

Many businesses use straight-line depreciation for internal accounting and reports to shareholders. You can also use straight-line depreciation under the current tax law, but salvage value is not counted. That option may be attractive for businesses that expect low earnings or losses in their early years.

Investment real estate must be depreciated by the straight-line method under the current tax law, but, again, salvage value is not taken into account. Only the structure may be depreciated, not the land on which it stands. The tax law specifies the life for various types of property. @SLN does not prorate depreciation for the first and last years, as required by the law.

Example: A piece of equipment costs $10,000 and should have a salvage value of $2,000 at the end of five years. What is the annual depreciation?

Answer: @SLN(10000,2000,5) = $1,600.

@SYD

The sum-of-the-year's digits method of calculating accelerated depreciation for tax purposes was used mainly before 1981. With this method, more depreciation expense occurs in earlier periods than in later ones (although not so much as when you use the double declining balance method). The method is now seldom used.

@SYD(*cost*,*salvage*,*life*,*period*) calculates the depreciation for a given year, using the sum-of-the-year's digits method.

Example: A piece of equipment costs $10,000 and should have a salvage value of $2,000 at the end of five years. What is the depreciation for the second year?

Answer: @SYD(10000,2000,5,2) = $2,133.33.

@VDB

@VDB, a variable declining balance function, is the only @Function capable of calculating depreciation under the Modified Accelerated Cost Recovery System (MACRS), the method currently required for tax calculations. You can also use @VDB to calculate accelerated depreciation by other methods.

@VDB provides three critical options, all necessary to calculate depreciation under MACRS:

1. It allows you to prorate depreciation for the first and last periods, as required under MACRS. Under the rules, equipment is depreciated for a half year in its first and last years unless you bought more than 40% of the depreciable assets placed in service during the year during the fourth quarter. In the latter case, you begin depreciating all equipment at the midpoint of the quarter in which it was placed in service.

2. You can specify the double-declining balance factor (200%) used by MACRS.

3. Although it does not require you to do so, @VDB allows you to switch to the straight-line method of depreciation at the point in an asset's life where straight-line depreciation yields a higher depreciation allowance than the double-declining balance method. This, too, is the method used by MACRS.

@VDB takes a rather elaborate argument:

@VDB(*cost,salvage,life,start period,end period,*
   [*depreciation factor*],[*switch*])

This is not as complicated as it might at first appear. In fact, the function is quite naturally suited to MACRS calculations. Cost is simply the original cost of a depreciable asset. Salvage value is not taken into account under MACRS, so that value will be 0. Life is also determined by the MACRS rules. Cars, light trucks, computers, typewriters, and other office equipment are depreciated over five years. Furnishings, such as desks, files, and refrigerators, are depreciated over seven. Only real estate and a few special categories of assets fall into different categories.

Start period and *end period* refer to the asset's age at the beginning and end of the fiscal period being analyzed. Under the midyear rule, the first year's *start period* is 0, and the *end period* is 0.5. Under the midquarter rule, the *start period* is also 0 the first year. The *end period* depends on the quarter the property was placed in service. You can enter it as either a fraction or as a decimal:

First Quarter	7/8 or	0.875
Second Quarter	5/8 or	0.625
Third Quarter	3/8 or	0.375
Fourth Quarter	1/8 or	0.125

For the next year, the *start period* is the previous year's *end period*; the *end period* is that value plus 1, and so on. Under the midyear convention, for example, the first year's *start period* is 0, and the *end period* is 0.5. For the second year, the *start period* is 0.5, and the *end period* is 1.5. And so on.

The last two elements of the argument are optional, and not required for MACRS calculations. [*Depreciation factor*] can be any value greater than 0, but the default is 2, or 200%, which is the double-declining balance factor used under MACRS. [*Switch*] can be either 0 or 1. If it is 0, @VDB switches to straight-line depreciation when it yields a higher depreciation allowance than double-declining balance depreciation. If [*switch*] is 1, @VDB does not switch to straight-line depreciation. Since MACRS does make the switch, you can omit the switch and accept the default.

Figure B.3 shows the annual depreciation under the MACRS midyear rule for a $10,000 asset with a life of five years. Note that only a half-year's depreciation is calculated in the first and last years.

```
        A                          B           C
 1  Equipment Depreciation under MACRS
 2
 3  Cost                       10000
 4  Life                           5
 5  First year                   0.5
 6
 7
 8  Year 1                      2000
 9  @VDB(B3,0,0.5,B5)
10  Year 2                      3200
11  @VDB(B3,0.5,1.5,B5)
12  Year 3                      1920
13  @VDB(B3,1.5,2.5,B5)
14  Year 4                      1152
15  @VDB(B3,2.5,3.5,B5)
16  Year 5                      1152
17  @VDB(B3,3.5,4.5,B5)
18  Year 6                       576
19  @VDB(B3,4.5,5,B5)
20                          ========
21  Total                      10000
```

Figure B.3. Calculating MACRS depreciation with @VDB.

Math Functions

The math @Functions help with a variety of basic calculations. Here, they are divided into three groups: Basic Math, Logarithms, and Trigonometry. For the most part, these functions are fairly self-explanatory if you understand the basic math. A few basic mathematical concepts are provided along the way.

Basic Math

The basic math functions perform basic mathematical tasks, such as finding absolute value, calculating a square root, rounding, and providing the value of *pi* to 10 decimal places. They are generally quite straightforward. Applications are suggested in the examples below.

@ABS

@ABS(x) calculates the absolute, or positive, value of x. @ABS(–10), for example, is 10.

@INT

@INT(x) returns the integer value of x. For example, @INT(10.7) = 10, and 10*@INT(10.7) = 100. This is in contrast to formatting a cell as Fixed, with 0 decimal places. In that case, the display will be 11, but if you multiply that value by 10, the result will be 107. @ROUND(10.7) will also display 11, but 10*@ROUND(10.7) = 110.

@MOD

@MOD(x,y) calculates the modulus, or remainder, of the division x/y. For example, @MOD(10,3) = 1, because 10/3 = 3 with a remainder of 1.

@MOD can be used with @DATE to calculate the day of the week. If you divide a date number by 7 and get a remainder of 1, the date falls on Sunday; 2 is Monday, 3 is Tuesday and so on. Saturday is 0.

Example: @MOD(@DATE(95,7,4),7) = 3. July 4, 1995, falls on a Tuesday.

@PI

@PI returns the value *pi*, about 3.141593. For example, the area of a circle with radius r is $pi*r^2$. Thus, the area of a circle with a radius of 3 meters is @PI*3^2=28.274334 square meters (rounded). You can also use @PI to convert angle measurements between degrees and radians.

@RAND

@RAND generates a random number between 0 and 1. You can copy it into a range of cells. You can use @RAND in combination with other functions and operators to generate numbers in any range. For example, @RAND*1000 generates random numbers between 1 and 1,000.

@RAND recalculates every time the worksheet recalculates. In many models, you will want to freeze the original random numbers. You can do this with the Edit Quick Copy command with the Convert to Values option selected. If you copy your @RAND calculations onto themselves, the values in the range are permanently frozen. If you copy the values to a new range, the new range will be frozen, but the original values will continue to recalculate.

@ROUND

@ROUND(x,n) rounds x to n decimal places. For example, @ROUND(@PI,2) rounds pi to two decimal places: 3.14.

x can be any value; n can be any value between 15 and -15. If n is positive, x is rounded to n decimal places. If n is negative, x is rounded to the positive nth power of 10. For example, @ROUND(x,-2) rounds to the nearest 100 (10^2). Thus, @ROUND(2333,-2) = 2,300; @ROUND(-2333,-2) = -2,300.

Note that @ROUND functions differently from decimal formats and @INT. @ROUND actually rounds the underlying value, not simply the display. Decimal formats, by contrast, round the display, but not the underlying values; other calculations are not affected. @INT actually doesn't round; it simply lops off the numbers to the right of the decimal.

@SQRT

@SQRT(x) finds the square root of x. For example, @SQRT(2) = 1.414214 (rounded). Of course, @SQRT(4) = 2 (exactly).

> Note: You can also use a fractional exponent to find the nth root of a number: the nth root of x=x^(1/n). Thus, the square root of 2 = @SQRT(2) = 2^(1/2) = 1.414214 (rounded). The cube root of 8 = 8^(1/3) = 2 (exactly). The root of 16 = 16^(1/4) = 2 (exactly).

Logarithms

Logarithms are a variation on exponential calculations. If $x = y^n$, then n is the logarithm of x to the base y, and x is the antilogarithm of n. In principle, y could be any value. In practice, only two values are used: base 10 and the theoretically derived constant e, which is approximately 2.718282. Logarithms to the base 10 are called common logarithms; those to the base e are called natural logarithms.

Many logarithmic calculations can be derived from three simple equations:

$\log (x*y) = \log (x) + \log (y)$

$\log (x/y) = \log (x) - \log (y)$

$\log (x^n) = n * \log (x)$

Logs are not necessary for ordinary multiplication and division in 1-2-3 because the program automatically makes those calculations anyway. However, they are sometimes useful in solving exponential equations. To calculate the term for a lump sum to reach a future value, for example, @CTERM uses this equation, where i is the interest rate:

$\ln(FV/PV)$

$\ln(1+i)$

@EXP

@EXP(x) calculates the value of the constant e (approximately 2.718282) raised to the power of x. @EXP(x) is the inverse of the natural logarithm function, @LN(x). That is, it converts a natural log back into an ordinary number. If @LN(x) = y, then @EXP(y) = x. (The calculation is subject to slight rounding errors if you enter the values directly, rather than making the first calculation on your worksheet, and then using a cell reference in the second.) You can also use @EXP to calculate the natural logarithm constant e: @EXP(1) = 2.718282 (rounded).

@LN

@LN(x) finds the natural logarithm of x (that is the log to the base e, the natural logarithm constant). The constant e is approximately 2.718282 (see @EXP). For example, @LN(2) = 0.693147 (rounded). That means that e^0.693147=2 (approximately).

@LOG

@LOG(x) calculates the common logarithm of x, or the log to the base 10. For example, @LOG(100) = 2 (exactly), because 100 = 10^2. Use @LOG in calculations that require a common logarithm, such as formulas for finding the root of a number.

Example: Find the cube root of 110,592.

Answer: @LOG(110592)/3 = 1.681241 (rounded) or 10^1.681241 = 47.999974. This is a slight rounding error. If you use a cell reference in the second calculation (or do the entire calculation in one cell), the answer is exactly 48.

Trigonometric Functions

Trigonometric functions are based on right triangles, but can be applied to any triangle. The three basic ratios used by 1-2-3's trig functions are based on an acute angle of a right triangle:

sine (angle) = opposite side/hypotenuse

cosine (angle) = adjacent side/hypotenuse

tangent (angle) = opposite side/adjacent side

There are no @Functions for the other three basic trigonometric ratios:

cotangent (angle) = adjacent side/opposite side

secant (angle) = hypotenuse/adjacent side

cosecant (angle) = hypotenuse/opposite side

These omissions are easily remedied with the following simple ratios:

cotangent = 1/tangent

secant = 1/cosine

cosecant = 1/sine

1-2-3's trig @Functions measure angles in radians. To convert from radians to degrees, multiply by 180/@PI. To convert from degrees to radians, multiply by @PI/180.

Example: 45(degrees)*@PI/180 = 0.785398 radians. 0.785398(radians)* 180/@PI = 44.99999 degrees. The reason the latter calculation does not equal 45 degrees exactly is that the measurement in radians is rounded to six decimal places.

@ACOS

@ACOS(x) calculates the arc cosine of x. This is the angle whose cosine is x, measured in radians. To convert to degrees, multiply by 180/@PI. The cosine of an acute angle in a right triangle is adjacent side/hypotenuse. Thus, when you know the lengths of the hypotenuse and another side, you can use @ACOS to find the angle in between.

Example: As an airplane takes off, it traverses 1,000 yards on the ground, but actually has traveled 1,100 yards through the air. What is its angle of ascent?

Answers: @ACOS(1000/1100) = 0.429600 radians. @ACOS(1000/1100)*180/@PI = 24.61997 degrees.

@ASIN

@ASIN(x) calculates the arcsine of x. This is the angle, measured in radians, whose sine is x. To convert to degrees, multiply by 180/@PI. The sine of an acute angle in a right triangle is opposite side/hypotenuse. If you know the hypotenuse and the opposite side, you can use @ASIN to find the angle.

Example: The airplane has now traveled 2,000 feet through the air and has reached an altitude of 1,000 feet. What is its average angle of ascent?

Answers: @ASIN(1000/2000) = 0.523599 radians. @ASIN(1000/2000)*180/@PI = 30 degrees (exactly).

@ATAN

@ATAN(x) figures the arctangent of x. The result is the angle, measured in radians, whose tangent is x. To convert to degrees, multiply by 180/@PI. The tangent of an acute angle in a right triangle is opposite side/adjacent side. If you know these values, you can use @ATAN to determine the angle.

Example: An airplane is at an altitude of 1,000 feet and has traveled 1,750 feet in ground distance. What is its angle of ascent?

Answers: @ATAN(1000,1750) = 0.519146 radians. @ATAN(1000, 1750)*180/@PI = 29.744881 degrees.

@ATAN2

@ATAN2(x,y) calculates the four-quadrant arctangent of the angle defined by x and y. This is the angle, measured in radians, of the angle whose tangent is y/x. To convert to degrees, multiply by 180/@PI.

x and y can be any values. If is 0, @ATAN2 returns 0. If both x and y are 0, the function returns an ERR message.

Example: Think of a circle divided in quadrants. The angle bisecting the upper right quadrant is 45 degrees and can be defined by the coordinates 2,2 (or any equal positive coordinates). Moving clockwise, the angle bisecting the next quadrant is - 45 degrees, defined by -2,2. The next quadrant is bisected by an angle of -135 degrees, defined by -2,-2. The final quadrant, the upper left, is bisected by a 135 degree angle, defined by 2,-2. The @ATAN2 calculations for these angles are shown in Table 9.1.

Formulas		Radians	*180/@PI	Degrees
@ATAN2(2,2)	=	0.785398	*180/@PI	= 45
@ATAN2(2,-2)	=	-0.785398	*180/@PI	= -45
@ATAN2(-2,-2)	=	-2.356194	*180/@PI	= -135
@ATAN2(-2.2)	=	2.356194	*180/@PI	= 135

Table B.1. Using @ATAN2 to calculate four-quadrant angles measured in radians and degrees.

@COS

@COS(x) finds the cosine of angle x, measured in radians. To convert from degrees to radians, multiply by @PI/180. For example, the cosine of a 30-degree angle is @COS(30*@PI/180) = 0.866025.

The cosine of an acute angle in a right triangle is adjacent side/hypotenuse. If you know the angle and one of these values, you can calculate the other.

Example: An airplane is climbing at a 30-degree angle and has traveled 1,500 feet through the air. How much ground distance has it covered?

Answer: First, convert degrees to radians and calculate the angle's cosine: @COS(30*@PI/180) = 0.866025. Then, calculate the distance travelled using the cosine: x/1500 = 0.866025. Thus, x = 1500*0.866025 = 1299.38016. (The airplane has traveled about 1,300 feet, measured on the ground.)

@SIN

@SIN(x) calculates the sine of x, where x is an angle measured in radians. To convert degrees to radians, multiply degrees by @PI/180. For example, the sine of a 30-degree angle is @SIN(30*@PI/180) = 0.5.

The sine of an acute angle in a right triangle is opposite side/hypotenuse. Thus, if you can measure an angle in degrees or radians and the length of the opposite side or the hypotenuse, you can calculate the third value.

Example: You are installing a television antenna on a flat roof. The instructions say that the guy wires should be installed at a 35-degree angle to a flat surface (the angle opposite the antenna). If the antenna is 20 feet tall, how long are the guy wires?

Answer: First, convert degrees to radians and calculate the angle's sine: @SIN(35*@PI/180) = 0.573576. Then, use the sine value to calculate how long the wires are: 20 feet/x = 0.573576. Thus, x = 20/0.573576 = 34.868936. The guy wires are about 35 feet long, so if you want to install three, you will need at least 105 feet of wire.

@TAN

@TAN(x) computes the tangent of angle x measured in radians. To convert degrees to radians, multiply by @PI/180. For example, the tangent of a 30-degree angle is @TAN(30*@PI/180) = 0.577350.

The tangent of an acute angle in a right triangle is opposite side/adjacent side. If you know the angle and one of these values, you can compute length of the other side.

Example: You are installing a 20-foot television antenna on a flat roof. The instructions say that the guy wires should be at a 55-degree angle to the antenna. How far away from the base of the antenna should you fasten the guy wires?

Answer: Convert degrees to radians and calculate the tangent of the angle: @TAN(55*@PI/180) = 1.428148. Then, use the tangent to find out how far away the guy wires should be fastened: x/20 = 1.428148. This gives x = 20*1.428148 = 28.562960. (The guy wires should be attached about 28.5 feet from the base of the antenna.)

Statistical Functions

The statistical functions perform a variety of ordinary mathematical tasks, such as finding the average (mean) or sum of the values in a range. In most cases, the argument is a range of values, such as monthly sales figures or test scores for students in a class. The range can be identified as a range address (e.g., A1..A20) or as a range name you have assigned using the Range Name Create command. Applications are generally straightforward. Blank cells within ranges are ignored, but it is important to note that labels and 0's evaluate to 0, which counts as an entry. This can cause unwanted results with any of the statistical functions except @SUM. (@SUM simply adds up the values in a range, so 0's don't matter.) If the range contains a NA or ERR message, any of the statistical functions will yield the same result.

This section is divided into two parts. The first covers the basic statistical functions. The second covers standard deviation and variance, which are somewhat more technical.

Basic Statistical Functions

The basic statistical functions include such commonplace calculations as average (mean), the maximum and minimum values in a range, and counting the number of entries in a range. The applications are largely self-explanatory.

@AVG

@AVG(*list*) finds the average, or mean, of the values in a range or list of ranges or values. For example, @AVG(12,19,11,20) = 11.5. You would get the same answer with @AVG(A1..A4) if those values occupied the range. @AVG (A1..A4, E7..E10) finds the average of all the values in the two ranges. @AVG ignores blank cells in a range, but labels evaluate to 0, thus affecting the calculation.

@COUNT

@COUNT(*list*) counts the number of entries in a range or list of ranges. Labels and 0's count as do ERRs and NAs, but blank cells do not. Note that if you include single-cell addresses in your @COUNT list, they *will* be counted, blank or not blank.

@MAX

@MAX(*list*) returns the highest value in a range or list of ranges or values. Labels count as 0 and so do cells that *seem* empty but contain spaces or a label prefix. Blanks are ignored unless your list includes single-cell references to blank cells. @MAX (A1..C3, D5..F10) finds the largest of all the values in the two ranges.

@MIN

@MIN(*list*) returns the least value in a range. As with @MAX, labels count as 0 as do cells that *seem* empty but contain spaces or a label-prefix. Blanks are ignored unless your list includes single-cell references to blank cells.

@SUM

@SUM(*list*) finds the total of values in a range or list of ranges or values. Blanks and labels count as 0. For example @SUM(1, 2,3,4) = 10. If the value in A1 is 5, and the value in B1 is 6, @SUM (A1..B1)=11.

@SUMPRODUCT

@SUMPRODUCT(range1,range2,range3...) multiplies the corresponding values in each range, and then totals the results. The ranges must be the same size and shape; otherwise @SUMPRODUCT returns an ERR message.

In Figure B.4, the values in column A are multiplied by the values in column B. @SUMPRODUCT does not return the values in column C, which are provided to illustrate how the function works. Here, the result is equal to 10*50+20*60+30*70+40*80. The @SUM version of the calculation solves the problem a step at a time; the @SUMPRODUCT formula makes the calculation in a single step.

> Note that if the ranges are columns, @SUMPRODUCT multiplies by rows; if the ranges are rows @SUMPRODUCT multiplies by columns. If each range is *more* than one column, @SUMPRODUCT multiplies by rows.

	A	B	C	D
1			AxB	
2	10	50	500	
3	20	60	1,200	
4	30	70	2,100	
5	40	80	3,200	
6			==========	
7	@SUM(C2..C5)			7,000
8	@SUMPRODUCT(A2..A5,B2..B5)			7,000

Figure B.4. @SUMPRODUCT multiplies the values in two or more ranges, and then totals the results.

Standard Deviation and Variance

Two statistical calculations, standard deviation and variance, require special attention. Both are measures of the variation of the data being analyzed from the average for a group. The higher the standard deviation or variance, the more widely values for the group vary around the group average.

In statistics, it is important to distinguish between an entire population and a sample of a population for these calculations. The Census Bureau, for example, would survey the entire population of a county, while a pollster would survey a random sample. Statisticians have found that sampling tends to create a downward bias in calculating the degree to which values vary. Thus, they use slightly different formulas for populations, as opposed to samples. If you use the same values, sample standard deviation and sample variance will be somewhat larger than comparable calculations for a population census. However, the difference is small when the size of the sample is greater than 30. @STD and @VAR calculate *population* standard deviation and variance. @STDS and @VARS calculate sample variance and sample standard deviation.

The next sections give a brief overview of 1-2-3's @Functions for calculations standard deviation and variance, based on the records from Porky's Pig Farm.

The Mathematics of Standard Deviation and Variance

Suppose Porky's Pig Farm wants to analyze the variation in the weights of its pigs. Figure B.5 shows calculations of sample variance, sample variance, standard deviation, and sample standard deviation, using the mathematical formulas, rather than @Functions. Standard deviation is the square root of the variance, so it is simplest to explain variance first. Here is the formula for calculating population variance:

$$\frac{\Sigma(V_I - avg)^2}{n}$$

where V_I is the fifth item on the list; avg is the average for the list; and n is the number of items in the list. The idea is quite a bit simpler than the equation looks. First, find the average for the group (in this case, the pigs' weights). This is 385.3, computed with @AVG in B21. Next, subtract the average from each pig's weight and square the difference. This is done in column C. (The average difference between individuals and the group average is 0 by definition. Although the calculation has more elaborate theoretical underpinnings, squaring the difference yields all positive values.) Finally, add up the sum of the squares and divide by the number of individuals in the population to determine the variance. This calculation appears in C24, using this formula: @SUM (C4..C19)/ @COUNT(C4..C19).

The population variance is 3,443.07, a number that makes direct sense only if you are comparing it to the variance of another pig population or using it for further calculations. Population standard deviation is simply the square root of the variance. In C27, Porky's makes this calculation using this formula: @SQRT(@SUM(C4..C19)/@COUNT)C4..C19).).

If data shown in Figure B.5 represents the entire population of Porky's Pig Farm, the standard deviation is 58.68 pounds. As a rule of thumb for a population with a normal distribution, about two-thirds of the population will fall within one standard deviation of the average, 95% within two standard deviations, and nearly all will fall within three standard deviations.

If the data in the example are merely a sample of the pigs on Porky's farm, Porky might want to calculate the sample variance and sample standard deviation of the pigs' weights. The mathematical equations are very similar to those for the calculations for a population. To compensate for the downward bias, $n-1$ is substituted for n in the denominator.

	A	B	C
1	Porky's Pig Farm		
2			
3		Weight	(B-avg)^2
4	Alberta	404.9	384.16
5	Alfreda	441.9	3203.56
6	Catbaby	375.2	102.01
7	Dusseldorf	366.9	338.56
8	Elvira	478.1	8611.84
9	Elvis	374.7	112.36
10	Emmanuel	422.0	1346.89
11	Fred	312.2	5343.61
12	Grunt	303.1	6756.84
13	Leon	321.0	4134.49
14	Madigan	316.7	4705.96
15	Napoleon	449.9	4173.16
16	Sam	308.7	5867.56
17	Smitty	411.5	686.44
18	Watanabe	397.3	144
19	Zapolski	481.1	9177.64
20			=========================
21	Average	385.3	
22	@AVG(B4..B19)		
23			
24	Population Variance		3,443.07
25	@SUM(C4..C19)/@COUNT(C4..C19)		
26			
27	Population Standard Deviation		58.68
28	@SQRT(@SUM(C4..C19)/@COUNT(C4..C19))		
29			
30	Sample Variance		3,672.61
31	@SUM(C4..C19)/(@COUNT(C4..C19)-1)		
32			
33	Sample Standard Deviation		60.60
34	@SQRT(@SUM(C4..C19)/(@COUNT(C4..C19)-1))		

Figure B.5. Calculating population standard deviation and variance without @Functions.

In C30, this calculation is made with the formula @SUM(C4..C19)/(@COUNT(C4..C19)-1). The result is 3,672.61, somewhat more than the population variance, as expected.

In C33, the sample standard deviation is calculated using the formula @SQRT(@SUM(C4..C19)/(@COUNT(C4..C19)-1)). The result is 60.60, again somewhat higher than the population standard deviation.

Standard Deviation and Variance @Functions

With 1-2-3's @Functions, you can calculate standard deviation and variance as well as sample deviation and variance without making the sum-of-the-squares calculation in the solutions just described.

@STD

@STD(*list*) returns the population standard deviation of the values in the range. Again, it is important to distinguish between population standard deviation and sample standard deviation.

Example: Using the data in Figure B.6 (without the calculations in column C), Porky's Pig Farm can calculate the population standard deviation of the pigs' weights as shown in Figure B.7. The answer is 58.68—the same, of course, as the result of making the calculation the long way.

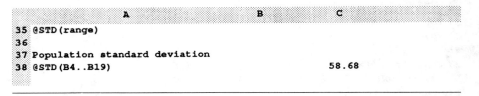

	A	B	C
35	@STD(range)		
36			
37	Population standard deviation		
38	@STD(B4..B19)		58.68

Figure B.6. Calculating population standard deviation with @STD.

@STDS

@STDS(*list*) calculates the sample standard deviation in a range or series of ranges or values. Statisticians have found that there is a downward bias in a sample of a population as opposed to a complete census of the population. Thus, a sample standard deviation will be somewhat higher than a population standard deviation, using the same values.

Example: Suppose that the pig weights shown in Figure B.5 represent a random sample of the pigs at Porky's Pig Farm. In Figure B.7, Porky's has calculated the sample standard deviation both ways. In the first, in C41, Porky's uses the @STDS function. In C44, the calculation is made using an equivalent formula. The answers, of course, are the same.

	A	B	C
39	@STDS(range)		
40			
41	Sample Standard Deviation		60.60
42	@STDS(B4..B19)		
43			
44	Sample Standard Deviation		60.60
45	@STD(B4..B19)*SQRT(@COUNT(B4..B19)/(@COUNT(B4..B19)-1))		

Figure B.7. Calculating sample standard deviation at Porky's Pig Farm (see Figure B.5) with the @STDS function and with an equivalent formula.

@VAR

@VAR(*list*) calculates the population variance of the values in a range or series of ranges or values. It is often important to distinguish between population variance and sample variance. Sample variance will be somewhat larger than population variance, but the difference is small when the sample is larger than 30.

Example: Suppose that the values for Porky's Pig Farm shown in Figure B.5 represent the entire population of pigs at the farm. Porky's has already calculated the variance for weights using the mathematical formula. The farm can make the calculation more simply using @VAR, as shown in Figure B.8. The answer, 3,443.07, of course, is the same.

	A	B	C
46	@VAR(range)		
47			
48	Population Variance		3,443.07
49	@VAR(B4..B19)		

Figure B.8. Calculating variance with @VAR.

@VARS

@VARS(*list*) computes the sample variance for the values in the range. The outcome of the sample variance calculation will be somewhat higher than the result of a population variance calculation, but the difference is small when the sample is more than 30.

Example: Suppose the pig weights for Porky's Pig Farm, shown in Figure B.5, represent a random sample of the pigs at the farm, rather than a census of the population. Porky's has already calculated the sample variance mathematically. Figure B.9 shows the same calculation using @Functions. The calculation in C52 uses the @VARS function. The calculation in C55 uses an equivalent formula. The 1/100th of a pound difference in the latter calculation is a result of rounding.

	A	B	C
50	@VARS(range)		
51			
52	Sample Variance		3,672.61
53	@VARS(B4..B19)		
54			
55	Sample Variance		3,672.61
56	@VAR(B4..B19)*(@COUNT(B4..B19)/(@COUNT(B4..B19)-1))		

Figure B.9. Calculating sample variance at Porky's Pig Farm with @VARS function and with an equivalent formula.

Database Statistical Functions

A 1-2-3 database is simply a range in which each row includes information about an individual item or person. This is called a *record*. Specific information about each item or person is entered across the columns of the database. The column entry for each record is called a *field*. For the database functions to work correctly, each column must be labeled with a heading.

The database statistical functions are similar to the statistical functions described above, except that they allow you to analyze information that meets certain criteria.

Example: Esmerelda's Weight Boutique wants to analyze the results for its patients in September. Each record includes fields recording the patient's name, sex, starting weight, ending weight, and loss, as shown in Figure B.10. Although you can set up more elaborate criteria, Esmerelda simply wants to distinguish between males and females, as indicated by m and f in the Sex column.

	A	B	C	D	E
1					
2			Esmerelda's Weight Boutique		
3			September Group		
4					
5	Patient	Sex	Start	End	Loss
6	Aaron, J.	f	178	173	5
7	Black, Q.	m	297	278	19
8	Bronstadt, D.	m	190	172	18
9	Dover, P.	m	240	203	37
10	Harpole, M.	f	145	124	21
11	James, R.	f	151	150	1
12	Kazutsky, B.	f	142	131	11
13	Kramer, A.	f	163	143	20
14	May, A.	m	265	243	22
15	Meltzer, R.	m	203	187	16
16	Ringwalt, F.	m	311	307	4
17	Rogers, L.	f	150	139	11
18	Vaden, R.	m	283	269	14
19	Willis, S.	f	132	122	10

Figure B.10. A database for Esmerelda's patients in September.

Using this database, Esmerelda can use all of 1-2-3's statistical functions to analyze her patients' progress for the month.

Database @Function Arguments

All database functions (except @DQUERY function) require the same argument: (*input, field, criteria*). Let's look at the components.

The *input range* is the range that defines the database, including column headings. In Esmerelda's case, this is A5..E19. You can refer to the input range by its address, or you can assign it a name, using the Range Name Create dialog. In the examples that follow, Esmerelda has assigned the name SEPTEMBER to the range A5..E19.

The *field* is either the name—in quotation marks—or the offset number of the field you want to analyze. (It can also be the address of the cell that contains the field name.) For the examples based on Figure B.10 that follow, Esmerelda will use the Loss field (cell E5, offset 4).

The *criteria* component of the argument is very flexible. You can use criteria to restrict the analysis to database records that meet one or more specifications. At a minimum, the criteria range consists of two cells—a column heading in one cell, with a value, label, or formula entered in the cell below.

In the examples here, Esmerelda uses two criterion ranges: the first, in D24..D25, identifies records with m, for male, in the Sex field. Esmerelda has assigned this range the name MEN. The second, in D27..D28, identifies records with f, for female, in the Sex field. This is named WOMEN in the examples below. Figure B.11 shows the criteria entries on the worksheet.

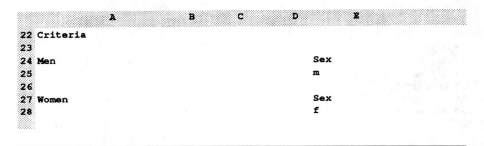

Figure B.11. Setting criteria for database @Functions.

In summary, most of Esmerelda's database calculations will use the argument (SEPTEMBER,"LOSS",MEN) or (SEPTEMBER,"LOSS",WOMEN). For example, @DAVG(SEPTEMBER,"LOSS",MEN) yields the average weight loss for men enrolled in the program during September.

@DAVG

@DAVG(*input, field, criteria*) finds the average of the values in a certain field for all of the records in a database that meet certain conditions—those specified in the criteria range.

Example: Esmerelda's Weight boutique wants to know the average weight loss of its patients for September, broken down by gender. Esmerelda can calculate the average loss for men by entering: @DAVG(SEPTEMBER,"LOSS", MEN). 1-2-3 returns the value 18.57. To calculate the average loss for women, she entered: @DAVG(SEPTEMBER,"LOSS",WOMEN). 1-2-3 returned 11.29.

Men lost an average of 18.57 pounds in September. Women lost an average of 11.29 pounds.

@DCOUNT

@DCOUNT(*input, field, criteria*) counts all the nonblank entries in a particular field of a database that meet certain criteria.

Example: Esmerelda's Weight boutique has already calculated the average weight loss for men and women. Esmerelda wants to count the number of men and women in the program in September. The field doesn't really matter in this case, since there are no blank cells in the database, but Esmerelda selects the LOSS field designating each patient's weight loss. To count the number of men she entered: @DCOUNT(SEPTEMBER,"LOSS",MEN). To count the number of women she entered: @DCOUNT(SEPTEMBER,"LOSS",WOMEN). There were seven men and seven women in the program in September.

@DGET

@DGET(*input, field, criteria*) returns a value or label from a database record that meets certain criteria. If there is more than one record that meets the criteria, @DGET returns an ERR message.

Example: Andrew May, a former patient at Esmerelda's Weight boutique, inquires how much weight he lost in September. Esmerelda uses the same database shown in Figure B.10 to look up the information. The input range is A5..E19, which is assigned the range name SEPTEMBER. The LOSS field is where each patient's weight loss is listed. She creates a criteria range in E48..E49 to find May's record and names it CLIENT.

Now she can find May's record by entering @DGET(SEPTEMBER,"LOSS", CLIENT). May lost 22 pounds in September. To find the record for another patient, Esmerelda can simply change the second line of the criteria range.

@DMAX

@DMAX(*input, field, criteria*) returns the largest value in a field of a database that meets the criteria specified in the criteria range. @DMIN(*input, field, criteria*) returns the smallest value in a field of a database that meets the criteria set up in the criteria range.

Example: Esmerelda's Weight Boutique wants to find the maximum and minimum weight losses for men and women during September.

Esmerelda can use @DMAX and @DMIN to extract the information from her database, as shown in Figure B.12.

	A	B	C	D
51	@DMAX(input,field,criterion)			
52	@DMIN(input,field,criterion)			
53				
54	Maximum loss, men			37
55	@DMAX(SEPTEMBER,"LOSS",MEN)			
56				
57	Minimum loss, men			4
58	@DMIN(SEPTEMBER,"LOSS",MEN)			
59				
60	Maximum loss, women			21
61	@DMAX(SEPTEMBER,"LOSS",WOMEN)			
62				
63	Minimum loss, women			1
64	@DMIN(SEPTEMBER,"LOSS",WOMEN)			

Figure B.12. Using @DMAX and @DMIN with Esmerelda's database. (see Figure B.10)

In September, the men in the program lost 4 to 37 pounds; the women lost 1 to 21.

@DQUERY

@DQUERY(*function,ext-arguments*) is used with Data External commands to send a command to an external database. @DQUERY is used in a criterion range to retrieve records from an external data base. The function argument is the name of a command in the external database. It can be a literal string, enclosed in quotation marks, a reference to a cell that contains a label, or a formula that evaluates to a string. The extension arguments list any arguments required by the external database command.

> Note: @DQUERY recalculates only when you use Data Query Delete; Data Query Extract; Data Query Modify Extract; or Data Query Modify Replace.

How might you use @DQUERY? Imagine you want to make use of an external database function called CENTIGRADE that converts degrees from Fahrenheit to Centigrade. The function requires one argument—the number of degrees to convert. To use the function in 1-2-3, enter +TEMP=@DQUERY ("CENTIGRADE",60) in a criteria range. This will let you extract all entries from the field TEMP in an external table that match the temperature in Centigrade equivalent to 60° Fahrenheit.

@DSTD

@DSTD(*input,field,criteria*) calculates the population standard deviation of a group that meets the criteria. Standard deviation is a measure of the degree to which individuals in a population vary from the average (mean) for the population. @DSTD treats the subgroup that meets the criteria as a population; the calculation is based on the average for the subgroup, *not on the average of the population as a whole*. For example, if you use @STD to segregate males from females in a population, @DSTD measures the degree to which individual males differ from the average for males and the degree to which individual females differ from the average for females. @DSTD produces the most accurate results when the number of observations is large.

Example: Esmerelda's Weight Boutique wants to compare the variation in weight loss for men, with that for women. Using the same worksheet shown in Figure B.10, Esmerelda makes the calculations shown in Figure B.13. Since the standard deviation for men is higher than the standard deviation for women, Esmerelda concludes that there is more variation for men than for women when weight loss is measured in pounds. (Actually, if you make an additional calculation to determine weight loss as a percentage of starting weight, standard deviation of the percentages for men and women turns out to be about the same.)

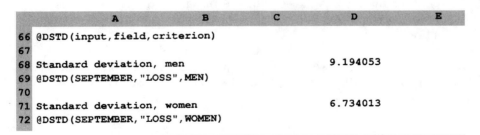

Figure B.13. Esmerelda's Boutique uses @DSTD to calculate the standard deviation of groups within a population.

@DSTDS

@DSTDS(*input,field,criteria*) calculates the sample standard deviation for a population sample that meets the criteria specified in the criteria range. As with @DSTD, the calculation is based on the average for the group within the sample that meets the criteria, not the average for the entire sample.

Example: Suppose that the data shown in Figure B.10 is a random sample of patients at Esmerelda's Weight Boutique, rather than a summary of patients' progress for September. Esmerelda has labeled the database SAMPLE. This allows her to make more general conclusions about her patients. To determine the sample standard deviation for men and women, Esmerelda makes the calculations shown in Figure B.14.

@DSUM

@DSUM(*input,field,criteria*) totals the values in a particular field for all the records in the database that meet the criteria.

Example: Esmerelda's Weight Boutique wants to know the total lost by men and the total by women in September. Using the practice database shown in Figure B.10, Esmerelda calculates the total weight lost by the men by entering: @DSUM(SEPTEMBER,"LOSS",MEN). She calculates the total weight lost by women in September by entering: @DSUM(SEPTEMBER,"LOSS",WOMEN). During the month, seven men lost a total of 130 pounds, and seven women lost a total of 79.

@DVAR

@DVAR(*input,field,criteria*) calculates the variance of the values in a specified field for the records in the database that meet the criteria. This is the subgroup's variance from the average of the subgroup, not from the average for the entire database.

Example: Esmerelda's Weight Boutique wants to determine the variance of weight loss for men and women during September. Using the practice database shown in Figure B.10, Esmerelda makes the calculations shown in Figure B.14.

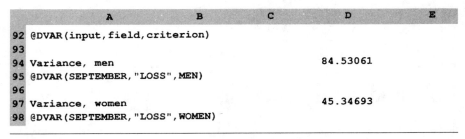

Figure B.14. Calculating variance for Esmerelda's database records that meet certain criteria.

As expected, the variance for men is higher than for women. This means that there was more variation in the number of pounds lost for men than for women.

@DVARS

@DVARS(*input,field,criteria*) calculates the sample variance of the values in a specified field for the records in a database that meet the criteria. Sample variance is a measure of the variation of a subset of a total population, as compared for the average for the subset that meets the criterion.

Example: Suppose Esmerelda's Weight Boutique database, shown in Figure B.10, represents a random sampling of patients, rather than a population census for September, and that Esmerelda has assigned the range name SAMPLE to the database. Using @VARS Esmerelda can calculate the sample variances for men and women as shown in Figure B.15.

```
        A                  B           C           D           E
100 @DVARS(input,field,criterion)
101
102 Sample variance, men                         91.30349
103 @DVARS(SAMPLE,"LOSS",MEN)
104
105 Sample variance, women                       52.90476
106 @DVARS(SAMPLE,"LOSS",WOMEN)
```

Figure B.15. Determining sample variance with @DVARS.

As expected, the sample variance for both groups is slightly higher than the variances calculated with @DVAR.

Date and Time Functions

1-2-3 assigns a serial date number between 1 (January 1, 1900) and 73050 (December 31, 2099) to every date in the 20th and 21st centuries. The program also assigns a time value between 0.000000 (midnight) and 0.999988 (11:59:59 p.m.). The time value is a decimal fraction of a day. Thus, 1:03.15 p.m., April 7, 1990 = 32970.543924, because 32970 is the serial number for the date and 0.543924 is the serial number for the time. Date and time @Functions allow you to manipulate these serial numbers for a variety of useful purposes. The most common application is probably calculating the interval between two dates or times. You could use a date function, for example, to calculate when an invoice is due, given today's date and due date of 30 days. With a time function, you can determine the interval between two times. Before Release 2.0, 1-2-3 offered date functions, but not time functions. Date and time serial numbers do not make much sense by themselves, but the display is easily converted into a more intelligible form with the Range Format command. The options are illustrated in Table B.2. (The same options are available with Worksheet Global Settings Format command.) In all cases, the date/time serial number is 32970.543924, representing 1:03.15 p.m., April 7, 1990.

Format	Example
Date 1 (DD-MMM-YY)	07-Apr-90
Date 2 (DD-MMM)	07-Apr
Date 3 (MMM-YY)	Apr-90
Date 4 (Long Intn'l)	04/07/90
Date 5 (Short Intn'l)	04/07
Time 6 (HH:MM:SS AM/PM)	01:03:15 PM
Time 7 (HH:MM AM/PM)	01:03 PM
Time 8 (Long Intn'l)	13:03:15
Time 9 (Short Intn'l)	13:03

Table B.2. Date and time formats.

Five date formats and four time formats are offered. With Time formats 6 and 7, time is calculated on a 12-hour clock. For the international time options, a 24-hour clock is used. To format a cell to display 07-Apr-90, for example, you would select Range Format 1 (DD-MMM-YY). To format for Short International time select Range Format (Short Intn'l). The following explanation of the time and date @Functions suggests practical applications.

@DATE

@DATE(*year,month,day*) returns the serial date number for the indicated year, month and day argument. If the cell is not assigned a date format, the date will appear as a serial number. If the cell is formatted, the result will appear in the date format selected, such as 17-Jan-91. The argument must meet these specifications:

- year can be any integer between 0 (1900) and 199 (2099).
- month can be any integer between 1 and 12.
- day can be any integer between 1 and 31. However, @DATE returns an ERR message if you enter an invalid date, such as February 31.

Examples : @DATE(91,1,10) = 33248 = 10-Jan-91 (when formatted in the Date 1 format). @DATE is often used to calculate the interval between two dates. For example, if you issue an invoice on January 10, due in 30 days, you can calculate the due date this way: @DATE (91,1,10)+30 = 33278 = 09-Feb-91. You can use a similar technique to calculate the number of days between July 4 and Christmas: @DATE(91,12,25)-@DATE(91,7,4) = 174 days. You can also use @DATE in conjunction with @MOD to calculate the day of the week a certain date falls on. When you divide the serial date number by 7, the remainder (or modulus) will be 0 if the date falls on Saturday, 1 for Sunday, and so on up to 6 for Friday. For example, @MOD(@DATE(91,2,9),7) = 0. February 9, 1991, falls on a Saturday, so you might give your customer in the earlier example until February 11 to pay the invoice.

@DATEVALUE

@DATEVALUE(*string*) returns the serial date number of a label that looks like a date. The label can be a literal string or a formula that evaluates to a string. It must be in one of the date formats listed in Table B.2. @DATEVALUE can be used with information imported from another program, such as a word processor, as well as with 1-2-3 data.

Example: Suppose you have entered '25-Dec-91 in A1 and '4-Jul-91 in B1. (Note the apostrophes designating labels.) To determine the number of days between July 4 and Christmas, you can enter @DATEVALUE(A1)-@DATEVALUE(B1) = 174 days.

@DAY

@DAY(*date number*) converts a serial date number to the day of the month, an integer between 1 and 31.

Examples : Here are three ways @DAY can be used: @DAY(32963) = 31, because 32963 is March 31, 1990; @DAY(@DATEVALUE("25-Dec-91")) = 25; @DAY(@NOW) = 4 if entered on July 4.

@D360

@D360(*start date,end date*) calculates the number of days between two date numbers based on a 360-day calendar (12 months of 30 days each). The 360-day calendar is used by some banks and other businesses for calculating interest, determining when payments are due, and so on. The start and end dates must be in a proper 1-2-3 date format. If the start date comes after the end date, @D360 returns a negative number.

Examples : You deposit $10,000 on September 15. If the bank pays 12% interest, compounded daily on a 360-day basis, how much will be in the account on November 1? First, determine the number of days your money earns interest: @D360(@DATE(91,9,15),@DATE(91,11,1)) = 46 days. Then, determine the daily interest rate: Daily interest rate = 0.10/360 = 0.033333%. Finally, calculate how much you will have: Future value = 10000*(1+0.033333%)^46 = $10,154.49. You can also use @D360 to determine whether invoices are overdue, based on a 360-day calendar. Suppose, for example, you have used @DATE to enter invoice dates in column A. The entry in A5 is @DATE(91,10,11).

You can use this formula to determine whether the invoice has been outstanding for more than 30 days: IF(@D360(A5,@TODAY)=30,"Overdue",""). If the invoice has been outstanding for more than 30 days, the formula returns Overdue. If not, it returns a blank.

@HOUR

@HOUR(*time number*) converts a serial time number to an hour, based on a 24-hour clock. A serial time number can be any value between 0.000000 (midnight) and 0.999988 (11:59:59 p.m.). Usually, the time number is supplied by another time @Function, such as @TIME or @NOW. @HOUR ignores numbers to the left of the decimal, which are reserved for date serial numbers.

@HOUR might be useful, for example, to calculate the frequency of transactions by hour. If a bank has a record of the times of transactions, for example, it might want to break the results down by hour to determine how many tellers to have on hand during various periods of the day.

Examples: @HOUR(@TIME(15,33,22)) = 15, because 15,33,22 represents 3:33:22 p.m., which falls in the 15th hour on a 24-hour clock. @HOUR (0.648171) also returns 15, because the decimal in the argument is the time serial number for 3:33:22 p.m. @HOUR(@NOW) returns the current hour.

@MINUTE

@MINUTE(*time number*) extracts the minute after the hour from a time serial number. Usually, the time number is supplied by another time @Function.

Examples: @MINUTE(@TIME(15,33,22)) = 33, because 15,33,22 represents 3:33:22 p.m. @MINUTE(0.648171) also returns 33, because the decimal in the argument is the time serial number for 3:33:22 p.m. @MINUTE(@NOW) returns the current minute.

@MONTH

@MONTH(*date number*) calculates the month from a serial date number, which is usually supplied by another Date @Function. The result can be any integer from 1 (January) to 12 (December).

Examples: @MONTH(32963) = 3, because 32963 is March 31, 1990. @MONTH(@DATEVALUE("25-Dec-91")) = 12. @MONTH(@NOW) = 7 if entered anytime in July.

@NOW

@NOW, which uses no argument, returns the current date and time serial number from your computer's clock. You can display the result in any of the date and time formats. @NOW is often used in conjunction with other date and time functions. It is important to remember that @NOW recalculates every time you recalculate your worksheet. If you have set calculation to Automatic, @NOW recalculates every time you enter a new value. In some situations, obviously, this will wreak havoc with your worksheet. You can use Edit Quick Copy and then the Convert to Values box to convert @NOW to a pure value and end the recalculations. You should do this immediately after entering a formula containing @NOW. Otherwise, @NOW may continue to recalculate when you don't intend for it to, and you may not be able to recover the original result.

Example: At 11:45:40 a.m. on March 30, 1990, you entered @NOW and froze the value with Edit Quick Copy with the Convert to Values option selected. The display depends on the cell format. Examples are provided in Table B.3. Regardless of the format, however, 1-2-3 continues to make calculations based on the full date and time serial number.

Format,	Result
General	32963.490046
6 (HH:MM:SS AM/PM)	11:45:40 AM
1 (DD-MMM-YY)	31-Mar-90

Table B.3. Sample displays for the display of @NOW.

@SECOND

@SECOND(*time number*) returns an integer from 0 to 59, indicating the seconds portion of a date-time number. The time number is usually provided by another time and date function.

Examples: @SECOND(@TIME(11,45,40)) = 40, because 40 is the seconds portion of the time argument 11,45,40. @SECOND(0.6455) = 31, because 0.6455 is the time number for 2:29:31 p.m.

@TIME

@TIME(*hour,minutes,seconds*) returns the time number, based on a 24-hour clock for the specified hour, minutes, and seconds. This function is often used to calculate elapsed time. Hours can be any integer between 0 (midnight) and 23 (11 p.m.). Minutes and seconds can be any integer between 0 and 59.

If the cell containing the formula is assigned the general format, the result will be a decimal between 0.000000 (midnight) and 0.999988 (11:59:59 p.m.). Note that these values represent a decimal fraction of a day. Thus, to convert elapsed time to hours, you must multiply by 24. Use the Range Format menu to display the result in a more intelligible format, such as 11:45:40 AM.

Example: An attorney works on a case from 9:30 a.m. to 11:45 a.m. How much is the bill if he or she charges $100 an hour?

Answer: To solve this problem, you must subtract the starting time number from the ending time number, multiply by 24 (to convert the time number to hours), and then multiply by $100 to determine the total bill: @TIME(11,45,0)-@TIME(9,30,0))*24*10 0 = $225.

If you simply want to display the elapsed time, however, the multiplication is not necessary: @TIME(11,45,0)-@TIME(9,30,0) = 0.1783.

This seemingly unintelligible number is actually a fraction of a 24-hour day. You can use the Range Format menu to convert it to a much more readable form: 02:15:00. However, the underlying value is still expressed as a fraction of a day, not as 2 hours and 15 minutes or 2.25 hours. Thus, further calculations can yield unexpected results if you do not fully understand the date and time functions.

@TIMEVALUE

@TIMEVALUE(*string*) converts a label that looks like a time into a serial time number so that you can use it in calculations. The string can be a literal string enclosed in quotation marks, a reference to a cell that contains a label, or a formula that evaluates to a string.

Example: @TIMEVALUE("11:45:00 AM") = 0.48958 in General format.

@TODAY

@TODAY returns the date number for the current date according to the computer's clock. In a format assigned a General format, it will be a number between 1 (January 1, 1900) and 73050 (December 31, 2099). If you have assigned a Date format to the cell, the result will be displayed in a more familiar form at, such as 31-Mar-90. Use @TODAY rather than @NOW when you only need to calculate with today's date as opposed to today's date and time.

@YEAR

@YEAR(*date number*) returns a two- or three-digit number representing the year indicated by a date number. (To convert an @YEAR calculation to a four-digit year, add 1900.) For example, a date number that falls in 1991 returns the value 91. A date number that falls in 2025, returns 125. The date number is usually supplied by another date function.

   Examples: @YEAR(33597) = 91, because 33597 is the date number for December 25, 1991. @YEAR(@DATE(91,12,25)) = 91, because the @DATE function also returns the date number for December 25, 1991. @YEAR(@TODAY) or @YEAR(@NOW) = the current year. @YEAR(33597)+1900 = 1991 and @YEAR(@DATE(125,12,25))+1900 = 2025 show how an @YEAR calculation can be changed to a four-digit year.

Logical Functions

Logical @Functions allow you to write conditional formulas and macros. The most common and useful logical @function is @IF. This function allows you to make one calculation if a condition is true and another if it is false. Most of the other logic functions basically test for certain conditions and are useful mainly in macros and complex formulas.

@FALSE

@FALSE returns the logical value 0 (false). @FALSE can be used in any logic calculation, but it is most often used in macros or in conjunction with other @Functions such as @IF or @CHOOSE. @FALSE takes no argument.

   Example: The formula @IF(E15>>1000,@TRUE,@FALSE) returns a 1 if the value in E15 is greater than 1,000, a 0 if it is not. You would get the same result if you entered @IF(E15>1000,1,0), but @TRUE and @FALSE make it clearer what the calculation means.

@IF

@IF(*condition,x,y*) returns x if the condition evaluates to true, y if it evaluates to false. The condition is usually a logical formula using the operators: =, <, >, <=, >=, <>, #AND#, #OR#, and #NOT#. 1-2-3 evaluates any condition that does not equal 0 (*zero*) as True and any condition that does not equal 0 as False. (Blank cells, text, ERR, and NA all equal 0 when used as a condition.)

Example: @IF(A5>10000,A5,0) returns the value in A5 if it is greater than 10,000; the formula returns 0 if the value in A5 is less than or equal to 10,000.

@IF(A5>10000#AND#B5<=5,A5*B5,@ERR) returns +A5*B5 if the value in A5 is greater than 10,000 and the value in B5 is less than or equal to 5. If either of the conditions is false, the formula returns an ERR message.

Within the argument for @IF, *x* and *y* can also be conditions. This is called nesting. Suppose, for example, that you are grading students' papers. Scores above 90 rate an A, scores above 80 rate a B, and scores above 70 rate a C. If a student's score is assigned the range name SCORE, you can use this formula to determine the grade: @IF(SCORE>=90,"A",@IF(SCORE>=80,"B",@IF(SCORE>=70,"C","Needs Work"))).

	A	B	C
1	Score	Grade	Calculations
2	85	+C2	@IF(SCORE>=90,"A",C3)
3			@IF(SCORE>=80,"B",C4)
4			@IF(SCORE>=70,"C","Needs Work")

Figure B.16. Breaking an @IF formula into its components.

This formula returns A if SCORE is greater than or equal to 90, B if SCORE is less than 90 but greater than or equal to 80, C if SCORE is greater less than 80 but greater than or equal to 70, and Needs Work if SCORE is less than 70. This formula is not hard to understand if you break it down into its components:

1. First the formula determines whether SCORE is greater than or equal to 90. If it is, it returns A. If not, it evaluates the next condition.

2. If SCORE is greater than or equal to 80, the formula returns B. If not, it moves to the next condition.

3. If SCORE is greater than 70, the formula returns C. If not, it returns Needs Work.

You can build quite elaborate formulas this way. However, it is often easier to break down conditional calculations into separate cells. Figure B.17 shows the same calculation. The result is the same, but the formulas are easier to follow.

@ISAAF

@ISAAF(*function name*) tests whether an add-in @Function is available. The function returns 1 (true) if the function is available, or a 0 (false) if it is not. @ISAAF is used in macros to branch to an error message or to a command to attach an add-in program if the function is not available. The function name can be a literal string, enclosed in quotation marks, a reference to a cell that contains a label, or a formula that evaluates to a string. Do *not* include the @ sign in the function name. For example, if you have an tax add-in program that includes the function @MRATE to calculate your marginal tax rate, you would enter @ISAAF("MRATE"), not @ISAAF("@MRATE").

Note: @ISAAF returns a 0 (false) if you ask for a regular @Function such as @SUM, because the 1-2-3 functions are not add-ins.

@ISAPP

@ISAPP(*name*) is used in macros to determine whether the named add-in program is attached (or currently in memory). If it is not, you can branch to an error message or to an attach command. @ISAPP returns 1 (true) if the named add-in is attached, or 0 (false) if it is not.

The *name* in the argument is the file name of the add-in program, enclosed in quotation marks *without* a file extension. The name can be a literal string, enclosed in quotation marks, a reference to a cell that contains a label, or a formula that evaluates to a string. For example, to test whether an add-in named Invoice is attached, you would enter @ISAPP("INVOICE").

Note: @ISAAP can identify only add-ins that you can load using Tools Add-in Load. It cannot recognize add-ins that contain only @Functions. In addition, some add-ins contain several files that have different names than the add-in itself. For example, an add-in called Finance might actually consist of files called LEASES.ADN and LOANS.ADN. In that case, you would have to test for LEASES and LOANS separately.

@ISERR

When a calculation returns an ERR message, the result ripples through the worksheet, so that all cells that are dependent on the original calculation also return ERR messages. You can use @ISERR to block this ripple effect or to set a condition for a branch command in a macro.

@ISERR(x) returns 1 (true) if x is the value ERR; otherwise it returns 0 (false). It is often used to eliminate ERR messages resulting from division by 0.

Example: You want to divide the value in E5 by the value in E6, then use the result in further calculations. If the value in E6 is 0, +E5/E6 returns an ERR message. However, if you replace E5/E6 with @IF(ISERR(E5/E6),0,E5/E6), the formula will return 0 if E6 is 0, or the result of the division if E6 is any other value. This way you can avoid getting ERR messages from any other formulas that depend on this calculation.

@ISNA

Like ERR messages, the effect of NA (not available) messages ripples through your worksheet. Any formula or cell reference that refers to a cell that returns NA also returns NA. See the discussion of @NA for how this can be useful. However, ERR messages we know can crop up for many reasons; NA will not appear unless you have entered @NA or a formula that evaluates to @NA. Thus, NA messages are less likely than ERR messages to turn up in unexpected places.

Nevertheless, if you need to test for NA messages, in either a formula or a macro, you must use @ISNA. @ISNA(x) returns 1 (true) if x is an NA message; otherwise, it returns 0 (false). A simple logical condition, such as E10=@NA will always evaluate to NA.

Example: @IF(@ISNA(E5),0,E5) returns 0 if E5 contains NA, or the contents of E5 if it does not.

@ISNUMBER

@ISNUMBER(x) determines whether x is a value. If x is a number or a blank, @ISNUMBER returns 1 (true). If x is a label or other string, the function returns 0 (false). @ISNUMBER is primarily used in macros to ensure that data referred to by a formula are of the appropriate type, but it can be used in any logical function.

Example: In A36, you enter @IF(@ISNUMBER(A35),A35,@ERR). If A35 contains a value, the formula returns that value. If A35 is blank, the formula returns 0. If A35 contains a label or other string, the formula returns ERR.

@ISRANGE

If you enter a formula that contains an invalid range address or range name, 1-2-3 returns an ERR message. @ISRANGE(*range*) is used to avoid errors in formulas caused by an incorrect range name. The function tests to determine whether the argument range is a valid range name or address. If it is, the function returns 1 (true); if not, it returns 0 (false). @ISRANGE is most naturally used in a logical formula, such as one using @IF function.

Examples: @ISRANGE(ZZ1..ZZ10) returns a 0, because ZZ is not a valid column address. @ISRANGE(TAX) returns a 1 if you have assigned the range name TAX to a range on your worksheet; otherwise it returns 0. Note that you should *not* enclose your range name argument in quotes, or precede the range address with the plus (+) sign.

If you are making a reference to a different worksheet, an @ISRANGE function might look like this: @ISRANGE(<<TAXES_90.WK3>>TAX). This formula will return a 1 if the worksheet named TAXES_90.WK3 includes a range named TAX; otherwise, it returns 0. @IF(@ISRANGE(TAX),@SUM(TAX), "Calculate") returns the total for the range named TAX if that is a valid range; otherwise, it returns Calculate, advising you that you must calculate your taxes by another method.

@ISSTRING

@ISSTRING(x) determines whether x is a label or text string. If x is a number ERR, NA, or a blank @ISSTRING returns 0 (false). If x is a label or a cell that contains a label, the function returns 1 (true). @ISSTRING is usually used in macros to ensure that data referred to by a formula are of the right kind, but it can be used in any logical formula.

Example: In A36, you enter @IF(@ISSTRING(A35),A35,@ERR). If the entry in A35 is a label or other string, the formula returns that string. If A35 contains a value or is blank, the formula returns ERR.

@TRUE

@TRUE returns the logical value 1 (true). @TRUE can be used in any logical formula, but it is most often used in macros or in combination with @Functions such as @IF or @CHOOSE.

Example: The formula @IF(E15>1000,@TRUE,@FALSE) returns a 1 if the value in E15 is greater than 1,000, a 0 if it is not. You would get the same result if you entered @IF(E15 1000,1,0), but @TRUE and @FALSE make it clearer what the calculation means.

String Functions

String functions allow you to manipulate strings within your worksheet. Generally, a string is a label; that is, any entry that is not a value. A string can be any text, including letters, numbers, punctuation marks, and special characters. If used directly in a formula or macro, the string must be enclosed in quotation marks. A string can also be a reference to a cell that contains a label, or a formula or @Function that evaluates to a string.

@CHAR

@CHAR(x) generates the character numbered x in the Lotus Multibyte Character Set (LMBCS). x can be any valid LMBCS code. Values outside of the range result in ERR messages. The LMBCS codes are listed in the appendix of your manual.

Examples: The English pound sign (£) is character 156, so you can generate this character by entering @CHAR(156).

You can also generate extended strings. To get £100, for example, you would enter @CHAR(156)&"100". Note that the string must be enclosed in quotation marks. In addition, the @CHAR function must be in the form of a formula. Thus, to use @CHAR to create a string that begins with a label, you must make the entry in this format: +"*label*"@CHAR(x).

@CODE

@CODE(*string*) returns the LMBCS code for the first character of a string. The string can be a literal string, enclosed in quotation marks, or the range name or address of a cell containing a label. It can also be a formula or an @Function that evaluates to a string.

Examples: @CODE("d") returns 100, the code for lowercase d. @CODE ("Lotus 1-2-3") returns 76, the code for an uppercase L.

See the appendix of your manual for more information on the Lotus Multibyte Character Set.

@FIND

@FIND(*search string,string,start number*) finds the position of the search string in a string. It begins the search at the position indicated by the start number. This function is most useful when used in conjunction with @LEFT, @MID, @REPLACE, or @RIGHT.

The *search string* and the *string* can be a literal string, enclosed in quotation marks, a reference to a cell that contains a label, or a formula that evaluates to a string. @FIND is case sensitive, which means that uppercase and lowercase letters are not interchangeable. If you ask @FIND to search for an "f", it will bypass "F".

The *start number* is the offset at which you want @FIND to begin counting. It is important to note that the offset for the first character in a string is 0. In the string William Faulkner, for example, W is start number 0, i is 1, the first l is 2, and so on.

Examples: @FIND("F","William Faulkner",0) = 8 because F occupies the 8th position in the string, starting with W as position 0. @FIND("f","William Faulkner",0) = ERR, however, because there are no lowercase f's in William Faulkner.

If you have entered William Faulkner in A1, you can use @MID and @FIND to extract the author's last name with this formula: @MID(A1,@FIND(" ",A1,0)+1,100) = Faulkner. This formula locates the space (" ") at offset 7, adds 1, taking you to the F in Faulkner, then returns the remainder of the string. See the entry under @MID for details.

@LEFT

@LEFT(*string,n*) extracts the left *n* characters from a string. The string can be a literal string (enclosed in quotation marks), the range name or address of a cell that contains a label, or a formula that evaluates to a string.

Example: @LEFT("ANTIDISESTABLISHMENTARIANISM",4) = ANTI.

@LEFT is most useful in combination with formulas or other functions. You may wish to combine the first three letters of a customer's last name with a Zip code to create an account number. If the entry in A4 is Abrams, Ann and the entry in D4 is the Zip code '019156, then @LEFT(A4,3)&D4 returns Abr019156. (Note that the Zip code must be entered as a label.)

@LEFT can also be usefully combined with other @Functions such as @VLOOKUP and criteria ranges for database statistical functions.

@LENGTH

@LENGTH(*string*) calculates the number of characters in a string, including spaces and punctuation. The *string* may be a literal string (enclosed in quotation marks) or the range name or address of a cell containing a label. It can also be a formula that evaluates to a string.
   Example: @LENGTH("ANTIDISESTABLISHMENTARIANISM") = 31.

@LOWER

@LOWER(*string*) converts a string to lowercase letters. Punctuation and numbers are not affected.
   Example: @LOWER("Joe's Bar & Grill #2") = joe's bar & grill #2.

@MID

@MID(*string,start number,n*) returns *n* characters in a string, beginning with the start number. The *string* can be a literal string, enclosed in quotation marks; a reference to a cell that contains a label; or a formula that evaluates to a string.
   The start number is the number of characters to the right occupied by the first character you want @MID to return. It is important to note that the first character in the string is 0, rather than 1. For example in the string TEST, T is position 0, E is 1, and S is 2.
   If you want to extract the end of a string but don't know exactly how many characters follow the start number, use a large number for *n*. @MID will return the remainder of the string. If you enter 0 for *n*, @MID returns an empty string.
   Examples: @MID("Joe's Bar & Grill",6,3) = Bar. @MID("Joe's Bar & Grill",6,100) = Bar & Grill.
   @MID can be used with @FIND to locate part of a string to the right of a particular character. Suppose, for example, that the cell A1 contains the string William Faulkner. You can use this formula to return the author's last name: @MID(A1,@FIND(" ",A1,0)+1,100), where A1 identifies the cell containing the string William Faulkner; @FIND sets up the function to find the first occurrence of a search string; " " tells @FIND to locate the first blank space in the string; +1 adds 1 to the result to move to the first character of the last name; 0

instructs @FIND to begin counting at offset 0 (i.e., the W in William); and 100 is a large number, so that @MID will return Faulkner's entire last name.

@N

@N(*range*) returns the first value in a range. If the first cell in the range contains a value, @N returns that value. @N returns a 0 if the first cell in the range contains a label, a blank or a 0. If the first-cell entry is @NA or @ERR, @N returns NA or ERR, respectively. @N is used primarily for error trapping in macros, to ensure that the range contains the appropriate type of data.

Example: The range D2..E2 contains the entries Smith and 100. @N(D2..E2) returns 0. The formula +600+@N(F6..H9) returns the value 700 if cell F6 contains the value 100.

@PROPER

@PROPER(*string*) converts the first letter of each word in a string to uppercase and all others to lower case. Numbers and punctuation marks are not affected, although punctuation can yield unexpected results. The string can be any literal string (enclosed in quotation marks). It can also be the range name or address of a cell that contains a label, or a formula, or an @Function that evaluates to a string.

Example: If cell A26 contains the label "*joe's bar & grill*" @PROPER(A26) yields Joe'S Bar & Grill. The S in Joe's is capitalized because @PROPER takes it to be the beginning of a new word.

@REPEAT

@REPEAT(*string,n*) duplicates a string *n* times. The string can be a literal string (in quotation marks). It can also be a cell that contains a label, or a formula, or an @Function that evaluates to a string. *n* can be any positive integer.

Examples: @REPEAT("Test ",5) yields Test Test Test Test Test. (Be sure to include the space within the quotation marks, or you will get TestTestTest TestTest.) REPEAT("=",10) yields ==========.

> Note: @REPEAT differs from the backslash (\) repeat command. The backslash repeats a character or string until the current cell is filled. @REPEAT generates the specified number of repetitions, regardless of column width.

@REPLACE

@REPLACE(*old string,start,n,new string*) removes *n* characters from the old string, beginning at start, and replaces them with a new string.

Old string can be a literal string, enclosed in quotation marks; a reference to a cell that contains a label; or a formula that evaluates to a string. The start number is the offset at which you wish to remove *n* characters. The left character of a string is offset 0. The new string is the string you want to insert.

Example: @REPLACE("William Faulkner",8,8,"Shakespeare") yields William Shakespeare. The replacement begins with offset 8, occupied by the F in Faulkner, and the eight characters in Faulkner are removed. The string Shakespeare is substituted in their place.

> Note: You can use @FIND to locate the start character.

@RIGHT

@RIGHT(*string,n*) returns the last *n* characters in the string.
Example: @RIGHT("University of Texas",5) = Texas.

@S

@S(*range*) returns the label in the first cell of a range. If the first cell in the range is blank or contains a value, @S returns an empty string. If the first cell in the range contains @NA or @ERR, @S returns NA or ERR, respectively. @S is used primarily for error trapping in macros, to make sure that a range contains the appropriate type of data.

Example: If the range D4..D5 contains the values 1 and 2, @S(D4..D5) returns a blank. If D4 contains the label Texas, @S returns Texas.

@STRING

@STRING(*x,n*) converts a value to a string with *n* decimal places, converting the value into a label.

Example: @STRING(987.654789,2) = 987.65. Also 2+@STRING(2,0) = 2 because the value of a string is 0. @STRING is useful when you need to incorporate a cell value in a string of text. If you had a dollar amount due in cell A5—say $697.95, you could enter this text formula: +"You currently owe $"&@STRING(A5,2)&"." to return: You currently owe $697.95.

Note that *@STRING* ignores any formatting characters such as currency symbols, etc. that 1-2-3 uses to display *X*.

@TRIM

@TRIM(*string*) removes extraneous spaces from a string. These include leading, trailing, and double spaces.

Example: @TRIM(" Joe's Bar & Grill ") = Joe's Bar & Grill.

@UPPER

@UPPER(*string*) converts all letters in a string to uppercase. Punctuation and numbers are unaffected.

Example: @UPPER("Joe's Bar & Grill #2") = JOE'S BAR & GRILL #2.

@VALUE

@VALUE(*string*) converts a string that looks like a value to its numerical value. You cannot include operators within the string. The string can be text in quotation marks or a label that contains only numbers.

Examples: @VALUE("26.75") = 26.75; @VALUE("$1.89") = 1.89; @VALUE ("15%") = 0.15; 2*@VALUE("26.75") = 53.5; @VALUE ("$2.95") = 2.95; @VALUE ("45 3/4") = 45.75; and @VALUE("2")+@VALUE ("2") = 4. However, @VALUE("2+2") = ERR, because it contains a non-numeric character.

Special Functions

Special functions serve a variety of purposes. @HLOOKUP and @VLOOKUP are extremely useful for extracting information from a table. Most of the special functions are used in macros to check on various conditions.

@@

@@(*location*) lets you indirectly obtain the contents of the cell specified in the location argument. This cell acts as a pointer, identifying *another* cell or range address. This pointer cell is an address entered as a label (e.g., A1, *not* the formula +A1) or a range name. @@(location) looks to the pointer cell label and then actually returns the *contents* of the cell or range identified by the pointer cell.

Example: Esmerelda's Weight Boutique has run up the worksheet shown in Figure B.17. The actual losses for women and men are shown in columns E and F. Esmerelda has assigned the range name WOMEN to E8..E14 and the range name MEN to F8..F14. These range names have also been entered as labels in B7..B10.

	A	B	C	D	E	F
1						
2		Esmerelda's Weight Boutique				
3		September Group				
4						
5	Calculation	Sex	Result		Women	Men
6	==============	=====	======		=====	===
7	@AVG(@@(B7))	Women	14			
8	@AVG(@@(B8))	Men	16		10	22
9	@AVG(B9)	Women	0		14	22
10	@AVG(B10)	Men	0		22	3
11					19	14
12					1	16
13					11	19
14					21	16

Figure B.17. Using @@ within formulas.

In A7, the formula @AVG(@@(B7)) looks to the label in B7 and returns the correct average for the range WOMEN. In A9, however, the formula @AVG(B9) returns 0, because, without the @@ function, the label Women in B7 evaluates to 0. The same applies to MEN.

@CELL

@CELL("*attribute*",*location*) returns information about the specified attribute of the first cell in the location specified. The nature of the information depends on which attribute you specify. You can use this in macros with other functions—usually @IF—to determine whether the target cell meets certain criteria. Table B.4 shows the attributes @CELL accepts.

Example: {IF@CELL("type";PROFIT)="b"}{BEEP}{QUIT} causes a beep and terminates the macro if the first cell of the range named PROFIT is blank.

Attribute	Result
"address"	Absolute cell address in abbreviated form (column letter and row number only).
"col"	Column number as a value, from 1 to 256 (e.g., 1 for column A, 5 for column E, and so on).
"color"	Returns 1 if the cell is formatted for negative numbers in color, and 0 if it is not.
"contents"	Contents of the cell.
"coord"	Returns absolute cell address, including worksheet letter, column letter, and row number.
"filename"	The name of the file that includes the cell, including the path.
"format"	Returns the cell format, with 0 to 15 decimal places as follows:
	C## Currency
	F## Fixed
	G General
	P## Percent
	S## Scientific notation
	,## Commas
	+/- Format
	D1-D9 Date formats
	T Text
	H, Hidden
	L Label
	A Automatic
	- Color for negative numbers
	() Parentheses

Table B.4. Attribute arguments for @CELL and @CELLPOINTER. *(continued)*

Attribute	Result *(continued)*
"parentheses"	Returns 1 if the cell is formatted for parentheses, and 0 if it is not.
"prefix"	Returns the leading symbol for the following cell formats:
	' Left-aligned label
	" Right-aligned label
	^ Centered label
	\\ Repeating label
		Nonprinting label
	No symbol if the cell is empty or contains a value.
"protect"	Returns 1 if the cell is protected, and 0 if it is not.
"row"	Returns the row number, from 1 to 8192.
"sheet"	Returns the worksheet letter as a number (1 for worksheet A, 2 for worksheet B, and so on).
"type"	Returns the type of data in the cell as follows:
b	blank cell
v	value
l	label
"width"	Returns the column width.

Table B.4. Attribute arguments for @CELL and @CELLPOINTER.

@CELLPOINTER

@CELLPOINTER("*attribute*") works exactly like @CELL, except that it returns information about the current cell instead of information about the cell at the address in the @CELL argument. "attribute" can be any of the arguments listed in Table B.4. The argument must be enclosed in quotation marks.

Example: {IF@CELLPOINTER("type")="b"}{BEEP}{QUIT} causes a beep and terminates the macro if the current cell is blank.

@CHOOSE

@CHOOSE(*n,list*) selects the nth item in a list. The first item in the list is number 0, so the second item is 1, the third is 2, and so on. The items in the list must be separated by commas, and they can be any combination of values, strings, and range references that return a value or a string. Unlike many other @Functions, however, @CHOOSE will not accept a simple range reference as a list.

Example: Figure B.18 shows a table of stock numbers, items, and prices. @CHOOSE(A4-1000,C3,C4,C5,C6) = 3.95. A4 is the stock number for hammers, 1001. That value minus 1000 = 1. Thus, @CHOOSE moves down one row and selects 3.95 in C5, which is the price of hammers, because C3 is offset 0, C4 is offset 1, and C5 is offset 2, and so on.

	A	B	C
1			
2	Stock #	Item	Price
3	1000	Mallets	10.95
4	1001	Widgets	3.95
5	1002	Chisels	5.95
6	1003	Screwdrivers	4.95
7			
8	@CHOOSE(A4-1000,C3,C4,C5,C6) =		3.95

Figure B.18. Using @CHOOSE to select an entry from a list.

> Note that while the argument (A4,C3..C6) would work in most @Functions calling for a list or range, @CHOOSE will not accept it.

@COLS

@COLS(*range*) counts the number of columns in a range. Range can be a range address or a range name. @COLS can be useful for determining the size of a range you want to print, for example: you might also use @COLS as a stop value in a {FOR} loop macro—one that repeats the same action on a series of columns.

Example: @COLS(A1..E6) returns 5. If A1..E6 is named TABLE, @COLS (TABLE) yields the same result.

@COORD

@COORD(*worksheet,column,row,absolute*) builds a cell address from the values in the argument. *Worksheet* and *column* can be any integers between 1 and 256; 1 represents worksheet A or column A, 2 represents B, and so on. *Row* can be any row number from 1 to 8,192.

The *absolute* argument, an integer from 1 to 8, determines which references within the argument are absolute and which are relative, as shown in Table B.5.

Value	Worksheet	Column	Row	Example
1	Absolute	Absolute	Absolute	$A:$A$1
2	Absolute	Relative	Absolute	$A:A$1
3	Absolute	Absolute	Relative	$A:$A1
4	Absolute	Relative	Relative	$A:A1
5	Relative	Absolute	Absolute	A:$A$1
6	Relative	Relative	Absolute	A:A$1
7	Relative	Absolute	Relative	A:$A1
8	Relative	Relative	Relative	A:A1

Table B.5. The effect of absolute arguments in @COORD.

@COORD is not very useful by itself, since it would be easier just to enter the cell address directly. However, in the argument you can use cell addresses and functions, such as @INDEX, @HLOOKUP, and @VLOOKUP, to determine the values from worksheet tables. Used in conjunction with @@ you can find the value in the cell address created by @COORD.

Examples: @COORD(3,2,10,1) = $C:$B$10 and @COORD(3,2,10,4) = $C:B10.

@ERR

@ERR is seldom used alone, but it is useful for error trapping, particularly in logic functions. For example, the formula @IF(B2>100,@ERR,B2) will return an ERR message if the value in B2 is more than 100 or the value of B2 if the value is 100 or less. The advantage is that @ERR ripples through your worksheet calculations, and an ERR message will appear in any cells that depend on the erroneous calculation.

Be aware of the difference between the label ERR and the value ERR in formulas. If you enter @ERR in cell B3, the formula +B3+92 evaluates to ERR. If you enter the label ERR in Cell B3, the same formula evaluates to 92, since the label is treated as a 0 (zero).

@EXACT

@EXACT(*string1,string2*) determines whether the two strings match exactly. The strings can be literal strings (as in our example), references to cells that contain labels, or formulas that evaluate to strings. If the strings do not match exactly, @EXACT returns 0 (false); if the strings do match, it returns 1 (True). @EXACT is more precise than the logical operator =, because it distinguishes between uppercase and lowercase letters. It also counts leading, trailing, and double spaces, as well as accents. @EXACT is often used to compare user input strings with valid responses.

Examples: @EXACT("Joe's Bar & Grill","Joe's Bar & Grill") = 1. However, @EXACT("Joe's Bar & Grill","joe's bar & grill") = 0.

@HLOOKUP

@HLOOKUP(*x,range,row offset*) looks up a value x, in a horizontal lookup table—a range with a top row consisting of values in ascending order, or labels in any order. The operation of @HLOOKUP is similar to that of @VLOOKUP, except that @HLOOKUP searches across the top row of the lookup table, while @VLOOKUP searches down the left column. A simple example is provided in the entry under @VLOOKUP. The example here suggests a practical application.

@HLOOKUP compares x to each cell in the top row of the table. When 1-2-3 locates a cell in the top row that contains x, it moves *down* that column according to the number of rows specified by the row offset and returns the contents of that cell as the answer. If the top row of the lookup table contains values, x can be greater than or equal to the first value in the table's top row. If x is smaller than the first value @HLOOKUP returns ERR. If x is larger than the last value in the top row of the lookup table, @HLOOKUP stops at the last cell in the row specified by the row offset number, and returns the contents of that row as the answer. If the top row of the lookup table contains labels, x can be a literal string enclosed in quotation marks, a reference to a cell that contains a label, or a formula that evaluates to a string. If x does not exactly match the contents of a cell in the top row of the lookup table, @HLOOKUP returns ERR.

Example: Porky's Pig Farm can use @HLOOKUP to calculate depreciation under the Modified Accelerated Cost Recovery System (MACRS) as shown in Figure B.19. The MACRS depreciation schedule for property depreciated under the half-year rule, provided by the IRS, is shown below the double line. MACRS divides most equipment into classes with lives of three, five, or seven years, as indicated by the entries in C12..E12. The depreciation for each class for each year is listed below. The range C12..E20 has been assigned the range name MACRS.

	A	B	C	D	E
1					
2	1990 MACRS Depreciation for Porky's Pig Farm				
3					
4	Item	Cost	Class	Year	Dep
5	Computer	10,000.00	5	2	3,200.00
6	Refrigerator	795.00	7	3	139.05
7	Farrowing eqpt.	32,500.00	3	2	14,446.25
8	Truck	15,250.00	5	7	0.00
9					
10	Total				7,358.55
11	==				
12		Year	3	5	7
13		1	33.33%	20.00%	14.29%
14		2	44.45%	32.00%	24.49%
15		3	14.81%	19.20%	17.49%
16		4	7.41%	11.52%	12.49%
17		5	0	11.52%	8.93%
18		6	0	5.76%	8.92%
19		7	0	0	8.93%
20		8	0	0	4.46%

Figure B.19. Calculating MACRS depreciation with @HLOOKUP.

Above the double line, depreciable assets are listed in column A, original cost is listed in column B, MACRS class (or life) is in column C, and the year for which depreciation is being calculated is listed in column D. Under MACRS, most equipment and light vehicles are classified as five-year property, so 5 is entered under Class for the computer and truck. Furnishings, including refrigerators, are depreciated over seven years, and certain equipment, including equipment used for hog breeding, is depreciated over three years. The entries for these items are made accordingly.

With this information in place, Porky's can use a simple @HLOOKUP formula to calculate the depreciation for each item. The formula in E5, depreciation for the computer, is +B5*@HLOOKUP(C5,$MACRS,D5). The formula breaks down like this:

+B5* recalls the cost of the computer, listed in B5, and sets up the multiplication by the rest of the formula

@HLOOKUP sets up the @HLOOKUP function.

C5 recalls the class from column C, in this case 5, because the computer is a five-year property; this is the value x we want to look up in the tables.

$MACRS is an absolute reference to the lookup table; the absolute reference allows you to copy the formula down column E; this is the range.

D5 recalls the depreciation year from column D, in this case year 2; this is the row offset.

Thus, the @HLOOKUP formula looks across the top row of the lookup table (MACRS) until it finds 5 (the class), drops down two rows (year), and returns 32.00%. This value is multiplied by the cost: 10,000*32.00% = 3,200.00.

You can copy the formula in E5 down column E, because the references to class and year are relative, but the reference to the lookup table ($MACRS) is absolute. The formula for the truck, now in its seventh year, returns 0, because the truck has aged out of the depreciation schedule.

@INDEX

@INDEX(*range,column offset,row offset,worksheet offset*) returns the value or label from the cell identified by the column, row, and worksheet offsets. The *range* is a range name or address that specifies the lookup range. The *column offset* is the number of columns to the right from which @INDEX retrieves an entry. The row offset is the number of rows down. As usual, the left column and top row of the range are 0. A column offset of 1 returns the entry from the second column, and so on.

Sometimes databases or tables do not lend themselves to using @HLOOKUP or @VLOOKUP. The first row and/or column, for example, may not contain values in ascending order. In these cases, you can use @INDEX to specify a column and row offset independently of the values and labels in the table. You can also use formulas to determine the offsets, based on calculations that are independent of the table.

Example: Esmerelda's Weight Boutique has set up a database that ranks its women and men patients for September by the amount of weight each has lost. Now Esmerelda can use @INDEX to extract the names and weights of the top losers, as shown in Figure B.20. She has assigned the range name WOMEN to

A13..E20 and the range name MEN to A23..E30. Note that the range names include the table headings Women and Men, so that the row offset for the first row of data is 1, but the column offset for column A, which contains the names, is 0.

	A	B	C	D	E
1					
2		Esmerelda's Weight Boutique			
3		September Group			
4					
5					
6	Top Losers				
7		Name		Loss	
8	Women	Harpole, M.		21	
9	Men	Dover, P.		37	
10					
11	Patient	Sex	Start	End	Loss
12					
13	Women				
14	Harpole, M.	f	145	124	21
15	Kramer, A.	f	163	143	20
16	Kazutsky, B.	f	142	131	11
17	Rogers, L.	f	150	139	11
18	Willis, S.	f	132	122	10
19	Aaron, J.	f	178	173	5
20	James, R.	f	151	150	1
21					
22					
23	Men				
24	Dover, P.	m	240	203	37
25	May, A.	m	265	243	22
26	Black, Q.	m	297	278	19
27	Bronstadt, D.	m	190	172	18
28	Meltzer, R.	m	203	187	16
29	Vaden, R.	m	283	269	14
30	Ringwalt, F.	m	311	307	4

Figure B.20. Using @INDEX to extract information from a database.

In B8, @INDEX(WOMEN,0,1) returns the name Harpole, M., the top female weight loser, because the offset 0,1 returns the entry from column A in the first record in the range WOMEN. Similarly, @INDEX(WOMEN,4,1) returns Harpole's weight loss, because column offset 4, is column D, where her loss is recorded, and 1 is the row offset for the first record in the range. For men, the formula in B9 is @INDEX(MEN,0,1) and returns the Name Dover, P., the top male loser. The formula in D9 is @INDEX(MEN,4,1) and returns Dover's weight loss: 37.

@INFO

@INFO("*attribute*") is a programmer's tool that allows you to check current system information in macros. For example, you can use @INFO to check whether there is enough RAM left to execute a macro, to check on current directory, or to check on the current recalculation mode.

In the argument, the attribute must be enclosed in quotation marks. The attributes available for @INFO are shown in Table B.6.

Attribute	Result
"dbreturncode"	Most recent error code returned by the Database driver
"dbdrivermessage"	Most recent Database message
"dbrecordcount"	Number of records extracted, modified, or inserted from the last query (in the worksheet or in an extended database)
"directory"	Current directory
"memavail"	Available memory
"mode"	Current mode:
	0 WAIT
	1 READY
	2 LABEL
	3 MENU
	4 VALUE
	5 POINT
	6 EDIT
	7 ERROR
	8 FIND
	9 FILES
	10 HELP
	11 STAT
	13 NAMES
	99 Other modes

Table B.6. Attribute arguments for @INFO. *(continued)*

Attribute	Result (continued)
"numfile"	Number of active files
"origin"	Cell at the top left corner of the screen, as of the most recent recalculation, as an absolute address
"osreturncode"	Value returned by the most recent System command or {SYSTEM} advanced macro command
"osversion"	Current operation system version
"recalc"	Returns the strings "Automatic" or "Manual", depending on the current recalculation mode
"release"	Release number, upgrade level, and version number of current 1-2-3 product
"selection"	Returns a range reference describing the current selection
"system"	Name of the operating system
"totmem"	Total memory available (both amount currently available and amount already used)

Table B.6.   Attribute arguments for @INFO.

@NA

@NA returns to the value @NA. It allows you to flag any calculations for which data are not available. Suppose, for example, that the range E1..E12 contains monthly sales but that sales for December are not yet available. Cell E14 contains the formula @SUM(E1..E12), to calculate sales for the year. If you enter @NA in E12 for December sales, NA will appear in E12. The @SUM calculation will also return NA, because the necessary information is not available. Like @ERR, @NA ripples through your worksheet. Any further calculations that depend on the annual total will also return NA.

You can also use @NA in logic formulas. For example, using the formula @IF(B> 50#OR#B5<0,B5,@NA) returns the value in B5 if B5 contains a value other than 0. The formula returns NA if B5 contains a 0, is blank, or contains a label.

@ROWS

@ROWS(*range*) counts the number of rows in a range. Range can be a range address or a range name.

Example: @ROWS(A1..A5) returns 5. If A1..A5 is named TABLE, @COLS (TABLE) yields the same result.

@SHEETS

@SHEETS(*range*) returns the number of worksheets in a given range. The range can be an address or a range name.

Example: @SHEETS(PAYROLL) = 4 if PAYROLL identifies the range A:A1..D:F20.

@VLOOKUP

@VLOOKUP(*x,range,column offset*) looks up x in a vertical lookup table—a range with a first column containing values in ascending order, or labels in any order. @VLOOKUP is particularly useful for tax and depreciation tables. The operation of @VLOOKUP is similar to that of @HLOOKUP, except that @VLOOKUP searches down the left column of a lookup table, while @HLOOKUP searches across the top row of the table. A simple lookup example is provided here; a more complex example is discussed under @HLOOKUP.

@VLOOKUP compares x to each cell in the first column of the table. When 1-2-3 locates a cell in the first column that contains x (or, if x is a value, the value closest to but not larger than x), it moves across that row by the number of columns specified by the *column offset* and returns the contents of that cell as the answer. Note that if the first column of the lookup table contains values, x can be any value greater than or equal to the first value in the column. If x is smaller than the first value in the column, @VLOOKUP returns ERR. If x is larger than the last value in the first column in the table, @VLOOKUP stops at the last cell in the column specified by the column offset and returns the contents of that cell as the answer.

If the first column of the lookup table contains labels, x can be a literal string enclosed in quotation marks, a reference to a cell that contains a label, or a formula that evaluates to a string.

If x does not exactly match the contents of a cell in the first column of the lookup table, @VLOOKUP returns the value ERR.

Example: Figure B.21 shows a database listing stock numbers in ascending order in column A, item labels in column B, and prices in column C. The range A3..C6 is assigned the range name STOCK. You can use @VLOOKUP to determine either the item name or price for any stock number, as shown below.

@VLOOKUP(1002,STOCK,1) = Widgets, because the function looks down column A until it finds 1,002, then returns the entry one column to the right.

@VLOOKUP(1003,STOCK,2) = 5.95, because the entry two columns to the right of 1003 is 5.95, which is the price of chisels.

```
       A          B              C
1
2   Stock #    Item           Price
3      1001    Mallets        10.95
4      1002    Widgets         3.95
5      1003    Chisels         5.95
6      1004    Screwdrivers    4.95
7
8   @VLOOKUP(1002,STOCK,1) =   Widgets
9   @VLOOKUP(1003,STOCK,2) =     5.95
```

Figure B.21. Using @VLOOKUP to retrieve entries from a lookup table.

Note: If you enter a number higher than 1004 as the criterion, @VLOOKUP will return the corresponding entry for 1004, Screwdrivers, because the function accepts the smallest number in the lookup column that is not greater than the criterion. For the same reason, a criterion of 1002.5 will return the corresponding entry for Widgets. @VLOOKUP returns an ERR message if the criterion is smaller than the lowest value in the lookup column.

Macros

Getting Started

Macro Key Names

Before you learn about the macro commands, you should know how to use the many special keys on your keyboard in a macro. Special keys are those keys other than the ones you use to type letters or numbers. For example, the Backspace key and the F5 (GOTO) key are special keys. The table below lists the macro key names that correspond to the 1-2-3 function keys, pointer-movement keys, and a few other special keyboard keys.

1-2-3 Key	Macro Instruction
~ (TILDE)	{~}
{ (OPEN BRACE)	{{}
} (CLOSE BRACE)	{}}
ALT	{ALT}, {MENUBAR}, or {MB}
ALT+F6 (ZOOM)	{ZOOM}
ALT+F7 (APP1)	{APP1}
ALT+F8 (APP2)	{APP2}
ALT+F9 (APP3)	{APP3}
BACKSPACE	{BACKSPACE} or {BS}
BACKTAB	{BACKTAB} or {BIGLEFT}
CTRL	{CTRL}
CTRL+END	{FILE}
CTRL+END CTRL+PGUP	{NEXTFILE}, {NF}, or {FILE}{NS}
CTRL+END CTRL+PGDN	{PREVFILE}, {PF}, or {FILE}{PS}
CTRL+END END	{LASTFILE}, {LF}, or {FILE}{END}
CTRL+END HOME	{FIRSTFILE}, {FF}, or {FILE}{HOME}

1-2-3 Key	Macro Instruction
CTRL+HOME	{FIRSTCELL} or {FC}
CTRL+LEFT	{BACKTAB} or {BIGLEFT}
CTRL+PGUP	{NEXTSHEET} or {NS}
CTRL+PGDN	{PREVSHEET} or {PS}
CTRL+RIGHT	{BIGRIGHT}
DEL	{DEL}
DOWN	{DOWN} or {D}
END	{END}
END CTRL+HOME	{LASTCELL} or {LC}
ESC	{ESCAPE} or {ESC}
F1 (HELP)	{HELP}
F2 (EDIT)	{EDIT}
F3 (NAME)	{NAME}
F4 (ABS)	{ABS}
F5 (GOTO)	{GOTO}
F6 (PANE)	{WINDOW}
F7 (QUERY)	{QUERY}
F8 (TABLE)	{TABLE}
F9 (CALC)	{CALC}
F10 (MENU)	{ALT}, {MENU}, or {MB}
HOME	{HOME}
INS	{INSERT} or {INS}
LEFTARROW	{LEFT} or {L}
PG UP	{PGUP}
PG DN	{PGDN}
RIGHTARROW	{RIGHT} or {R}
TAB	{TAB} or {BIGRIGHT}
UP	{UP} OR {U}

The {MB} Keystroke Instruction. {MENUBAR} or {MB} makes the 1-2-3 main menu active. Thus the macro instruction {MB}FS~ saves the current file.

The {CE} Keystroke Instruction. {CLEARENTRY} or {CE} clears the current data from the edit line or in a text box when 1-2-3 is in EDIT mode. For example, the macro {MB}FO{CE}my file .WK3~ brings up the File Open dialog box, clears the default path, then enters the name of the file to open (my file .WK3) and opens it.

Missing Keystroke Instructions. Note that 1-2-3 does not have macro key names for the following keys: ALT+BACKSPACE (UNDO), ALT+F1 (COMPOSE), ALT+F2 (STEP), ALT+F3 (RUN), CAPS LOCK, NUM LOCK, PRINT SCREEN, SCROLL LOCK, and SHIFT. Therefore, you cannot use these keystrokes in a macro.

Use a Number To Repeat Key Names. In 1-2-3 Release 2.0 and all subsequent releases of 1-2-3, you have the option to designate any number of repetitions of a keystroke represented by a key name. {LEFT}{LEFT}{LEFT}{LEFT} and {LEFT 4} are equivalent.

- You cannot use this technique to repeat the Return key. You must represent the Enter key with a tilde, and a tilde will not accept an argument.

- You can provide a range name to substitute for the numeric argument. For example, {left REPEAT} has the same effect as {l 6} if the cell named Repeat contains the value 6. If the referenced cell contains a zero, is empty, or contains a string, when 1-2-3 reads the key name in a macro, the key name will have no effect. If the value in the referenced cell contains a fraction (perhaps it was calculated), only the integer portion of the number will be significant: {left 6.99999} and {left 6} will have the same effect.

Macro Commands

Before we introduce macro commands, let's take a moment to review each of their components—keywords, arguments, and separators.

Keywords. Like the macro special key names (such as {edit} or {right}), all macro commands begin and end with braces. Don't confuse braces {} with brackets [] or parentheses (). You can't use them interchangeably in macros. In the advanced macro commands, the keyword is typically the first word following the opening brace. For example, in the {quit} command, the keyword is *quit*.

Remember, don't assign any range names that duplicate the keyword used by an advanced macro command. For example, avoid assigning to a range the name *wait*, since *wait* is the keyword for the command {wait}.

Arguments. Some advanced macro commands either can or must contain one or more arguments. Arguments specialize the action of a command. For example, in the command {branch A12}, the cell address A12 is an argument that specializes how 1-2-3 will respond to the {branch} command—it will branch to cell A12.

Arguments are also variables. In the previous example, we could have used any other cell address besides A12, or we could have used a range name.

While some macro commands take one argument, others take more than one argument, still others take none at all.

The contents of an argument consist of one of four things:

1. A numeric value or numeric formula. In the syntax descriptions that follow, numeric arguments are represented as [number]. You can substitute a cell reference (in the form of a cell address or range name) for a numeric argument. In that case, the referenced cell should contain the appropriate value, or a formula that returns that value.

2. A string value or string-valued formula. In the syntax descriptions that follow, string-valued arguments are represented either as [string] or ["string"]. In most cases, you can substitute a cell reference (in the form of a cell address or range name) for a string argument. If you do, the referenced cell should contain the appropriate string, or a formula that returns that string value.

Whenever you supply a string directly as an argument, as opposed to using a cell reference or a string formula to supply the argument, we recommend that you enclose that string in quotation marks. Doing so will guarantee that 1-2-3 will interpret the string as a string, and not construe it as a range name.

3. A location on the worksheet. In the syntax descriptions that follow, location arguments are represented as [location]. You can represent them through a cell address or range name.

4. A logical expression or other formula evaluating to either zero or one, or the values zero or one. In the syntax descriptions that follow, logical arguments are represented as [logical]. You can substitute a cell reference (in the form of a cell address or range name) for a logical argument. In that case, the referenced cell should contain the value zero, the value one, or a formula that returns either of those values.

Format of the Command Definitions. Since the arguments possible with each command can vary so widely, we'll begin the explanation of each command with an explicit description of its possibilities. If you've already learned the commands and just need a reminder on how to write a particular command, you'll probably only need to consult that definition. If you're reading about these commands for the first time, a detailed description of the arguments and uses of the command follows each definition.

Here's an overview of the structure we'll use to explain each command to you.

Purpose: Briefly defines the primary purpose of the command.

Format: Describes the syntax of the command. Square brackets [ ] enclose arguments; omit the square brackets when you write the command. A one word descriptor appears within the brackets to represent each argument. A brief explanation of the allowable forms of the argument follows each format diagram.

Sample: To clarify the syntax described above, the sample demonstrates how you might write the command.

Complements: Lists other advanced macro commands, if any, that either must be or are normally used with this command.

See also: Lists macro commands that implement related functions.

Description: A statement of common uses for the command, the context in which it's used, and a list of any factors that affect your use of it. Here's where you'll find the most detailed explanation of each command.

Example: A working example of the command to illustrate it's usage and purpose. All examples include named and commented macros.

Controlling the Screen

These commands control the sounding of the computer's bell and the different parts of the 1-2-3/W screen display, including the mode indicator.

{Beep}

Purpose: Use {beep} to provide auditory feedback to the user of a macro.

Format: {beep [tone-number]}
Where [tone-number] is an integer from 1 to 4, inclusive. [Tone-number] may be a number, a formula, a cell address, or a range name describing a single cell.

Sample: {beep 2}

Description: {Beep} sounds one of 1-2-3's four standard tones on the computer's speaker and is most often used to signal the end of a macro, the end of a waiting period within a macro, alert the user that an error has occurred, or that an on-screen message has appeared.

Used without its optional numeric argument, {beep} sounds the same tone you hear when you attempt to move the cell pointer past the end of the worksheet. That is also the tone produced by {beep 1}. The tone of the computer's speaker ascends with the value of the {beep} command's argument; 1 is the lowest, 4 the highest.

{Beep} does *not* sound a tone if the computer bell has been turned off by the Tools User Setup dialog.

Example:

{beep} {beep 4}

{?}

This macro sounds the bell twice, with two different tones, to alert the user that the program awaits input.

{Frameoff}

Purpose: {Frameoff} suppresses display of the inverted "L" worksheet frame.

Format: {frameoff}

Sample: {frameoff}

Complements: {frameon}

See also: {paneloff}, {indicate}

Description: {Frameoff} suppresses display of the inverted "L" worksheet frame until the macro either reads a {frameon} command or terminates.

This command is useful primarily in turnkey applications. By turning off the worksheet frame, you make an environment that looks less like the familiar 1-2-3 worksheet. This way you can create a visual environment that users will associate more closely with *your* application.

You can achieve an even greater effect by using this command in concert with two other commands, {paneloff} and {indicate}. {Paneloff} lets you clear the display of the control panel. {Indicate} lets you eliminate the mode indicator or change it to an indicator of your choice.

> Note: If you give have frozen the worksheet screen with a {Windowsoff} command in your macro and you want to use {Frameoff} or {Frameon}, you must precede either command with a {Windowson} command. {Frameoff} and {Frameon} will have no visible effect unless screen redrawing is *on*.

Example:

```
{frameoff}            Clear frame
{paneloff "clear"}    Clear control panel
{goto}MSG1~           Show message
{windowsoff}          Freeze screen
{return}              Return to caller
```

{Frameon}

Purpose: {Frameon} redisplays the worksheet frame after that frame has been suppressed with the {frameoff} command.

Format: {frameon}

Sample: {frameon}

Complements: {frameon}

See also: {panelon}, {indicate}

Description: {Frameon} redisplays the inverted "L" worksheet frame after a macro has read a {frameoff} command.

If you want to redisplay the frame only when the macro finishes, you need not use the {frameon} command. If the worksheet frame has been suppressed by the {frameoff} command, 1-2-3 will automatically redisplay that frame when the macro terminates.

{Graphoff}

Purpose: {Graphoff} clears from the screen a graph displayed using the {graphon} command.

Format: {Graphoff}

Sample: {graphoff}

Complements: {graphon}

Description: With a graph displayed on the screen that was selected using the {graphon} command, use {graphoff} to redisplay the worksheet.

{Graphoff} will not affect a graph that was displayed using the {graph} key name, the Graph View command, or the Graph Name Use command. A graph displayed using any of those methods suspends a macro. It requires that the user press a keystroke in order to clear it from the screen and cause the macro to resume operation.

{Graphon}

Purpose: {Graphon} can redisplay the most recently displayed graph, display any named graph, or make current a given named graph's settings without displaying the graph.

Format: {Graphon ["graph_name"], ["nodisplay"]}

Where ["graph_name"] is the name of a named graph and ["nodisplay"] is the string *nodisplay* in quotation marks. You may use in place of either or both strings a cell address, range name, or formula that evaluates to that string.

Sample: {graphon "QTR_1";"nodisplay"}

Complements: {graphoff}

Description: {Graphon} is the only way to make a given graph's settings current without displaying that graph. Displaying a graph with the {graphon} command is also the only way to have 1-2-3 continue reading a macro while a graph displays.

If you want to have a macro continue reading while a graph displays, use {graphon} to display the current graph. Use {graphon ["graph_name"]} to make the named graph of your choice the current graph and display it-full screen. Either use of {graphon} will let the macro continue running while the graph is on the screen. The graph will remain on the screen until one of several things happens: until the macro reads another {graphon} command, until the macro reads a {graphoff} command, or until the macro reads a command that requires it to display something in the control panel, such as a custom prompt command, a custom menu command, or an {indicate} command.

If you want to make a named graph *current*, without displaying that graph to the user, use {graphon ["graph_name"];"nodisplay"} where ["graph_name"] is the name of a named graph.

Example:

{graphon "SALES_COMP"}	Display graph
{sort}~	Sort database
{return}	Return to caller

{Indicate}

Purpose: {Indicate} changes 1-2-3's mode indicator.

Format: {indicate [string]}

Where [string] is any text that can fit in the format line (the third line from the top of the 1-2-3 screen). [String] can also consist of a cell address, a range name reference, or a string formula.

Sample: {indicate "ENTRY"}

{indicate MESSAGE} displays the contents of a cell named MESSAGE as the mode indicator.

Description: 1-2-3's mode indicator appears at the right of the third line in 1-2-3's control panel (it often displays the word *Ready*). Depending on how you use it, the {indicate} command either changes the mode indicator to a string of your choice up to 240 characters long (though usually limited to 80 characters, depending on the display adapter you're using), removes the mode indicator entirely, or restores the mode indicator to 1-2-3's control.

{Indicate} is most often used to provide the user with a context for the operation currently underway. For example, when you point to a cell while writing a formula, 1-2-3 changes the mode indicator to Point. You can provide that same kind of feedback to users of macro applications that you write. For example, during a data-entry operation you might want to change the indicator to the word Entry. You must issue another {indicate} command each time you wish to change the mode indicator's prompt from one string to another.

{Indicate} is the only command through which a macro can post a message in 1-2-3's control panel without awaiting user input of some kind. That is, it is the only command with which you can post a message and have the macro continue processing.

Unlike the action of most other macro commands, {indicate} remains in effect after the macro has relinquished control to 1-2-3. For example, if you change the mode indicator to Enter, after the macro terminates, the mode indicator will continue to display Enter, irrespective of the mode in which 1-2-3 is operating. Even if 1-2-3 encounters an error, if you've used {indicate} to set the mode indicator, you won't see the flashing Error indicator 1-2-3 would otherwise display. (However, the error message that normally appears at the bottom of the screen when an error occurs will display.) {Indicate} differs from {paneloff} in this way. Errors override {paneloff}.

You can return control of the mode indicator to 1-2-3 either by saving and retrieving the file or by issuing the {indicate} command with no argument: *{indicate}*.

- If you've written an autoexecute macro and want to maintain control over the mode indicator from the time the file is retrieved, the {indicate} command should be one of the first commands you invoke.
- If you want your macro to reset the mode indicator to its default state, use the {indicate} command without any arguments: *{indicate}*.
- To remove the mode indicator entirely, specify a blank string: *{indicate ""}*.

The mode indicator resides on the third line from the top of the 1-2-3 screen, whereas prompts generated by commands such as {getlabel} reside in the 1-2-3 Classic window. Therefore, even if you use the full width of the screen as your indicator, that indicator won't conflict with prompts generated by other kinds of commands. If you invoke the {paneloff "clear"} command, {indicate} will still superimpose its prompt on the control panel.

If the string you specify as an indicate message duplicates the name of a single-cell range and you fail to enclose that string in quotation marks, 1-2-3 will do one of two things. If the range contains a label, 1-2-3 will display that label in the indicator. If the range is empty or contains a value, the macro will terminate and 1-2-3 will issue the error message *Macro: Invalid string value in INDICATE* followed by the cell address of the {indicate} command—this cannot be trapped with {onerror}.

If the named range you specify for the {indicate} message consists of more than one cell, the macro will treat the string as if it had had quotation marks around it.

Example:

{indicate "-1-"}	Change mode indicator
{getnumber "Enter 1st number. ";FIRST}	Get first entry
{indicate "-2-"}	Change mode indicator
{getnumber "Enter 2nd number. ";SECOND}	Get second entry

{Paneloff}

Purpose: {Paneloff} freezes the control panel (consisting of the top four lines of the screen) and the status line (the bottom line of the screen).

Format: {Paneloff ["clear"]}
Where ["clear"] is an optional string contained in quotation marks, a cell address, a range name, or a string formula that evaluates to that string.

Sample: {paneloff}

Complements: {panelon}

See also: {windowsoff}, {frameoff}

Description: While a macro is running, {paneloff} prevents 1-2-3 from updating both the status line (the bottom line of the screen) and the control panel (the top four lines of the screen). You may also use the optional argument "clear" in the {paneloff} command to erase the contents of the control panel and the status line before freezing them. In either case, {panelon} will cause 1-2-3 to once again continuously refresh the control panel.

{Paneloff} is useful when the macro makes a lot of command-menu selections, which might confuse or distract the user. The command will also help speed up the macro. If 1-2-3 doesn't have to update the control panel, it can process the macro more quickly. (The {windowsoff} command, however, will speed it up a great deal more.)

Macro commands that ordinarily display something in the control panel are unaffected by {paneloff}. For example, if the macro reads the command {indicate "Processing"} after reading a {paneloff} command, you will still see the mode indicator *Processing* in the control panel.

If an entry is in the edit line of the control panel (such as occurs when you are typing an entry or editing one) at the time that 1-2-3 reads the {paneloff} command, 1-2-3 will cease to display that entry on the edit line. Although invisible, the entry itself will remain in the edit line unless otherwise removed.

Unlike the {indicate} command, the effect of {paneloff} terminates as soon as the macro does. That means that if you retrieve another worksheet file you must reinvoke the {paneloff} command to continue to suppress updating of the control panel. The same holds true if you trap an error with the {onerror} command. Since an error will reset the status of the control panel, you must include another {paneloff} command in the routine to which the {onerror} command branches. {Paneloff} differs from {indicate} in this regard. {Indicate} will override the error indicator.

Example:

{windowsoff}{paneloff}	Freeze screen
{goto}DATA~	Go to top of database
/dsd{bs}.{r}{end}{d}{r 5}~	Redefine sort range
g	Sort it

{Panelon}

Purpose: The {panelon} command reverses the effect of the {paneloff} command; it reenables 1-2-3 to update the control panel and the bottom line of the screen.

Format: {panelon}

Sample: {panelon}

Complements: {paneloff}

See also: {windowson}, {borderson}, {frameon}

Description: {Panelon} reverses the effect of {paneloff}, allowing the control panel and status line to be refreshed continuously during a macro.

Unlike the {indicate} command, {paneloff} has no effect after a macro ends, so you need not issue a {panelon} command at the end of a macro to restore the control panel. Use the {panelon} command only when you want 1-2-3 to resume continuously updating the control panel while the macro is still running.

{Windowsoff}

Purpose: Use {windowsoff} to freeze the worksheet portion of the screen during macro processing.

Format: {windowsoff}

Sample: {windowsoff}

Complements: {windowson}

See also: {paneloff}, {bordersoff}, {frameoff}

Description: {Windowsoff} prevents the worksheet portion of the screen (lines 5 through 24 on an 80 by 25 display) from being updated while a macro is running.

Use {windowsoff} to:

- Suppress screen activity that the user has no need to view.
- Increase the speed of macros that generate a lot of screen activity (by freeing 1-2-3 from the job of updating the screen, you enable it to process macro instructions more quickly).

Just as {paneloff} does not clear the control panel, {windowsoff} does not clear the screen before freezing it, so you might want to first move the screen to display something you want the user to see while {windowsoff} is in effect. For example, if it will be a while before you resume updating the screen, you might display a screen containing a message telling the user approximately how long the operation will take.

{Windowsoff} remains in effect until the macro ends or until 1-2-3 reads a {windowson} command.

Example:

{windowsoff}{paneloff}	Freeze screen
{for COUNT;1;ITEMS;1;PROCESS}	Run once for each item
{panelon}{windowson}	Restore screen

{Windowson}

Purpose: Use {windowson} to reenable 1-2-3 to update the worksheet portion of the screen during a macro after you've used {windowsoff} to suppress that capability.

Format: {windowson}

Sample: {windowson}

Complements: {windowsoff}

See also: {panelon}

Description: {Windowson} reverses the effect of {windowsoff}, allowing 1-2-3 to continuously refresh the screen display during a macro. {Windowsoff} has no effect after a macro ends, so you need not issue a {windowson} command at the end of a macro; 1-2-3 will automatically resume continuously updating the control panel. Use {windowson} only when you want 1-2-3 to resume continuously updating the worksheet screen while the macro is still running.

Allowing Keyboard Interaction

These commands suspend macro execution for user input, control macro interuption and the timing of macro execution, and they create custom dialog boxes.

{Break}

Purpose: Use {break} to clear the edit line when data is being edited, or to leave the current dialog box during the selection of a 1-2-3 command and return 1-2-3 to Ready mode.

Format: {break}

Sample: {break}

Description: While a macro is underway, the {break} command will return 1-2-3 to Ready mode under two circumstances. They are, first, if a cell entry is underway—that is, it appears on the edit line but not yet in the cell itself—and, second, if 1-2-3 is in the midst of a menu selection. In either case, the macro will remain in control of the worksheet.

When you use 1-2-3 interactively (not under macro control), the Control-Break key combination (also known as the Break key sequence) performs the same function as the {break} command does while a macro is running. So, if you use 1-2-3 interactively to type something into the edit line, for example, and press the Break key sequence, 1-2-3 will cancel the entry and return to Ready mode.

However, if you use the Break key sequence when a macro is running: it terminates the macro. When you use the {break} command instead, the macro itself will continue to run although any cell entry or command sequence in progress will be cancelled.

You might use {break} to ensure that 1-2-3 is in Ready mode when the macro begins. If you're uncertain as to what mode 1-2-3 will be in when the user invokes your macro, and you want to guarantee that 1-2-3 will be in Ready mode from the outset of the macro, simply begin that macro with the {break} command.

Example:

{break}	Cancel any menu
{goto}HELP_MESSAGE	Go to range named HELP_MESSAGE

{Breakoff}

Purpose: Use {breakoff} to disable the Break key (Ctrl-Break) while the macro is running.

Format: {breakoff}

Sample: {breakoff}

Complements: {breakon}

Description: {Breakoff} prevents users from terminating your macro with the Break key sequence (Ctrl-Break). For that reason, {breakoff} is particularly useful for securing applications against abuse. You can use {breakoff} in conjunction with a prompt (see {getlabel}) to implement an effective password system. {Breakoff} has no effect on the function of the {break} command. {Breakoff} affects only the Break key sequence.

As you develop and test your macros, {breakoff} should be nearly the last—if not the very last—command you add to your macro before its completion. Once you add the {breakoff} command, if the macro errs, even *you* will be unable to stop it. For that reason, we recommend that you test and debug all other portions of the macro before you add the {breakoff} command. While it's a good idea to save the worksheet before running any macro for the first time, it's imperative that you do so before testing a macro that contains {breakoff}.

When macro execution comes to a halt, 1-2-3 restores the function of Ctrl-Break. Thus, if you want to continuously disable the Break key, you must use {breakoff} every time you activate a new macro. If you are merely transferring control from one location to another with a command such as {branch} or {menubranch}, {breakoff} remains in effect. {Breakoff} also remains in effect during an interactive pause in a macro (initiated with the {?} command).

Example: Here is a macro for a password security system.

{goto}PASSWD_SCREEN~	Display password screen
{breakoff}	Disable break key
{getlabel "Enter Password: ";ANS}	Ask for password
{if @upper(ANS)=@upper(PW)}{branch GO}	If match, GO
{branch STOP}	If not, STOP

{Breakon}

Purpose: Use {breakon} to reenable the Break key (Ctrl-Break) after it has been disabled with {breakoff}.

Format: {breakon}

Sample: {breakon}

Complements: {breakoff}

Description: The sole purpose of {breakon} is to restore the function of the Ctrl-Break key sequence after it has been disabled by the {breakoff} command.

Since 1-2-3 restores the function of the Break key after a macro ends, you do not need to use {breakon} to do that job at the end of a macro. If a macro reads {breakon} while the Ctrl-Break key sequence is enabled, {breakon} will simply have no effect.

{Form}

Purpose: Use {form} to display an entry blank that lets you enter and edit data in unprotected cells in a specified range.

Format: {form [input-location],[call-table],[include-list],[exclude-list]}

Where [input-location] is the range where data is to be entered. It can be of any size and should contain unprotected cells. [Input-location] cannot include any hidden columns or worksheet. [Call-table] is an optional argument that specifies a two-column range. The first column contains the name of a key. Each adjacent cell in the second column contains a set of macro instructions that 1-2-3 performs when the user presses the key listed in the first column. [Include-list] is an optional argument that specifies a range that contains a list of allowable keystrokes. [Exclude-list] is an optional argument that specifies a range that contains a list of keystrokes to ignore. You cannot specify both an [include-list], and an [exclude-list]. If you specify both an [include-list] and an [exclude-list], 1-2-3 uses the [include-list] and ignores the [exclude-list]. To use an optional argument without using the ones that precede it you must include a comma or semicolon for each argument you skip. For example, to use a [call-table] and an [exclude-list] without an [include-list], use this syntax:

{form [input-location],[call-table],,[exclude-list]}.

The extra comma between [call-table] and [exclude-list] tells 1-2-3 that you omitted [include-list].

Sample: {form datanew,,okkeys}

Complements: {formbreak}

See also: {appendbelow}, {appendright}, {getlabel},{getnumber},{get}, {?}

Description: The {form} command starts by moving the *cell pointer* to the first unprotected cell in [input-location]. It then suspends macro execution, and waits for you to press a key. The {form} commands optional arguments determine what happens when you a press a particular key.

If the {form} command does not use optional arguments, you can press any typewriter or pointer-movement key and any of the following keys: Enter, Esc, F1 (HELP), F2 (EDIT), Home, End, Backspace (while typing or editing an entry), and (if the entry is a value) F9 (CALC). If [input-location] is a *3-D range*, you can also use Ctrl+Pg Up and Ctrl+Pg Dn. If you are typing or editing a formula, you can use F4 (ABS) and F3 (NAME).

When you end the {form} command (by pressing either Enter or Esc from ready mode, the macro continues.

If the {form} command uses a [call-table] argument, 1-2-3 checks the first column of the [call-table]. If the keystroke is listed, 1-2-3 executes the instructions in the second column as a *subroutine*, and then returns to the {form} command and waits for you to press another key.

> Note: Including {ESC} or ~ (tilde) in a [call-table] subroutine, at a point in the subroutine when the mode indicator displays READY, temporarily suspends the {form} command, letting you move the cell pointer out of the [input-range] unprotected area and use all 1-2-3 keys and menus for their standard functions for the rest of the subroutine.

When the [call-table] subroutine ends, 1-2-3 moves the cell pointer back to wherever it was when the [call-table] subroutine started (unless the cell pointer is within the [input-range] unprotected area when the subroutine ends, in which case 1-2-3 leaves the cell pointer where it is) and reinstates use or 1-2-3 keys as defined by the {form} command.

To end a macro from within a [call-table] subroutine, use *{restart}* or *{quit}* in the subroutine. To end a {form} command from within a [call-table] subroutine but continue the macro, use {formbreak} to leave the {form} command and continue macro execution at the instruction immediately following the {form} command.

If the {form} command uses an [include-list] argument, 1-2-3 checks [exclude-list]. If the keystroke appears in [include-list], 1-2-3 performs the keystroke. Otherwise, 1-2-3 ignores the keystroke.

If the {form} command uses an [exclude-list] argument, 1-2-3 checks [exclude-list]. If the keystroke appears in [exclude-list], 1-2-3 ignores the keystroke. Otherwise, 1-2-3 performs the keystroke.

[Call-table], [include-list], and [exclude-list] are case-sensitive for letters typed at the keyboard. For example, if [include-list] contains an uppercase B but not a lowercase b, 1-2-3 allows only uppercase B's during the {form} command; lowercase b's are ignored.

Example: The {form} command in the following example uses a [call-table] and an [exclude-list]. This {form} command processes inventory orders in a database table using an entry form in a range named ENTRYFORM.

{form entryform,sigkeys,,badkeys}

stops the macro temporarily so the user can enter an order in the entry form. The [call-table], SIGKEYS, includes two key names: {INS}, and {QUERY}.

- If you press INS during the {form} command, 1-2-3 appends the data in INPUT to the order database table (ORDERS), erases INPUT, and returns to the {form} command.
- If you press F7 (QUERY) during the {form} command, 1-2-3 branches to subroutine CONFIRM, which uses a {getlabel} command to confirm that you want to stop entering orders. If you enter y at the {getlabel} prompt, the {quit} command ends the macro. If you enter any other letter, 1-2-3 returns to the {form} command.

{Formbreak}

Purpose: {Formbreak} is used to end a {form} command.

Format: {formbreak}

Sample: {formbreak}

Complements: {form}, {appendbelow}, {appendright}

Description: After executing a {formbreak} command, 1-2-3 continues macro execution at the instruction immediately following the {form} command.

If you use {formbreak} to end a nested {form} command, 1-2-3 returns you to the location from which the {form} command you are ending was issued and continues the macro there.

Use {formbreak} only within a [call-table] subroutine or a subroutine to which you transfer control with {branch} or {dispatch}. Using {formbreak} anywhere else causes the macro to terminate with an error.

Example: The {form} command in the following example uses a [call-table] and an [exclude-list]. This {form} command processes inventory orders in a database table using an entry form in a range named ORDERFORM.

{form orderform,keytable,,nokeys}

Here the {form} command stops the macro temporarily so you can enter an order in the entry form. The [call-table], KEYTABLE, includes two key names: {INS} and {END} and looks like this:

{INS}   {appendbelow neworder,newentry} {blank newentry}
{END}   {formbreak}

- If you press INS during the {form} command, 1-2-3 appends the data in NEWENTRY to the order database table (NEWORDER), erases NEWENTRY, and returns to the {form} command.
- If you press END during the {form} command, the {formbreak} command ends the {form} command and 1-2-3 continues to any instructions that immediately follow the {form} command.

{Get}

Purpose: Use {get} to capture a keystroke from the user.

Format: {get [location]}

Where [location] is the name or address of the range to store the keystroke. [Location] may be a cell name or address, a range name or address.

Sample: {get ANS}
{if @upper(ANS)="N"}{branch STOP}{branch CONTINUE}

See also: {getlabel}, {getnumber}, {look}, {?}, {form}

Description: Use the {get} command to fetch a keystroke from the keyboard buffer and enter it into a worksheet cell. After executing a {get} command, 1-2-3 continues to the cell immediately below the {get} command, ignoring any instructions in the same cell as the {get} command. Note that you must use two {get} commands to record these keystrokes: Ctrl-End Home, End Ctrl-Home, Ctrl-End End, Ctrl-End Ctrl-PgUp, and Ctrl-End Ctrl-PgDn.

{Get} is particularly useful in the following three applications:

- Posting a message to the user with the instruction to press any key. Since {get} will interrupt macro processing until the user enters a keystroke, it will leave the message on the screen until the user presses the key to continue.

- Creating a full-screen menu. Such menus can include more than eight choices (the limit of the {menubranch} and {menucall} commands).
- Capturing and filtering each keystroke that a user types to maintain macro control at all times.

The {get} command moves a single keystroke from the keyboard buffer to a worksheet cell and enters it there as a label. The keystroke is stored in the range designated in the sole argument to the {get} command. If there are no keystrokes in the keyboard buffer, the {get} command will suspend macro processing until the user provides one. (It will not however, provide a prompt to the user regarding what it is waiting for.)

{Get}'s results are not posted to the screen automatically. If you wish to update the screen after a {get}, include a tilde (~) in the macro just after the {get} command. Also 1-2-3 does not automatically recalculate formulas after executing a {get} command, even when worksheet calculation is set to automatic. To force recalculation, follow the {get} command with ~ (tilde) or with {calc}.

Whether you force 1-2-3 to update the screen or not, 1-2-3 will respond to the presence of the captured, though invisible, keystroke if you test for it just after the {get} command. For example, if the command following the {get} command tests the value of the cell designated in the {get} command, 1-2-3 will use the value that would appear in the cell had the screen been updated.

Example:

{goto}MSG_SCREEN~	Display message screen
{get ANS}	Pause for key
{branch CONTINUE}	Continue macro

{Getlabel}

Purpose: Use {getlabel} to prompt the user and store the user's input as a label in a worksheet cell.

Format: {getlabel ["prompt"],[location]}

Where ["prompt"] is an optional string, and [location] is the cell in which to store the user's response. ["Prompt"] can be the literal text for a prompt, enclosed in quotation marks; it can also be the address or name of a cell that contains a label or it can be a string formula that proceeds the prompt. It *cannot* be a blank cell, a cell that contains a value or a multiple-cell range. [Location] may be a cell address, a range address, or a range name.

Sample: {getlabel "Enter your city: ",CITY}

See also: {get}, {getnumber}, {?}, {form}

Description: {Getlabel} pauses for user input. If you have supplied the optional prompt string, it also displays a one-line prompt in the 1-2-3 Classic window. The user may type a response up to 511 characters long; in any event, the user must click OK or press Enter and 1-2-3 will store that entry in a worksheet cell as a label. If the user doesn't enter anything before pressing Enter, 1-2-3 will enter just an apostrophe (the left-alignment label prefix) in the designated cell.

{Getlabel} is particularly useful for controlling the data type of the cell entry that results from user input. For example, if you are entering zip codes, {getlabel} frees you from having to enter a label prefix before each entry.

1-2-3 uses the mandatory [location] argument to determine the cell in which to store the entry. You can supply a range with either a cell name or address, or a range name or address. If that range consists of more than one cell, 1-2-3 will store the entry in the top left cell of the range.

Although {getlabel} changes the contents of cells, 1-2-3 does not automatically recalculate formulas after executing a {getlabel} command when worksheet recalculation is set to Automatic. To force recalculation after a {getlabel} command, follow the command with ~ (tilde) or {CALC}.

Example: This macro allows you to easily enter data in the current cell, move to another cell, and enter data there. Note that the line +ENTRY{calc}{home}'~ enters a label prefix at the beginning of the edit line and is appropriate for use only with the {getlabel} command, not the {getnumber} command.

\A	{getlabel "Enter first item: ",ENTRY}	Get entry
	{ENTER}	Call entry routine
	{getlabel "Enter second item: ",ENTRY}	Get next entry
	{ENTER}	Call entry routine
	{quit}	End
ENTER	+ENTRY{calc}{home}'~	Enter into cell
	{d 2}	Move down 2 cells
	{return}	Return to main routine
ENTRY		Store entry

{Getnumber}

Purpose: Use {getnumber} to prompt the user for number input to be stored in a worksheet cell.

Format: {getnumber ["prompt"],[location]}

Where ["prompt"] is an optional string, and [location] is a cell on the worksheet. [Location] may be a cell name or address, or a range name or address. ["Prompt"] can be the literal text for a prompt, enclosed in quotation marks; it can also be the address or name of a cell that contains a label or it can be a string formula that results in the prompt. It *cannot* be a blank cell, a cell that contains a value or a multiple-cell range.

Sample: {getnumber "Enter number of branch offices: ";OFFICES}

See also: {get}, {getlabel}, {?}, {form}

Description: {Getnumber} is most often used for form-type data entry. It allows you to prompt a user for data and specify the cell where 1-2-3 will enter it on the worksheet.

{Getnumber} pauses for user input. If you have supplied the optional prompt string, it also displays a one-line prompt in the 1-2-3 Classic window. The user may type a response of up to 511 characters in length; in any event, the user must press Enter before the macro will proceed.

If the user types anything before pressing Enter—a number, a numeric formula, or the address or name of a cell that contains a value—1-2-3 will store that entry in a worksheet cell as a value. If the user doesn't enter anything in that cell before pressing Enter, or if the user enters a label, or presses the Escape key, 1-2-3 will enter the value ERR in the designated cell.

1-2-3 uses the mandatory [location] argument to determine the cell in which to store the entry. You can supply a range with a cell name or address and with a range name or address. If that range consists of more than one cell, 1-2-3 will store the entry in the top left cell of the range. Although {getnumber} changes the contents of cells, 1-2-3 does not automatically recalculate formulas after executing a {getnumber} command, follow the command with ~ (tilde) or {calc}.

Example: This macro allows you to easily enter data in the current cell, move the cell pointer to another cell, and enter data there. Note that the statement +ENTRY{calc}~ is appropriate for use only with the {getnumber} command, not with the {getlabel} command.

\A	{getnumber "Enter first number: ",ENTRY}	Get entry
	{ENTER}	Call entry routine
	{getnumber "Enter second number: ",ENTRY}	Get next entry
	{ENTER}	Call entry routine
	{quit}	End
ENTER	{if @iserr(ENTRY)}{branch FIX}	Test entry
	+ENTRY{calc}~	Enter into cell
	{d 2}	Move down two cells
	{return}	Return to main routine
FIX	{getnumber "Enter a valid number: ",ENTRY}	Reprompt
	{branch ENTER}	Test again
ENTRY		Store entry

{Look}

Purpose: Use {look} to capture a keystroke from the user.

Format: {look [location]}

Where [location] is the location to store the keystroke. [Location] may be a cell name or address or a range name or address. If you specify a multi-cell range, 1-2-3 records the keystroke in the first cell in the range.

Sample: {look ANS}{if @length(ANS)>0}{get ANS}

See also: {get}, {getlabel}, {getnumber}

Description: {Look} examines the keyboard buffer for a keystroke. If it finds a keystroke stored there, it stores that keystroke as a label entry in the location specified by the range argument. If the keyboard buffer contains more than one keystroke, {look} will store only the first of those keystrokes. Thus, if the macro contains the command {look E1} and the Enter key is the keystroke stored in the buffer, then after the macro finishes and the worksheet has been updated, a tilde will appear in cell E1.

{Look} will not cause the macro to pause if there is no keystroke waiting in the buffer (unlike {get}, which will). If the buffer is empty, {look} will enter a null string (consisting of an apostrophe label-prefix character) in the designated cell. Here's how to test to see if there has been no keystroke. First, before the {look} command, use the {blank} command to clear the cell you will be testing. Second, test for a null string, as in {if CHAR=""}, or for the opposite condition, as in {if CHAR<>""}.

{Look} doesn't clear the keystroke from the buffer, unlike {get}, which does. Thus a second, subsequent {look} command will record the same keystroke. You might say that {look} *copies* the keystroke from the buffer to the worksheet (so the keystroke resides in both places), while {get} *moves* it.

{Look} is among the commands that do not update the worksheet automatically. Therefore, you will not see the keystroke appear in the designated cell as a character until you force 1-2-3 to update the worksheet by some other means. Nonetheless, the label is immediately available to any commands that may require it. For example, if you use the {look} command to store a keystroke in cell E1 in one line of a macro and in the next line test for its presence, {look} will update the cell immediately and the test will respond to the presence of the keystroke.

You can force 1-2-3 to update the screen by including a tilde or cell pointer movement command after the {look} command. Any movement of the cell pointer after the macro has ended will also update the worksheet.

Example:

KEYCH	{look KEY}{if #not#KEY- ""}{TEST}	Check keystroke buffer
	{return}	If empty, return
TEST	{get KEY}	Clear keystroke buffer
	{if KEY="{ESC}"}{restart}{branch HALT}	If key = ESC, run HALT
	{return}	Run previous routine

{Menubranch}

Purpose: Use {menubranch} to branch to a custom menu.

Format: {menubranch [location]}

Where [location] is the first cell of a row that contains menu items. [Location] may be a cell name or address or a range name or address, a range name.

Sample: {menubranch PMENU}

See also: {menucall}, {branch}

Description: Use the {menubranch} command to display a custom menu in the 1-2-3 Classic window and to interrupt processing of the macro until the user selects an option from the menu. When the user selects an option, the macro will branch to the macro instructions associated with the selected menu item.

[Location] is the upper left cell in a range containing entries representing menu choices and their associated explanation or description lines. At a minimum, the cell designated in [location] must include a label number or formula as the menu item. (If you enter a formula, 1-2-3 displays the formula's result as the menu item.) Entries representing additional menu option(s) and explanation line(s) are optional.

The labels you wish to represent menu options should be entered in *consecutive cells* beginning with the cell designated in [location] and continuing to the right. Leave the cell after the final menu item blank. 1-2-3 will represent up to eight consecutive entries as menu choices in the 1-2-3 Classic window when it reads the {menubranch} command in a macro. If you make any more entries than that, 1-2-3 will ignore them. If an empty cell appears to the right of one of these label entries, the label directly to the left of the empty cell will be the last menu item displayed.

Each menu item can include up to 512 characters. However, if the total number of characters in all the menu items, plus the spaces on either side of each item, exceeds the width of the window, 1-2-3 displays as many of the menu items as possible and uses an arrow at the end of the menu line to indicate that more items are off to the right. Also, if the number of characters in any single menu item exceeds the screen width, 1-2-3 truncates the item when displaying the menu.

You may also enter descriptive labels in the cells beneath each of the labels representing menu options. When 1-2-3 displays the menu, it will use each of the lower entries as explanation lines for the menu choice entered in the cell above it. When the menu pointer highlights a given menu choice, the associated explanation label will appear in the second line of the 1-2-3 Classic window. In the example below, when 1-2-3 reads the {menubranch} command, the menu pointer by default highlights the choice Post, and the explanation line reads *Post entries*. If you move the menu pointer to highlight the choice Clear, the explanation line reads *Clear entries*.

A menu-item description can include up to 512 characters. However, you should limit the description to the width of the window because 1-2-3 truncates descriptions whose length exceeds the width of the window.

When 1-2-3 displays the menu in the control panel, it will function like a 1-2-3 menu: The user may select an option by positioning the menu pointer and pressing Enter or by typing the number or first letter of an option. If the macro contains more than one choice that begins with the same character and the user types that character to select a choice, the option located farthest to the left will be selected.

While the menu displays in the control panel, the flow of control remains stopped at the {menubranch} command. When the user selects a menu option, the macro branches to the cell located two cells *below* the cell containing the selected menu choice. In the example below, if the user selected Clear from the menu, control would move from {menubranch MEN1} to {branch CLEAR}.

If the user presses the Escape key while the menu displays, the {menubranch} command is cancelled, and control will continue beyond the {menubranch} command to the next instruction in the macro.

Note that a macro menu will appear in the 1-2-3 Classic window even after a {paneloff} command.

Example:

\M	{menubranch MEN1}		Display menu
MEN1	Post	Clear	Menu options
	Post entries	Clear entries	Explanation lines
	{branch POST}	{branch CLEAR}	Macro instructions

{Menucall}

Purpose: Use {menucall} to call a custom 1-2-3 style menu as a subroutine.

Format: {menucall [location]}
Where [location] is the address or name of the first cell of a row that contains menu items and prompts.

Sample: {menucall PMENU}

Complements: {return}

See also: {menubranch}

Description: {Menucall}, like {menubranch}, displays a custom menu in the 1-2-3 Classic window. The two commands differ in the way they transfer control to other macros when a user selects a menu choice. Unlike {menubranch}, {menucall} only temporarily transfers control to another location after the user makes a menu choice. When the selected routine finishes, 1-2-3 returns control to the command directly following the {menucall} command. In other words, {menucall} treats the other macro commands as a subroutine.

[Location] is the left cell in a row containing entries that represent menu choices. In the row below appear explanation lines for each of the menu options. At a minimum, the cell designated in [location] must include a label number or formula entry. (If you enter a formula, 1-2-3 displays the formula's result as the menu item.) Label entries representing additional menu option(s) and explanation line(s) are optional. See the {menubranch} discussion for more details on how to set up a macro menu.

While the menu displays in the control panel, the control flow remains stopped at the {menucall} command. When the user selects a menu option, the control flow jumps to the cell located two cells beneath the cell containing the label representing the selected menu choice. In the example below, if the user selects Clear, control moves from {menucall MEN1} to {branch CLEAR}. However, 1-2-3 treats the change in control as a *call* rather than a *branch* (the {menubranch} command treats the change of control as a branch). So, in our example, when either the Post or Clear routine ends, the macro will next read the instructions immediately following {menucall MEN1}.

In a branch, once the macro control flow has begun reading at a new location, it continues there unless further modified. In a call, control continues at the new location only until 1-2-3 reads a {return} command, an empty cell, or a cell containing a value; at this point control will return to the command directly following the {menucall} command.

Note that if the macro encounters a {quit} command in the called subroutine, macro control will terminate completely—control will not return to the calling routine as it would if the macro encountered a {return} command.

In the example below if someone selects Clear, control will have moved from the cell containing the {menubranch} command to the cell that reads {branch CLEAR}. We strongly recommend that you place a {branch} command there to redirect control to a macro residing in the macro column. Otherwise, you'll be writing macros in as many columns as there are menu items in your menu and, because they'll be written side by side, those macros will be impossible to document and very difficult to read.

If the user presses the Escape key while the menu displays, control returns to the macro instruction that immediately follows the {menucall} command to the next label in the macro. Thus, whether the user presses Escape or chooses a menu option, control returns to the same instruction. Since it is highly unlikely you want the macro to process the same instruction if a person presses Escape as you want processed at the end of the subroutines, you have to make a decision as to what instruction should follow the original {menucall}. The more important of the two choices is the command you use to continue processing after the subroutines terminate. That means that you should plan to subsequently offer the user—who may have pressed Escape mistakenly—the choice to return to this menu. The menu must contain an option the user can select to exit from the loop you've created with the {menucall} command.

Example:

\M	{menucall MEN1}		Display menu
	{branch REPORTS}		Reporting routine
MEN1	Post	Clear	Menu options
	Post entries	clear entries	Explanation lines
	{branch POST}	{branch CLEAR}	Macro instructions

{Wait}

Purpose: Use {wait} to cause 1-2-3 to wait until a specific date and time before creating the next command in the macro. 1-2-3 displays WAIT as the mode indicator until the specified time.

Format: {wait [time-number]}

Where [time-number] is a date and time serial number. [Time-number] may be a number, a formula, a cell address, or a range name describing a single cell. If [time-number] represents a non-existent time, or a time that has already passed, {wait} has no effect.

Sample: {wait @now+@time(0;0;5)}

See also: {?} (interactive command)

Description: {Wait} causes 1-2-3 to suspend reading the current macro until DOS's built-in clock matches the date and time specified in the {wait} command. You can use {wait} to pause either until a given time (such as 11:30 p.m. on January 3, 1991) or for a certain length of time (such as 1 hour).

To cause 1-2-3 to suspend creating the current macro until a certain time, you must first translate that time into 1-2-3's means for specifying it. For example, to suspend the macro until 11:30 p.m. on January 3, 1991, use the command: {wait@date(91;1;3)+@time(23;30;0)}. The command combines the @date and @time functions. the @date function uses the arguments year, month, day, so @date(91;1;3) translates to January 3, 1991. The @time function uses the arguments hours, minutes, seconds, so @time(23;30;0) is 11:30 p.m.

If you want to suspend macro execution until some time later today, you could use either of two methods—either tell the macro to wait for a certain length of time, or tell it to wait until a certain time. To tell the macro to wait a certain length of time, use an argument that consists of the @now function added to a certain length of time. To wait ten minutes for instance, use: {wait@now+@time(0;10;0)}. To wait five seconds use: {wait @now+@time(0;0;5)}.

{Wait} is most often used to set the length of time a message will display to the user. For example, an error or information screen can be made to appear on the screen for thirty seconds, and then the macro can continue.

Example:

{let ANS;@cellpointer("address")}	Store current address
{goto}INFO_SCREEN~	Display info screen
{wait @now+@time(0;0;3)}	Wait for 3 sec
{goto}{ANS}~	Return to original address

{?} (interactive command)

Purpose: Use {?} to return control of the macro to the user temporarily—until the user presses Enter.

Format: {?}

Sample: {?}

See also: {get}, {getlabel}, {getnumber}

Description: Known as either the interactive command or the pause command, the {?} command does both. When 1-2-3 reads {?} in a macro, it temporarily interrupts the macro's processing (thus, the name "pause") and returns control to the keyboard (thus, the name "interactive"). As soon as the user presses Enter, the macro resumes control and continues reading with the next command.

There are a number of ways you might use the {?} command. In simple macros, you can use it to allow the user to read a message. If you are testing a macro, insert {?} commands where you want the macro to pause so that you can verify that the macro has performed properly (don't forget to remove them later). You can also use it to return control of 1-2-3 to the keyboard in the midst of a macro. You might want to allow the user to move the cell pointer or menu pointer, enter data, or make menu selections. The user can also click OK with the mouse to enter data and the {?} command will remain in effect, allowing further entry before proceeding with the macro.

When you use the {?} to turn control of 1-2-3 back to the user, you do so unconditionally. You cannot prevent a user from doing things you don't want done; the macro has suspended all control.

You should also beware that the first time the user presses Enter, the macro will continue processing where it left off. If the user has just done something that requires a Enter to complete that operation, the macro must provide the Return in the form of a tilde directly following the {?}.

For example, if during an interactive pause in the macro, the user types some data and presses Return, the Return keystroke, which would normally enter the data in a cell, will not do so. Instead, it will trigger the macro to continue reading keystrokes. Since the typed data will still be in the control panel (with 1-2-3 in Edit mode) when the macro resumes, it falls to the macro to enter the data. Typically, you would include a tilde as the first character after the {?} command to do so. If you have to move the cell pointer next, you can omit the tilde and just follow the {?} command with the cell pointer movement command—it'll move the cell pointer and enter the data.

Example:

\A	{?}{r}	Data entry sequence
	{?}{r}	
	{?}{r}	
	{1 3}	Return to start of next row
	{d}	
	{branch \A}	Repeat macro

Controlling Program Flow

These commands direct the path of macro execution, using subroutines, branches, calls, for loops, and conditioned processing.

{subroutine}

Purpose: Use {*subroutine*} to temporarily redirect macro flow of control from the current location to another location.

Format: {subroutine [parameter1],[parameter2],[parameter*N*]}
Where subroutine is a range name (or a range address) to which control will be temporarily transferred; the range name can refer to the first cell of the subroutine or to the entire subroutine. [Parameter1] is an optional data element to be used by one of the commands in that location. {*subroutine*} passes the parameters to the subroutine, which *must* begin with a {define} command if parameters are used.

By default, each [parameter] is treated as a string. However, if the {define} command in the corresponding subroutine specifies that a [parameter] is to be a value (:v), it may be a number, a formula, a cell address, or a range name describing a single cell. Curiously, [parameter] need not evaluate to a number if it is a formula, a cell address, or a range name.

Sample: {WIDTH} or {WIDTH 30}

Complements: {return}

See also: {define}, {menucall}, {for}, {dispatch}, {branch}

Description: {*subroutine*} instructs 1-2-3 to temporarily discontinue reading macro instructions in the current cell and begin reading in the top left cell of the specified named range. {*subroutine*} can also pass one or more labels or values (called parameters) to be used by macro commands in the new location.

Like entire macros, subroutines are commonly referred to by the name of the cell containing their first instruction. However, you do not activate a macro with the first line of a subroutine; you transfer control of an already operating macro to that line.

You transfer control to a subroutine by including the name of the subroutine within curly braces in the macro. If cell B10 has been named Print, and the first line of a printing subroutine begins in cell B10, when 1-2-3 reads the command {PRINT} in a macro, it will transfer macro control to that subroutine.

The macro commands in the new location to which control has been redirected are known as a subroutine. A subroutine is a good place to store commonly used macro operations. Instead of repeating those operations within each macro, you can simply redirect control temporarily to the subroutine (that's known as "calling" a subroutine). When the subroutine finishes its work, it will return control to the macro that called it. Specifically, control will return to the command directly following the {*subroutine*} command in the calling macro. In that way, different macros can use the services of just a single subroutine.

Let's look at an example of a subroutine call. Suppose you frequently use the command sequence {windowsoff}{paneloff} to freeze the current contents of the display. Instead of writing the commands {windowsoff}{paneloff} repeatedly, you place them into a subroutine called Off. Likewise, you could store the complementary commands {windowson}{panelon} in a subroutine called On. when you use either Off or On in the macro, you'll enclose them in the subroutine command so they look like this, {OFF} and {ON}.

Here's the macro:

\A	{goto}MESSAGE2~	Display message
	{OFF}	Freeze display
	/dsg	Sort list
	/cENTRY1~ENTRY2~	Copy entries
	{ON}	Update screen
	{menubranch MEN2}	Display menu
OFF	{windowsoff}{paneloff}	Freeze display
	{return}	Return to main routine
ON	{windowson}{panelon}	Thaw display
	{return}	Return to main routine

A calling routine can send data to the subroutine it calls in order to specialize the way in which that subroutine works. The data it sends may be labels, values, or both, and are known collectively as parameters. The process of sending this data to a subroutine is known as passing parameters.

In the next macro, the main routine (\A) uses a series of calls to a subroutine named Test to test each of the four entries in a column of sales figures. However, instead of simply calling the subroutine as {TEST}, each subroutine call also includes a number, such as {TEST 10}. The number 10 in {TEST 10} is a parameter. Directly following each subroutine call is the cell pointer movement key name {d}, which moves the cell pointer down to the next entry in the column.

Example:

\A	{TEST 10}{d}
	{TEST 15}{d}
	{TEST 12}{d}
	{TEST 25}{d}
	{TEST 45}{d}
	{quit}
TEST	{define BUDGET:v}
	{if @cellpointer("contents")>=Budget}{return}
	{r}
	Too low
	{l}
	{return}
BUDGET	

The subroutine named Test does the work of testing each entry.

The first command, {define}, stores the passed parameter as a value in a cell named Budget. (Without the :v at the end of the {define} command, the passed parameter would be stored as a label.)

The second line of the subroutine evaluates whether the current cell is greater than or equal to the amount stored in the cell named Budget.

If so, the {if} statement is true and the macro reads the {return} command located to its right. The {return} command returns control to the main routine just after the command that called the subroutine. That next command is {down}, which moves the cell pointer to the next sales figure in the list. The command that follows in yet another subroutine call with another parameter.

But what happens if the entry being tested is less than the amount stored in the cell named Budget? The {if} command in the second line of the subroutine will evaluate to false. Rather than read the {return} command to its right, macro control will skip directly to the next line.

The macro moves the cell pointer one cell to the right, types the label *Too low*, moves left again (and, in the process, enters the label on the worksheet), and returns control to the main routine.

For more information on the relationship between passing parameters and the {define} command, see the {define} command.

Each time a macro makes a subroutine call, 1-2-3 must make a note of where that call came from in order to return to that location when the subroutine ends.

As you may have already discovered, you can call subroutines within subroutines. This is called *nesting*. Using nested subroutines lets you create large macro applications that are clearly structured, and easy to revise. Each time you call a subroutine within a subroutine, 1-2-3 adds the latest location of the subroutine call to the list of places it must remember. Collectively, that list of locations is known as the subroutine stack or the subroutine chain.

Each time a macro calls a subroutine, the number of subroutines in the stack increases by one level. Each time a subroutine returns control to the calling routine, that stack decreases by one level. Another way to describe the status of the subroutine stack is to say that there are currently a certain number of levels of subroutines nested in the chain.

1-2-3 can accommodate 31 levels of subroutine calls before the stack fills to its capacity. If your macro encounters a 32nd subroutine call, it will terminate in an error, and 1-2-3 will display the message *Too many nesting levels in macro calls*.

{Branch}

Purpose: Use {branch} to redirect macro control flow from the current location to another location.

Format: {branch [location]}
Where [location] refers to the location of the macro commands to execute. [location] may be a cell name or address or a range name or address.

Sample: {branch NEXT}

See also: {subroutine}, {for}, {dispatch}, {onerror}, {menubranch}

Description: {Branch} instructs 1-2-3 to discontinue reading macro instructions in the current cell and resume reading in the top left cell of the specified location. {Branch} is equivalent to the GOTO command in the BASIC programming language. {branch} is not, however, the same as {goto}. {Goto} moves the cell pointer to another cell, while {branch} transfers macro control to the commands that begin in the location designated.

{Branch} is the command through which you can implement a simple loop; that is, make the macro repeat itself by branching to a cell above the {branch} command in the same macro. If you want to write a loop with a counter, either use the {for} command or use {branch} as part of a counter routine.

Example:

{if ANS>30}{branch NEXT}	If more than 30, run NEXT
{branch LOOP}	Otherwise, try again

{Define}

Purpose: Use {define} to designate a range in which to store one or more arguments to be passed to a subroutine. You must include a {define} command in any subroutine to which you pass arguments, and the {define} command must appear *before* the part in the subroutine where the arguments are used.

Format: {define [cell1]:[type1],...,[cell$N$]:[type$N$]}
Where [cell] represents the location in which to store the parameter and each optional [type] argument may be either *value* (or simply *v*), or *string* (or simply *s*). If no type is specified, 1-2-3 assumes a string. [Cell] may be a cell name or address or a range name or address.

Sample: {define ANS:value}

Complements: {subroutine}

Description: When you call a subroutine (see the {subroutine} command), you have the option of passing arguments or parameters to that subroutine to specialize the way in which it works. A parameter could be a label or a value, and you can pass more than one parameter at a time.

The {define} command stores those parameters in worksheet cells so that the subroutine can reference them. Since the calling routine will do the work of changing the parameters it passes, the subroutine need to never be changed.

When a parameter is a value, which is frequently the case, you must specify it as a value in the {define} command. When you write the {define} command, you can do that by writing the entire word *value* as a suffix to the cell location or by writing only the first letter of that word, v.

Example: let's suppose you need to set columns to a variety of widths during your application. The commands to set column width are /Worksheet Column Set-Width followed by a value representing a number of spaces, and Enter. If you wanted to set the column to 25 spaces wide, the macro would be /wcs25~. You could write one routine for each column-width setting, but that would involve a lot of rewriting of routines that are essentially the same. Instead, you could write just one subroutine to vary the width of a column and pass to that subroutine the appropriate width setting each time you use it.

If the column-setting subroutine is called Width, then the command {WIDTH 30} in the calling macro would call the Width subroutine and pass it to the parameter 30. The Width subroutine would then look like the one shown in the example below:

```
WIDTH      {define SIZE}
           /wcs{SIZE}~
           {return}
```

The first command in the subroutine, {define}, stores the parameter (in this case, 30) as a label in a cell named Size. The next line of the macro uses that cell as a subroutine to supply the width setting to the /wcs command. Finally, the {return} command returns the flow of control to the calling routine.

{Dispatch}

Purpose: Use {dispatch} to indirectly branch to a macro at some other location.

Format: {dispatch [range]}

Where [range] is the name or address of range1. Range1 in turn contains a reference to range2. Range2 contains the macro commands to execute.

[Range] may be a cell name or address or a range name or address. [Range] may also be a formula that returns a cell address, a range address, or a range name.

Sample: {dispatch CHOICE}

See also: {branch}, {*subroutine*}

Description: {Dispatch} transfers macro control from one routine to another by way of an intermediary range. This intermediary range contains the name or address of the range containing the actual macro commands to execute.

For example, suppose you want to offer the user a menu with more than eight choices. Rather than write a two-level menu with the {menubranch} or {menucall} command, you decide to write the menu choices on the worksheet, along with a message instructing the user to choose a menu choice by highlighting the cell containing a menu letter and pressing Enter.

That menu screen (SCREEN_MENU) might appear like this:

To select a choice: Move the pointer to the letter of your choice and press the Return key
A   Post monthly entries.
B   Produce Reports.
C   Retrieve another file.

The macro code you might use to control that operation appears as follows:

\M	{goto}SCREEN_MENU~	Show menu
	{?}	Pause for user choice
	{Let CHOICE;@CELLPOINTER("CONTENTS")}	Store choice
	{dispatch CHOICE}	Branch through CHOICE
CHOICE	Variable storage	
A	{goto}SCREEN_ONE~	Routine A
	{quit}	
B	{goto}SCREEN_TWO~	Routine B
	{quit}	
C	{goto}SCREEN_THREE~	Routine C
	{quit}	

In this macro the first command displays the portion of the worksheet containing the menu; the second line uses the interactive command to temporarily return control to the user. the user is expected to read the menu, move the cell pointer to the letter beside a menu choice, and press Enter to select that choice. When the user does this, the {dispatch} command will cause the macro to branch to the named location matching the menu letter.

In the macro, the cell named Choice stores a copy of the letter on which the cell pointer sat when the user pressed Enter. The {dispatch} command transfers the macro control flow to the location named in Choice.

Note that {dispatch} does not return control to the calling macro. To return control to the calling macro, use {branch} or another {dispatch} in the called macro.

{For}

Purpose: Use {for} to implement a counter. It will run a macro subroutine any number of times you specify.

Format: {for [counter],[start],[stop],[step],[location]}

Where [counter] is a cell in which {for} will increment a value; [start] is the number at which to begin counting; [stop] is the number at which to stop counting; [step] is the number by which to increment the counter with each repetition of the subroutine that begins at the location specified by [location].

[Counter] may be a cell name or address or a range name or address. It should be a blank cell since anything in {counter} is replaced. Each of [start], [stop], and [step] may be a number, a formula, a cell address, or a range name describing a single cell. [Location] may be a cell name or address or a range name or address.

Sample: {for NUM,1,10,1,BELL}

Complements: {forbreak}

See also: {forbreak}, {*subroutine*}, {branch}, {dispatch}

Description: {For} enables you to control the number of repetitions of a given subroutine. The {for} command passes control to a subroutine; when control returns, {for} increments a counter and compares it against a preset limit (the stop value). If the counter value is less than the limit value, {for} passes control back to the subroutine and the process repeats. If the counter value is equal to or greater than the limit value, control passes from the {for} command to the next command in the macro (instead of to the subroutine).

The arguments to the {for} command define how the counter will work. The first of them, [counter], identifies the cell used to store the counter value; the second, [start], sets an initial value for that cell.

The third argument, [stop], establishes the stop value. Each time the subroutine called by {for} returns control to {for} and 1-2-3 increments the counter cell, 1-2-3 will also compare the stop value to the counter value. If the stop value is equal to or greater than the counter value, instead of running the subroutine again, the {for} command will relinquish macro control to the next command in the macro.

The fourth argument, [step], sets the amount by which to increment the counter each time macro control returns to the {for} command. Obviously, if [step] is 0, the number in [counter] will never exceed the stop value, and the {for} loop becomes an infinite loop. Finally, the fifth argument, [location], identifies the first cell of the subroutine that the {for} command will call.

The {for} command allows you to start counting with any value you wish. For example, if the second argument in the {for} command is a one, then the first value that the {for} command will assign to the counter cell is one. The difference between a start value of one and a start value of zero is significant. Given the same value for the upper limit argument, a counter that begins at value zero will process the loop once more than a counter that begins at the value one. To make the number of loops equal to the stop value (as most situations call for), use a one as your start value.

Remember that because {for} calls a subroutine, it's a good idea to end that subroutine with a {return} command to explicitly return control to the {for} command that called it.

Because {for} calls a subroutine, that call increases the subroutine chain by one. However, that subroutine also decrements the subroutine chain when it ends and returns control to the {for} command. So, {for} increases the subroutine chain by only one—regardless of how many times the {for} command repeats the subroutine it calls.

Example:

\A	{for COUNTER;1;LIMIT;1;WIDEN}	Set up counter
	{branch ENTRY}	Do data entry
	COUNTER	Store current count
	LIMIT 5	Store limit value
	WIDEN /wcs18~	Widen column
	{r}	Move right
	{return}	Return to \A

> Note: Don't use the {for} command—or any other form of loop—when the routine you want to repeat consists only of a macro key name (for example, {r} or {pgdn}). Key names all accept numeric arguments that describe how many times 1-2-3 should repeat them when they're in a macro (e.g., {r 10}, {pgdn 2}), and they operate much faster than implementing the same scheme through a loop.
>
> If you need to repeat a key name and want to be able to vary the number of times that 1-2-3 does so, use a range name as the key name argument ({r NUM}), then use a {let} or {getnumber} command to assign the contents of the range name. For example:
>
> {getnumber "Move to the right how many columns? ";NUM}
>
> {r NUM}

{Forbreak}

Purpose: Use {forbreak} to prematurely end the execution of a {for} loop.

Format: {forbreak}

Sample: {if VALUE>MAX}{forbreak}{branch OVERMAX}

Complements: {for}

See also: {restart}, {return}

Description: {Forbreak} cancels a subroutine called by a {for} statement and returns control to the macro instruction that immediately follows the {for} command. If the macro reads a {forbreak} when no {for} loop is in effect, an irrecoverable error will occur accompanied by the error message *Invalid FORBREAK*.

{Forbreak} differs from a {return} command in a subroutine called by a {for} routine. {Return} ends only the current iteration of the {for} loop and returns control to the {for} statement, whereupon {for} will increment its counter and decide if it should rerun the subroutine. {Forbreak} terminates the current iteration of the subroutine, seizes control from the {for} command, and transfers control to the next macro instruction following the {for} statement.

Another related command, {restart}, does yet another thing. {Restart} severs all ties between the currently executing subroutine and the routine(s) that called it. If a macro encounters {restart} in a {for} loop, 1-2-3 will clear the subroutine stack and continue reading in the current location. It will never return control to the main routine.

Since {restart} will entirely cancel the subroutine nesting chain, including any subroutine calls made by {for} commands, any {restart} command will render any {forbreak} commands unnecessary.

Because {for} increments the subroutine nesting chain by one, {forbreak} reduces it by one. For that reason, if you've nested {for} commands (where one {for} statement calls a subroutine that uses yet another {for} statement to call a second subroutine), the {forbreak} command will cancel only the last {for} subroutine.

Higher-level subroutine calls (i.e., subroutine calls that precede the {for} subroutine call in the subroutine nesting chain) will remain unaffected by {forbreak}. {Forbreak} is often used as an "escape hatch" from a {for} loop. To implement such an escape, place an {if} statement in the subroutine called by the {for} command. Structure the {if} statement so that one branch continues the subroutine while the other reads {forbreak} to break out of the loop.

{If}

Purpose: Use {if} to test a condition and direct program flow accordingly.

Format: {if [condition]}

Where [condition] is a numeric value. [Condition] is usually a logical formula or the name or address of a cell that contains a logical formula.

Sample: {if @cellpointer("row")<60}

See also: {branch}

Description: The {if} command generally contains an expression that evaluates to 0 or 1. The expression is usually a logical condition containing at least one of 1-2-3's relational operators =, <, >, <=, >=. If the condition is true, the conditional expression returns a 1; if false, the expression returns a 0. Here's an example of a conditional expression: Test1=Test2.

The {if} command will evaluate the conditioned expression and if it finds that expression to be false (that is, the expression returns a 0), it will modify the normal macro control flow by skipping over any remaining macro instructions in the same cell, and jumping directly to the next line. If the condition is true (the expression returns a 1), the macro will continue with the next instruction immediately following the {if} command in the same cell.

{If} is most useful when you use it as part of an "if-then-else" construct. An if-then-else construct enables the macro to test an expression and if it's true, then perform one set of instructions; or else (if it's false), perform a different set of instructions.

Let's look at an example. The routine shown below checks to see if a user has entered the letter Y and either runs the routine named Yes if the user did so, or runs the routine named No in the user entered any other letter or no letter at all.

{get ANS}	Capture user's keystroke
{if @upper(ANS)="Y"}{branch YES}	If it's "Y", run YES
{branch NO}	Otherwise, run NO

Line one of the macro captures a keystroke from the user and stores it in a cell named ANS. Line two contains two commands—an {if} command followed by a {branch} command. The {if} command checks to see if the keystroke, stored in ANS, is equal to a *Y*. Since 1-2-3 discriminates between uppercase and lowercase in conditional formulas, but you want either *Y* or *y*, this conditional formula first converts the string value in ANS to uppercase: @upper(ANS). Whether the keystroke was uppercase or lowercase, you can now test for an uppercase Y.

If the conditional formula is true, the macro will continue reading in normal fashion with the command {branch YES}. When it does, that command will transfer control directly to the routine named Yes, skipping the next line. If the conditional formula is false, the macro will skip any commands following the {if} command on the same line and transfer control directly to the line below. That line contains the command {branch NO}, which will transfer control to a routine named No.

In sum, the {if} command evaluates a condition and transfers control to one routine if the condition is true, or transfers control to another routine if the condition is false.

However, there's a potential for a problem with an if-then-else construct in a macro. Suppose that to the right of the {if} command you used some other command *besides* a {branch} command. For example, suppose you wanted the application to record the label *Yes* if the keystroke stored in ANS is a *Y*, and the label *No* if the stored keystroke is anything else or no keystroke at all. Here's the macro:

{get ANS}	Capture user's keystroke
{if @upper(ANS)+"Y"}Yes~	If it's "Y", enter Yes
No~	Otherwise, enter No

If the condition is false, the macro works fine: it skips the instructions to the right of the {if} command, reads the instructions on the line below, and enters the label *No*. However, if the condition is true, the macro won't perform as intended: The condition is true, so the macro continues reading instructions on the same line and enters the label *Yes* in the current cell. However, *it then continues reading on the next line*, and enters the label *No* over the label *Yes* in the current cell. In other words, no matter what the condition is, the end result will be the label *No*.

The only way an {if} command can properly perform its if-then-else mission is if its writer includes on the same line as the {if} command an instruction to transfer control elsewhere or an instruction that ends the macro. In short, if the instructions that follow the {if} command on the same line are read, they must prevent macro control from reaching the next line.

{Onerror}

Purpose: Use {onerror} to specify a macro routine to be run in the event the macro encounters an error.

Format: {onerror [branch-location],[message-location]}

Where [branch-location] is a cell name or address, or a range name or address that contains the macro instructions to which 1-2-3 should branch after an error occurs. If you use a multicell range, 1-2-3 branches to the first cell in that range. [Message-location] is an optional argument; it can be a cell name or address, or a range name or address specifying a location in which to store 1-2-3's error message.

Sample: {onerror RECOVER}

See also: {return}, {branch}, {subroutine}

Description: {Onerror} enables a macro to recover gracefully from many errors that would otherwise cause it to terminate in Error mode. Such errors include *Printer error, File does not exist,* and *Disk drive not ready.* {Onerror} cannot trap macro syntax errors (e.g., typing errors within a macro). When it encounters macro syntax errors, it ends the macro and displays a message that describes the error.

The first argument, [branch-location], supplies a location to which macro control will branch in the event of an error. The optional second argument tells 1-2-3 where to store its error message.

If you use the second argument, you'll probably want to do one of two things, or both. You can include an instruction to display the designated location, to inform the user of the nature of the error, and to enable him to do something to correct it. You might also have the macro test the contents of that location, perform a table lookup on a table of error messages, and use the result to determine the proper error-handling routine to run.

{Onerror} not only prevents 1-2-3 from terminating macro control when one of the errors it can trap occurs, it suppresses 1-2-3's normal display of the error message at the bottom of the screen and the beep that normally accompanies such errors. Consequently, you may wish to display the error message on the worksheet and use the {beep} command to alert the user of the problem before initiating corrective action.

Once invoked, {onerror} remains in effect until the macro encounters an error and executes the {onerror} command's instructions, or until another {onerror} command supersedes it, or until macro control ends. Each time 1-2-3 reads a new {onerror} command, 1-2-3 cancels the old {onerror} command's instructions and stores the new command's instructions.

When 1-2-3 encounters an error and branches according to the instructions in the last {onerror} command, the subroutine chain is completely canceled, no matter how many levels of subroutines that chain may have contained. If the macro subsequently reads a {return} command, for example, macro control will end—just as it will any time the macro reads a {return} when the subroutine chain is empty.

The routine you designate in the {onerror} command—the one macro will branch to in the event of an error—should help you to correct the source of the trouble.

Such a macro can either show the user the error message and expect the user to figure out the problem, or it can test for any of several likely error messages and specifically instruct the user how to correct the problem.

Example:

PRINT	{onerror ERR1,ANS}	Setup error trap
	/ppagpq	Print
	{return}	Return to caller
ANS		Store Err message
ERR1	{if @mid(ANS;11;6)="driver"}{branch NO_DRV}	No Drvr, No Printer,
	{if @mid(ANS;0;7)="Printer"}{branch NO_PRN}	and No Print Range
	{if @mid(ANS;9;5)="range"}{branch NO_RING}	errors

{Quit}

Purpose: Use {quit} to force the macro to stop and return keyboard control to the user.

Format: {quit}

Sample: {quit}

Description: {Quit} stops the processing of the current macro and returns control of 1-2-3 to the user at the keyboard. {Quit} returns control to the keyboard unconditionally—the command ends the entire macro, not just a subroutine.

Because {quit} provides an explicit terminator to a macro, it eliminates the need to place a blank row between different macros. It's advisable to use the {quit} command wherever you want to end a macro. You can end the macro by leaving a blank cell below the last command of that macro, but if you later inadvertently enter a label there, the macro will read that label—whether or not it was intended as part of the macro.

{Restart}

Purpose: Use {restart} to prevent subroutine from returning to the main routine when it's finished.

Format: {restart}

Sample: {restart}

See also: {subroutine}, {forbreak}, {return}, {quit}

Description: {Restart} clears the subroutine nesting chain, thereby severing the relationship between a subroutine and its calling routine.

Recall that each time a macro makes a subroutine call, 1-2-3 remembers where that call came from so as to return control to that location when the subroutine ends. You can also call subroutines within subroutines. Each time you do, 1-2-3 adds the location of the latest subroutine call to the list of places it must remember. Collectively, that list of locations is known as the subroutine stack or the subroutine nesting chain. Each time a macro calls a subroutine, the number of subroutines in the nesting chain increases by one. each time a subroutine returns control to the calling routine, that chain decreases by one.

{Restart} returns the nesting chain to level zero; that is, at the time that 1-2-3 reads the {restart} command in a macro, it immediately releases any nested subroutine calls.

When 1-2-3 encounters the {restart} command, it executers the remaining instructions in the current subroutine, but instead of returning control to the calling macro after the current subroutine ends, the macro ends.

Example:

\A	{getnumber "Enter value: ";ENTRY}	Prompt for entry
	{TEST 100}	Test entry
	+ENTRY{calc}~	Put entry on sheet
	{d}	Move down one
	{branch \A}	Repeat macro
TEST	{define LIMIT:v}	Store param. as value
	{if ENTRY>LIMIT}{branch ERROR	Perform test
	{return}	Return to caller
ERROR	{goto}ERRORMSG1~	Explain problem
	{wait @now+@time(0:0:20)}	Pause 20 seconds
	{restart}	Clear subrt stack
	{goto}DATA_SCRN~	Restore display
	{branch \A}	Begin again
ENTRY		Store entry
LIMIT		Store limit parameter

In this example, the main routine prompts the user for an entry, and then the subroutine named Test checks it. If the entry is within bounds, the subroutine returns control to the main routine. The main routine places an entry in the current cell on the worksheet and prompts the user for the next entry.

However, if the entry is out of bounds, the subroutine branches to a routine called Error. Even though subroutine Test has transferred control to Error, 1-2-3 still regards the entire operation as a subroutine initiated by the second line of the macro \A. If the macro encounters a {return} command or a blank cell, control will immediately return to the command directly following the subroutine call in the second line of macro \A.

{Return}

Purpose: Use {return} to return control from a subroutine to the calling macro.

Format: {return}

Sample: {return}

Complements: {system}, {menucall}, {for}

See also: {restart}, {forbreak}

Description: When a subroutine encounters a {return} command, control returns to the calling macro—to the command directly following the one that called that subroutine. The subroutine chain is decremented by one. (Refer to the *{subroutine}* entry for an explanation of the subroutine chain.)

If a macro reads a {return} command when the subroutine chain is empty, {return} will return control to the keyboard; the macro will end just as if a {quit} command had been read.

{Return} always returns control to the command directly following the most recent subroutine call, no matter if it was called by a {subroutine}, a {menucall}, or a {for} command. If the subroutine chain is three levels deep, the first {return} command will return control to the third calling routine. The next {return} will return control to the second calling routine. The final {return} will return control to the first calling routine. If the macro encounters another {return} command before another subroutine has been called, macro control will end immediately.

Example:

\A	{WIDE}	Call subroutine
	{branch PRINT}	Branch to print
WIDE	/wcs35~	Widen column
	{r}	Move right one cell
	{return}	Return to caller

{System}

Purpose: Use {system} to suspend the worksheet session, exit to DOS, run some DOS program or batch file from DOS, and return to the worksheet.

Format: {system ["program"]}

Where ["program"] is the name of a DOS program, command, or batch file that can be run from the current directory, or a range name, cell address, or formula that evaluates to such a name. The string that makes up ["program"] can also include any parameters for that command, such as a file you wish to load with that program (refer to the sample below).

Sample: {system "payroll"}

Description: The {system} command temporarily sets aside the worksheet session, loads DOS, and loads any other program for which sufficient memory remains. When the program, batch file, or DOS command you've initiated finishes, if it fails to pass control to some other process, the worksheet returns and control returns to the command following {system}.

The {system} command differs from selecting /System from the 1-2-3 Classic menu in that the latter merely loads DOS and presents the DOS prompt, whereas the former passes control to some DOS-based program, batch file, or command. If that program, batch file, or command is unavailable to accept control, if there is insufficient memory available for it to run, or if it finishes running, control *returns to 1-2-3 and the calling macro.*

You do not have to enter the command Exit to return to 1-2-3 as you do when you invoke the /System command.

You can use {system} to dramatically extend the scope of your macros. With sufficient memory in your computer, your macro applications can now include dBASE programs, sophisticated batch files, and BASIC, PASCAL, and C programs. You might, for example, call dBASE, run a dBASE accounting program, save one of the accounting database files in comma-delimited format, return to 1-2-3, use the File Import From Numbers command to import it onto the worksheet, and have the macro analyze the file.

The {system} command requires an argument. You might use the command to call a DOS batch file maned Trans.bat ({system "trans"}) or run a dBASE program maned Payables.prg ({system "dBASE payables"}).

Manipulating Data

These commands Enter, Edit and recalculate data.

{Appendbelow}

Purpose: Use {appendbelow} with the [form] command to transfer records from an entry form to a database table. {Appendbelow} copies the contents of a source-location to the rows immediately below a target-location.

Format: {appendbelow[target-location],[sourcelocation]}

Where [target-location] and [source-location] are ranges of any size. If you use named ranges, the range name definition of [target-location] expands to include the rows that contain the appended data.

Sample: {appendbelow ORDERS,NEWORDER}

Complements: {form}

See also: {appendright}

Description: To use the {appendbelow} command you should set up an entry form (as your source location) and a database table (as your target location). {Appendbelow} will copy the current labels and values in the same range and attach them to the last row of the database table. When source-location contains formulas, {appendbelow} copies the current values of the formulas to target-location, not the formulas themselves. The range address defining the database table will expand one row each time a new record is appended.

{Appendbelow} will fail and the macro will stop if it encounters these errors:

- The number or rows in source-location exceeds the number of rows in the worksheet below target-location.
- The area below the target-location contains data that would be overwritten.
- When rows below target-location are protected.

Example:

The following macro lets you enter new customer information in an unprotected range named NEWCUST in an entry form named CUSTFORM. It then appends the information in NEWCUST to the customer database table named CUSTDB and expands CUSTDB to include the new record.

{FORM CUSTFORM}
{appendbelow CUSTB,NEWCUST}

{Appendright}

Purpose: Use {appendright} to add a new field to a database table or a column of data to a spreadsheet application. {Appendright} copies the contents of a source-location to the columns immediately to the right of a target-location.

Format: {appendright[target-location],[source-location]}

Where [target-location] and [source-location] are ranges of any size. If you use named ranges, the range name definition of [target-location] expands to include the columns that contain the appended data.

Sample: {appendright} SALES, WESTSALES}

Complements: {form}

See also: {appendbelow}

Description: {Appendright} is generally used to copy periodic columnar data such as monthly or annual figures to the right of an existing table of data for the month or year to date. (e.g. adding the column of April's sales figures to the columns for January, February and March). Note that when the source data contains formulas, {appendright} copies just the current values of the formulas to the target location, and not the formuals themselves. {Appendright} will fail and stop the macro if the number of columns in source-location exceeds the number of columns in the worksheet to the right of target-location.

- The appending source-location will write over existing data.
- The columns to the right of target-location are protected.

Example: In a sales record-keeping system, the macro below copies July sales totals (JULTOT) to the right of the monthly sales totals (MONTOT), and expands MONTOT to include the appended totals.

{appendright MONTOT,JULTOT}

{Blank}

Purpose: Use {blank} to erase a range on the worksheet.

Format: {blank [range]}
Where [range] is a cell name or address, or range name or address.

Sample: {blank FORM1}

Description: {Blank} erases a designated range on the worksheet. {Blank} differs from Edit Clear and the Classic range Erase in two ways:

- The Edit Clear command (and /Range Erase) must be invoked from Ready mode. {Blank} is much more flexible; it can be invoked in the middle of a menu, a formula, and so on.

- The Edit Clear command (and /Range Erase) will immediately update the screen, where as the {blank} command won't. If you want 1-2-3 to update the screen immediately after reading a {blank} command, place a tilde directly after {blank} in the macro. Otherwise, 1-2-3 will not update the screen until after the macro ends and you move the cell pointer or press Enter, or until some other command forces a screen update.

Example:

{blank FORM}	Erase data entry form
{branch ENTRY}	Begin data entry

{CONTENTS}

Purpose: Use {contents} to place a formatted number into a cell and convert it to a label.

Format: {contents [destination],[source],[width],[format]}

Where [destination] is a cell in which to store the label entry produced by the command; [source] is a cell from which to copy the appearance of an entry; [width] is the length of the resulting label; and [format] is a code representing the range format to impose on the resulting label. (See the table below for format code numbers.) [Width] and [format] are optional arguments.

Each of [destination] and [source] may be a cell name or address or a range name or address. Each of [width] and [format] may be a number, a formula, a cell address, or a range name describing a single cell.

Sample: {contents DEST1,SOURCE1,12;78}
{contents DEST2,SOURCE2,,113}

See also: {let}, {put}

Description: {Contents} copies the appearance of a given source cell and places that copy into a given destination cell as a label. You can modify the appearance of the original cell contents by specifying a width other than that of the source cell, and if the source cell contains a value, you may also specify a different format. When the source cell contains a value, {contents} can adopt any of 1-2-3's Range Formats as part of the label it enters into the destination cell. If you do not specify a width or format code in the {contents} command, it will use the same width and format display of the source cell.

{Contents} always produces a left-aligned label entry in the destination cell. If the entry in the source cell is a value, the {contents} command will convert it to a label. If the entry in the source cell is a label, only the portion of the label that displays *within* the current column will be copied to the destination cell; portions of the label that overwrite adjoining cells won't be copied to the destination cell. Therefore, if you want to copy the entire label, adjust the width of the column containing the source cell so that it accommodates the entire label to be copied.

If you specify a destination width smaller than that needed to accommodate a source *value*, 1-2-3 will display asterisks in the destination cell, just as it would anytime a cell width prevents a value from fully displaying. If you specify a destination width smaller than that needed to accommodate a source *label*, 1-2-3 will truncate the label it enters into the destination cell, leaving off characters farthest to the right in the original entry.

The foregoing problem affects labels in a curious way. If the source cell is insufficiently wide to display the whole label, you know that the label merely writes over the cell directly to its right, provided that cell is empty. However, if the destination is insufficiently wide, 1-2-3 will truncate the label to fit the cell and will not write over the cell to the right, even if that cell is empty. To copy a label with the {contents} command in this case, you must specify a width large enough to accommodate the whole label. (Only then will 1-2-3 let the label spill over to the cell directly to the right of the destination cell.)

Although the label in the destination cell will be left-aligned, {contents} may pad it with blank spaces to make it appear as it did in the source cell. Therefore, suppose the source cell is 15 spaces wide and contains the centered label *Hello*. If you use the {contents} command to copy it to a destination cell, the destination cell will contain a left-aligned label consisting of five blank spaces, the string *Hello*; and five more blank spaces. The actual width of the destination cell is irrelevant. If the source cell was still 15 spaces wide but the label it contained was right-aligned, the label in the destination cell would consist of the string *Hello* preceded by 10 blank spaces.

Since values are right-aligned on the worksheet, when {contents} reproduces a value as a label, it will display it one space to the left of the right border of that label.

If the source cell is empty, {contents} will enter an apostrophe label-prefix in the destination cell.

If the source cell is a label and you have supplied a format argument, 1-2-3 will ignore that format argument.

If you want to convert a value entry into a label entry, you can specify the same range for both the destination and source ranges. When you execute the {contents} command, the macro will change the entry in the source cell into a label with the designated formatting.

Use the following table to select the value you should use as the last argument of the {contents} command to produce the corresponding format.

0 to 15	Fixed, 0-15 decimal places	
16 to 31	Scientific, 0-15 decimal places	
32 to 47	Currency, 0-15 decimal places	
48 to 63	Percent, 0-15 decimal places	
64 to 79	Comma, 0-15 decimal places	
112	+/-	
113	General	
114	DD-MM-YY (D1)	
115	DD-MMM (D2)	
116	MMM-YY)D3)	
117	Literal	
118	Hidden	
119	HH:MM:SS: AM/PM (D6)	
120	HH:MM AM/PM (D7)	
121	MM/DD/YY Full international date (D4)	
122	MM/DD Partial international date (D5)	
123	HH:MM:SS Full international time (D8)	
124	HH:MM Partial international time (D9)	
127	Current Worksheet Global Format	

Example:

{let TODAY;@now}	Enter date serial no.
{contents DATE1;TODAY;10;114}~	Date stamp the sheet
{quit}	End of macro

{Let}

Purpose: Use {let} to place a number or a left-aligned label into another cell.

Format: {let [destination],[entry]}

Where [destination] is the cell in which to store data and [entry] is the data to be placed in the cell. [Destination] may be a cell name or address, or a range name or address. If you specify a range, 1-2-3 enters the number or label in the first cell of the range. [Entry] may be text, a number, a formula, a cell address, or a range name describing a single cell.

You can add one or two suffixes—:string or :value (or an abbreviation of string or value, as long as the first letter is s or v, respectively)—to [entry]. The suffix tells 1-2-3 explicitly whether to treat the argument as a literal string (enter the argument verbatim) or to evaluate the argument before entering it.

The :string suffix tells 1-2-3 to store the argument as a left aligned label, even if the argument looks like a number, formula, or cell or range address.

The :value suffix tells 1-2-3 to evaluate the argument before storing it. If the argument is a number, 1-2-3 stores it as a number. If the argument is a formula, 1-2-3 evaluates the formula, and stores the result either as a left-aligned label (for a text formula) or a number (for a numeric formula). If the argument is a cell address or range name, 1-2-3 evaluates the contents of the referenced cell and stores the result as a label or number.

Sample: {let DATE,@now}

Complements: {if}

See also: {contents}, {put}

Description: Use {let} to store data in a cell. The data that {let} places in the destination cell may be either a value or a label.

{Let} will accept either a source range or a source expression. The expression may consist of a string, a value, or a formula. If the source expression contains a formula, {let} will evaluate it and enter the result as a simple value in the destination cell.

{Let} will accept expressions and store the result of such expressions in a cell. The statement {let TOTAL,4+5} enters the value *9* in the cell named Total. The statement {let GREETING; "Hi "&"John!"} produces the label *Hi John!* in a cell (although, most often you'd use a reference to another cell to supply at least part of each expression).

One of the most common ways to use {let} is to modify an existing entry—perhaps to increment a value or to add to an existing string. For example, if the cell named Counter contains the value *5*, then the command {let COUNTER;COUNTER+1} will change that to *6*. If the cell named Name contained the label *John*, then {let NAME1;+NAME1&" Jones"} will change that to *John Jones*.

Although {let} changes the contents of cells, 1-2-3 does not automatically recalculate formulas after executing a {let} command when worksheet recalculation is set to Automatic. To force recalculation after a {let} command, follow the command with ~ (tilde) or {calc}.

Example:

{let TODAY,@now}	Enter date serial no.
{contents DATE1;TODAY;10;114}~	Date stamp the sheet
{quit}	End of macro

{Put}

Purpose: Use {put} to enter a value or left aligned label into a table on the worksheet.

Format: {put [destination],[col_offset],[row_offset],[entry]}

Where [destination] is the range that contains the cell in which to store data; [col_offset] describes how many columns the cell is from the left extent of the range; [row_offset] describes how many rows the cell is from the top of the range; [value] is the data to be placed in the cell.

[Destination] may be a cell name or address or a range name or address. Each of [col_offset] and [row_offset] may be a number, a formula, a cell address, or a range name describing a single cell. [Entry] may be a string, a number, a formula, a text formula, a cell address, or a range name describing a single cell.

You can add one or two suffixes—:string or :value (or an abbreviation of string or value, as long as the first letter is s or v, respectively)—to [entry]. The suffix tells 1-2-3 explicitly whether to treat the argument as a literal string (enter the argument verbatim) or to evaluate the argument before entering it.

The :string suffix tells 1-2-3 to store the argument as a left aligned label, even if the argument looks like a number, formula, or cell or range address.

The :value suffix tells 1-2-3 to evaluate the argument before storing it. If the argument is a number, 1-2-3 stores it as a number. If the argument is a formula, 1-2-3 evaluates the formula, and stores the result either as a left-aligned label (for a text formula) or a number (for a numeric formula). If the argument is a cell address or range name, 1-2-3 evaluates the contents of the referenced cell and stores the result as a label or number.

Sample: {put TABLE;1;1;@sum(SALES_APR)}

See also: {let}, {contents}

Description: {Put} enables you to build tables or modify them. {Put} is a variant of {let}. In a {let} command you specify the target cell by its name or address. In a {put} command, you identify the target cell by its row-and-column position in a table.

Using the row and column position of any cell within a given range, {put} enables you to enter data into that cell. That entry can be a label or value produced by a string, a value, a formula, or a reference to any cell on the worksheet.

The {put} command consists of four arguments, beginning with the table range into which you want to place the entry. The next two arguments consist of values that identify the row offset and the column offset of the destination cell. To calculate the row offset, beginning with zero, count the number of rows from the top of the table range to the row in which the destination cell resides. To calculate the column offset, beginning with zero, count the number of columns from the left side of the table to the column containing the destination cell. The final argument supplies the source data.

To provide more detail, let's develop an example. Suppose your table looks like:

	APRIL	MAY	JUNE	TOTAL
Apples	100	110	110	320
Oranges	250	225	250	725
Tomatoes	90	90	90	270

The table resides in cells A3..E6, so that forms the first argument in the {put} command: *{put A3..E6,*. If you assigned the range name TABLE1 to that range, the {put} command would begin *{put TABLE1,*.

If you want to change the figure in cell D5 (June's sales of oranges), you'll next need to calculate the offset values for the row and column in which that cell resides. The table range is A3..E6, so you begin counting with zero, column A is offset 0, column B is 1, C is 2, and D (which contains the destination cell) is offset 3. Likewise, row 3 is offset 0 because it's the top row in the range A3..E6. That makes row 5—which contains the destination cell—offset 2.

Thus far, the {put} command consists of *{put TABLE1,3,2*. We next have to supply some source data. Suppose the data you want is stored in a cell called Entry. As long as you are sure that the named range Entry will exist at the time you activate the macro containing this {put} command, you can use Entry as your final argument. Here's the final {put} command: *{put TABLE1;3;2;ENTRY}*. If the named range Entry does not exist at the time you use this macro, 1-2-3 will instead enter the word ENTRY in cell D5.

The tables you produce with {put} consist exclusively of static cell entries in the form of labels or values. They never consist of cell references or formulas. Consequently, there is no active link between the table you produce or modify with {put} and the data you used in the process. If the source data changes after you use the {put} command, the destination data will not change unless you rerun the macro containing the {put} command.

Although {put} changes the contents of cells, 1-2-3 does not automatically recalculate formulas after executing a {put} command when worksheet recalculation is set to Automatic. To force recalculation after a {put} command, follow the command with ~(tilde) or {calc}.

{Recalc}

Purpose: When worksheet recalculation has been set to Manual, or during the course of a macro, use {recalc} to perform a rowwise recalculation of a range of cells.

Format: {recalc [range],[condition],[iteration]}

Where [range] is the range to be recalculated, [condition] is usually a logical formula evaluating to zero or one, and [iteration] is a number. [Condition] is an optional argument that tells 1-2-3 to repeat the recalculation until [condition] is true. [Iteration] is an optional argument that tells 1-2-3 to perform the specified number of reiteration passes. If [iteration] is 0, 1-2-3 performs the recalculation once.

[Range] may be a cell name or address or a range name or address. Each of [condition] and [iteration] may be a number, a formula, a cell address, or a range name describing a single cell.

Sample: {recalc TEST_RANGE}

See also: {recalccol}

Description: {Recalc} recalculates a range of cells on a row-by-row basis. {Recalc} is used primarily to force the recalculation of a selected portion of the worksheet *when recalculation mode has been set to Manual*. {Recalc} is also used to force 1-2-3 to update formulas that refer to cells that were modified by a macro. Because {recalc} does not recalculate the entire worksheet, it is usually able to perform a recalculation in less time than it would take were you to use the {calc} key. Use {recalc} to recalculate formulas located *below and to the left of* the cells on which they depend.

If you are using string formulas in your macros, you may use {recalc} to selectively update them.

If you want only to update the screen after using one of the advanced macro commands, such as {let} (which may change the worksheet), simply follow that command with a tilde in the macro.

Not only does {recalc} recalculate only a selected portion of the worksheet, it does not follow the natural order of recalculation.

That imposes two limits that may cause you to obtain results other than those you expect. The natural order of recalculation—1-2-3's default mode—automatically determines all cell dependencies and recalculates each cell in the proper order to resolve those dependencies correctly.

{Recalc} follows a row-by-row order of recalculation, irrespective of the dependencies of the cells within the specified range. This may cause you to obtain unexpected results.

{Recalc} will optionally repeat the recalculation until a specified condition has been satisfied or until a specified number of iterations has been reached. Note that if you use both a condition and an iteration count, 1-2-3 will stop recalculating as soon as it satisfies either argument, not both. You can use the [iteration] argument without the [condition] argument by including an extra argument separator as follows: *{recalc range,,iteration}*

Example: Assume a value in cell F5 is changed, and that a formula in A9 depends on cell F5. Both of these cells are in the range named FORM1. Because recalculation proceeds row by row, 1-2-3 recalculates F5 before A9 and the printout is accurate.

/riFORM1~	Accept data
{recalc FORM1}	Update form range
/ppcrrFORM1~agpq	Print form
{quit}	End

{Recalccol}

Purpose: Use {recalccol} to perform a columnwise recalculation of a range of cells.

Format: {recalccol [range],[condition],[iteration]}

Where [range] is the range to be recalculated, [condition] is usually a logical formula evaluating to zero or one, and [iteration] is a number. [Condition] is an optional argument that tells 1-2-3 to repeat the recalculation until [condition] is true. [Iteration] is an optional argument that tells 1-2-3 to perform the specified number of reiteration passes. If [iteration] is 0, 1-2-3 performs the recalculation once.

[Range] may be a cell name or address or a range name or address. Each of [condition] and [iteration] may be a number, a formula, a cell address, or a range name describing a single cell.

Sample: {recalccol TEST_RANGE}

See also: {recalc}

Description: {Recalccol} recalculates a range of cells on a column-by-column basis. {Recalccol} is used to force the recalculation of a selected portion of the worksheet *when recalculation mode has been set to Manual.* Because {recalccol} does not recalculate the entire worksheet, it is usually able to perform a recalculation in less time than it would take were you to use the {calc} key. Use {recalccol} to recalculate formulas located *above and to the right* of the cells on which they depend.

If you are using string formulas in your macros, you may use {recalccol} to selectively update them.

If you want only to update the screen after using one of the advanced macro commands, such as {let} (which may change the worksheet), simply follow that command with a tilde in the macro.

{Recalccol} does not follow the natural order of recalculation. It recalculates cells one column at at time, and only the cells within a specified range. Both of those factors may cause you to obtain unexpected results.

{Recalccol} will optionally repeat the recalculation until a specified condition has been satisfied or until a specified number of iterations has been reached.

Example: Assume a value in cell A9 is changed and that a formula in F6 depends on cell A9. Both of these cells are in the range named FORM1. Because recalculation proceeds column by column, 1-2-3 recalculates A9 before F6 and the printed report is accurate.

/wgrm	Manual recalc
/riFORM1~	User input
{let INPUT,@sum(DATA)}	Fill in statistics
{let INPUT2,@afg(DATA2)}	
{recalccol FORM1}	Update worksheet
{branch PRINT}	Next routine

File Manipulation

These macros commands work with text files (also known as ASCII print files).

{Close}

Purpose: In some circumstances, use {close} to terminate your work with a text file previously opened with the {open} command.

Format: {close}

Sample: {close}

Complements: {open}

Description: Under certain circumstances, if you do not explicitly close an open file, you will lose some of the data you have written to that file. The {close} command is one way to close an open file.

1-2-3 can open only one ASCII file at a time. If you write to an open file with the {write} or {writeln} commands, 1-2-3 will leave the file open for more input unless one of the following things happens:

1. You open another file

2. You invoke the /System command.

3. You retrieve another worksheet file.

4. You use the File Exit command to leave 1-2-3.

5. You use the {close} command to close it.

If, after opening an ASCII file with the {write} or {writeln} command, the macro ends and none of the above events has occurred, the file will remain open, and you face two possible problems.

The first problem occurs if you then try to use the File Import From command to import the text the file contains. Depending on circumstances, one of two things will happen. If you have opened the file in write mode (such as with the command {open "TEST.BAT";"w"}), you will import nothing. If you opened the file in append mode (such as with the command {open "TEST.BAT";"a"}) or in modify mode (such as {open "TEST.BAT";"m"}), you will get only the text written to the file prior to opening it this time. You will not get any text written to it since you opened it.

The second problem occurs if you shut your computer off or lose power without closing the file. Depending on circumstances, one of two things will happen. If you opened the file in write mode you will lose the entire file. Your disk will show a file of that name, but it will contain nothing. If you opened the file in append mode or in modify mode, you will lose only the text written to the file prior to opening this time. You will not lose the text written to it before you opened it.

For these reasons, you may wish to avoid leaving a file in the open condition. It takes but one {close} command to close it, and just another {open} command to open it again later.

Note that the termination of macro control does not close a file. If the macro ends and the file is still open, you can activate another macro and continue to manipulate the same file without issuing another {open} command.

Once a file has been reopened in write, read, or modify mode (refer to the listing for the {open} command for an explanation of these modes), 1-2-3 repositions the byte pointer to offset zero. Whether that change occurs at the time of closing or opening the file is a moot point. Every time you open an ASCII file in one of these modes, the byte pointer will be repositioned to offset zero. If you open the file in append mode, the byte pointer will be positioned at the end of the file.

After it successfully executes a {close} command, 1-2-3 goes directly to the next cell in the macro, ignoring any macro instructions after {close} in the same cell. If {close} returns an error, the macro continues in the same cell as {close}.

Example:

{open "BGT1.PRN","r"}	Open file in read mode
{filesize SIZE}	Get size of file
{setpos SIZE-10}	Goto 10 before end
{readln LAST}	Read that line
{close}	Close the file
/fitBGT1~	Import file
{quit}	Quit

{Filesize}

Purpose: Use {filesize} to determine and store the number of bytes in an open text file.

Format: {filesize [location]}

Where [location] is the address or name of a cell or range. If you specify a range, 1-2-3 enters the number in the first cell of the range.

Sample: {filesize SIZE}

Complements: {open}

See also: {getpos}, {setpos}

Description: {Filesize} is one of the macro file-manipulation commands that works reliably with any text file. Use it to determine the number of bytes a file occupies on a disk. Before you use the {filesize} command, you must first have used the {open} command to open that file.

{Filesize} is useful in two ways. First, if you are reading in lines from a file, you'll need to know when to stop. After reading each line, use {getpos} to obtain the current position of the byte pointer. Compare that offset to the result of the {filesize} command (see {getpos} for more information). Second, if you have been writing data to a file, you may want to move the byte pointer to the end of the file in order to write data there. Use the {setpos} command to set the byte pointer to the position returned by the {filesize} command (see {setpos} for more information).

If the specified file does not exist, the {filesize} command will fail, as will the {open} command that precedes it. Like other macro file-manipulation commands, when the {filesize} commands fails, macro control proceeds with the next command directly to its right—if any. If the command succeeds, control jumps directly to the cell below and 1-2-3 will not process any commands on the same line following the {filesize} command.

Example: Here's an example of a routine to read the last record in an ASCII file.

{open "REPORT.PRN","r"}	Open file in read mode
{filesize SIZE}	Get size of file
{setpos SIZE-10}	Goto 10 before end
{readln LAST}	Read that line
{close}	Close the file

{Getpos}

Purpose: Use {getpos} to determine the current position of the byte pointer in the file.

Format: {getpos [location]}

Where [location] is the address or name of a cell or range. If you specify a range, 1-2-3 enters the number in the first cell of the range.

Sample: {getpos LOCATION}

Complements: {open}

See also: {setpos}

Description: {Getpos} stores, in the specified cell, the location of the byte pointer in the currently open file. (You must open a text file with {open} before using {getpos}.) The location will be stored as a value and can be referenced by the {setpos} command to reposition the byte pointer, or it can be compared with the file size to determine when the byte pointer has reached the end of the file. The first position in a text file is reported as 0, not 1. Thus, if the byte pointer is on the first byte in the file, {getpos} enters 0 in location; if the byte pointer is on the tenth byte, {getpos} enters 9, and so on.

After it successfully executes a {getpos} command, 1-2-3 goes directly to the next cell in the macro, ignoring any macro instructions after {getpos} in the same cell. If {getpos} returns an error (for example, if no text file is open), the macro continues in the same cell as {getpos}.

Although {getpos} changes the contents of cells, 1-2-3 does not automatically recalculate formulas after executing a {getpos} command when worksheet recalculation is set to Automatic. To force recalculation after a {getpos} command, follow the command with ~ (tilde) or {calc}.

Here's an example of a macro to read an ASCII file onto the worksheet.

READ_FILE	{open"REPORT.PRN","R"}	Open file in read mode
	{filesize SIZE}	Get size of file
LOOP	{readln $M$42}	+"(readln"@cellpointer("address")}"
	{getpos LOCATION}	Store location
	{if SIZE=LOCATION}{QUIT}	If at end of file, stop
	{d}	Otherwise, blank cell
	{branch LOOP}	Repeat read operation

{Open}

Purpose: Use {open} to open a text file prior to reading it, writing to it, or ascertaining its size. (An open text file does not appear on screen. It is open only in the sense that 1-2-3 can use it.)

Format: {open [filename],[x]}

Where [filename] is the full name of a text file, including the extension, or the address or name of a cell that contains a text file name. Unless the text file is in the current directory, you must specify its path as part of [filename] and enclose the argument in " " (quotation marks). [X] is one of the letters r, w, m, or a, or a cell that contains one of those characters.

Sample: {open "SPREAD.PRN","w"} or, with a pathname:
  {open "C:\DBASE\PARTS.TXT","r"}

See also: {close}

Description: Use {open} to open a file prior to ascertaining its size, reading it, or writing to it.

When you use 1-2-3 in interactive mode, you don't need to know of any distinction between an open and a closed file. When you retrieve a worksheet file with 1-2-3, the program automatically opens the worksheet file, reads a copy of the worksheet into memory, and then closes the file. When you save a worksheet, 1-2-3 opens the worksheet file, writes a copy of the worksheet in memory over the worksheet file on disk, and closes the file.

When you use the macro file input/output commands to manipulate ASCII text files, you must perform each of these steps with separate commands. The {open} command opens the file, the {read} and {readln} commands read from it, the {write} and {writeln} commands write to it, and the {close} command closes it.

The mode in which you open the file determines what you can do with that file once it's open, and how 1-2-3 will change the file in response to the commands that follow.

You have a choice of four modes: read (r), write (w), modify (m), or append (a). Read mode enables you to read the file but not write to it. Write enables you to write to the file but not read it. Write mode also erases the contents of existing files before the macro does any writing. Modify mode enables you to read and write to the file interchangeably. Unlike write mode, it will retain an existing file's contents. Append mode enables you to add new data to the end of an existing file but not read the file.

Although modify mode would seem to encompass write mode, when you issue {write} or {writeln} commands, the commands work differently. When you open an existing file in modify mode, if the byte pointer is positioned anywhere but at the end of the file, either command will overwrite existing bytes in the file with the new bytes written by these commands. The file will otherwise remain unchanged. In write mode, the entire file will be erased first. The macro will write to the file, but no matter the location of the byte pointer, nothing of the original contents of the file will remain. If the location of the byte pointer is anywhere else but at the beginning of the file, 1-2-3 will fill the offsets preceding that location with random characters already present on the disk.

You cannot open a new file in append mode. You can open only an existing file in append mode. If you try to open a new file in append mode, the {open} command will fail, and control will pass to the next command on the same line.

After opening a file in one mode, you can at any time change modes by issuing another {open} command and specify another mode. You don't have to close the file before doing so; 1-2-3 will do that for you.

Whether you supply it through a string, a string expression, or a reference to a cell containing a string, the first argument in the {open} command must consist of, at minimum, both a file name and an extension (that is, if the subject file has and extension; most do).

If the file is stored somewhere outside 1-2-3's current file directory, then you must specify the path to that file with a valid DOS pathname preceding the file name. If you use a pathname you *must* enclose the pathname and file name in quotation marks.

Example: Here's an example of writing a line of data to a file.

{open "LIST>PRN","a"}	Append to List.prn
{writeln "12,10,15,19,58"}	Comma separated values
{close}	Close the file
{return}	Return to main routine

{Read}

Purpose: Use {read} to read a portion of a text or a sequential data file. (You must open a text file with the {open} command before using {read}.

Format: {read [count],[location]}

Where [count] is a value from 0-511 and [location] is a cell. [Count] may be a number, a formula, a cell address, or a range name describing a single cell. [Location] may be a cell name or address or a range name or address.

Sample: {read 10TARGET}

Complements: {open}

See also: {readln}, {write}, {writeln}

Description: From the currently open ASCII file, the {read} command reads from the current byte forward a specified number of bytes, the {count}, and copies the characters stored in those bytes to a specified cell, the [location]. If the byte count is greater than the number of bytes remaining in the file, {read} copies all the remaining bytes to the specified location.

If the location specified is a range encompassing more than one cell, 1-2-3 will enter those characters into the top left cell in that range. The entry will always appear as a left-aligned label entry.

The {read} command differs from the {readln} command in that {read} can read forward any number of bytes from the current location, whereas {readln} will read only through the character directly preceding the carriage return that terminates the current line.

If you want to read through an entire ASCII file, in most cases {readln} is a more appropriate command than is {read}. If you want to read the entire file onto the worksheet, chances are you want to divide that file into lines, and {readln} does so automatically; {read} does not. {Read} simply copies the carriage return and line-feed characters at the end of text lines. However, you can use {read} to read through a file, and you may find a situation that warrants it.

If you choose to use the {read} command to read through an entire file, you'll need to know when it has read to the end of the file. Unlike {readln}, {read} will not fail if it tries to read beyond the end of the file, it will merely continue to read the last byte in the file.

You can test for the end of the file using the advanced macro commands {filesize}, {getpos}, and {if}. {Filesize} will return the number of bytes in the entire file. {Getpos} will return the offset number of the current position of the byte pointer. When the offset number of the byte pointer equals the total number of bytes in the file, the byte pointer is at the end of the file. You can use the {if} command to test to see if that is true.

After it successfully executes a {read} command, 1-2-3 goes directly to the next cell in the macro, ignoring any macro instructions after {read} in the same cell. If {read} returns an error (for example, if no text file is open), the macro continues in the same cell as {read}.

Although {read} changes the contents of cells, 1-2-3 does not automatically recalculate formulas after executing a {read} command when worksheet recalculation is set to Automatic. To force recalculation after a {read} command, follow the command with ~ (tilde) or {calc}.

Example: The following macro will read the specified number of bytes from the file into the current cell (the location of the cell pointer), then move the cell pointer down one cell and repeat the operation until it has read the entire file.

\A		{open "SAMPLE.PRN","r"}	Open file
		{filesize SIZE}	Check size
		{paneloff}	Turn off menu display
	LOOP	{read 5;ANS}	Read five bytes into ANS
		/cANS~~	Copy ANS to current cell
		{getpos POS}	Check position
		{if POS<SIZE}{d}{branch LOOP}	If EOP, stop
		{close}	Close file
		{quit}	
	POS		Store position
	ANS		Store data

This macro happens to read five bytes at a time; you can specify any number that suits you (up to a maximum of 239).

{ReadIn}

Purpose: Use {readln} to copy an entire line from an ASCII file on to the worksheet.

Format: {readln [location]}

Where [location] is a cell. [Location] may be a cell name or address or a range name or address.

Sample: {readln TAX}

Complements: {open}

See also: {read}

Description: In the currently open ASCII file, {readln} reads from the current position of the byte pointer to the end of the current line and enters that data into the specified cell.

If the location specified is a range encompassing more than one cell, 1-2-3 will enter the characters it reads into the top left cell in that range. The entry will always appear as a left-aligned label entry.

{ReadIn} begins reading at the current byte and advances the byte pointer to the beginning of the next line in the file. If the macro reads another {readln} command at that time, it will read the entire next line. While with the {read} command you must specify the number of bytes for {read} to read, {readln} almost always reads from the current byte through the end of the current line.

The {readln} command differs from the File Import From Text command (or the classic /fit) in that File Import From Text will read only the entire file on to the worksheet; {readln} will read individual lines (or portions thereof) from the file.

If you intend to read every line in a file and stop at the end, you could simply use the File Import From Text command. However, if you want to direct each line of the file to a different cell (instead of reading them into successive cells in a column), or if you want to begin reading somewhere after the beginning of the file, the File Import From Text command can't help. Use {readln} instead.

If you intend to use {readln} to read through the file, you need to know when you've reached the end of the file. After reading each line of the file, the byte pointer will move to the beginning of the next line. After reaching the last line of the file, the byte pointer will reside on a special byte that demarcates the end of the file. If the macro at that time reads another {readln} command, that command will fail.

As with all file I/O commands, if {readln} succeeds, it immediately directs the macro control to the next line of the macro, bypassing any instructions that may remain on the same line. If the command fails, control continues in normal fashion. If there are any instructions to the right of the {readln}, the macro will read them.

With that in mind, you might wish to include a {branch} command directly to the right of the {readln} command. The {branch} command would direct control to the routine you want to start once 1-2-3 reaches the end of the file.

Example: This macro shows a sample application that tests for the end of the file. If opens a file and reads through it line by line.

\A	{open "SAMPLE.PRN","r"}	Open file
	{paneloff}	Turn off menu display
LOOP	{readln ANS}{branch STOP}	Read a line into ANS
	/cANS~~	Copy ANS to current cell
	{d}{branch LOOP}	Move down, read more
STOP	{close}	Close file
	{quit}	
ANS		Store data

{Setpos}

Purpose: Use {setpos} to change the position of the byte pointer in an ASCII file.

Format: {setpos [offset-number]}

Where [offset-number] is a number that specifies the position in the file (relative to the first byte in the file) to which you want to move the byte pointer. [Offset-number] may be a number, a formula, a cell address, a range name describing a single cell.

Sample: {setpos 8}

Complements: {open}

See also: {getpos}

Description: Use {setpos} to reposition the byte pointer in an ASCII file. You must have opened the file with the {open} command prior to using the {setpos} command. Remember that the first byte-pointer position in a text file is reported as 0, not 1. Also note that 1-2-3 does not prevent you from placing the byte pointer past the end of a file. If necessary, use {filesize} to determine the size of a file before using {setpos}.

After it successfully executes a {setpos} command, 1-2-3 goes directly to the next cell in the macro, ignoring any macro instructions after {setpos} in the same cell. If {setpos} returns an error (for example, if no text file is open), the macro continues in the same cell as {setpos}.

Example: This macro will (1) open the file Sample.prn, (2) check the size of the file, (3) set the position of the byte pointer to two bytes before the end of the file, (4) write some new text at the end of the last line, and (5) close the file.

{open "SAMPLE.PRN","a"}	Open file for both
{filesize SIZE}	Determine file size
{setpos SIZE-2}	Goto end of last line
{write " This is new!"}	Write new text there
{close}	Close file

{Write}

Purpose: Use {write} to write a string of characters to an ASCII file, starting at the current byte-pointer position.

Format: {write [text]}

Where [text] is a string of characters. [Text] may be a string, a formula, a cell address, or a range name describing a single cell. If [text] is a text formula, 1-2-3 evaluates the formula and writes the resulting text in the file. If [text] is a value, the macro terminates with an error.

Sample: {write "December 1988"} or {write ENTRY}

Complements: {open}

See also: {writeln}, {read}, {readln}

Description: {Write} enables you to write one or more characters to the currently open file. {Write} will commence writing bytes at the current position of the byte pointer, and advance the byte pointer to the position just beyond the last character written. If necessary, 1-2-3 extends the length of the file to accommodate the incoming string.

Suppose you open an existing file in modify mode, which is the mode in which you can write to an existing file without the macro erasing everything in it first. In modify mode, {write} will overwrite bytes already stored in the locations to which it writes. For example, suppose you have the following ASCII file:

```
Washers:      100       200       250
Faucets:      50        25        75
```

Let's superimpose our own offset counter above and below the file:

```
01234567890123456789012345
Washers:      100       200       250
Faucets:      50        25        75
567890123456789012345678 9
```

Let's further suppose that the byte pointer is at offset 10. Remember, you begin counting with 0, so offset 10 is actually the 11th byte in the file. In this case, that's the second 0 in the offset counter. If the macro reads the command {write "125   210   255"}, then the file would look like this:

```
Washers:      125       210       255
Faucets:      50        25        75
```

The string in the {write} command overwrites the bytes in the file, beginning with the current byte. If you attempted to write a longer string of characters, you'd begin to overwrite the hidden characters at the end of the first line, the carriage return and linefeed.

Quotation marks surrounding the string will ensure that it will be treated as a string. 1-2-3 will always attempt to treat a string not enclosed in quotation marks as a location. If the string cannot be treated as a cell address, a formulaic expression, or a range name (because the string is not a cell address or formula and no such range name exists), 1-2-3 will then treat it as a string. The danger in not enclosing a string of literal text in quotation marks is that someone may later create a range name that duplicates the string. The next time after such an event, the macro would malfunction.

If you are writing to a file that already exists, you should open that file in modify mode. In that mode, {write} begins writing at the current position of the byte pointer and writes over each succeeding byte until it has finished writing the specified string. If data was stored in any of the bytes written to with a {write} command, 1-2-3 will overwrite the data stored in those bytes.

After it successfully executes a {write} command, 1-2-3 goes directly to the next cell in the macro, ignoring any macro instructions after {write} in the same cell. If {write} returns an error (for example, if no text file is open), the macro continues in the same cell as {write}.

{Writeln}

Purpose: Use {writeln} to write a complete line to an ASCII file.

Format: {writeln [text]}
Where [text] is a string of characters. [Text] may be a string, a formula, a cell address, or a range name describing a single cell. If [text] is a text formula, 1-2-3 evaluates the formula and writes the resulting text in the file. If [text] is a value, the macro terminates with an error.

Sample: {writeln TEXT}

Complements: {open}

See also: {write}, {readln}, {read}

Description: {Writeln} enables you to write an entire line to the currently open file. {Writeln} will write the new line at the current position of the byte pointer, and add a carriage return and a line feed.

If you open a new file and write to it, but do so at some offset from position zero, 1-2-3 will pad the opening of the file with random characters that appear to be from the disk. To avoid such "random" padding, include blank spaces in the string you write to the current line. This applies also if you open an existing file in write mode, which erases the current contents of the file before it begins writing the new data.

If you wish to precede the current line with one or more blank lines, first use one {writeln} command with a null string for each blank line you wish to create. Used in that manner, the {writeln} command will enter a carriage return/linefeed (abbreviated together as CRLF) on each line, then advance the byte pointer to the next line. After it successfully executes a {writeln} command, 1-2-3 goes directly to the next cell in the macro, ignoring any macro instructions after {writeln} in the same cell. If {writeln} returns an error (for example, if no text file is open), the macro continues in the same cell as {writeln}.

Example: If you wanted to open a new file and write the string Happy Birthday! indented five characters to the left of the margin on the third line, you would use this macro:

{open "NEW.PRN","w"}	Open new file
{writeln ""}	CRLF
{writeln ""}	CRLF
{write " Happy Birthday!"}	Write a line
{close}	Close file
{quit}	Quit

DDE Commands

There are several commands built to help you exploit Windows' DDE feature so that you can create hotlinks between applications. When data changes in the source application, it can automatically update the target application.

The DDE commands are for the true Windows hacker. They let you manage the conversation between applications at a very low level.

{DDE-advise}

Purpose: {DDE-advise} specifies what macro to execute when a particular data item (in a particular format) changes in the server application.

Format: {DDE-advise [branch-location], [item-name], [format]}

Where [branch-location] is the address or name of a cell or range that contains macro instructions. It is often the name of another macro or subroutine. [Item-name], is the item in the application file whose data you want transferred through the link. [Format] is an optional argument that specifies one of the clipboard formats (for example, Text or Rich Text Format). [Item-name] and [format] can be any text enclosed in quotation marks, a formula that results in text, or the address or name of a cell that contains a label, or a formula that results in a label.

Sample: {DDE-advise range1,"item1","text"}

Description: {DDE-advise} causes the macro in a specified location, the [branch-location], to execute each time the item specified by [item-name] is updated by the server application. A DDE conversation must be open for {DDE-advise} to work. If a [format] is not specified, 1-2-3 assumes Text format.

{DDE-close}

Purpose: {DDE-close} terminates the current conversation with a Windows application. If no conversation is open, {DDE-close} does nothing.

Format: {DDE-close}

Sample: {DDE-close}

Complements: {DDE-open}

Description: Use {DDE-close} to close the current conversation—the one opened by the most recent {DDE-open} or {DDE-use} command. Note that {DDE-close} terminates any advises that may be currently associated with items in the conversation. Also note that {DDE-close} does not terminate execution in the current cell like the file {close} macro.

{DDE-execute}

Purpose: {DDE-execute} sends a command to a Windows application.

Format: {DDE-execute [execute-string]}

Where [execute-string] represents any command from another Windows application, including macros. [Execute string] is any text enclosed in quotation marks, a formula that results in text, or the address or name of a cell that contains a label, or a formula that results in a label.

Sample: {DDE-execute "update"}

Description: {DDE-execute} sends an execute string to the current conversation. {DDE-execute} reports an error if the conversation isn't open, or if the server application cannot complete the command represented by the execute string, or if it times out, or is busy.

{DDE-open}

Purpose: {DDE-open} initiates a conversation with a Windows application, making that the current conversation.

Format: {DDE-open [app-name],[topic-name],[location]}
Where [app-name] is the name of an open Windows application. [Topic-name] is the name of the application file to link to. [App-name] and [topic name] can be any text enclosed in quotation marks, a formula that results in text, or the address or name of a cell that contains a label, or a formula that results in a label. [Location] is an optional argument that specifies the address or name of a cell or range. If you specify a range, 1-2-3 enters the identification number in the first cell of the range.

Sample: {DDE-open "amipro","myfile",range1}

Description: {DDE-open} opens a conversation with the application and on the topic specified by the [app-name] and [topic-name] arguments. If you include a [location] argument, 1-2-3 will provide the specified cell with a unique number to identify the conversation being opened. You can then use the {DDE-use} macro to make a particular conversation current *by its unique number*, selecting from the various conversations opened by {DDE-open}.

If a conversation is successfully opened with {DDE-open}, macro execution continues with the next macro in the column. If the conversation could not be opened, macro execution continues with the rest of the current cell and the returned conversation number will be zero. {DDE-open} will fail to open a conversation if it encounters invalid application or topic names, if the named application isn't running, or if the named topic isn't available. Note that unlike {link-create}, {DDE-open} does not auto-launch. You must start an application with the {launch} command before using {DDE-open}. Because 1-2-3 allows you to use more than one {DDE-open} command in a macro, use {DDE-use} to make a particular conversation current.

{DDE-poke}

Purpose: {DDE-poke} sends a range of data to a server application during the current conversation.

Format: {DDE-poke [range],[item-name],[format]}
Where [range] is the address or name of the range that contains the data you want to send to the server application. [Item-name] is the name of the range to link to. [Format] is an optional argument that specifies one of the clipboard formats (for example, Text, Metafilepict, or Rich Text Format). [Item-name] and [format] can be any text enclosed in quotation marks, a formula that results in text, or the address or name of a cell that contains a label, or a formula that results in a label.

Sample: {DDE-poke myrange, "filenew", "text"}

Description: In the current conversation, {DDE-poke} sends your specified source range of data to a server application *as* the specified item. {DDE-poke} will return an error if the source range isn't valid, if the conversation isn't open, if the server application is busy, or if the server application cannot accept source data. Note that if you do not include the [format] argument, 1-2-3 uses the clipboard Text format.

{DDE-request}

Purpose: {DDE-request} transfers data from a Windows application to 1-2-3. 1-2-3 enters the data in the specified range.

Format: {DDE request [range],[item-name],[format]}

Where [range] is a range address or range name. [Item-name] is the name of the topic item to link to. This is the item in the application file whose data you want transferred through the link. [Format] is an optional argument that specifies one of the clipboard formats (for example, Text, Metafilepict, or Rich Text Format). [Item-name] and [format] can be any text enclosed in quotation marks, a formula that results in text, or the address or name of a cell that contains a label, or a formula that results in a label.

Sample: {DDE-request formulas,"newstuff","Rich Text Format"}

Description: {DDE-request} fetches the identified data item ([item-name]) and then places it in the location you specify. It does this through the conversation most recently opened by {DDE-open} or selected by {DDE-use}. {DDE-request} will fail and generate an error if the conversation is not open, if the server application cannot service the data request, or if the destination range is invalid. {DDE-request} does not pre-clear the destination range before depositing the fetched data into the worksheet. Use {edit-clear} to clear all data and formatting from the specified range before using {DDE-request}. Unlike links being refreshed (see {link-create}, {link assign}, and {link-update}), {DDE-request} does not deposit ERR or NA cells if an error occurs or if the conversation isn't running. Use {onerror} to detect these conditions.

{DDE-unadvise}

Purpose: {DDE-unadvise} cancels a {DDE-advise} command.

Format: {DDE-unadvise [item-name],[format]}

Where [item-name] is the name of the topic item whose data is transferred. [Format] is an optional argument that specifies one of the clipboard formats (for example, Text, Metafilepict, or Rich Text Format). [Item-name] and [format] can be any text enclosed in quotation marks, a formula that results in text, or the address or name of a cell that contains a label, or a formula that results in a label.

Sample: {DDE-unadvise "newstuff","Rich Text Format"}

Description: {DDE-unadvise} ends the association of a macro location and the link established by a DDE-advise. {DDE-unadvise} tells 1-2-3 to no longer trigger the advise macro when data changes in the server application. {DDE-unadvise} returns an error if the conversation is not open or if the item does not currently have an advise active. Note that if the original advise specified a [format] argument, then the same [format] argument must be supplied in the {DDE-unadvise} command.

{DDE-use}

Purpose: {DDE-use} makes a specified conversation the current conversation.

Format: {DDE-use [conversation-number]}
Where [conversation number] is the identification number Windows assigns to the conversation.

Sample: {DDE-use 3}

Description: {DDE-use} identifies the conversation you want to make current so that it can be manipulated by the other low-level DDE macros. Because you can open more than one conversation in a macro, you need to use {DDE-use} to make a specific conversation the current conversation. {DDE-use} returns an error if the indicated conversation is not open. The conversation number should be the same value returned by {DDE-open}. (Note that if you use the optional [location] argument in {DDE-open}, 1-2-3 will enter the identification number in the worksheet.)

{Launch}

Purpose: {Launch} loads a Windows application and specifies the state of its window.

Format: {launch [command],[window]}
Where [command] is the command string requested to run the Windows application. And [window] is an optional argument that controls the initial state of the application ("minimize", or "maximize").

Sample: {launch "amipro myfile.Sam","maximize"}

Description: {Launch} spawns another Windows task and invokes the other application using the specified string as the command line. Note that if you do not specify a window argument, 1-2-3 tries to minimize the application upon starting it, and 1-2-3 will remain the active application.

{Link-assign}

Purpose: {Link-assign} associates a destination range with a link.

Format: {link-assign [link-name],[range],[property1],[property2],...[property$n$]}
Where [link-name] is the name for the link specified in {link-create}. [Range] is a range address or name that specifies the destination range. [Property1] and [property2] are each optional arguments that specify what to clear from the destination range before every update. The [link-name] and [property] arguments can be text enclosed in quotation marks, or they can be formulas that result in text, or they can be the address or name of a cell that contains a label, or a formula that results in a label.

Sample: {link-assign "hotlink",rangenew,"formats","styles"}

Description: {Link-assign} specifies a destination range for updated data received through a link. You cannot assign more than one destination range for any one link. Note that when the destination range is not big enough to hold the incoming data, 1-2-3 clips the incoming data to fit into the destination range; it will also resize a graph that is too big for the destination range.

The optional property parameters may have the same values as the property argument in {edit-clear}. These properties specify what to clear from the destination range before each update. If you do not include property arguments, 1-2-3 clears *all* properties in the destination range. Here is a table that lists the property arguments:

Argument	Action
contents	deletes the contents of all cells in the selected ranges but leaves cell format intact
formats	deletes all cell formats created with Range Format for the selected range and resets the cell formats to the default set for the worksheet with Worksheet Global Settings Format.
styles	deletes all formatting done with the Style commands for the selected range; returns the font settings to the default font set for the worksheet file with Style Font; returns the color setting to the defaults set for the worksheet window with Window Display Options; and returns the label alignment to the default set for the worksheet with Worksheet Global setting Align labels.
graphs	deletes a graph from the selected range, but does not delete the graph from memory or from disk, and does not affect the data on which the graph is based.

{Link-assign} returns an error if you assign more than one destination range to a link, or if you refer to a link-name that does not exist.

{Link-create}

Purpose: {Link-create} creates a DDE link between the current worksheet file and another worksheet file or between the current worksheet file and another Windows application file assuming that the application supports DDE as a server.

Format: {link-create [link-name],[app-name],[topic-name],[item name],[format],[mode], [branch]}

Where [link-name] is a name you specify to identify the link. [Link-name] can be up to 15 characters long. It should not start with an exclamation point (!), nor should it contain any of the following characters: +, *, -, /, &, >, <, @, #, {, or ?. [Link-name] should also not look like a cell address such as AA45 or AB6, nor should it begin with a number such as 13FEB. Do not use @function names, key names or macro command keywords as link names. [App-name] is the name of the Windows application. [Topic-name] is the name of the application worksheet or file to link to. [Item-name] is the name of the topic item to link to. This is the item in the application worksheet or file whose data you want transferred through the link. [Format] is an optional argument that specifies one of the valid clipboard formats. [Mode] is an optional argument that specifies when data is updated. (It can be either Manual or Automatic.) [Branch] is an optional argument that specifies a location where macro execution will start when the data from the link is updated. [Branch] can be the address or name of a cell or range. [Link-name], [app-name], [topic-name], [item-name], [format], and [mode] are entered as text enclosed in quotation marks, or can be a formula that results in text, the address or name of a cell that contains a label, or a formula that results in a label.

Sample: {link-create "hotlink","amipro","doc1","text",,branch2}

Description: Use {link-create} to create a new DDE link with a data source that you identify by application, topic, and item names. If the macro encounters no errors, the link is created, regardless of whether the conversation was established or not. If the conversation for this link is successfully created, the macro skips the commands remaining in the cell and moves to the next line. If the conversation cannot be established execution continues within the current cell.

If the conversation implied by the application and topic arguments cannot be established, and if the auto-launch flag in the .ini file settings is non-zero, {link-create} will try to *launch* the application: it will concatenate the application and topic names to form a command-line and then try a second time to establish the conversation. Conversation creation can fail if the application does not exist or if the specified topic is not available. Note also that if a specified [link-name] is already in use, an error results.

The {link-create} command's [mode] argument is a string with the value of Automatic or Manual. The mode indicates whether the link should be a warm/hot link (where data is transferred through the link *whenever* it changes in the server) or a cold-link (where the data is only transferred when the user requests a link update). If the server application cannot supply data in the requested mode, the appropriate mode will be selected for the user. The default mode is Automatic for the cell-oriented formats such as "Text", "WK1", and "WK3"; the default mode is Manual for the graphic formats such as "Bitmap" and "MetafilePict". "Rich Text Format" defaults to Automatic.

The [branch] location argument tells 1-2-3 where macro execution will start when data from the link is updated. If a destination range has been specified for this link with the {link assign} command, the data from the link is deposited in the sheet *before* macro execution begins at the [branch] location. If the link is explicitly updated and it happens that the link is not active (for example, the conversation for this link is not available), then the macro at [branch] will not be executed.

{Link-deactivate}

Purpose: {Link-deactivate} temporarily deactivates a DDE link in the current worksheet, but leaves the link intact.

Format: {link-deactivate [link-name]}

Where [link-name] is the name for the link specified in {link-create}. [Link-name] can be entered as text enclosed in quotation marks, or it can be a formula that results in text, the address or name of a cell that contains a label, or a formula that results in a label.

Sample: {link-deactivate "hotlink"}

Description: {Link-deactivate} temporarily suspends message traffic for a particular DDE link. When a link is deactivated, 1-2-3 does not update values in the destination range. Use {link-deactivate} in macro applications for performance enhancement. Links can be reactivated using {link-update}.

{Link-delete}

Purpose: {Link-delete} erases a link in the current worksheet, but leaves the values obtained through the link in the worksheet.

Format: {link-delete [link-name]}

Where [link-name] is the name for the link specified in {link-create}. [Link-name] is entered as text enclosed in quotation marks, or it can be a formula that results in text, or the address or name of a cell that contains a label, or a formula that results in a label.

Sample: {link-delete "hotlink"}

Description: {Link-delete} deletes an existing link. As a convenience, if a destination range assignment is in effect for the named link, a {link-remove} is executed automatically. Note that when the last link in a particular conversation is deleted the conversation is terminated. {Link-delete} reports an error if the [link-name] does not refer to an existing link.

{Link-remove}

Purpose: {Link-remove} removes the currently assigned destination range for a DDE link.

Format: {link-remove [link-name]}
Where [link-name] is the name for the link specified in {link-create}. [Link-name] should be text enclosed in quotation marks, or it can be a formula that results in text, or the address or name of a cell that contains a label, or a formula that results in a label.

Sample: {link-remove "hotlink"}

Description: {Link-remove} breaks the association of a destination range with a particular link. It does not delete the link itself. {Link-remove} reports an error if the link does not exist, or if no destination range is currently assigned.

{Link-table}

Purpose: {Link-table} creates a table of all DDE links associated with the current file.

Format: {link-table [location]}
Where [location] is the address or name of the top left cell of the range to receive the table.

Sample: {link-table range1}

Description: {Link-table} creates a table describing all the links associated with the current file. The table will occupy several columns and as many rows as there are links associated with the file, modifying the sheet in a way similar to the Range Name Table command. Remember that 1-2-3 writes over any existing data when it creates the table, so make sure the range does not contain any data you need.

{Link-update}

Purpose: {Link-update} updates a DDE link when the link update mode is Manual; it will also activate and update a link that has been deactivated with {link-deactivate}.

Format: {link-update [link-name]}
Where [link-name] is the name for the link specified in {link-create}. [Link-name] should be should be text enclosed in quotation marks, or it can be a formula that results in text, the address or name of a cell that contains a label, or a formula that results in a label.

Sample: {link-update "hotlink"}

Description: {Link-update} refreshes the data from a link. If you have assigned a destination range to the link, the data received from the link is placed there.

If the conversation for this link is not running, {link-update} will attempt to restart the conversation. If the conversation cannot be established, macro execution continues in the same cell. If the conversation is running or is successfully established, macro execution proceeds to the next macro instruction in the column—one cell down.

If there is a destination range assigned to the link and a conversation could not be established, {link-update} will place NA cells in the destination range. If there is an error in fetching the data (for example, the item specified in the link creation is not recognized by the server application or if the requested format is not supported by the server application), the destination range is filled with ERR cells.

Window Control

The window control commands allow you to control the size and position of windows: the 1-2-3/W application window and the document windows within it.

{App-adjust}

Purpose: {App-adjust} lets you alter the size of the 1-2-3/W application window.

Format: {App-adjust [x-pos],[y-pos],[width],[height]}

Where [x-pos] specifies the horizontal position, in pixels, measured from the left side of the screen to the left side of the 1-2-3 window. [Y-pos] specifies the vertical position, in pixels, measured from the top of the screen to the top of the 1-2-3 window. [Width] specifies the window width, in pixels, from the left border to the right border. [Height] specifies the window height, in pixels, from the top border to the bottom border. [X-pos], [y-pos], [width], and [height] are values, formulas that result in values, or the addresses or names of cells that contain a value or a formula that results in a value.

Sample: {app-adjust 20,20,100,100}

Complements: {window-adjust}

Description: Use {app-adjust} to position the 1-2-3 window on the screen. {App-adjust} can also be used to reduce and enlarge the 1-2-3 window. Reducing the window lets the user see more of the other open application windows, and enlarging the window lets the user see more of the files displayed in the 1-2-3 window. Note that if you specify too large a value for [x-pos] or [y-pos], the window moves partly or completely out of view.

Example: This macro places the 1-2-3 window 30 pixels from the top of the screen and 30 pixels from the left edge of the screen, and makes the window 200 by 200 pixels in size.

{App-adjust 30,30,200,200}

{App-state}

Purpose: The {app-state} command lets you change the status of the 1-2-3/W application window.

Format: {app-state [state]}
Where [state] is either Maximize, Minimize, or Restore; [state] can be text enclosed in quotation marks, or it can be a formula that results in text, the address or name of a cell that contains a label, or a formula that results in a label.

Sample: {app-state "minimize"}

Description: Use {app-state} to maximize, minimize, or restore the 1-2-3/W window—just as you would click on the Maximize, Minimize, or Restore buttons.

{Window-adjust}

Purpose: {Window-adjust} lets you alter the size of the active document window. The active document can be a Worksheet, Graph, or Transcript window.

Format: {window-adjust [x-pos],[y-pos],[width],[height]}
Where [x-pos] specifies the horizontal position, in pixels, measured from the left side of the 1-2-3 window to the left side of the window being moved. [Y-pos] specifies the vertical position, in pixels, measured from the top of the 1-2-3 window to the top of the window being moved. [Width] specifies the window width, in pixels, from the left border to the right border. [Height] specifies the window height, in pixels, from the top border to the bottom border. [X-pos], [y-pos], [width], and [height] are values, formulas that result in values, or the addresses or names of cells that contain a value or a formula that results in a value.

Sample: {window-adjust 20,30,180,180}

Description: Use {window-adjust} to position a document window in the 1-2-3 window. For example, you can move a Worksheet window to see the Graph window, perform some formatting tasks in the Graph window, then move the Worksheet window back. You can also use {window-adjust} to reduce and enlarge windows. Reducing a window lets the user see more of the other open windows, and enlarging a window lets the user see more of the file shown in the enlarged window. Remember that if you specify too large a value for x or y, the window moves partly or even entirely out of view. To bring the window back into view, use Window Tile.

Example: This macro places the current window 30 pixels from the left and 30 pixels from the top of the 1-2-3 window, and makes the window 200 by 200 pixels in size.
{window-adjust 30,30,200,200}

{Window-select}

Purpose: {Window-select} activates a specified Worksheet or Graph window. You identify the window by the name that appears in its title bar.

Format: {window-select [window-name]}
Where [window-name] is the name of an open window, as it appears in the *title bar*, or the address or name of a cell that contains the name of an open window.

Sample: {window-select myfile}

Description: When you use {window-select} in a macro, 1-2-3 activates the window you specify and then continues executing the macro. Remember that the menu that is available after a {window-select} command depends on whether the active window is a Worksheet window, a Graph window, or the Transcript window.

You do not need to include the file extension as part of [window-name] unless files with the same name but different extensions are open (for example, plan91.wk1, and plan91.wk3).

{Window-select} returns an error if you specify a window that is not open.

Example: This macro activates the Graph window market.onf and uses Chart Type Bar to change the graph type from a line graph to a bar graph.

{window-select market.onf}{alt}ctb~

{Window-state}

Purpose: {Window-state} lets you change the status of the active Worksheet, Graph, or Transcript window.

Format: {window-state [state]}

Where [state] is either Maximize, Minimize, Restore; [state] can be text enclosed in quotation marks, or it can be a formula that results in text, the address or name of a cell that contains a label, or a formula that results in a label.

Sample: {window-state "restore"}

Description: Use {window-state} to minimize, maximize, or restore the active document window—be it a worksheet, document, or transcript window.

Example: This macro minimizes the active Worksheet window before displaying the graph named DYNAMO in the Graph window.

{window-state "minimize"}{alt}gv{alt"g"}DYNAMO~

External Tables

These commands control how 1-2-3 handles transactions with external databases.

{Commit}

Purpose: {Commit} commits (or finalizes) pending external database transactions.

Format: {commit [driver-name],[database-name]}

Where [driver-name] is an optional argument that specifies the name of the driver. [Database-name] is an optional argument that specifies the name of the external database. [Driver-name] and [database-name] can be any text enclosed in quotation marks, a formula that results in text, the address or name of a cell that contains a label, or a formula that results in a label.

Sample: {commit "sql_server","budget"}

Complements: {Rollback}

Description: {Commit} currently works with the SQL driver only. With {commit} you must use both the [driver-name] and [database-name] argument, or neither. {Commit} *with* arguments commits only the transaction pending for the driver and database you specify. {Commit} with no arguments commits all pending transactions.

{Rollback}

Purpose: {Rollback} cancels pending external database transactions.

Format: {rollback [driver-name],[database-name]}
Where [driver-name] is an optional argument that specifies the name of the driver. [Database-name] is an optional argument that specifies the name of the external database. [Driver-name] and [database-name] can be any text enclosed in quotation marks, a formula that results in text, the address or name of a cell that contains a label, or a formula that results in a label.

Sample: {rollback "sql_server","busplan"}

Complements: {commit}

Description: {Rollback} currently works with the SQL driver only. With {rollback} you must use both the [driver-name] and [database-name] argument, or neither. {Rollback} *with* arguments cancels only the transaction pending for the driver and database you specify. {Rollback} with no arguments cancels all pending transactions.

Edit/Clipboard

The clipboard commands, in their simplest form, mimic commands you can choose from the Edit menu. Most of these commands use the clipboard to perform common editing tasks. You can use these commands as more-readable substitutes for {alt} commands using {edit-copy} instead of {alt}ec, for example.

Most of these commands have an optional format argument. This argument lets you can determine which of several data formats should be used when 1-2-3/W puts information onto the clipboard or copies it from the clipboard.

{Edit-clear}

Purpose: {Edit-clear} permanently removes data and related formatting from the worksheet *without* moving it to the clipboard.

Format: {edit-clear [source-range],[property]}
Where [source-range] is an optional argument that specifies the range whose contents you want to delete. If you do not include the [source-range] argument, 1-2-3 deletes the contents of the current source-range. [Property] is an optional argument that is one of the words from the table below. [Property] can be text enclosed in quotation marks, a text formula, or the address or name of a cell that contains a label or text formula.

Sample: {edit-clear range1,"formats"}

Complements: {blank}

Description: {Edit-clear} erases the data (as dictated by the cell [property] argument) for all the cells in the [source-range]. The contents of the clipboard are not modified in any way. {Edit-clear} is equivalent to choosing Edit Clear Special. When you remove the contents of a range with {edit-clear}, you cannot paste them back into the worksheet since they are not on the clipboard. The [source-range] may be from any file in memory. If a [source-range] is not specified, the current [source-range] selection is used. If no selection is in effect, the cell at the current cell pointer is cleared.

[Property] is a string argument which must evaluate to one of the following:

Contents	deletes the contents of all cells in the selected range but leaves the cell format intact.
Formats	deletes all formatting done with the Range Format command for the selected range and resets the number format to the worksheet default (set with Worksheet Global Settings Format).
Styles	deletes all formatting done with the Style commands for the selected range; it returns the font settings to the default font (set for the worksheet file with Style Font); it also returns the color settings to the worksheet window default (set with Window Display Options); and it returns the label assignment to the default (set with Worksheet Global Settings Align Labels).
Graphs	deletes a graph from the selected range, but does not delete the graph from memory or from disk; and it does not affect the data on which the graph is based.

Note that "contents" is equivalent to the 1-2-3 Classic /Range Erase. "Formats" is equivalent to the 1-2-3 Classic /Range Format Reset. "Styles" is equivalent to the Wysiwyg :Format Reset; and "graphs" works like a :Graph Remove. The cell property is not case sensitive. If the cell-property argument is not specified, all four cell properties are cleared.

{Edit-clear} reports an error if any cells in the clear range are protected or read-only or if a property string is supplied that does not match one of the above property names.

{Edit-copy}

Purpose: {Edit-copy} copies the cells in the source range to the clipboard; it is equivalent to the 1-2-3/W Edit Copy menu command.

Format: {edit-copy [source-range],[format]}

Where [source-range] is an optional argument specifying the range to be copied to the clipboard. [Format] is an optional argument that specifies a clipboard format such as Text, Metafilepict, or Rich Text Format; [format] can be text enclosed in quotation marks, a formula that results in text, the address or name of a cell that contains a label, or a formula that results in a label. If you do not include the [format] argument, 1-2-3 places all appropriate formats on the clipboard.

Sample: {edit-copy newrange, "Rich Text Format"}

Complements: {edit-cut}, {edit-paste}

Description: {Edit-copy} copies the contents, formats, and styles of all the cells in the source-range onto the clipboard. It also copies any on-sheet graphs which are in the current selection. {Edit-copy} is equivalent to choosing Edit Copy. After copying the contents of a range with {edit-copy}, you can paste them repeatedly with {edit-paste} commands.

The [source-range] argument specifies the source-range of the data. It can be any range from any file in memory. If the source-range is not specified, 1-2-3 copies the current selection. If there is no current selection, the current cell is copied. If the source range is successfully copied to the clipboard and a [format] argument is *not* specified, {edit-copy} places a special "link" object on the clipboard which records the application, topic, and item names required to request the selected data using a DDE link.

Note that all clipboard and DDE functions support two graph selection mechanisms: *single-cell* graph selection and *fully-enclosed* graph selection. Single cell graph selection means that if the source-range is a single cell, the topmost graph of all the graphs that contain *that one cell* will be selected. In the case of {edit-copy}, this one graph will be copied to the clipboard without the user having to enclose it within the selection. Single-cell selection applies only to "cell" oriented clipboard formats, like Lotus 123Private.

Fully enclosed graph selection means that you must explicitly select the exact rectangle that you desire on the clipboard (as a range of cells). You must "fully enclose" the graph selection with display oriented clipboard formats (such as Metafilepict and Bitmap). These formats will represent *only* the selected region of the worksheet on the clipboard.

{Edit-copy-graph}

Purpose: The {Edit-copy-graph} command copies the current graph to the clipboard. It is the equivalent of choosing Edit Copy from a Graph window.

Format: {edit-copy-graph}

Sample: {edit-copy-graph}

Complements: {edit-copy}

Description: The {edit-copy-graph} macro places the graph in the current graph window on the clipboard. It returns an error if a graph window is not selected.

Example: This macro makes the Graph window named buspres.onf the active window and then copies the graph to the clipboard.

{window-select buspres.onf}

{edit-copy-graph}

{Edit-cut}

Purpose: {Edit-cut} cuts data and related formatting from the worksheet to the clipboard.

Format: {edit-cut [source-range],[format]}

[Source-range] and [format] are optional arguments. [Source-range] is the range to be cut to the clipboard. If you do not include the source-range argument, 1-2-3 cuts the contents of the current source-range. [Format] specifies a clipboard format such as Text, Metafilepict, or Rich Text Format. It can be text enclosed in quotation marks, a formula that results in text, the address or name of a cell that contains a label, or a formula that results in a label. If you do not include the [format] argument, 1-2-3 places all appropriate formats on the clipboard.

Sample: {edit-cut 92fore}

Complements: {edit-copy}, {edit-paste}

Description: {Edit-cut} places a copy of the source data onto the clipboard and then clears the source-range of all of its cell properties. {Edit-cut} is equivalent to choosing Edit Cut. After cutting the contents of a range with {edit-cut} you can paste them repeatedly with {edit-paste} commands. If the source-range is protected, {edit-cut} reports an error and neither the data on the clipboard nor the data in the source-range are modified.

{Edit-paste}

Purpose: {Edit-paste} copies data and related formatting from the clipboard into the active worksheet file.

Format: {edit-paste [selection],[format]}
Where [selection] is an optional argument that specifies the target range in which you want to paste the clipboard contents. If you do not include the [selection] argument, 1-2-3 pastes the contents of the clipboard into the current selection. [Format] is an optional argument that specifies one of the clipboard formats (for example, Text, Metafilepict, or Rich Text Format). [Format] can be any text enclosed in quotation marks, a formula that results in text, the address or name of a cell that contains a label, or a formula that results in a label.

Sample: {edit-paste fillrange}

Complements: {edit-copy}, {edit-cut}

Description: {Edit-paste} is equivalent to choosing Edit Paste. It copies the cell data from the clipboard to the destination range. The optional [selection] argument controls the clipping, replication and graph-sizing behavior of {edit-paste} in the destination range. The [format] string allows the user to select only data in a particular clipboard format from the clipboard. If you do not include the [format], 1-2-3 pastes using its own private format, Lotus 123Private.

The destination range may be any range in any file in memory. There are two kinds of pastes, depending on whether or not there is a destination range specified (or preselected): *constrained* and *unconstrained*.

If the destination range is supplied, 1-2-3 executes a *constrained* paste. This will first clear the destination range of all cell contents, formats, styles, and selected graphs. Then the data from the clipboard is copied into the destination range with clipping, replication, and graph-sizing as follows. If the data on the clipboard does not match the size of the destination range *and* if the clipboard only contains cell-data (that is, non-graphic data), the cell-data is clipped or replicated (in the style of /copy) to fit the destination range. If the data being pasted contains graphs or is a mixture of cell-data and graphs, the cell-data will be clipped, if necessary, but *will not* be replicated; the graph-data will be sized to fit the destination range.

If the destination range is not supplied and there is no current pre-selection, 1-2-3 executes an *unconstrained* paste. Here, 1-2-3 attempts to copy the clipboard data into the sheet without clipping, replication, or graph-sizing. In an unconstrained paste, the cell-pointer is used as the anchor point for a *single instance* of all data in the clipboard. (Note that in an unconstrained paste, any graphs (or metafiles or bitmaps) that contain no intrinsic size information when they were copied to the clipboard will be sized to fit the single cell at the current cell-pointer.) If the clipboard data would extend beyond the edges of the spreadsheet, or if it extends to a depth greater than the remaining number of sheets in the current file, {edit-paste} reports an error and the data in the spreadsheet are not modified. All cell contents, formats, styles, and graphs that would underlie the *implied* destination range are cleared.

If the [format] string argument is present, it selects the specific clipboard format that will be pasted from the clipboard. {Edit-paste} generates an error if any cells in the destination range of a constrained paste or in the *implied* destination range of an unconstrained paste are protected.

Also, if the optional specified [format] is not supported or is not on the clipboard, an error is generated.

Example: The following macro cuts the contents of cell A:H1 and pastes them into each of the cells B:A1, C:A1, and D:A1:

{edit-cut A:H1}

{edit-paste B:A1}

{edit-paste C:A1}

{edit-paste D:A1}

{Edit-paste-link}

Purpose: {Edit-paste-link} creates a link between a 1-2-3 for Windows worksheet file and the file referenced on the clipboard.

Format: {edit-paste-link [destination-range]}

Where [destination-range] is an optional argument that specifies the range into which the linked data should be pasted.

Sample: {edit-paste-link rangenew}

Description: {Edit-paste-link} is equivalent to choosing Edit Paste Link. It creates a DDE link from the application, topic, and item names on the clipboard (extracted from the "link" clipboard format) and uses the range argument as the destination range for the link. The name of the link is created automatically without user intervention (automatic link names are of the form "LINK1", "LINK2", ...). You can use {edit-paste-link} only when the clipboard contains data copied from a valid source file—that is, from another worksheet file or from a file created with another Windows application that supports DDE.

The destination range may refer to any range in any of the files in memory. If the destination range is not supplied, the current selection is used. If a current selection is not available, the cell pointer is used as a single cell destination range and all the incoming data from the link will be clipped into that single cell range. Unlike {edit-paste}, {edit-paste-link} does not implement any form of unconstrained data transfer.

Note that when you copy data from a valid source file to the clipboard, the link reference (for example, a range address) is also stored on the clipboard. {Edit-paste-link} links the active worksheet file to the source file from which you copied the data. Initially, 1-2-3 creates this new link with the update mode set to Automatic (which automatically updates the link whenever the source file changes).

The clipboard format and the update mode (Automatic or Manual) of the DDE-link are selected automatically based on what the server application can supply. 1-2-3 determines the format and update mode by repeatedly trying to establish a link with the server application using the different formats in a priority order until the link is established. The priority order is the same priority used in extracting formats from the clipboard and may be modified by the user in the .ini file.

{Edit-paste-link} reports an error if any cells in the destination range are protected or if the link with the server application can not be established or if the clipboard does not contain a "link" format.

Index

A

About Program Manager command, 44
@ABS function, 150, 516
ABS key (F4), 61
    for entering dollar signs, 188
    as preselection key, 119–20, 122
{ABS} key name, 421
absolute cell references, 186, 188–89
accelerator keys, 35, 120
@ACOS function, 520
active window, 21
Addition operator, 134
address box, 54
Adobe Type Manager (ATM), 7
    fonts, 80, 283–84
Advanced Macro Commands, 399, 403
aggregate columns, 340, 342–44
Align labels options, in Worksheet Global Settings dialog box, 201
alignment of labels (or text), 92–95.
   See also label prefixes
    in header or footer, 268
    new features in 1-2-3/W, 93–95
    nonprinting text, 126
    SmartIcons for, 125
Align-over-columns option, 93, 94, 127
All edges option, 88, 89
Allways, 6
Alt-F10 key, 121
Alt-F3. *See* RUN key
Alt-F4, to close applications, 34
Alt-F6 (ZOOM key), 122, 209, 218
Alt key
    for shortcut keys, 33, 35
    to use menus, 33
{ALT} key name, 420
amortizing loan template, 496–98
anchoring, 118–20
{ANCHOR} key name, 421
#AND# operator, 134, 136, 365
annuities, @function for, 507–9
apostrophe (') label prefixes, 92, 125

apostrophe vertical-bar ('|) label prefixes, 126–27
{APP-ADJUST} macro command, 417
{APPENDBELOW} macro command, 605-6
{APPEND-RIGHT} macro command, 606–7
application design. *See* designing spreadsheets
application icons, 21
applications. *See* spreadsheets; templates
application windows, 19–20, 22–23
    closing, 24
{APP-STATE} macro command, 418
area graphs, 307
arithmetic operators, 134
Arrow keys
    in macros, 403
    navigating worksheets with, 115–17
    uses of, 33, 35
ASCII files, importing, 347
@ASIN function, 520
asterik (*), in criteria, 363
@ATAN function, 520
@ATAN2 function, 520–21
@functions *are alphabetized under F*
at-sign SmartIcon, 146
autoexecuting macros, 203, 402, 457
Automatically Fit to Page option, in File Page Setup dialog box, 271
Automatic format, 130, 139, 143
@AVG function, 156, 162–63, 359, 523

B

Back button, in Help window, 108
backslash (\) label prefixes, 92
Backsolver, 9, 463–68
    budget projection example, 466–67
    @functions and, 466
Backspace key, 36
{BACKTAB} key name, 421

bar graphs, 308. *See also* histograms
    horizontal, 309
    mixed line and, 310
Beep-on-error option in Tools User
    Setup dialog box, 202–3
BigLeft key, navigational use of, 115
BigRight key, navigational use of, 115
{BIGRIGHT} key name, 421
bitmaps, 438. *See also* BMP files;
    Paintbrush, designing your own
    SmartIcon with
{BLANK} macro command, 607
BMP files. *See also* SmartIcons,
    creating your own
boldface, 84
Bookmark, in Help window, 108, 121
Border option, in File Page Setup dialog
    box, 269–70
borders, 87–89
boxes, 323
{BRANCH} macro command, 595
{BREAK} macro command, 579–80
{BREAKOFF} macro command, 580
{BREAKON} macro command, 580–1
Browse backward button, in Help
    window, 108
Browse forward button, in Help
    window, 108
browsing through menus and on-screen
    hints, 110–12

C

CALC indicator, 205
Calendar SmartIcons, 435–36
Cancel button, 54
caret (^) label prefixes, 92, 125
cascading windows, 21–22, 235
@CELL function, 555–57
@CELLPOINTER function, 151–52, 557
cells
    editing, 54–59
        EDIT key (F2), 55
        edit line, 54
        Edit mode, 55–56
        techniques, 56–59
    numbers of characters in, 55
{CE} macro command, 570
center alignment, 92, 125
    across multiple columns, 93
    of long labels, 95, 126
CGM files (Metafiles), 317–20

@CHAR function, 158, 549
Chart Axis Options command, 303
Chart Borders/Grids command, 305
Chart Data Labels command, 303
Chart Heading command, 300–2
charts. *See also* graphs
    pie, 312
Chart Type command, 298
Cheat Sheet, 111
check boxes, 32
check reconciliation template, 494–96
check register template, 492–93
@CHOOSE function, 153–55, 558
CIRC indicator, 161
circles, 323
circular references, 161
{CLEARENTRY} or {CE} macro
    commands, 570
clearing data, 179–82
Clipboard, 38–39, 166, 167
    macro commands, 418–19
    macro commands for, 628–31
    moving and, 176
    moving graphics with, 319–20
    with multiple files, 248, 249
    using, 60–61
Clock Display option, in Tools User
    Setup dialog box, 204
Close command, in document control
    menu, 236
{CLOSE} macro command, 614–15
closing files, 73
CLP files, 167
@CODE function, 159, 549–50
colors, 90–91
    global settings, 206
Colors options, in Window Display
    Options dialog box, 206
@COLS function, 558
column headings, printing, 269–70
columns
    aggregate, 340, 342–44
    border, for printing, 269–70
    computed, 340–42
    deleting
        formulas and, 190–91
        graphics and, 326
    hidden, graphics and, 325–26
    inserting, 182–84
        formulas and, 189
        graphics and, 326

Column-width box, in Worksheet Global Settings dialog box, 202
column widths, 95–99
   changing, 69
   graphics and changes in, 325
Comma format, 68, 139–40
command buttons, 31
{COMMIT} macro command, 419
compatibility of 1-2-3/W with other releases of 1-2-3, 9
compound-growth template, 502–4
compound interest, @function for, 506–7
Compression options, in File Page Setup dialog box, 271, 282
computed columns, 340–42
Concatenation operator, 134
Confirm button, 54
{CONTENTS} macro command, 607–9
Control key. *See* Ctrl key
Control menus, 23–26, 235–36
control panel, 54, 59
   format in, 141
Control Panel utility in Windows' Main group, 42
converting data. *See* importing data into 1-2-3
Convert-to-values option, Edit Quick Copy command's, 171
@COORD function, 559
/Copy command, 62, 174
COPY command (DOS), 75
copying, 165–75. *See also specific copying commands*
   across multiple files, 248
   across programs, 167
   with Clipboard, 4. *See also* Clipboard
   graphics from another file, 326–27
   from one cell to several, 169–70
   pattern, 172–73
   program item icons, 43
   rows and columns, SmartIcons for, 449–57
   SmartIcons for, 65–66, 166, 169–70
   styles, 170
   transposing data and, 171–72
   values and not the underlying formulas, 171
@COS function, 150–51, 521

@COUNT function, 156, 162–63, 359, 523
CPYDOWN SmartIcon, 449–57
CPYRIGHT SmartIcon, 449–57
Criteria ranges. *See also* databases
   criteria for queries and @D functions, 367–70
   in formulas, 367
   creating, 334
cross-tabulation, 378–80
@CTERM function, 507
Ctrl-clicking the mouse, 17
Ctrl-dragging the mouse, 17
Ctrl-F4, to close document, 34
Ctrl-F6, to navigate documents, 33
Ctrl key
   to activate macros, 196
   to extend navigation range, 35
{Ctrl} MACRO key, 401
Ctrl-Tab, to navigate documents, 33
cutting and pasting operations, 61. *See also* Clipboard
Currency format, 68, 139, 141

D

data analysis, 371–98
   cross-tabulation, 378–80
   frequency distributions, 381–82
   Histograms, 382–83
   matrix multiplication, 383–90
      business applications of, 389–90
      changing a column by a percentage with, 385
      simultaneous equations and, 387–88
   regression analysis, 390–98
      multiple regression models, 395–98
      predicting results with, 393–94
   simultaneous equations, 387–88
   what-if analyses, 371–78
      Backsolver and, 463–68
      with one-way what-if tables, 373–74
      Solver and. *See* Solver
      with three-way what-if tables, 376–78
      with two-way what-if tables, 375–76

database functions, 147
databases, 8–9, 329–70
   computed and aggregate columns in, 340–42
   creating, 330
   criteria for queries and @D functions, 363–70
      formulas in the Criteria range, 367–70
      multiple conditions, 365–66
      operators, 364–65
      specific date, finding a, 369
      specific string, finding a, 367–69
   deleting records in, 338
   extracting records in, 336–38
      dBase files, 353
   finding records in, 333–36
   managing data from mainframes and other programs, 346–56. *See also* Data External commands
      /Data External commands, 354–55
      @DQUERY function, 355–56
      parsing data, 348–49
   QUERY key (F7), 339–40
   sorting data in, 331–33
   statistical functions for, 530–38
      arguments required by, 531–32
      @DAVG, 532
      @DCOUNT, 533
      @DGET, 533
      @DMAX, 533
      @DMIN, 533–34
      @DQUERY, 534–5
      @DSTD, 535
      @DSTDS, 536
      @DSUM, 536
      @DVAR, 536–37
      @DVARS, 537
database tables
   definition of, 329, 351
   joining, 344–46
Data Distribution command, 381–82
   recalculation and, 411–12
Data External commands, 8, 347, 349–56
   Connect to External options, 351, 352
   DataLens and, 350
   macro commands, 419–20
   Options Paste Fiels command, 352–53
   setting up a link with, 352
   table definition with, 352
/Data External commands, 354–55
/Data External List Tables command, 355
/Data External Other Refresh command, 355
/Data External Other Translation command, 355
data labels, in graphs, 303
DataLens, 249, 349–50
Data Matrix commands, 383
Data Matrix Inverse command, 387–88
Data Matrix Multiply command, 383–90
Data Parse command, 247, 348–49
Data Query commands, 175, 334–35
   with dBase files, 353
   QUERY key (F7) and, 339
Data Query Delete command, 338
Data Query Extract command, 336–38
   with computed and aggregate columns, 340–44
   joining tables with, 344–46
Data Query Find command, 335–36
/Data Query Parse command, 348
Data Query Unique command, 342
data ranges, graph, 295
Data Regression commands, 392–98
Data Sort command, 331–33
data tables for what-if analyses, 371–78
   one-way, 373–74
   three-way, 376–78
   two-way, 375–76
Data What-if Table command, 372
   cross-tabulation and, 378–80
Data What-if Table 1-Way command, 374, 378
Data What-if Table 2-Way Table command, 375
date and time @functions, 147–48, 538–44
   @DATE, 539
   @DATEVALUE, 539–40
   @DAY, 540
   @D360, 540
   @HOUR, 531
   @MINUTE, 531
   @MONTH, 531

@NOW, 541–42
@SECOND, 542
@TIME, 542–43
@TIMEVALUE, 543
@TODAY, 543
@YEAR, 544
Date format, 139, 141–42
@DATE function, 137, 369–70, 539
dates
    finding records that contain specific, 369–70
    in header or footer, 268
@DATEVALUE function, 137, 539–40
@DAVG function, 162–63, 360, 532
@DAY function, 147–48, 370, 540
DBASE driver, 351–54
dBASE IV files, 351–54
@DCOUNT function, 162–63, 360, 533
@DDB function, 512
{DDE-ADVISE} macro command, 419, 624
{DDE-CLOSE} macro command, 419, 624
{DDE-EXECUTE} macro command, 419
{DDE-OPEN} macro command, 419, 625
{DDE-POKE} macro command, 419, 625–26
{DDE-REQUEST} macro command, 419, 626
{DDE-UNADVISE} macro command, 419, 626
{DDE-USE} macro command, 419, 627
debugging macros, 422
{DEFINE} macro command, 595–96
Delete key, 36
deleting. *See also* removing
    records, 338
        with QUERY key (F7), 340
    rows and columns, 185–86
        formulas and, 190–91
        graphics and, 326
    several characters, 56
    worksheets, 217
        formulas and, 190–91
depreciation
    @function for, 512–15
    template, 500–2
designing spreadsheets, 77–102, 251–55. *See also* fonts

alignment of labels, 92–95
assessment of needs and, 252
column widths, 95–99
documentation and, 255
finishing touches, 100–2
guidelines for, 79
learning about the features of 1-2-3/W and, 253
row heights, 99–100
testing and, 254, 255
desktop (Windows), 13–14
@D functions, 357, 359–61
    aggregate columns versus, 343–44
@DGET function, 361, 533
dialog boxes, 30–32
    file-related, 51, 74
    navigating, 34, 35
    repositioning, 62
    shortcut keys in, 35
directories, switching among, 74
Directories list box, 74
disk drives, switching among, 74
{DISPATCH} macro command, 596–97
:Display command, 206
:Display Default Update command, 206
Division operator, 134
@DMAX function, 533
@DMIN function, 533–34
documentation of applications, 255
document windows, 20, 22–23
    closing, 24
DOS applications, under Windows, 41–42
DOS prompt, 41
    SmartIcon for bringing up, 437–38
double-caret (^^) label prefixes, 126
double-quote ("") label prefixes, 92, 126
@DQUERY function, 355–56, 534–5
Draw menu, 321–23
drop-down list boxes, 31
    Alt-DownArrow to open, 35
Drop shadow option, 88
@DSTD function, 360, 535
@DSTDS function, 360, 536
@DSUM function, 360, 536
@D360 function, 540
duplicating graphics, 320
@DVAR function, 536–37
@DVARS function, 360, 537

Dynamic Data Exchange (DDE), 5, 167, 249
    macro commands, 419

E

edit box, 54
Edit Clear command, 58–59, 180–81
    SmartIcon for, 181
{EDIT-CLEAR} macro command, 418, 634-35
Edit Clear Special command, 59, 181, 325
Edit Clear Special Styles command, 127
Edit Copy command, 60–61, 166–67, 176–77
    accelerator key for, 61
    SmartIcon for, 65, 166
{EDIT-COPY-GRAPH} macro command, 418
{EDIT-COPY} macro command, 418, 635-36
Edit Cut command, 61, 176–77, 325
    accelerator key for, 61
    removing data with, 180
    SmartIcon for, 65, 176–77
{EDIT-CUT} macro command, 418, 636-37
Edit Find command, 59
editing cells, 54–59
    EDIT key (F2), 55
    edit line, 54
    Edit mode, 55–56
    techniques, 56–59
EDIT key (F2), 55
edit line, 54
Edit Link Options Update command, 249
Edit menu macro commands, 418–19
Edit mode, 55–56
    in Help window, 108
Edit Move Cells command, 177–79
    Styles-only option, 179
{EDIT-PASTE} macro command, 637-38
Edit Paste command, 61, 166–67, 176–77
    accelerator key for, 61
    SmartIcon for, 65, 166, 176–77
Edit Paste Link command, 59, 167

{EDIT-PASTE-LINK} macro command, 419, 638-39
{EDIT-PASTE} macro command, 419
Edit Quick Copy command, 62, 167–69
    convert-to-values option, 171
    with multiple files, 248
    SmartIcon for, 65, 66, 169
Edit Quick Styles-only option, 170
Edit Undo command, 58, 112
    Alt-Backspace as accelerator key for, 35
    SmartIcon for, 65
ellipses, 323
EMPLOYEE.DBF practice file, 351–54
Enable Edit Undo option, in Tools User Setup dialog box, 203
End key, navigational use of, 116–17
Enter key, to confirm, 33
Equals operator, 134
erasing data, 179–82
ERR conditions, 163
@ERR function, 559–60
Escape key, to cancel, 33
even alignment, 126–27
@EXACT function, 159, 560
exclamation point (!), 163
Exit command, 74
exiting 1-2-3/W, 74
@EXP function, 518
Exponentiation operator, 134
exporting data. *See* Data External commands
extracting records, 336–38
    with computed and aggregate columns, 340–42
    from dBase files, 353

F

F3. *See* NAME key
F6. *See* PANE key
F10 key, to use menus, 33
@FALSE function, 544
field names, 330
fields, 330
File Administration Paste Table command, 236
File Administration Update Links command, 233
File Allocation Table (DOS), 41

Index

File Combine command, 246
File Combine From command, 175
File commands, 74
File Delete command, Program
  Manager's, 44
/File Erase command, 111
file extensions, 75
File Extract command, 247
File Extract-to-all command, 175
File Import commands, 247–48
File Import From command, 175
File Import From Numbers command,
  248, 347–48
File Import From Text command,
  347–48
File Import Styles command, 248
file linking, 231–32. *See also* multiple
  (linked) files
  basic techniques, 232
  range names and, 232–33
file-linking formulas, 231–33, 238.
  See also multiple (linked) files
    file specification in, 236
    setting up, 237
File Manager (Windows), 41, 44
File menu, 30
  in Help window, 108
File Name box, 74
file names, 51
File New command, in Program
  Manager, 43
File Open command, 73
File Page Setup command, 71, 266–73
  borders option, 269–70
  Compression options, 271, 282
  Header and Footer options, 267–69
  Landscape or Portrait orientation,
    272
  Margins option, 271
  Options, 272–73
  Restore button, 267
File Preview command, 71, 230, 262–63
  SmartIcon for, 71
File Print command, 72, 231, 258–59
  Pages options, 263
  Preview, 262–63
  Range(s) option, 260, 263
  SmartIcon for, 72
File Printer Setup command, 70–71

File Properties command
  in Program Manager, 43
File Run command (Windows), 41
File Save As command, 49–51, 113
  Password-protect option, 250
File Save command, 49, 73, 113
{FILESIZE} macro command, 615–16
Files list box, 74
file management
  basic techniques of, 73–74
  closing files, 73
  exiting 1-2-3/W, 74
  opening files, 73
file specification, 236
  default, 51
financial @functions, 148–49, 506–15
  for annuities, 507–9
  for compound interest, 506–7
  @CTERM, 507
  @DDB, 512
  for depreciation, 512–15
  @FV, 507–8
  for internal rate of return and net
    present value, 509–11
  @IRR, 509–10
  @NPV, 510–11
  @PMT, 508
  @PV, 508–9
  @RATE, 507
  @SLN, 512–13
  @SYD, 513
  @TERM, 509
  @VDB, 513–15
@FIND function, 159, 367–69, 550
finding
  records, 333–36
  a specific date, 369–70
  a specific string, 367–68
Fixed format, 139, 141
flush-right alignment, 126
FM3 files, 75
fonts, 80–87, 274
  Adobe Type Manager (ATM),
    283–84
  definition of, 80
  problems with, 283–84
  replacing, 85–87
  serif, 80
font set, customizing, 85–87

footers. *See* headers and footers
{FORBREAK} macro command, 599–600
{FOR} loops, 414
{FOR} macro command, 597–99
format bar, 59
Format button, in Worksheet Global Settings dialog box, 202
:Format Color Reverse command, 91
format files, 75
:Format Reset command, 182
formats, 129–30, 138–45. *See also specific formats*
   control panel display of, 141
   names and descriptions of, 139
   parentheses and, 143
   SmartIcons for, 138
   values not affected by changing, 144
formatting ranges, 138
formatting characters, entering values and, 129
{FORMBREAK} macro command, 582–83
{FORM} macro command, 581–82
Formula option, in File Extract dialog box, 247
formulas, 130–37
   absolute cell references in, 186, 188–89
   characters that can start, 132
   circular references in, 161
   converting to values, 130
   counting or averaging, 162–63
   in Criteria range, 367
   entering, 59–61
   file-linking, 231–33, 238. *See also* multiple (linked) files
      file specification in, 236
      setting up, 237
   hierarchy of operations in, 161–62
   logical, 135–36, 365
   moving and, 175
   parentheses in, 162
   problems with, 160–63, 186–91
      absolute cell references, 186, 188–89
      deleting a referenced row, column, or sheet, 190–91
      inserting rows, columns, or sheets, 189–90

   moving a referenced cell, 190
   relative cell references, 186–87
   relative cell references in, 186–88
   starting, 132–33
   string, 135
   time and date, 137
   types of entries in, 133
{FRAMEOFF} macro command, } 573–74
{FRAMEON} macro command, 574
Frame options, in Window Display Options dialog box, 207
free corner, 118
frequency distributions, 381–82
function keys, 120–22
@functions, 9, 145–60, 505–67
   Backsolver and, 466
   database, 147, 530–38
      arguments required by, 531–32
      @DAVG, 532
      @DCOUNT, 533
      @DGET, 533
      @DMAX, 533
      @DMIN, 533–34
      @DQUERY, 534–5
      @DSTD, 535
      @DSTDS, 536
      @DSUM, 536
      @DVAR, 536–37
      @DVARS, 537
   date and time, 137, 147–48, 538–44
      @D360, 540
      @DATE, 539
      @DATEVALUE, 539–40
      @DAY, 540
      @HOUR, 531
      @MINUTE, 531
      @MONTH, 531
      @NOW, 541–42
      @SECOND, 542
      @TIME, 542–43
      @TIMEVALUE, 543
      @TODAY, 543
      @YEAR, 544
   displaying a list of, 63
   @FALSE, 544
   financial, 148–49, 506–15
      for annuities, 507–9
      for compound interest, 506–7
      @CTERM, 507

Index **649**

@CTERM function, 507
@DDB, 512
 for depreciation, 512–15
@FV, 507–8
 for internal rate of return and net present value, 509–11
@IRR, 509–10
@NPV, 510–11
@PMT, 508
@PV, 508–9
@RATE, 507
@SLN, 512–13
@SYD, 513
@TERM, 509
@VDB, 513–15
help on, 107, 145
list of, how to display, 146
logical, 149–50, 149–50, 544–49
 @IF, 544–45
 @ISAAF, 546
 @ISAPP, 546
 @ISERR, 546–47
 @ISNA, 547
 @ISNUMBER, 547
 @ISRANGE, 548
 @ISSTRING, 548
 @TRUE, 548–49
mathematical, 150–51, 515–22
 @ABS, 516
 @ACOS, 520
 @ASIN, 520
 @ATAN, 520
 @ATAN2, 520–21
 basic, 516–17
 @COS, 521
 @EXP, 518
 @INT, 516
 @LN, 518
 @LOG, 519
 logarithms for, 518–19
 @MOD, 516
 @PI, 516
 @RAND, 517
 @ROUND, 517
 @SIN, 522
 @SQRT, 517
 @TAN, 522
 trigonometric, 519–22
 plus sign not needed for, 132

Solver and, 487
special, 151–55, 554–67
 @CELL, 555–57
 @CELLPOINTER, 557
 @CHOOSE, 558
 @COLS, 558
 @COORD, 559
 @ERR, 559–60
 @EXACT, 560
 @HLOOKUP, 560–62
 @INDEX, 562–63
 @INFO, 564–65
 @LOOKUP, 566–67
 @NA, 565
 @ROWS, 565–66
 @SHEETS, 566
 @@f, 555
statistical, 155–57, 357–60, 523–38
 @AVG, 523
 basic, 523–25
 @COUNT, 523
 database. *See* database *above*
 @MAX, 524
 @MIN, 524
 standard deviation and variance, 525–30
 @STD, 528
 @STDS, 528–29
 @SUM, 524
 @SUMPRODUCT, 524–25
 @VAR, 529
 @VARS, 529–30
string formulas and, 135
string, 157–60, 549–54
 @CHAR, 549
 @CODE, 549–50
 @FIND, 550
 @LEFT, 550–51
 @LENGTH, 551
 @LOWER, 551
 @MID, 551
 @N, 552
 @PROPER, 552
 @REPEAT, 552
 @REPLACE, 553
 @RIGHT, 553
 @S, 553
 @STRING, 553–54
 @TRIM, 554

@UPPER, 554
@VALUE, 554
time and date, 137
@FV function, 507–8

G

General format, 139, 141
{GETLABEL} macro command, 405–6, 584-85
{GETNUMBER} macro command, 405, 585–86
{GETPOS} macro command, 616-17
global settings, 198–208. *See also* Worksheet Global Settings command
  in 1-2-3W.INI file, 208
  local settings that can be turned into, 208
  for panes, 209–12
  Tools User Setup command, 58, 202–5
    Beep-on-error option, 202–3
    Clock Display option, 204
    Enable Edit Undo option, 203
    International button, 204
    Iterations option, 205
    Recalculation dialog box, 204–5
    Run Autoexecute Macros option, 203
    Worksheet Directory option, 205
  Window Display Options command, 91, 205–8
    Colors options, 206
    Options settings, 207
    Palette button, 207
    Restore button, 208
    Update button, 208
    Zoom setting, 207
  Worksheet Global Settings command, 198–202
    Align labels options, 93, 201
    Column-width box, 202
    Format button, 202
    group mode, 201
    Protection option, 201, 250
    Zero display options, 200, 226
GOTO key (F5), 116–17
  using a named range, 195–96
:Graph Add Metafile command, 319
:Graph Add Named command, 299

Graph Add-to-sheet command, 299, 318–19
graph data ranges, 295
:Graph Edit Edit Arrowheads command, 322
:Graph Edit Edit Smoothing None command, 323
graphical user interface (GUI), 3–4, 10
graphic objects, 318
  adding to a worksheet, 320–24
  for annotating a range, 324
  arrows, 322–23
  editing, 324
  ellipses, circles and ovals, 323
  lines, 322–23
  rectangles, 323
  text, 321–22
graphics, 317–27. *See also* graphic objects; graphs
  adding explanatory text to, 321–22
  changes in column widths or row heights and, 325
  copying from another file, 326–27
  definition of, 317
  duplicating, 320
  hidden columns and, 325–26
  inserting and deleting rows and columns and, 326
  moving, 319–20
  problems with, 325–26
  removing, 325
  SmartIcons for, 460
Graph Import command, 319
GRAPH key (F10), 121, 293
:Graph Move command, 320
Graph (New or View) Draw Text command, 321–22
Graph (New or View) Chart Axis Options command, 303
Graph (New or View) Chart Borders/ Grids command, 305
Graph (New or View) Chart Data Labels command, 303
Graph (New or View) Chart Heading command, 300–2
Graph (New or View) Draw command, 321
{GRAPHOFF} macro command, 574–75
{GRAPHON} macro command, 575
:Graph Remove command, 182, 325

graphs, 6–7, 289–315. *See also* charts
   as analytical tools, 291–92
   analytical versus presentation, 290
   area, 307
   bar, 308
   columnwise versus rowwise data in, 297–98
   creating, 295–96
   critical points to creating, 294–95
   data labels in, 303
   grid lines for, 305
   High-Low Close-Open (HLCO), 314–15
   line, 296, 305–7
   notes and 2nd notes of, 301
   placing in worksheet, 298–300
   removing, 182
   scaling, 304
   settings for, 292
   as stored in worksheet and format files, 293
   titles and subtitles of, 301
      x-axis, 303
   XY, 311
/Graph Save command, 319
:Graph Settings Range command, 320
Graph Style Display Options
   Transparent command, 299
:Graph Zoom command, 319
Greater than operator, 134
Greater than or equal to operator, 134
Greater than or less than operator, 134
gridlines, 89
   for graphs, 305
group icon, 15
GROUP indicator, 221
Group mode
   dangers of, 221–22
   3-D worksheets in, 221, 230
   in Worksheet Global Settings dialog box, 201
groups, Program Manager, 15
group windows, 43

H

headers and footers, printing, 267, 269, 276, 280–81
Help command, in Help window, 108
Help Edit Annotate command, 108
Help Edit Copy command, 108
Help For Upgraders command, 107
Help How Do I? command, 107
HELP key (F1), 35, 107
Help window, 107–110
Hidden format, 139, 143
hierarchy of operations, 161–62
High-Low Close-Open (HLCO) graphs, 314–15
Histograms, 382–83
@HLOOKUP function, 153, 560–62
Home key, navigational use of, 115–16
horizontal bar graphs, 309
@HOUR function, 531

I

I-beam, 36
icons
   assigning, 43
   group, 15
   program item, 15
      copying, 43
identity matrix, 384
@IF function, 136, 149–50, 544–45
{IF} macro command, 416, 600–1
importing data into 1-2-3. *See also*
   databases, managing data from
   mainframes and other programs;
   Data External commands
      into databases, 346–48
Index button, in Help window, 108
@INDEX function, 562–63
{INDICATE} macro command, 575–76
@INFO function, 146, 151–52, 564–65
inserting
   rows or columns, 182–84
      formulas and, 189
      graphics and, 326
   worksheets, 216–17
      formulas and, 189
      SmartIcon for, 217
insertion point, 36, 56
International button, in Tools User Setup dialog box, 204
@INT function, 370, 516
@IRR function, 372, 509–10
@ISAAF function, 546
@ISAPP function, 546
@ISERR function, 546–47
@ISNA function, 547
@ISNUMBER function, 547

@ISRANGE function, 548
@ISSTRING function, 548
italics, 84
Iterations option, in Tool User Setup Recalculation dialog box, 205

J

joining database tables, 344–46

K

keyboard
    navigating worksheets with, 115–16
    preselection of cells with, 119–20
    techniques, 33–36
key names, 399, 569–71
    repeating, 571
keywords. *See* macro keywords

L

Label format, 139, 143
label prefixes, 92, 124–27
    extra, 128
    macro names and, 127
    methods of choosing, 124–25
    preventing problems with, 127–29
labels, 123–29
    alignment of. *See* alignment of labels (or text)
    that start with a number or a character that ordinarily starts a formula, 128
    too long to fit in a cell, 129
Landscape orientation, 272
LANs. *See* networks
{LAUNCH} macro command, 420, 627
left alignment, 125. *See also* alignment of labels (or text)
@LEFT function, 159, 550–51
@LENGTH function, 159, 551
Less than operator, 134
Less than or equal to operator, 134
{LET} macro command, 609–10
linear equations, 384
line graphs, 296, 305–7
    mixed bar and, 310
{LINK-ASSIGN} macro command, 419, 627–28
{LINK-CREATE} macro command, 419, 628–29

{LINK-DEACTIVATE} macro command, 629
{LINK-DELETE} macro command, 419, 629–30
linked files. *See* file linking; multiple (linked) files
{LINK} macro, 6
Link Options command, 59
{LINK-REMOVE} macro command, 419, 630
{LINK-TABLE} macro command, 419, 630
{LINK-UPDATE} macro command, 419, 630–31
list boxes, 31
LMBCS (Lotus Multibyte Character Set), 158
@LN function, 518
loan amortization template, 496–98
logarithms, @functions for, 518–19
@LOG function, 519
logical formulas, 135–36, 365
logical functions, 149–50, 544–49
    @IF, 544–45
    @ISAAF, 546
    @ISAPP, 546
    @ISERR, 546–47
    @ISNA, 547
    @ISNUMBER, 547
    @ISRANGE, 548
    @ISSTRING, 548
    @TRUE, 548–49
logical operators, 364
{LOOK} macro command, 586–87
@LOOKUP function, 566–67
lottery, macro for producing random numbers for use in, 407–16
Lotus Applications group, 15
@LOWER function, 159, 551

M

MAC files, 435
macro commands, 571–639
    arguments of, 571–72
    data manipulation, 605–14
        {APPENDBELOW}, 605–6
        {APPEND-RIGHT}, 606–7
        {BLANK}, 607
        {CONTENTS}, 607–9
        {LET}, 609–10

Index

{PUT}, 610–12
{RECALC}, 612–13
{RECALCCOL}, 613–14
file manipulation and editing, 614–39
   {CLOSE}, 614–15
   {DDE-ADVISE}, 624
   {DDE-CLOSE}, 624
   {DDE-EXECUTE}, 624–5
   {DDE-OPEN}, 625
   {DDE-POKE}, 625–26
   {DDE-REQUEST}, 626
   {DDE-UNADVISE}, 626
   {DDE-USE}, 627
   {EDIT-CLEAR}, 634-35
   {EDIT-COPY}, 635-36
   {EDIT-CUT}, 636-37
   {EDIT-PASTE}, 637-38
   {EDIT-PASTE-LINK}, 638–39
   {FILESIZE}, 615–16
   {GETPOS}, 616–17
   {LAUNCH}, 627
   {LINK-ASSIGN}, 627–28
   {LINK-CREATE}, 628–29
   {LINK-DEACTIVATE}, 629
   {LINK-DELETE}, 629–30
   {LINK-REMOVE}, 630
   {LINK-TABLE}, 630
   {LINK-UPDATE}, 630–31
   {OPEN}, 617–18
   {READ}, 618–20
   {READLN}, 620–21
   {SETPOS}, 621
   {WRITE}, 622–23
   {WRITELN}, 623
keyboard interaction, 579–92
   {?} (Interactive command), 591–92
   {BREAK}, 579–80
   {BREAKOFF}, 580
   {BREAKON}, 580-81
   {FORM}, 581–82
   {FORMBREAK}, 582–83
   {GET}, 583–84
   {GETLABEL}, 584–85
   {GETNUMBER}, 585–86
   {LOOK}, 586–87
   {MENUBRANCH}, 587–88
   {MENUCALL}, 589–90
   {WAIT}, 590–91

list of, 112
program flow, 592–605
   {BRANCH}, 595
   {DEFINE}, 595–96
   {DISPATCH}, 596–97
   {FOR}, 597–99
   {FORBREAK}, 599–600
   {IF}, 600–1
   {ONERROR}, 601–2
   {QUIT}, 602–3
   {RESTART}, 603–4
   {RETURN}, 604
   {SUBROUTINE}, 592–95
   {SYSTEM}, 604–5
screen control, 573–79
   {BEEP} macro command, 573
   {FRAMEOFF}, 573–74
   {FRAMEON}, 574
   {GRAPHOFF}, 574
   {GRAPHON}, 575
   {INDICATE}, 575–76
   {PANELOFF}, 577
   {PANELON}, 578
   {WINDOWSOFF}, 578
   {WINDOWSON}, 579
MACRO key (Ctrl), 401
macro key names, 403, 569–71
   repeating, 571
macro keywords, 403
macro names, label prefixes and, 127
macros, 6, 399–423
   Advanced Macro Commands, 399, 403
   autoexecuting, 203, 402, 457
   cell location and, 404
   GUI versus 1-2-3 Classic commands in, 421
   help with, 415
   new commands in 1-2-3/W, 417–21
      Clipboard/Edit commands, 418–19
      Data External commands, 419–20
      Dynamic Data Exchange (DDE), 419
      for navigating menus, dialog boxes, and worksheets, 420–21
      window control commands, 417–18
   with a pause for data-entry, 407

for random-number generation, 407–16
range names and, 196–97, 406, 422
reasons to use, 400–1
with Solver, 480–81
stopping from running, 405
Transcript window for creating, 409–12
troubleshooting problems with, 422
MACRS (Modified Accelerated Cost Recovery System), @function for, 513–15
Main group (Windows), 15
margins, in File Page Setup dialog box, 271
mathematical @functions, 150–51, 515–22
    @ABS, 516
    @ACOS, 520
    @ASIN, 520
    @ATAN, 520
    @ATAN2, 520–21
    basic, 516–17
    @COS, 521
    @EXP, 518
    @INT, 516
    @LN, 518
    @LOG, 519
    logarithms for, 518–19
    @MOD, 516
    @PI, 516
    @RAND, 517
    @ROUND, 517
    @SIN, 522
    @SQRT, 517
    @TAN, 522
    trigonometric, 519–22
mathematical optimization, 467–68. *See also* Solver
matrix multiplication, 383–90
    business applications of, 389–90
    changing a column by a percentage with, 385
    simultaneous equations and, 387–88
@MAX function, 156, 359, 524
Maximize command, in Windows control menus, 24, 235
maximize icon, 24
{MB} key name, 420
menu bar, 28–29, 59

{MENUBAR} key name, 420, 570
{MENUBRANCH} macro command, 587–88
{MENUCALL} macro command, 589–90
menus
    browsing through, 110–12
    graphical user interface (GUI) vs. 1-2-3 Classic, 10
Metafiles (CGM files), 317–20
Microsoft Windows. *See* Windows environment
@MID function, 159, 551
@MIN function, 156, 524
Minimize command, in control menus, 25, 235
minimize icon, 21
minimizing windows, 21
@MINUTE function, 531
@MOD function, 516
@MONTH function, 147–48, 370, 531
mouse, 15–19
    clicking the, 16
    double-clicking the, 16
    dragging the, 16
    menu bar and, 28–29
    selecting a range with, 119–20
    Shift-clicking and Ctrl-clicking with a, 17
    Shift-dragging and Ctrl-dragging with a, 17
    in 3D spreadsheets, 115
mouse pointer, 19
/Move command, 177, 179
Move command, in Windows, 25, 236
moving, 175–79
    a referenced cell, formulas and, 190
    graphics, 319–20
    SmartIcon for, 178
multiple (linked) files, 8, 233–45. *See also* file linking; file-linking formulas
    making files work together, 237–45
    navigating among open worksheets, 234–35
    performing the lookup, 243
    preparing for a lookup, 239–40
    switching among windows, 240–41
    updating links, 233
    window-management techniques, 235–36

multiple regression analysis, 395–98
multiplication, matrix, 383–86
Multiplication operator, 134

N

@NA function, 565
NAME key (F3), 112, 122
   to enter range names, 196
navigating
   with keyboard, 33–35
   macro key names, 420–21
   among open worksheets, 234–35
   with scroll bars, 27
   through Help system, 107–8
   worksheets, 114–20
      End key, 116–17
      with keyboard, 115–16
      keyboard preselection, 119–20
      mouse movements, 114–15
      1-2-3 Classic vs. Windows
         techniques, 10
      range references, 118–20
      3-D worksheets, 219–20
negative numbers, entering, 129
networks, file access on, 250–51
Next command, in Windows control
   menus, 25, 236
@N function, 552
nonprinting text, alignment of, 126
#NO# operator, 134, 136
notes, graph, 301
@NOW function, 147–48, 370, 541–42
@NPV function, 372, 510–11
Numbers option, in File Import dialog
   box, 248
numeric keypad, 60

O

{ONERROR} macro command, 601–2
1-2-3 for Windows
   benefits of, 11
   features of, 7–9
   order of selecting data and issuing
      commands in, 19
   starting, 49
      with a mouse, 18
1-2-3W.INI, 208
one-way what-if tables, 373–74
opening files, 73
{OPEN} macro command, 617–18

operators, 133–34
   in criteria for database queries and
      @D functions, 364–65
   hierarchy of, 162
optimization, 467–68. *See also* Solver
option buttons, 32
Options settings, in Window Display
   Options dialog box, 207
Oracle, 351
order of precedence, 161–62
#OR# operator, 134, 136–137, 366
Outline border option, 88
Output range, 336–38
   creating, 336
   extracting records to, 338
ovals, 323

P

page breaks, 264, 266, 278–79
   manual, 264–66, 285
   soft, 264–265
page number, in header or footer, 268
Page Setup dialog box. *See* File Page
   Setup command
PageUp and PageDown keys,
   navigational use of, 115
Paintbrush, 434
   designing your own SmartIcon with,
      438–46
      assigning the macro, 444–45
      color palette, 441
      painting the icon, 442–44
      starting Paintbrush, 439
      text tool, 443
      Tool Palette, 440
   tips on using, 458–61
      bigger canvas, 458–59
      OS/2-based bitmap editor, 460
      right mouse button, 459
      screen-capture facility, 459–60
Palette button, in Window Display
   Options dialog box, 207
PANE key (F6), 122, 218
{PANELOFF} macro command, 577
{PANELON} macro command, 578
panes, 209–12
   basic techniques, 209
   horizontal and vertical, 210–11
   synchronized or unsynchronized,
      209

parentheses, in formulas, 162
parsing data, 348–49
passwords, 250
pattern copying, 172–73
percentage, changing a column by a, 385–86
percentage values, entering, 130
Percent format, 139, 141
   confusion about the, 144
Perspective view, 211–12, 217–18, 227
PIC files, 317–20
pie charts, 312
PIF files, 41
@PI function, 516
pixels, 441
+/- format, 139
plus sign (+), entering formulas with, 132
@PMT function, 148–49, 508
Point mode, 160
Portrait orientation, 272
PostScript-compatible fonts, 80
precedence, order of, 161–62
predicting results with regression analysis, 393–94
preselecting cells, 119–20
present value template, 498–500
previewing a printout, 262, 275
Preview SmartIcon, 262
:Print command, 259
/Print command, 259
printer ports, 285
printing, 257–86. *See also* File Print command
   basic techniques, 70–72
   borders, 269–70
   commands used for, 258–59
   headers and footers, 267, 269, 276, 280–81
   a large spreadsheet, 261
   more than one copy of worksheet, 285
   order of processing pending printouts, 283
   page breaks for, 264, 266, 278–79
   page number, 268
   page setup for. *See* File Page Setup command
   previewing before, 262, 275
   procedures for, 274–83

questions and answers about, 283–86
slowing down of computer and printer when, 283
SmartIcon for, 260–261
3-D worksheets, 230–31
Print Manager Utility (Windows), 283
PrintScreen key, 459
program item icons, 15
   copying, 43
Program Manager (Windows), 14
   groups in, 15
   navigating, 33
   tips on using, 43–44
@PROPER function, 552
protection of data, 250, 254–55
Protection option, in Worksheet Global Settings dialog box, 201
{PUT} macro command, 613–14
@PV function, 508–9

Q

QUERY key (F7), 339–40
   for fast queries, 339–40
question mark (?)
   in criteria, 363
   as interactive macro command, 405, 591–92
{QUIT} macro command, 602–3
quotation mark (") label prefixes, 125

R

radio buttons, 32
@RAND function, 517
Range Annotate command, 324
/Range Erase command, 181–82
Range Format command, 138, 225
/Range Format command, 138
Range Format Reset command, 182
Range Go To command, 117
/Range Label-Alignment command, 125
Range Name Create command, 193–94
/Range Name Create command, 194
Range Name Delete command, 197
Range Name Label Create command, 195
/Range Name Note command, 197–98
Range Name Paste Table command, 197
range names, 193–98
   assigning, 193–95

with file links, 232–33
helpful hints on, 197–98
macros and, 196–97, 406, 422
using a named range and, 195–96
Range Protect command, 182
range references, single cell references as, 163
ranges. *See also* range names
anchoring, 118
Criteria. *See also* databases
criteria for queries and @D functions, 367–70
in formulas, 367
creating, 334
formatting, 138
selecting, 118–20
in 3-D worksheets, 118, 220
Range Search commands, 59
Range Transpose command, 171–72
/Range Transpose command, 172, 175
/Range Values command, 171, 174
@RATE function, 507
{READLN} macro command, 620–21
{READ} macro command, 618–20
rebooting your computer, 41
{RECALCCOL} macro command, 613–14
{RECALC} macro command, 612–13
recalculation, Data Distribution command and, 411–12
Recalculation dialog box, in Tools User Setup dialog box, 204–5
records. *See also* databases
definition of, 329–30
deleting, 338
with QUERY key (F7), 340
extracting, 336–38
computed and aggregate columns, 340–42
finding, 333–36
sorting, 331–33
regression analysis, 390–98
multiple regression models, 395–98
predicting results with, 393–94
relative cell references, 186–88
removing. *See also* deleting
data, 179–82
graphics, 325
icons from the current palette, 432

@REPEAT function, 159, 552
@REPLACE function, 553
replacing selected characters, 56, 57
resizing a window with a mouse, 18
{RESTART} macro command, 603–4
Restore command, in Windows, 25, 208, 235
restoring a window, 21, 22
{RETURN} macro command, 604–5
reverse text, 91
right alignment, 92, 125
of long labels, 94–95, 126
Right-alignment SmartIcon, 69
@RIGHT function, 553
{ROLLBACK} macro command, 420
@ROUND function, 145, 150–51, 517
rounding, 144–45
row headings, printing, 269–70
row heights, 99–100
graphics and changes in, 325
rows
border, for printing, 269–70
deleting, 185–86
formulas and, 190–91
graphics and, 326
inserting, 182–84
formulas and, 189
graphics and, 326
@ROWS function, 565–66
Run Autoexecute Macros option, in Tools User Setup dialog box, 203
RUN key (Alt-F3), 122
for macros, 402

S

sample group, in regression analysis, 390–91
sans serif fonts, 80
saving files, 49, 113
frequency of, 53
scale indicator, 304
scaling graphs, 304
Scientific format, 139, 142
screen-capture facility, 459–60
scroll arrows, 27
scroll bars, 114–15
scroll box, 27
scrolling, 26–28
Search button, in Help window, 108

Search-for box, 108
secondary key, sorting data with, 331–33
@SECOND function, 542
2nd notes, graph, 301
serif fonts, 80
{SETPOS} macro command, 621
@S function, 553
shading, 89–90
sheet letter, 53, 114
@SHEETS function, 566
Shift-clicking the mouse, 17
Shift-dragging the mouse, 17
Shift key, 34
Show Grid lines, in File Page Setup dialog box, 273
Show Worksheet frame, in File Page Setup dialog box, 272
@SIN function, 522
Size command, in Windows, 25, 236
@SLN function, 512–13
/ (slash) menu options, 111
SmartIcon Palette, 64, 425–61
   altering, 426–34
      adding standard icons and custom icons, 432–34
      choosing the current icons, 430–34
      floating window, displaying palette as, 429–30
      hiding the palette, 430
      position of palette, 66, 427–29
   graphs and, 318
SmartIcons, 5–6, 64–69, 112
   adding to the current palette, 432–34
   for alignment of labels (or text), 125
   at-sign, 146
   for copying, 65–66
   for copying commands, 166
   creating your own, 434–61. See also Paintbrush, designing your own SmartIcon with
      allocating worksheet space to SmartIcon macros, 449
      anatomy of SmartIcons, 435–37
      for copying rows and columns, 449–57
      DOS prompt, SmartIcon for bringing up, 437–38
      single-celled nature of SmartIcon macros, 447–48
      steps in, 446
   in current palette, 430–34
   for formats, 138
   for graphics, 460
   for label alignment, 92
   prompt that describes, 66, 426
   standard versus custom, 435
   for @SUM, 65
   using, 426
Solver, 9, 146, 468–87
   adjustable cells in, 470
   answer window in, 472–73
   changing a constraint in, 477
   @functions and, 487
   guess values in, 482
   guidelines for learning, 487
   inconsistent problems in, 477–78
   macros and, 480–81
   more complex problem in, 474–77
   optimatl cell in, 471
   problems not meant for, 481–82
   progress window in, 472
   reporting options, 478–79
   simple optimization problem with, 469–74
   whole-number solutions in, 482–86
@SOLVER function, 146, 480–81
sorting data, 331–33
   SmartIcons for, 333
spacebar, to select a control, 34
:Special Copy command, 170, 174
:Special Move command, 179
splitter icons, 210
spreadsheet design. See designing spreadsheets
SQL-based relational databases, 351
@SQRT function, 150–51, 517
standard deviation, 525–29
starting a worksheet, 48–53
starting 1-2-3 for Windows, 49
   with a mouse, 18
statistical functions, 155–57, 357–60, 523–38
   @AVG, 523
   basic, 523–25
   @COUNT, 523
   database, 530–38
      arguments required by, 531–32

@DAVG, 532
@DCOUNT, 533
@DGET, 533
@DMAX, 533
@DMIN, 533–34
@DQUERY, 534–5
@DSTD, 535
@DSTDS, 536
@DSUM, 536
@DVAR, 536–37
@DVARS, 537
@MAX, 524
@MIN, 524
standard deviation and variance, 525–30
@STD, 528
@STDS, 528–29
@SUM, 524
@SUMPRODUCT, 524–25
@VAR, 529
@VARS, 529–30
status indicator, 110
@STD function, 156, 528
@STDS function, 156, 359, 528–29
string formulas, 135
{GETLABEL} macro command and, 406
@STRING function, 159, 553–54
string functions, 157–60, 549–54
@CHAR, 549
@CODE, 549–50
@FIND, 550
@LEFT, 550–51
@LENGTH, 551
@LOWER, 551
@MID, 551
@N, 552
@PROPER, 552
@REPEAT, 552
@REPLACE, 553
@RIGHT, 553
@S, 553
@STRING, 553–54
@TRIM, 554
@UPPER, 554
@VALUE, 554
Style Alignment Align-over-columns command, 127
Style Alignment commands, 92–95

Style Border dialog box, 88
Style Color command, 90–91
Style Font dialog box, 80, 82–87
Style Font Replace dialog box, 85–87
styles, copying, 170
Style Shading command, 89
Styles-only option, Edit Move Cells command's, 179
Styles option, in File Import dialog box, 248
{SUBROUTINE} macro command, 592–95
subroutines, 407
    breaking macros into, 413
subtitles, graph, 301
Subtraction operator, 134
@SUM function, 156–57, 359, 524
    SmartIcon for, 65
@SUMPRODUCT function, 157, 524–25
Switch To command, in Windows, 25
@SYD function, 513
Symphony, 122
/System command, 111
    SmartIcon for, 437–38
{SYSTEM} macro command, 604–5

T

Tab key, to navigate a dialog box, 34
{TAB} key name, 421
tables, database. *See* database tables
    definition of, 329, 351
    joining, 344–46
@TAN function, 522
Task List, 39–40
templates, 491–504
    amortizing loan, 496–98
    check reconciliation, 494–96
    check register, 492–93
    compound growth, 502–4
    depreciation, 500–2
    present value, 498–500
@TERM function, 509
testing an application, 254–55
:Text Align Center command, 93
:Text Align command, 125
Text attribute, Align-over-columns option and, 127
text boxes (fields), 32
:Text Clear command, 127

text files. *See* ASCII files
Text format, 139, 143
Text option, in File Extract dialog box, 247
:Text Set command, 127
text tool, Paintbrush, 443
3-D worksheets, 8, 113, 215–31
   adding sheets to, 216–17, 226–27
   creating and using, 222–30
   in Group mode, 221, 230
   inserting sheets, 185
   navigating, 219–20
   in Perspective view, 211–12, 217–18, 227
   printing, 230–31
   range references in, 118, 220
   reasons to use, 216
   setting up first sheet of, 223–25
   sheet letter in, 53
three-way what-if tables, 376–78
tiling windows, 21–22, 235
time and date formulas, 137
time and date @functions, 147–48, 538–44
   @DATE, 539
   @DATEVALUE, 539–40
   @DAY, 540
   @D360, 540
   @HOUR, 531
   @MINUTE, 531
   @MONTH, 531
   @NOW, 541–42
   @SECOND, 542
   @TIME, 542–43
   @TIMEVALUE, 543
   @TODAY, 543
   @YEAR, 544
Time format, 139, 141–42
@TIME function, 137, 542–43
@TIMEVALUE function, 543
title bar, 21
   of control panel, 59
titles, 212–13
   graph, 301
      x-axis, 303
@TODAY function, 137, 147–48, 543
Tool Macro Show Transcript command, 409–12
Tools Add-in command, 121

Tools Icon Palette command, 64, 66, 427
Tools Icon Palette Customize command, 430–31
   Assign Macro button, 436, 444
Tools Macro Debug command, 422
Tools User Setup command, 58, 202–5
   Beep-on-error option, 202–3
   Clock Display option, 204
   Enable Edit Undo option, 203
   International button, 204
   Iterations option, 205
   Recalculation dialog box, 204–5
   Run Autoexecute Macros option, 203
   Worksheet Directory option, 205
training users, 255
Transcript window, 409–11
Translate, 250
Translate utility, 347
trigonometric @functions, 519–22
@TRIM function, 554
@TRUE function, 548–49
TSR programs, 42
two-way what-if tables, 375–76
typefaces. *See* fonts

U

underlined text, 84
underscore (_), to separate words in a range name, 194
Undo feature, 58, 203
Unrecoverable Application Error message, 53
Update button, in Window Display Options dialog box, 208
@UPPER function, 554

V

@VALUE function, 159, 554
values
   converting formulas to, 130
      with Edit Quick Copy commands, 171
   copying, with Edit Quick Copy command's Convert-to-values option, 171
   entering, 129–30
Values option, in File Extract dialog box, 247

@VAR function, 156, 359, 529
variables, solving simultaneously for several, 467
variance, 525–26, 529–30
@VARS function, 156, 359, 529–30
@VDB function, 513–15
vertical bar (|) label prefix, 92, 126
@VLOOKUP function, 152–53, 238, 243, 566

W

{WAIT} macro command, 590–1
what-if analyses, 371–78
    Backsolver and, 463–68
    with one-way what-if tables, 373–74
    with Solver, 9, 146, 468–87
        adjustable cells in, 470
        answer window in, 472–73
        changing a constraint in, 477
        @functions and, 487
        guess values in, 482
        guidelines for learning, 487
        inconsistent problems in, 477–78
        macros and, 480–81
        more complex problem in, 474–77
        optimatl cell in, 471
        problems not meant for, 481–82
        progress window in, 472
        reporting options, 478–79
        simple optimization problem with, 469–74
        whole-number solutions in, 482–86
    with three-way what-if tables, 376–78
    with two-way what-if tables, 375–76
whole-number requirement in Solver, 482–86
wild-card characters, in criteria, 363
{WINDOW-ADJUST} macro command, 418, 632
Window Cascade command, 235
window control macro commands, 417–18
Window Display Options command, 91, 205–8
    Colors options, 206
    frame options, 207
    Options settings, 207
    Palette button, 91, 207
    Restore button, 208
    Update button, 208
    Zoom setting, 207
windows. *See* panes; multiple (linked) files
{WINDOW-SELECT} macro command, 418, 632–3
Windows environment, 13–44
    active window in, 21
    application and document windows in, 19–20, 22–23
    benefits of, 3–5
    cascade or tile arrangement of windows in, 21–22
    Clipboard, 38–39, 166–67, 176
        macro commands for, 418–19, 634–39
        moving graphics with, 319–20
        with multiple files, 248–49
        using, 60–61
    Control menus in, 23–26
    customizing, 42–44
    dialog boxes in, 30–32
    DOS applications under, 41–42
    keyboard techniques in, 33–36
    maximizing an application window in, 24
    minimizing windows in, 21
    mouse techniques and maneuvers in, 15–19
    moving among applications in, 39–41
    preselection method in, 19
    Program Manager, 14
        groups in, 15
    resizing a window, 18
    restoring a window in, 21, 22
    scroll bars in, 26–27
    Setup utility, 42–43
    starting, 13–15
    Task List in, 39–40
    text-editing operations in, 36–37
{WINDOWSOFF} macro command, 578
{WINDOWSON} macro command, 579
Window Split Clear command, 209
{WINDOW-STATE} macro command, 418, 633
Window Tile command, 235
Window Titles Clear command, 213

Window Titles command, 213
WK3 files, 75
word processors, 5
Worksheet Delete command, 185–86, 217
/Worksheet Delete File command, 186
Worksheet Directory option, in Tool User Setup Recalculation dialog box, 205
worksheet files, 75
/Worksheet Global Col-Width command, 202
/Worksheet Global commands, 198–99
/Worksheet Global Format command, 138
Worksheet Global Settings commands, 198–202
    Align labels options, 93, 201
    Column-width box, 202
    Format button, 202
    group mode, 201
    Protection option, 201, 250
    Zero display options, 200, 226
Worksheet Insert command, 182–84, 216
    SmartIcon for, 183
/Worksheet Insert command, 183
Worksheet Insert Sheet command, 185, 226–27
:Worksheet Page command, 266
/Worksheet Page command, 266
Worksheet Row Height command, 99–100
worksheets
    deleting, 217
        formulas and, 190–91
    inserting, 216–17
        formulas and, 189
        SmartIcon for, 217
    navigating, 114–20
        End key, 116–17
        with keyboard, 115–16
        keyboard preselection, 119–20
        mouse movements, 114–15
        1-2-3 Classic vs. Windows techniques, 10
        range references, 118–20
        3-D worksheets, 219–20
3-D. *See* 3-D worksheets
Worksheet Split Perspective command, 218
/Worksheet Titles command, 209
/Worksheet Windows command, 209
{WRITELN} macro command, 623
{WRITE} macro command, 622–23
Wysiwyg, 6, 10, 111. *See also specific commands*
    printing with, 259

X

x-axis titles, 303
XY graphs, 311

Y

y-axis titles, 303
@YEAR function, 370, 544

Z

Zero display options, 200, 225–26
ZOOM key (Alt-F6), 122, 209, 218
Zoom setting, in Window Display Options dialog box, 207

The 1-2-3 for Windows Application Disk

Send now for the disk that accompanies *The Lotus Guide to 1-2-3 for Windows*! You'll find six practical applications to help you save valuable time and put 1-2-3 to work immediately. Included is a quick check register and check reconciliation template, plus an amortizing loan template to help you calculate a home mortgage or business loan. Also included is a compound growth template, plus two other business templates—one for depreciation and another to help you evaluate the present value of future payments.

In addition, you'll find all the exercises described in this book—all the keyboarding's been done for you! Finally, you'll get some handy SmartIcons to start you off on your own indispensable SmartIcon library.

Just send a check or money order for $20.00 with this order form to:

DISK OFFER
P.O. Box 2009
Cambridge, MA 02238

Please make checks payable to DISK OFFER. (Massachusetts residents please include $1.00 sales tax.)

☐ 5 1/4" diskette   ☐ 3 1/2" diskette

Name _____

Address _____

City _____ State _____ Zip _____

Telephone _____